D1687474

INFORMATION LAW SERIES – 11

THE COMMODIFICATION OF INFORMATION

International Board of Editors

EDITOR-IN-CHIEF

Prof. P. Bernt Hugenholtz
Institute for Information Law
University of Amsterdam
The Netherlands

MEMBERS

Prof. Eric Barendt
University College London
England

Prof. Martin Bullinger
Albert-Ludwigs-Universität Freiburg
Germany

Prof. Herbert Burkert
Institut für Medien und Kommunikationsmanagement
University of St. Gallen
Switzerland

Prof. Egbert J. Dommering
Institute for Information Law
University of Amsterdam
The Netherlands

Prof. Michael Lehmann
Max-Planck Institute for Foreign and International Patent, Copyright and Competition Law
University of Munich
Germany

Prof. André Lucas
Université de Nantes
France

Prof. Ejan Mackaay
Centre de recherche en droit public
Université de Montréal
Canada

Prof. Eli M. Noam
Colombia Institute for Tele-Information
Columbia University, New York
USA

The titles in this series are listed at the back of this volume.

INFORMATION LAW SERIES – 11

THE COMMODIFICATION OF INFORMATION

Editors

Niva Elkin-Koren
Faculty of Law, University of Haifa

and

Neil Weinstock Netanel
The University of Texas School of Law

Contributors

C. Edwin Baker
Yochai Benkler
David Dranove
Rochelle Cooper Dreyfuss
Rebecca S. Eisenberg
Niva Elkin-Koren
Neil Gandal
Wendy J. Gordon
P. Bernt Hugenholtz
Jessica Litman
Ejan Mackaay

David McGowan
Eben Moglen
Neil Weinstock Netanel
David Nimmer
Helen Nissenbaum
Eli Noam
Margaret Jane Radin
Pamela Samuelson
Anselm Kamperman Sanders
David Vaver
Jonathan Weinburg

Published by
Kluwer Law International,
P.O. Box 85889, 2508 CN The Hague, The Netherlands
sales@kli.wkap.nl
http://www.kluwerlaw.com

Sold and distributed in North, Central and South America by
Kluwer Law International,
101 Philip Drive, Norwell, MA 02061, USA
kluwerlaw@wkap.com

In all other countries, sold and distributed by
Kluwer Law International,
Distribution Centre, P.O. Box 322, 3300 AH Dordrecht, The Netherlands

DISCLAIMER: The material in this volume is in the nature of general comment only. It is not offered as advice on any particular matter and should not be taken as such. The editor and contributing authors expressly disclaim all liability to any person with regards to anything done or omitted to be done, and with respect to the consequences of anything done or omitted to be done wholly or partly in reliance upon the whole or any part of this volume without first obtaining professional advice regarding the particular facts and circumstances at issue. Any and all opinions expressed herein are those of the particular author and are not necessarily those of the editor or publisher of this volume.

A C.I.P. Catalogue record for this book is available from the Library of Congress.

Printed on acid-free paper

ISBN 90-411-9876-8
© 2002 N. Netanel and N. Elkin-Koren

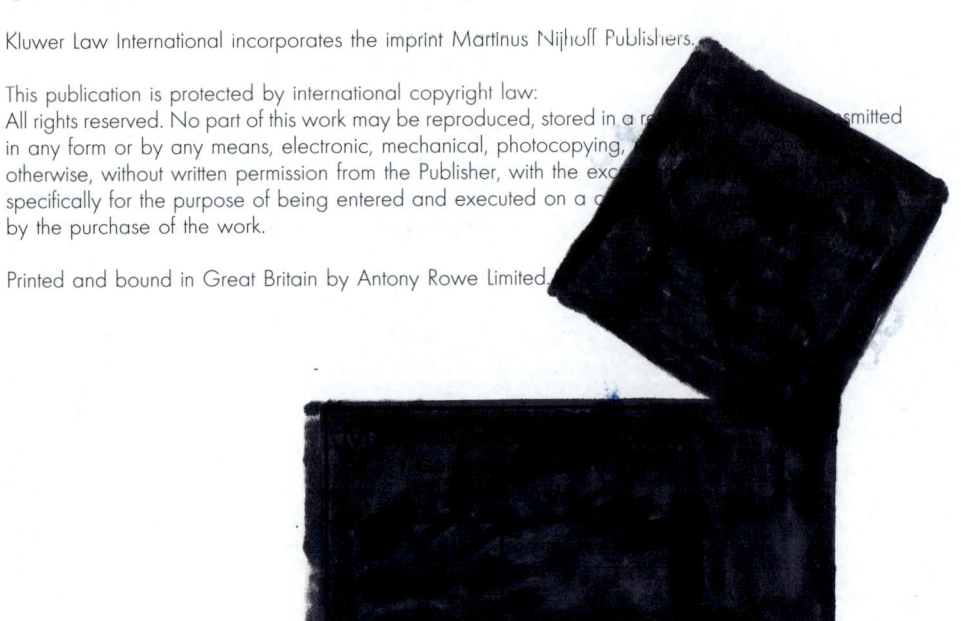

Kluwer Law International incorporates the imprint Martinus Nijhoff Publishers.

This publication is protected by international copyright law:
All rights reserved. No part of this work may be reproduced, stored in a retrieval system, or transmitted in any form or by any means, electronic, mechanical, photocopying, recording or otherwise, without written permission from the Publisher, with the exception of any material supplied specifically for the purpose of being entered and executed on a computer system, for exclusive use by the purchase of the work.

Printed and bound in Great Britain by Antony Rowe Limited.

Contents

Introduction: The Commodification of Information   vii
   Neil W. Netanel & Niva Elkin-Koren

I. Foundations   1
   Incomplete Commodification in the Computerized World   3
   Margaret Jane Radin
   Electronic Commerce and Free Speech   23
   Jessica Litman
   Two Cheers for the Commodification of Information   43
   Eli Noam

II. Copyright and Commodification: Broad Trends   61
   Copyright, Commodification, and Censorship: Past as Prologue – But to What Future?   63
   Pamela Samuelson
   It's All About Control: Rethinking Copyright in the New Information Landscape   79
   Niva Elkin-Koren
   Anarchism Triumphant: Free Software and the Death of Copyright   107
   Eben Moglen
   Intellectual Property and the Internet: The Share of Sharing   133
   Ejan Mackaay

III. Copyright and Commodification: Doctrine and Doctrinal Developments   147
   Excuse and Justification in the Law of Fair Use: Commodification and Market Perspectives   149
   Wendy J. Gordon
   How Much Solicitude for Fair Use is There in the Anti-Circumvention Provision of the Digital Millennium Copyright Act?   193
   David Nimmer

Copyright Developments in Europe: The Good, the Bad
and the Harmonized 223
David Vaver
Copyright and Freedom of Expression in Europe 239
P. Bernt Hugenholtz

IV. Media and Telecommunications 265
International Trade in Media Products 267
C. Edwin Baker
A Speakers' Corner Under the Sun 291
Yochai Benkler
The Commercial Mass Media's Continuing Fourth
Estate Role 317
Neil W. Netanel

V. Information Aggregation 341
Hardware-Based ID, Rights Management, and
Trusted Systems 343
Jonathan Weinberg
Databases – In Search of the Free Flow of Information 365
Anselm Kamperman Sanders

VI. Collaborative Production and Scientific Research 395
Commodifying Collaborative Research 397
Rochelle Cooper Dreyfuss
Patents on DNA Sequences: Molecules and Information 415
Rebecca S. Eisenberg
New Research Norms for a New Medium 433
Helen Nissenbaum

VII. Market Practices 459
Network Effects, Standardization, and the Internet:
What Have We Learned From the DVD v. DIVX Battle? 461
David Dranove & Neil Gandal
Vaporware, The Internet, and Consumer Behavior 479
David McGowan

About the Contributors 493

Index 501

Introduction: The Commodification of Information

Neil Netanel & Niva Elkin-Koren

Information has been subject to the rough and tumble of the marketplace at least since the invention of the printing press. Indeed, the rise of commercial booksellers and newspapers played an integral role in the early capitalist revolution. Just as the market enabled merchants to throw off feudal restraints, it empowered authors and their publishers to look directly to audiences rather than aristocratic and ecclesiastical patronage for financial sustenance. The early modern market spawned an outpouring of industry and invention. So did it underwrite a new sphere of public discourse imbued with the values of nascent liberal democracy.

But information and expression have never been completely commodified. In fact the development of a market economy and growth of democratic political institutions have drawn support no more from a commercial authorship and press than from those speakers and those aspects of speech that have remained largely outside the market domain. The commercial mass media have traditionally been seen to make up the backbone of the celebrated Fourth Estate. But much of the commercial mass media has until quite recently consisted of cottage industries, driven by ideological and artistic predilection as much as the bottom line. Moreover, the commercial press has comprised only a portion of our system of free expression. In democratic countries, the commercial press has always been supplemented — and, to a significant degree, countered — by political party press, government subsidized media, civic associations, and street corner pamphleteers. These institutions and individuals have made decisions about which speech to create and disseminate out of concern for communicative import, not market dictate.

Copyright law has also straddled the border between market and nonmarket. Copyright provides the legal groundwork for the propertization of original

---

N. Elkin-Koren and N.W. Netanel (eds.), *The Commodification of Information*, vii–xi.
© 2002 *Neil Netanel and Niva Elkin-Koren. Printed in Great Britain.*

expression. Yet in so doing, it has always accorded authors a decidedly limited set of exclusive rights. Copyright facilitates markets in cultural works. But, as traditionally conceived, it aims ultimately to undergird a rich and varied public domain, a realm of largely noncommodified expression in which all can share in transmitting, receiving, and reconfiguring our cultural heritage.

So, too, in the area of scientific research. Patent and trade secret laws accord monopolies in information. But these monopolies are limited in scope. And traditionally, propertized, privately funded research has co-existed with a large government-funded and university-supported research sector dedicated to sharing information with no expectation of royalty or exclusive claim.

We now stand at the cusp of a new social, economic, and, some would argue, political revolution. As numerous commentators and pundits have proclaimed, information stands at its center. Goods and services in which the primary value is information and expression have come to comprise a major portion of domestic commerce and world trade. But at the same time, digital technology and the Internet have created vast new possibilities for decidedly noncommercial production and sharing of information. These competing trends threaten to upend the rough accommodation between commodity and noncommodity, market and nonmarket, that has characterized the production and dissemination of information since the early modern era.

Digital technology and the Internet hold the promise for some of an unprecedented, global realm of decentralized public discourse and information exchange, free from the hegemony of both commercial mass media and overbearing state institutions. But whatever the Internet's actual potential for unleashing such a creative maelstrom, our system of expression and information may be moving solidly in the opposite direction, toward ever greater commercialization, commodification, and propertization. Mega entertainment and telecommunications conglomerates have absorbed cottage-industry publishers and journalists, subordinating artistic and editorial discretion to overall corporate strategy and investor demands. Government funding of broadcasting, the press, the arts, and scientific research has steadily dwindled in relation to the rapidly growing, avaricious sector of market-driven speech and science. Copyright and other intellectual property has dramatically expanded in scope and duration, giving content providers unprecedented proprietary control over expression and information and threatening the continued viability of the public domain. Indeed, personal decisions regarding the sorts of information and expression one receives and creates have themselves been transformed into marketable data, creating an enormous industry in personal profiling and data collection, aggregation, and management.

The essays collected in this book address various aspects and ramifications of this multifarious trend. The book opens with an exploration of some of the fundamental issues underlying the commodification of information. Margaret Jane Radin, whose seminal work on the conflicts between market and nonmarket rhetoric, activity, and values helped to inspire our project, examines "Incomplete Commodification in the Computerized World." She presents examples, ranging from copyright to data privacy, in which the doctrine and rhetoric of "private property/free contract" might foreclose uses of the cultural commons that we need to constitute ourselves as autonomous persons and engage in democratic dialogue. Jessica Litman's essay, "Electronic Commerce and Free Speech," discusses the tension between commercial speech and "free" speech, in the double sense of non-market driven and near-zero cost speech. She depicts the American entertainment and information industries' successful takeover of the Internet and imposition of market and legal barriers before "free" speech. Eli Noam's essay "Two Cheers for the Commodification of Information," takes issue with the argument presented by other contributors and, indeed, with some of the basic themes of this book. Noam contends that the concerns raised by others in this book are overblown, that the commercialization of information is epiphenomenal to much larger trends of a knowledge-based society and economy, and that such commercialization has brought us an unprecedented abundance and diversity of expression.

Part II of this book addresses copyright law's relation to the commodification of expression. Pamela Samuelson's essay, "Copyright, Commodification, and Censorship: Past as Prologue — But to What Future?," finds commonalities between copyright's censorsial "pre-modern" precursor, the notorious registry of the English Stationers' Company, and today's capacious "post-modern" copyright. Niva Elkin-Koren's chapter, "It's All About Control: Rethinking Copyright in the New Information Landscape," limns copyright's transition from a regime designed to provide a narrowly tailored incentive for expressive creativity to one that accords content providers with "market control." Elkin-Koren cautions that copyright's new paradigm may be incompatible with democracy and civic virtue. In his chapter, "Anarchism Triumphant: Free Software and the Death of Copyright," Eben Moglen presents a non-propertarian theory and practice of the digital society. He contends that the free software movement, of which the GNU/Linux operating system is its best-known component, is fast overwhelming the copyright-centered regime of proprietary control and serves as a precursor for other forms of collaborative, non-proprietarian cultural and scientific production. Ejan Mackaay, in contrast, argues that the viability of some sharing arrangements, such as Java, Linux and sharing amongst scientists, does not justify abandoning intellectual property rights altogether. In "Intellectual Property and the Internet: The Share of Sharing," he contends that the institutions developed by interested persons in the new information environment suggest that property regimes still enjoy legitimacy.

Part III further develops the themes discussed in Part II, but in greater doctrinal detail. In her essay, "Excuse and Justification in the Law of Fair Use: Commodification and Market Perspectives," Wendy Gordon extends and refines her seminal work on fair use as market failure. Drawing upon policies regarding commodification, she differentiates between uses deemed fair use for reasons of "excuse" and uses deemed fair use because they are "justified." She contends that the former should not be available if, because of new licensing mechanisms or other institutional or technological change, the excusing circumstances disappear, whereas the latter should remain free from copyright owner control despite such changes. David Nimmer's essay, "How Much Solicitude for Fair Use is There in the Anti-Circumvention Provision of the Digital Millennium Copyright Act?," concludes that the anti-circumvention provision contains insufficient solicitude for fair use. He asserts, indeed, that the DMCA provides a legal framework for universal pay-per-use and de facto perpetual protection for digital content. In "Copyright Developments in Europe: The Good, the Bad and the Harmonized," David Vaver sketches recent expansions of copyright and related rights in European Union law. Concomitantly, in "Copyright and Freedom of Expression in Europe," Bernt Hugenholtz argues that recent court decisions from Europe suggest that the free speech provisions of the European Convention on Human Rights might, under certain circumstances, impose limits to such expansion.

Part IV turns to the area of media and telecommunications. Ed Baker's chapter, "International Trade in Media Products," argues that democratic countries are justified in protecting the availability of domestic media and cultural products in the face of a flood of American imports. Baker demonstrates that international free trade exacerbates systemic market failures in the production and dissemination of cultural products and contends that local democratic institutions require a strong domestic media. In his essay, "A Speakers' Corner Under the Sun," Yochai Benkler argues that a communications commons would better serve the democratic values of autonomy (in both its personal autonomy and political self-governance senses) than would contemporary alternative approaches to communications infrastructure regulation, including proprietary, common-carriage, and publicly owned regimes. In "The Commercial Mass Media's Continuing Fourth Estate Role," Neil Netanel compares the commercial media with party press, government-financed media, and peer-to-peer alternatives for gathering and distributing information and opinion to citizens of advanced liberal democracies. He contends that those partly nonmarket alternatives ought to supplement, rather than supplant, the commercial media in its traditional Fourth Estate role.

Part V examines commodification in the arena of information aggregation. In "Hardware-Based ID, Rights Management, and Trusted Systems," Jonathan Weinberg explores the ramifications of technology that content providers can use to identify Internet users and thus track and better control users' receipt of information via the Internet. In "Databases — In Search of the Free Flow of Information," Anselm Kamperman Sanders examines the extension of property rights in databases. He also highlights a possible conflict between such rights and the right of free speech contained in the European Convention on Human Rights.

Part VI addresses issues in collaborative production and scientific research. In her essay, "Commodifying Collaborative Research," Rochelle Cooper Dreyfuss explores the special challenges that information commodification presents to participants in collaborative projects, including works of joint authorship and scientific research. Rebecca Eisenberg's chapter discusses the commodification of genomic information. In "Patents on DNA Sequences: Molecules and Information," Eisenberg analyzes the risks involved in patenting DNA sequence information while stressing some advantages involved in patenting DNA molecules. In "New Research Norms for a New Medium," Helen Nissenbaum analyzes the effect of commodification and electronic publication on the attribution norms that have traditionally governed research and scholarship.

In Part VII, the book concludes with a case study of market practices and the Internet, focusing on "vaporware" and network effects. In their essay, "Network Effects, Standardization, and the Internet: What Have We Learned from the DVD v. DIVX Battle?," David Dranove and Neil Gandal note that market forces often result in suboptimal standardization in the presence of network effects, which are ubiquitous in information and communication markets, but that commentators disagree on whether and how regulation should counter such market failure. In that regard, they suggest that unhindered, "bottom-up" communication on the Internet can sometimes blunt the power of "vaporware," product preannouncements that play on network effects to induce consumers to defer buying competitors' information products even when the announcer's product does not yet exist. In "Vaporware, the Internet, and Consumer Behavior," David McGowan concludes that while antitrust law will not generally prevent "vaporware," unfair competition law might legitimately be applied to prevent consumers from being sandbagged by such preannouncements.

The idea for this book and many of the essays that it presents originated in a conference, The Commodification of Information: Political, Social, and Cultural Ramifications, which took place at the University of Haifa Faculty of Law in May 1999. We are grateful to our co-organizer of that conference, Dr. Victor H. Bouganim, for his many contributions to that conference and this book. We also acknowledge the financial support of the University of Haifa and the United States-Israel Science and Technology Commission, without which neither the conference nor this book would have come to fruition. We thank Yossi Edrey, former Dean of the University of Haifa Faculty of Law, for his unwavering support of this project. Last but not least, we thank Jill Garbi for her dedicated and excellent work as our copy editor and Yael Bregman for her assistance in research and manuscript preparation.

I. FOUNDATIONS

Incomplete Commodification in the Computerized World

*Margaret Jane Radin**

Introduction: Commodification in Cyberspace

One emerging focus of debate about policy in the world of cyberspace is how to reconcile theories and practices of intellectual property with theories and practices of freedom of expression. (I will refer to these complexes of theories and practices as "realms.") Within the realm of intellectual property lies another debate: what is the proper extent of propertization and what is the proper extent of the public domain? Other essays in this volume make important contributions to these debates.[1]

Unless one conceives of the public domain wholly in economic terms, these two debates are connected because the scope of the public domain is related to the scope of freedom of expression. But there are now many people who do conceive of the scope of propertization – hence the scope of nonpropertization, what is left over after propertization, the public domain – wholly in economic terms. That is, many people now conceive of the public domain in terms of the conceptual scheme of the market, in what I like to call market rhetoric. Market rhetoric is part of the conceptual scheme of commodification, as I will explain shortly. The prevalent tendency to think about the public domain in market rhetoric introduces the questions about commodification, and especially incomplete commodification, that I want to raise in this essay. To set the stage for the questions I want to talk about, I will first recapitulate the way that I see the general issues of commodification.

In some kinds of human activity, market transactions are well accepted. In

---

* Thanks to Neil Netanel for very helpful comments on an earlier draft; and thanks to Kevin E. Collins and Corynne McSherry for research assistance.
[1] Among others, see the contributions of C. Edwin Baker and Yochai Benkler.

N. Elkin-Koren and N.W. Netanel (eds.), The Commodification of Information, 3–21.
© *2002 Margaret Jane Radin. Printed in Great Britain.*

others, they are avoided, or at least deplored. In some activities and practices, though, the appropriateness of market transactions is hotly contested. The contest plays out in the reality of how the practices operate; but at the same time it plays out in the rhetoric or conceptual schemes for describing them, interpreting them, and reasoning about them. Market rhetoric is the practice of describing things in terms of markets and reasoning about them as one reasons about the functioning of a market: supply and demand functions, profit-maximization, monetary cost-benefit analysis. I have called the market practices, and the market thought system, commodified; and the nonmarket practices and thought systems, noncommodified.[2]

The touchstone of commodification is the organized activity of exchange, supported by the legal infrastructure of private-property-plus-free-contract (abbreviated "PPFK").[3] The touchstones of noncommodification involve (when the focus is the value of individual personhood) human dignity, autonomy, and self-constitution; and (when the focus is the value of community or group identity) unpropertized, unmonetized sharing, connectedness, and communicative interaction.

I have argued that the area of contestedness over markets and market rhetoric is greater than has generally been thought. Noncommodified understandings coexist with commodified understandings even in circumstances where the existence of markets is well accepted. In light of this pervasive coexistence, I have urged that the best way to describe much of our economic, political and social practice is incomplete commodification.[4] In this essay I will urge this thesis in light of three examples of contested commodification in the computerized world.

Cyberspace, the world of computerized interactions, is an optimal field in which to explore commodification. The Internet has evolved rapidly from a resolutely noncommercial modality to a largely commercial one. In the earlier noncommercial phase of the Internet, only a few years ago, propertization was eschewed; now, in the commercial phase, propertization of knowledge keeps growing.[5]

---

[2] See Margaret Jane Radin, Contested Commodities (1996).
[3] I took this useful abbreviation from Duncan Kennedy & Frank Michelman, Are Property and Contract Efficient?, 8 Hofstra L. Rev. 711 (1980).
[4] See Radin, Contested Commodities, supra note 2.
[5] All of the main intellectual property regimes – copyright, patent, and trademark – have increased in scope in the past few years. See, e.g., Margaret Jane Radin, The Transformation of Property and Contract in the Digital Environment. [Available as the Cecil A. Wright Lecture at University of Toronto, <www.law.utoronto.ca;> specifically at the Centre for Innovation Law and Policy, <http://www.innovationlaw.org/video/laws01–1.ram>] to be published in a forthcoming book.

Legislative developments have recently spearheaded the increase in copyright scope. The Sonny Bono Copyright Term Extension Act of 1998, extended the protected term by twenty years, while the Digital Millennium Copyright Act of 1998 adds anti-circumvention and anti-trafficking rights to the rights already held by copyright owners. Digital Millennium Copyright Act, Pub. L. No. 105–304, ß 103(a), 112 Stat. at 2865, 17 U.S.C. ß 1201 (a)(3)(B)). See Pamela

As propertization of knowledge grows, there has been a shift in rhetoric. Knowledge understood as a commodity is known as "content," or "information property," or simply "information." These words now have the connotation primarily of fungible objects bearing market value. Indeed, the locution "information object" is common. "Information" is traded for money in markets just like the proverbial widgets; and "content" is fungible; it is all interchangeable for other "content" bearing the same market value. Other locutions – "ideas," "conversation," "communication," or "knowledge" itself – are less clearly part of a commodified conceptual scheme.[6]

Perhaps the word "expression" has the most ambiguity. In the context of the realm of freedom of expression, it is most often thought of as noncommodified; though there is a strand of commodified thought in that realm too, having to do with the so-called "marketplace of ideas."[7] On the other hand, in the realm of copyright, expression represents the propertizable, commodifiable aspect of a work (as opposed to nonpropertizable, noncommodifiable "ideas").[8] One may think of copyright itself as a regime of incomplete commodification because of its commitment to the noncommodification of ideas, and also because of certain limitations on the commodification of expression, which I will touch upon later.

(cont.)
Samuelson, Intellectual Property and the Digital Economy: Why the Anti-Circumvention Regulations Need to Be Revised, 14 Berkeley Tech. L. J. 519. The increasing reach of patent law has also been pushed legislatively, most notably via the Bayh-Dole Act of 1980 encouraging universities to patent inventions resulting from federally funded basic research. The courts have been equally if not more active in facilitating assertions of patent rights in ever wider fields. In 1980 and 1981, the U.S. Supreme Court opened the patentability door for living material and computer software inventions. Diamond v. Chakrabarty, 444 U.S. 1028 (1980); Diamond v. Diehr 450 U.S. 175 (1981). Business methods have recently been found to be patentable subject matter, ending a decades-old belief that such "inventions" were too abstract to be patentable, State Street Bank and Trust Co. v. Signature Financial Group, Inc, 149 F.3d 1368 (1998). In ATT v. Excel, the Court of Appeals for the Federal Circuit took its position one step further by declaring the traditional condition that an invention work a "physical transformation" to be not a requirement but merely a way of demonstrating utility. 172 F. 3d 1352 (1999). See also G. J. Maier and R. C. Mattson, State Street Bank in the context of the software patent saga. In 8 George Mason Law Review 307 (1999). In the trademark arena, the Federal Anti-Dilution Act of 1995, 15 USC 1125(c), recognized dilution as a federal cause of action for "famous" trademarks, greatly expanding the reach of this branch of trademark doctrine. The Act is but one instance of a broader movement toward severing trademark doctrine's traditional commitment to territoriality and market compartmentalization. See Margaret Jane Radin and R. Polk Wagner, The Myth of Private Ordering: Rediscovering Legal Realism in Cyberspace, 73 Chi.-Kent. L. Rev. 1295 (1998).

[6] This insight was suggested to me by C. Edwin Baker's essay for this volume, International Trade in Media Products.
[7] See Contested Commodities, supra note 2, chapter 12.
[8] Thanks to Neil Netanel for making me see how the notion of commodification relates in a complex way to the idea/expression dichotomy.

II. THE QUESTION OF OVERPROPERTIZATION AND THE VISION OF DYSTOPIA

In light of the increasing propertization of knowledge and communication, many observers have begun to think about the perils of overpropertization. When does propertization become overpropertization? In a noncommodified understanding of the world of value, too much propertization exists when commodification of "content" forecloses the kind of use of the cultural commons that we require in order to constitute ourselves as autonomous persons, or forecloses the kind of communicative give-and-take that we require to foster democratic dialogue and human creativity.[9]

Overpropertization is salient in the market conceptual scheme, too. In the rhetoric of PPFK, too much propertization exists when the costs of the property system outweigh its benefits. The costs of "information property" systems are twofold: monopolization of (commodified) "information," which, once produced, could just as well be used by everyone as by a single owner; and the increased cost of creating new works when the already existing "information" one needs to draw on cannot be used without paying for it. The benefit of "information property" systems is supposed to be supplying enough incentive for profit-maximizing producers to create "information" in the first place. As propertization increases, at a certain point the costs due to monopolization and necessary upstream acquisition begin to outweigh the benefits of increasing incentives.

No empirical analysis has seriously shown how much incentive would be optimal. Such an empirical analysis faces great complexity in its variables. For one thing, even those who believe that the premises of "economic man" are appropriate in policy reasoning – that we are, at least for purposes of policy formation, best viewed as relentless profit-maximizers – realize that certain fields of creative endeavor are less prone to profit-maximizing motivation than others (for example, fine art drawings vs. greeting card drawings). Moreover, even if we assume that the profit-maximizing assumption is the right one, it seems clear that the needed incentive would be different in different fields of endeavor, because of the different risks and costs involved (for example, developing new drugs vs. developing greeting card verses). Earlier scholarship was dubious about the utility of copyright and patent.[10] The systems have ratcheted upward – increased their scope of coverage – quite a bit since that time, and never de-escalated. De-escalation would be quite difficult because of the political weight of vested interests in existing property rights, and because of the ability of businesses to

---

[9] See Yochai Benkler's essay for this volume, A Speaker's Corner Under the Sun.
[10] Stephen Breyer, The Uneasy Case for Copyright: A Study of Copyright in Books, Photocopies, and Computer Programs, 84 Harvard Law Review 281 (1970). See generally Fritz Machlup and Edith Penrose, The Patent Controversy in the Nineteenth Century, 10 J Econ Hist 1, 10–20 (1950); Fritz Machlup, An Economic Review of the Patent System, Subcomm. on Patents, Trademarks, and Copyrights of the Senate Comm on the Judiciary, Study No 15, 85th Cong, 2d Sess (GPO, 1958).

migrate out of jurisdictions that restrict their "information" assets and into jurisdictions that expand those assets. The risk of overpropertization stands in urgent need of investigation, even from economic premises, and a fortiori in light of pervasive commitments to noneconomic values.

Though the transition to commercialization is largely complete, competing visions of the nature of cyberspace, and its future, still vie for our attention and commitment. One vision reflects a noncommodified conception of digitized knowledge and communication, the other a commodified conception of digitized information and content. One is utopian, the other dystopian.

The utopian vision extrapolates from the old Internet ideal, which might be called early cyberspace. In this vision, a worldwide digital network transcends national borders and provincial sovereignties, promoting open dialogue, cooperation, sharing, and self-regulation. It is a vision of free and robust scientific, artistic, educational, and political interaction. It is a model of "any to any," in which any recipient can also be a producer and distributor of knowledge. It brings to the fore a hitherto submerged noncommercial tradition of freedom of expression and extends it: it transforms politics by making true dialogue and free debate available to everyone. It makes concrete the intellectual and social infrastructure of cooperative inquiry and undominated dialogue that democratic theorists from John Dewey to Jurgen Habermas have argued is needed as the basis of ideal democracy.[11] It transforms our lives, making them more creative and interactive.

Meanwhile, the competing dystopic vision of the future of cyberspace makes our lives more passive and flat. It is a commodified model that could be nicknamed the couch potato model. In this dystopian vision, vast networks deliver lowest-common-denominator "content" to passive recipients. It is an apolitical vision, a vision of lowered intellectual horizons and of manipulation and mind-control. Advertising and content coalesce. Their fusion forms the profit-making logic of the companies that own the conduits of information, the content flowing through them, and the products the conduits and content flow are being used to sell. Everything that we want to look at must be paid for; it is all commodified content. Even our attention is commodified – our eyeballs are sold to advertisers. The dystopic vision transforms our lives, making them less political, less social, and ultimately less human.

Many who think the utopian vision can win out tend to think of cyberspace as its own free country;[12] tend to say that property is dead;[13] tend to think that

---

[11] For an interpretation of democratic dialogue in the context of copyright law and policy, see Neil Netanel, Copyright in a Democratic Society, 106 Yale L. J. 283 (1996).

[12] See, e.g., David R. Johnson and David Past, Law and Borders – The Rise of Law in Cyberspace, 48 Stanford Law Review 1367 (1996).

[13] See, e.g., Esther Dyson, Intellectual Value, Wired, July 1995; Nicholas P. Negroponte, Being Digital 58–61 (1995); John Perry Barlow, The Economy of Ideas, Wired, March 1994, at 84; John Perry Barlow, Stopping the Information Railroad, available at < http://www.ora.com/gnn/bus/ora/features/barlow/index/html. >

"good" hackers will always beat those who try to cabin this freedom.[14] On the other hand, many who think the dystopian vision is winning tend to say that property is not dead but stronger than ever;[15] tend to think that technological locks will benefit the powerful commodifiers even more than the beefed-up property rules they have obtained from governments;[16] tend to think that the interests of governments will be allied with the interests of multinational conglomerates in putting a stop to "good" hackers, and that this alliance will prevail. The maxim, "follow the money," does turn out to be a rather successful predictor of political results.[17] Because "the money" is mostly underwriting the dystopian vision, I tend to think it will succeed – is already succeeding – to a great extent. Nevertheless, commodification is always incomplete, perhaps because while we remain human a stubborn commitment to a noncommodified realm of human value remains. It is important, therefore, to explore how commodified and noncommodified visions of life coexist in cyberspace as elsewhere; to describe areas where each vision is strong or weak; to consider what mixtures might be desirable; and to consider how to get there – to a better mixture – from here.

In the rest of this essay I will begin this project by describing three loci of debate over digitized knowledge and communication: the "fair use" defense to copyright liability; the open source movement; and data privacy. In each of these arenas of debate, I believe the interpretive conceptual framework I have outlined – commodification, noncommmodification, incomplete commodification – will prove at least somewhat clarifying. (Of course, mine is only one take on a complex emerging world.)

III. COMMODIFICATION AND THE DISAPPEARANCE OF FAIR USE

The doctrine of "fair use" in U.S. copyright law is an affirmative defense to infringement liability. If a court finds that a defendant's activity is in fact unauthorized copying (or a violation of one of the other owner's rights, such as distribution or display), nevertheless, on a case by case basis, the unauthorized activity may be excused if the court deems the activity to be fair use. Fair use

---

[14] See e.g., Custom Levels and Scenarios Under Siege, Computer Gaming World, Jan. 1, 1997, at 20 ("For every code, there is a cracker."); this view is often expressed by students in my classes, and may be seen as well by lurking for a while on any listserv frequented by crypto types.

[15] See text accompanying note 5 and note 5, supra; see also Mark Lemley, Romantic Authorship and the Rhetoric of Property, 75 Texas L. Rev. 873, 902 (1997).

[16] See, e.g., Julie E. Cohen, Lochner in Cyberspace: The New Economic Orthodoxy of "Rights Management," 97 Michigan L. Rev. 462 (1998).

[17] Taken to its logical extreme, the maxim leads to a commodified vision of politics, usually known as public choice theory. I do not want to take it to the extreme, because in politics as elsewhere, I think commodified forms coexist with noncommodified forms. See Contested Commodities, supra note 2, chapter 14.

began as a judge-made doctrine, one that some said was required in order for copyright, which restricts communication and dissemination of knowledge, to comport with the right of free expression in the U.S. Constitution.[18]

Fair use became part of the governing statute when copyright was legislatively revamped by the U.S. Congress in 1976. The statute, perhaps in keeping with the supposed underpinnings of the doctrine in ideals of free expression, provides that "the fair use of a copyrighted work ... for purposes such as criticism, comment, news reporting, teaching (including multiple copies for classroom use), scholarship, or research, is not an infringement of copyright."[19] In determining whether an otherwise infringing use is or is not fair use, the statute directs judges to "include" consideration of four factors. The factors nicely illustrate how copyright is responsive both to commodified and noncommodified understandings of its purpose and effects. The first factor ("the purpose and character of the use, including whether such use is of a commercial nature or is for nonprofit educational purposes"[20]) can be read as shoring up noncommodified activity by privileging the noncommercial. Yet the fourth factor ("the effect of the use upon the potential market for or value of the copyrighted work")[21] can be read as wholly in the commodified realm of market-based monetary cost-benefit analysis.

In my mind it is questionable whether first amendment values would be satisfied by this statute even if it were interpreted straightforwardly. The status of fair use as an affirmative defense to prima facie infringement means that whoever loses on fair use is liable for infringement (absent some other defense). The case-by-case balancing approach means it is fairly unpredictable which way a particular court will come down in a particular case. This legislative structure engenders a chilling effect: a would-be speaker is likely to think, "When in doubt, leave it out." Thus, a legislature more attuned to free speech values[22] and less in the grip of "the money" – the copyright industries – might have delineated specific categories of exemption. Nevertheless, the fair use exemption is made even narrower because the statute has not been interpreted straightforwardly.

Case law has made clear that making multiple copies for classroom use is generally not privileged, in spite of specific mention in the statute as a purpose that could be privileged.[23] The same is true of noncommercial use, which is not privileged (unless it makes no inroads on the market of paying customers for the

---

[18] See, e.g., Time, Inc. v. Bernard Geis Assocs., 293 F. Supp. 130 (S.D.N.Y. 1968).
[19] Copyright Act of 1976, 17 U.S.C. sec. 107.
[20] Id.
[21] Id.
[22] The Copyright Act was drafted with such a tin ear for free speech values that it authorizes ex parte prior restraint injunctions without even directing judges to weigh first amendment values. 17 U.S.C. sec. 502. See, e.g., Mark A. Lemley and Eugen Volokh, Freedom of Speech and Injunctions in Intellectual Property Cases, 48 Duke L.J. 157 (1998).
[23] See, e.g., Princeton Univ. Press v. Michigan Document Servs., Inc., 99 F.3d 1381, 1400 (6th Cir. 1996); Basic Books, Inc. v. Kinko's Graphics Corp., 758 F. Supp. 1522 (S.D.N.Y. 1991).

work);[24] ditto for news reporting.[25] In spite of the third factor, which directs the court to weigh the amount and substantiality of the use, taking an insubstantial portion of the work is not necessarily privileged.[26] Finally, to make a long story short, case law has made clear in recent years that the fourth factor (market harm) is the most important; and this factor is also the one that most embodies the commodified side of copyright. Although the U.S. Supreme Court carved out a niche for parody by holding that undermining the demand for a work by ridiculing it rather than supplanting it can count as a fair use,[27] most recent cases have interpreted fair use quite narrowly.

Concomitant with these narrowing interpretations, an economic interpretation of fair use has been gaining favor. The interpretation of fair use has, in other words, turned toward commodification. In the commodified interpretation, the only purpose of the fair use doctrine is economic efficiency. According to this interpretation, the doctrine is only invoked (or should only be invoked) as a substitute for licensing when licensing cannot take place because transaction costs are too high.[28] For example, if a great many users would have to negotiate with a copyright holder for short excerpts or a few copies, the cost of the negotiations might deter the parties from entering into licenses; yet if the users were allowed to use the material the losses to the owner would be far outweighed by the gains to the user, resulting in a net social gain. In such a case, according to the commodified argument, a court should accomplish the next-best substitute for the transactions that cannot take place, by allowing the use to proceed as a fair use.

Conversely, the commodified argument holds that a court should refuse to judge a use fair, no matter what kind of use it is, if the use could have been licensed. The commodified argument was the underpinning of an important case holding that it was not fair use for researchers to make individual file copies of journal articles for their own use, on the ground that an efficient licensing market, although it did not exist, could in fact be brought into existence through the use of a collecting agency.[29]

The commodified argument leads inexorably to one conclusion. Wherever a

---

[24] See, e.g., Encyclopaedia Britannica Educational Corp. v. Crooks, 542 F. Supp. 1156 (W.D.N.Y. 1982).
[25] See, e.g., Harper & Row Publishers Inc. v. Nation Enterprises, 471 U.S. 539 (1985). Of course, reporting of "facts" is still permissible because "facts" are not original works of authorship and therefore not protected by copyright law in the U.S. More inroads on the public domain status of "facts" (in the U.S.) can be expected when database protection legislation is enacted, as is overwhelmingly expected as this essay goes to press.
[26] Id.
[27] Campbell v. Acuff-Rose, 501 U.S. 569 (1994).
[28] In an article published in the Columbia Law Review, Wendy Gordon proposed this interpretation of fair use, though I do not believe she would approve of all of the uses to which it has been put. See Wendy Gordon, Fair Use as Market Failure: A Structural and Economic Analysis of the Betamax Case and Its Predecessors, 82 Columbia Law Review 1600 (1982). For Professor Gordon's attempt to cabin this argument, see her contribution to this volume, 'Excuse and Justification in the Law of Fair Use: Commodification and Market Perspective'.
[29] American Geophysical Union v. Texaco, Inc., 37 F.3d 881 (2d Cir. 1994).

licensing market is possible in the economic sense – cheap enough to establish and maintain so that the difference between proceeds and costs will be positive – fair use should cease to exist. (Just say yes to licensing, said the White Paper promulgated by the U.S. government a few years ago.[30])

The commodified argument is sweeping indeed in the context of the networked digital environment. Transaction costs are dramatically lowered for all kinds of "content" transactions. With the advent of digital rights management systems and digital payment mechanisms that can efficiently handle micropayments, it will be economically possible for a "content" originator to charge users even for short quotations, passages read once, and passages downloaded only for personal reference. If the commodified argument is the right way to look at fair use, then fair use is a thing of the past. It is an outmoded doctrine that evolved to deal with a problem – high transaction costs in licensing – that we no longer have. Now there is no transaction costs barrier preventing "content" owners from charging people for everything they read, nor is there any transaction costs barrier to paying people for everything they say.

But what about freedom of expression? The ethos of freedom of expression, especially in the political arena, but also in the realms of artistic productions and in other kinds of knowledge production, conflicts with the ethos of propertization. The ethos of freedom of expression involves treating information as a public good: sharing information and learning, engendering waves of political debate and criticism, drawing on a huge public domain of accumulated cultural artifacts to argue, interact, and create.[31] The mainstream rationale of copyright has hitherto included the notion that the commodification of expression for a limited term is in the service of ultimate contribution to the realm of uncommodified knowledge in the public domain.[32] Contrary to these strands of thought, the ethos of propertization involves treating information as a private asset and attempting to internalize all benefits to the owner of the asset.[33]

---

[30] Information Infrastructure Task Force, Intellectual Property and the National Information Infrastructure: the Report of the Working Group on Intellectual Property Rights (1995). See also, Tom W. Bell, Fair Use vs. Fared Use: The Impact of Automated Rights management on Copyright's Fair Use Doctrine, 76 North Carolina L. Rev. 557 (1998).

[31] Freedom of expression is itself a contested concept, however; and, in addition to this noncommodified version, in the U.S., at least, there is a commodified version, described in market rhetoric, as "the marketplace of ideas." See Contested Commodities, supra note 2, chapter 12. Perhaps the ambiguity in the realm of freedom of expression itself renders the first amendment less capable of delineating a check on the commodification of knowledge and communication by means of intellectual property regimes.

[32] But once the importance of an uncommodified public domain is weakened, perhaps through the advent of a commodified vision of the realm of freedom of expression, the traditional rationale for placing limits on copyright's commodification of expression is undermined. (I owe this point to colloquy with Neil Netanel.)

[33] At least, this is the commodified version of the ethos of property. Although commodification is the dominant ethos of propertization, property too has other, less commodified, ethical underpinnings. See, e.g., Margaret Jane Radin, Reinterpreting Property (1994).

In the past it has often been said that the legal system has successfully mediated the conflict between the realm of freedom of expression and the realm of propertization, primarily by protecting only "expression" and not "ideas," but also because the fair use doctrine supposedly functioned as a safety valve for the values of freedom of expression.[34] In my opinion there is much reason for skepticism about whether the doctrine of fair use, together with the idea/expression dichotomy, was ever adequate to this task, but fair use was probably better than nothing.

Fair use symbolically undergirded a noncommodified aspect of political culture. It enabled citizens to maintain a background understanding that portions of texts could be copied for criticism, news reporting, and education. That background understanding is changing. The advent of technological control systems, and the advent of legal protection for control systems that foreclose otherwise permissible fair use, are hastening the change.[35] If the commodified interpretation of fair use causes the doctrine to die, right now we do not have a strong mediating doctrine to replace it.

IV. THE OPEN SOURCE MOVEMENT AND ITS COMMODIFIED LEGAL INFRASTRUCTURE

Open source licensing refers to transactions involving use of computer programs under contractual terms providing that source code, including improvements contributed by users, must not be propertized, at least not in the usual sense of private property under the sole control of the user. Instead, the users form a distributional community having access to the source code in common. An important feature of these distributional communities is that each user who makes improvements to the program must contribute the source code for the improvements back to the community.[36] The structure for accomplishing this goal differs in different open source programs. Possibilities include having all users agree explicitly with the original licensor with respect to the open source conditions; having each user in the chain of distribution "agree" to make source code for improvements available to the original licensor; having each user "agree" to make source code for improvements available to all users upstream in the chain of distribution; or having each user "agree" to make the source code for

---

[34] See, e.g., Paul Goldstein, Copyright and the First Amendment, 70 Columbia L. Rev. 983 (1970).
[35] This trend is greatly enhanced by the Digital Millennium Copyright Act of 1998, which prohibits the use or sale of devices that circumvent technological access controls. See 17 U.S.C. § 1201. So far, judges have not been sympathetic to the idea that fair use is a defense to that prohibition. See, e.g., Universal City Studios, Inc. v. Corley, 273 F.3d 429 (2nd Cir. 2001).
[36] See < www.opensource.org; > see also, Chris Di Bona, Mark Stone and Sam Ockman (eds), Opensources: Voice from the Open Source Revolution (2000).

improvements available to everyone in a distributional community, i.e., everyone who has ever used the software or who ever will use it in the future. (I have put the word "agree" in quotes in the latter three scenarios to signify that in these circumstances it is unclear whether an actual binding agreement would be found if the matter came before a court.)

The basic open source license depends upon copyright (i.e., on private property). The original licensor grants copyright permission to subsequent users, upon condition that improvements in the source code be made available. The licensor wants the license to be interpreted as lapsing with respect to anyone who fails to fulfill the condition and make source code available to the distributional community. In a sense, this is an attempt to use private property against itself, to maintain a commons, a public domain; and that is why this type of license was christened "copyleft."[37] In my view there is an important question whether the largely commodified tool of copyright can succeed in undermining itself in this way.

The danger is not only that the copyleft license will be legally unenforceable (see below). In addition there is in my opinion a serious risk of backlash. The types of activities that the open source license wants to construe as imposing obligations on all users – e.g., the travel of a digital "information object" down a chain of distribution – could also be used by ideologues of an opposite stripe, propertization maximalists, to impose extra obligations on users of the same kinds of "information objects." Consider, for example, a license conditional upon waiving all rights of fair use by anyone into whose hands the information object came; or conditional upon waiving all rights to criticize the information object. If copyleft obligations are held valid, then these supercopyright obligations might well be valid too.

There is an ideological split in the open source movement, which is interesting to view in light of positions with respect to commodification. In the noncommodified wing are Richard Stallman, the founder of the Free Software Foundation, and his followers, who believe that PPFK for computer software is bad, period. According to this view, not only is private property in computer programs not needed for economic incentives, it hampers freedom and communication and the nonmonetary rewards of programming. In the commodified wing, the value of open source schemes for the economic system is stressed. Proponents are eloquent about the advantages of such regimes for efficient software development.

Simply put, the open source regime is supposed to produce better software in less time. Eric Raymond likens proprietary software development to a cathedral

---

[37] For more information about copyleft, which was developed by the Free Software Foundation, see its site, <www.gnu.org/fsf/fsf.html.> See also Marcus Maher, Open Source Software: The Success of an Alternative Intellectual Property Incentive Paradigm, 10 Fordham Intellectual Property, Media & Entertainment L.J. 619.

and open source development to a bazaar.[38] The problem with the cathedral model is that it is difficult to test and predict what can go wrong with the program out there in the world of users. In the bazaar model, bugs are quickly found by users and communicated to everyone; they are quickly fixed by someone in the community, not necessarily the same member as the finder. Linux and other open source programs are known to be very robust and to crash much less frequently than proprietary programs such as those of Microsoft.

Because it produces a better product, at least in some cases, and produces it more quickly, at least in some cases, the open source model has a chance of becoming more and more prevalent. But that will depend upon whether the bazaar model is scalable and whether it will hold up against economic and legal challenges. The bazaar model depends upon a nucleus of volunteer engineers who are willing (and/or whose employers are willing) to contribute their work to the distributional community. It is said that these volunteers are rewarded by reputation rather than money. Employers who are software users, not in the business of supplying the software to the market, could find it in their interest to allow their employees to improve the software and increase their firm's reputation along with the employee's personal reputation. If these conjectures are right, then the volunteers' motives may be noncommodified – though not if their pursuit of reputation is profit-oriented résumé building. Their employers' motives are largely commodified (enhancing market share through enhancing the firm's reputation). The production of open source software is an interesting mixture of commodified and noncommodified motives and processes, not yet fully explored.

One of the main questions facing the open source movement is what will happen if the community ceases to be so cohesive, and someone defects and tries to keep improvements proprietary. At least if the propertized improvements relate to an important piece of software, and relate to a significant improvement, all users will have to pay for a license from the defector. Once defections start, the community could quickly collapse: contributors would not keep contributing if defectors could take private possession of their contributions. As discussed below, the conditions in the license contract that are aimed at preventing defection may prove to be unenforceable, or, even if enforceable, unavailing to stop such a collapse.

The open source model fits into a more general economic pattern in the networked environment. The features of this economic logic include lock-in, network externalities, and easy proliferation of information. Open source licensing seems to fit this network economic logic in several respects. In most cases the licensing contract is intended to be "viral" – it is supposed to attach itself to a software "object" and govern rights and obligations with respect to that

---

[38] Eric. S. Raymond, The Cathedral and the Bazaar, <www.tuxedo.org/~esr/writings/cathedral-bazaar/>

information "object" no matter who is using it.[39] In other words, the terms of the contract are intended to proliferate through a chain of distribution.[40] In addition, the attractiveness of the model to the programming community can help lock in a user base and help reach the crucial tipping point. For example, when Netscape released its browser under an open source license, it was with the hope that equipment manufacturers and important users would standardize on it because they could trust that bugs would be fixed and that it would be rapidly improved, and that they could in fact contribute to that improvement. Netscape's strategy was not in furtherance of a noncommodified ideology of sharing, but rather an attempt to get the jump on Microsoft's product, Internet Explorer.

If open source development proves the most efficient method of producing a certain commodity (software), then the logic of the competitive market may make its adoption imperative. In that case, its legal infrastructure – its particular instantiation of PPFK – may be tested. Except in situations where all users must come to explicit agreement with the original licensor, firms and entities that promulgate open source licenses intend the terms of the license to be binding on everyone in the chain of distribution, not just the immediate recipient who would be the promisor in traditional contract law. A recipient who is remote in the chain of distribution, that is, not the original promisor, could argue that a purported contract of this viral variety cannot operate to impose obligations on such a recipient.

Viral contracting is legally dubious. A picture of autonomous consent between contracting parties has hitherto been the policy basis of contract (even though modern contracting often attenuates autonomous consent in practice). The category of terms that one inherits automatically from a predecessor in interest is hard to assimilate to the picture of autonomous consent. In some ways the purported contract is analogous with land obligations – servitudes – of real property law. The analogy can pinpoint the difficulty with viral obligations.

---

[39] See Margaret Jane Radin, Humans, Computers, and Binding Commitment, 75 Indiana L.J. 1125, 1132 (2000).

[40] I should note here that in referring to the license as a contract I am taking one side of a debate. Most legal practitioners do think of copyright licenses as contractual; and, indeed, most licenses of traditional property interests are thought of as contracts, too. The proponents of the "copyleft" license wish to claim that the license is not contractual, however, but rather merely a conditional grant of a property right. The purpose of this characterization is to make the claim that the license grants a defeasible property right, defeasible upon happening of the condition that the user fails to make the source code available or fails to include this condition when entering into a sublicense with another user. Then, the argument runs, the right to use the underlying digital object ceases immediately upon attempted propertization of improvements. The argument has a certain formal logic, usually referred to as the greater includes the lesser, and relied on by conservative ideologues to enlarge the scope of dead hand control: if I can grant you the whole property interest, surely I can grant you a lesser interest, namely that interest that doesn't include the right to keep the interest if you fail to perform my conditions. This formal logic has not been persuasive to courts in the past, because the promise of the recipient to perform affirmative conditions has not been seen as merely part of a property right, but rather the imposition of a burden on the recipient, which must stand or fall under traditional rules of contract.

One of the most difficult issues the common law faced with respect to schemes of servitudes is who has the standing to enforce the obligations. Under certain circumstances it is possible to use a third-party beneficiary theory. Someone who buys a plot and agrees to a servitude may be supposed to intend to benefit those who have previously bought plots. But suppose one owner in the community (or his predecessor in interest) purchases from the original developer later in time than another owner (or her predecessor in interest) against whom he wishes to enforce the obligation. Then there is no contractual nexus between the would-be beneficiary and the owner against whom he wishes to enforce the obligation. The common law solved this problem by requiring that in order to enforce obligations by one remote owner against another, a plan for a scheme of mutual servitudes had to have existed at the time the original sales were made. Thus, whoever bought first would know how many owners he would eventually be obligated to, because the number of plots in the development was determined.

The same is not the case with most varieties of open source licenses. The number of possible users is not fixed at the outset. The inherited obligations impose unknown risk on each user, because the number of other users to whom one becomes obligated remains open-ended and could increase exponentially. In these circumstances, a third-party beneficiary theory might not work. Thus, there is a viable argument that one licensee cannot be held contractually liable to another for violating the restrictions. If so, the current PPFK infrastructure will not support the commodified use of the open source model. Those who are interested in the particular form of incomplete commodification it represents would be well counseled to develop a different legal infrastructure to support it.

V. DATA PRIVACY: HUMAN RIGHT OR PROPERTY RIGHT?

There are many aspects of the privacy debate.[41] I believe it will be helpful to cast portions of the debate in terms of commodification. In my opinion, in this arena

---

[41] In order to clarify the debate, we should at least disaggregate categories of privacy. There is no prima facie reason why one set of descriptions or prescriptions would fit disparate categories involving privacy: medical records; data relating to professional competence and integrity; data that can constitute trade secrets; data about people's buying habits and preferences; data constituting communications between people, or between firms and people. In the case of medical records, a data subject might want every care provider in the world to be able to call up her records at a moment's notice in case she is struck with a serious illness while traveling in a remote locale, yet she would not wish her insurance company or her employer to be able to make adverse judgments based upon them, and would not want to find dozens of spams for diabetic products in her mailbox the day after she is diagnosed with diabetes. In the case of marketing data, it may be more offensive to record and use data on all of someone's information browsing and purchases than on her purchases of most kinds of tangible goods. If I were engaged in a research project that had me searching neo-Nazi hate sites, for example, it would be deeply disturbing to find in my mailbox dozens of spams offering to sell me hate literature. In fact, such a possibility would have a chilling effect on my research.

rhetoric makes a big difference. It makes a big difference whether privacy is thought of as a human right, attaching to persons by virtue of their personhood, or as a property right, something that can be owned and controlled by persons. The difference has to do with the rhetorical significance of alienability. Human rights are presumptively market-inalienable, whereas property rights are presumptively market-alienable.[42]

Consider the situation if some particular type of privacy, for example data regarding a person's information buying habits, is conceived of and treated as a human right. Then to gain access to and use the private data, in ways other than sanctioned by society, violates a human right. We could think of such violation as a tort, if we have in mind torts against personal integrity rather than against business interests. If a defendant wanted to argue that the data subject had waived or transferred the right, probably by means of a contract, such an argument would face an uphill battle. As a human right, at least presumptively the right would be non-waivable and non-transferable. Human rights are rooted in a noncommodified understanding of personhood and the attributes and context necessary to constitute and maintain personhood. Because the rhetoric of human rights tends to assume inalienability, whoever wants to argue for alienability has a substantial burden. It is not the case, of course, that such rights are never in practice held to have been waived. Rather, because the rhetoric leans toward inalienability, such holdings at least require some argumentative footwork. (Of course, too, if such footwork comes to be routinely performed, then the concept of inalienable human rights will be undermined.)

The situation is reversed if data privacy is conceived of and treated as a property right of the data subject. In that case, to gain access to and use the private data, in ways other than those sanctioned by society, is a violation of a property right. We could think of this violation as a tort, if we have in mind torts against property or business interests – like theft of trade secrets – rather than against personal integrity. In this case, a defendant who wanted to argue that the subject's privacy rights had been transferred or waived would have a much easier time. In the PPFK system, transferability (alienability) of property rights is presumed. The market system depends both upon private property and free contract; neither can function without the other to support a market. They are tightly connected rhetorically as well as in the actual world of exchange. Some thinkers believe that alienability is inherent in the concept of private property. At minimum, once something is conceived of as private property, arguing for market-inalienability is an uphill battle.

The difference in the presumptive starting points of these two rhetorical perspectives may say a lot about the difference between the EU and the U.S. when

---

[42] See Contested Commodities, supra note 2, chapter 2; see also, Margaret Jane Radin, Market-Inalienability, 100 Harvard L. Rev. 1849 (1987).

it comes to privacy. The data marketers in the U.S. argue that data they have collected (by the sweat of their corporate brows) belongs to them, not to the subjects. Thus, some consumer advocates in the U.S. believe that legislation declaring that the property right belongs to the data subject will provide protection for privacy. According to the EU view, which treats privacy more like a noncommodified human right and less like a commodified property right, this would be inadequate to protect data subjects.[43]

Indeed, defeating the property claims of the data marketers and vesting the property right in the data subject instead would be a Pyrrhic victory. In either case the issue of waiver and transferability – market-alienability – is paramount. It appears that online commerce will be governed more and more by contracts between providers and users, and less by a priori (default) entitlement structures.[44]

Of course, there will be lots of issues about whether what purports to be a contract actually is one. For example, if a website has an interior page of fine print that says that anyone who accesses the site waives data privacy rights, would that be binding? If the site has a box saying "I accept these terms," and you must click it before having access to the site, does that make the fine print binding? If the site offers you $2 off its product if you agree to waive all your privacy rights, is that binding? In the PPFK framework, we would presume the waiver is valid. If you want to argue that it is not, you have an uphill battle; you can try to argue unconscionability, for example. On the other hand, in a human rights framework, we (at least if we are true to the premises of the underlying conceptual scheme) would presume the waiver is invalid. As mentioned above, if you want to argue that it is valid, you have an uphill battle. You could try to argue that the person understood all the particular conditions under the circumstances, and autonomously chose to relinquish her right.

It might appear that the difference in rhetorical perspectives can be understood in terms of opting in versus opting out. It seems that opting in to a regime of sharing one's personal data is more consonant with the idea that data privacy is a personal or human right, and having to opt out is more consonant with the idea that data privacy is a property right. Yet both opt-in and opt-out can be part of a PPFK scheme; it just depends on whether the property rights start out with the

---

[43] Under the Rome Convention for The Protection of Human Rights and Fundamental Freedoms, Article 8(1), "Everyone has the right to respect for his private and family life, his home and his correspondence." For an elaboration of the basis of the EU's view of information privacy, see Paul M. Schwartz & Joel R. Reidenberg, Data Privacy Law: A Study of United States Data Protection 39-42 (1998); Neil Netanel, Cyberspace Self-Governance, 88 Calif. L. Rev. 395, 474–75 (2000).

[44] This is true, I think, for two reasons: (1) non-harmonization of entitlement structures in the fact of globalization; (2) standardization of terms. For discussion of standardization of terms, see Radin, Humans, Computers, and Binding Commitment, supra note 78 at 1150–1153; and Margaret Jane Radin, Online Standardization and the Integration of Text and Machine, 70 Fordham L. Rev. 1125 (2002).

data subject (in an opt-in scheme) or start out with the data aggregators and marketers (in the opt-out scheme). Because waiver or transfer can be easy if standardized contracts are held valid, waivers or transfers can turn out to be ubiquitous, in which case it will not much matter where the rights started out. What will matter is where they end up.

In some circumstances even an opt-in regime will be troublesome for those who see privacy as a human right. Consider this opt-in regime: Bank says an account will cost you $5 per month, and its site contains a privacy statement promising non-use of your data, but if you click a box that says Bank can use your data at its discretion, the account will be free. Now consider the corresponding opt-out regime: The account is free, but the Bank's fine print says that it will use your data at its discretion, or you can click a box to pay $5 per month for non-use of your data. Especially if the bank is providing a service that you cannot do without (and it has no competitors with better terms, perhaps because terms are standard in the industry), then there may be little to choose between these two: either way, you will pay $5 to keep your data private. True, cognitive research on the offer-asking problem suggests that when you possess the entitlement at the outset you are more likely to hang on to it.[45] Yet cognitive research also suggests that the initial entitlement regime could be troubling too, undervalued by the holders because of simple lack of information, distributional concerns, and possible heuristic biases (other than offer-asking asymmetry).

I can perhaps unpack this with a more familiar type of example.

Suppose the seller was asking people to waive tort liability for a dangerous product (opt-in to a regime of bearing risk of personal injury) or to purchase personal injury protection (opt-out of a regime in which otherwise user bears risk). If there is simple lack of information, then consumers just don't know what they are risking, so they may mistakenly check the box and take the $5.[46] If we suspect distributional bias, we might think only poor people would opt in to the risky regime, because the money is worth it to them; or that they would stay in the risky regime even if opt-out is available, because they do not have the money to opt out. If we suspect heuristic bias, we might think people who opt into taking the risk might not understand exactly what it means to them until the risk

---

[45] See, e.g., Cass Sunstein, Incommensurability and Valuation in Law, 92 Mich. L. Rev. 779 (1994).

[46] In the data privacy case, information asymmetry may be prevalent. The user may not realize the extent to which data relating to her will become a commodity in market transactions, nor the scope of the personal data that is divulged. A user who opts into divulging limited sets of information on a variety of what appear to be distinct sites may be unaware of aggregation and data mining. Can a user, prompted at several points to consent to commodification of discrete chunks of information, be deemed to have consented to the revelation of traits discernable only as emergent properties after aggregation and mining?

actually comes to pass.[47] Is loss of privacy rights significantly analogous to injury from a dangerous product? That may depend upon whether one conceives of privacy invasion more in terms of a human right or in terms of a property right.

As the debate proceeds about how to conceive of and protect digital data, at least we should realize that we have had these arguments before, in the offline world, about such things as whether consumers can waive product liability, or whether form leases can have tenants waive implied warranty of habitability and live in a cheaper but unsafe and unhealthy dwelling. On the one side, PPFK rhetoric argues that users have the right to waive or transfer whatever rights they have, for a consideration; on the other side, human rights rhetoric argues that users cannot waive rights that are important to personal integrity and self-constitution, at least unless we are very sure that they are doing so in possession of full understanding of the consequences. Debate will be advanced if we work on what sort of an incomplete commodification is appropriate for various aspects of privacy; that is, which aspects of the individual's interests in various kinds of data privacy are more appropriately conceived of as human (personal) rights and which are more appropriately conceived of as property (economic) rights.

Conclusion

In the U.S., even scholars who are committed to preserving a public domain and a realm of human freedom of communication and interaction often seem to couch arguments in terms of property rights. This could be partly due to the political attractiveness of private property in the U.S. and the entrenched general notion that nominally private-law solutions to problems are preferable. It could be partly due to the notion that it takes a strong right to beat another strong right. For example, if, taking the commodification of free speech to its limit, data aggregators argue that they have a "free speech" right to use the data they collect however they wish, it might appear that one could juxtapose against that a "property right" of the data subject to prevent them from doing so.[48] These strategic concerns may explain the property rhetoric of the U.S. advocates for fair use, open source licensing, and data privacy, but the rhetoric seems puzzling to

---

[47] See Robert E. Scott, Error and Rationality in Individual Decisionmaking: An Essay on the Relationship between Cognitive Illusions and the Management of Choices, 59 S. Cal. L. Rev. 329 (1986); Ward Edwards and Detlof Von Winterfeldt, Cognitive Illusions and their Implications for the Law, 59 S. Cal. L. Rev. 225 (1986).

[48] See the enlightening – and frightening – discussion in Julie E. Cohen, Examined Lives: Informational Privacy and the Subject as Object, 52 Stanford L. Rev. 1373 (2000).

non-U.S. colleagues. While I do not want to argue that such strategic concerns can never justify propertization, I do want to argue that propertization brings with it the conceptual structures of commodification, and should at least give us pause. I hope that this essay might engender further thought about the conflicting conceptual schemes – commodification and noncommodification – reflected in our political and cultural commitments surrounding control and use of knowledge and communication. I hope the notion of pervasive incomplete commodification might help us begin to think through what mixtures will improve our situation, without collapsing rhetorically into either one pole or the other.

Electronic Commerce and Free Speech

Jessica Litman*

Internet historians studying the end of the 20th century will probably conclude that 1998 was the year that American entertainment and information industries achieved their initial objectives in their takeover of Netspace. In 1998, while the public's attention on Internet-related issues was absorbed with smut control, and the media debated the pros and cons of censorship and hard-core porn, big business persuaded politicians of both political parties to transfer much of the basic architecture of the Internet into business' hands, the better to promote the transformation of as much of the Net as possible into a giant American shopping mall. 1998 was the year that the White House handed over the keys to the Internet domain name system to the private sector, conditioned on a promise that domain name space would henceforth be more hospitable to trademark owners.[1] That same year, the United States Patent Office gave out patents covering Internet-based coupon-delivery systems that targeted specific recipients based on user preferences calculated from clickstream data, and the technology underlying P3P, a privacy protocol developed by the World Wide Web Consortium.[2] 1998 was the year that copyright owner interests persuaded Congress to enact a codicil to the copyright law giving copyright holders new tools to control the public's uses of their works.[3] Also in 1998, American industry convinced the U.S. government that

---

* An earlier version of this paper appeared in 1 Ethics and Information Technology 213 (1999). I'm grateful to Jon Weinberg for his many perceptive suggestions. I'd also like to thank James Boyle, Perry Cook, Larry Lessig, Stanley Katz and Ejan Mackaay for their helpful comments on earlier drafts. Internet citations were current as of June 21, 2000.

[1] See Memorandum of Understanding Between the U.S. Department of Commerce and the Internet Corporation for Assigned Names and Numbers, Nov. 25, 1998, URL: <http://www.ntia.doc.gov/ntiahome/domainname/icann-memorandum.htm>.

[2] See U.S. Pat. No. 5,761,648; U.S. Pat. No. 5, 848, 396; U.S. Pat. No. 5,862,325; U.S. Pat. No. 5, 832, 212. The Internet patent gold rush has continued. See Seth Shulman, Software Patents Tangle the Web, Technology Review, March/April 2000, at URL: <http://www.techreview.com/articles/ma00/shulman.htm>; Rochelle Cooper Dreyfuss, Are Business Method Patents Bad for Business?, 16 Santa Clara Computer & High Tech'y L.J. 263 (forthcoming 2000).

[3] See Digital Millennium Copyright Act, Pub. L. No. 105–304, 112 Stat. 2861 (1998).

N. Elkin-Koren and N.W. Netanel (eds.), The Commodification of Information, 23–42.
© 2002 *Jessica Litman. Printed in Great Britain.*

avoiding the enactment of new legal protections for data privacy was worth the risk of a trade war with Europe.[4] A key theme running through the transformation was the expectation that the Internet could be used as a medium for the advertisement of (American) goods and services worldwide, and, moreover, could itself become a marketplace for the worldwide sale of (American) information and entertainment to consumers.

Back in 1992, the United States had feared it was a fading world power, hobbled by its budget deficit. The U.S. might have built the Internet, but it couldn't afford to *run* the Internet. If the Internet were to be developed into a new engine of economic growth, the private sector would need to bear the expense.[5] The Clinton administration devised an Internet policy based on supplying incentives for American business to invest in what it called the "National Information Infrastructure," and smoothing the way for commercial exploitation of its possibilities.[6] Throughout the Clinton administration, under the aegis of the U.S. Department of Commerce, the government identified aspects of the Internet that might be transferred to private sector control, did what it could to make those aspects attractive targets for private sector capture, and adopted policies designed to facilitate the transfer.[7] Clinton administration policy documents emphasized the new potential for electronic commerce in information products.[8] To realize that potential, the administration supported measures to enhance the degree to which valuable information and ideas could be treated as proprietary.[9] Meanwhile, a number of businesses worked to make sure that the Internet would be a comfortable and familiar environment in which established conventional companies could do business; and one that would not be unduly receptive to new, upstart high-tech businesses that might take market share away from 1998's market leaders.

---

[4] See Edmund L. Andrews, European Law Aims to Protect Privacy of Personal Data, N.Y. Times, Oct. 26, 1998, at URL: <http://www.nytimes.com/library/tech/98/10/biztech/articles/26privacy.html>; Joel Reidenberg, Restoring Americans' Privacy in Electronic Commerce, 14 Berkeley Tech. L. J. 771 (1999). Eventually, Europe blinked. See, e.g., Privacy Safe Harbor Privacy Agreement Seen As Only the Beginning of Global Policy Debate, 5 Electronic Commerce & Law 625 (June 14, 2000).

[5] See White House Information Infrastructure Task Force, The National Information Infrastructure: Agenda for Action, Oct. 19, 1994, URL: <http://metalab.unc.edu/nii/NII-Agenda-for-Action.html>.

[6] See, e.g., Remarks by Vice President Al Gore at National Press Club, December 21, 1993, URL: <http://www.iitf.nist.gov/documents/speeches/gore_speech122193.html>; The National Information Infrastructure: Agenda for Action, supra note 5.

[7] See U.S. White House, The Framework for Global Electronic Commerce (July 1, 1997), URL: <http://www.whitehouse.gov/WH/New/Commerce/read.html>.

[8] See, e.g., The National Information Infrastructure: Agenda for Action, supra note 5.

[9] See, e.g., Information Infrastructure Task Force, Intellectual Property and the National Information Infrastructure: The Report of the Working Group on Intellectual Property Rights 211–238 (1995).

I.

If you look at which Internet-related bills have made it through Congress and which have not;[10] if you read the White House's *First Annual Report on Electronic Commerce*;[11] if you follow the trade press accounts of who is suing whom, it's hard to miss a pronounced slant toward making commercial speech the favored flavor of discourse on the Internet. The signs that things were moving in that direction were there several years ago,[12] but most of us didn't take them very seriously. In our everyday milieu, after all, commercial speech had long been ubiquitous. Ads were everywhere: in our magazines, schools, newspapers and hospitals. Some of them were explicit; others were rendered more coyly. Manufacturers, for instance, paid huge sums for the privilege of being the candy that ET eats, the shades that the Men in Black wear, or the car that James Bond drives.[13] The idea that vast expanses of ads and shopping opportunities would be just a mouse click away seemed uninteresting.

In thinking about the effect of networked digital technology on the flow of information in general and freedom of expression in particular, most of us were struck instead by its implications for noncommercial speech. The most important factor seemed to be that the Internet enabled people to speak inexpensively. Once the capital investment of building the Internet in the first place had been sunk, people could speak to people all over at essentially no marginal cost, and they did.[14] A large number of the speakers were different people from the folks who spoke in conventional media, and what they had to say was often not the same stuff that gets said in conventional media.[15] Most obviously, there were lots of volunteers eager to express themselves to anyone willing to read or view what they

---

[10] See Courtney Macavinta, Congress passes slew of high-tech bills, C|net News.com, Nov. 24, 1999, at URL: <http://news.cnet.com/news/0-1005-200-1463637.html>; Internet and Tech Bills Become Law, Tech L. J., Oct. 22, 1998 at URL: <http://www.techlawjournal.com/internet/81022omn.htm>; Tech Bills that Failed in the 105th Congress, Tech L.J., Oct. 26, 1998, at URL: <http://www.techlawjournal.com/internet/81026.htm>.

[11] U.S. Government Working Group on Electronic Commerce, First Annual Report (1998).

[12] See, e.g., Michael Goldberg, Why Jim Clark Loves Mosaic, WIRED 2.10, Oct. 1994, at 118; Joshua Quittner, Billions Registered, WIRED 2.10, October 1994 at 50.

[13] See Jessica Litman, Breakfast with Batman: The Public Interest in the Advertising Age, 108 Yale L.J. 1717, 1731-35 (1999).

[14] That sort of pricing structure isn't hardwired into the architecture, of course, and there's no particular reason why the price structure couldn't change to a more exclusionary schedule of tariffs if it turned out to be profitable to do so. Major media businesses might well welcome such a change, because of the entry barriers it would erect to speakers that are not (or not yet) major media businesses.

[15] See Jessica Litman, Copyright Noncompliance (Or Why We Can't "Just Say Yes" to Licensing), 29 N.Y.U. J. Int'l L. & Politics 237, 247-52 (1997).

posted.[16] And even when the search tools for finding the content one wanted on the Internet were unbelievably primitive, one could, with a little work and ingenuity, find all sorts of content that was worth reading and viewing.

Much of this was due to the magic of large numbers. It may seem to me as if I'm the only person out there who wants to make vegetable soup but is allergic to carrots, celery and beans, say, but it isn't true. You network together enough people, and you find several of me; we can trade recipes.[17]

Some of this was the magic of what Eugene Volokh has called "cheap speech."[18] I might have a half dozen recipes that I'd like to share with the world. They're good recipes, but not good enough to persuade some publisher to bring out a cookbook full of recipes like them, and, even if they were, I'm not going to try to shop them to a publisher, since that takes time and money and effort and I have a day job. But typing them up and sending them off to some recipe archive in the sky is incredibly easy.[19] It's precisely what I want to do on some rainy afternoon when I'm putting off grading exams, and I'm bored with computer solitaire. While I'm there, I can read someone else's.

Some of this derived from the magic of digital technology. Hypertext makes it possible to say some things in some ways that would be difficult without hypertext. Online chat is different from a conference call. The ability to interact with the content you're reading changes your relationship with the content and that, eventually, changes both the way the content is written and displayed and what the content means.[20] The ability to interact with the recipients of your content inspires distinct expression.[21]

In any event, in relatively short order, there was lots of content on the Internet that was different from stuff available in conventional media.[22] Many of the

---

[16] Even before the invention of the World Wide Web, there were thousands of Usenet news newsgroups, covering almost every conceivable subject, some of which received hundreds of posts each day from all over the world. See Ed Krol, The Whole Internet 151–185 (1994). See generally Lost In Usenet, URL: <http://www.faqs.org/usenet/>.

[17] See the Usenet food group rec.food.recipes, URL: <news:rec.food.recipes>. See also, e.g., alt.bread.recipes; alt.food.chocolate; alt.recipes.babies; alt.recipes.hawaii; rec.food.cuisine.jewish; rec.food.recipes.babies; rec.food.recipes.cats; rec.food.recipes.dogs.puppies.

[18] Eugene Volokh, Cheap Speech and What It Will Do, 104 Yale L.J. 1805 (1995).

[19] See, e.g., URL: <http://recipes.alastra.com/soups/fresh-mushroom.html>; URL: <http://recipes.alastra.com/microwave/poached-pears.html>.

[20] See M. Ethan Katsh, Rights, Camera, Action: Cyberspatial Settings and the First Amendment, 194 Yale L.J. 1681 (1995). It takes a little while to adjust to the implications of the new medium. You need to develop new criteria for evaluating the reliability of the content you're reading: nifty graphics, for instance, don't necessarily mean that the speaker knows whereof she speaks.

[21] Opportunities for sharing material have proved unexpectedly compelling. The wildly successful Napster software was invented by a college freshman seeking to combine music file sharing with the features of Internet Relay Chat. See Napster (Company Profile) at URL: <http://www.napster.com/company.html>. Napster acquired 10 million registered users in its first eight months of operation. See Matt Richtel, Napster Has a New Interim Chief and Gets a $15 Million Investment, New York Times, May 23, 2000, at C27.

[22] See Litman, Copyright Noncompliance, supra note 15, at 247–50.

speakers on the Internet were different from the market leaders in the conventional media. We started hearing talk about the vast possibilities of a world in which everyone was her own publisher, in which distributors and other intermediaries were unnecessary, in which citizens need no longer rely on the news media in order to make political decisions, but could engage in true participatory democracy.[23]

Legal scholars responded with a crop of scholarship on how the Internet would advance freedom of expression unless the government clamped down on all sorts of speech because it was afraid of smut.[24] The media portrayed the Internet as a vast source of accessible pornography,[25] and Congress moved to plant anti-pornography flags in the sand.[26] Lawmakers came up with an endless series of heavy-handed proposals to stop porn.[27] Whether Internet services, web sites, libraries, or schools should be permitted or required to protect children (or adults) from noxious content was an accessible issue, easily debated in the popular press.[28] Conventional and digital news media, along with libraries and schools, became parties in lawsuits challenging Internet censorship, and reported copiously on the suits' details.[29] We paid too much attention to those.[30] We were so busy watching

---

[23] See, e.g., Volokh, supra note 18.

[24] See, e.g., Jerry Berman and Daniel J. Weitzner, Abundance and User Control: Renewing the Democratic Heart of the First Amendment in the Age of Interactive Media, 104 Yale L.J. 1619 (1995).

[25] See, e.g, Sex Finds Lucrative Home on the Web, USA Today, Sept. 3, 1997, URL: <http://www.usatoday.com/life/cyber/tech/ctb128.htm>; Philip Elmer-Dewitt, On a Screen Near You: Cyberporn, Time Magazine, July 3, 1995, at 38.

[26] See Communications Decency Act of 1996, Pub. L. No. 104–104, 110 Stat. 56 (1996) [CDA]; Reno v. ACLU, 521 U.S. 844 (1997).

[27] See CDA; Child Online Protection Act, Pub. L. No. 105–277, 112 Stat. 2681 (1998); S. 1482, 105th Cong., 1st Sess. (1997); S. 97, 106th Cong., 1st Sess. (1999). The Clinton administration cleverly recast the debate over content controls as an opportunity for private sector investment in content control software products. See Jonathan Weinberg, Rating the Net, 19 Hastings Comm/Ent L.J. 453 (1997).

[28] See American Library Association v. Pataki, 969 F. Supp. 160 (S.D.N.Y. 1997); Pamela Mendels, Michigan Law Leaves Library's Internet Filters Open to Debate, N.Y. Times CyberTimes, Aug. 6, 1999 at URL: <http://www.nytimes.com/library/tech/99/08/cyber/articles/06michigan.html>.

[29] See, e.g., ACLU v. Reno, 31 F. Supp. 2d 473 (E.D.Pa. 1999), aff'd, 2000 U.S. App. LEXIS 14419 (3d Cir 2000); Cyberspace v. Engler, 55 F. Supp. 737 (E.D. MI 1999); Mainstream Loudoun v. Loudoun Country Library Board of Trustees, 24 F. Supp. 2d 552 (E.D.Va. 1998); American Library Association v. Pataki, 969 F. Supp. 160 (S.D.N.Y. 1997).

[30] Lest it seem that I am minimizing the threat to public decency and morals posed by the availability of pornography on the Internet, I should clarify my views: I don't think the threat to public decency and morals is especially significant, and see no particular reason for deeming it more pressing than the threat posed by other sorts of content that is prohibited by other nations but routinely tolerated, even celebrated, in the U.S. See, e.g., German Criminal Code § 130; German Law on the Dissemination of Publications Morally Harmful to Youth; Swedish Personal Data Act (1998:204); Singapore Broadcasting Authority, Internet Code of Practice, URL: <http://www.sba.gov.sg/internet.htm>. See generally Amber Jene Sayle, Note: Net Nation and The Digital Revolution: Regulation of Offensive Material for a New Community, 18 Wis. Int'l L.J. 257 (2000).

the smut laws that we didn't pay enough attention to the other stuff going on at the same time.

II.

The talk about a world without publishers, record companies, motion picture studios, and software distributors also came to the attention of publishers, record companies, motion picture studios, and software distributors, who understandably didn't like that picture. While most of us were watching the smut bills on their constitutional journey, the representatives of commercial media managed to accomplish a fair amount to protect themselves from being eclipsed any time soon.

Commercial media found the Internet frightening, and with good reason. Entertainment and information merchants tend to express that fear as a fear of massive piracy, but piracy turns out to be not so hard a nut to crack. Piracy over digital networks leaves incriminating electron trails; you can track it down and avenge it.[31] Increasingly, moreover, there are tools to prevent it. A variety of technological locks, booby-traps and other devices have been deployed that make unauthorized use difficult for the huge majority of users, few of whom are

---

Even those who believe that Internet pornography causes incalculable harm, however, would probably concede that porn makes irresistible politics. A vote to punish pornography is cheap and risk-free. Perhaps for that reason, arguments against Internet pornography have been offered in support of a wide variety of legislation with no intrinsic pornography connection. See, e.g., 145 Cong. Rec. S.9749 (July 29, 1999) (statement of Senator Hatch introducing the Domain Name Piracy Prevention Act of 1999).

[31] See Software and Information Industry Association, Seven Warning Signs of Piracy: How ISPs Can Protect Themselves, URL: < http://www.siia.net/piracy/policy/int_7.asp >. BMI, for example, has dispatched a "Musicbot" to sniff out and measure the incidence of unlicensed music on the Internet. See BMI MusicBot℠ Version 2.0 Announced, July 14, 1998, at URL: < http://www.bmi.com/iama/webcaster/technology/musicbot.asp >. The Association of American Publishers has introduced a digital watermarking project that it characterizes as "branding" texts so that their owners can always find them. See The Digital Object Identifier, at URL: < http://www.doi.org >. The Recording Industry Association of America has persuaded consumer electronics manufacturers to incorporate copyright-protection technology into portable digital music players that will "detect illegitimately distributed music." See Secure Digital Music Initiative, Guide to the SDMI Portable Device Specification Part 1, Version 1.0 (July 8 1999) at 3, URL: < http://www.sdmi.org/download/port_device_spec_guide.pdf >. The RIAA also touts its ability to identify and shut down online music pirates. See RIAA, Education, Innovation and Enforcement, URL: < http://www.riaa.org/Protect-Online-3.cfm >. The Napster litigation has demonstrated the ease with which the massive unauthorized exchange of digital files may be tracked, and the identity of individual infringers may be traced. See, e.g., John Borland, Metallica fingers 335,435 Napster Users, May 1, 2000 at URL: < http://news.cnet.com/news/0-1005-200-1798138.html >; Napster, Information About Metallica's Request to Disable Napster Users, URL: < http://www.napster.com/metallica-notice.html >.

dedicated hackers.[32] The really scary thing was not, I think, piracy, but obsolescence. In the long term, other media might grow up and eclipse the current market leaders, just as player pianos yielded to radios in the 1920s, and movies superseded live theatre in the 1930s and 1940s.[33] Even in the short term, the Internet posed a threat, because it facilitated an enormous amount of free speech that could divert potential consumers from the speech they had to pay for.

When I speak of free speech, I mean speech that doesn't cost any money. To distill it down to the simplest formulation: free speech has the potential to squeeze out expensive speech. Not completely, of course. There's plenty of information out there that isn't fungible. I buy hardcover books. I subscribe to particular periodicals and wouldn't be happy with their competitors. But a lot of information is fungible enough. I don't really care who tells me the weather. All of the weather reporters get their data from the National Weather Service, and if I have a choice between free weather and pay weather, I'll take the free weather every time. Free, after all, is free. If I can get similar information from a free database and a proprietary database, I'll usually pick the free one, at least if I'm the person who's paying. If some scholarly work exists both in expensive bound form and free digital form, I may well be willing to buy the book to have it on my shelf. But I surely won't buy two copies to keep one at home and another at work. And when it comes to assigning it to my students, I'm likely to pick the free electronic version.[34]

Free speech may drive out speech people have to pay for. At first, that doesn't seem like a problem. Our entire free-expression jurisprudence is built on the premise that the more speech easily available to the most people, the better.[35] If, however, you happen to be in the business of selling speech, a glut of free stuff (especially high quality free stuff) has the potential to run you out of business. If you are a publicly-traded company that employs a bunch of people, pays your taxes, gives back to your community, and makes campaign contributions to your elected representatives, then it's easy to persuade policymakers that your financial health is important to the general welfare, and anything that threatens to drive you out of business is a threat to the public interest.

So, we have a puzzle. Do we continue to advance the free expression agenda at the cost of significant economic consequences, or do we moderate our commitment to free speech with a generous dollop of economic realism? We haven't had to worry about this before, because speaking in a meaningful way to a large audience was expensive, and people couldn't afford to do serious mass

---

[32] See Julie Cohen, Copyright and the Jurisprudence of Self Help, 13 Berkeley Tech. L.J. 1089 1092–96 (1998).

[33] See Jessica Litman, Revising Copyright Law for the Information Age, 75 Ore. L. Rev. 19, 27–30 (1995).

[34] The hornbook I recommend to my copyright students, for example, is Terry Carroll, Copyright F.A.Q. (1994), URL: <http://www.tjc.com/copyright/>, available only online and only for free.

speaking for free for very long.[36] Now that it's much cheaper, though, it doesn't take much to give out information to the whole world, every day, for free, for years, and people do. Of course much of it is dreck. But, there's the magic of large numbers again: some of it is excellent by any standard.[37] When we were imagining the Internet, we didn't fully appreciate the implications of that. Representatives of conventional media saw it before we did.

Conventional media wanted to market their own brands of new improved digital media, but many discovered that they couldn't persuade readers to pay for them. They tried a variety of different strategies. One popular scheme was to give out free samples: "this online publication will be free for a trial period, but then you'll have to buy a subscription."[38] The date for paying kept slipping. Some electronic publications initiated a paid subscription policy, and then decided to discontinue it when their readership dropped.[39] They tried advertising. That works okay, if the ads don't take too long to load. Some people actually read them. But, you know what? The small upstart speakers can sell advertising, too. And they do. Go surf some college students' web pages – you'll find banner ads.[40] Or check out individual home pages on geocities.com, an Internet service provider that inserts ads into all its subscribers' web sites.[41] Here's the bottom line: If you are a distributor of information or entertainment who wants to sell content over the Internet, it isn't going to be enough to arm yourself with advanced weapons to prevent piracy. There are too many volunteers out there. You need to get rid of them, or marginalize them, or make life difficult for them, in order to compete on your own terms.

Academics and civil libertarians have been watching the pornography follies, so many of us didn't notice when commercial content owners scored some significant progress in herding free speakers off the Net. There's an important synergy between persuading the government to give your industry some friendly new laws or regulations, and using new and old legal tools to make life more difficult or expensive for inconvenient competitors who aren't necessarily doing anything

---

[35] See Whitney v. California, 274 U.S. 357, 372 (1927) (Brandeis, J. concurring); Cohen v. California, 403 U.S. 15, 24 (1971); Reno v. ACLU, 521 U.S. at 874–82.

[36] See Jonathan Weinberg, Questioning Broadcast Regulation, 86 Mich. L. Rev. 1269, 1271–85 (1988).

[37] See Litman, Copyright Non-Compliance, supra note 15, at 247–251.

[38] See Ashley Dunn, Surf & Turf: In the Free Web Orchard, Who Will Pay for Fruit?, N.Y. Times CyberTimes, July 24, 1996.

[39] See Alex Kuczynski, Slate Ends Its 10-Month Experiment With Subscriptions, N.Y. Times, Feb. 15, 1999, at C11.

[40] Banner ad swap networks and sponsor-supported banner ad placement services have sprung up all over the web to facilitate free or low cost banner advertising on any web site willing to volunteer to host ads. See, e.g., Banner Network, URL: < http://adnetwork.linkexchange.com/ >; BannerSwap, URL: < http://www.bannerswap.com/ >.

[41] See Yahoo! GeoCities Terms of Service ¶ 11, URL: < http://docs.yahoo.com/info/terms/geoterms.html >.

illegal. What's been notable about the past few years is that businesses have been able to combine the two strategies to make the Internet a much safer place to sell.

III.

On the regulation front, once we look past the familiar high drama over pornography, it appears that both the Clinton administration and Congress have been falling all over themselves to help business move its business onto the Internet.[42] The dynamic relied on the government's conception of the Internet as an engine to drive the United States economy. What the engine was supposed to do was to transform the existing Internet infrastructure into a giant American shopping mall and multiplex in the sky. The government's regulatory strategy was to identify what needed to be done to facilitate electronic commerce, to do that, and to do as little as possible except for that.[43]

The rhetoric deployed to support this strategy changed over time. Back in the early years of the Clinton administration, when the only folks who actually used the Internet were students and geeks, it was common to describe the Internet as if it were a collection of empty pipes, with no content anyone would want to read, just waiting to be turned into a 500-channel television transmission machine.[44] People insisted that nobody would subscribe to an Internet service unless there were something to see there, and nobody would post any content worth reading unless the poster believed it would make a profit, so we needed to redesign the legal infrastructure to ensure that folks had control over what they posted and were confident of making money.[45]

While that story was making the rounds, of course, millions of people signed up

---

[42] See, e.g., Framework for Global Electronic Commerce, supra note 7; Cybersquatting and Consumer Protection: Ensuring Domain Name Integrity: Hearing on S. 1255 Before the Senate Comm. on the Judiciary, 106th Cong, 1st Sess. (July 22, 1999).

[43] See U.S. Government Working Group on Electronic Commerce, supra note 11.

[44] See, e.g., United States Patent & Trademark Office, United States Department of Commerce, National Information Infrastructure Task Force Working Group on Intellectual Property, Public Hearing on Intellectual Property Issues Involved in the National Information Infrastructure Initiative (Thursday, November 18, 1993) (testimony of Steven J. Metalitz, Information Industry Council); Information Infrastructure Task Force, Intellectual Property and the National Information Infrastructure: A Preliminary Draft of the Report of the Working Group on Intellectual Property Rights 6–7 (1994).

[45] See, e.g., Bruce A. Lehman, Copyright Fair Use and the National Information Infrastructure (address delivered at George Mason University, Feb. 23, 1996), Red Rock Eater News Service (Feb. 25, 1999), URL: <http://commons.somewhere.com/rre/1996/Copyright.Fair.Use.and.t.html>; Copyright Protection on the Internet: Hearing Before the Courts and Intellectual Property Subcomm. of the House Comm. on the Judiciary, 104th Cong, 2d Sess. (Feb. 7, 1996) (testimony of Barbara Munder for the Information Industry Association).

for Internet access, Internet-related stocks went through the roof, advertisers started buying banner ads on college students' homemade web pages, and company after company included a URL for its own web page in its television commercials. Then we began to hear a new story about how, since the Internet was borderless, folks from other countries were stealing American stuff, and we needed to change the legal infrastructure to foil the pirates.[46] To stop all those foreigners from stealing valuable intellectual property from important companies, we needed to show our trading partners that we were also taking an unyielding stance against domestic pirates (and, anyway, the domestic pirates were stealing valuable intellectual property from important companies, too.)[47]

That story sold. A coalition of conventional media interests persuaded Congress to enact the *Digital Millennium Copyright Act* to help them out.[48] The effect (and, I would argue, the intent) of that law is to give commercial content owners a break in the form of entry barriers against upstart new competitors.[49] The law has a cornucopia of measures that are supposed to prevent piracy, and a large number of narrow, detailed carve-outs for identified interests who are scrupulous about crossing a bunch of Ts and dotting a slew of Is. Of course, you have to know about the Ts and the Is. Among other things, what that means is that it is now exceedingly perilous to do any sort of business over the Internet unless you have a copyright lawyer looking over your shoulder.

The *Digital Millennium Copyright Act* is, by any measure, an ugly law. I defy anyone to understand its major provisions on a first (or fifth) careful reading.[50] It

---

[46] See NII Copyright Protection Act of 1995: Hearing on H.R. 2441 Before the Subcomm. On Courts and Intellectual Property of the House Comm. on the Judiciary, 104th Cong., 2d Sess. (Feb. 8, 1996) (opening statement of Rep. Carlos Moorehead); id. (testimony of Jack Valenti, Motion Picture Association of America).

[47] See WIPO Copyright Treaties Implementation Act and Online Copyright Liability Limitation Act: Hearing on H.R. 2281 and H.R. 2180 Before the Subcomm. On Courts and Intellectual Property of the House Comm. on the Judiciary, 105th Cong., 1st Sess. (Sept. 17, 1997)(testimony of Robert Holleyman, BSA); id. (testimony of Hilary B. Rosen, RIAA).

[48] Digital Millennium Copyright Act, Pub. L. No. 105-304 (1998), codified at 17 U.S.C. § 101 et. seq. [DMCA]. See Jessica Litman, Digital Copyright and Information Policy, in Kraig M. Hill et. al., Globalization Of Intellectual Property In The 21st Century (CASRIP Publication Series # 4) 299 (1999).

[49] Along with dozens of other copyright law professors, I spent time and energy over the past six years trying to influence the shape of the copyright law Congress enacted to expand copyright to networked digital technology. And, along with my compatriots, I have to confess that we were snookered. We were outbid, outplayed and outclassed. Although some would debate the point, I have absolutely no hesitation in confessing that the Digital Millennium Copyright Act enacted by Congress in 1998 is kinder to commercial content owners and much, much worse for the public in general than the original law proposed by Bruce Lehman's infamous White Paper. Compare H.R. 2441, 104th Cong., 1st Sess. (1995) with DMCA, Pub. L. No. 105-304, 112 Stat. 2861 (1998).

[50] The most comprehensible summary of the DMCA comes from the Register of Copyrights and is available on the Copyright Office web site. See United States Copyright Office, The Digital Millennium Copyright Act of 1998: U.S. Copyright Office Summary, URL: <http://lcweb.loc.gov/copyright/legislation/dmca.pdf>.

takes general principles, like "fairness," and translates them into exceptionally long, complicated, wordy, counter-intuitive and internally inconsistent proscriptions. One example is the act's newfangled substitute for the traditional copyright fair use privilege, which requires a triennial formal administrative proceeding in order to gain a legal privilege to make unauthorized uses that, because of other provisions in the act, will not be technically feasible in any event.[51]

Another example is the supposed safe harbor for Internet service providers whose subscribers, without the service providers' knowledge, post material that turns out to infringe someone's copyright. The service provider safe harbor provisions of the DMCA[52] were billed as a codification of the sensible standards for service provider liability articulated by a trial court in *Religious Technology Center v. Netcom On-line Communications Services*.[53] The DMCA's version of *Netcom*, however, has little to do with common sense. There are different rules for avoiding liability for different sorts of subscriber conduct. The statute identifies distinct categories of problematic events that *may* be able to qualify for a privilege: transitory communications, system caching, hosting of subscribers' files, and technical infringements committed through the use of search engines and other information location tools.[54] It sets different rules and conditions for absolution, depending on which category the offending conduct fits into. There are further special rules and conditions for non-profit educational institutions. None of the categories, rules and conditions make much sense on their own terms. Rather, each set gives the wary ISP an opportunity to jump through a long, complicated series of hoops and thereby avoid liability.[55] Finding all of the hoops requires the services of a very attentive copyright lawyer.

But, while this stuff was going on, one of the things the bill's supporters said

---

[51] I refer, here, to the provisions of the new 17 U.S.C. § 1201(a)(1), which prohibit consumers from circumventing technological devices that restrict access to works, but exclude from the prohibition works of a class that is determined by the Librarian of Congress in a periodic rulemaking to be entitled to a temporary exception on grounds not made explicit in the statute. Section 1201(a)(2), however, prohibits anyone from offering to the public or otherwise trafficking in any technology, product, service, or device designed to circumvent technological access restrictions, even for works ruled exempt in the administrative proceeding. See also Universal City Studios v. Reimerdes, 82 F. Supp. 2d 211, 219 (S.D.N.Y. 2000) ("If Congress had meant the fair use defense to apply to such actions, it would have said so.").

[52] Online Copyright Infringement Liability Limitation Act, DMCA § 202, codified at 17 U.S.C. § 512.

[53] 907 F. Supp. 1361 (N.D. Cal. 1995). In Netcom, the Church of Scientology sought to hold Internet service providers strictly liable for the infringing posts of their subscribers, disgruntled former Scientologists. The court refused to impose liability on an Internet service provider for infringement it had no reason to know about and no ability to control. The House Judiciary Committee Report explains: "[T]he bill essentially codifies the result in the leading and most thoughtful judicial decision to date: Religious Technology Center v. Netcom On-line Communications Services, Inc." H.R. Rep. No. 551, part 1, 105th Cong., 2d Sess. 11 (1998).

[54] See DMCA § 202, codified at 17 U.S.C. § 512.

[55] See U.S. Copyright Office Summary, supra note 50, at 8–14; A&M Records v. Napster, Inc., 2000 U.S. Dist. LEXIS 6243 (N.D. Cal. 2000).

was, "Hey, it's not so bad, because all the stuff that's available on the Internet today will still be there tomorrow, alongside the commercial stuff, and you can still read the free stuff if you want to."[56] That may yet turn out to be true, but the early signs aren't encouraging. The new copyright law puts in place a complex system of entry barriers that will discourage amateurs who know the law is there, and that is, I believe, intended to do so.[57] It also gives content owners a bunch of new tools to stop piracy. Now that those tools exist, though, they are being used to stop free speakers who are not pirates.

The highest profile dispute of this sort is between the recording industry and anyone who wants to use a digital file format called MP3.[58] MP3 allows the transmission of high quality music recordings over the Internet. You can download the music and play it through your computer's speakers. You can keep a whole music library on your hard disk. MP3 can of course be used for unauthorized recordings. It also can be used for authorized recordings; it is, after all, just a file format.[59] Independent bands have been distributing their music directly to consumers in MP3 format, some for free and others for money. Bigger bands have posted files containing free samples. There are advertising-supported sites out there devoted to MP3 hype and MP3 tips and MP3 files. Companies have brought out portable MP3 players that let you take an hour's worth of music with you wherever you go.

The recording industry tried to shut this all down. All of it. Not only the pirate sites, but also the authorized sites.[60] Bands who posted MP3 files on their web

---

[56] A number of witnesses gave testimony to this effect in the Hearing before the House Telecommunications and Trade Subcommittee. See Intellectual Property: Hearing Before the Telecommunications, Trade And Consumer Protection Subcommittee Of The House Commerce Committee, 105th Cong., 2d Sess. (June 5, 1998) (testimony of George Vradenburg III, America Online); id. (testimony of Robert Holleyman, Business Software Alliance).

[57] See Litman, Digital Copyright and Information Policy, supra note 48; Jessica Litman, New Copyright Paradigms in Laura A. Gassaway, Growing Pains: Adapting Copyright for Libraries, Education and Society 63, 66–80 (1997).

[58] See MP3 Rocks the Web, WIRED News, at URL: <http://www.wired.com/news/news/mpthree/>; Jon Pareles, With a Click, a New Era of Music Dawns, N.Y. Times, Nov. 15, 1998, section 2 at 1.

[59] Thus, a number of musicians without recording contracts have used MP3 to distribute their recorded performances directly to potential fans. See URL: <http://www.mp3.com>. Those authorized recordings are legal. The RIAA has argued that the number of authorized MP3 files is dwarfed by the number of unauthorized files. The majority of unauthorized consumer-created MP3 files, however, are arguably legal under current law. In Recording Industry Association v. Diamond Multimedia, 180 F.3d 1072 (9th Cir. 1999), the Court of Appeals for the 9th Circuit concluded that making personal copies of recorded music on the hard disk of a computer was permitted under the statute. See also 17 U.S.C. § 1008 (shielding consumers from liability for noncommercial reproduction of music).

[60] See Music Download Debate Continues, C|Net News.Com, Dec. 16, 1998, at URL: <http://www.news.com/News/Item/0,4,29980,00.html>. See also Electronic Frontier Foundation, Electronic Frontier Foundation Digital Audio and Free Expression Policy Statement, May, 1999, at URL: <http://www.eff.org/cafe/eff_audio_statement.html>.

pages were ordered to take them down or lose their recording contracts.[61] When the first portable player came out, the recording industry filed suit to stop it.[62] MP3 sites received a variety of threatening bigfoot letters demanding that they take down any information that discussed ways to convert proprietary files into MP3.[63] The recording industry perceived that many consumers wouldn't buy pay-per-listen music if free music were readily available. From that viewpoint, it's completely reasonable for it to try to sweep all the free music off the Net.

The tools the recording companies used in this campaign were the tools the copyright statute gave them, but they employed those tools to try to elbow legitimate as well as illegitimate activity out of the online market. The Recording Industry Association used its infringement lawsuit against the manufacturer of the Rio portable MP3 player as a threat against all consumer electronics manufacturers, and demanded that no business market a portable device capable of playing MP3 files. Instead, the Recording Industry Association insisted, portable digital players should be compatible only with secure, encrypted recording formats. The courts, however, ruled that the lawsuit against the Rio was meritless.[64] Meanwhile, the recording industry failed to come up with a competing digital specification. Thus, in the spring of 1999, as consumer electronics manufacturers geared up their production lines for the Christmas season, there was little secure encrypted musical content available for download, and lots of MP3 files. A device designed to play scarce content but to be incompatible with the content consumers wanted to play was unlikely to make it into a lot of Christmas stockings.

The Recording Industry Association began looking for a fallback position. It proposed that manufacturers market portable devices temporarily capable of playing MP3 files. The devices would incorporate a trigger, however, which could be activated remotely once the recording industry's Secure Digital Music Initiative was up and running, to disable MP3 compatibility. As described in the popular press, the compromise would mean that consumers could run out and buy portable digital players that would allow them to listen to downloaded music in the MP3 format as well as such music as they might be able to find in the encrypted SDMI format. One day in the not so far future, the recording industry would direct manufacturers to press some virtual button, sending a signal to all portable digital players, wherever they might be. The signal would suddenly disable the device from playing any MP3 files at all, forcing the consumer to either

---

[61] See Neil Strauss, Free Web Music Spreads From Campus to Office, NY Times, April 5, 1999, at A1.
[62] See Recording Industry Association v. Diamond Multimedia, 29 F. Supp. 2d 624 (C.D. CA 1998), aff'd, 180 F.3d 1072 (9th Cir. 1999).
[63] See, e.g., Liquid Audio Hits MP3.com with Cease and Desist (Nov. 1, 1998), URL: <http://www.mp3.com/news/122.html>.
[64] Recording Industry Association v. Diamond Multimedia, 180 F.3d 1072 (9th Cir. 1999), aff'g 29 F. Supp. 2d 624 (C.D. CA 1998).

toss her player in the trash or run to her computer and download encrypted replacements.[65] That proposal proved unpopular with device manufacturers. Without a robust, secure digital music specification, the recording industry has so far been unable to muscle unencrypted music out of the marketplace. Record companies have settled for a two-stage rollout in which Stage 1 machines will be MP3 compatible, but will be subject to a voluntary future software upgrade that will allow them to play SDMI music, and also prevent them from playing a still vaguely defined category of other music.[66]

As the SDMI effort bogged down, a 19-year-old college freshman invented Napster, which may be the recording industry's worst nightmare. Napster is software that permits individuals to locate and share files across the Internet.[67] Shawn Fanning developed the software to make it easier to find, share and talk about music files with other music fans. He made the software available for free download; millions of people installed Napster and began trading MP3 files with one another. The recording industry filed suit against Napster even before the company could officially launch the product.[68] Napster and many of the individuals who use its software to exchange MP3 files have credible arguments that they are doing nothing illegal under current law.[69] The recording industry has pursued its lawsuit fervently, in the face of bad press from normally supportive sources,[70] because, from its vantage point, it would be intolerable that Napter be legal.

The recording industry's campaign to banish MP3 from the Internet has so far failed because the industry has consistently overplayed its hand. It demanded too much in return for too little. It asked consumers, websites and consumer electronics manufacturers to shun a popular format in favor of a specification that was, and is still, vaporware. This temporary defeat, however, may not mean much in the long term. The most prominent MP3 sites have already succumbed to

---

[65] See Christopher Jones, Music Biz Builds a Time Bomb, WIRED News, May 14, 1999, at URL: < http://www.wired.com/news/news/technology/story/19682.html >.

[66] See SDMI Guide, supra note 31. The rollout of SDMI-compliant devices has thus far failed to proceed on schedule.

[67] See Peter Lewis, Napster Rocks the Web, New York Times, June 29, 2000 (Nat'l ed.) at D1.

[68] See A&M Records v. Napster, Inc., 54 U.S.P.Q.2D (BNA) 1746 (N.D. Cal. 2000).

[69] Napster has a strong argument under Sony v. Universal City Studios, 464 U.S. 417 (1984), that it cannot be held liable for contributory infringement because its service is capable of substantial non-infringing use. Individuals' exchange of MP3 files are an unlikely candidate for fair use, but may fall within the statutory exemption for specified noncommercial consumer reproductions of musical recordings. 17 U.S.C. § 1008. In addition, Napster has asserted that it fits the statutory definition of a "service provider" in section 512 of the statute, and is therefore entitled to claim the benefit of the service provider safe harbor. See supra notes 52 – 55 and accompanying text. Napster's activities seem to fit within the literal language of the statute. On May 5, 2000, however, Judge Patel denied Napster's summary judgment motion on its asserted 512 defense. 2000 U.S. Dist. LEXIS 6243 at 29–30.

[70] See Napster Agonistes, Wall Street Journal, June 19, 2000; Why Block Free Exchange of Records and Movies?, USA Today, June 23, 2000, at 16A.

Internet IPO fever.[71] They, too, are looking for ways to make money fast selling digital music. They aren't volunteers any more, and they have stockholders to please.

IV.

We are in the end stages of a takeover of domain name space, in which control over Internet domain names is being handed over to the private sector.[72] The domain name system, which pairs unique numbers corresponding to computers connected to the Internet with easy-to-remember alphanumeric strings, originated for the convenience of human users. The Internic, under contract to the U.S. government, handed out domain names on a first-come, first-served basis.[73] The first applicant for the domain acme.com, for example, was neither Acme Auto Repair nor Warner Brothers, but a fellow named Jef Poskanzer who has long been a fan of Wile E. Coyote;[74] the first applicant for candyland.com was not Hasbro, but the proprietor of a sexually explicit Web site.[75] Outraged trademark owners filed trademark infringement suits against occupiers of domains they wanted for themselves.[76] Some won;[77] some lost.[78] The trademark bar insisted that the only legitimate domain name use of an alphanumeric string that was also a trademark was a trademark use by the trademark owner. They demanded a system that allowed trademark owners to oust non-trademark owners of domain names incorporating their marks, and that permitted trademark owners to prevent any subsequent registration of any domain name incorporating their marks in any top-level domain.[79]

Trademark owners' legitimate concerns could have been resolved by expanding the number of generic top-level domains to give multiple claimants access to

---

[71] See Joanna Glasner, Musicmaker IPO Hits High Note, WIRED News, July 7, 1999, at URL: <http://www.wired.com/news/news/politics/mpthree/story/20606.html>; Beth Lipton, Net music gets louder next week, C|net News.Com, July 16, 1999, at URL: <http://www.news.com/News/Item/0,4,39310,00.html>; Richtel, supra note 21.
[72] See Larry Lessig, Governance and the DNS Process, URL: <http://cyber.harvard.edu/works/lessig/cpsr.pdf>; U.S. Government Working Group on Electronic Commerce, supra note 11, at 12–13.
[73] See generally Ellen Rony & Peter Rony, The Domain Name Handbook 15–244 (1998).
[74] See Acme Laboratories, URL: <http://www.acme.com>.
[75] See Hasbro, Inc. v. Internet Entertainment Group, 40 U.S.P.Q.2d 1479 (W.D. Wash. 1996).
[76] See Rony & Rony, supra note 73, at 299–378.
[77] See, e.g., Cardservice International, Inc. v. McGee, 950 F. Supp. 737 (E.D. Va. 1997); Hasbro, Inc. v. Internet Entertainment Group, 40 U.S.P.Q.2d 1479 (W.D. Wash. 1996); Intermatic Inc. v. Toeppen, 40 U.S.P.Q.2d 1412 (N.D. Ill. 1996).
[78] See, e.g., Gateway 2000 v. Gateway.com, 1997 U.S. Dist. LEXIS 2144 (W.D.N.C. 1997); Maritz v. Cybergold, 947 F. Supp. 1338 (E.D. Mo. 1996).

domains containing the same alphanumeric strings. Jef Poskanzer could keep acme.com, and Warner Brothers could take acme.biz, while the Acme glass company could have acme.glass and so forth.[80] That struck the trademark bar as absolutely unacceptable: the owner of the mark trademark® not only wanted (and argued that it was entitled to) a domain name featuring trademark, but needed and (was entitled) to be the *only* entity on the Internet that had a domain name containing trademark. Multiplying the top-level domains, trademark owners argued, would merely multiply the potential for confusion.[81]

As a prediction, that one is flawed. Consumers know that there are lots of different businesses named Acme, and don't expect any given Acme to be the particular Acme they have in mind. If consumers learned that there were lots of Acme-based domain names on the web, they wouldn't expect any particular one to belong to either Poskanzer or Warner Brothers. They wouldn't be confused. Of course, a powerful potential marketing tool might thereby be lost, but that, without more, seems an insufficient reason to structure the Internet domain name system around trademark owners' demands. Trademark owners have insisted that they need to control any domain names containing words over which they claim trademark rights, but they want not to dilute the value of that asset by multiplying it. Instead, they demanded a way to preemptively reserve domain names containing their marks across all top-level domains.[82]

Congress was sympathetic.[83] The Clinton administration had committed itself to restructuring the legal infrastructure of the Internet to facilitate electronic commerce,[84] and the trademark bar insisted that a trademark-friendly domain

---

[79] See Craig Simon, Overview of the DNS Controversy (May 19, 2000), URL: <http://www.flywheel.com/ircw/overview.html>.

[80] See Jonathan Postel, Memorandum: New Registries and the Delegation of International Top-level Domain (June 1996), online at URL: <http://www.newdom.com/archive/draft-postel-iana-itld-admin-01.txt>; Generic Top-level Domain Memorandum of Understanding § 9, Feb. 28, 1997, at URL: <http://www.gTLD-MoU.org/gTLD-MoU.html>.

[81] See International Trademark Association, INTA Response to the U.S. Government Paper on the Improvement of Technical Management of Internet Names and Addresses (March 18, 1998), URL: <http://www.ntia.doc.gov/ntiahome/domainname/130dftmail/scanned/INTA.htm>; Continued Oversight Hearing before the Subcomm. On Courts and Intellectual Property of the House Comm. on the Judiciary, 105th Cong., 2d Sess. (Feb. 12, 1998) (testimony of David C. Stimson, INTA).

[82] See World Intellectual Property Organization, Interim Report on the WIPO Internet Domain Name Process, Chapter 4 at ¶¶ 202–244, URL: <http://wipo2.wipo.int/process/eng/processhome.html>.

[83] See generally Intellectual Property: Oversight Hearings on Internet Domain Trademark Protection Before the Subcomm. On Courts and Intellectual Property of the House Comm. on the Judiciary, 105th Cong., 1st & 2nd Sess. (1998); Internet Domain Names: Hearing Before the Subcomm. On Basic Research of the House Science Comm., 105th Cong., 1st & 2nd Sess. (1998).

[84] See U.S. Government Working Group on Electronic Commerce, supra note 11.

name system was a crucial part of that transition.[85] Trademark owners pushed hard, in both international and domestic fora, to recast the domain name system into something more hospitable to the owners of valuable trademarks, and downright hostile to folks who select their domain names with something other than trademark rights in mind.[86]

The White House directed the Commerce Department to supervise the privatization of the administration of the Domain Name System in a fashion that resolved trademark owners' concerns.[87] Working closely with a variety of different industry interests, the Commerce Department came up with ICANN – the "Internet Corporation for Assigned Names and Numbers."[88] ICANN has generated an enormous amount of controversy for a range of reasons, most of them related to a perception that it is neither broadly representative of the universe of Internet users nor designed in a way to make it accountable to its constituents.[89] The fact that ICANN's assurances to the Commerce Department incorporate explicit and implicit promises that established commercial speakers will find it easy to take valuable domain names away from small companies, amateurs and volunteers (and will further be able to limit them in their efforts to get new ones) has not yet been high on the list of popular objections.[90] That may change. With the Department of Commerce's approval, ICANN adopted an organizational structure that gives representatives of intellectual property interests an influential role in any decisions.[91] In 1999 ICANN adopted a mandatory arbitration procedure to permit owners of trademarks and service marks to oust prior domain name registrants.[92] Although ICANN's initial charge included responsibility for

---

[85] See, e.g, International Trademark Association, supra note 81; International Trademark Association, Harmonizing Domain Names and Brand Protection, URL: < http://www.inta.org/harmdom.htm >.

[86] See Jessica Litman, The DNS Wars: Trademarks and the Internet Domain Name System, 4 J. Small & Emerging Bus. L 149 (2000).

[87] See U.S. Government Working Group on Electronic Commerce, supra note 11, at 12.

[88] See Lessig, supra note 72; ICANN Home Page, URL: < http://www.icann.org >.

[89] See Domain Name System Privatization: Is ICANN Out of Control?: Hearing Before the Subcomm. On Oversight and Investigations of the House Comm. on Commerce, 106th Cong., 1st Sess. (July 22, 1999) (testimony of Jonathan Weinberg, Wayne State University); Ellen Roney & Peter Rony, The Domain Name Handbook, URL: < http://www.domainhandbook.com/ >; Berkman Center for Internet & Society, ICANN Public Meetings, URL: < http://cyber.law.harvard.edu/icann/ >.

[90] But see Domain Name System Privatization, supra note 89 (testimony of Mikki Barry, Domain Name Rights Coalition); A. Michael Froomkin, A Critique of WIPO's RFC 3 (February, 1999) at URL: < http://www.law.miami.edu/~amf/ >; Jonathan Weinberg, Comments on WIPO RFC-3, URL: < http://www.law.wayne.edu/weinberg/rfc3.pdf >.

[91] See ICANN Organizational Chart (modified 4/23/00), URL: < http://www.icann.org/general/icann-org-chart_frame.htm >; Milton Mueller, ICANN and Internet Governance: sorting through the debris of "self-regulation", 1 info, No. 6, December 1999 at 497, 519–520.

[92] See ICANN, Uniform Domain name Dispute Resolution Policy, URL: < http://www.icann.org/udrp/udrp.htm >; see, e.g., Fiber-Shield Industries v. Fiber Shield (Toronto) Ltd., NAF # FA1000092054 (Feb. 29, 2000); J. Crew International v. crew.com, WIPO # D2000-0054 (April 30, 2000); Hewlett-Packard Co. v. Burgar, NAF # FA2000093564 (April 10, 2000).

creating new generic top-level domains to compete with .com,[93] ICANN has thus far confined itself to studying whether to do so.[94] Trademark interests, meanwhile, have insisted that any introduction of a new top-level domain be preceded by an opportunity to give trademark and service mark owners the ability to preempt the registration of any domain name similar to any trademark or service mark in any generic top-level domain.[95]

As ICANN put its dispute resolution procedure in place, impatient trademark owners persuaded Congress to enact the *Anticybersquatting Consumer Protection Act,* giving trademark owners a sheaf of new remedies against registrants of domain names alleged to infringe or dilute their trademarks.[96]

These developments would be less troubling if we didn't already have plenty of evidence that trademark owners were using the legal tools at their disposal to persuade legitimate users of contested alphanumeric strings to forgo lawful uses. Trademark owners have threatened litigation against amateurs, critics, fans, children and coincidental adopters of domain names claimed to be too close to valuable marks.[97] Trademark litigants have insisted that because Internet search engines index sites according to all of the words that they contain, use of a trademarked word on a site, or even in the meta tags to a site, constitutes infringement and dilution.[98] The idea, here, is that if a customer seeking, say,

---

[93] See United States Department Of Commerce, Management of Internet Names and Addresses, 63 Fed. Reg. 31741 (Jun. 10, 1998).

[94] See ICANN Yokohama Meeting Topic: Introduction of New Top-Level Domains (June 13, 2000), at URL: <http://www.icann.org/yokohama/new-tld-topic.htm>; ICANN DNSO Names Council, Consideration of Introducing New Generic Top-Level Domains (April 20, 2000), at <http://www.icann.org/dnso/gtld-topic-20apr00.htm>.

[95] See ICANN/DNSO Intellectual Property Constituency, Sunrise Proposal Plus 20 (April 14, 2000), at URL: <http://ipc.songbird.com/IPC_Sunrise_Proposal.htm>; ICANN DNSO Names Council Working Group B Final Report ,URL: <http://www.dnso.org/dnso/notes/20000515.NCwgb-report.html>.

[96] Anticybersquatting Consumer Protection Act, P.L. 106–113, div b, § 1000(a)(9), 113 stat. 1536 (1999), codified at 15 U.S.C. 1125(d) (2000). see Sporty's Farm L.L.C., v. Sportsman's Market, Inc., 202 F.3d 489 (2d Cir. 2000); Caesars World v. Caesars-Palace.Com, 54 U.S.P.Q.2d (Bna) 1121 (E.D. Va 2000); Morrison & Foerster v. Wick, 94 F. Supp. 2d 1125 (D. Colo. 2000).

[97] The well-publicized cases of two-year-old Veronica Sams's "Little Veronica" website at <http://www.veronica.org> and 12 year-old Chris "Pokey" Van Allen's web page at <http://www.pokey.org> pitted trademark owners against children whose parents had registered their children's names in the .org domain. The registration and operation of the web sites was unquestionably innocent, and there was no plausible likelihood that consumers would be misled. Nonetheless, in both cases, the trademark owners demanded that the children's web sites be taken down. A flood of negative publicity persuaded the trademark owners in both cases to back down. Publicity also persuaded the Colgate Palmolive Company to drop its legal action against Benjamin Kite, operator of a noncommercial site at www.ajax.org named after the Greek warrior. See Paul Festa, Ajax.org Wins Trademark Fight, C|Net News.Com, Oct. 20, 1998 at URL: <http://www.news.com/News/Item/0,4,27742,00.html>; How We Got Colgate Palmolive to Back Down, URL: <http://www.ajax.org/ajax/colpal/>.

[98] See, e.g., Playboy v. Welles, 7 F. Supp. 2d 1098 (SD Cal. 1998); Brookfield Communications v. West Coast Entertainment, 174 F.3d 1036 (9th Cir. 1999); Oppedahl & Larson v. Advanced Concepts, Civil Action No. 97-Z-1592 (D. Colo. 1997), URL: <http://www.patents.com/ac/

PLAYBOY® ONLINE, types the word "playboy" into a search engine, and receives a list of links including a page maintained by someone who used to be a Playboy Playmate, and another by someone who insists the erotic pictures at the site are better than Playboy's, that Playboy's mark is thereby infringed and diluted.[99] Even worse, Playboy complains, on top of the list is a paid banner ad from some pornographic business that isn't Playboy's.[100] So far, the courts have, in the main, treated such claims cautiously, but plenty of threatened sites have chosen to close down or to conform their page to lawyers' demands rather than be dragged into court.[101] That is, we are perilously close to conceding that ownership of a trademark gives one the exclusive right to use the word on the Internet.

V.

In the past few years, we've seen a lot of something that used to be very rare, which is big companies going after little fish (college students, critics, amateurs and other volunteers) and threatening them with ruinous intellectual property litigation if they don't remove their stuff from the web, or if they don't vacate a particular domain name, or if they don't buy a license and stop giving away their content for free. Entertainment companies are even cracking down on fan websites, apparently sufficiently concerned about volunteer competition to be willing to bite the hands that feed them.[102] Now, most of the little fish roll over and play

---

cont.
   index.sht >; Carl Kaplan, Cyberlaw Journal: Lawsuits Challenge Search Engines' Practice of 'Selling' Trademarks, N.Y. Times CyberTimes, February 12, 1999, at < http://www.nytimes.com/library/tech/99/02/cyber/cyberlaw/12law.html >.

[99] See Playboy v. Welles, 7 F. Supp. 2d 1098 (SD Cal. 1998); Playboy Enterprises v. Asia Focus, 1998 WL 724000 (ED Va 1998); Playboy Enterprises v. Calvin Designer Label, Civil Action No. 97–3204 CAL (filed 9/27/97). See also, e.g., Bensusan Restaurant Corp. v. King, 126 F.3d 25 (2d Cir. 1997).

[100] See Playboy Enterprises v. Netscape Communications, 55 F. Supp. 2d 1070 (C.D. Cal.), aff'd, 202 F.3d 278 (9th Cir. 1999).

[101] See, e.g., Washington Post v. TotalNEWS, No. 97 Civ. 1190 (PKL). See generally Ellen Roney, Domain Name Handbook Domain Diaries, URL: < http://www.domainhandbook.com/dd.html >.

[102] See, e.g., DC Comics Crackdown: A Heroes Special Report, Heroes May, 1999, at URL: < http://victorian.fortunecity.com/belvedere/223/archive/hsr1/ >; Webmasters for a Free La Femme Nikita, URL: < http://www.geocities.com/TelevisionCity/9932/index.htm >; Keeping the Menace Down, WIRED News, April 27, 1999 at URL: < http://www.wired.com/news/business/0,1367,19355,00.html >. One can spin the recent crackdowns on fan sites in different ways. Some (although not all) of the targeted sites were created by fans on Internet services, like Geocities.com and Tripod.com, that add banner advertisements to all subscriber web pages. The subscribers get none of the advertising revenue, but instead are given free or low-cost access to the Internet. One can sympathize with intellectual property owners who wish to ensure that only they receive such advertising revenue as is generated by their properties. On the other

dead. You would too, if it were going to cost you half a million dollars to get a court to say that what you'd been doing was perfectly legal. Some of them take their sites down,[103] some give up their domain names,[104] some buy licenses and start selling stuff they used to offer for free. But, if they decide to litigate, the new laws have a lot of sneaky legal tools in them that favor the big content owners.[105]

So, we have a trend. To make the Internet into a viable shopping mall, merchants need to evict the riff-raff who are hanging around and giving out free stuff. It's reminiscent of the behavior that goes on over rent-controlled apartments. We can't actually throw the occupants out, but we can make their lives unpleasant. We can make them all need to hire lawyers if they want to stick around. We can jigger the rules so that it's hard for them to win. In order to transform the Internet into an engine of economic growth, we have reformed the legal infrastructure in a host of ways to favor commercial speech over its noncommercial sisters.

Several years ago, when the news media spoke breathlessly of the Information Superhighway or the National Information Infrastructure as if it was going to be a hugely enhanced and expanded version of commercial subscription television augmented by lots of home shopping opportunities,[106] I chalked that vision up to a failure of imagination. Lately, I've been wondering whether I might not have underestimated it. Increasingly, it's looking like a blueprint for an edifice that's well under construction.

---

cont.
    hand, the effect of a no-unauthorized-advertising policy, if that's what the recent crackdowns reflect, is to increase the cost of putting up fan sites by preventing their appearance on low-cost or free advertising-supported Internet access services.
[103] According to the RIAA, 60% of the sites it shut down in 1997 were college or university web pages. See Strauss, supra note 61.
[104] See Rony & Rony, supra note 73, at 299–378.
[105] See, e.g., 17 U.S.C. § 1201; 15 U.S.C. § 43(d).
[106] See, e.g., Paul Farhi, TCI's Malone Quietly Assembling an Empire, Washington Post, Oct. 14, 1993 at A1; Benjamin J. Stein, More Channels, More Laziness, Washington Post, Nov. 2, 1993, at A19.

Two Cheers for the Commodification of Information

Eli Noam

1. Introduction[1]

This essay takes issue with the notion of "information commodification," a staple of communications scholarship and advocacy. It concludes that the term has been used in contradictory and non-factual ways. It concludes further that a system of economic transactions in information is, in fact, essential to the future information environment. The reason is not because such transactions establish financial incentives for the creation of information, which is the traditional rationale for intellectual property rights. Instead, it is because transactions in information enable the coordination of numerous activities involving information[2] flows. This changes the terms of the debate from one of private vs. public ownership to one of distributed vs. centralized transactions. The essay sketches how such a system of information transactions would look like. It concludes that it would not only permit the coordination of information but also provide policy makers with a tool to pursue various goals of social and cultural policy. Thus, embedding information in a "commodified" economic system of transactions is actually helpful to its creation, flow, and widespread distribution.

The expression "commodification of information" is trendy. But what does it mean, exactly? It seems to be a broad umbrella that shelters various views, mostly critical, about information, media, and knowledge. The term is used by the academic left[3] as well as the capitalist right, often to mean different things.

---

[1] This essay is dedicated to the memory of Herbert Schiller, who would not have liked the answer, but would have enjoyed the argument.
[2] "Information" as used in this article means "data subjected to organization".
[3] Schiller, Dan. "From Culture to Information and Back Again: Commoditization as a Route to Knowledge." *Critical Studies in Mass Communication*, Vol. 11.11, (1994), pp. 93–115. Mosco, Vincent and Janet Wasko eds. The Political Economy of Information The U. of Wisconsin Press:Winconsin 1988 pp. 27–43.

N. Elkin-Koren and N.W. Netanel (eds.), *The Commodification of Information*, 43–59.
© 2002 Eli Noam. Printed in Great Britain.

Microsoft's leaked "Halloween memos" that were featured in the government's antitrust case against the company included the internal conclusion that it should "decommoditize protocols and applications" by "extending these protocols and developing these protocols[4]" In other words, the company should seek a proprietary strategy, likely to involve the exercise and creation of market power, in order to *prevent* a commodification that lowers profitability. In a similar way, McKinsey consultants warn their business clients, in an article entitled *Shedding the Commodity Mind Set* that "with true commodities, you don't get a price premium."[5] Madison Avenue, too, bemoans commodification where advertising is bought in bulk without concern with the surrounding content.[6] Such commodification leads to advertisers viewing different publications as interchangeable, and the ill-fated energy giant Enron, consequently, consided creating a trading market for generic advertising space, including futures contracts, etc. Wall Street has concluded that long distance service has become commodified,[7] and AT&T and MCI WorldCom have been dropped like hot potatoes.

In contrast, the usual scholarly assumption is that proprietary approaches to information are exactly what *causes* commodification by creating ownership and control relations in the information environment, making it unaffordable and under-supplied with respect to the poorer and weaker parts of the population, as well as controlled by large media companies that commercialize its use.

These perspectives on commodification are significantly at odds with each other. Business types do not like commodification because it reduces profits. They pursue "branding" strategies and seek market power in order to offset commodification. Academic and activist critics do not like it because it encroaches on the public sphere. The common element of these perspectives is a negative interpretation of commodification. In contrast, I will argue that commodification is actually a positive and necessary element of the information environment, and not for the usual reasons of incentives and reward advanced by the traditional owners of intellectual property rights in their efforts to expand these proprietary rights. (Because these efforts are retarding the development of the information environment, commodification gets only two cheers in this article).

When a term such as "commodity" gets bandied about loosely to criticize a collection of trends that people do not seem to like, loose thinking inevitably follows. Let us therefore look at the term more closely. It goes back to the Latin

---

[4] Cohen, Josh and Vinod Valloppillil, *The Halloween Documents,* Nov 1998, <http://www.opensource.org/halloween/index.html>

[5] Forsyth, John E., Alok Gupta, Sudeep Haldar, and Michael V. Marn, "Shedding the commodity mind-set" *The McKinsey Quarterly,* 2000 No. 4.
Garcia, Jon C. and Jon Wilkins, "Cable Is Too Much Better To Lose." *The McKinsey Quarterly* April 9, 2001.

[6] Jim Meskauskas, "The Commodification of Online Media," http:/www.clickz.com/article/cz.3768.html, April 17th, 2001.

[7] Uhland, Vicky, "Switchin' To Go." *Interactive Week.* January 15, 2001.

commodus, "useful." In English, its first meaning was benign, "A thing of use or advantage to mankind," according to the Oxford English Dictionary. The earliest extant use, taking that meaning, goes back to the year 1400:[8] "The land of Inde es the maste plentifous land of folk that es owerwhare, by cause of the grete *commodietez* that it has therein." Use of the term in the sense of a convenience or of something useful dates to at least 1430. Shakespeare uses it in 1592 to denote something of value and advantage. "I will turn diseases to commodity."[9] From there, the term acquired the meaning of an economic good as an article of commerce. Soon, it was anything that one trades or deals in, and by 1608 negative meanings began to be associated, too. "The whore who is called the commodity."[10] The negative meaning was later elevated by Karl Marx, for whom the commodity concept was central, and who saw it constituting "social things whose qualities are at the same time perceptible and imperceptible by the senses"[11] This was sufficiently cloudy to let the senses of subsequent generations of scholars perceive almost anything into it.

As an economic good, commodity became associated with abundant, mass-produced goods, like cotton, cocoa, minerals or pork bellies traded on exchanges in Chicago or London. "It must be ... an homogeneous substance of consistent quality throughout so that it may be sold by sample."[12] From mass product it was only a small step to a meaning of an inferior item, of low quality. It often signifies a highly competitive market in which suppliers are interchangeable. To others, the process of commodification is associated with control by business, especially big firms, of activities that are otherwise not part of market mechanism. This accords with the meaning of the term commodification, by 1970: "the act of turning something into, or treating something as, a (mere) commodity; commercialization of an activity, etc., that is not by nature commercial."[13] A few years ago, the term began to be applied also to information,[14] especially to the control of communication by large media firms,[15] and to the expansion of intellectual property laws.

---

[8] *Oxford English Dictionary*, Oxford University Press, 1989, Mandeville (Roxb.xxii.101.)
[9] *Henry IV*. 2, I, II, 1592.
[10] *Oxford English Dictionary*, Oxford University Press, 1989, Dekker, Belman Lond.
[11] Marx, Karl, *Capital, A Critique of Political Economy*. Vol. 1. p. 83, C. H. Kerr & Co., Chicago: 1919.
[12] "Dictionary of Banking and Finance: A Commentary on Banking, Financial Services, and Corporate and Personal Finance," London; Marshfield, Mass.: Pitman Pub. 1985.
[13] *Oxford English Dictionary*, Oxford University Press, 1989.
[14] Allen, Beth, "Information as an Economic Commodity." "*American Economic Review.*" 80, 1980, pp. 268–273.
[15] Schiller, Herbert I. *Who Knows: Information in the Age of the Fortune 500*, Ablex Publishing Corp, NJ, 1982.

2. The Meaning of Commodification

Thus, several quite disparate and contradictory elements are thrown together in the term commodity and to its application to information. We will now discuss the various meanings in turn. We will not attempt to determine which meaning is the most appropriate; rather, we will try to evaluate the validity of the negative connotation associated with each.

2.1 COMMODITY AS A MASS PRODUCED GOOD

The first meaning of commodification is that of a *massification* of information and its production with the implicit belief that mass-produced information has a lower quality than more selectively created information.

Obviously, there has been a huge increase in information production and producers. Already 40 years ago it was observed that 90 percent of all scientists who ever lived were still alive.[16] Most branches of science show exponential growth of about 4–8 percent annually with a doubling period of 10–15 years. There are more than 80,000 scientific and technical journals, and more than 1,500 scientific abstracting periodicals. To get a sense of the trend: At the beginning of the 20th century, *Chemical Abstracts* took 32 years of publication (1907 to 1938) to list one million abstracts. The fifth million, near the end of the century, took only three years and four months, 1/10 of the time.[17] Wherever one looks, more book titles are published than ever before, 60,000 in the U.S. in 2000, compared with 15,000 in 1950 and 8,000 in 1900. More magazines are published, about 22,000 in the U.S., with 1,000 new titles each year. There are fewer newspapers than before, but those that have survived are thicker than ever. For television, where once about five channels were available to the American viewer, there are now more than 200 different channels offered by cable and satellite. Similar trends can be observed in all developed countries.

According to one study,[18] unique information produced annually in the world is 1–2 exabytes (1–2 billion gigabytes). This translates to about 250 megabytes produced per human being. (Of these, printed documents comprise only .003 percent. One country alone, the U.S., produces about 25 percent of all textual information and 30 percent of the photographic information).

---

[16] Price, Derek J. de Solla. *Little Science, Big Science*. New York: Columbia University Press, 1963, pp. 73–74.
[17] Noam, Eli, "Electronics and the Dim Future of the University," *Science*, Vol. 270. p. 247–249, 1995.
[18] Lyman, Peter. And Varian, Hal R. "How Much Information?" *The Journal of Electronic Publishing*, Vol. 6.2, December 2000.

An increase in the creation of information should be viewed as a positive trend, unless it means a reduced quality of information. Information does not decline in usefulness just because there is more of it. But is the quality aggregate of newly created information declining over time? This is a difficult question to answer, starting with the very definitions of "quality" and "information." In the past, too, much inferior information was created, but most of it has, mercifully, not been preserved. One should expect mostly exemplary of work to be culled, saved and transmitted across generations. We remember the best of Shakespeare and have forgotten almost all of his contemporary wordsmiths. A viewing of a typical movie from the '40s or TV show from the '50s should quickly dispel any romanticization of past quality of media content. One empirical study, by the author, measured the increase of TV programs by content categories, in particular of quality categories.[19] Since 1969, total program hours per week offered over TV and cable TV has increased in New York City to more than a half million program hours per year.[20] Compound annual growth rate has been more than 10 percent for at least 30 years. Growth in the supply of TV content has been above average for several content categories usually associated with quality, such as documentaries, news magazines, health/medicine, and science/nature. All of these show annual growth rates of about 12 percent. Below average – but still substantial – growth rates exist for quality children programs (7.6%), foreign language programs (9.5%) and education (9.4.%).

It is always difficult to define and measure quality of content. But from the limited evidence, it does not appear that the mass production of information that is one meaning of commodification has led to low quality of information. Where such decline in TV has occurred it was based on the loss of exclusivity of public service TV in Europe.[21] To demonstrate a further reduction based on quantity, it would require substantial empirical evidence rather than assertion. Of course, more garbage programs are being produced; but so is high-quality information, as well as any other content category.

2.2 COMMODITY AS HOMOGENEITY

A second meaning of the term "commodity" is homogeneity – undifferentiated and largely interchangeable products, like orange juice futures traded in Chicago. As mentioned, the commercial characteristic of a commodity is being sold by a sample. Yet for information, the opposite is the case. The more information there is, the more specialized it must become, and the *less* homogenous it therefore is.

---

[19] Noam, Eli. "Public Interest Programming in American Television," in Eli Noam and Jens Waltermann eds., *Public Television in America*. Bertelsmann, 1998, pp.145–175.
[20] In terms of channel capacity, New York City is in the top third among cable areas but by no means near the top.

This should be obvious if one looks at the increasing specialization of scientific journals, music formats, or web sites. Yet many people believe that the evolution of the commercial TV environment has simply led to "more of the same", to a multiplication of commoditized content. But it would not make sense to duplicate content even within a profit-maximizing paradigm. A commercial broadcaster maximizes advertising revenue by maximizing desirable audiences. This is the case at the peak of a normally distributed audience. Additional commercial broadcasters will position themselves slightly differentiated relative to the incumbent broadcaster. They do not offer quite the same programming type. As the process continues with additional channels, the total range of program types widens.[22] A gradual differentiation rather than homogeneity is the rational strategy.

When commercial TV in the U.S. was limited to a handful of channels, aiming at a minimum of 25 percent of the audience for a program to survive, programming was indeed centrist in orientation. This, indeed, was "commodity TV." But this has given way to narrowcasting to audience slices of less than one percent, and, in the near future, to customized and individualized programming over the Internet to still narrower audiences.[23]

The offering of new program networks has accelerated. Whereas in 1992, 20 new program channels were concretely proposed or offered to the cable operators, in 1993 it was more than 40, and in 1998 more than 100.[24] These include channels on a wide variety of increasingly specialized topics, including wrestling and astrology, but also programs on more respectable topics, such as art performances, books, computers, classic arts, programs for the deaf and disabled, the environment, health, history, human development, independent films, jazz, lectures, museums and exhibitions, and public affairs. Thus, we cannot conclude that homogeneity in the information created has occurred. Quite to the contrary.

2.3 COMMODITY AS CHEAPNESS OF INFORMATION

Another set of meanings associated with the term commodity is "inexpensive" and "highly competitive." This is the negative meaning given by the supplier industry and reflected in the quotes from Microsoft and McKinsey provided earlier. From a consumer and public perspective, why should a low price be considered a problem? Paperbacks and cheap paper made books widely affordable. Inexpensive

---

[21] Noam, Eli. *Television in Europe*. 395 pp., Oxford University Press 1991.
[22] Noam, Eli, "A Public and Private-Choice Model of Broadcasting," *Public Choice*, 55, 1987, pp. 163–187.
[23] Noam, Eli. "The Stages of Television: From Multi-Channel Television to the Me-Channel," Contamine, Claude, & van Dusseldorp, Monique, eds., *European Institute for the Media*, 1994, pp. 49–58.
[24] Noam, Eli. "Public Interest Programming in American Television," in Eli Noam and Jens Waltermann eds., *Public Television in America*. Bertelsmann, 1998, pp. 145–175.

movies and records brought performances and music to the masses. A typical cable TV system provides almost 10,000 hours of programs per week. On a per hour basis it costs the subscribers less than one tenth of one cent. Newspapers provide hundreds of up-to-date stories written by some of the best journalists, produced and delivered within a few hours, at a cost of less than one cent per page. Internet service provides access to largely free information at a connectivity price, on average, for Internet and telephone of less than one cent per minute.

That information should become cheaper makes economic sense in a long-term way. More information than ever is being created and distributed, while the ability of individuals and society to use and absorb it does not rise as fast.[25] In consequence, one should expect prices for information to fall, in the same way that the price of food has declined over the past centuries as its production increased faster than aggregate appetites. And as information becomes cheaper, more of it is used by more people. It becomes more widely affordable and more broadly disseminated across the social spectrum and, due to its sheer quantity, less easy to control. All this should delight the users of information content and of its distribution channels. If anyone should be unhappy about this form of commodity it is the creators, producers, and distributors of information. They find their profit margins lowered by competition for audience's attention. This is the type of commodification they dread. They counter it by attempts to reduce competition through concentration in the market structure. They try to differentiate (rather than homogenize) and to create "brand" images for products and producers that enable the changing of higher prices.

Thus, if anything, the goals of public policy should be to uphold this kind of commodification in its meaning of competitive and inexpensive.

2.4 COMMODITY AS COMMERCIALIZATION

Perhaps the major meaning of the term "commodity" in academic critique is its commercial dimension. Information becomes a private good, produced and sold according to profit criteria. To Herbert Schiller, it was becoming "something which, like toothpaste, breakfast cereals and automobiles, is increasingly bought and sold." [26] It enters the stream of commerce without special consideration for the intellectual content behind it. It is part of a larger commodification process of the capitalist system. The expansion of the market to information and its unequal distribution makes many people uneasy. Jeremy Rifkin worries that "when the

---

[25] Noam, Eli. "Overcoming the Last Communications Bottleneck", *Optics and Photonics*, 1993, pp. 23–25

[26] Schiller, Herbert I. *Who Knows: Information in the Age of the Fortune 500*, Ablex Publishing Corp, NJ, 1982.

culture itself is absorbed into the economy, only commercial bonds will be left to hold society together."[27]

The meaning of commodification as privatization and commercialization goes back to Marx. Under capitalism everything becomes a commodity; everything can be bought and sold. Under capitalism, production is not determined primarily by "use value", e.g., some intrinsic merit of the work, but of "exchange value", i.e. of how markets evaluate it, which in turn is defined and created by the societal power and class relationships of the production process.[28] If one accepts this, it suggests that the commodification of information is not really new, not really part of the digital revolution or of recent media concentration, but that it has existed for centuries.[29]

Gutenberg printed his bibles to sell them as part of a commercial venture. His unabashed goal was not religion but personal enrichment. The Globe Theatre in London charged admission to Shakespeare plays. Rembrandt sold his paintings and they were resold to others. It is not easy to locate a golden past when information of value to many was not jealously guarded or meted out as a special privilege, but rather freely given away with no expectation for reward. We know about Gutenberg mostly from the court records of his litigations against the unauthorized users of his various inventions. Thus, the criticism inherent in the meaning of commodity as commercialization is inconsistent and ahistorical.

The fundamental forces at work today are the transformation of advanced societies into information-based economies, with information becoming a major input of economic and societal activities, and the main activity of individuals and organizations the production of information or of instrumentalities that assist in that process. Given the increase in the quantity of information produced, and the relatively static amount of attention available for its absorption, the information needs to be of increasing attractiveness to the user. All this – quantity and quality – requires considerable and rising effort, organization, and investment. In consequence, the individuals and organizations involved will not usually give the product away freely. Even if much of the information were to be created by public entities and distributed freely, in any free society there would still be many independent creators and media outlets outside the public system, and commercialization would remain even if its scope is reduced.

---

[27] Rifkin, Jeremy, "Behind Merger Hype: Hypercapitalism; Business: AOL-Time Warner marriage shows just how far we've come toward commodifying culture." *The Los Angeles Times*; Los Angeles, CA; January 13, 2000.

[28] Böhm-Bawerk, Eugen von. *The Exploitation Theory Of Socialism-communism*. South Holland, Ill.: Libertarian Press, 1975.
Perry, John. An Evaluation of the Practitioner-team Ethic towards developing the Concept of the Learning Organization, 1998, < http://www.cultsock.ndirect.co.uk/MUHome/medintro.htm >

[29] Some people try to get around this problem by distinguishing the container of information, e.g., the artifact "book," from the information itself, but that is distinction without much difference.

While the commercialization of information and its means of distribution has existed for centuries, it has expanded in scope, as will be described below. It is classic that any expansion of the realm of the market leads to objections against encroachment of the "realm of rights". Markets in credit were or are still prohibited by some religions as sinful. Markets for air pollution elicit howls of protest. Most societies oppose the selling of justice,[30] health, babies, sex, public offices, and legal rights. In almost all cases these transactions take place anyway.

This is not to denigrate those objections, but to put them into a larger perspective. Legal rights, in a democracy, are distributed in a more egalitarian fashion than markets would distribute them. But rights are only a first distribution, followed by subsequent exchange transactions in which participants try to better their situation. Information, similarly, even if distributed freely, would be "enhanced" by private efforts, as happens to most governmental information, and subject to market forces.

The trend toward markets is by no means uni-directional. Military and civilian officers used to be formally for sale, but are not anymore. Conversely, the "rights" regime of the universal male military draft has given way to a market system of recruitment. In information too, trends and counter-trends exist. If anything, today in the age of the Internet, information of value is shared as a principle. The amount of useful but free information on the Internet is entirely without precedence.

Many categories of information would be adequately produced under a private commercial regime. But in other cases, such as basic research, a commercialization would lead to an underproduction since only the information's value to the private producer is factored in. Basic research has a considerable multiplier value, which a private firm would not consider in its investment decision. This is the reason for the public financing of much of basic research. University researchers do not truly give away information as a gift. They create the information as part of their employment deals with universities that are funded largely by public monies, and later distribute it as part of their status and career advancement.

The alternatives to intellectual property would not be palatable, either. In the absence of property rights, creators of information are not likely to give it away freely, but would engage in various stratagems of secrecy, contractual obligations[31] to non-disclose, etc. The alternative to property rights has been in the past based on benefactors, rewards, or an employment relation, with an associated dependency status for creators.

A commercial system of information does not negate parallel models. Happily, direct financial incentives are not the only motivator for humans to create and

---

[30] Mohr, Richard. "Commodification of Justice and the 'Re-Privatization' of Private Property." Prepared for the conference *Commodification: Theories, Practices, Histories and Representations*. University of Wollongong, February 19–20, 1998.

[31] Libecap, Gary D. *Contracting for Property Rights*. Cambridge, UK: Cambridge University Press, 1989, p. 10.

contribute information. Information can be given away as a gift, exchanged, shared as a community, or donated to the public. This means that one can maintain non-commercial forms of information exchange without negating commercial ones.

Under most circumstances, information is most likely to be freely offered when it has only limited value to a wider audience; as part of an eleemosynary distribution; and when it is part of a collaborating community. There is room for all these arrangements but they are not likely to serve as a foundation of an economy based on information.

2.5 COMMODIFICATION AS CONTROL BY BIG MEDIA COMPANIES

The real fear of commercialization is embodied in the meaning of commodification as the control of information by media giants.[32] In that view, the commercialization of information takes place because large media companies push it. But this is loose reasoning. Large firms are not primarily the cause for commercialization of information but just as much its result, though of course there is an interaction, as will be discussed below. The commercialization of information as based on the much larger secular trends of a knowledge-based society and economy.

The basic economic problem of information is how to cover the cost of its creation when reproduction costs are low while its initial creation (first copy cost) is expensive. The concentration and expansion of media companies is the result of the desire to extract higher returns from the information than would be possible in a competitive market structural when prices are driven to the low incremental cost. As Geoffrey Mulgan points out, "unless information can be kept scarce it cannot command a price. Without a price, private capital has no incentive to provide it. If production industries are unable to control the commodity form of what they produce the end result will be massive underproduction."[33]

Libraries, in particular, have vocally complained about market power in the serials they acquire. Their main problem, however, is the relentless expansion in production of titles, which face ever-narrower slices of individual subscribers, hence increasing the cost share and, thus, price to cover the cost for an increasing

---

[32] Schiller, Herbert I. *Who Knows: Information in the Age of the Fortune 500*, Ablex Publishing Corp, NJ, 1982.
Mosco, Vincent and Janet Wasko eds. The Political Economy of Information The U. of Wisconsin Press:Winconsin 1988; Sunstein, Cass. "Television and the Public Interest," *California Law Review* (2000); Baker, Edwin C. "The Media that Citizens Need" 147 U. of Penn L.Rev. 317 (1998).
[33] Mulgan, Geoffrey J. *Communications and Control: Networks and the New Economies of Information*. Guilford, NY, 1991.

number of publications. Market power is merely a problem on top of a problem. And the solution – the electronic publishing of serials – is at hand.

The desire by firms to form oligopolies for the purpose of keeping prices high is not unique to the information sector, but is prevalent across industries. The response to oligopolistic gasoline prices is not, however, to give it away for free, but to deal with the underlying oligopolistic market structure, such as through antitrust enforcements. The same holds true for information. The problem of high prices for music is not due to the fact that recordings are not given away freely or that musicians and composers are over-compensated, but primarily due to the highly concentrated industry structure for recorded music, where five firms dominate and engage in efforts to reduce that number further. Private firms have incentives to try to create oligopolies, and the purpose of governmental antitrust actions is to maintain competition in the instances where market forces do not. This is particularly true in those instances where network effects and compatibility requirements enable the leveraging of market power in one segment of the information sector to control other segments, too. Microsoft is an example of such a situation, and it has led to government antitrust action. Local cable TV distribution has some elements of this potential, and it has led to various regulated access requirements for distribution and content.

2.6 COMMODIFICATION AS THE EXPANSION OF INTELLECTUAL PROPERTY

Clearly, there has been a relative expansion of the scope of intellectual protection laws, which suggests a widening of the commercial sphere of information at the relative expense of the public sphere.[34] Words of the language are becoming owned by trademark holders. Business ideas can be patented.[35] Fair use gets squeezed. Distribution architecture gets controlled.[36] University researchers cease circulating results and start patenting them.[37] Genetic life forms are being owned. These are disturbing trends, though one should not lose perspective. It is grating if words like "polo" are claimed by a textile designer and his aggressive lawyers; but the English language has more than one million words, most of which are under-utilized and

---

[34] Bettig, Ronald. "Critical Perspectives on the History and Philosophy of Copyright." Critical Studies in Mass Communication (1992).
[35] State Street Bank & Trust Co. v. Signature Financial Group, Inc., 149 F.3d 1368 (Fed. Cir. 1998). Merges. Robert P. "As Many as Six Impossible Patents Before Breakfast: Property Rights for Business Concepts and Patent System Reform," 14 Berkeley Tech. L.J. 577 (Spring 1999), at < http://www.law.berkeley.edu/institutes/bclt/pubs/merges/ >
[36] Fitzgerald, Brian F. "Software As Discourse: The Power Of Intellectual Property In Digital Architecture" 18, *Cardozo Arts & Entertainment Law Journal* 337, 2000. Lessig, Lawrence, *Code and Other Laws of Cyberspace*. New York, NY: Basic Books, 1999.
[37] Kahin, Brian, "The Expansion of the Patent System: Politics and Political Economy," *First Monday*, < http://www.firstmonday.dk/issues/issue6_1/kahin/ >, December 2000.

wide-open, and each year probably more new words are created freely than subtracted commercially.

Similarly, while some academic research is being privatized – as it always had been – there is also more research taking place than ever. In the past, even life forms were protected: silk worms had to be smuggled out of China into the West, at pain of death.

Clearly, the traditional pragmatic balance between private incentive and public sphere has shifted. However, this imbalance may eventually right itself as stakeholders inevitably over-reach and reaction sets in.

The expansion of intellectual property has been likened to an encroachment by the market (sanctioned by courts and legislatures) on the public "commons." The image of the enclosure of the commons has been powerful on early socialist writers. In Britain, common lands for grazing were enclosed and appropriated by private owners, especially in the early years of the industrial revolution, leading to the plight of small farmers and their migration to the industrial cities. This image is now being transferred to information. But is it apt? Enclosure or not, it is clear that agriculture was greatly over-staffed, and employment had nowhere to go but to shrink. Industrial factories provided the major alternative for work, aside from emigration. In contrast, information is a booming and expanding sector.

Furthermore, the public sphere of the commons should not be romanticized. If truly open in terms of access, a commons attracts the kind of over-utilization described in Hardin's *The Tragedy of the Commons*.[38] It will thus not literally be open to all and free from restrictions. This makes the commons subject to the political process of allocation. In the U.S., grazing land, timber, and mineral deposits have notoriously been regulated to benefit favored constituencies. Free access to cable TV has been primarily granted to established commercial broadcasters. Furthermore, openness is not the only value to uphold but has to be weighed against others, such as privacy. Thus, declaring something a commons is not the end of a debate over access rights and obligations but only its beginning where conflicting uses and values exist, as they invariably do.

As applied to information, the concept of the commons, in contrast to land or resources, is vague. To some it means a rollback in the reach of copyrights, trademarks, and patents. To others, it means a public access to private media of distribution such as cable TV. To others it means the creation of a publicly financed or owned infrastructure dedicated to public access.[39] To still others it is the absence of private licenses for spectrum and their replacement by user fees[40] or

---

[38] Hardin, Garrett, "The Tragedy of the Commons," *Science*, 162,1968. pp.1243–1248.

[39] Benkler, Yochai. "Property, Commons, and the First Amendment: Towards a Core Common Infrastructure." White Paper for the First Amendment Program, Brennan Center for Justice at NYU School of Law, 2001

[40] Noam, Eli. "Taking the Next Step Beyond Spectrum Auctions: Open Spectrum Access." *IEEE Communications Magazine*, (December 1995), pp. 66–73.

no charges.[41] In principle, it is not clear why a public ownership of infrastructure is needed when most of its functions can be met by common carriage,[42] the traditional form of opening transportation and communication, and/or by principles of non-discriminatory "Third Party Neutrality," proposed by the author.[43]

A classic instant for the commons was the Internet in its early "frontier" years. As with any frontier situation, soon individuals begin to carve up profitably parts for themselves.[44] The early web browser, Mosaic, was developed at the University of Illinois. An entrepreneur recruited the core development team, upgraded Mosaic into the incompatible Netscape browser, and became a billionaire. Such expropriators of the commons became folk heroes as paragons of entrepreneurship. But one should also recognize that the huge wealth thus created also provided a powerful incentive to an astonishing burst of energy in various industries, regions, and countries. Thus, the Internet was accelerated beyond its otherwise likely trajectory of a government project by both greed and voluntarism. Both are at odds with each other, yet each seemed to have been indispensable to the Internet.

3. Why transactions in information are essential

So far we have described the weakness in the negative interpretations of the various meanings of "commodification of information." We will now argue in favor of such commodification as an essential part of an environment in which huge amounts of information get created, distributed, processed, and used. If anything, transactions in information will inevitably increase. They will do so as part of a wider transaction mechanism because this will be by far the best way to coordinate activities involving information.

---

cont.
  Noam, Eli. "Spectrum Auctions: Yesterday's Heresy, Today's Orthodoxy, Tomorrow's Anachronism." *Journal of Law and Economics*, December 1998. pp. 765–790.
[41] Gilder, George, "Auctioning the Airways," *Forbes*, April 11, 1994.
  Benkler, Yochai, and Lessig, Lawrence, "Will Technology Make CBS Unconstitutional? Net Gains." *The New Republic*, 2000.
[42] Noam, Eli. "The Tragedy of the Common Network: Theory for Formation and Breakdown Public Network," in *Private Networks, Public Objectives*, Elsevier Science B.V., Amsterdam. (1996) pp. 51–64. Noam, Eli. *Interconnecting the Network of Networks*, Cambridge, MA: MIT Press, 2001.
[43] Noam, Eli. *Interconnecting the Network of Networks*, Cambridge, MA: MIT Press, 2001.
[44] Bollier, David, "Public Assets, Private Profits: Reclaiming the American Commons in an Age of Market Enclosure." *New America Foundation*, Washington, DC. 2001. <http://www.newamerica.net/events/transcripts_texts/PA_Report.pdf>

The key fact about information is that it has increased in volume and applications, and in consequence there is so much of it moving around in ever-increasing complex arrangements that it becomes difficult to control directly. In consequence, information is increasingly channeled by and to machines rather than people. Soon, automobiles will be communicating directly with highways, packages with shippers, suitcases with airlines, light bulbs with utilities, and TV sets with film distributors. The information flows over wires and fibers, over the air, navigating various and shifting technical, economic, and legal bottlenecks.

How can such a system function in operational and economic terms? Not by human control except on the macro level of basic principles and rules of full-time supervision. Not by giant firms dealing with each other to account for trillions of transactions. Not by centralized machines. Not even by networked machines controlling from a distance. Too much transmission and processing would be used up by each piece of information having to be controlled from the distance, report back, receive instructions, account for itself, etc.

Computer scientists begin to recognize that the only feasible way to manage these information flows is by decentralizing and decomposing the control into numerous small and automated transactions.[45] Decentralized "invisible hand mechanisms"[46] function as huge information processing machines for the myriad of transactions of society in a way that centralized decision-makers in government or industry cannot.[47]

In earlier times the decentralization of information was accomplished by pushing the decision mechanisms down the hierarchy, from the state level to that of companies, institutions, and individuals. But now, with the increasing complexity of the environment, it becomes necessary to push them down again, to the level of the information itself. Information needs to be engaged in direct transactions that involve it.

What does this mean and how could it be accomplished?

The key here is to understand that information and its transmission networks are moving from continuous streams of analog or digital signals, to discrete

---

[45] Davis, Randall & Smith, Reid G. "Negotiation as a Metaphor for Distributed Problem Solving," *Artificial Intelligence* (1983); Waldspurger, Carl A. "A Distributed Computational Economy for Utilizing Idle Resources," Master's thesis, Massachusetts Institute of Technology, (1989); Wellman, Michael P. "A Market-Oriented Programming Environment and its Application to Distributed Multi-commodity Flow Problems" *Journal of Artificial Intelligence Research*, 1:1–23, (1993); Miller, Mark S. & Drexler, K. Eric. "The Agoric Papers," *The Ecology of Computation*, Amsterdam: Elsevier Science Publishers, B. V. (1998); Bogan, Nathaniel. "Economic Allocation of Computation Time with Computation Markets" (1994); Ferguson & Yemini. "Economic Models for Allocation Resources in Computer Systems" mimeo (1996); Sairmamesh et al. "E-Marketplaces: Architecture, Trading Models, and Their Role in Bandwidth Markets" mimeo (2000).

[46] Nozick, Robert. *Anarchy, State, and Utopia,* New York: Basic Books, 1974

[47] Hayek, Friedrich A. von. *The Road to Serfdom.* University of Chicago Press. 1944.

packets transmitted discontinuously. The information is labeled by sender, location within a document, and other operational data.[48]

This principle of identifiable information associated with an address is an enormously powerful concept. The next step would be to add payment mechanisms and other instructions. Thus, information could operate on its own in a decentralized fashion, without continuous control and guidance, and engage in "nano-transactions" for access, transmission, storage, processing, and other information.

3.1 SOCIAL POLICY GOALS

One implication of such identifiable packets is that information can be treated in a highly differentiated fashion. Counter to the claim of information becoming an undifferentiated commodity or that technologically "a bit is a bit,"[49] actually quite the opposite will be happening. Each packet has an address, sender and recipient, and soon other identifiable information. This means that different packets can be treated quite differently.

The ability to identify has significant implications for future public policy. It opens entirely new avenues for various mechanisms on the level of information. (We can call this "nano-regulation.") For example, one could establish – if that were the policy decision – price differentiation in favor of certain uses or users, such as education of rural users or students. Subsidy mechanisms could be established in which some users, such as the poor, would get free or cheaper access. Various meritorious content could receive preferential treatment, etc. This would deal with the most objectionable aspect of any market mechanism, its distributional impact. For almost any purpose, government has at its disposal a tool that is quite powerful for whatever purpose the public decision process determines is desirable. The scope of these policies is based on legal, constitutional, and political considerations, not on technical or practical ones. Of course, there will be resourceful people who keep a step ahead of enforcement capabilities; but that does not negate the basic point: the mechanism of transactions in information enable control and liberation, concentration and openness.

4. CONCLUSION

In light of the expansion, differentiation, diversity, and increasing affordability of information, it is hard to understand on what data the thesis of information

---

[48] Baran, Paul. "History, Alternative Approaches, and Comparisons," RM-3097-PR. 1964.
[49] Negroponte, Nicholas. *Being Digital*. Knopf, New York, 1995.

commodification is based on, other than on pressures to expand intellectual property rights into areas where they did not exist before.

Our discussion finds multiple meanings for "commodity" and "commodification" that are at odds with each other. For some it means cheap, to others expensive. To some it means homogenous, to others proprietary. To some it means excessive control, to others excessive competition. Yet neither of these views is especially persuasive.

The debate over the commodification of information needs to be seen in context. Information used to be a scarce good. It is now abundant. From this many consequences flow. For a long time information was controlled by the state. It was produced and disseminated by state-controlled institutions like monasteries, schools, universities, telecom networks and television networks. The underlying organizational logic was that information was scarce and hence valuable, and had to be produced, distributed, and shared under some public control. A body of theory provided the intellectual underpinnings, such as those of natural monopoly, public goods, industrial policy, and economic development planning.

With information becoming plentiful, its production and distribution grew in volume and complexity. The system became too complicated for any single organization, whether a school system, a monopoly telecom provider, a broadcaster, or a cable TV firm, to run well, and for government to supervise. The state control model broke down. This called for a different treatment.

The new model was one of markets and property rights. The basic idea was that anybody could enter the information sector, that markets would provide the control functions, and that property rights would provide incentives.[50] This transition created losers, such as traditional public service broadcast organizations that had functioned as the gatekeepers for the creativity of entire societies. It also created winners, such as major media companies. The debate over commodification is part of this struggle. But it is not forward-looking. The property rights perspective is dominant in the present, but not for the future.

The property rights approach worked best in the information sector when it dealt with "old economy" physical assets, such as wire line networks competing with each other. It had only spotty explanatory power when it came to the new digital environment. Its thinking could not help with the most interesting new developments in communications, except in a labored way. Network externalities and communities do not fit into the property rights analysis, just as economics in general had a difficult time with externalities. The whole Internet must be a property rights advocate's intellectual nightmare.

---

[50] Posner, Richard A. *Economic Analysis of Law*. Aspen Publishers,. 5th ed. January 1998. Barzel, Yoram *Economic Analysis of Property Rights*, 2nd ed. New York, NY: Cambridge University Press, 1997. Demsetz, Harold "Toward a Theory of Property Rights," *American Economic Review*, v. 57, 1967, pp. 374–359. Umbeck, John R., *A Theory of Property Rights* Ames, Iowa: State University Press, 1981.

The reason why the property rights approach has hit its limitations is that just as the state approach before, it, too, cannot deal with the new levels of complexity that the digital environment is rapidly creating. But most of the critics of the property rights system and its co-modification are also reacting to the past. The key to thinking about the next stage of the information economy is not property but transactions.[51]

This essay concludes that the expansion of a transaction-based system of information creation and distribution will be an essential – and beneficial – part of the information environment, and that it will enhance the ability to create information. Furthermore, it will enable the distribution of information according to societal policy determinations. Thus, such a transaction-oriented commodification deserves our cheers, not condemnation.

---

[51] This transaction approach goes back to Oliver Williamson see Graff, Jamison. *An Introduction to the Work of Oliver Eaton Williamson.* < http://users.iems.nwu.edu. > June 1995, with some credit to Ronald Coase ("The Problem of Social Cost." Journal of Law and Economics, 1960). Williamson explained organizations' size and structure by their desire to minimize transaction cost. Hierarchical control of internal transactions reduced their costs below those of market coordination. This led to large firms and other organizations. Today, for information, external transaction and internal coordination costs are radically changing, and their relative magnitude should greatly affect the size and structure of firms and industries.

II. COPYRIGHT AND COMMODIFICATION: BROAD TRENDS

Copyright, Commodification, and Censorship: Past as Prologue – But to What Future?

*Pamela Samuelson**

Copyright, commodification, and freedom of expression have often been viewed as harmonious and complementary concepts. In *Harper & Row Publishers, Inc. v. Nation Enterprises*, for example, the Supreme Court characterized copyright law as the "engine of free expression."[1] Holding a left-leaning news magazine liable for copyright infringement for publishing excerpts from Gerald Ford's forthcoming memoirs did not, in the Court's view, condone an act of private censorship. It was in harmony with first amendment principles because copyright incentives would ensure that these memoirs would reach the public through the normal operation of the marketplace.[2] Copyright scholars such as Neil Netanel and Niva Elkin-Koren have emphasized copyright's contribution to democratic discourse in providing rights that enable independent writers and artists to make a living from their expression.[3]

In the mainstream view, one reason copyright and free expression are harmonious is because copyright protection extends only to an author's

---

[*] An earlier version of this paper was included in a binder of papers presented for a conference on the Commodification of Information held at Haifa University in May of 1999. My thanks to Niva Elkin-Koren and Neil Netanel for the opportunity to participate in this conference.

[1] 471 U.S. 539, 558 (1985).

[2] Cutting against fair use were The Nation's attempt to "scoop" the part of Ford's memoir about the Nixon pardon and the allegedly "purloined" nature of the manuscript from which the Nation's editors drew the excerpts as cutting against The Nation's fair use defense. Id. at 562–64.

[3] See, e.g., Neil W. Netanel, *Copyright and a Democratic Civil Society*, 106 Yale L.J. 283 (1996); Niva Elkin-Koren, *Cyberlaw and Social Change: A Democratic Approach to Copyright*, 14 Cardozo Arts & Ent. L.J. 215 (1996).

N. Elkin-Koren and N.W. Netanel (eds.), *The Commodification of Information*, 63–77.
© 2002 *Pamela Samuelson. Printed in Great Britain.*

"expression," not to her "ideas" or information the work may contain.[4] Other authors are always free to express the same idea or reuse information derived from a protected work in a subsequent work as long as he expresses the ideas or information in a different way. This substantially limits the potential for private censorship in copyright. Also contributing to the compatibility of copyright and freedom of expression principles has been the fair use doctrine.[5] When Howard Hughes acquired copyright in a magazine article about his life and tried to use it to stop publication of an unauthorized biography, an appellate court rebuffed the effort to use copyright to accomplish private censorship by finding that the biographer had made fair use of the article.[6] Acuff-Rose Music, Inc., which owned a copyright in the popular song "Pretty Woman," may similarly have hoped to stop Two Live Crew from selling its rap parody version of the song because of its distaste for the parody. However, the Supreme Court was persuaded that this parody was the kind of critical commentary on a protected work that the fair use doctrine should permit.[7] In these and other cases, courts have invoked fair use to prevent the exercise of copyright as a means of censoring content of which the copyright owner disapproved.

Occasionally, fair use and the idea/expression distinction have failed to preserve as much harmony between copyright and free expression principles as society deems desirable. In the aftermath of the Supreme Court's *Harper & Row* decision, for example, biographers and historians perceived themselves to be at risk of private censorship if they quoted from unpublished letters or manuscripts of public figures, such as those by the famously private J.D. Salinger or the controversial founder of the Scientology movement.[8] Congress responded to these concerns by amending the fair use provision to clarify that the unpublished nature of copyrighted works did not preclude the exercise of fair use.[9] A seeming deviation between copyright and freedom of expression principles was thus mended, and historians and biographers, among others, breathed a sigh of relief.[10]

On other occasions, the common law adjudication process has taken care to

---

[4] See, e.g., Melville B. Nimmer, *Does Copyright Abridge the First Amendment Guarantee of Free Speech and Free Press?*, 17 UCLA L. Rev. 1180, 1186–89 (1970). Nimmer also regarded the limited duration of copyright as important to the consistency of copyright and the First Amendment. Id. at 1193.

[5] See, e.g., Paul Goldstein, *Copyright and the First Amendment*, 70 Column. L. Rev. 983, 1011–15, 1017–22 (1970). See also Robert C. DeNicola, *Copyright and Free Speech: Constitutional Limitations on the Protection of Expression*, 67 Cal. L. Rev. 283 (1979).

[6] See Rosemont Enterp. v. Random House, Inc., 366 F.2d 303 (2d Cir. 1966).

[7] See Campbell v. Acuff-Rose Music, Inc., 510 U.S. 569 (1994).

[8] See, e.g., Pierre Leval, *Toward a Fair Use Standard*, 103 Harv. L. Rev. 1105 (1990) (discussing cases).

[9] See 17 U.S.C. sec. 107, as amended.

[10] Yet concerns persist about chilling effects on free expression of visual artists from rulings such as Rogers v. Koons, 751 F. Supp. 474 (S.D.N.Y. 1990), aff'd, 960 F.2d 301 (2d Cir.), cert. denied, 113 S.Ct. 365 (1992). See, e.g., Louise Harmon, *Law, Art, and the Killing Jar*, 79 Iowa L. Rev. 367 (1994).

allay concerns about copyright being in conflict with freedom of expression principles. Some years ago, for example, Fred Yen expressed concern that the "total concept and feel" test for software copyright infringement was so vague as to threaten freedom in computer programming expression.[11] Later cases repudiated the broad "look and feel" claims,[12] and so, this conflict between copyright and First Amendment principles was resolved.

These doctrines and developments seem to have bred some complacency among copyright professionals about the compatibility of copyright and freedom of expression principles. Oddly enough, there has been to date remarkably little scholarship produced by First Amendment scholars on the compatibility of copyright and free expression principles. Such literature as exists has largely been produced by copyright scholars who have tended to visit the First Amendment literature to find support for their arguments on specific copyright issues. Copyright professionals may have been blinded by familiar doctrines from perceiving certain threats to free expression values that a First Amendment scholar would easily perceive.

Shaking off the field's complacency is a new generation of scholars – Yochai Benkler, Julie Cohen, Niva Elkin-Koren, Lawrence Lessig, Mark Lemley, Neil Netanel, and Eugene Volokh, among them – who recognize a greater potential for disharmony between copyright and freedom of expression principles than their predecessors.[13] The need for this work arises from the fact that the rights of copyright owners have expanded considerably in recent years and that fair use principles have been under attack.[14] These young scholars have looked to First Amendment and other constitutional principles to shore up limiting doctrines of copyright law and to make policy recommendations about how copyright law should evolve. As admirable as this new literature is, it largely ignores the fact that

---

[11] See Alfred C. Yen, *A First Amendment Perspective on the Idea/Expression Dichotomy and Copyright in a Work's "Total Concept and Feel,"* 38 Emory L.J. 393 (1989). The principal case endorsing this concept was Whelan Assoc., Inc. v. Jaslow Dental Lab., Inc., 797 F.2d 1222 (3d Cir. 1986), cert. denied, 479 U.S. 1031 (1987).

[12] See, e.g., Apple Computer, Inc. v. Microsoft Corp., 35 F.3d 1435 (9th Cir. 1994) (rejecting "look and feel" claim for user interface); Lotus Dev. Corp. v. Borland Int'l, Inc., 49 F.3d 807 (1st Cir. 1995), aff'd by equally divided court, 116 S.Ct. 804 (1996) (rejecting "look and feel" claim).

[13] See, e.g., Yochai Benkler, *Free As the Air to Common Use: First Amendment Constraints on the Enclosure of the Public Domain,* 74 N.Y.U. L. Rev. 354 (1999); Julie E. Cohen, *A Right to Read Anonymously: A Closer Look at Copyright Management in Cyberspace,* 28 Conn. L. Rev. 981 (1996); Niva Elkin-Koren, *Copyright Law and Social Dialogue on the Information Superhighway: The Case Against Copyright Liability of Bulletin Board Operators,* 13 Cardozo Arts & Ent. L. J. 345 (1995); Mark A. Lemley and Eugene Volokh, *Freedom of Speech and Injunctions in Intellectual Property Cases,* 48 Duke L.J. 147 (1999); Lawrence Lessig, *Code and Other Laws of Cyberspace* (2000); Netanel, supra note 3.

[14] See, e.g., Report of the Working Group on Intellectual Property, Intellectual Property and the National Information Infrastructure 63–84 (Sept. 1995) (hereinafter "White Paper") (expansively interpreting copyright's exclusive rights and criticizing fair use).

copyright has at least as long a history of being a handmaiden of censorship as it has a history of being the so-called "engine of free expression."[15] Understanding this history may be valuable in assessing whether this past may be a prologue to a future in which copyright and censorship will once again be conjoined.

So let us briefly visit this history: The Anglo-American copyright regime arose out of practices and policies of the English Stationers' Guild in the late 15th and early 16th centuries.[16] To ensure harmony within the ranks, the guild established a registry system for staking claims in books. Members entered into the guild register the names of books in which they claimed printing rights,[17] whereupon other guild members were expected to refrain from publishing the same book. A private enforcement system enabled guild members to resolve disputes amongst themselves over rights in particular books. While some stationers in this era were surely noble fellows who sought to enlighten the public, the private copyright system of the pre-modern era mainly functioned to regulate the book trade to ensure that members of the guild enjoyed monopolies in the books they printed.

This system was, however, conducive to taking on a second function. Conveniently for English authorities, the guild's practices provided an infrastructure for controlling (i.e., suppressing) publication of heretical and seditious materials. The English kings and queens were quite willing to grant to the Stationers' Guild control over the publication of books in the realm in exchange for the guild's promise to refrain from printing such dangerous materials.[18] Until its abolition, the Star Chamber was available to enforce judgments emanating from the stationers' private adjudication system.

The pre-modern copyright system undoubtedly promoted freedom of expression by making books more widely available. However, this was an incidental byproduct of the market for books, not an intended purpose of the then-prevailing copyright system. Far more harmonious was the relationship between copyright and censorship in that era. Men burned at the stake for writing texts that were

---

[15] See supra note 1 and accompanying text. For a history of the pre-modern era of copyright, see, e.g., L. Ray Patterson, *Copyright in Historical Perspective* (1968). See also Mark Rose, *Authors and Owners: The Invention of Copyright* (1993); John Feather, *A History of British Publishing* (1988). Rather than heavily footnoting the text's discussion of what I call the pre-modern era of copyright, as in a law review article, I am citing here the three works from which I drew this history. Readers wishing to engage in further investigation should consult these works.

[16] The guild included not only the printers of books, but others involved in the book trade, such as book-binders and booksellers. English kings and queens also granted letters patent to certain printers conferring on them exclusive rights to print certain types of works was an auxiliary system of regulating the printing trade that in time was folded into copyright. Over time, the Stationers' Company became the predominant copyright system.

[17] Rights to print these books were regarded by guild members as perpetual in duration; they could, however, be assigned or licensed to other guild members.

[18] That the Licensing Acts were integrally interrelated with the Stationers' copyright system is demonstrated in part by the fact that the Stationers Company emphasized the valuable role of these acts in suppressing dangerous speech when arguing that Parliament should reinstate the Licensing Acts after they expired in the late 17th century.

critical of the Crown or of established religion, and printers of such books could expect no better fate. The stationers' copyright regime was part of the apparatus aimed at ensuring that these texts would not be printed or otherwise be made widely accessible to the public.

The principal development that ushered in the modern era of copyright was the English Parliament's passage of the Statute of Anne in 1710.[19] On its face, this statute was both a repudiation of several principal tenets of the stationers' copyright system and a redirection of copyright's purpose away from censorship and toward freedom of expression principles. In addition, it sought to promote competition among printers and booksellers – that is, to break the stranglehold that major firms within the Stationers' Company had had over the book trade.

The Statute of Anne achieved these goals in several ways: First, the act granted rights to authors, not to publishers. Second, it did so for the utilitarian purpose of inducing learned men to write and publish books. Third, the act established a larger societal purpose for copyright, namely, to promote learning. Fourth, it granted rights only in newly authored books. Thereafter, ancient books were in the public domain and could be printed by anyone. Fifth, it limited the duration of copyright protection to fourteen years (renewable for another 14 years if the author was living at the end of that term), thus abolishing perpetual copyrights.[20] Sixth, the statute conferred rights of a limited character (not to control all uses, but to control the printing and reprinting of protected works). Seventh, it imposed a responsibility on publishers to deposit copies of their works with designated libraries. Eighth, it provided a system for redressing grievances about overpriced books.

While it took an additional 50 years or so for the pre-modern copyright system to die away,[21] the modern law of copyright emerged from the Statute of Anne's precepts. Censorship held no place of honor in this new copyright system. The modern copyright system embraced Enlightenment values that influenced the framers of the U.S. Constitution.[22] Article I, sec. 8, cl. 8 of the Constitution, which empowers Congress to promote the progress of science and the useful arts by securing to authors and inventors for limited times an exclusive right in their respective writings and discoveries, should be viewed in historical context as an American endorsement of England's repudiation of the speech-suppressing, anti-competitive and otherwise repressive pre-modern copyright system that the English Parliament meant to reshape through the Statute of Anne. Core elements of the Statute of Anne are reflected in that clause's purpose ("to promote

---

[19] See, e.g., Rose, supra note 15 (discussing the Statute of Anne).
[20] A "grandfather" provision allowed holders of existing copyrights some additional time to exploit the rights, but the duration was limited. Id.
[21] See, e.g., id. (discussing litigation about the implications of the Statute of Anne on common law rights).
[22] See, e.g., Office of Technology Assessment, Intellectual Property Rights in an Age of Electronics and Information 37–39 (1986).

Science"), in the persons to whom rights were to be granted ("authors"), and in the duration of rights ("for limited times").

Marci Hamilton has sometimes asserted that the Constitution did not include a provision on freedom of speech because the framers had done everything necessary to ensure a healthy system of free expression by authorizing enactment of a copyright law.[23] Though I would not go that far, I would agree that the copyright clause of the Constitution, properly construed, embodies first amendment and anti-monopoly principles. Because of this, I agree with Professor Hamilton that there is a "dormant copyright clause" waiting to be reawakened in the case law – and hopefully in Congress – after a long sleep in which the clause has become a meaningless cliché.[24]

To understand why rejuvenation of this clause may be desirable, it may be worth considering some parallels between copyright in the pre-modern era and copyright as it has evolved in the past decade or so, the trend toward which I will call "post-modern copyright."

- **Consolidation in the Copyright Industries:** The rise of publishing and media giants, such as Reed Elsevier, AOL-Time-Warner, and Disney, harkens back to the dominance of certain London booksellers in the Stationers' Company and their influence on pre-modern copyright policy. As the work of James Boyle has shown, major copyright industry players have been remarkably successful in recent years in promoting a high protectionist agenda in the national policy arena, as though theirs were the only interests worthy of concern.[25] This should be of concern in part because the work of Yochai Benkler suggests that strengthening intellectual property rights does not broadly advance the interests of all creators, but rather advantages large vertically integrated content providers while disadvantaging small scale firms and individual creators.[26] Consolidation in the copyright industries also affects the ability of freelance writers to negotiate fair contracts with major media firms who tend to want writers to assign all rights in their works for a one-time payment.[27]
- **The Decline of the Author/The Rise of the Work:** As in the pre-modern era, the post-modern copyright emphasis is on "the work," "the copyright," and "the rights holder," rather than on "authors."[28] The post-modern copyright system

---

[23] Address to the Section on Defamation and Privacy, Association of American Law Schools, San Francisco CA, January 1998.
[24] Marci Hamilton, *The Dormant Copyright Clause* (manuscript on file with the author).
[25] See, e.g., James Boyle, *The Politics of Intellectual Property: Environmentalism for the Net?*, 47 Duke L.J 87 (1997).
[26] See, e.g., Benkler, supra note 13, at 400-08.
[27] See, e.g., P. Bernt Hugenholtz, *The Great Copyright Robbery: Rights Allocation in a Digital Environment*, presented at New York University Law School (April 2000), available at < http://www.ivir.nl/medewerkers/hugenholtz-uk.html >.
[28] See Peter Jaszi, *Toward a Copyright Theory: The Metamorphoses of Authorship*, 1991 Duke L. J. 455 (1991).

promotes the interests of rights holders in their works more than it promotes the interests of individual authors. The "major labels" in the recording industry, for example, have systematically advanced their interests in a way that has worked to the disadvantage of many individual performers, including by seeking legislation to designate sound recordings as "works for hire" so that individual creators would not be able eventually to exercise termination of transfer rights.[29]

- **A Decline in the Utilitarian and Learning Purposes of Copyright/The Rise of Profit Maximization:** From the standpoint of dominant players in the content industries, the purpose of copyright law is to maximize revenues for the benefit of rights holders, not to provide the minimum level of protection necessary to incent a desirable level of investments in creative activity, let alone to promote learning or innovation.[30] Hollywood firms may have recouped its investments in films many times over, but they nevertheless wish to exploit whatever residual value exists in those films. That the utilitarian rationale for granting authors limited rights in their works has given way to pure rent-seeking behavior is especially evident in the Congressional decision in 1998 to extend the copyright term for another 20 years.[31]

- **A Predicted Demise of Fair Use and Other Copyright Limitations:** The pre-modern copyright system had no fair use or other public interest exceptions to the scope of publisher rights, nor did it seek to promote science, innovation, or freedom of expression, values which in the modern era have given rise to fair use and other exceptions.[32] Historically fair use and related limitations on the scope of copyright have been regarded as part of the social bargain of the U.S. copyright system.[33] In the postmodern era, U.S. policymakers have sometimes spoken of fair use and other limitations as a "tax" on publishers.[34] They have predicted that fair use will fade away because copyright owners are developing new licensing schemes through which they can be compensated for access to and uses of their works.[35] The 1994 Agreement on Trade-Related Aspects of Intellectual Property Rights (TRIPS) arguably limits national authority to create exceptions and limitations that interfere with the ability of rights holders

---

[29] See, e.g., Courtney Love, *Courtney Love Does the Math*, Salon Magazine, <http://www.salon.com/tech/feature/2000/06/14/love/>; Shawn Zeller, Compromise, Hell!, 32 Nat'l Law J. 3668 (11/18/00) (discussing the recording industry's success in obtaining legislation naming sound recordings as works for hire).

[30] See, e.g., Netanel, supra note 3.

[31] See, e.g., Pub. L. No. 105-298 (1998). A constitutional challenge to this extension of the copyright term was rejected at the trial court level. See Eldred v. Reno, 74 F.Supp.2d 1 (D.D.C. 1999).

[32] See, e.g., 17 U.S.C. secs. 107-121 (copyright exceptions).

[33] See, e.g., Jessica Litman, *Revising Copyright Law for the Information Age*, 75 Or. L. Rev. 19, 31-35 (1996).

[34] See, e.g., White Paper, supra note 14, at 84.

[35] Id. at 49-53, 82.

to control exploitations of their works.[36] Some representatives of the copyright industries have already expressed a desire to use this agreement to challenge copyright exceptions in national copyright laws.[37]

- **Perpetual Copyrights:** In the pre-modern era, copyrights were perpetual. In the modern era, copyrights have been limited in duration, intended to be long enough to enable authors and their progeny to benefit from any commercial value deriving from the author's work, and enriching the public domain thereafter.[38] The willingness of Congress to extend the copyright term to save Mickey Mouse and other valuable intellectual creations from being consigned to the public domain suggests that copyright in the post-modern era may be on its way to becoming perpetual again – this time on the installment plan, as Peter Jaszi so wittily observed.[39] The public domain may also be threatened by the use of technical measures to protect works whose copyright is nearing expiration because the technical measures will not cease limiting access and use when the copyright expires. Technical measures may, moreover, be used to control access to and uses of public domain works. This may mean that works that copyright law officially conceives of as being in the public domain may instead be perpetually protected by technology, backed up by the anti-circumvention rules discussed below as long as rights holders use the same technical measures to protect works in copyright as well as works out of copyright.[40]

- **The Decline of Originality as a Meaningful Constraint on Publisher Rights:** If major information industry players such as Reed Elsevier have their way in the U.S. as they did in the European Union, Congress will soon adopt a new form of intellectual property protection for collections of information that will, in essence, obviate the need to show any creative "originality" for an

---

[36] See Final Act Embodying the Results of the Uruguay Round of Multilateral Trade Negotiations, Apr. 15, 1994, reprinted in *The Results of the Uruguay Round of Multilateral Trade Negotiations – The Legal Texts 2–3* (Gatt Secretariat ed. 1994); Marrakesh Agreement Establishing the World Trade Organization, Apr. 15, 1994, Annex 1C: Agreement on Trade-Related Aspects of Intellectual Property Rights, reprinted in *Results of Uruguay Round*, supra at 6–19, 365–403. See TRIPS, art. 13.

[37] See, e.g., Eric Smith, *Worldwide Copyright Protection Under the TRIPS Agreement*, 29 Vand. J. Transn'l L. 559, 577–78 (1996). But see Pamela Samuelson, *The U.S. Digital Agenda at WIPO*, 37 Va. J. Int'l L. 369, 398–409 (1997) (arguing that existing copyright exceptions and limitations are compatible with TRIPS).

[38] See, e.g., Peter Jaszi, *Goodbye to All That: A Reluctant (and Perhaps Premature) Adieu to a Constitutionally Grounded Discourse of Public Interest in Copyright Law*, 29 Vand. J. Transn'l L. 595, 597–600 (1996).

[39] Statement of Professor Peter Jaszi, Washington College of Law, American University, On S. 4839. The Copyright Term Extension Act of 1995, Before the Senate Judiciary Committee, Sept. 20, 1995.

[40] See infra notes 68–70 and accompanying text. Development of a tool to bypass a technical measure used to protect a public domain work will be illegal under these rules as long as copyright owners use the same measure to protect works in copyright. See 17 U.S.C. sec. 1201(a)(2) and (b)(1).

informational work to receive copyright-like protection.[41] Some digital media firms have been claiming copyright protection in digitized versions of public domain works.[42] If public domain works in digital form cannot be fully controlled by copyright because of lingering questions about the sufficiency of their originality, one can expect such firms to use technical protection measures to control access to and use of these works and/or to obtain intellectual property-like protection through mass-market licenses governed by the law of jurisdictions that have adopted the Uniform Computer Information Transactions Act (formerly known as Article 2B of the Uniform Commercial Code).[43]

- **Excessive Pricing:** In the post-modern era, as in the pre-modern era, complaints about excessive pricing of copyrighted works have become common. Universities have been especially vocal about excessive pricing of science journals sold by publishing giants such as Reed Elsevier.[44] Noticeably absent from public discourse about intellectual property in the U.S. is any serious consideration of the possibility of imposing compulsory licenses, legal licenses, or obligations to license on fair and reasonable terms as a way to counteract this problem, although some scholars have raised these possibilities.[45]

- **Unclear Origins of Rights:** In the post-modern, as in the pre-modern era, there is noticeable fuzziness about the source of authority firms have when claiming certain rights in informational works. It is unclear, for example, whether asserted rights to license works or to technically protect them derive from ownership or possession of a particular artifact, from intellectual property law, or from some other source. In the pre-modern era, stationers considered rights in their "copies" to derive from their possession of manuscripts and any investments they may have made in printing those manuscripts.[46] In the post-modern era, claims of seemingly absolute rights to license works on all but

---

[41] H.R. 354, 106th Cong., 1st Sess. (1999). See, e.g., J.H. Reichman & Pamela Samuelson, *Intellectual Property Rights in Data?*, 50 Vand. L. Rev. 51 (1997) (explaining genesis of this legislation); J.H. Reichman & Paul F. Uhlir, *Database Protection at the Crossroads: Recent Developments and Their Impact on Science and Technology*, 14 Berkeley Tech. L.J. 793 (1999) (analyzing H.R. 354).

[42] See, e.g., Pamela Samuelson, *The Originality Standard For Literary Works Under U.S. Copyright Law*, 42 Am. J. Compar. Law 393 (1994) (discussing such claims).

[43] This model law is discussed at length in law review symposium issues. See, e.g., Symposium, *Intellectual Property and Contract Law in the Information Age: The Impact of Article 2B of the Uniform Commercial Code on the Future of Transactions in Information and Electronic Commerce*, 13 Berkeley Tech. L.J. 809 (1998); Symposium, *Intellectual Property and Contract Law in the Information Age: The Impact of Article 2B of the Uniform Commercial Code on the Future of Transactions in Information and Electronic Commerce*, 87 Calif. L. Rev. 1 (1999). UCITA has thus far been enacted in Virginia and Maryland.

[44] See, e.g., Stanley Chodorow & Peter Lyman, "The Future of Scholarly Communication", in *The Mirage of Continuity* (Brian Hawkins & Patricia Battin, eds. 1998).

[45] See, e.g., J.H. Reichman & Jonathan Franklin, *Privately Regulated Intellectual Property Rights: Reconciling Freedom of Contract with Public Good Uses of Information*, 147 U. Penn. L. Rev. 875 (1999).

[46] See sources supra note 15.

unconscionable terms and to use technical protection measures to control access to protected works have an unclear provenance. Jessica Litman has pointed out that UCITA posits the existence of property rights in information other than those arising from intellectual property law without specifying exactly what those rights are or how far they extend.[47]

- **Private Ordering/Private Enforcement:** Also evident in the post-modern copyright era is a renewed romance with private ordering and private enforcement efforts. The rhetoric employed by high protectionists about the desirability of trusting the market to work out appropriate arrangements resembles, as Julie Cohen has cogently pointed out, the rhetoric once employed in a now discredited Supreme Court decision that challenged public policy limitations on freedom of contract.[48] Yet high protectionists in the post-modern era have employed this rhetoric with considerable success. When considering the impact of private ordering and enforcement, it is also worth reflecting on the stationers' copyright system. The history of this regime reveals why leaving the exploitation of informational works solely to private ordering can have serious deleterious consequences for society, in particular, for innovation, competition, and the dissemination of learning.[49] As in the pre-modern era, industry groups in the post-modern era have played significant roles in policing compliance with copyright norms. A well-known example is the "hotline" the Software Publishers Association provides through which disgruntled employees and the like can inform on their employers for unlicensed software.

- **The Rhetoric of "Piracy" and "Burglary":** Characterizing unauthorized copying as "piracy" has both pre- and post-modern roots. In the pre-modern era, the so-called "pirates" were printers who did not belong to the Stationers' Company but dared to publish works in which stationers claimed copyright.[50] Today "pirates" seem to come in many shapes and sizes. Increasingly common is the use of the term "piracy" to refer to single acts of infringement by individuals. Major firms in post-modern copyright industries are using, or planning to use, technical protection systems to protect their works from such "piracy."[51] These firms are unwilling to rely solely on private ordering to protect their interests, however. In 1998, they persuaded Congress to make it illegal to bypass a technical protection measure used by copyright owners to control access to their works and to make or distribute technologies that can be

---

[47] See Jessica Litman, *The Tales That Article 2B Tells*, 13 Berkeley Tech. L.J. 931 (1998).
[48] See Julie E. Cohen, *Lochner in Cyberspace: The New Economic Orthodoxy of "Rights Management,"* 97 Mich. L. Rev. 462 (1998).
[49] See sources cited supra notes 15.
[50] See, e.g., Rose, supra note 15.
[51] See, e.g., Mark Stefik, *Shifting the Possible: How Trusted Systems and Digital Property Rights Challenge Us To Rethink Digital Publishing*, 12 Berkeley Tech. L.J. 137 (1997) (discussing the concept of trusted system technology).

used to bypass technical access- or use-controls.[52] They liken circumvention to "burglary" and the technologies that enable circumvention to "burglar's tools."[53] The anti-circumvention provisions of the Digital Millennium Copyright Act (DMCA), while ambiguous in some key respects, provide legal reinforcement for technical protection of rights, with criminal penalties available to punish willful violators of these norms.[54]

- **Increased Criminal Sanctions:** The rhetoric of piracy lends itself to increased use of criminal penalties to enforce copyright interests. Post-modern copyright, like pre-modern copyright, increasingly looks to criminal sanctions to punish "bad" actors in the copyright space. In the modern era, only large-scale commercial infringers were at risk of criminal liability for copyright infringement. In the post-modern era, criminal copyright liability provisions are proliferating and casting a far wider net. For example, the No Electronic Theft Act for the first time imposes criminal liability on willful infringers without regard to commercial purpose.[55] Consider also the anti-circumvention provisions of the DMCA, which seemingly allow a circumventor or maker of a circumvention tool to be held criminally liable without any showing of an underlying act of infringement.[56] Mere potential to enable infringement seemingly suffices.

Many things, of course, distinguish the post-modern from the pre-modern era of copyright, including the social, political, and economic context within which these post-modern developments are occurring. Many members of the judiciary, including members of the Supreme Court, continue to believe in modern copyright precepts. Because of this, it would be unduly alarmist to suggest that post-modernism has totally captured copyright law or that copyright law will get divorced from freedom of expression principles in order to remarry censorship. What may save copyright's second marriage from doom may well be this larger

---

[52] See Digital Millennium Copyright Act, Pub. L. No. 105–304. The anti-circumvention provisions are now codified at 17 U.S.C. sec. 1201. These rules partly reinscribe the pre-modern Licensing Acts by requiring cryptographers to seek advance permission before attempting to circumvent a technical protection scheme used by copyright owners to protect their works. See id., sec. 1201(g).

[53] See, e.g., Testimony of Allan Adler, Hearing Before the Subcommittee on Courts and Intellectual Property of the House Judiciary Committee on H.R. 2281, 105th Cong., 1st Sess., Sept. 17, 1997.

[54] See 17 U.S.C. sec. 1201, 1204. For history of this provision and an analysis of many of its ambiguities, see, e.g., Pamela Samuelson, *Intellectual Property and the Digital Economy: Why the Anti-Circumvention Regulations Need To Be Revised*, 14 Berkeley Tech. L.J. 519 (1999).

[55] No Electronic Theft Act, Pub. L. No. 105–147, 111 Stat. 2678 (1997), codified at 17 U.S.C. sec. 506(a)(2).

[56] See, e.g., Universal City Studios, Inc. v. Corley, 111 F. Supp.2d 294 (S.D.N.Y. 2000) (liability for violating the anti-trafficking provisions of DMCA anti-circumvention provisions do not depend on proof—or absence thereof—of infringements arising from the availability of a circumvention technology). See also 17 U.S.C. sec. 1204 (criminal liability provision).

context. Yet, it would be naïve not to notice the drift toward a renewed flirtation with pre-modern concepts and do nothing to stop it.

Among the strategic efforts needed to arrest post-modern developments are, first, a renewed and refreshed discourse about "modern" copyright concepts, such as fair use, and second, an elucidation of constitutional principles for defending modern copyright from post-modern incursions. Proponents of "modern" copyright principles have sought to do this in amicus briefs in prominent cases such as A&M Records, Inc. v. Napster, Inc.[57] and Universal City Studios, Inc. v. Corley.[58] In the *Napster* case, for example, amici criticized the trial court's interpretation of the Supreme Court's decision in Sony Corp. of Am. v. Universal City Studios, Inc.[59] and the breadth of the preliminary injunction that, in essence, would have required Napster to prove that every digital music file exchanged with aid of its peer-to-peer software was a noninfringing copy.[60] In *Corley*, amici have questioned the application of the DMCA's anti-circumvention rules to a journalist who linked to sites where a decryption program could be found in the course of news coverage about a controversy about the program, as well as challenging the constitutionality of these rules if they eliminate fair use for technically protected works.[61]

Working against adoption of post-modern legislative proposals, such as UCITA, is also important. UCITA works off the base of copyright, finding in it "informational rights" that then can be licensed under its aegis. But UCITA seems to treat copyright limitations as presumptively precatory and capable of being overridden by license terms.[62] In response to strong criticism of UCITA from intellectual property law experts, the drafters of UCITA have somewhat lessened this presumption.[63] UCITA now expressly empowers courts to withhold enforcement of contract clauses that violate "fundamental public policy."[64] However, this limitation on licensor authority may be too vague to give comfort to persons whose licenses include a term that limits free expression or fair use rights. Computer scientists, for example, are likely to be deterred from posting on

---

[57] 114 F. Supp.2d 896 (N.D. Cal. 2000).
[58] 111 F. Supp.2d 294 (S.D.N.Y. 2000).
[59] 464 U.S. 417 (1984)(no liability for contributory infringement for selling Betamax machines because machines of substantial noninfringing uses, including home taping of television programs for time shifting purposes).
[60] Brief Amicus Curiae of Copyright Law Professors and Brief Amicus Curiae of American Civil Liberties Union In Support of Reversal, on appeal to Ninth Circuit Court of Appeals in A&M Records, Inc. v. Napster, Inc. (2000) (on file with the author).
[61] Brief Amicus Curiae of American Civil Liberties Union in Support of Reversal, on appeal to the Second Circuit Court of Appeals in Universal City Studios, Inc. v. Corley (2001) (on file with the author).
[62] See, e.g., Charles McManis, *The Privatization (of "Shrinkwrapping") of American Copyright Law*, 87 Calif. L. Rev. 173 (1999).
[63] See, e.g., David Nimmer et al., *The Metamorphosis of Contract into Expand*, 87 Calif. L. Rev. 17 (1999).
[64] See UCITA, sec. 105.

the Internet the results of performance tests they've run on database programs when license prohibits public dissemination of test results. Even if these scientists are convinced that public policies favoring the free exchange of ideas and information are fundamental enough to make such clauses unenforceable, they may still not be keen to invite litigation to challenge these restrictions. A chilling effect may accordingly set in.

Also troublesome in UCITA mass-market licenses are clauses aimed at maintaining trade secrecy-like limitations on use of licensed information.[65] Such terms might include prohibitions on reverse-engineering, pledges not to disclose information, or assertions of the unpublished (and presumably secret) nature of that information. Terms of this sort may be unobjectionable in the context of individually negotiated licenses between sophisticated commercial firms possessing relatively equal bargaining power. However, they become disturbing if the licensed work has been the subject of a mass-market transaction. Even though reverse-engineering object code may be lawful as a matter of copyright law,[66] license restrictions may inhibit exercise of this copyright-based privilege. It remains to be seen whether anti-criticism/anti-reverse engineering clauses will continue to proliferate and how courts will deal with them.[67] The potential certainly exists for UCITA to be used to accomplish acts of private censorship that copyright and freedom of expression principles, left to their own devices, would disfavor.

Also threatening freedom of expression principles are the new anti-circumvention provisions of the DMCA. They make it illegal to circumvent a technical protection system used by a copyright owner to control access to its work[68] and to make or distribute technologies that circumvent access controls.[69] Major movie studios relied on the latter provision when they sued a journalist named Corley because he posted a computer program known as DeCSS, which can be used to bypass the Content Scrambling System (CSS) embedded in mass-marketed DVD movies, on the website of 2600 magazine in the course of covering the controversy about this program. After being enjoined from posting this program, Corley decided instead to link to sites where DeCSS could be found as part of his continuing coverage of the story. The trial court ultimately ruled that linking too violated the anti-circumvention provisions of the DMCA, even though the movie studios had offered no proof that it had ever been used to make an infringing copy of a DVD movie. Indeed, they stipulated that they had no such proof.

If Corley can be enjoined merely for linking to sites where allegedly illegal

---

[65] See, e.g., Mark A. Lemley, *Intellectual Property and Shrinkwrap Licenses*, 68 S. Cal. L. Rev. 1239 (1995) (questioning the enforceability of such licenses).

[66] See, e.g., Sega Enterp. Ltd. v. Accolade, Inc., 977 F.2d 1510 (1992).

[67] See, e.g., Mark A. Lemley, *Beyond Preemption: The Law and Policy of Intellectual Property Licensing*, 87 Calif. L. Rev. 111 (1999).

[68] Id., sec. 1201(a)(1)(A).

[69] Id., sec. 1201(a)(2). See also sec. 1201(b)(1)(similar ban of other kinds of circumvention technologies).

information can be found, then so too can the San Jose Mercury News, and so can Jane Ginsburg, who linked to sites about DeCSS so that students enrolled in her copyright course could understand the controversy about this program and analyze the application of the DMCA to it.[70] Also at risk are those who wear T-shirts bearing DeCSS source code or scientists who write articles about DeCSS, discussing its algorithm and CSS. In the post-modern era, free speech and fair use may become subsidiary values to the preeminent value of protecting the business models and technologies that copyright owners adopt for their works.

The *Corley* case is on appeal, and so perhaps Judge Kaplan's post-modern decision will be overturned if the appellate court interprets the scope of the anti-circumvention provisions less broadly than he did[71] or because it finds merit in the constitutional concerns that Kaplan brushed aside. The appellate court could, for example, decide that Corley cannot be held liable for violating the anti-circumvention rules under the First Amendment or under a subsection of the DMCA that states that "[n]othing in this section shall enlarge or diminish any rights of free speech or the press for activities using consumer electronics, telecommunications, or computing products."[72] By including this subsection in the DMCA, Congress seems to have realized the potential for the anti-circumvention rules to conflict with free speech/free press principles and provided courts with a statutory basis for limiting its application when free speech rights would be diminished.[73] It must be said, however, that Congress provided almost no guidance on how to mediate or resolve the tension between the interests of free speech and those underlying the anti-circumvention rule.

For copyright law to remain true to its modern aspiration to live in harmony with freedom of expression principles and to remain divorced from censorship principles, those who deeply believe in its second ("modern") marriage will need to be steadfast in monitoring the evolution of copyright and related policies and practices in the commercial market. Post-modernism has made considerable headway. However, the struggle is far from over.

Copyright's past will unquestionably be a prologue to its future. The principal question is: to which of its pasts shall we chart its course? The choice we make will have profound consequences on the kind of information society in which we will be living in the twenty-first century. My choice would be to retain the modern concept of copyright and reject post-modern tendencies. To do this, we believers in the modern concept of copyright must work together to develop a more powerful rhetoric with which to preserve constitutionally grounded values in copyright law

---

[70] See, e.g., Jane C. Ginsburg, Copyright Use and Excuse on the Internet, 24 Colum.-VLA J. L. & Arts (forthcoming 2000) (discussing fair use and free speech issues raised by linking).

[71] See, e.g., Samuelson, supra note 54, at 537–56 (discussing ways in which courts could narrow the reach of DMCA's anti-circumvention rules by interpretation).

[72] 17 U.S.C. sec. 1201(c)(1).

[73] See, e.g., Benkler, supra note 13, at 414–29 (discussing First Amendment implications of the anti-circumvention regulations).

and policy. Rhetoric alone, however, will not suffice. We must also show policymakers how these values can be specifically implemented in copyright rules that will truly "promote the progress of science and the useful arts" and preserve an open and democratic society.[74]

---

[74] See, e.g., Lawrence Lessig, *Reading the Constitution in Cyberspace*, 45 Emory L.J. 869 (1996)(suggesting ways to translate constitutional values into the new information environment). See also Lessig, supra note 13, Chapter 11 (translating constitutional values specifically as to copyright).

It's All About Control: Rethinking Copyright in the New Information Landscape

Niva Elkin-Koren

Introduction

Copyright law became popular at the turn of the 21st century. The heavy news coverage of the Napster case was the peak of a process that turned copyright law from a relatively exotic legal discipline practiced by a limited group of experts into a subject of vigorous public debate regarding the future of content industries in the digital online age.

The copyright story, which emerges from this public debate, is the official story told by the courts and the literature; that is the "incentive paradigm". Copyright law, we are told, must secure incentives for potential creators to assure their continuous investment in the creation of copyrighted works. We are further told that it would be unfair to rip off the revenues produced by works and deprive creators from their just compensation.

Yet, a closer look at recent copyright disputes and legislative amendments reveals a different story. While the public debate over copyright issues focuses on remuneration, "just compensation" and pirating, the overall effect of the new copyright regime on the information environment is often overlooked. To fully appreciate the ramifications of recent copyright developments, one must examine the larger picture and look at some characteristics of the information age. In this context two observations are due: the first has to do with the nature of competition in the new information markets, and the second relates to the central role of information in the information society.

In the new information economy entry barriers are lower and market power is no longer measured by ownership of tangible goods. Furthermore, the potentially

---

N. Elkin-Koren and N.W. Netanel (eds.), *The Commodification of Information*, 79–106.
© 2002 *Niva Elkin-Koren. Printed in Great Britain.*

decentralized nature of online information markets increases pressure on the legal system to produce means of market control. In the absence of a central bottleneck in the infrastructure, market players increasingly rely on legal rights for exercising control over information markets and protecting market domination. Intellectual property laws have turned out to be a major means of expanding market power, reducing competition and concentrating control over production and distribution of information. Copyright law in recent years became a vehicle of control, and copyrights are being claimed for accomplishing strategic ends.

At the same time, however, information became more central to the human experience. The information society is characterized by an increasing significance of representations. Many basic human experiences, such as learning and transacting, turn out to be information processing. Social interactions are turned into information exchanges on email, chats, and online portals. Informational works, including entertainment products, computer programs, and data, occupy an increased share of overall consumption. Furthermore, we no longer consume merely commodities, but also representations such as images, labels, and signs. Representations are the very element of culture and affect processes of constructing identities, ideologies and meaning.

So, while copyright laws are increasingly exercised to gain control over diffused information markets, and the copyright regime is providing more powerful means of control, this body of law becomes relevant to many aspects of life in the information age and could affect individual autonomy and freedom.

Robust copyrights facilitate the turning of the public sphere into a concentrated market for goods dominated by economic conglomerates. I argue that such a process could be detrimental to democracy. Turning the public sphere into a concentrated marketplace could limit opportunities for meaningful participation in social dialogue, and could restrict freedom and autonomy. By strengthening commercialization and concentration of the market for content, this process may also produce alienation and weaken civic virtue.

This paper examines how the new copyright regime structures the information markets, and how this economic structure may affect the tenets of democracy. Focusing on copyright law as a market control mechanism may disclose what we are missing by using the property discourse in the context of copyright debates. It may also help us better understand the interconnection between copyright law and other laws affecting the exploitation of market power, such as antitrust laws. The paper begins by demonstrating how copyright law has served in recent years to centralize control over the information market. After briefly discussing the new role undertaken by copyright law in the information economy, I turn to discuss the ramifications for democracy. I examine whether such an information market could provide an adequate basis for a democratic public discourse: how does the "information market" shaped by copyright affect our freedom and autonomy? How does it affect our ability to participate in democratic life? And what effects does it have on civic virtue?

I. The New Copyright Regime

It is not by coincidence that copyright law has become the main focus of many of the legal battles among businesses that seek to build up their dominating position in emerging markets of electronic commerce. In retrospect, what we have been witnessing in the copyright arena in recent years seems inevitable. The increased pressure on legislators, both domestically and internationally, to expand copyright[1] and the intensive litigation and legalization of electronic commerce seem to be necessary outcomes of the information economy.

The 'information economy' transformed the meaning of market power.[2] Economic power is no longer based on possessing and controlling tangible assets, but is increasingly defined in terms of control over the production and distribution of information. Consequently, it is only natural that competition in the market for content is focused on gaining control over production and distribution of cultural artifacts.[3] Market players seek to control decisions regarding which works would be produced, in what format, when, where and how these works would become available to the public. Copyright laws provide a set of exclusive rights allowing owners to restrict potentially competitive behaviors; and they therefore become essential.

In the past, control over distribution channels (such as television stations or motion picture studios) was central for acquiring control over content. Whoever controlled the production of copies and distribution channels could precondition distribution in the assignment of intellectual property rights.[4] Furthermore, the high costs involved in producing copies and maintaining distribution channels resulted in a relatively concentrated information market governed by few publishers and distributors. Mass production of records or books required large-scale industrial enterprises.

Information flow over the Internet is decentralized and adheres to a different

---

[1] Pamela Samuelson, "Intellectual Property and the Digital Economy: Why the Anti-Circumvention Regulations Need to Be Reviewed", 14 *Berkeley Technology Law Journal* 1 (1999); Jessica Litman, *Digital Copyright* (2001).

[2] For further discussion of the term "Information Economy" *see* Ian Miles, *Mapping and Measuring the Information Economy, A Report Produced for the Economic and Social Research Council's Programme on Information and Communication Technologies* (1990); James Martin, "From After the Internet Alien Intelligence", *Capital Press*, Washington D.C., 2000; Denis McQuail & Sven Windahl, *Communication Models for the Study of Mass Communication*, p. 201–204 (2d ed., 1995); Dan L. Burk, "Symposium on the Internet and Legal Theory: Virtual Exit in the Global Information Economy", 73 *Chicago Kent Law Review* 943 (1998).

[3] Ronald V. Bettig, *Copyrighting Culture, The Political Economy of Intellectual Property*, p. 36 (1996) (arguing that capitalists seek to eliminate competition in order to reduce the costs and risks that competition engenders).

[4] Thus, musicians who sought to distribute their music on records or compact discs were dependent on recording companies and were often required to assign their copyright to the recording company. Similarly, authors were required to assign their rights to publishers.

set of economic rules. Technically anyone can post their content and make it available through various channels independently of music producers or large publishers. Entry barriers are presumably lower.[5] The Internet is a highly dispersed communication network with live competition among various means of access such as telephone lines, cables, cellular and satellite networks. In the absence of a central bottleneck in the infrastructure, the significance of control over the content via copyright laws is growing.

The potentially decentralized nature of the Internet further increases pressure on the legal system to produce means of market control. The increased pressure to expand copyright law resulted in robust copyrights. Copyright law has become more pervasive as it was stretched to cover more behaviors and regulate more aspects of our use of informational goods. Heavy pressure from the content industry resulted in the anti-circumvention provisions in the 1996 Geneva Internet Treaties. Similar pressure on the U.S. Congress led to the enactment of the Digital Millenium Copyright Act (DMCA) in 1998.[6] The anti-circumvention legislation expands the coverage of copyright law beyond the set of exclusive rights defined by standard copyright legislation.[7] It introduces novel rights related to copyright management systems, allowing rightholders to act against any competing technology. The DMCA prohibits the development, manufacturing and distribution of technologies designed to circumvent protection measures employed by rightholders to control access to information distributed digitally. Thus the privileged status awarded to copyright management systems under the DMCA gives rightholders much stronger legal protection than the rights they held under traditional copyright regime.[8] Moreover, copyright management systems are self-enforced and therefore are free of any legal scrutiny. Once adopted by a rightholder, these technological self-help means are no longer vulnerable to circumventing technologies because these technologies are now prohibited by law.

Copyright law not only covers new practices to which it was previously irrelevant, but it also regulates the behavior of an increasing number of individuals

---

[5] Not only the costs of distribution are significantly low, but also the costs of production are going down. Indeed, the production of content still involves the high cost of human skills, but means of production are cheaper than they used to be. It is no longer necessary to own a high-tech studio, for instance, in order to record a song. The necessary equipment is now more widely available, and at a reasonable price.

[6] Digital Millenium Copyright Act, Pub. L. No. 105–304, 112 Stat. 2860 (1998). A similar legal framework was adopted by the European Union: Parliament and Council Directive 2001/29/EC of 22 May 2001 on the Harmonization of Certain Aspects of Copyright and Related Rights in the Information Society available at: < http://europa.eu.int/comm/internal_market/en/intprop/news/index.htm >

[7] In the U.S. these include the exclusive right of reproduction, the right to make derivative works, the right of public performance and public display, and the right of public distribution. 17 U.S.C § 106.

[8] *See* Pamela Samuelson, "The Copyright Grab", *Wired*, 4.01, 1996.

and small businesses.⁹ Since potential threats to commercial interests are increasingly posed by individual users rather than exclusively by competitors, enforcement efforts are also directed at a large number of users involved in the production and distribution of content over the Internet.

In recent years there is also an increased displacement of copyright law by other common law doctrines such as contract law. Copyright laws provide the legal infrastructure to control the use of information upon which private mechanisms are built. Contracts are employed to restrict or prohibit altogether certain uses of the work that are otherwise permissible under copyright law.¹⁰ The enforceability of automated contracts is still uncertain, and there are conflicting authorities on this matter.¹¹ Other legal doctrine such as unfair competition, misappropriation and, recently, trespass to chattel are gaining an increasing importance.¹²

Copyright law had always facilitated the commercialization of culture by enabling rightholders to circulate copies of their works for a fee. Yet, information was never turned into a perfect commodity, and the law allowed owners to control only a limited number of uses.¹³ What we witness in recent years is the turning of

---

⁹ The latter is due to the nature of e-commerce. E-commerce involves information processing and informational goods. Consider for instance a retail store that engages in selling clothing fashions off-line. This would rarely involve any intellectual property questions (often dealt with by the PR company). By contrast, operating a website would involve creating content (such as interfaces or product presentations) using various computer programs to execute the transaction (processing orders, billing, and sometimes the delivery itself such as in the case of information products that are downloaded directly from a website), and facilitating content created by others (such as messages and materials posted by customers on public forums).

¹⁰ For instance, a contractual provision may limit the use of mere data (such as search results of a search engine or listings of entertainment shows) that may not be copyrighted. *Feist Publications v. Rural Tel. Services Co.*, 499 U.S. 340 (1991).

¹¹ Several courts rejected the enforceability of such license. See *Ticketmaster Corp. v. Tickets.com, Inc.*, 2000 U.S. Dist. LEXIS 4553 (2000) (holding that terms of use posted on a homepage, which prohibited commercial use of plaintiff's information, do not create a contract with anyone using the website); *Specht v. Netscape Communications Corp.*, 2001 U.S. Dist. Lexis 9073 (distinguishing between "shrink-wrap licenses", "click-wrap licenses" and "browse-wrap licenses", and holding that while the first two could be enforceable browse-wrap licensing is not). Other courts, however, found such posted terms to constitute an enforceable contract. See *Register.com, Inc. v. Verio, Inc.*, 2000 U.S. Dist. Lexis 18846 (holding that defendant manifested its assent to be bound by the terms of use posted on plaintiff's website by proceeding to submit a WHO IS query). See also *Caspi v. Microsoft Network, L.L.C.*, 732 A.2d 528, 532 (N.J. Super. Ct. App. Div. 1999) (holding that a choice of forum clause in a click-on agreement was enforceable). Finally, state legislation adopting the Uniform Computer Information Transaction Act ('UCITA') facilitates the enforcement of such contracts.

¹² *eBay, Inc. v. Bidder's Edge, Inc.*, 100 F. Supp. 2d 1058 (N.D. Cal. 2000) (Holding that conducting automated searches by defendant on eBay's website without permission constituted trespass to chattel).

¹³ The term *commodification* seems inconsistent with the rather incorporeal nature of informational works. Information is intangible and lacks any physical boundaries. While tangible assets have physical boundaries and could be fenced to prevent unauthorized access, we cannot physically prevent others from playing music at a pub or copying our manuscript.

The commodification of information thus refers to the process of turning an intangible informational work into an object of trade that could be bought and sold. See *The Oxford American Dictionary of Current English* (*commodity*) 1999.

information into a perfect commodity, granting rightholders a set of powerful legal rights to control every access and use of such information.

The legal regime is thus transformed from a relatively narrow set of rights necessary to guarantee incentives to create new works, into a claim for the protection of owners' expectations to maximize their profits and utilize every economic potential related to their work.[14] If copyright law had once created *islands* of information, which are subject to the sovereign control of copyright owners, these *islands* are now turning into a continent leaving little available space in between. Copyright law thus becomes a very powerful means for accumulating control.

II. Strategic Use of Copyrights: It's All About Control

As the official copyright story tells us, copyright laws are about royalties. The law seeks to protect owners' expectations of selling copies in the market and of making a return on their investment. Copyright law has done so by turning works of art (a movie, play, or musical title) into an asset that could be sold in the marketplace. The mechanism for securing royalties under the copyright paradigm is therefore based on property law principles. Rightholders are granted a set of exclusive rights, and the state intervenes by injunction to protect the holder from an involuntary transfer. Consequently, license of use can materialize only through voluntary transactions.

Entitlement to compensation is independent, of course, of the method by which such entitlement ought to be protected.[15] Property methods, rather than the compensation itself, enable concentration in the information market and make commodification of information so risky. Increasingly, copyrights are being used as a strategic corporate asset allowing content providers to increase barriers on entry (that are otherwise low) and reduce the risks of competition. The new copyright regime allows rightholders to expand their market power and accumulate control over the production and circulation of information.

Control rather than remuneration becomes the focus of legal disputes concerning copyright. Copyright law is exercised to gain control over how content becomes available to the public. Recent cases demonstrate the nature of control battles in information markets and the strategic use of copyright law by

---

[14] Jeremy Waldron, "From Authors to Copiers: Individual Rights and Social Values in Intellectual Property", 68 *Chicago-Kent Law Review* 851 (1993).

[15] *See* Guido Calabresi & Douglas Melamed, "Property Rules, Liability Rules and Inalienability: One View From the Cathedral", 85 *Harvard Law Review* 1089 (1972) (specifying three types of protections – property rules, liability rules and inalienability rules).

rightholders to protect their dominating market status. Such control is significant for keeping a competitive lead in traditional information markets, and for reducing competition in emerging online markets. Control over the production, circulation and adoption of representations is also crucial, however, for democracy. Centralized decision-making power in information markets could affect what is made available for reception and reinterpretation by the public. Examining these legal disputes from the perspective of control may therefore highlight some ramifications of the current pervasive copyright regime.

CONTROLLING THE DISTRIBUTION CHANNELS: WHO DECIDES WHAT TO DISTRIBUTE AND WHEN?

Control over distribution channels is a major concern in the content market. For rightholders it is essential to maintain control over decisions as to when and how content is to be delivered. While the capacity to administer supply and demand is always valuable for gaining market domination, this is particularly significant for content in the information market. The market for content lacks rigid demand, and all releases are competing for the scarce attention of the audience.[16] Consequently, rightholders must exercise control over the number of releases, the timing of shows, and the frequency in which access to content becomes available.

Newcomers who introduced new online distribution methods have threatened the dominating position of traditional players. Consequently, copyright laws are increasingly employed to prevent newcomers from entering the market. Many of the copyright suits during the end of the 90s and the beginning of the 21st century were initiated by major rightholders, such as the Motion Picture Association and the Recording Industry Association of America.[17] This legal campaign for copyright enforcement was not so much about remuneration, but rather focused on controlling new distribution methods. Analyzing the legal campaign launched by the major rightholders demonstrates these strategic goals.

---

[16] That is evident in the entertainment industry, for instance, where every film competes with all other films released in the marketplace. *See* Eileen R. Meehan, "Holy Commodity Fetish, Batman!": The Political Economy of a Commercial Intertext", in *The Many Lives of the Batman* (Roberta E. Pearson & William Uricchio eds., 1991).

[17] The RIAA is a non-profit trade group which represents the largest companies in the sound recording industry, including Sony Music Entertainment, Inc., MCA Records, Inc., Altantic Recording Corporation, Capitol Records, Inc., BMG Music d/b/a, The RCA Records Label, Universal Records, Inc., Elektra Entertainment Group, Inc., A&M Records, Inc., Arista Records, Inc., Polygram Records, Inc., Motown Record Company, Virgin Records America, Inc., and Warner Brothers Records, Inc.

Internet streaming

The conflict over Internet retransmission of television broadcasts is one example. Simultaneous retransmission of television programs apparently doesn't compromise revenues in existing markets. Broadcasters derive revenues from selling show time to advertisers, where the selling price pretty much depends on the size of the intended audience. In fact, when the expected audience of a television program is larger, the price would arguably be higher.[18] Therefore, when retransmission expands the rating for television programs, broadcasters suffer no direct monetary harm and have no reason to object to retransmission other than for strategic purposes.

Internet streaming allows the delivery of television programs to Internet users. iCraveTV.com offered its users the option of viewing their favorite television programs over the net.[19] The service captured the broadcasts off the air, digitized them and made them available to users by streaming. Access to the service was limited to Canadians only (identified by their telephone area code), namely, the intended receivers of the original, off the air broadcasts.[20]

The Motion Picture Association filed a suit against iCraveTV.com claiming that it violates their exclusive right of public performance under copyright law and that Internet streaming must be subject to authorization. Rightholders further alleged that since iCraveTV.com is available worldwide it interferes with their licensing schemes, which require that programs be licensed separately in many local markets. The court granted a preliminary injunction and a temporary restraining order, holding that iCraveTV.com operation infringed upon MPA members' copyright.[21]

The issue at stake was not remuneration. It went beyond an attempt to simply capture a share in the benefits made available by new technologies. In fact iCraveTV.com offered to pay the copyright fees and did not deny that rightholders should be paid for their works. At stake was control over Internet streaming of TV signals, and whether those could be picked up without authorization and retransmitted over the net. Even though the movie studios didn't suffer an

---

[18] For further discussion of this standard business model of broadcasting *see* Michael Botein, *Regulation of the Electronic Mass Media Law and Policy for Radio, Television, Cable and the New Video Technologies*, p. 11 (3d ed., 1998); For a review of alternative business models *see* McQuail & Windahl, *supra* note 2.
[19] The business model for iCraveTV.com was based on selling advertisements on banners that appeared on the screen simultaneously with the copyrighted programs that were being streamed.
[20] The court found that the system could be easily circumvented and allow access to non-Canadian viewers. This should not have changed the legal analysis. If infringing nature of the service was based merely on its potential to allow transmission outside the region, then the court could have authorized the service contingent upon an upgraded security system.
[21] *Twentieth Century Fox Film Corp. v. icraveTV*, 2000 U.S. Dist. Lexis 11670. iCraveTV.com has since reached a settlement and has ceased its streaming service.

immediate loss, they sought to maintain their decision-making power over the distribution of their works: at what timing, in what format, and in which context their works may be made available to the public. Internet streaming offers a whole new range of business opportunities that challenge existing licensing schemes and allow international coverage, interactivity and customization. Rightholders sought to govern this new distribution method.[22]

Interestingly, retransmission by cable operators was also controversial during the 1970s and 1980s. U.S. copyright holders similarly claimed that such retransmission is pirated and interferes with the owners' rights to authorize use of their works. However, that controversy was resolved differently. Although simultaneous retransmission of broadcast was not subject to royalties until January 1978, under the 1976 Copyright Act it was eventually subject to a compulsory licensing system, which successfully separated remuneration and control.[23]

New distribution methods do not always replace the more traditional types of distribution and uses. Often such methods are expanding the overall market, introducing a wider range of available uses for each particular content. Some legal disputes thus focus on whether rightholders are legally entitled to control such new distribution methods.

The RIAA launched a series of lawsuits against online distributors who facilitated

---

[22] Cellular transmission (*cellecast*) of Internet content through cellular phones raises similar issues. Should it be considered an extension of Internet circulation or does it constitute retransmission? In *CNN, L.P. v. GOSMS, Inc.*, 2000 U.S. Dist. Lexis 16156 CNN filed a suit against GOSMS for allowing its users to receive information from the Internet on various devices such as mobile telephones and computers. GOSMS offers Short Messages Service to users of cellular companies, allowing them to define the scope of their interest (i.e., NBA news, cellular technology, NASDAQ, world news). GOSMS converts the selected content into a short message that strips the content of all non-text material, such as advertisements and graphics. Plaintiff argued that while doing so, GOSMS has copied the trademark and copyrighted content from plaintiffs' websites. The court found that the plaintiffs' allegations were insufficient to plead direct copyright or trademark infringement or either contributory infringement or vicarious liability.

[23] *See* 17 U.S.C. sec. 111 (subjecting cable operators to compulsory copyright fees). The courts first viewed cable systems as passive intermediaries and found their service was not a "performance for profit". *See Fortnightly Corp. v. United Artists Television, Inc.*, 392 U.S. 390, 401 (1968). Thus, cables could carry broadcast programming without obtaining permission from the copyright owners. *See* Botein, *supra* note *18* at 401–404; Donald E. Lively, *Modern Communication Law*, p. 161 (1991).

It is interesting to note that retransmission by Canadian cable operators was also controversial during the 1980s. U.S. copyright holders similarly claimed that such retransmission is pirated and interferes with the owner's rights to authorize use of their works. As part of the U.S-Canada Free Trade Agreement (Jan 1989), the Canadian law was amended subjecting retransmission to a compulsory licensing system similar to the U.S law. *See* Copyright Act Retransmission, R.S.C. 1985, c. C-42, sec. 31 (stating that retransmission of signals is not an infringement of copyright if the signal is local or distant; the retransmission is lawful under the Broadcasting Act; The signal is transmitted simultaneously and is permitted under the laws of Canada; and in the case of distant signal – the retransmitted has paid royalties and complied with any terms and conditions fixed under the act).

access to recorded music in MP3 format. In UMG Recording, Inc. v. MP3.COM, Inc.,[24] the RIAA sought to stop streaming of music over the Internet by services such as those offered by MP3.com. The MY.MP3.com service allowed owners of CDs to store and listen to recorded music contained on their CDs from any place where they have Internet connection. The new service did not rip off the charges collected by the record companies and did not threaten to reduce the profitability of existing plaintiff's markets. MP3.com compiled its library of sound recordings by legally acquiring CDs. Furthermore, the service was made available to subscribers who already had a CD version of the recording, and sought to listen to their music via the Internet.[25] Consequently, the service did not substitute the purchasing of CDs, but simply offered new ways for utilizing the purchased copies. The record companies were therefore able to collect compensations for the use by individual consumers. They further collected compensation from MP3.com, which had purchased the CDs to create the digital library.[26] Nevertheless, the court enjoined the service, holding that unless authorized, it infringes the copyright of copyrightholders.

Acquiring control over peer-to-peer distribution

Peer-to-peer is the sharing of computer resources and services by direct exchange between computer systems. This architecture takes advantage of existing desktop computing power and networking connectivity. P2P networks can eliminate the need for servers and considerably enhance the efficient use of network resources.[27] Peer-to-peer and file-sharing technologies have become increasingly popular. These distribution methods are decentralized, and allow direct exchange of content among members of online communities. They do not require central management and control. Control in such networks is diffused, and therefore gaining market domination is getting tricky. Such methods are challenging existing business models in the content market.

The effectiveness of copyright law for attaining exclusive control over

---

[24] *UMG Recording, Inc. v. MP3.COM, Inc*, 92 F. Supp. 2d 349 (S.D. N.Y. 2000).
[25] Subscribers were required to either purchase a CD from MP3.com affiliated online retailers, or verify possession of a CD through the "Beam-it Service": inserting a copy of the relevant CD into the computer CD-Rom drive for a few seconds. The fact that there might be users who didn't purchase their disks but rather copied them is irrelevant to the service provided by MP3.com. Copying of such disks is not made available by MP3.com service. This situation may be analogous to users who counterfeit a license to convince a distributor that they are authorized to use a computer program.
[26] The court refused to consider such positive impact on plaintiffs' market, holding that: "[a]ny allegedly positive impact of defendant's activities on plaintiffs' prior market in no way frees defendant to usurp a further market that directly derives from reproduction of the plaintiffs' copyrighted work." *UMG Recording, Inc.* 92 F. Supp. 2d, at 352.
[27] *See*: <www.peer-to-peerwg.org/whatis/index.html> and also: <http://compnetworking.about.com/cs/peertopeer/index.htm>

distribution channels was evident in the legal campaign held by leading rightholders associations against file-sharing services. The most notable example is the Napster case. Napster designed and operated a system that permits the transmission and retention of sound recordings employing digital technology. Napster facilitated the transmission of MP3 files among its users, using the P2P file sharing process. Users of Napster made available MP3 music files stored on their individual computer hard drives for copying by other Napster users. Napster further allowed searching for MP3 music files stored on other users' computers and transferring these files from one computer to another via the Internet. Napster was sued for contributory and vicarious copyright infringement.[28]

In A&M Records, Inc. v. Napster, Inc.[29] the district court issued a preliminary injunction enjoining Napster "from engaging in, or facilitating others in copying, downloading, uploading, transmitting, or distributing plaintiffs' copyrighted musical compositions and sound recordings, protected by either federal or state law, without express permission of the rights owner." The Court of Appeals for the Ninth Circuit affirmed in part the district court decision.[30] The court found sufficient evidence of contributory infringement for the purpose of preliminary injunction, holding that Napster's peer-to-peer file sharing service facilitated the direct infringement committed by its users. The court found that Napster had actual knowledge that specific infringing materials are available throughout its system, and that although it could block access to suppliers of such materials, it refused to do so.[31] Rejecting Napster's defense that its users engaged in fair use, the court held that retransmiting an entire copyrighted work in a different medium is not deemed a fair use. The court reasoned that repeated downloading of music files by individual users was commercial since it was made to save the expense of purchasing authorized copies. The court found that copying by Napster's users not only harmed plaintiffs' CD sales, but also had a "deleterious effect on the present and future digital download market", thus holding the fourth fair use factor, the effect of the use on the market, to weigh against fair use.[32] Similar suits have been filed against other operators of file sharing services.[33]

---

[28] *A&M Records, Inc. v. Napster, Inc.* 239 F. 3d 1004, 1010–1011 (9th Cir. 2001).
[29] *A&M Records, Inc. v. Napster, Inc.*, 114 F. Supp. 2d 896, 927 (N.D. Cal. 2000).
[30] *A&M Records, Inc.* 239 F. 3d, at 1011, 1029.
[31] The court found that the "mere existence of the Napster system, absent actual notice, and Napster's demonstrated failure to remove the offending materials, is insufficient to impose contributory liability." The court held that contributory liability may only be imposed to the extent Napster "1) receives reasonable knowledge of specific infringing files containing copyrighted 2) knows or should know such files are available on the system, and 3) fails to act to prevent viral distribution of the works." *A&M Records, Inc.*, id. at 1027.
[32] The court further held that "lack of harm to an established market cannot deprive the copyright holder of the right to develop alternative markets." *A&M Records, Inc.*, id. at 1017.
[33] *See Twentieth Century Fox Film Corp. V. Scour, Inc.* (MPAA sued Scour, Inc. for its Exchange service which enabled users to find and download music, image and video files. Scour Inc.

Hyperlinks

Hyperlinks constitute a fundamental part of the Internet infrastructure and are shaping the decentralized nature of online information flow. Content could be stored and posted by various providers, sometimes outside the jurisdiction, and accessed by users through various paths and in various contexts. It should therefore come as no surprise that the legality of links was contested in copyright litigation. If popular portals or Internet locating tools could be held liable for materials posted on the linked destination site, this could effectively reduce diffused dissemination of information and strengthen the ability of rightholders to efficiently supervise online distribution channels.

Liability for links to infringing materials was the focus of a legal dispute between RIAA and MP3Board.com.[34] The MP3Board.com website provides access to various search engines and indexing programs and posts lists of hypertext links automatically generated by search engines as a response to an inquiry entered by a user. The links refer users to publicly accessible websites on the Word Wide Web, which post music files or other materials related to music. In Intellectual Reserve, Inc. v. Utah Lighthouse Ministry Inc.[35] the court held that the defendant could be liable for referring its users to sites containing allegedly infringing materials, under the doctrine of contributory infringement.[36]

Rightholders further succeeded in establishing that linking to circumventing means might be prohibited under the DMCA. Defendants in Universal City Studios v. Reimerdes posted links to a computer program that allowed circumventing the DVD encryption scheme ("DeCSS"). The court enjoined defendants from linking to copies of the DeCSS posted on other sites, holding that

---

cont.
    declared bankruptcy and shut down its website). The RIAA also sent a cease and desist letter to Aimster threatening legal action if Aimster didn't remove copyrighted musical compositions from its file trading directories (*see* <www.wired.com/news/mp3/0,1285,43496,00.html>). Aimster, in response, filed a law suit, asking the court to declare that its service is not a violation of the copyright act, *see Abovepeer, Inc. v. Recording Industry Association of America, Inc.* available at: <www. Boycott-riaa.com/pdfs/complaint_of_AbovePeer.PDF>.

    The defendants' motion to dismiss the case was denied. Defendants were also enjoined from prosecuting or participating in the actions before the United States District of New York (*Abovepeer, Inc. v. Recording Industry Association of America, Inc.*, 2001 U.S. Dist. Lexis 8810).

[34] In *MP3Board v. RIAA*, MP3Board sought a declaratory judgment stating that hypertext linking, automated searching and automated indexing of hypertext links do not constitute copyright infringement even if the link is to a website containing infringing materials. *MP3Board v. Recording Industry Association of America, Inc.*, 2001 U.S. Dist. Lexis 6883 (RIAA's motion to dismiss the case was denied).

[35] *Intellectual Reserve, Inc. v. Utah Lighthouse Ministry Inc.*, 75 F. Supp. 2d 1290 (D. Utah, 1999).

[36] *Intellectual Reserve, Inc.,* Id. at 1292–1293. It must be emphasized that the court's reasoning went beyond defendant's linking activity and was also based on defendant's posting emails encouraging distribution of the infringing materials, and instructing users how to download infringing copies from the linked sites.

defendants' linking was the "functional equivalent" of actual posting.[37] The court recognized that exposing people to liability for linking under the DMCA could have a chilling effect, and therefore applied a high standard of culpability. It held that an essential element of trafficking is "a desire to bring about the dissemination".[38] Under this standard, liability for links would require proof of intent and knowledge that the link was made to a circumvention device, by clear and convincing evidence. The court concluded, however, that even if linked sites offer additional content, linking could still be enjoined if defendants' main purpose was to provide the circumventing software to their users.

The overall effect of the recent line of cases significantly expands the ability of rightholders to control online distribution channels. It subjects emerging distribution methods to the exclusive discretion of copyright owners, who are free to determine whether a license is granted or refused, under what terms and conditions, and in what circumstances.

There is nothing new in the interpretation of copyright as comprising of a right to protect current markets, including the capacity to refuse licensing altogether.[39] Yet, in the wake of online global distribution channels and the pervasiveness of copyrights under DMCA and common law doctrines, this approach should be reconsidered. Such robust rights allow rightholders to significantly reduce competition in the market for content, and thereby preserve their dominating role. It thus facilitates concentration in the information market.

Controlling the Format to Govern Access

While in the past, control over distribution channels facilitated control over copyrights, it is now possible to accumulate control over distribution means through the copyright system.

Consider the DVD case for instance.[40] The DVD (Digital Versatile Disk) allows the distribution of full motion picture on a disk. DVDs are distributed in an encrypted form called CSS (Content Scrambling System), which is designed to prevent copying of the DVD. The CSS is an encryption-based security system that

---

[37] *Universal City Studios, Inc. v. Reimerdes*, 111 F. Supp. 2d 294, 325 (S.D. N.Y. 2000).
[38] *Universal City Studios, Inc.*, id. at 341.
[39] See *Stewart v. Abend*, 495 U.S. 207, 228–229 (1990) (the Copyright Act grants a copyright owner "the capacity arbitrarily to refuse to license one who seeks to exploit the work"). *See also, UMG Recording, Inc.*, 92 F. Supp. 2d, at 352 (holding that the exclusive rights of a copyrightholder includes the right "to curb the development of such derivative market by refusing to license a copyrighted work or by doing so only on terms the copyright owner finds acceptable").
[40] The attempt to impede the market penetration of MP3 format for music files provides another example. *Recording Industry Association of America v. Diamond Multimedia Systems, Inc.*, 180 F.3d 1072 (9 Cir. 1999).

requires the use of specific hardware (DVD player or computer DVD drive) to decrypt, unscramble and play back copies of the motion picture on DVDs. The key that is installed on the DVD becomes operative if it is accessed by an algorithm licensed by the DVD Copy Control Association (CCA) and installed in DVD players or in various programs available for PCs. DeCSS is a computer program that emulates the CSS algorithm, which operates the "key" and thus enables users to play a DVD even in the absence of the CSS algorithm. In fact, it allows a non-CSS-Compliant DVD player to play copies with DVD content.

Several international producers and distributors of films, television programs, and home videos filed a suit against a number of distributors of DeCSS under the anti-circumvention provisions of the DMCA. In Universal City Studios v. Reimerdes[41] (the "DVD case") the court granted a preliminary injunction ordering the defendants to remove all copies of DeCSS from their websites. The court held that CSS is a technological measure limiting the users' ability to make unauthorized copies of DVDs, and that the DeCSS is a circumventing device within the language of the DMCA.[42]

The DVD Copy Control Association further filed a compliant in a California court against 72 defendants, some of whom were unnamed. The compliant asserted that the creator of the DeCSS violated the terms of a clickwrap license that prohibit reverse engineering and the disclosure of trade secrets embodied in the CSS. The court was therefore asked to enjoin the defendants from posting, disclosing or distributing the DeCSS. The court accepted CCA's argument that CSS was a reverse engineered in violation of CSS license and that the trade secrets embodied in CSS were obtained unlawfully.[43] The California State Appeals Court reversed, holding that the DeCSS is "pure speech" and therefore the preliminary injunction violated the defendant's First Amendment rights.

The DVD case of course begs for a comparison with another challenge posed by technology to the motion pictures industry about 20 years ago. The challenges posed by the DeCSS to the DVD are pretty much the same as those presented by the VCR concerning domination of the motion picture industry during the 1980s. In the DVD case the Motion Picture Association (MPA) claimed that it was struggling for its survival in the digital world. It was further claimed that if DeCSC were to be allowed, it would destroy the home distribution of films and would severely injure the movie industry. These exact claims were raised by the movie industry when the VCR was introduced and was challenged by the studios in the

---

[41] *Universal City Studios, Inc. v. Reimerdes*, 82 F. Supp. 2d 211 (S.D. N.Y. 2000) aff'd Universal City Studio, Inc. v. Corley, 273 F.3d 429 (2nd Cir. 2001).
[42] 17 U.S.C § 1201(a)(2).
[43] *DVD Copy Control Association, Inc. v. McLaughlin, et al.* no. CV – 786804, (Sup. Ct. Cal., Jan. 20, 2000) available at: < www.eff.org/IP/Video/DVDCCA_case/20000120-pi-order.html > reversed DVD Copy Control Association, Inc. v. Andrew Bunner, 2001 Cal. App. Lexis 1179.

Sony case.[44] A comparison of the two legal regimes, under which these two cases were litigated, highlights the extent to which copyright law has become a pervasive means of control.

In Sony, as in the DVD case, the Hollywood studios were fighting a device that allowed copying, some of which may have been infringing on the studios' copyrights while other types of copying probably not. Circumventing devices are blind to usage. They may be used for various purposes. Copyright law does not prohibit all copying. It incorporates checks and balances by recognizing instances in which copying may be privileged.

Under the DMCA once an owner employs a technical device for controlling access to their work, the law prohibits developing and distributing any devices that would allow access by avoiding such technological protection. In other words, the DMCA allows owners to control access to their works regardless of the scope of their copyright.

The fact that protection devices (CSS) were employed by studios is insignificant under traditional copyright law. Let us assume that in the Sony case, studios were able to employ encryption for broadcasting, making sure that no film could be recorded by VCR, and that VCRs were equipped to decrypt such security measures. This would not have changed the outcome in the Sony case – the reason being that Sony was litigated under copyright law. In the case of Sony, the court identified a legitimate use for the VCR, namely copying by television viewers for time shifting. Such use, the Court held, constitutes fair use and therefore Sony could not be liable for contributory infringement merely by making VCRs available to the public. In the DVD case the court refused to consider the fair use of the DeCSS, holding that fair use is not available under the DMCA. The DMCA, as interpreted by the court, not only provides new powerful rights, but also lacks the checks and balances of copyright law.

One of the claims raised by the defendants was that DeCSS allows users to make use of a legitimate copy of a DVD on operating systems such as Linux, which are not authorized by the rightholders. This claim was dismissed by the court,[45] even though it is a claim of great importance. If all DVDs are protected so that they require a key-player, and that key-player is only available under the Windows operating system – then rightholders obtain the right to control not only the use of their works, but also the devices by which their works are accessed and distributed.

The motion picture industry tried to exercise its copyright to gain control over distribution in the past. Yet rightholders were never equipped with equivalent robust copyrights. The outcome of the DVD case demonstrates that rightholders

---

[44] *Sony Corp. of America v. Universal City Studios, Inc.*, 464 U.S. 417 (1984).
[45] *Universal City Studios, Inc.*, 111 F. Supp. 2d, at 319 [The court states that even if this claim is true (and that is questionable – p. 311, footnote 79) defendant is still responsible under the DMCA].

can now limit access to content, and subject it to whatever restrictions they choose. They are able to use contracts and also technological measures for this purpose. The law enforces this choice and protects it. Rightholders can control the format in which their work is distributed and the hardware on which it is to be played. They are therefore able to control how the work is being used outside the relatively narrow scope of exclusive rights granted to them under copyright law.

When rightholders govern the format of the work they are able to control what individuals can do with cultural texts. They can determine whether individuals can only passively consume cultural artifacts or whether they could actively use the texts and adopt them to reflect their own agenda.[46] When individuals can use artistic works in a context of their choice, and adopt it to reflect their own agenda, they are able to contest the original meaning attached to it. Copies detached from their original context could be experienced (heard, read, watched) differently and allow individuals to create a new meaning.[47] Information represented digitally, that is disentangled from physical formats, could adapt itself to its surroundings, and facilitate a plurality of voices.

CONTROL OVER VIRTUAL GATEKEEPERS: ON SEARCH ENGINES AND PROPERTIZING INFORMATION

In an age of information overload, search engines are becoming a focal point for controlling access to information. Search engines are becoming the new virtual gatekeepers of cyberspace and, consequently, they turn out to play a key role in shaping the information environment. Information that is undetectable, or otherwise remains unlisted on the search results, is almost nonexistent on the web. In an age of information overload, control over such virtual gatekeepers may give one the power to filter information, that is, to locate some information while avoiding another.

One example of control battles in the information markets is the eBay case. eBay, the largest online person-to-person auction site, objected to the unauthorized use of its database by metacrawlers and data aggregators. Bidder's Edge, an

---

[46] One example for control stemming from the format of distribution is the distribution of computer programs. Most software publishers distribute mass market software without the source code. This does not allow modifying the program, fixing bugs, learning its operation, and adopting it to perform new functions. This is notwithstanding the claim made by various commentators that the open source model would produce technically superior software. *See* Eric Raymond, *A Brief History of Hackerdom, in Opensources* (Chris DiBona ed., 1999).

[47] Walter Benjamin, "The Work of Art in the Age of Mechanical Reproduction", in *Illuminations* 219, 223 (Hannah Arendt ed. & Harry Zohn trans., 1970) clearly describes this liberating potential of mechanical reproduction of works of art ("One might generalize by saying: the technique of reproduction detaches the reproduced object from the domain of tradition... in permitting the reproduction to meet the beholder or listener in his own particular situation, it reactivates the object reproduced").

auction aggregation site, allowed its users to search for items simultaneously across numerous online auctions by conducting a single search and without having to search each auction site individually.[48] Like many search engines, eBay prohibited the automated use of its database in its users' agreement, and further employed technical means to block access to Bidder's Edge. Eventually eBay brought a suit against Bidder's Edge and was granted a preliminary injunction enjoining Bidder's Edge from accessing eBay's systems by use of any automated querying program without eBay's written authorization.[49]

The reasons behind eBay's objection to Bidder's Edge activity are intriguing. Like many search engines and data aggregators, Bidder's Edge was not directly competing with eBay. eBay is a person-to-person trading site that allows sellers to list items for sale, and potential buyers to search the listings and bid on items. eBay collects commissions for sales. In fact, eBay's subscribers could benefit from the use of metacrawlers such as Bidder's Edge since they increase their listings' exposure. A greater number of potential bidders would tend to increase the likelihood of closing transactions at a higher price.[50] Such contingency could potentially increase eBay's revenues, since eBay's commission is based on the closing price.[51] If eBay's goal was to maximize profits, why did eBay object to the use by Bidder's Edge?

eBay sought to preserve its dominance in the online auction industry.[52] If metacrawlers like Bidder's Edge are crawling around, then eBay may lose its key assets. These assets include its control over the community of users that occupies its site since they will no longer be captured and restricted to a single site. Another business advantage is the power to shape preferences and affect actual choices made by users, by determining what alternative transactions are made available to them. Finally, there were opportunities for branding and establishing a distinctive

---

[48] Bidder's Edge created a database of information compiled from various auction sites. On March 2000 the site compiled information on items auctioned on more than 100 auction sites. Similarly, AuctionWatch offers for free a Universal Search function which allows users to send a single query and search for items available for auction over a couple hundred sites. *eBay, Inc.*, 100 F. Supp. 2d.

[49] *eBay, Inc.*, id. Similarly, MySimon (www.MySimon.com) a popular Internet shopping search engine, sued Priceman.com meta-search engine, which was searching shopping engines, for using its search results and infringing its copyright. MySimon claimed that its search results are reprinted on the site with no attribution to the source. Brian Banks, "Builder Beware", *Canadian Business*, (October 29, 1999) available at < http://www.canadianbusiness.com/magazine_items/1999/oct22_99_builderbeware.shtml >.

[50] Indeed, posting the items for sale on data aggregators may normally introduce competition with sellers from other sites and push down the price. Yet, due to the method of auction such competition would not necessarily lower the closing price of any particular deal.

[51] www.pages.ebay.com/help/sellerguide/selling-fees.html: In addition to an insertion fee, eBay.com charges a Final Value Fee – between 1.25% to 5% of the final sale price.

[52] eBay further argued that it sought to protect its interest in the auction data compiled through its relationship with its customers. Steven Bonsiteel, "eBay Hints Other Auction Aggregators Could Be Blocked – Update", *Newsbytes* (Novermber 4, 1999) (citing eBay's spokesman kevin Pursglove).

reputation. Owning a powerful online brand would usually allow sellers to charge a higher price for identical products. When users are searching via bargain finders, competition turns to focus on price alone.[53] Under such circumstances there are less opportunities for cashing the benefits of branding. To secure its brand, eBay objected to the display of its results next to those of its competitors.

While a right to exclude publicly available data is explicitly exempted under copyright law, claims based on other legal doctrines were raised by eBay, such as contract, unfair competition, misappropriation and trespass to chattel. The displacement of copyright law by other common law doctrines for establishing a right to control access to information is worrisome.[54] Copyright law was designed to regulate use of information, and therefore it includes some checks and balances informed by the unique character of informational works and their social significance. Information policy could be easily obscured when general legal doctrines are strictly applied to create a new type of control over access to information.

Rejecting Bidder's Edge's claim that it cannot trespass eBay's website because it is publicly accessible, the court held that eBay's servers and their capacity are private property and therefore access is conditioned upon the owner's permission. The court held that Bidder's Edge searches constituted an unauthorized use of this property, depriving eBay of the ability to use the occupied portions of its personal property for its own purpose.[55] The newly created right to exclude indexers, established by the eBay decision, is strengthening a trend of propertizing information in recent years. The eBay rule opens new opportunities for accumulating control and interfering with competition in the search engines market. This rule may allow search engines to legally prevent the use of their search results, thus requiring anyone who wishes to use such results to acquire a license.

A right to exclude information mining and indexing is likely to hinder, rather than encourage, competition in the search engines market. Such a legal right may affect both vertical relationships between sites and search engines in which they are listed, and competition among search engines, metacrawlers and data aggregators.

At the site-search engine level, when search engines must acquire a license to

---

[53] *See* J. Bradford DeLong & A. Michael Froomkin, "Speculative Microeconomics for Tomorrow's Economy", *at* < http://personal.law.miami.edu/~froomkin/artciles/spec.htm >.

[54] The eBay rule allows far-reaching, expansive restrictions on the use of information. Indeed, we sometimes allow restrictions on the use of information that is publicly available, to protect certain entitlements, such as proprietary rights, individual privacy, individuals' right to their good name, or the right of some individuals to control their public image. All these rights are subject to restrictions such as free speech. The eBay rule facilitates control over information that incorporates no such balances. We may wish to prevent information mining when it is necessary to protect the individuals to which information is pertained. Yet, when rather than protecting entitlements (such as users' privacy) the court instead creates a broad right to control access to information, it also allows private parties to legally control other aspects of information that should be left uncontrolled, such as its informative value or its meaning.

[55] The court held that "[t]he law recognizes no such right to use another's personal property." *eBay, Inc.*, 100 F. Supp. 2d, at 1071.

locate and refer to posted information, the cost of the search increases. That is due to higher transaction costs involved in negotiating and acquiring the necessary licenses and paying the license fees. The commercialization of the reference process would increase barriers on entry and allow a considerable advantage to commercial engines.

The eBay rule further creates dependency of the indexer on the subject of indexing. Sites could condition licensing in exchange for receiving a higher ranking, specific presentation on the search results, or the exclusion of others on search results. Such dependency of indexers in their subjects, created by law, would hardly contribute to the reliability of the search engines market. Once again, this is likely to give an advantage to commercial sites.

Search engines themselves could rely on the eBay rule to object to the use of their output search results. They could use licensing search schemes to acquire market domination, force business alliances when they are not technically necessary, and limit the operation of competitors. Those business interests, however, are not necessarily compatible with the public interest. It could undermine the feasibility of introducing new, independent metacrawlers in the search engines market.

Finally, a legal right to exclude, as opposed to the technical ability to do so, is propertizing the search results. It is turning search results into a corporate asset. An exclusive right to use search results, such as under the eBay rule, protects a market share. Search results as a corporate asset could be accumulated. It could be used strategically to prevent indexing by competitors, or restrict indexing to advance commercial interests. A right to exclude indexing could therefore serve to hinder competition among search engines and would facilitate centralization of the search engines marketplace.[56]

The eBay rule introduces a broad right to control access. Information is abstract and normally detached from any physical presence. Information in digital form, however, requires some sort of electronic access to make it intelligible and instrumental. Consequently, paradoxically, the virtual space accompanied by the newly created rights to exclude access reconstructs the physicality of information.

Apparently the preliminary injunction issued in the eBay case allowed eBay to deny only a particular type of access. It is arguable that access is technically available to all information that is posted on the web, and that it remains so even under the eBay rule. The court explicitly restricted the scope of the injunction to automated search,[57] excluding other forms of search from its scope: "[n]othing in

---

[56] Niva Elkin-Koren, "Let the Crawlers Crawl: On Virtual Gatekeepers and the Right to Exclude Indexing", 26 *Dayton Law Review* 179 (2001).

[57] The court issued a preliminary injunction enjoining Bidder's Edge "from using any automated query program, robot, web crawler or other similar device, without written authorization, to access eBay's computer systems or networks, for the purpose of copying any part of eBay's auction database." *eBay, Inc.*, 100 F. Supp. 2d, at 1073.

this order precludes Bidder's Edge from utilizing information obtained from eBay's site other than by automated query program, robot, web crawler or similar device."[58] Nevertheless, physical access is not sufficient to guarantee actual access to information. Access to information in cyberspace is enabled by search engines, and controlling such enablers and their use determines what information is actually made available.

The fact that in eBay, access was denied to otherwise publicly available search results suggests that *control over the terms of access,* rather than *access per se,* was at stake. Therefore, the legal right to exclude granted to eBay facilitates control over the terms of access.

Decentralized competition among search engines is essential for keeping a competitive market in electronic commerce.[59] But in addition to their extraordinary commercial significance, search engines also affect the organization of information and the meaning it pertains to. Therefore search engines may potentially shape positions, concepts, and ideas by defining what information becomes available for each query. They create a type of virtual bottleneck governing access to information. Expensive limits on the use of search engines may reduce competition and result in an exclusionary information system.

IV. On Copyright Laws and Centralization in Information Markets

Some believe that even though rightholders won the legal disputes they lost the battle over online dissemination.[60]

This rather naïve view overlooks some serious consequences and ancillary effects of a pervasive copyright regime. Recent legal developments may have a chilling effect on decision makers, such as legal advisors of high-tech companies advocating avoiding the development of potentially infringing technological applications due to the perceived high legal risk. Similarly, recent litigation and court decisions could chill investors away from what would be perceived as legally risky technologies, thus shrinking the invested resources in the development of

---

[58] *eBay, Inc.,* id. at 45.
[59] Elkin-Koren, *supra* note 56. Competition alone, however, may be an insufficient remedy for the biases created by search engines. See Lucas D. Introna & Helen Nissenbaum, "Shaping the Web: Why the Politics of Search Engines Matters", 16 *The Information Society* 169, (2000) (arguing that competition alone cannot guarantee access to the Web, because search engines would still give prominence to popular and wealthy sites at the expense of others, either through their algorithms or by selling prominence for a fee).
[60] The aftermath of Napster could teach us that Napster lost but the p2p and file swapping technology won. *See* John Perry Barlow, "The Next Economy of Ideas", *Wired* 8.10 2000.

new technologies and business practices, which might threaten the rightholders' position.

Recent case law may also affect access to infrastructure for controversial online services. For instance, online service providers might refuse to make some services available to the public over their facilities frightened of being sued. Rightholders often demand that Online Service Providers cease providing controversial services, threatening legal action against such providers.[61]

Increased pressure to expand control over information via copyright law further lead to judicialization of the use of information. Pervasive copyright legislation and aggressive litigation policy of rightholders are turning more issues related to the use of information into legal questions and of making everything a matter of law. Indeed, new technologies also allow technical control of access, which could have resulted in less regulation. However, as it is apparent from recent anti-circumvention legislation, the introduction of technical protection devices induced a massive regulation governing anti-circumvention measures.

Judicialization of information usage may further centralize control over information and reduce competition in the information market. The anti-circumvention legislation increases potential legal exposure involved in developing new technologies. Legal considerations are implemented at an early stage of the creation process, completely prohibiting the development of some technologies. This in turn increases the cost of entry and reduces competition. Robust legislation such as the DMCA is also extremely complex and obscure, therefore the format of legislation communicates and maintains power. This type of regulation is in fact accessible only to wealthy businesses that can afford legal advice, thus creating a barrier on entry to the market.

Another outcome of judicialization is the increased cost of privileged use, which creates a chilling effect. Judicialization of information creates pressure to further regulate the use of information. That is because copyright laws that create abstract "fences" around (abstract) informational goods, are particularly dependent on legal definitions, government enforcement, and public compliance with the law. Intensive regulation and economic power associated with copyright law may lead to social alienation. This in turn increases enforcement efforts to ensure compliance by declaring certain infringements as criminal, increasing fines, and expanding the scope of liability to apply to contributors. Furthermore, since copying and distribution may be done by individual users and not merely by competitors, enforcement efforts are increasingly directed against individual users.

---

[61] *See for instance*, a cease and desist letter sent on October 1999 to the Online Service Providers of MP3Board (AboveNet Communication and Metromedia Company), demanding the removal, delete or disabling of the allegedly infringing site. Similarly, after receiving a cease and desist letter AbovePeer filed a suit against RIAA asking the court to declare that they are not infringing the copyright act. *See* complaint, *Abovepeer, Inc.* (available at: www. Boycott-riaa.com/pdfs/complaint_of_AbovePeer.PDF).

This again reinforces alienation and resistance. The process is circular and may partly explain the robust copyright legislation developed in recent years.

V. Centralized Information Markets and the Information Society

The new copyright regime structures the market so that rightholders can accumulate power and control over the use of information. Centralized information markets cannot provide sufficient outlets for democratic participation. The information market is not just another outlet for ordinary commodities. It also constitutes our cultural life and the public sphere in our communities. Consequently, the way information markets are structured is of great importance to our democratic life. I will highlight these ramifications by discussing two organizing concepts: *participation* and *civic virtue*. This analysis departs from the classical balance struck by copyright law between incentives and use, control and access. It is further distinguishable from other attempts to balance copyright claims and freedom of speech principles, which seek a resolution between conflicting entitlements. My interest is the way in which copyright laws shape our public sphere and thereby design the environment in which political freedom is exercised.

Democracy as Participation in the Public Sphere

Democracy requires that people would have a reasonable opportunity to participate in political affairs on equal terms. The liberal ideal of "one person one vote" emphasizes voting as the prominent act of participation in democratic life, and thus focuses on neutrality and equal weight of voting rights. From this perspective the democratic scene is perceived as a competitive marketplace of ideas that must be kept free so it can best reflect the aggregated citizens' choice.

A growing awareness of the limits of the liberal model in recent years led commentators to acknowledge that politics cannot be reduced to voting. It has been increasingly recognized that preferences and values are not prior and exogenous to the political process.[62] Instead, preferences are a by-product of a

---

[62] Daniel A. Farber & Philip P. Frickey, *Law and Public Choice: A Critical Introduction*, p. 61–62 (1991) (rejecting the view of democracy as a black box intended to produce strict majority rule, and arguing that "a viable democracy requires that preferences be shaped by public discourse and processed by political institutions so that meaningful decisions can emerge."); Cass R. Sunstein, "The Republican Civic Tradition: Beyond the Republican Revival" 97 *Yale Law Journal* 1539, 1541 (1988); Jon Elster, *Sour Grapes: Studies in the Subversion of Rationality*, p. 35 (1983) (arguing that the central concern of politics should be the transformation of preferences rather than their aggregation).

political process that takes place in the public sphere and are shaped by deliberation or sometimes the inability to deliberate. Citizens develop their ideas, shape their positions, identify their interests, and ascertain their identity in the public sphere. The public sphere is thus the main scene of our democratic life. That is where our public decision-making process occurs and where the output of elections is in fact determined. The tenets of democracy must therefore apply to the public sphere in its various shapes and forms in modern life. Accordingly, to guarantee equal access to the political process, it is not sufficient to secure equal voting rights. It is necessary to guarantee reasonable access to will formation processes in the public sphere.

Elsewhere I argued that the notion of the *public sphere* should be given a broad understanding.[63] It should not be limited to public debates on controversial political issues, but rather be understood as a discursive will formation process that takes place in our cultural life. Interaction and exchange in the public sphere create meaning. They affect one's views regarding living the good life, shape people's values and identity, and help them prioritize preferences and distinguish between good and bad.

Will formation processes occur through exposure to headline news, public debates on television shows and radio programs, editorials, and review articles. People are exposed to information, positions and analyses and react by adopting, rejecting, avoiding or denying such information.[64] Will formation processes also occur through various media forms by consuming and interacting with cultural artifacts such as fictional super heroes and narratives created through different media manifestations such as films, television series, comic books, audio-visual clips, and toys. Individuals may create meaning by identifying or reinterpreting a fictional character or by challenging themes and ideas relevant to their social life.[65] Such interactive processes consequently affect our preferences in the broad sense of the word. The production and circulation structures of popular cultural products therefore affect potential participation in the public sphere.

Participation in the public sphere thus refers to the ability of any individual to take an active part in this will formation process. Although there may always be disparities in participating power, it is necessary to guarantee reasonable access to means of participation. For this purpose it is necessary to eliminate extreme disparities in the ability to participate. Disparities of power – and not just absolute power – may affect opportunities for meaningful participation. Focus on participation is thus a focus on decentralizing the production of content and facilitating meaningful access to cultural production means.

Disparities of power are not necessarily disparities of wealth. Indeed, exercising

---

[63] Niva Elkin-Koren, "A Democratic Approach to Copyright in Cyberspace", 14 *Cardozo Arts & Entertainment Law Journal* 215 (1996).
[64] Pierre Bourdie, *On Television* (1996).

central control over information markets serves the financial needs of content producers and increases inequality of wealth. Yet, the issue is not simply inequality of wealth, but rather the distribution of power – legal power – to determine what content is being produced and published. Aside from distributional consequences, such legal power may lead to cultural domination, which could affect personal autonomy and freedom.[66]

PARTICIPATION AND CENTRALIZATION

Securing sufficient participation in the democratic sense discussed above requires decentralization of the will formation processes. Accumulation of control over content, facilitated by copyright law in its recent comprehensive form, may interfere with this principle. When power accumulated in the market is used in the public sphere, it tends to distort equal participation and reduce fair access to participation means. Powerful economic bodies that control the means of production are better positioned to express their own agendas and thereby marginalize diversity. Corporate agenda must not be specific to have an impact on public discourse. It reflects an ideology of consumerism and consumption. Content in such an environment is no longer perceived as an authentic reflection of one's beliefs and autonomy, but as a product created with the purpose of being marketed as a commodity. Concentration of ownership and control over content may reduce pluralism and result in a "marginal" or "meaningless" diversity of the type of content created. Thus, pervasive copyright regime could affect the type of content that is being produced. While the focus of traditional copyright controversies is whether content will be created and distributed, the more interesting question, often overlooked by these discussions, is what type of creation is facilitated by this regime.[67]

It is arguable that users could participate in the "market for content", understood as a site for contesting ideologies and meanings reflected in artifacts. When information is traded as an article of commerce, readers and viewers in their capacity as consumers could affect the content that is being produced by creating demand for certain content, thus affecting decisions regarding the production and circulation of content. Producers of content must be attentive to demand and rating and are likely to shape the type of content that is produced accordingly.

This perception has several significant limitations. First, a centralized content market could determine what is made available. Individuals are likely to adapt

---

[65] *See generally* Meehan, *supra* note 16.
[66] On cultural domination see Nancy Fraser, "From Redistribution to Recognition? Dilemmas of Justice in a "Post Socialist" Age", 212 *New Left Review* 68, 70–74 (1995).
[67] Debora J. Halbert, *Intellectual Property in the Information Age: The Politics of Expanding Ownership Rights*, p. 144 (1999).

their preferences to the available choices and opportunities.[68] Consequently, it would be inappropriate to take existing preferences as reflecting what individuals really want, since their choice was constrained by what was made available to them. It cannot be said to reflect individual autonomy, or what individuals would ideally prefer if the options were structured by the market differently.

Furthermore, information is not an ordinary commodity and the so-called "market for information" does not function as a regular market for goods. Information does not play by the old rules of offer and demand. Informational products affect their own demand. Consequently, centralized power in such a marketplace could be very powerful in shaping preferences and agendas.[69] It could limit opportunities for meaningful participation in social dialogue, and restrict freedom and autonomy for ordinary participants.

Participation may take the form of actively communicating one's positions, preferences, taste, values and ideas. Participation may also involve viewing, reading, listening, absorbing and making use of content that reflects one's ideas, or those with which an individual identifies. Control over content may affect the extent to which people can appropriate content and adapt it to reflect their own agenda. When production of content is centralized, few bodies determine what becomes available to the public, and thus of the variety from which the public can decide what values, identities and positions to adapt.

Democracy and Civic Virtue

Participation in the public sphere is further viewed as an independent good capable of constituting a civic virtue, a shared sense among citizens in pursuit of the public good, and an ability to actively participate and affect the outcome of some processes.[70] This perspective assumes a significant distinction between the way people form and express their preferences in their capacity as citizens and the way in which they hold their preferences as consumers.[71] In their role as

---

[68] Ian Ramsay, *Advertising, Culture and the Law: Beyond Lies, Ignorance and Manipulation*, p. 37 (1996) (discussing adaptive preferences).

[69] On the affect of art on demand for new technologies *see* Benjamin, *supra* note 47 at 239 ("One of the foremost tasks of art has always been the creation of a demand which could be fully satisfied only later. The history of every art form shows critical epochs in which a certain art form aspires to effects, which could be fully obtained only with a changed technical standard, that is to say, in a new art form").

[70] Sunstein, *supra* note 62 at 1556.

[71] *See* Cass R. Sunstein, "Endogenous Preferences, Environmental Law", 22 *Journal of Legal Studies* 217, 242–243 (1993); Cass R. Sunstein, "Social Norms and Social Roles", 96 *Columbia Law Review* 903, 923–925 (1996); Elizabeth Anderson, *Value in Ethics and Economics*, p. 144–147, 158–159, 203–210 (1993); For a critical view of this dichotomy *see* Daphna Zamir-Levinson, "Consumer Preferences, Citizen Preferences, and the Provision of Public Goods", 108 *Yale Law Journal* 377 (1998).

consumers, citizens try to maximize their private interests. In their capacity as citizens deliberating and reasoning about polity, people may establish a civic virtue, namely the willingness to "subordinate their private interests to the general good."[72]

Civic virtue describes an *other-regarding* rather then a purely *self-interest* approach – a willingness to give priority to the communal interest. Civic virtue is thus significant to democratic life in that it enables participants in their capacity as citizens to undertake responsible decisions that are informed by, and respectful of, the claims of other groups and individuals. This may also enhance the well-being of individuals by creating a sense of communal belonging and social solidarity. [73]

Social dialogue is dependent on these virtues for its continuing existence. When the public sphere replicates the market for goods, citizens replicate their role as consumers rather than acting as citizens.

CENTRALIZATION AND ALIENATION

Concentration of power in the public sphere may weaken the sense of civic virtue, for when the public sphere reflects the views of few – and is driven by pure commercial interests – there is less trust, and therefore less commitment to shared goals. In this sense, the alienation created by recent developments in intellectual property laws has a potentially destructive effect.

When decisions regarding the production of content tend to mirror commercial interests, culture is turned into a market. Culture is thus ruled by economic considerations that are irrelevant to the public sphere. Decisions regarding what would be produced, and when and where it would be distributed, are governed by the commercial interests of private companies seeking to maximize profits. When a movie, book or television show are manufactured and sold as commodities, their content is determined by their sales potential.[74]

There is very little room for civic virtue when what appears to be social dialogue in the public sphere turns out to be merely a market for goods. This result is not merely the outcome of less access to information and opportunities for participation. It is also the outcome of a lower sense of trust. When cultural artifacts such as movies and television series are sold they cannot be taken as reflecting authentic views and concerns, ideas and agendas.

When production and distribution of content is centrally governed by few

---

[72] Cass R. Sunstein, "Interest Groups in American Public Law", 38 *Stanford Law Review* 29, 31 (1985).
[73] Sunstein, *supra* note 62, p. 1547: "a system lacking widespread participation will suffer from the failure to cultivate the various qualities that may accompany political life – self-development, feeling of empathy, social solidarity, and so forth".
[74] Bourdie, *supra* note 64; Bettig, *supra* note 3 p. 36.

commercial businesses, the public sphere is structured, and increasingly understood, as a market for information rather than a forum of exchange. When music, films, and news stories are produced and traded as commodities that must be purchased rather than expressions that could be shared, we are not only losing the free flow of information but we are also diminishing trust. Such an attitude promotes separate self-interest rather then communal exchange. Trust is a social capital that may improve communal and civic life, benefiting society by strengthening solidarity.[75]

When culture is turned into a market it reduces citizens into potential consumers of goods, and sometimes treats them as goods themselves (such as in the case of advertisers-supported television and increasingly also the Internet). Consequently citizens become suspicious and lose trust in social dialogue. A public sphere that is merely a market for informational goods focuses on private profits and control rather than on public goals. It therefore supports cynicism and alienation regarding public discourse and thereby weakens civic virtue. Consequently, turning our entire culture into a market for goods leaves very little room for political action of individuals as citizens rather than as consumers.

Summary

While modern legal systems recognized the risks involved in centralized communication markets, awareness of the centralization of information market has not yet matured.

Copyright law has come a long way from its origins. Copyrights are perceived as a legitimate claim of individual creators for "just reward", a return on investment, a claim for royalties, and a share in profits. Realistically, however, copyright law must serve content production by profit-oriented corporations. Thus copyright is a mechanism for inducing corporations to invest in innovation and distribution of informational goods. Copyright in this sense protects a market share. It defines rights to exploit the commercial potential of the work.[76] The issue concerning copyright law is therefore the extent to which commercial expectations in the information market ought to be protected.

Copyright law now allows complete commodification of content in a way that was not available before. During the last couple of years copyright law was

---

[75] Robert D. Putnam, *Making Democracy Work: Civic Tradition in Modern Italy 169–170* (1993).
[76] Christopher Lind, "The idea of capitalism or the capitalism of ideas? A moral critique of the Copyright Act", 7 *Intellectual Property Journal* 65, 69 (1991) ("What is being stolen is not the object nor a property of the object, but rather a market for the object or the possibility of being able to exploit the commercial potential of the object").

transformed (if not revolutionized) to provide owners with a substantially more powerful right to control information. This transforms copyright law from a law that sought to serve policy goals and secure incentives for creators into a law that facilitates control in information markets.

I argue that copyright law has gone too far. This argument is neither a claim against capitalism, nor is it a claim against a capitalist market as a mechanism for producing informational goods and cultural artifacts. In fact, private incentives have many advantages when compared with other alternatives for creating content.[77] If copyright returned to serving its original purpose, it may well be able to provide an adequate basis for cultural creation and social dialogue. It may well be that copyright law should be adjusted to undertake such new roles in the information economy.

Furthermore, the significance of control over information in the information economy calls for reconsidering the traditional balance drawn between copyright and freedom of speech. Copyright law in its current form and role in the information economy challenges freedom of speech. This may not be apparent when the analysis stops at the *right to free speech*. The challenge posed by copyright law to freedom of speech is structural and is concerned with the actual power to participate. Freedom of speech can no longer be understood as merely a negative right against government interference in a complex world of information managed by various producers and private owners of distribution channels.[78] It is therefore necessary to develop a better understanding of freedom of speech, which goes beyond the rights discourse, and could encompass the notion of participating in social dialogue in a meaningful way.

Finally, drawing the balance between copyright law and freedom of speech in the new information environment may require transforming copyright law from its property paradigm into a liability rule that secures compensation but does not provide control. The use of copyright law as a means of control is related to the property paradigm of copyright law. As long as copyrights are protected as a property right, they require the owner's consent prior to the use of the work. When prior authorization is required, copyright law ends up as a means of control. A liability model would entitle rightholders to monetary compensation only, leaving the issue of control outside their reach.

---

[77] Alternatives to a copyright system include sponsorship by advertisers (selling audiences to advertisers rather than selling informational goods to consumers) patronage. Such alternatives are also suffering from significant shortcomings.

[78] An analysis of the legal opinion of Judge Kaplan in the DVD case reveals the shortcomings of the current freedom of speech discourse. The court's discussion examined violation of the legal right of free speech rather than the actual ability to exercise rights. It also focused on a particular expression rather than on availability of information and ability to participate.

Anarchism Triumphant: Free Software and the Death of Copyright

Eben Moglen

Software as Property: The Theoretical Paradox

Software: no other word so thoroughly connotes the practical and social effects of the digital revolution. Originally, the term was purely technical, and denoted the parts of a computer system that, unlike "hardware," which was unchangeably manufactured in system electronics, could be altered freely. The first software amounted to the plug configuration of cables or switches on the outside panels of an electronic device, but as soon as linguistic means of altering computer behavior had been developed, "software" mostly denoted the expressions in more or less human-readable language that both described and controlled machine behavior.[1]

That was then and this is now. Technology based on the manipulation of digitally encoded information is now socially dominant in most aspects of human culture in the "developed" societies.[2] The movement from analog to digital

---

[1] The distinction was only approximate in its original context. By the late 1960s certain portions of the basic operation of hardware were controlled by programs digitally encoded in the electronics of computer equipment, not subject to change after the units left the factory. Such symbolic but unmodifiable components were known in the trade as "microcode," but it became conventional to refer to them as "firmware." Softness, the term "firmware" demonstrated, referred primarily to users' ability to alter symbols determining machine behavior. As the digital revolution has resulted in the widespread use of computers by technical incompetents, most traditional software – application programs, operating systems, numerical control instructions, and so forth – is, for most of its users, firmware. It may be symbolic rather than electronic in its construction, but they couldn't change it even if they wanted to, which they often – impotently and resentfully – do. This "firming of software" is a primary condition of the propertarian approach to the legal organization of digital society, which is the subject of this paper.

[2] Within the present generation, the very conception of social "development" is shifting away from possession of heavy industry based on the internal-combustion engine to "post-industry" based on digital communications and the related "knowledge-based" forms of economic activity.

N. Elkin-Koren and N.W. Netanel (eds.), *The Commodification of Information*, 107–131.
© 2002 *Eben Moglen. Printed in Great Britain.*

representation – in video, music, printing, telecommunications, and even choreography, religious worship, and sexual gratification – potentially turns all forms of human symbolic activity into software, that is, modifiable instructions for describing and controlling the behavior of machines. By a conceptual backformation characteristic of Western scientific thinking, the division between hardware and software is now being observed in the natural or social world, and has become a new way to express the conflict between ideas of determinism and free will, nature and nurture, or genes and culture. Our "hardware," genetically wired, is our nature, and determines us. Our nurture is "software," establishes our cultural programming, which is our comparative freedom. And so on, for those reckless of blather.[3] Thus "software" becomes a viable metaphor for all symbolic activity, apparently divorced from the technical context of the word's origin, despite the unease raised in the technically competent when the term is thus bandied about, eliding the conceptual significance of its derivation.[4]

But the widespread adoption of digital technology for use by those who do not understand the principles of its operation, while it apparently licenses the broad metaphoric employment of "software," does not in fact permit us to ignore the computers that are now everywhere underneath our social skin. The movement from analog to digital is more important for the structure of social and legal relations than the more famous if less certain movement from status to contract.[5] This is bad news for those legal thinkers who do not understand it, which is why so much pretending to understand now goes so floridly on. Potentially, however, our great transition is very good news for those who can turn this new-found land into property for themselves. Which is why the current "owners" of software so strongly support and encourage the ignorance of everyone else. Unfortunately for them – for reasons familiar to legal theorists who haven't yet understood how to apply their traditional logic in this area – the trick won't work. This paper explains why.[6]

---

[3] Actually, a moment's thought will reveal, our genes are firmware. Evolution made the transition from analog to digital before the fossil record begins. But we haven't possessed the power of controlled direct modification. Until the day before yesterday. In the next century the genes too will become software, and while I don't discuss the issue further in this paper, the political consequences of unfreedom of software in this context are even more disturbing than they are with respect to cultural artifacts.

[4] See e.g., *Jack M. Balkin, Cultural Software: A Theory of Ideology* (1998).

[5] See *Sir Henry Sumner Maine, Ancient Law: Its Connection With the Early History of Society, and its Relation to Modern Ideas* (J. Murray, 1st ed., 1861).

[6] In general I dislike the intrusion of autobiography into scholarship. But because it is here my sad duty and great pleasure to challenge the qualifications or *bona fides* of just about everyone, I must enable the assessment of my own. I was first exposed to the craft of computer programming in 1971. I began earning wages as a commercial programmer in 1973 – at the age of thirteen – and did so, in a variety of computer services, engineering, and multinational technology enterprises, until 1985. In 1975 I helped write one of the first networked email systems in the United States; from 1979 I was engaged in research and development of advanced computer

We need to begin by considering the technical essence of the familiar devices that surround us in the era of "cultural software." A CD player is a good example. Its primary input is a bitstream read from an optical storage disk. The bitstream describes music in terms of measurements, taken 44,100 times per second, of amplitude in each of two audio channels. The player's primary output is analog audio signals.[7] Like everything else in the digital world, music as seen by a CD player is mere numeric information; a particular recording of Beethoven's Ninth Symphony recorded by Arturo Toscanini and the NBC Symphony Orchestra and Chorale is (to drop a few insignificant digits) 1276749873424, while Glenn Gould's peculiarly perverse last recording of the Goldberg Variations is (similarly rather truncated) 767459083268.

Oddly enough, these two numbers are "copyrighted." This means, supposedly, that you can't distribute another copy of these numbers, once fixed in any physical form, unless you have licensed them. And you can't turn 767459083268 into 2347895697 for your friends (thus correcting Gould's ridiculous judgment about tempi) without making a "derivative work," for which a license is necessary.

At the same time, a similar optical storage disk contains another number, let us call it 7537489532. This one is an algorithm for linear programming of large systems with multiple constraints, useful for example if you want to make optimal use of your rolling stock in running a freight railroad. This number (in the U.S.) is "patented," which means you cannot derive 7537489532 for yourself, or otherwise "practice the art" of the patent with respect to solving linear programming problems no matter how you came by the idea, including finding it out for yourself, unless you have a license from the number's owner.

Then there's 9892454959483. This one is the source code for Microsoft Word. In addition to being "copyrighted," this one is a trade secret. That means if you take this number from Microsoft and give it to anyone else you can be punished.

Lastly, there's 588832161316. It doesn't do anything; it's just the square of 767354. As far as I know, it isn't owned by anybody under any of these rubrics. Yet.

At this point we must deal with our first objection from the learned. It comes from a creature known as the IPdroid. The droid has a sophisticated mind and a

---

cont.
programming languages at IBM. These activities made it economically possible for me to study the arts of historical scholarship and legal cunning. My wages were sufficient to pay my tuitions, but not – to anticipate an argument that will be made by the econodwarves further along – because my programs were the intellectual property of my employer, but rather because they made the hardware my employer sold work better. Most of what I wrote was effectively free software, as we shall see. Although I subsequently made some inconsiderable technical contributions to the actual free software movement this paper describes, my primary activities on its behalf have been legal: I have served for the past nine years (without pay, naturally) as general counsel of the Free Software Foundation.

[7] The player, of course, has secondary inputs and outputs in control channels: buttons or infrared remote control are input, and time and track display are output.

cultured life. It appreciates very much the elegant dinners at academic and ministerial conferences about the TRIPs, not to mention the privilege of frequent appearances on MSNBC. It wants you to know that I'm committing the mistake of confusing the embodiment with the intellectual property itself. It's not the number that's patented, stupid, just the Kamarkar algorithm. The number *can* be copyrighted, because copyright covers the expressive qualities of a particular tangible embodiment of an idea (in which some functional properties may be mysteriously merged, provided that they're not too merged), but not the algorithm. Whereas the number isn't patentable, just the "teaching" of the number with respect to making railroads run on time. And the number representing the source code of Microsoft Word can be a trade secret, but if you find it out for yourself (by performing arithmetic manipulation of other numbers issued by Microsoft, for example, which is known as "reverse engineering"), you're not going to be punished, at least if you live in some parts of the United States.

This droid, like other droids, is often right. The condition of being a droid is to know everything about something and nothing about anything else. By its timely and urgent intervention the droid has established that the current intellectual property system contains many intricate and ingenious features. The complexities combine to allow professors to be erudite, Congressmen to get campaign contributions, lawyers to wear nice suits and tasseled loafers, and Murdoch to be rich. The complexities mostly evolved in an age of industrial information distribution, when information was inscribed in analog forms on physical objects that cost something significant to make, move, and sell. When applied to digital information that moves frictionlessly through the network and has zero marginal cost per copy, everything still works, mostly, as long as you don't stop squinting.

But that wasn't what I was arguing about. I wanted to point out something else: that our world consists increasingly of nothing but large numbers (also known as bitstreams), and that – for reasons having nothing to do with emergent properties of the numbers themselves – the legal system is presently committed to treating similar numbers radically differently. No one can tell, simply by looking at a number that is 100 million digits long, whether that number is subject to patent, copyright, or trade secret protection, or indeed whether it is "owned" by anyone at all. So the legal system we have – blessed as we are by its consequences if we are copyrights teachers, Congressmen, Gucci-gulchers or Big Rupert himself – is compelled to treat indistinguishable things in unlike ways.

Now, in my role as a legal historian concerned with the secular (that is, very long term) development of legal thought, I claim that legal regimes based on sharp but unpredictable distinctions among similar objects are radically unstable. They fall apart over time because every instance of the rules' application is an invitation to at least one side to claim that instead of fitting in ideal category A the particular object in dispute should be deemed to fit instead in category B, where the rules will be more favorable to the party making the claim. This game – about whether a typewriter should be deemed a musical instrument for purposes of railway rate regulation, or whether a steam shovel is a motor vehicle – is the frequent stuff of legal ingenuity. But when the conventionally approved legal categories require judges to distinguish among the identical, the game is infinitely lengthy, infinitely costly, and almost infinitely offensive to the unbiased bystander.[8] Thus parties can spend all the money they want on all the legislators and judges they can afford – which for the new "owners" of the digital world is quite a few – but the rules they buy aren't going to work in the end. Sooner or later, the paradigms are going to collapse. Of course, if later means two generations from now, the distribution of wealth and power sanctified in the meantime may not be reversible by any course less drastic than a *bellum servile* of couch potatoes against media magnates. So knowing that history isn't on Bill Gates' side isn't enough. We are predicting the future in a very limited sense: we know that the existing rules, which have yet the fervor of conventional belief solidly enlisted behind them, are no longer meaningful. Parties will use and abuse them freely until the mainstream of "respectable" conservative opinion acknowledges their death, with uncertain results. But realistic scholarship should already be turning its attention to the clear need for new thoughtways.

When we reach this point in the argument, we find ourselves contending with the other primary protagonist of educated idiocy: the econodwarf. Like the IPdroid, the econodwarf is a species of hedgehog,[9] but where the droid is committed to logic over experience, the econodwarf specializes in an energetic and well-focused but entirely erroneous view of human nature. According to the econodwarf's vision, each human being is an individual possessing "incentives," which can be retrospectively unearthed by imagining the state of the bank account at various times. So in this instance the econodwarf feels compelled to object that without the rules I am lampooning, there would be no incentive to create the things the rules treat as property: without the ability to exclude others from music there would be no music, because no one could be sure of getting paid for creating it.

Music is not really our subject; the software I am considering at the moment is the old kind: computer programs. But as he is determined to deal at least cursorily with the subject, and because, as we have seen, it is no longer really possible to

---

[8] This is not an insight unique to our present enterprise. A closely-related idea forms one of the most important principles in the history of Anglo-American law, perfectly put by Toby Milsom in the following terms: "The life of the common law has been in the abuse of its elementary ideas. If the rules of property give what now seems an unjust answer, try obligation; and equity has proved that from the materials of obligation you can counterfeit the phenomena of property. If the rules of contract give what now seems an unjust answer, try tort. ... If the rules of one tort, say deceit, give what now seems an unjust answer, try another, try negligence. And so the legal world goes round". Stroud F.C. Milsom, *Historical Foundations of the Common Law* 6 (Butterworths, 2nd ed., 1981).
[9] See Isaiah Berlin, *The Hedgehog and the Fox; an Essay on Tolstoy's View of History* (1953).

distinguish computer programs from music performances, a word or two should be said. At least we can have the satisfaction of indulging in an argument *ad pygmeam*. When the econodwarf grows rich, in my experience, he attends the opera. But no matter how often he hears *Don Giovanni* it never occurs to him that Mozart's fate should, on his logic, have entirely discouraged Beethoven, or that we have *The Magic Flute* even though Mozart knew very well he wouldn't be paid. In fact, *The Magic Flute*, the *St. Matthew's Passion*, and the motets of the wife-murderer Carlo Gesualdo are all part of the centuries-long tradition of free software, in the more general sense, which the econodwarf never quite acknowledges.

The dwarf's basic problem is that "incentives" is merely a metaphor, and as a metaphor to describe human creative activity it's pretty crummy. I have said this before,[10] but the better metaphor arose on the day Michael Faraday first noticed what happened when he wrapped a coil of wire around a magnet and spun the magnet. Current flows in such a wire, but we don't ask what the incentive is for the electrons to leave home. We say that the current results from an emergent property of the system, which we call induction. The question we ask is "what's the resistance of the wire?" So Moglen's Metaphorical Corollary to Faraday's Law says that if you wrap the Internet around every person on the planet and spin the planet, software flows in the network. It's an emergent property of connected human minds that they create things for one another's pleasure and to conquer their uneasy sense of being too alone. The only question to ask is, what's the resistance of the network? Moglen's Metaphorical Corollary to Ohm's Law states that the resistance of the network is directly proportional to the field strength of the "intellectual property" system. So the right answer to the econodwarf is, resist the resistance.

Of course, this is all very well in theory. "Resist the resistance" sounds good, but we'd have a serious problem, theory notwithstanding, if the dwarf were right and we found ourselves under-producing good software because we didn't let people own it. But dwarves and droids are formalists of different kinds, and the advantage of realism is that if you start from the facts the facts are always on your side. It turns out that treating software as property makes bad software.

Software as Property: The Practical Problem

In order to understand why turning software into property produces bad software, we need an introduction to the history of the art. In fact, we'd better start with the

---

[10] See Eben Moglen, The Virtual Scholar and Network Liberation, Address Before the Association of American Law Schools, New Orleans, 5 January 1995, at http://emoglen.law.-columbia.edu/my_pubs/nospeech.html

word "art" itself. The programming of computers combines determinate reasoning with literary invention.

At first glance, to be sure, source code appears to be a non-literary form of composition.[11] The primary desideratum in a computer program is that it works, that is to say, performs according to specifications formally describing its outputs in terms of its inputs. At this level of generality, the functional content of programs is all that can be seen.

But working computer programs exist as parts of computer systems, which are interacting collections of hardware, software, and human beings. The human components of a computer system include not only the users, but also the (potentially different) persons who maintain and improve the system. Source code not only communicates with the computer that executes the program, through the intermediary of the compiler that produces machine-language object code, but also with other programmers.

The function of source code in relation to other human beings is not widely grasped by non-programmers, who tend to think of computer programs as incomprehensible. They would be surprised to learn that the bulk of information contained in most programs is, from the point of view of the compiler or other language processor, "comment," that is, non-functional material. The comments, of course, are addressed to others who may need to fix a problem or to alter or enhance the program's operation. In most programming languages, far more space is spent in telling people what the program does than in telling the computer how to do it.

The design of programming languages has always proceeded under the dual requirements of complete specification for machine execution and informative description for human readers. One might identify three basic strategies in language design for approaching this dual purpose. The first, pursued initially with respect to the design of languages specific to particular hardware products and collectively known as "assemblers," essentially separated the human- and machine-communication portions of the program. Assembler instructions are very close relatives of machine-language instructions: in general, one line of an assembler program corresponds to one instruction in the native language of the machine. The programmer controls machine operation at the most specific possible level, and (if well-disciplined) engages in running commentary alongside

---

[11] Some basic vocabulary is essential. Digital computers actually execute numerical instructions: bitstrings that contain information in the "native" language created by the machine's designers. This is usually referred to as "machine language." The machine languages of hardware are designed for speed of execution at the hardware level, and are not suitable for direct use by human beings. So among the central components of a computer system are "programming languages," which translate expressions convenient for humans into machine language. The most common and relevant, but by no means the only, form of computer language is a "compiler." The compiler performs static translation, so that a file containing human-readable instructions, known as "source code" results in the generation of one or more files of executable machine language, known as "object code."

the machine instructions, pausing every few hundred instructions to create "block comments," which provide a summary of the strategy of the program, or document the major data structures the program manipulates.

A second approach, characteristically depicted by the language COBOL (which stood for "Common Business-Oriented Language"), was to make the program itself look like a set of natural language directions, written in a crabbed but theoretically human-readable style. A line of COBOL code might say, for example "MULTIPLY PRICE TIMES QUANTITY GIVING EXPANSION." At first, when the Pentagon and industry experts began the joint design of COBOL in the early 1960s, this seemed a promising approach. COBOL programs appeared largely self-documenting, allowing both the development of work teams able to collaborate on the creation of large programs, and the training of programmers who, while specialized workers, would not need to understand the machine as intimately as assembler programs had to. But the level of generality at which such programs documented themselves was wrongly selected. A more formulaic and compressed expression of operational detail "expansion = price × quantity," for example, was better suited even to business and financial applications where the readers and writers of programs were accustomed to mathematical expression, while the processes of describing both data structures and the larger operational context of the program were not rendered unnecessary by the wordiness of the language in which the details of execution were specified.

Accordingly, language designers by the late 1960s began experimenting with forms of expression in which the blending of operational details and non-functional information necessary for modification or repair was more subtle. Some designers chose the path of highly symbolic and compressed languages, in which the programmer manipulated data abstractly, so that "A × B" might mean the multiplication of two integers, two complex numbers, two vast arrays, or any other data type capable of some process called "multiplication," to be undertaken by the computer on the basis of the context for the variables "A" and "B" at the moment of execution.[12] Because this approach resulted in extremely concise programs, it was thought, the problem of making code comprehensible to those who would later seek to modify or repair it was simplified. By hiding the technical detail of computer operation and emphasizing the algorithm, languages could be devised that were better than English or other natural languages for the expression of stepwise processes. Commentary would be not only unnecessary but distracting, just as the metaphors used to convey mathematical concepts in English do more to confuse than to enlighten.

---

[12] This, I should say, was the path that most of my research and development followed, largely in connection with a language called APL ("A Programming Language") and its successors. It was not, however, the ultimately-dominant approach, for reasons that will be suggested below.

How We Created the Microbrain Mess

Thus the history of programming languages directly reflected the need to find forms of human-machine communication that were also effective in conveying complex ideas to human readers. "Expressivity" became a property of programming languages, not because it facilitated computation, but because it facilitated the collaborative creation and maintenance of increasingly complex software systems.

At first impression, this seems to justify the application of traditional copyright thinking to the resulting works. Though substantially involving "functional" elements, computer programs contained "expressive" features of paramount importance. Copyright doctrine recognized the merger of function and expression as characteristic of many kinds of copyrighted works. "Source code," containing both the machine instructions necessary for functional operation and the expressive "commentary" intended for human readers, was an appropriate candidate for copyright treatment.

True, so long as it is understood that the expressive component of software was present solely in order to facilitate the making of "derivative works." Were it not for the intention to facilitate alteration, the expressive elements of programs would be entirely supererogatory, and source code would be no more copyrightable than object code, the output of the language processor, purged of all but the program's functional characteristics.

The state of the computer industry throughout the 1960s and 1970s, when the grundnorms of sophisticated computer programming were established, concealed the tension implicit in this situation. In that period, hardware was expensive. Computers were increasingly large and complex collections of machines, and the business of designing and building such an array of machines for general use was dominated, not to say monopolized, by one firm. IBM gave away its software. To be sure, it owned the programs its employees wrote, and it copyrighted the source code. But it also distributed the programs – including the source code – to its customers at no additional charge, and encouraged them to make and share improvements or adaptations of the programs thus distributed. For a dominant hardware manufacturer, this strategy made sense: better programs sold more computers, which is where the profitability of the business rested.

Computers, in this period, tended to aggregate within particular organizations, but not to communicate broadly with one another. The software needed to operate was distributed not through a network, but on spools of magnetic tape. This distribution system tended to centralize software development, so that while IBM customers were free to make modifications and improvements to programs, those modifications were shared in the first instance with IBM, which then considered whether and in what way to incorporate those changes in the centrally-developed and distributed version of the software. Thus in two important senses the best computer software in the world was free: it cost nothing to acquire, and the terms on which it was furnished both allowed and encouraged experimentation, change, and improvement.[13] That the software in question was IBM's property under prevailing copyright law certainly established some theoretical limits on users' ability to distribute their improvements or adaptations to others, but in practice mainframe software was cooperatively developed by the dominant hardware manufacturer and its technically sophisticated users, employing the manufacturer's distribution resources to propagate the resulting improvements through the user community. The right to exclude others, one of the most important "sticks in the bundle" of property rights (in an image beloved of the United States Supreme Court), was practically unimportant, or even undesirable, at the heart of the software business.[14]

After 1980, everything was different. The world of mainframe hardware gave way within ten years to the world of the commodity PC. And, as a contingency of the industry's development, the single most important element of the software running on that commodity PC, the operating system, became the sole significant product of a company that made no hardware. High-quality basic software ceased to be part of the product-differentiation strategy of hardware manufacturers. Instead, a firm with an overwhelming share of the market, and with the near-monopolist's ordinary absence of interest in fostering diversity, set the practices of the software industry. In such a context, the right to exclude others from participation in the product's formation became profoundly important. Microsoft's power in the market rested entirely on its ownership of the Windows source code.

To Microsoft, others' making of "derivative works," otherwise known as repairs and improvements, threatened the central asset of the business. Indeed, as subsequent judicial proceedings have tended to establish, Microsoft's strategy as a

---

[13] This description elides some details. By the mid–1970s IBM had acquired meaningful competition in the mainframe computer business, while the large-scale antitrust action brought against it by the US government prompted the decision to "unbundle," or charge separately, for software. In this less important sense, software ceased to be free. But – without entering into the now-dead but once-heated controversy over IBM's software pricing policies – the unbundling revolution had less effect on the social practices of software manufacture than might be supposed. As a fellow responsible for technical improvement of one programming language product at IBM from 1979 to 1984, for example, I was able to treat the product as "almost free," that is, to discuss with users the changes they had proposed or made in the programs, and to engage with them in cooperative development of the product for the benefit of all users.

[14] This description is highly compressed, and will seem both overly simplified and unduly rosy to those who also worked in the industry during this period of its development. Copyright protection of computer software was a controversial subject in the 1970s, leading to the famous CONTU commission and its mildly pro-copyright recommendations of 1979. And IBM seemed far less cooperative to its users at the time than this sketch makes out. But the most important element is the contrast with the world created by the PC, the Internet, and the dominance of Microsoft, with the resulting impetus for the free software movement, and I am here concentrating on the features that express that contrast.

business was to find innovative ideas elsewhere in the software marketplace, buy them up and either suppress them or incorporate them in its proprietary product. The maintenance of control over the basic operation of computers manufactured, sold, possessed, and used by others represented profound and profitable leverage over the development of the culture;[15] the right to exclude returned to center stage in the concept of software as property.

The result, so far as the quality of software was concerned, was disastrous. The monopoly was a wealthy and powerful corporation that employed a large number of programmers, but it could not possibly afford the number of testers, designers, and developers required to produce flexible, robust and technically innovative software appropriate to the vast array of conditions under which increasingly ubiquitous personal computers operated. Its fundamental marketing strategy involved designing its product for the least technically sophisticated users, and using "fear, uncertainty, and doubt" (known within Microsoft as "FUD") to drive sophisticated users away from potential competitors, whose long-term survivability in the face of Microsoft's market power was always in question.

Without the constant interaction between users able to repair and improve and the operating system's manufacturer, the inevitable deterioration of quality could not be arrested. But because the personal computer revolution expanded the number of users exponentially, almost everyone who came in contact with the resulting systems had nothing against which to compare them. Unaware of the standards of stability, reliability, maintainability and effectiveness that had previously been established in the mainframe world, users of personal computers could hardly be expected to understand how badly, in relative terms, the monopoly's software functioned. As the power and capacity of personal computers expanded rapidly, the defects of the software were rendered less obvious amidst the general increase of productivity. Ordinary users, more than half afraid of the technology they almost completely did not understand, actually welcomed the defectiveness of the software. In an economy undergoing mysterious transformations, with the concomitant destabilization of millions of careers, it was tranquilizing, in a perverse way, that no personal computer seemed to be able to run for more than a few consecutive hours without crashing. Although it was frustrating to lose work in progress each time an unnecessary failure occurred, the evident fallibility of computers was intrinsically reassuring.[16]

None of this was necessary. The low quality of personal computer software could have been reversed by including users directly in the inherently evolutionary

---

[15] I discuss the importance of PC software in this context, the evolution of "the market for eyeballs" and "the sponsored life" in other chapters of my forthcoming book, *The Invisible Barbecue*, of which this essay forms a part.

[16] This same pattern of ambivalence, in which bad programming leading to widespread instability in the new technology is simultaneously frightening and reassuring to technical incompetents, can be seen also in the primarily-American phenomenon of Y2K hysteria.

process of software design and implementation. A Lamarckian mode, in which improvements could be made anywhere, by anyone, and inherited by everyone else, would have wiped out the deficit, restoring to the world of the PC the stability and reliability of the software made in the quasi-propertarian environment of the mainframe era. But the Microsoft business model precluded Lamarckian inheritance of software improvements. Copyright doctrine, in general and as it applies to software in particular, biases the world toward creationism; in this instance, the problem is that BillG the Creator was far from infallible, and in fact he wasn't even trying.

To make the irony more severe, the growth of the network rendered the non-propertarian alternative even more practical. What scholarly and popular writing alike denominate as a thing ("the Internet") is actually the name of a social condition: the fact that everyone in the network society is connected directly, without intermediation, to everyone else.[17] The global interconnection of networks eliminated the bottleneck that had required a centralized software manufacturer to rationalize and distribute the outcome of individual innovation in the era of the mainframe.

And so, in one of history's little ironies, the global triumph of bad software in the age of the PC was reversed by a surprising combination of forces: the social transformation initiated by the network, a long-discarded European theory of political economy, and a small band of programmers throughout the world mobilized by a single simple idea.

Software Wants to Be Free; or, How We Stopped Worrying and Learned to Love the Bomb

Long before the network of networks was a practical reality, even before it was an aspiration, there was a desire for computers to operate on the basis of software freely available to everyone. This began as a reaction against propertarian software in the mainframe era, and requires another brief historical digression.

Even though IBM was the largest seller of general purpose computers in the mainframe era, it was not the largest designer and builder of such hardware. The telephone monopoly, American Telephone & Telegraph, was in fact larger than IBM, but it consumed its products internally. And at the famous Bell Labs research arm of the telephone monopoly, in the late 1960s, the developments in computer languages previously described gave birth to an operating system called Unix.

---

[17] The critical implications of this simple observation about our metaphors are worked out in Eben Moglen, "How Not to Think about 'The Internet'," in *The Invisible Barbecue (forthcoming)*.

The idea of Unix was to create a single, scalable operating system to exist on all the computers, from small to large, that the telephone monopoly made for itself. To achieve this goal meant writing an operating system not in machine language, nor in an assembler whose linguistic form was integral to a particular hardware design, but in a more expressive and generalized language. The one chosen was also a Bell Labs invention, called "C."[18] The C language became common, even dominant, for many kinds of programming tasks, and by the late 1970s the Unix operating system written in that language had been transferred (or "ported," in professional jargon) to computers made by many manufacturers and of many designs.

AT&T distributed Unix widely, and because of the very design of the operating system, it had to make that distribution in C source code. But AT&T retained ownership of the source code and compelled users to purchase licenses that prohibited redistribution and the making of derivative works. Large computing centers, whether industrial or academic, could afford to purchase such licenses, but individuals could not, while the license restrictions prevented the community of programmers who used Unix from improving it in an evolutionary rather than episodic fashion. And as programmers throughout the world began to aspire to and even expect a personal computer revolution, the "unfree" status of Unix became a source of concern.

Between 1981 and 1984, one man envisioned a crusade to change the situation. Richard M. Stallman, then an employee of MIT's Artificial Intelligence Laboratory, conceived the project of independent, collaborative redesign and implementation of an operating system that would be true free software. In Stallman's phrase, free software would be a matter of freedom, not of price. Anyone could freely modify and redistribute such software, or sell it, subject only to the restriction that he not try to reduce the rights of others to whom he passed it along. In this way free software could become a self-organizing project, in which no innovation would be lost through proprietary exercises of rights. The system, Stallman decided, would be called GNU, which stood (in an initial example of a taste for recursive acronyms that has characterized free software ever since), for "GNU's Not Unix." Despite misgivings about the fundamental design of Unix, as well as its terms of distribution, GNU was intended to benefit from the wide if unfree source distribution of Unix. Stallman began Project GNU by writing components of the eventual system that were also designed to work without modification on existing Unix systems. Development of the GNU tools could thus proceed directly in the environment of university and other advanced computing centers around the world.

The scale of such a project was immense. Somehow, volunteer programmers had to be found, organized, and set to work building all the tools that would be

---

[18] Technical readers will again observe that this compresses developments occurring from 1969 through 1973.

necessary for the ultimate construction. Stallman himself was the primary author of several fundamental tools. Others were contributed by small or large teams of programmers elsewhere, and assigned to Stallman's project or distributed directly. A few locations around the developing network became archives for the source code of these GNU components, and throughout the 1980s the GNU tools gained recognition and acceptance by Unix users throughout the world. The stability, reliability, and maintainability of the GNU tools became a by-word, while Stallman's profound abilities as a designer continued to outpace, and provide goals for, the evolving process. The award to Stallman of a MacArthur Fellowship in 1990 was an appropriate recognition of his conceptual and technical innovations and their social consequences.

Project GNU, and the Free Software Foundation to which it gave birth in 1985, were not the only source of free software ideas. Several forms of copyright license designed to foster free or partially free software began to develop in the academic community, mostly around the Unix environment. The University of California Berkeley began the design and implementation of another version of Unix for free distribution in the academic community. BSD Unix, as it came to be known, also treated AT&T's Unix as a design standard. The code was broadly released and constituted a reservoir of tools and techniques, but its license terms limited the range of its application, while the elimination of hardware-specific proprietary code from the distribution meant that no one could actually build a working operating system for any particular computer from BSD. Other university-based work also eventuated in quasi-free software; the graphical user interface (or GUI) for Unix systems called X Windows, for example, was created at MIT and distributed with source code on terms permitting free modification. And in 1989–1990, an undergraduate computer science student at the University of Helsinki, Linus Torvalds, began the project that completed the circuit and fully energized the free software vision.

What Torvalds did was to begin adapting a computer science teaching tool for real life use. Andrew Tannenbaum's MINIX kernel,[19] was a staple of Operating Systems courses, providing an example of basic solutions to basic problems. Slowly, and at first without recognizing the intention, Linus began turning the MINIX kernel into an actual kernel for Unix on the Intel x86 processors, the engines that run the world's commodity PCs. As Linus began developing this kernel, which he named Linux, he realized that the best way to make his project

---

[19] Operating systems, even Windows (which hides the fact from its users as thoroughly as possible), are actually collections of components, rather than undivided unities. Most of what an operating system does (manage file systems, control process execution, etc.) can be abstracted from the actual details of the computer hardware on which the operating system runs. Only a small inner core of the system must actually deal with the eccentric peculiarities of particular hardware. Once the operating system is written in a general language such as C, only that inner core, known in the trade as the kernel, will be highly specific to a particular computer architecture.

work would be to adjust his design decisions so that the existing GNU components would be compatible with his kernel.

The result of Torvalds' work was the release on the net in 1991 of a sketchy working model of a free software kernel for a Unix-like operating system for PCs, fully compatible with and designed convergently with the large and high-quality suite of system components created by Stallman's Project GNU and distributed by the Free Software Foundation. Because Torvalds chose to release the Linux kernel under the Free Software Foundation's General Public License, of which more below, the hundreds and eventually thousands of programmers around the world who chose to contribute their effort toward the further development of the kernel could be sure that their efforts would result in permanently free software that no one could turn into a proprietary product. Everyone knew that everyone else would be able to test, improve, and redistribute their improvements. Torvalds accepted contributions freely, and with a genially effective style maintained overall direction without dampening enthusiasm. The development of the Linux kernel proved that the Internet made it possible to aggregate collections of programmers far larger than any commercial manufacturer could afford, joined almost non-hierarchically in a development project ultimately involving more than one million lines of computer code – a scale of collaboration among geographically dispersed unpaid volunteers previously unimaginable in human history.[20]

By 1994, Linux had reached version 1.0, representing a usable production kernel. Level 2.0 was reached in 1996, and by 2002, with the kernel at 2.5.12 and available not only for x86 machines but for a variety of other machine architectures, GNU/Linux – the combination of the Linux kernel and the much larger body of Project GNU components – and Windows NT were the only two operating systems in the world gaining market share. A Microsoft internal assessment of the situation leaked in October 1998 and subsequently acknowledged by the company as genuine concluded that "Linux represents a best-of-breed UNIX, that is trusted in mission critical applications, and-due to it's [sic] open source code-has a long term credibility which exceeds many other competitive OS's."[21] GNU/Linux systems are now used throughout the world, operating everything from web servers at major electronic commerce sites to "ad-hoc supercomputer" clusters to the network infrastructure of money-center banks. GNU/Linux is found on the space shuttle, and running behind-the-scenes computers at (yes) Microsoft. Industry evaluations of the comparative reliability

---

[20] A careful and creative analysis of how Torvalds made this process work, and what it implies for the social practices of creating software was provided by Eric S. Raymond in his seminal 1997 paper *The Cathedral and the Bazaar*, http://firstmonday.org/issues/issue3-3/raymond/index.html, which itself played a significant role in the expansion of the free software idea.

[21] This is a quotation from what is known in the trade as the "Halloween memo," which can be found, as annotated by Eric Raymond, to whom it was leaked, in Vinod Vallopillil, Linux OS Competitive Analysis: The Next Java VM? (Halloween II), at http://www.opensource.org/halloween1.html

of Unix systems have repeatedly shown that Linux is far and away the most stable and reliable Unix kernel for personal computers, with a reliability exceeded only by the GNU tools themselves. GNU/Linux not only out-performs commercial proprietary Unix versions for PCs in benchmarks, but is renowned for its ability to run, undisturbed and uncomplaining, for months on end in high-volume, high-stress environments without crashing.

Other components of the free software movement have been equally successful. Apache, far and away the world's leading web server program, is free software, as is Perl, the programming language which is the lingua franca for the programmers who build sophisticated websites. Netscape Communications now distributes its Netscape Communicator 6.0 browser as free software, under a close variant of the Free Software Foundation's General Public License. Major PC manufacturers, including IBM, have announced plans or are already distributing GNU/Linux as a customer option on their top-of-the-line PCs intended for use as web- and fileservers. Samba, a program that allows GNU/Linux computers to act as Windows NT fileservers, is used worldwide as an alternative to Windows NT Server, and provides effective low-end competition to Microsoft in its own home market. By the standards of software quality that have been recognized in the industry for decades – and whose continuing relevance will be clear to you the next time your Windows PC crashes – the news at century's end was unambiguous. The world's most profitable and powerful corporation comes in a distant second, having excluded all but the real victor from the race. Propertarianism joined to capitalist vigor destroyed meaningful commercial competition, but when it came to making good software, anarchism won.

Anarchism as a Mode of Production

It's a pretty story, and if only the IPdroid and the econodwarf hadn't been blinded by theory, they'd have seen it coming. But though some of us had been working for it and predicting it for years, the theoretical consequences are so subversive for the thoughtways that maintain our dwarves and droids in comfort that they can hardly be blamed for refusing to see. The facts proved that something was wrong with the "incentives" metaphor that underprops conventional intellectual property reasoning.[22] But they did more. They provided an initial glimpse into the future of human creativity in a world of global interconnection, and it's not a world made for dwarves and droids.

---

[22] As recently as early 1994 a talented and technically competent (though Windows-using) law and economics scholar at a major US law school confidently informed me that free software couldn't possibly exist, because no one would have any incentive to make really sophisticated programs requiring substantial investment of effort only to give them away.

My argument, before we paused for refreshment in the real world, can be summarized this way: Software – whether executable programs, music, visual art, liturgy, weaponry, or what have you – consists of bitstreams, which although essentially indistinguishable are treated by a confusing multiplicity of legal categories. This multiplicity is unstable in the long term for reasons integral to the legal process. The unstable diversity of rules is caused by the need to distinguish among kinds of property interests in bitstreams. This need is primarily felt by those who stand to profit from the socially acceptable forms of monopoly created by treating ideas as property. Those of us who are worried about the social inequity and cultural hegemony created by this intellectually unsatisfying and morally repugnant regime are shouted down. Those doing the shouting, the dwarves and the droids, believe that these property rules are necessary not from any overt yearning for life in Murdochworld – though a little luxurious co-optation is always welcome – but because the metaphor of incentives, which they take to be not just an image but an argument, proves that these rules – despite their lamentable consequences – are necessary if we are to make good software. The only way to continue to believe this is to ignore the facts. At the center of the digital revolution, with the executable bitstreams that make everything else possible, propertarian regimes not only do not make things better, they can make things radically worse. Property concepts, whatever else may be wrong with them, do not enable and have in fact retarded progress.

But what is this mysterious alternative? Free software exists, but what are its mechanisms, and how does it generalize toward a non-propertarian theory of the digital society?

The Legal Theory of Free Software

There is a myth, like most myths partially founded on reality, that computer programmers are all libertarians. Right-wing ones are capitalists, cleave to their stock options, and disdain taxes, unions, and civil rights laws; left-wing ones hate the market and all government, believe in strong encryption no matter how much nuclear terrorism it may cause,[23] and dislike Bill Gates because he's rich. There is doubtless a foundation for this belief. But the most significant difference between political thought inside the *digirati* and outside it is that in the network society, anarchism (or more properly, anti-possessive individualism) is a viable political philosophy.

---

[23] This question too deserves special scrutiny, encrusted as it is with special pleading on the state-power side. See my brief essay, "*So Much for Savages: Navajo 1, Government 0 in Final Moments of Play*", http://emoglen.law.columbia.edu/publications/yu-encrypt.html

The center of the free software movement's success, and the greatest achievement of Richard Stallman, is not a piece of computer code. The success of free software, including the overwhelming success of GNU/Linux, results from the ability to harness extraordinary quantities of high-quality effort for projects of immense size and profound complexity. And this ability in turn results from the legal context in which the labor is mobilized. As a visionary designer Richard Stallman created more than Emacs, GDB, or GNU. He created the General Public License.

The GPL,[24] also known as the copyleft, uses copyright, to paraphrase Toby Milsom, to counterfeit the phenomena of anarchism. As the license preamble expresses it:

> When we speak of free software, we are referring to freedom, not price. Our General Public Licenses are designed to make sure that you have the freedom to distribute copies of free software (and charge for this service if you wish), that you receive source code or can get it if you want it, that you can change the software or use pieces of it in new free programs; and that you know you can do these things.
>
> To protect your rights, we need to make restrictions that forbid anyone to deny you these rights or to ask you to surrender the rights. These restrictions translate to certain responsibilities for you if you distribute copies of the software, or if you modify it.
>
> For example, if you distribute copies of such a program, whether gratis or for a fee, you must give the recipients all the rights that you have. You must make sure that they, too, receive or can get the source code. And you must show them these terms so they know their rights.

Many variants of this basic free software idea have been expressed in licenses of various kinds, as I have already indicated. The GPL is different from the other ways of expressing these values in one crucial respect. Section 2 of the license provides in pertinent part:

> You may modify your copy or copies of the Program or any portion of it, thus forming a work based on the Program, and copy and distribute such modifications or work ..., provided that you also meet all of these conditions:
>
> b) You must cause any work that you distribute or publish, that in whole or in part contains or is derived from the Program or any part thereof, to be licensed as a whole at no charge to all third parties under the terms of this License.

Section 2(b) of the GPL is sometimes called "restrictive," but its intention is liberating. It creates a commons, to which anyone may add but from which no one

---

[24] See GNU General Public License, Version 2, June 1991, http://www.fsf.org/copyleft/gpl.txt

may subtract. Because of §2(b), each contributor to a GPL'd project is assured that she, and all other users, will be able to run, modify and redistribute the program indefinitely, that source code will always be available, and that, unlike commercial software, its longevity cannot be limited by the contingencies of the marketplace or the decisions of future developers. This "inheritance" of the GPL has sometimes been criticized as an example of the free software movement's anti-commercial bias. Nothing could be further from the truth. The effect of §2(b) is to make commercial distributors of free software better competitors against proprietary software businesses. For confirmation of this point, one can do no better than to ask the proprietary competitors. As the author of the Microsoft "Halloween" memorandum, Vinod Vallopillil, put it:

> The GPL and its aversion to code forking reassures customers that they aren't riding an evolutionary 'dead-end' by subscribing to a particular commercial version of Linux.
> The "evolutionary dead-end" is the core of the software FUD argument.[25]

Translated out of Microspeak, this means that the strategy by which the dominant proprietary manufacturer drives customers away from competitors – by sowing fear, uncertainty and doubt about other software's long-term viability – is ineffective with respect to GPL'd programs. Users of GPL'd code, including those who purchase software and systems from a commercial reseller, know that future improvements and repairs will be accessible from the commons, and need not fear either the disappearance of their supplier or that someone will use a particularly attractive improvement or a desperately necessary repair as leverage for "taking the program private."

This use of intellectual property rules to create a commons in cyberspace is the central institutional structure enabling the anarchist triumph. Ensuring free access and enabling modification at each stage in the process means that the evolution of software occurs in the fast Lamarckian mode: each favorable acquired characteristic of others' work can be directly inherited. Hence the speed with which the Linux kernel, for example, outgrew all of its proprietary predecessors. Because defection is impossible, free riders are welcome, which resolves one of the central puzzles of collective action in a propertarian social system.

Non-propertarian production is also directly responsible for the famous stability and reliability of free software, which arises from what Eric Raymond calls "Linus' law": With enough eyeballs, all bugs are shallow. In practical terms, access to source code means that if I have a problem I can fix it. Because I can fix it, I almost never have to, because someone else has almost always seen it and fixed it first.

---

[25] V. Vallopillil, Open Source Software: A (New?) Development Methodology, http://www.opensource.org/halloween1.html

For the free software community, commitment to anarchist production may be a moral imperative; as Richard Stallman wrote, it's about freedom, not about price. Or it may be a matter of utility, seeking to produce better software than propertarian modes of work will allow. From the droid point of view, the copyleft represents the perversion of theory, but better than any other proposal over the past decades it resolves the problems of applying copyright to the inextricably merged functional and expressive features of computer programs. That it produces better software than the alternative does not imply that traditional copyright principles should now be prohibited to those who want to own and market inferior software products, or (more charitably) whose products are too narrow in appeal for communal production. But our story should serve as a warning to droids: The world of the future will bear little relation to the world of the past. The rules are now being bent in two directions. The corporate owners of "cultural icons" and other assets who seek ever-longer terms for corporate authors, converting the "limited Time" of Article I, §8 into a freehold have naturally been whistling music to the android ear.[26] After all, who bought the droids their concert tickets? But as the propertarian position seeks to embed itself ever more strongly, in a conception of copyright liberated from the minor annoyances of limited terms and fair use, at the very center of our "cultural software" system, the anarchist counter-strike has begun. Worse is yet to befall the droids, as we shall see. But first, we must pay our final devoirs to the dwarves.

Because It's There: Faraday's Magnet and Human Creativity

After all, they deserve an answer. Why do people make free software if they don't get to profit? Two answers have usually been given. One is half-right and the other is wrong, but both are insufficiently simple.

The wrong answer is embedded in numerous references to "the hacker gift-exchange culture." This use of ethnographic jargon wandered into the field some years ago and became rapidly, if misleadingly, ubiquitous. It reminds us only that the economeretricians have so corrupted our thought processes that any form of non-market economic behavior seems equal to every other kind. But gift-exchange, like market barter, is a propertarian institution. Reciprocity is central to these symbolic enactments of mutual dependence, and if either the yams or the fish are short-weighted, trouble results. Free software, at the risk of repetition, is a

---

[26] The looming expiration of Mickey Mouse's ownership by Disney required, from the point of view of that wealthy "campaign contributor," for example, an alteration of the general copyright law of the United States. See Eben Moglen, "Not Making it Any More? Vaporizing the Public Domain," in *The Invisible Barbecue (forthcoming)*.

commons: no reciprocity ritual is enacted there. A few people give away code that others sell, use, change, or borrow wholesale to lift out parts for something else. Notwithstanding the very large number of people (tens of thousands, at most) who have contributed to GNU/Linux, this is orders of magnitude less than the number of users who make no contribution whatever.[27]

A part of the right answer is suggested by the claim that free software is made by those who seek reputational compensation for their activity. Famous Linux hackers, the theory is, are known all over the planet as programming deities. From this they derive either enhanced self-esteem or indirect material advancement.[28] But the programming deities, much as they have contributed to free software, have not done the bulk of the work. Reputations, as Linus Torvalds himself has often pointed out, are made by willingly acknowledging that it was all done by someone else. And, as many observers have noted, the free software movement has also produced superlative documentation. Documentation-writing is not what hackers do to attain cool, and much of the documentation has been written by people who didn't write the code. Nor must we limit the indirect material advantages of authorship to increases in reputational capital. Most free software authors I know have day jobs in the technology industries, and the skills they hone in the more creative work they do outside the market no doubt sometimes measurably enhance their value within it. And as the free software products gained critical mass and became the basis of a whole new set of business models built around commercial distribution of that which people can also get for nothing, an increasing number of people are specifically employed to write free software. But in order to be employable in the field, they must already have established themselves there. Plainly, then, this motive is present, but it isn't the whole explanation.

Indeed, the rest of the answer is just too simple to have received its due. The best way to understand is to follow the brief and otherwise unsung career of an initially grudging free software author. Microsoft's Vinod Vallopillil, in the course of writing the competitive analysis of Linux that was leaked as the second of the famous "Halloween memoranda," bought and installed a Linux system on one of his office computers. He had trouble because the (commercial) Linux distribution

---

[27] A recent industry estimate puts the number of Linux systems worldwide at 7.5 million. See Josh McHugh, Linux: The Making of a Global Hack, Forbes, August 10, 1998. <http://www.forbes.com/forbes/98/0810/6203094s1.htm> Because the software is freely obtainable throughout the net, there is no simple way to assess actual usage.

[28] Eric Raymond is a partisan of the "ego boost" theory, to which he adds another faux-ethnographic comparison, of free software composition to the Kwakiutl potlatch. See Eric S. Raymond, Homesteading the Noosphere, http://www.tuxedo.org/esr/writings/homesteading. But the potlatch, certainly a form of status competition, is unlike free software for two fundamental reasons: it is essentially hierarchical, which free software is not, and, as we have known since Thorstein Veblen first called attention to its significance, it is a form of conspicuous waste. See *Thorstein Veblen, The Theory of the Leisure Class* 75 (Viking, 1967) (1899). These are precisely the grounds which distinguish the anti-hierarchical and utilitiarian free software culture from its propertarian counterparts.

he installed did not contain a daemon to handle the DHCP protocol for assignment of dynamic IP addresses. The result was important enough for us to risk another prolonged exposure to the Microsoft Writing Style:

> A small number of web sites and FAQs later, I found an FTP site with a Linux DHCP client. The DHCP client was developed by an engineer employed by Fore Systems (as evidenced by his email address; I believe, however, that it was developed in his own free time). A second set of documentation/manuals was written for the DHCP client by a hacker in *Hungary,* which provided relatively simple instructions on how to install/load the client.
>
> I downloaded & uncompressed the client and typed two simple commands:
> Make – compiles the client binaries
> install – installed the binaries as a Linux Daemon
> Typing "dhcpcd" (for DHCP Client Daemon) on the command line triggered the DHCP discovery process and voila, I had IP networking running.
>
> Since I had just downloaded the DHCP client code, on an impulse I played around a bit. Although the client wasn't as extensible as the DHCP client we are shipping in NT5 (for example, it won't query for arbitrary options & store results), it was obvious how I could write the additional code to implement this functionality. The full client consisted of about 2600 lines of code.
>
> One example of esoteric, extended functionality that was clearly patched in by a third party was a set of routines that would pad the DHCP request with host-specific strings required by Cable Modem/ADSL sites.
>
> A few other steps were required to configure the DHCP client to auto-start and auto-configure my Ethernet interface on boot but these were documented in the client code and in the DHCP documentation from the Hungarian developer.
>
> I'm a poorly skilled UNIX programmer, but it was immediately obvious to me how to incrementally extend the DHCP client code (the feeling was exhilarating and addictive).
>
> Additionally, due directly to GPL plus having the full development environment in front of me, I was in a position where I could write up my changes and email them out within a couple of hours (in contrast to how things like this would get done in NT). Engaging in that process would have prepared me for a larger, more ambitious Linux project in the future.[29]

"The feeling was exhilarating and addictive." Stop the presses: Microsoft experimentally verifies Moglen's Metaphorical Corollary to Faraday's Law. Wrap the Internet around every brain on the planet and spin the planet. Software flows

---

[29] See Vinod Vallopillil, supra note 21. Note Vallopillil's surprise that a program written in California had been subsequently documented by a programmer in Hungary.

in the wires. It's an emergent property of human minds to create. "Due directly to the GPL," as Vallopillil rightly pointed out, free software made available to him an exhilarating increase in his own creativity, of a kind not achievable in his day job working for the Greatest Programming Company on Earth. If only he had emailed that first addictive fix, who knows where he'd be now?

So, in the end, my dwarvish friends, it's just a human thing. Rather like why Figaro sings, why Mozart wrote the music for him to sing to, and why we all make up new words: Because we can. *Homo ludens*, meet *Homo faber*. The social condition of global interconnection that we call the Internet makes it possible for all of us to be creative in new and previously undreamed-of ways. Unless we allow "ownership" to interfere. Repeat after me, ye dwarves and men: Resist the resistance!

Their Lordships Die in the Dark?

For the IPdroid, fresh off the plane from a week at Bellagio paid for by Dreamworks SKG, it's enough to cause indigestion.

Unlock the possibilities of human creativity by connecting everyone to everyone else? Get the ownership system out of the way so that we can all add our voices to the choir, even if that means pasting our singing on top of the Mormon Tabernacle and sending the output to a friend? No one sitting slack-jawed in front of a televised mixture of violence and imminent copulation carefully devised to heighten the young male eyeball's interest in a beer commercial? What will become of civilization? Or at least of copyrights teachers?

But perhaps this is premature. I've only been talking about software. Real software, the old kind that runs computers. Not like the software that runs DVD players, or the kind made by the Grateful Dead. "Oh yes, the Grateful Dead. Something strange about them, wasn't there? Didn't prohibit recording at their concerts. Didn't mind if their fans rather riled the recording industry. Seem to have done all right, though, you gotta admit. Senator Patrick Leahy, isn't he a former Deadhead? I wonder if he'll vote to extend corporate authorship terms to 125 years, so that Disney doesn't lose The Mouse in 2004. And those DVD players – they're computers, aren't they?"

In the digital society, it's all connected. We can't depend for the long run on distinguishing one bitstream from another in order to figure out which rules apply. What happened to software is already happening to music. Their recording industry lordships are now scrambling wildly to retain control over distribution, as both musicians and listeners realize that the middlepeople are no longer necessary. The Great Potemkin Village of 1999, the so-called Secure Digital Music Initiative, will have collapsed long before the first Internet President gets inaugurated, for simple technical reasons as obvious to those who know as the ones that dictated the triumph of free software.[30] The anarchist revolution in music is different from the one in software *tout court*, but here too – as any teenager with an MP3 collection of self-released music from unsigned artists can tell you – theory has been killed off by the facts. Whether you are Mick Jagger, or a great national artist from the third world looking for a global audience, or a garret-dweller reinventing music, the recording industry will soon have nothing to offer you that you can't get better for free. And music doesn't sound worse when distributed for free, pay what you want directly to the artist, and don't pay anything if you don't want to. Give it to your friends; they might like it.

What happened to music is also happening to news. The wire services, as any U.S. law student learns even before taking the near-obligatory course in Copyright for Droids, have a protectible property interest in their expression of the news, even if not in the facts the news reports.[31] So why are they now giving all their output away? Because in the world of the net, most news is commodity news. And the original advantage of the news gatherers, that they were internally connected in ways others were not when communications were expensive, is gone. Now what matters is collecting eyeballs to deliver to advertisers. It isn't the wire services that have the advantage in covering Afghanistan, that's for sure. Much less those paragons of "intellectual" property, their television lordships. They, with their overpaid pretty people and their massive technical infrastructure, are about the only organizations in the world that can't afford to be everywhere all the time. And then they have to limit themselves to ninety seconds a story, or the eyeball hunters will go somewhere else. So who makes better news, the propertarians or the anarchists? We shall soon see.

Oscar Wilde says somewhere that the problem with socialism is that it takes up too many evenings. The problems with anarchism as a social system are also about transaction costs. But the digital revolution alters two aspects of political economy that have been otherwise invariant throughout human history. All software has zero marginal cost in the world of the net, while the costs of social coordination have been so far reduced as to permit the rapid formation and dissolution of large-scale and highly diverse social groupings entirely without geographic limitation.[32] Such fundamental change in the material circumstances of life necessarily produces equally fundamental changes in culture. Think not? Tell it to the Iroquois. And of course such profound shifts in culture are threats to existing

---

[30] See Eben Moglen, "They're Playing Our Song: The Day the Music Industry Died," in *The Invisible Barbecue (forthcoming)*.

[31] International News Service v. Associated Press, 248 U.S. 215 (1918). With regard to the actual terse, purely functional expressions of breaking news actually at stake in the jostling among wire services, this was always a distinction only a droid could love.

[32] See Eben Moglen, "No Prodigal Son: The Political Theory of Universal Interconnection," in *The Invisible Barbecue (forthcoming)*.

power relations. Think not? Ask the Chinese Communist Party. Or wait twenty-five years and see if you can find them for purposes of making the inquiry.

In this context, the obsolescence of the IPdroid is neither unforseeable nor tragic. Indeed it may find itself clanking off into the desert, still lucidly explaining to an imaginary room the profitably complicated rules for a world that no longer exists. But at least it will have familiar company, recognizable from all those glittering parties in Davos, Hollywood, and Brussels. Our Media Lords are now at handigrips with fate, however much they may feel that the Force is with them. The rules about bitstreams are now of dubious utility for maintaining power by co-opting human creativity. Seen clearly in the light of day, these Emperors have even fewer clothes than the models they use to grab our eyeballs. Unless supported by user-disabling technology, a culture of pervasive surveillance that permits every reader of every "property" to be logged and charged, and a smokescreen of droid-breath assuring each and every young person that human creativity would vanish without the benevolent aristocracy of BillG the Creator, Lord Murdoch of Everywhere, the Spielmeister and the Lord High Mouse, their reign is nearly done. But what's at stake is the control of the scarcest resource of all: our attention. Conscripting that makes all the money in the world in the digital economy, and the current lords of the earth will fight for it. Leagued against them are only the anarchists: nobodies, hippies, hobbyists, lovers, and artists. The resulting unequal contest is the great political and legal issue of our time. Aristocracy looks hard to beat, but that's how it looked in 1788 and 1913 too. It is, as Chou En-Lai said about the meaning of the French Revolution, too soon to tell.

Intellectual Property and the Internet: The Share of Sharing

Ejan Mackaay[1]

Just when we thought we knew everything we always wanted to know about intellectual property and had it properly organised, it explodes again. We thought we had answered the call that information wants to be free and shown that intellectual property is not the divine right of thugs.[2] We agreed on an international convention for adapting copyright to the Internet.[3] The Americans worked it into a piece of political compromise pompously called the Digital Millennium Copyright Act and blissfully unreadable. Yet now there is a call for the "right to read",[4] for limiting copyright in order to preserve an "information-rich environment",[5] for music to be exchanged freely in MP3 format. Further *contestataires* are putting video decryption software (DeCSS) at multiple spots on

---

[1] My thanks to Pierre Garello and participants at the European Association for Law and Economics in Ghent (14–16 September 2000 and at the *Premières Journées internationales du droit du commerce électronique* in Nice (23–25 October 2000) for comments on an earlier version of the paper, and to Niva Elkin-Koren and Neil Netanel for comments on the current version.

[2] Barlow, John Perry, "The Economy of Ideas – A framework for rethinking patents and copyrights in the Digital Age (Everything you know about intellectual property is wrong)", (1994) 2.03 *Wired* 84–90, 126–129.

[3] WIPO Copyright Convention, Geneva, 20 Dec. 1996. (Convention on Certain Copyright and Neighbouring Rights Questions).

[4] Jessica Litman, The Exclusive Right to Read, (1994) 13 *Cardozo Arts & Ent. L.J.* 29; Cohen, Julie, A Right to Read Anonymously: A Closer Look at "Copyright Management" In Cyberspace, (1996) 28 *Conn. L. Rev* 981.

[5] Yochai Benkler, for instance, in various recent articles defends the idea of limiting the reach of copyright to preserve an information rich environment: Benkler, Yochai, "Constitutional Bounds of Database Protection: The Role of Judicial Review in the Creation and Definition of Private Rights in Information", (2000) 15 *Berkeley Technology Law Journal* 535–603; Benkler, Yochai, "From Consumers to Users: Shifting the Deeper Structures of Regulation toward Sustainable Commons and User Access", (2000) 52 *Federal Communications Law Journal* 561–579; Benkler, Yochai, "Internet Regulation: A Case Study in the Problem of Unilateralism", (2000) 11 *European Journal of International Law* 171–185; Benkler, Yochai, "Net Regulation: Taking Stock and Looking Forward", (2000) 71 *University of Colorado Law Review* 1203–1261.

N. Elkin-Koren and N.W. Netanel (eds.), The Commodification of Information, 133–146.
© 2002 Ejan Mackaay. Printed in Great Britain.

the Internet, leading American officials to seek extraterritorial reach for their law in a frustrating effort to stop it. GNU/Linux is rapidly eating market share from commercial players in the operating system market, ostensibly demonstrating that the share economy can work and is even more creative, its proponents claim, than the developers of Windows. Scholarship accounts for such phenomena with the idea of the anti-commons: too much property right concentrated in a single object is counterproductive.[6] Respectable scholars lend their voice to the idea that folk art should not be open to appropriation and subsequent exclusive exploitation by any comer.[7] Must we yet resign ourselves to dance on the grave of copyright?[8]

To answer that question, we do well to return to the core ideas of copyright (and intellectual property rights generally) (A). This should allow us to discuss the suggestion of abandoning intellectual property rights altogether. The main critical voices, however, do not call for total abandonment, but rather for forms of sharing, sometimes called limited common property. We must look at the circumstances in which such a formula is viable as well as desirable (B).

A. The classical picture of intellectual property

1. INTELLECTUAL PROPERTY AS A SPECIES OF PROPERTY

In the classical picture, intellectual property is a species of property right, albeit a peculiar one. Property rights are a standard answer to scarcity; it is hardly worth establishing them on what is abundant. Scarcity arises with multiple competing uses for a single object. Emergent scarcity may be signalled by conflict amongst persons pursuing different uses for the same object.[9] Property rights reserve the

---

[6] Heller, Michael A., "The Tragedy of the Anticommons: Property in the Transition from Marx to Markets", (1998) 111 *Harvard Law Review* 621–688; Heller, Michael A., "The Boundaries of Private Property", (1999) 108 *Yale Law Review* 1163–1223; Heller, Michael A. and Rebecca S. Eisenberg, "Can Patents Deter Innovation? The Anticommons in Biomedical Research", (1998) 280 *Science* 698. In an as yet unpublished paper, Parisi et al. propose a formal model for this concept: Parisi, Francesco, B. Norbert Schulz and B. Ben Depoorter, *Duality in Property:Commons and Anticommons*, rapport, George Mason University, 2000.

[7] Rose, Carol M., Evolution of Property Rights, in: *The New Palgrave Dictionary of Economics and the Law, Vol. 2,* Peter Newman (ed.), London, MacMillan, 1998, pp. 93–98; Rose, Carol M., "The Several Futures of Property: Of Cyberspace and Folk Tales, Emission Trades and Ecosystems", (1998) 83 *Minnesota Law Review* 129–181.

[8] Barlow, *op. cit.*

[9] Demsetz, Harold, "Towards a Theory of Property Rights", (1967) 57 *American Economic Review* 347–373; Demsetz, Harold, Property Rights, in: *The New Palgrave Dictionary of Economics and the Law, Vol. 3,* Peter Newman (ed.), London, MacMillan, 1998, pp. 144–155; Mackaay, Ejan, The Economics of Emergent Property Rights on the Internet, in : *The Future of*

power to decide what is to be done with an object to a single person or group of persons, to the exclusion of all others, preferably with the right to transfer that power to someone else. They are expected to have the effect of creating incentives for carefully husbanding known resources and for inventing better ways of using them or discovering new ones. Granting the creator the spoils of an invention or creation, but also the losses if it flops, is a decentralised system for encouraging creation.

Intellectual rights, being a species of property rights, inherit this logic, but with a twist, because of the special nature of information. In many instances, information is costly to produce, but cheap to reproduce. This would mean, by standard economic reasoning, that it should be distributed at very low cost, making it difficult to recover the cost of creation. Often it is difficult to exclude people from using information once available; use by one person does not preclude use by another. The two features characterise a public good, with notorious difficulties for creating property rights and markets. Moreover, information embodied in one person's creation or invention is often used by someone else in developing a further creation or invention. This gives information a cumulative character which ill comports with the exclusivity a property right requires. All of these characteristics lead to the conclusion that property rights in information must be limited. They reflect a trade-off between incentives necessary for creating information and the monopolising effect, i.e. the cost of restricting access for other creators and the public in general.[10]

There is a substantial literature examining intellectual property rules with a view to determining whether they reflect an optimal trade-off and are in that sense "efficient". Enlightening though this analysis may be for rationalising rules, it does not show how rules reflecting such a trade-off come about. The origin of intellectual property rules is worth looking into, considering that legislatures can scarcely be expected to develop a balanced view in relying on groups making themselves heard in front of them, that is, as the public choice literature has shown, organised interests seeking firmer protection for their products. Nor is it the role of the courts to create novel rights from scratch.

2. EXTENSION OF INTELLECTUAL PROPERTY TO NEW OBJECTS

When new objects are invented or discovered for hitherto unprofitable objects, how do property rights come to govern these new objects? They are rarely created

---

cont.
  Copyright in a Digital Environment, P. Bernt Hugenholtz (ed.), The Hague, Kluwer Law International, 1996, pp. 13–25, at p. 16 s.

[10] Landes, William M. and Richard A. Posner, "An Economic Analysis of Copyright Law", (1989) 18 *Journal of Legal Studies* 325–363.

ex nihilo by legislation or judicial decision. Preferably legislation or judicial decision would acknowledge and codify institutions developed by interested persons themselves. In such a process of recognition the initiative falls to persons who stand to gain from using or commercialising the new object. Marie-Angèle Hermitte has described such a development for plant-breeder rights in France.[11] I would expect that a similar process has been at work leading up to the enactment of property rights in apartments. Enactment of individual property rights in apartments facilitates such operations as establishing mortgages (hypothecs) on them.

Property rights presuppose control over an object, i.e. the possibility of reserving its use to one person, to the exclusion of others. So the first step in the process is to secure control over the object. This may be achieved through physical fences or ditches, through encryption and "watermarking", but also through other forms of barrier including legal ones and marketing techniques, such as regular updates and tying arrangements like on-line assistance for legitimate clients of software. Contractual arrangements may also act as fences: you agree to give someone access to your technological know-how, specifying in the contract what measures he or she must take to keep it secret. Fences need not be foolproof, but they must be secure enough for the owner to find it profitable to use the property. Where fences are ineffective or altogether absent, the good is left in open access and is likely to be overused. This is the "fencing" aspect of property.[12]

Fencing techniques are themselves scarce goods like the objects they fence in. They are subject to property rights. Advances in fencing techniques may make new objects of property or new forms of exploitation viable.[13] Through exchange, the inventor of a new fencing technique can cash in on part of the gains the fence makes possible for property owners. Hence the incentives the property system creates for owners extend to builders and inventors of fences. Technological innovation may not only lead to new fences, however, but also undo fences that were effective under older technology, as cheap photocopying did to copyright restrictions on printed works. On the Internet, technology plays yet another trick on copyright protection. Since any use on the Internet implies some form of

---

[11] Hermitte, Marie-Angèle, Histoires juridiques extravagantes: La reproduction végétale, *in:* *L'homme, la nature et le droit,* Bernard Edelman and Marie-Angèle Hermitte (eds), Paris, Christian Bourgois éditeur, 1988, pp. 40–82, at 49, referred to in Mackaay, Ejan, "Economic incentives in markets for information and innovation", (1990) 13 *Harvard Journal of Law & Public Policy* 867–909, at 902–903.

[12] Mackaay, Ejan, The Economics of Emergent Property, *op. cit.*; Mackaay, Ejan, "L'économie des droits de propriété émergents sur l'Internet", (1997) 9 *Cahiers de propriété intellectuelle* 281–300.

[13] As barbed wire did for ranching in the American west. Ellickson, Robert C., "Property in Land", (1993) 102 *Yale Law Journal* 1315–1400. At p. 1330, Ellickson relates how the invention of barbed wire changed the economics of land use for cattle breeding by making smaller lots viable. Historical observation confirmed what economic theory predicted here.

copying, the balance between use (free) and copying (restricted) struck under legislation reflecting older technology is no longer satisfactory.

The first step in the emergence of property rights is for prospective owners to erect their own fence. If you are able to fence something in, you lay the foundation for your property right. This is a fundamental principle of civil and common law alike: possession is the root of title.[14] Conversely, without a fence you have no claim to a right. The legal system should not be on call to enforce rights owners cannot by and large make stick themselves. The contrary thesis would open the door to rent-seeking.

The "freedom to fence" has a limit. In fencing in new objects, you may not (substantially) interfere with existing rights of others. This principle explains why the legal system disallows "mere fence-cutting" inventions such as unscrambling equipment (television signals), domain name squatting and encryption circumvention technology. But this restriction on freedom to fence is bounded: you are free to use inventions that serve legitimate purposes and incidentally allow fence-cutting. The boundary should be defined by something like the test developed in the Sony-decision by the U.S. Supreme Court.[15]

If new technology results in old fences becoming more permeable, this problem falls to the owner. It is not the mission of state law enforcement to shore up outdated fences. Leaks in fences provide the spur for inventing new and better fences. Does this open the door to wasteful technology races? Not quite, since, as we saw, mere fence-cutting will be disallowed.

Ownership without the possibility of openly using the object is not good for business. So the next step is to ensure that the object can be used openly and given in use to other persons, without the owner permanently losing control over it. For most purposes contracts can do the job, provided one can fashion them as the context requires. Freedom of contract normally makes this possible. One can specify in a contract what users may and may not do with what is being given in use and under what conditions: copying, reverse engineering, developing extensions and improvements, incorporating the object in novel ones, and so on.

Contract also allows the object to be transferred. Contracts could provide for usage restrictions to run with the main object when transferred to a third person. In competitive markets, these contractual conditions may be expected to strike a reasonable balance between the parties on either side of the contract. In examining contracts they are asked to enforce, courts can insist that even in standard form agreements customers are given all essential rights necessary to pursue the main

---

[14] For instance, Epstein, Richard A., "Possession as the Root of Title", (1979) 13 *Georgia Law Review* 1221. It can be traced back to Locke (Locke, John, *Two Treatises of Government*, Cambridge, Cambridge University Press (1690), 1960), 2nd treatise, § 25, who qualifies the principle by the proviso, that in appropriating things by "admixing' them with one's labour, there is "at least [...] enough, and as good left in common for others'. (§ 27 in fine).

[15] *Sony Corp. v. Universal City Studios*, 464 U.S. 417 (1984).

purpose of the contract. In a contract for software, for instance, this would entail the right to make back-up copies, now codified as a fair use/fair dealing defence. Similarly one may presume that permission for private copying would generally be given – it does not preempt a sale – but under older technology (high transaction costs) would have been too costly to solicit. Hence that permission was granted by law as fair use/fair dealing.

As regards the cumulative nature of information, contracts, in the form of association rules, may also regulate the extent to which existing information may be used to develop further creations, designs or inventions. A most revealing context for such rules would be one in which the contracting parties would be now "borrowers" of new ideas, now "lenders". They would act under a sort of veil of ignorance, warranting the fairness of the rules so reached. Associations of persons active in the same trade might be taken as a reasonable approximation of such a situation, as they were in the case of the regional plant growers associations in France in Marie-Angèle Hermitte's study mentioned earlier.[16] Subject to field observation, it is plausible to think that such club rules would leave ideas, principles and laws of nature, as well as stock elements (scènes à faire) open for use by anyone, whilst reserving the spoils of specific inventions to the inventors. This could stand model for the way the public domain is defined in most legislation. By way of example, in microchip legislation, reverse engineering an invention for purposes of research is allowed.[17] Incorporating the fruits of such analysis into a new design is allowed and will lead to a right in this new design, provided it is original, i.e. makes a contribution beyond the older technology.[18]

The final institution we need for this process to work correctly is a technique to stop "leaks" to the outside world. These leaks are situations in which club goods are secretly sold by a club member to third persons, who can then "undersell" the club or otherwise free ride on the efforts of loyal club members. If the whole process is to be recognised as a legitimate way of discovering how the property order should be extended to new objects, the club arrangements should not be struck down as anticompetitive cartels nor leaks condoned for that reason. In practice liability rules and injunctions against the profiteurs of such leaks have been applied under legal doctrines such as unfair competition or parasitical behaviour. The courts intervene here only at the margin and as a temporary measure while the discovery process goes on and before it is codified into law.

---

[16] MA Hermitte, *op. cit.*; also Merges, Peter, "Of Property Rules, Coase, and Intellectual Property", (1994) 94 *Columbia Law Review* 2655–2673, p. 2662 ff. There is a risk of conspiracy against the public, as Adam Smith already knew. The answer lies in the right to set up a competing association.
[17] Sct. 6(2)(a). *Canadian Integrated Circuit Topography Act*, R.S.C. 1985, c. I–14.6
[18] id., sct. 6(2)(b) read with 4(2) and 4(3).

3. The Framework of Discovery

The formula "control + contract + leak control = (prototype) property" sums up succinctly how we discover the way in which the property order can be extended progressively to new objects at the initiative of primarily interested persons.[19] It is an open-ended process, applicable in principle to an infinite variety of objects at the margin of the existing order. It is decentralised, which means that it can be set in motion by anyone who sees the possibility for gain from new property rights.

In the logic whereby the property order extends itself to new objects at the initiative of prospective owners, the quality of the fence available to secure property is the owner's responsibility. The state guards against outright fraud and violence; for the remainder you are on your own. You make your calculations of whether property is worthwhile based on the revenue you can draw from it given a foreseeable rate of slippage. This logic would imply that on the Internet, where slippage is substantial, having done your sums and put up your product in the expectation that there is enough in it for you, you live with the slippage that your choice implies. For any product you sell on the Internet (software, text, music, video) you have to allow far more by way of sharing or "pirating" amongst your users than you were used to under older technology. But the cost of producing an extra copy is next to zero and you also have more ways of capturing what users do and hence of price-discriminating. While we learn this new reality, the proper policy seems to be: don't listen too much to complaints, don't try to stamp out all piracy, but sweep the market clean enough for business and let actors decide how to maximise their revenue.[20]

As a broad generalisation, such a decentralised discovery process is to be preferred over legislative fiat or forms of regulation, which are open to capture by rent-seeking interests. It offers the best incentives we know for the main actors involved to take the initiative and get the solutions right, even as legislation or judicial decisions are later called upon to codify the results and to correct at the margin what are perceived to be flaws (severe information asymmetries, exploitation of local monopolies, hold-out situations, and so on).

For this system to work, the law needs a set of background or meta-rules to circumscribe the process. These could be summarised as follows:

1. Freedom to fence in unowned objects.
2. Subject to prohibition of mere fence-cutting (attack on other persons' ownership)

---

[19] On this general logic: Libecap, Gary D., *Contracting for Property Rights*, Cambridge, Cambridge University Press, 1989 JDGD L694c 1989.
[20] Shapiro, Carl and Hal R. Varian, *Information Rules: A Strategic Guide to the Network Economy*, Cambridge, MA, Harvard Business School Press, 1998, p. 102.

3. But permission to use technology with useful applications and incidental fence-cutting properties.
4. What you control may become your property (possession as the root of title).
5. No fence, no right.
6. Leaks in older fences are the owner's responsibility (subject to protection against outright violence and fraud).
7. Freedom of contract.
8. Contract clauses must be interpreted so as not to prevent the accomplishment of the essential purpose of the contract.
9. Freedom to form associations and adopt internal rules.
10. Association rules may restrict output only as a means of preserving a jointly used or produced scarce resource.
11. Deliberately creating and exploiting "leaks" in the fence, by a club member's secretly transferring club goods to outsiders, should be curtailed by the courts. This may be accomplished through doctrines such as unfair competition or parasitical acts.

The point I wish to make is that these principles are sufficient for interested persons to set up the arrangements with their restrictions and limitations and to demonstrate their viability. They can account for most rules we find codified in copyright law and other intellectual property legislation. The justification for such rules does not stem from mere theoretical argument, but relies on being demonstrated by actors in the field or being amenable to such demonstration. This should be a proper safeguard against rent-seeking legislation. The rules for such a decentralised discovery process can be part of civil law codified law systems as much as of common law based legal systems.

The question we must now ask is whether such a test can be applied to the sharing arrangements proposed in the literature as a means to cure supposed forms of "market failure", which would develop as a result of excessive privatisation.

B. Sharing

Why should owners live with slippage if they have the technical means to curtail it? If all slippage is illegitimate within an otherwise legitimate property order, one cannot blame owners for looking for better fences: encryption, watermarking and the like, and insisting on having fence-cutting techniques outlawed, as they are in the American Digital Millennium Copyright Act. It is the very logic of property rights that the order extends that way. If slippage reflects a limiting principle of the property order, whose effect is magnified on the Internet, we may yet want to legitimise that slippage (as fair use/fair dealing for instance) and tell owners to live with it, not as a matter of good business practice, as Shapiro and Varian do, but as a matter of law.[21]

How to decide? Parisi and others make a theoretical argument for limiting private rights and, in the domain of copyright, for allowing fair use, on the basis of the anti-commons idea put forth by Heller.[22] An anti-commons is thought to arise when too many decision rights (property rights) on the same object lead to abuse of veto and hold-out situations, which in turn entail suboptimal use of the object. It is the opposite of the commons, where open access – the absence of sufficient property rights – leads to overuse of a resource. In a later paper, Depoorter and Parisi amplify this idea, stating that the anti-commons idea provides a justification for fair use in American copyright legislation independently of that provided by technical transactions costs.[23] The transactions costs defence of fair use has been most forcefully put forth by Gordon, but it would tend to evaporate as the cost of reaching copyright holders or their clearinghouse representative dwindles on the Internet.[24] Parisi and Depoorter in essence argue that the transactions costs stemming from opportunistic behaviour are not at all likely to vanish in the Internet environment. Strategic hold-out can, in their view, still be a problem. It might interfere with adequate access to information and this in turn, given the cumulative nature of much knowledge, might lead to welfare losses, justifying compulsory access to copyright information through the institution of fair use.

While the papers show an elegant symmetry with the commons and associated dangers, I am not persuaded that the theoretical argument alone is sufficient to justify fair use. Should not the empirical refutation of the public goods/externality arguments for lighthouses and bees give us pause?[25] Instead I propose to look for a justification in line with the argument developed in the first section of the paper. In

---

[21] Lessig, Lawrence, "Constitution and Code", (1997) 27 *Cumberland Law Review* 1–15, at 9–10: "The point is this: code could in principle make intellectual property unstealable—meaning unusable except in the ways the owner wants. But as it is understood just now, intellectual property is not supposed to be perfectly unstealable; it's not supposed to be perfectly protected. For the right that intellectual property grants is a compromised right: the holders of the right to intellectual property do so subject to a public use exception, called fair use."

[22] Parisi, Francesco, B. Norbert Schulz et B. Ben Depoorter, *Duality in Property: Commons and Anticommons*, rapport, George Mason University, unpublished paper, 2000; Heller, Michael A., "The Tragedy of the Anticommons: Property in the Transition from Marx to Markets", (1998) 111 *Harvard Law Review* 621–688; Heller, Michael A. et Rebecca S. Eisenberg, "Can Patents Deter Innovation? The Anticommons in Biomedical Research", (1998) 280 *Science* 698.

[23] Depoorter, Ben and Francesco Parisi, The Price Theory of Copyright Protection (The Doctrine of Fair Use and the Tragedy of the Anticommons), unpublished paper presented at the EALE Conference in Ghent 14–16 September 2000.

[24] Gordon, Wendy J., "Fair Use as Market Failure: A Structural and Economic Analysis of the *Betamax* Case and Its Predecessors", (1982) 82 *Columbia Law Review* 1600–1657.

[25] Cheung, Steven N.S., "The Fable of the Bees: An Economic Investigation", (1973) 16 *Journal of Law and Economics* 11–33; Coase, Ronald H., "The Lighthouse in Economics", (1974) 17 *Journal of Law and Economics* 357–376; and for a furthe debunking story: Liebowitz, Stan J. et Stephen E. Margolis, "The Fable of the Keys", (1990) 33 *Journal of Law and Economics* 1–25.

the discovery logic set out there, the initiative for extending the order falls to interested persons. They would have to demonstrate the viability of the arrangement they favour before it would be put into law. This principle is a precaution against rent-seeking through which some groups' preferences are legislated into law at the expense of other groups or the public at large. Can we find examples of interested persons demonstrating the viability of sharing arrangements?

1. RECORDED EXPERIENCES WITH TANGIBLE COMMON PROPERTY

In the tangible world, sharing arrangements may stem from difficulties in fencing. In the case of fishing communities for instance, as Ostrom has demonstrated,[26] it is difficult to reserve free-swimming fish to individual members, but one can reserve it to the community as a whole as against the outside and evolve within the community the rules regulating how much each member is allowed to catch, while maintaining the fish stock. The general thesis here is that where fencing is insufficient for establishing individual property rights, resources will not be left in open access. Limited common property regimes avoid the dangers of overuse and underproduction. These sharing arrangements are set up not primarily for the pleasure of sharing, but for want of better property rights because of fencing problems, while one must yet manage scarcity. They fulfil a useful function and must not be dismissed as merely anti-competitive cartels, as appears to have been the view of the Canadian government with respect to the fishery community arrangements on the Eastern seaboard.[27]

2. OPEN ACCESS GOODS IN THE NEW ECONOMY

The Java programming language

Let us look for similar arrangements in the new economy. A first example is the Java language. Sun has developed it as a platform independent tool. Program anything in Java and it can be run on any computer that accepts the language.

---

[26] Ostrom, Elinor, *Governing the Commons – The evolution of institutions for collective action*, Cambridge, Cambridge University Press, 1990; Yandle, Bruce, "Antitrust and the Commons – Cooperation or Collusion", (1998) 3 *Independent Review* 37–52. Carol Rose gives a scala of forms of common property with increasingly severe restrictions on what members can use the property for: Rose, Carol M., Evolution of Property Rights, dans : *The New Palgrave Dictionary of Economics and the Law, Vol. 2*, Peter Newman (dir.), London, MacMillan, 1998, pp. 93–98, at 96.

[27] Ostrom, *op.cit.*, p. 177; Yandle, *op. cit.*, p. 45.

There are economies of scale to be had from such initiatives, as there are from any norm or standard. Once the particular product has become an accepted standard, one might fear monopolistic practices, but the very possibility of entry of a competing standard would seem to limit the danger, and experience seems to confirm this.

A common standard runs counter, however, to implicit fences which Microsoft creates around its operating system. So Microsoft implemented in its operating systems a version of Java which created incompatibilities with the general version. This in fact counteracts the effect of the common norm. In litigation, Sun invoked its copyright in order to prevent the implementation of incompatible versions of Java. Copyright is used here in order to preserve an open-access good. Presumably, Sun would control any changes or improvements proposed for Java by third persons in order to maintain common access. An exclusive right (copyright) is used here deliberately to keep a good non-exclusive.

The GNU/LINUX operating system

A second case within the new economy to consider is the GNU/LINUX operating system. Here too software is deliberately kept non-exclusive by means of copyright. Marketing the GNU/LINUX operating system by third persons is allowed, provided the price be set to recover only the cost of marketing, whilst the software itself is free and left in open access. The arrangement here appears to be a direct reaction to Windows' virtual monopoly position. The promoters of this solution, for instance Richard Stallman's Free Software Foundation,[28] maintain that a network of independent programmers working together are more creative than a behemoth like Microsoft. Bugs found in the software will be more quickly corrected, new possibilities more quickly exploited.

This argument flies directly in the face of received wisdom in matters of property rights. Open access is generally resisted on the grounds that it will lead to overuse and underproduction along the lines of Hardin's tragedy of the commons. Overfishing as well as air and water pollution are given as evidence.[29] Common property is thought undesirable because of the cost of reaching decisions (hold-out problem). Civil codes have numerous examples showing caution with respect to common property. Generally institutions such as partnerships must be set up by explicit agreement; there are rules for overcoming lack of consensus by majority vote or other techniques; partnerships may be dissolved, if all else fails, by the court.

Private property is commonly expected to create stronger incentives for good management and for innovation and to outperform common property and open

---

[28] See Benkler papers quoted above.
[29] Hardin, Garrett, "The Tragedy of the Commons – The population problem has no technical solution; it requires a fundamental extension in morality", (1968) 162 *Science* 1243–1248.

access property. The GNU/Linux experience is illuminating in that it is currently gaining market share quickly, apparently contradicting this alleged all-round superiority of private property. The proponents of the GNU/Linux experience point to overriding benefit of sharing the discovery burden amongst a worldwide community of hackers. The open source code movement capitalises on this advantage. But, one may object, how do the proponents of GNU/Linux earn their keep? They do it in particular through offering paid services for implementing the system or particular programs compatible with it, or for programming altogether new applications. The arrangement is reminiscent of the practice of the Grateful Dead, as related by John Perry Barlow: let "dead" information be freely copied, but charge for "live" information.[30]

6. SHARING OF SCIENTIFIC KNOWLEDGE

Just why this sharing should be decisive is intriguing. Perhaps the experience of scientists sharing scientific discoveries through working papers and other informal techniques is illuminating.[31] Scientists working in the same field are in a relationship somewhat like a veil of ignorance. They do not know who will make the big discoveries, but know that they will do better with easy access to one another's results. Scientific research has historically been a community affair, in that scientists networked by working physically together (monasteries, institutes, laboratories) and through letter writing and conferences. Over the past century, especially since the Second World War, scientific publication has been transferred to commercial book publishers, operating on the basis of exclusive rights and requiring payment for the right to read. Recently, patenting scientific inventions, in biotechnology for example, has become accepted practice, indeed mandatory for research financing. So in the world of scientific research the two models are now available for use.

Have scientists turned their back to the share economy in favour of a trade economy? The answer is clearly no. Sharing is still standard practice, even though scientists rely on exclusive rights, contracts and other aspects of the trade economy when dealing with commercial outsiders.[32] Of course, incentives for scientists come in the form of reward for reputation (invitations to prestigious posts, prizes,

---

[30] Barlow, op. cit.
[31] Merges, Robert P., "Property Rights Theory and the Commons: The Case of Scientific Research", (1996) 13 *Social Philosophy & Policy* 145–167; Mackaay, Ejan, Scientific publishing without publishers, in: *Universiteit en auteursrecht – Wetenschappelijke informatievoorziening in een digitale omgeving* (*University and copyright – The circulation of scientific information in a digital environment*), P.B. Hugenholtz, J.J.C. Kabel and G.A.I. Schuijt (eds), Amsterdam, Otto Cramwinckel, 1999, pp. 21–40; Mackaay, Ejan, "L'édition électronique par et pour la communauté scientifique", (1999) 12 *Cahiers de propriété intellectuelle* 159–184.
[32] Merges 1996, *op. cit.*

research grants etc.). Where reputations are established through recognition by one's colleagues, sharing one's papers is a form of early advertising on which one hopes to cash in later. Within the sharing economy, acknowledging one's colleagues' contributions (i.e. respecting their reputation) is very much *de rigueur*. Community norms are designed, here as elsewhere, to allow use of the common resource by all members, while preserving what is scarce, here the reputation of the members. The trade economy, leading to costly borrowing, is a costlier set-up for scientific exchange. Of course, those who have established reputations may well decide they do best through the trade economy and require payment for all of their publications and public appearances.

Conclusion

The calls for a sharing economy and against a trade economy based on intellectual property rights invite us to re-examine the basis for different forms of property rights. One approach is to study the efficiency characteristics of various rules. This leaves in the dark the process through which we discover such rules and then recognise them in law. The approach taken in this paper is that understanding the discovery process is essential and indeed that the nature of that process provides a legitimation for the rights so discovered.

The process relies on interested persons securing control over an object and contracting with others about its use or to transfer it. Control presupposes reasonably effective fences. Basic principles involved are: Build your own fence; no fence, no right; technology solely to cut fences is not allowed. State enforcement is available to prevent outright fraud and violence, not to maintain ineffective fences.

The arrangements worked out in this process of control + contract + stopping leaks can serve to model how the new property right is to be codified in law. The reason for relying on such a process is that it guards us against recognising rights as a result of mere rent seeking. It provides for a decentralised and open-ended way of discovering how the "property rights order" should be extended.

If the discovery process works as suggested here, why codify rights in law at all? For the prospective rights holder, there is a gain in enforcement costs. Legally recognised rights can be enforced, drawing on state judicial and police services. Part of the burden of making one's rights "stick" is shifted to the population at large. This makes such rights more readily knowable and more secure than mere claims based on physical control and contract.

What can be the justification for such a shift, short of abuse of power, arbitrariness or rent-seeking? It must be that the rights to be codified promise viable, long term gains to the population at large beyond the enforcement costs. The promise of gains for all corresponds to the idea of a Pareto gain, which is the intuition behind the economist's notion of "efficiency". The legitimacy of rights stems from this feature. How to ensure such legitimacy? Public choice should make one wary of mere legislative fiat as a measure of it, given the risk of capture by interest groups. The discovery procedure highlighted in the previous pages not merely reveals the form in which rights should be codified, but at the same time serves to establish their legitimacy. Only legitimate rights should be codified and benefit from public justice and enforcement services. To recognise a sharing or (limited) open access order, a similar safeguard would be apposite. It will not do to recognise an open access order simply because some people have come up with a new "fence cutting" technology. We would like to see the viability of open access orders demonstrated. For some features of existing intellectual property rights, such a test seems plausible enough. Open access to ideas, principles and other elements of the public domain could plausibly result from standard contracts amongst interested persons, preferring easy sharing. Some forms of fair use can be similarly justified by high transaction costs or as necessary implications of contracts. The current trend in the U.S. to grant patents on business methods and software should make us wary of the limits of this argument.

To push the investigation further, we examined several instances of broad-based open-access arrangements for forms of information, such as Java, Linux and sharing amongst scientists. In each case, the sharing arrangement is maintained in the face of options to privatise (i.e. establish individual property rights). In the examples open access arrangements were set up either to establish uniform standards, entailing economies of scale, or amongst people who are now borrowers, now lenders of ideas and for whom easy sharing facilitates creation. Sharing is then an element of establishing one's reputation, a phenomenon akin to advertising. These sharing arrangements are viable side by side with private property arrangements (trade economies). It may be helpful to facilitate their establishment (create standard contracts, provide standard sharing clauses under copyright and other intellectual property rules) and to look at the function of sharing arrangements before condemning them as cartels.

The viability of some sharing arrangements does not, however, justify in my eyes the conclusion that we can do without the incentives of private property rights or discovery logic that comes with exclusive control (fences). Trade economies and share economies have different characteristics as to quality, creativity and cost and may serve different publics for different functions. I see little ground to curtail private rights on the mere argument for an information-rich environment, and a substantial danger that such a call will serve as a cover for rent-seeking and will be detrimental for innovation. It is important to let experience driven by interested persons in the field tell us which type of rights or arrangements we prefer for what purpose.

III. COPYRIGHT AND COMMODIFICATION: DOCTRINE AND DOCTRINAL DEVELOPMENTS

Excuse and Justification in the Law of Fair Use: Commodification and Market Perspectives

*Wendy J. Gordon**

Introduction

In American copyright law, the doctrine of "fair use" has long been problematic. Every plausible litmus test that might simplify the "fair use" inquiry has proven inadequate,[1] and copyright commentators have long sought an algorithm or

---

* Copyright 2002 by Wendy J. Gordon. For helpful comments I am grateful to workshop participants at the American Law & Economics Association, the Society for Economic Research on Copyright Issues, the University of Arizona, the Australian National University Faculty of Law, the Boston University Faculty Workshop and the B.U. Intellectual Property Discussion Group, the University of California (Berkeley) the Cardozo School of Law Conference on Copyright Law as Communications Policy, the Cardozo-DePaul First Annual Intellectual Property Scholars Conference (at DePaul), the Copyright Society of Australia (Sydney), the University of Montreal, St. Catherine's College in the University of Oxford (U.K.), the University of Sydney and, of course, the Conference on the Commodification of Information at the University of Haifa (Israel). In particular I thank Ed Baker, Linda Bui, Tyler Cowen, Tamar Frankel, Mike Harper, Gary Lawson, Mark Lemley, David Lyons, Mike Meurer, Neil Netanel, David Nimmer, Richard Posner, Margaret Jane Radin, Megan Richardson, Anne Seidman, Bob Seidman, Seana Shiffrin, Ken Simons, Avishalom Tor, David Vaver and the members of my seminar in intellectual property theory. Able students Michael Burling, Peter Cancelmo and Alisa Hacker provided research assistance.

[1] A court will deem a defendant's copying or other use of the plaintiff's work "fair" when, by and large, the use is non-commercial, involves a quantitatively small amount of copying, serves the public interest, and causes little or no harm to the owner of the copyright. See 17 U.S.C. section 107. Yet there are cases that give the lie to each of these factors standing alone: Cases where "fair use" was found potentially available for a use that is commercial, *Campbell v. Acuff-Rose Music*, 510 U.S. 569, 585 (1994); for a use that copies 100 percent of the copyrighted work, *Williams & Wilkins Co. v. U.S.*, 203 Ct. Cl. 74, 89–90 (1973), *aff'd by an equally divided court*, 420 U.S. 376 (1975) (per curiam); for a use of trivial aesthetic or public importance, *Sony Corp. of America v. Universal City Studios, Inc.*, 464 U.S. 417, 440 (1983) (copying of, *inter alia*, television entertainment programs); and for a use that harmfully diminishes the demand for the copyrighted work, *cf.* Fisher v. Dees, 794 F.2d 432, 437–38 (9th Cir. 1986) (for fair use purposes, only substitutional harm is relevant; other kinds of harm do not weigh against fair

N. Elkin-Koren and N.W. Netanel (eds.), *The Commodification of Information*, 149–192.
© 2002 *Wendy J. Gordon. Printed in Great Britain.*

heuristic to lend predictability and conceptual coherence to the doctrine. In an article whose recommendations are now sometimes misapplied, I suggested that the key to understanding the protean forms of "fair use" could best be found in the notion of market failure.[2] In the instant essay I extend and refine my market failure analysis in a way that should clarify its implications.

First, I here suggest that fair use cases can be usefully separated into two categories of market failure, which I dub "market malfunction" and "inherent limitation". Briefly, "market malfunction" identifies instances where there is a failure of perfect market conditions, but where economic norms appropriately govern. This is the category most law and economics scholars mean by "market failure". However, there is an additional set of circumstances where we cannot rely on markets to function as socially satisfactory institutions for the distribution of resources. These are the many instances where market norms themselves fail to provide fully suitable criteria for resolving a dispute. This kind of market failure I call "inherent market limitation". As will appear below, policies regarding commodification can help us distinguish when a court should treat a given interaction as appropriately governed by market norms, and when instead the court should treat such norms as fully or partly inadequate.

Second, I suggest that the distinction between these kinds of market failure can be illuminated by drawing on the distinction between "excuse" and "justification". That distinction, so far best developed in the context of criminal law, is capable of more general application.

"Excuse" connotes "if only" – *if only* some discrete fact were different, we could apply the law as written. In instances of "market malfunction" we are in the

---

cont.
use). Similarly, when the Supreme Court put great stress on the unpublished nature of a plaintiff's work, Harper & Row, 471 U.S. 539 (1985), Congress fairly quickly passed an amendment to the fair use statute to clarify that the unpublished status of a work should not be determinative. *See* the last sentence of 17 U.S.C. section 107.

[2] Wendy J. Gordon, *Fair Use as Market Failure: A Structural and Economic Analysis of the Betamax Case and its Predecessors*, 82 Colum. L. Rev. 1600 (1982) (hereinafter "Fair Use as Market Failure".)

The typical misunderstanding has been to interpret me as arguing that "the impossibility of arriving at bargains [is] the essential justification for the doctrine of fair use." David Lindsay, *The Future of the Fair Dealing Defense to Copyright Infringement* at 62 (Research Paper No 12, University of Melbourne Centre for Media, Communications and Information Technology Law, November, 2000); *accord,* Robert P. Merges, *The End of Friction? Property Rights And Contract In The "Newtonian" World Of On-Line Commerce*, 12 Berkeley Tech. L.J. 115 at 130–31 (1997). To the contrary, of course, the impossibility of arriving at bargains is only one of the types of market failure I explored in *Fair Use as Market Failure*. Other types of market failure can arise, inter alia, in the presence of nonmonetizable interests, anti-dissemination motives, and positive externalities generated by users. See *id.* at 1630–35.

Nevertheless, Lydia Pallas Loren suggests that many courts as well as some scholars have taken the erroneously narrow view of the market failure defense. Lydia Pallas Loren, *Redefining the Market Failure Approach To Fair Use in an Era of Copyright Permission Systems*, 5 J. Intel. Prop. L. 1, 26–27 (1997). I applaud most of the discussion in the Loren article as helping to avert further misunderstanding, and hope that the instant essay will help clarify further.

world of "if only": we would *prefer* the market to govern if only the market could function well, but when it fails to do so (because of, e.g., transaction costs), a court may *excuse* a participant from adhering to the usual market rules. Therefore, the "market malfunction" category corresponds, in a loose but useful way, to the legal concept of "excuse". It is based on the nonappearance of conditions that the governing model views as normal,[3] and is thus a conditional defense.

By contrast, a defense of "inherent limitation" would not be conditional in this way. If market norms are inherently inadequate in the particular context, then even were the market to function perfectly, a court might approve a departure from market procedures as *justified* under these other norms. Thus I suggest that this second category of market failure is analogous to the established concept of "justification". When we come up against the market's inherent limitations, we don't yearn toward what the market could do "if only" some fact were changed. We turn to other norms.

(Note the distinction parallels criminal law only in part. Criminal law parses "excuse" as pertaining largely to state of mind, and "justification" largely to a defendant's act. The way I use the terms, the core of the distinction is seen more generally: "Excuse" is a matter of factual divergence from the standard; "justification" is a matter of norms; and acts can be justified *or* excused.)

Third, I point out that in all tort cases – and copyright infringement is no exception – excuse and justification can apply at any of three levels: to the defendant's *behavior*, to the defendant's failure to obtain the plaintiff's *permission*, and/or to the defendant's failure to *compensate*. (This, too, is different from criminal law.) I show how the single "fair use" inquiry in fact contains all three inquiries.

Fourth, I suggest that courts should and do treat cases where a lack of permission and compensation are excused (market malfunction) differently from cases where absence of permission and compensation are justified (market limitation). The difference in treatment is summarized at the end of this Introduction.

Finally, I argue that significant societal dangers lurk in responding to defendants' claims of fair use with judicially created compulsory licenses. This latter option – denying the plaintiff an injunction but making the defendant pay – may look like a wonderful compromise that satisfies both free speech and incentive concerns, but data from psychology and behavioral law and economics suggests that it has costs of its own.

* * *

---

[3] Admittedly, the market is never fully "perfect". What counts as market malfunction is a matter of degree. This too bears a good analogy to the criminal law treatment of "excuse". The overall criminal law model assumes persons are rational actors who respond to incentives such as fear of imprisonment, even though all people are sometimes irrational and sometimes immune from incentives. It is only when the divergence from the normal grows great enough that someone is declared "insane", that he may be excused for criminal acts he performs.

My earlier work, linking fair use generally to notions of market failure, is consistent with making the proffered distinction between excused and justified fair uses.[4] Where I diverge from my earlier writing, however, is in my current belief that not all cases of market failure should be treated alike. Most notably, in my earlier work I had argued that even in the presence of market failure, fair use should generally be denied if recognizing the defense would cause substantial injury to the copyright owner.[5] I now recognize that condition as overly restrictive.[6] Substantial injury to the plaintiff is a factor that should be treated differently by "excuse" cases and by "justification" cases.

I will here argue as follows:

1. A case of "justification" can occur when we would not object if others emulated a defendant's having no permission and/or her having paid no compensation.[7] For free speech purposes, for example, it appears actively undesirable to require an iconoclast to obtain the permission of the entity she is ridiculing. We would want iconoclasts like her to speak[8] without obtaining permission from their targets.[9] If so, the iconoclast's failure to ask permission is justified.[10]

---

[4] As mentioned, in *Fair Use as Market Failure, supra* note 2, I presented "nonmonetizable interests" as a form of market failure. *Id.* at 1630. As discussed below, the presence of nonmonetizable interests can constitute a "justification" for fair use. In *Fair Use as Market Failure* I argued that transaction costs high enough to impede bargaining constituted another form of market failure. *Id.* at 1628. As discussed below, the presence of high transaction costs between owner and user can constitute an "excuse" for a court providing fair use treatment. Thus the use of the "excuse" and "justification" categories refines but does not contradict my earlier definition of the market failures that can trigger fair use treatment.

[5] *Fair Use as Market Failure, supra* note 2 at 1618–27 and *passim*.

[6] One of the important influences stimulating me to rethink this issue was Neil W. Netanel, *Copyright and a Democratic Civil Society*, 106 Yale L.J. 283 (1996) at 330–331. I thank Neil Netanel for the excellent and helpful criticism.

[7] Heidi M. Hurd, *Propter Honoris Respectum: Justification and Excuse, Wrongdoing and Culpability*, 74 Notre Dame L. Rev. 1551, 1555 (1999) ("A ... well-known test of when actions are justified holds that an action is justified if and only if we are willing to recommend that others emulate it in similar circumstances. In contrast, an action is eligible only for an excuse when we wish that the actor had acted differently and hope that others do not emulate the actor's unfortunate conduct in the future")

[8] I am following the convention that uses "speech" to embrace all acts of communication. Nevertheless, for those who identify "speech" with "talking", please note that quoting from copyrighted works in one's private talk does not require permission under copyright law, no matter how extensive the quotation may be. That is because "private performance" is outside a copyright owner's control. By contrast, giving a public talk is a "public performance" which is governed by section 106 of the Copyright Act. 17 U.S.C. section 106(4).

[9] Should the law require the iconoclast to obtain the permission of the person whose oeuvre she is attacking, such a requirement would likely block the critique altogether, or blunt its point and effectiveness. The target's dislike of being attacked is not a technical problem that can be easily *cured* by tweaking institutions or technology.

[10] Issues can arise on the borderline between excuse and justification, as will appear below. For one example, consider policies of redistribution. One scholar arguing that redistribution should be a relevant fair use policy is Robert Merges, *supra* note 2 at 133–36. Conceivably this could give rise to an "excuse", in the sense that correcting the maldistribution might eliminate the fair

2. For fair use, a potential "excuse" arises when something occurs that we do *not* want to have emulated – a behavior, lack of permission, or lack of compensation – but which we allow without imposing liability because of the particular facts of that case. A paradigmatic example is presented when high transaction costs between owner and possible licensee are so large that they swamp any possibility of bargaining.[11] The social good that could be furthered by the blocked transaction, coupled with the incapacity of the participants to use the market, can "excuse" the defendant from going forward without asking permission.[12] But if transaction costs were lower, we would want the defendant's use to occur only if voluntarily licensed by the copyright owner.
3. In cases of "excuse", fair use should and does disappear if, because of institutional or technological change, the excusing circumstances disappear. By contrast, in cases of "justification" a change in circumstances would not change the availability of the fair use defense.[13]
4. In cases of "excuse", it is defensible to deny fair use treatment if it would do significant harm to the plaintiff's interests and to the incentives of similarly situated copyright owners. In cases of "justification", however, harm to the owner should be given much more limited importance.[14]

The instant essay will explain the relevant concepts, explore the logical connections between them, and provide some examples. In addition, it will use concepts of both excuse and justification to explore a problem area that straddles the distinction: attempts by copyright owners to use intellectual property law as a tool of private censorship.

I begin by offering a partial conceptual map of excuse and justification.

---

cont.
  use. Alternatively, this could be conceptualized as a case of justification, where the market's monetary measure will be unable to accomplish social ends.
[11] The importance of transaction costs depends on their size *relative to* the benefits to be reaped from a transaction. A potential license will likely be blocked whenever the copyright owner and putative copier face transaction costs that are higher than any net gains that could result from a consummated transaction. See *Fair Use as Market Failure, supra* note 2 at 1627–30.
[12] This is how I interpret the court's decision in Williams & Wilkins Co. v. U.S., 203 Ct. Cl. 74 (1973), *aff'd by an equally divided court*, 420 U.S. 376 (1975) (per curiam). See *Fair Use as Market Failure, supra* note 2.
[13] The only thing that would change the availability of the defense in cases of justification is a change in *norms*.
[14] Please note that point (3), regarding change in circumstance, is true of all "excuses" by definition. An excuse is a defense based on special circumstances, which is applicable only when the circumstances are present. The next factor discussed – point (4), substantial injury to the copyright owner – is not definitional in the same way, and applies to many but not all cases of excuse.
  Presenting a full development would be beyond the scope of this summary. The article's purpose is to show the connections between fair use, "justification", and commodification.

Excuse and justification

In common lawyer's parlance, an act or omission is said to be "justified" if we would not object to its being emulated.[15] An act or omission is said to be "excused" if we would not want it to be emulated, but we have reasons *other than* the merits of the act or omission itself to relieve the defendant of liability. Thus, one might say that "justifying" an act or omission goes to the merits of the defendant's choice, while giving the defendant an "excuse" does not go to the merits.[16] Usually, an "excuse" arises because of some kind of institutional lack of fit between the circumstances and what the applicable law seeks to accomplish.

To illustrate, consider self-defense in the ordinary common law of crime. If someone in using reasonable force to repel a violent attack unavoidably breaks her attacker's arm, the attacker will not be able to sue the arm-breaker successfully for battery, nor will the arm-breaker be criminally liable. Her acts will not give rise to liability because it is desirable for innocent parties to defend themselves. The use of reasonable force is proper, and what the arm-breaker has done is *justified*. Even if it is not the best thing that she could have done (we may have preferred her to run away), the action is morally acceptable. We would not object to its being emulated by persons similarly situated.

By contrast, consider an arm-breaker who was delusional in thinking she was being attacked. In a criminal trial, she might escape conviction for battery, but not because her actions were justified. Rather, the delusional arm-breaker might be found "not guilty by reason of insanity". Such a verdict reflects an *excuse*. We do not want her action emulated. Rather, the criminal law merely chooses not to impose a criminal sanction because of particular circumstances that cause a lack of fit between the defendant's state of mind, on the one hand, and, on the other, the purposes and functioning of criminal law and its sanctions. A different result

---

[15] See Hurd, *supra* note 7. Or, as stated in the classic treatment by H.L.A. Hart: "In the case of 'justification' what is done is regarded as something which the law does not condemn, or even welcomes." H.L.A. Hart, *Prolegomenon to the Principles of Punishment*, in PUNISHMENT AND RESPONSIBILITY: ESSAYS IN THE PHILOSOPHY OF LAW 13 (Oxford 1968) (footnote omitted).

[16] For this useful simplification, I am indebted to Tamar Frankel. It allows me to sidestep the fascinating question of whether there is some definable essence, other than "not on the merits," that motivates excuses in civil tort law. As will appear below, I argue that most "excuses" in the tort of copyright are linked to deviations from what would be needed for the neoclassical Invisible Hand to operate. But as this intuition has a great deal of openness, a sidestep is useful.

In criminal law, it is often argued that "justification" goes to the defendant's *act*, while "excuse" goes to the defendant's culpability as a person. *See* Hart, *supra* note 15 at 13–14 ("psychological state of the agent"); *cf.* George Fletcher, RETHINKING CRIMINAL LAW at 577–78, 734 and chapter 10 (Little, Brown & Co. 1978) (excuse as lack of "accountability" or attribution). In my schema, the acts of refusing to pay, or of refusing to seek compensation, can be excused as well as justified.

might well be reached by a judge applying the civil law of torts,[17] with its different purposes and function.

If one evaluates the purposes and function of copyright, what do we find? Copyright sets up a market system in which, it is hoped, copyright owners, publishers, new creators and consumers will enter into transactions which will both disseminate the creative works and provide incentives for their creation.[18] Ownership is given to the class of persons – creators – from whose hands a market will most easily evolve and which will result in a desirable degree of internalization.[19] It is hoped that the result will maximize social welfare as well as the welfare of the participants. (Of the many ways to measure welfare, most legal scholars follow Judge Posner's classic approach, and seek to "maximize value

---

[17] Many states whose criminal law might excuse the delusional defendant would nevertheless impose civil (tort) liability on her.

[18] This standard language of "incentive and dissemination" is sometimes misinterpreted. Copyright is granted as a monopoly to subsidize creativity and *not* as a monopoly to subsidize physical production or physical dissemination. This was true historically as well. The publishers who benefited under the first copyright statute, the Statute of Anne, were those who had *paid* authors for an exclusive right to copy. Statute of Anne, 1710, 8 Anne, ch. 19. Thus, although publisher pressure may have helped that first copyright act come into being, the publishers were not subsidized *as* publishers, but rather as persons who had supported the authorial enterprise.

Had the publishers not paid for copyrights, their mere physical costs of printing and distribution would not have supported a claim for governmental aid. Normal competition applies to those physical processes. Copyright does not aim to make the physical act of dissemination more profitable than other physical processes. Copyright merely aims to encourage the creation of works – and the fixed costs of creation having been met, authors can then license the newly made works, providing access to the public.

[19] Even if it is decided that the law should adopt a rule of deference to property owners, it still remains necessary to specify who is the owner. Who will *receive* an ab initio right to use the resource, as compared with the non-owning people who must *purchase* a privilege to use the resource? From a moral perspective, we might want authors and inventors to have initial ownership in their intangibles if they *deserve* ownership. Debate would then center on the proper nature and bases of desert. It would be in part empirical (who does what?), but mostly normative (what significance should be given to what is done?). From a neoclassical economic perspective, however, ownership is placed not where it is morally deserved, but instead where benefits and costs can best be internalized. Debate then would center on how the dynamics of human behavior would be affected by different starting points. For example, if authors and inventors are given initial ownership rights, what is likely to follow? Or if the public is given rights to copy, what is likely to follow?

For economic purposes, ownership should be allocated according to whatever starting point is most likely to internalize benefits in a way that will give adequate incentives to produce socially-valuable products without causing excessive deadweight loss and administrative burdens. This involves essentially empirical inquiry, but some armchair inferences can be drawn from general patterns of human behavior. Thus, I have argued elsewhere that intellectual property markets and consequent internalization evolve most easily when, inter alia, copiers have an incentive to identify themselves. If so, giving ownership to the author or inventor indeed makes more economic sense than privileging all copiers. Conversely, I have argued that in most instances giving the public an entitlement to copy would be a cumbersome starting point, causing immense problems of coordination from which to reach a socially desirable level of production. If so, a starting point that presumptively gives ownership to authors and inventors, rather than to the public, appears preferable. Wendy J. Gordon, *Of Harm and Benefits: Torts, Restitution, and Intellectual Property*, 21 J. Legal Studies 449 (1992).

as measured by willingness to pay."[20]) Market transactions are thought a desirable way to pursue such maximization because, inter alia, decentralized market actors such as buyers and sellers have incentives to reveal some of their preferences, and need less data than a centralized entity would need in order to operate effectively. Second-guessing individual owners has high dangers of inaccuracy, as well as being administratively expensive.[21] Thus, enforcing a market system is one of the best ways of being sure that efficiency will be achieved, assuming of course that transaction costs are low and other conditions of perfect competition are adequately met. Thus, in cases where economic value is at stake, we ordinarily *want* a potential user to seek permission from the copyright owner and pay a price they negotiate. A copyist who fails to obtain consent and to pay is considered an infringer.

Sometimes, however, the goals of the law cannot be achieved through the market. If so, market logic suggests this is a good occasion for a defense: a doctrine or rule that permits the defendant to act without obtaining permission or paying compensation.[22] The market perspective can be used not only to identify the occasion when a defense may be needed to achieve social goals, but can also help classify the possible defenses into excuses and justifications, as follows:

---

[20] The instant article takes as its target model the classic Posnerian approach of "maximizing wealth as measured by willingness to pay". For an approach less used by lawyers but more similar to that used by academic economists, see Louis Kaplow & Steven Shavell, *Fairness Versus Welfare*, 114 Harv. L. Rev. 961 (2001). As Kaplow and Shavell point out, Judge Posner has himself amended his stance. *Id.* at note 68.

[21] This section is obviously indebted to the analysis in Guido Calabresi and A. Douglas Melamed, *Property Rules, Liability Rules, and Inalienability: One View of the Cathedral*, 85 Harv. L. Rev. 1089 (1972).

[22] A system of private law that puts the maximization of economic value above the maintenance of market "forms" will find either an excuse or a justification – or a prima facie limitation on owners' rights – in all those situations where markets cannot be relied on to function as socially satisfactory institutions for the distribution of resources. This statement is a virtual tautology. After all, a system that aims at value maximization by using markets will have to find some means to transfer resources *other than* through owners' voluntary consent when that economic goal is unreachable through markets.

Despite the tautology, the "market failure" language is useful: the economic paradigm provides a checklist and a structure for inquiry. It helps us identify many of the occasions on which the usual market-based system, where the owner's will is law, will not reliably maximize social value.

Note, incidentally, that the instant argument must alter if markets are desired *for their own sake* because, e.g., they contribute to an owner's autonomy. The instant analysis will assume that markets are desired because of their ability to contribute to value-maximization. For an exploration of alternative norms, see Ralph S. Brown, *Eligibility for Copyright Protection: A Search for Principled Standards*, 70 Minn. L. Rev. 579 (1985). Also see, e.g., Netanel, *supra* note 6 (copyright should serve the norm of encouraging democratic civil society).

Excuse

Sometimes the law's goal is economic, but a market malfunction is present in the sense that the current conditions diverge strongly from those needed for perfect competition. For example, high transaction costs may make it impractical for plaintiff and defendant to deal with each other. In such a case, allowing the defendant to proceed with his copying may produce a higher level of value than enforcing the copyright by enjoining the use. In such a case a court might allow a defendant fair use.[23]

However, allowing free use in such cases is distinctly a second-best solution. Recall that a criminal court might excuse an insane defendant, but *want* him to have acted differently. Similarly, a copyright court in the presence of high transaction costs might *excuse* the defendant, but if the transaction-cost problem were eliminated, would *want* the defendant to proceed through the market. This notion of "we would prefer otherwise' is near the essence of excuse.

Justification

Sometimes, by contrast, going outside the market is a first-best solution. In particular, where non-economic values are at stake, we might feel very uneasy trusting that market transactions could achieve the desired goals. In such a case, a judge might well decide that a defendant could be *justified* in proceeding without consent or compensation: that even if market conditions were perfect, it would be normatively appropriate to proceed outside the market's ordinary process of consent and payment.

For example, we might *want* a biographer to be able to quote from his subject's letters without obtaining the subject's consent. Similarly, we might *want* someone who is exposing the foibles of another's work to be able to quote from it without paying that other author compensation for the decrease in consumer demand that might follow. There can even be cases of copyright self-defense, where someone photocopies an attack that another wrote in order to refute it.[24] Under many views of fairness, we would not *want* the photocopier to pay his attacker or be subject to the attacker's veto power.

In such a case, because the inherent limitations of the market prevent it from implementing desired values, justification may appear. In these cases, the lack of permission or compensation may indeed be something we would want emulated.

---

[23] *See Fair Use as Market Failure, supra* note 2.
[24] *Cf.* Hustler Magazine Inc. v. Moral Majority Inc., 796 F.2d 1148 (9th Cir. 1986), discussed *infra* at notes 69–73 and accompanying text.

Three tiers of inquiry

I argue that potentially tortious acts contain at least three components that must be assessed in terms of both excuse and justification. These components are (1) the defendant's ultimate *behavior* in the world, that is, the defendant's use of the affected party's resource, (2) the defendant not having asked the affected party for her *consent,* and (3) the defendant not paying *compensation* to the affected party. Excuse and justification can go to any one level of inquiry, or all three. In order to make best use of the distinction between excuse and justification, we need to examine *what* is being excused or justified.

Although it is not generally stated in precisely this fashion,[25] all torts embody these three different levels of possible limitation. The tort of copyright infringement is no different. Consider the following examples, drawn both from common law and copyright, which illustrate the three tiers of inquiry. Note that the answers to any of the three-tier inquiries can be expressed either in terms of defenses, or in terms of limitations on the plaintiff's initial right of action.

Behavior

Is the defendant's *behavior* desirable and/or excused? Learned Hand's negligence calculus reflects this kind of inquiry. If it is economically more efficient to neglect a precaution than to take it, negligence law imposes no liability on the defendant who fails to take the precaution. The privilege of self-defense also reflects this inquiry: it is desirable for persons to preserve themselves from attack. In copyright law, the desirability of the defendant's behavior – the use she makes of the plaintiff's copyrighted work – also plays an obvious role.[26] One illustration is the

---

[25] The classic treatment is Calabresi and Melamed, *supra* note 21. They distinguish between rules that protect a right-holder's veto (a "property rule") and rules that give him only a right to be compensated (a "liability rule"). *Id.* at 1092. They also discuss how the law might decide where to place an entitlement in the first instance. *Id.* at 1096–1106.

[26] Fair use is an area that breaks or bends the usual copyright rules. For example, in the ordinary case, judicial diffidence is the rule, set down by Holmes: judges are supposedly ill equipped to evaluate art. Bleistein v. Donaldson Lithographing Co., 188 U.S. 239, 251–52 (1903). Some courts take this as an indicator they should not inquire into the social value of the works before them. In fair use, however, the social value of the defendant's use is often key.

Similarly, in fair use cases the usual rule that "creativity is no defense" is turned on its head. In the ordinary case where the defendant has published a work that transforms plaintiff's work without plaintiff's permission, the defendant's creativity is no defense: his creativity merely makes his product an infringing "derivative work". Further, as Learned Hand said, "no plagiarist can excuse the wrong by showing how much of his work he did not pirate." Harper & Row, 471 U.S. at 565 (quoting Sheldon v. Metro-Goldwyn Pictures Corporation, 81 F.2d 49, 56 (2nd. Cir. 1936), *cert. denied*, 298 U.S. 669 (1936)). Yet creativity and the extent of transformation are often key in fair use cases.

classic *Time v. Geis* case where an author was permitted fair use of copyrighted films showing the Kennedy assassination. The defendant had copied the films to illustrate a publicly valuable argument contesting the conclusions of the Warren Commission, and the court in granting fair use stressed the value of the defendant's behavior.[27]

LACK OF PERMISSION

If the defendant has not sought the property owner's *permission,* is that lack of deference to the plaintiff's property interest socially desirable and/or excused? Again negligence law and self-defense provide useful illustrations. When an injury is unintentional, as in negligence law, no blame attaches for failing to obtain advance permission from the injured party. That person's identity was not knowable in advance. In order to state a prima facie case in negligence, therefore, plaintiff must show something more than he suffered an unconsented injury.[28] As for self-defense, if we focus on the person who initiated the attack, we think the attacker through his aggression against another has (within reason) forfeited his ordinary right to be consulted about what happens to his body. In copyright's fair use doctrine, too, a copyright owner can forfeit his normative right to be consulted. This was intimated by the Supreme Court in *Acuff-Rose*: since a copyright owner will not ordinarily license someone to lampoon him, a parodist may be justified in not seeking the owner's permission.[29]

LACK OF COMPENSATION

When the defendant has taken, used, invaded or injured something belonging to the property owner, is it justifiable or excusable that he not pay *compensation* for it? In the famous case of *Vincent v Lake Erie,* a boat owner acted desirably in keeping his ship tied to the dock during a roaring storm, but the court nevertheless

---

[27] Time, Inc. v. Bernard Geis Assocs., 293 F.Supp. 130, 145–46 (S.D.N.Y. 1968) (finding "a public interest in having the fullest information available on the murder of President Kennedy"). As will appear below, however, virtually all uses of intangibles are justified. The harder questions are whether a lack of compensation and/or permission can be excused or justified.
[28] My "permission" category follows Calabresi & Melamed fairly closely. See their *Property Rules, supra* note 21 at 1106–09.
[29] *Campbell v. Acuff-Rose Music,* 510 U.S. 569 (1994); also see *infra* at text accompanying notes 99–113 (endowment effect and pricelessness).

made him pay for damage done to the dock.[30] The view of the law of Nuisance expressed in the Second Restatement reflects a similar approach: a failure to pay can make otherwise reasonable behavior "unreasonable."[31] This contrasts with the more traditional tort approach, under which rightful behavior brought no need to pay, and wrongful behavior could trigger both monetary and injunctive relief.

As for copyright, its core tradition too unites injunctive and monetary relief. In the typical case where infringement is found, both remedies are available, and in the typical case where fair use is found, both remedies are denied. Nevertheless, for copyright also, the question of copyright owner's consent is sometimes separated from questions of compensation. This is seen most explicitly in the many compulsory licenses set up by copyright legislation.[32]

In the judicially formed doctrine of fair use, too, the Supreme Court has suggested that sometimes an injunction should be denied (suggesting that the permission of the copyright owner need not be sought), but payment should nevertheless be made.[33] Thus, a use may be socially desirable, and it may be unnecessary to obtain the owner's consent, but payment may nevertheless be ordered.

---

[30] Vincent v. Lake Erie Transp. Co., 124 N.W. 221 (Minn. 1910).

	Potentially Justified	Potentially Excused	Defendant loses
No permission	X		
No compensation	No	No	X
Behavior	X		

[31] *See* Restatement 2d of Torts § 826(b) ("An intentional invasion of another's interest in the use and enjoyment of land is unreasonable if ... (b) the harm caused by the conduct is serious and the financial burden of compensating for this and similar harm to others would not make the continuation of the conduct not feasible.") (The official comment on clause (b) is somewhat clearer: "It may sometimes be reasonable to operate an important activity if payment is made for the harm it is causing, but unreasonable to continue it without paying.")

Dividing the desirability of *payment* from the desirability of *behavior* and from the desirability of *asking permission* is most familiar from the "takings" area of Constitutional law. Under the Fifth Amendment, sometimes government must pay those whom it has adversely affected, even when the effect was a by-product of socially beneficial action and even when the government permissibly failed to obtain the affected citizen's permission.

There are many applications of the notion that a defendant might appropriately receive a gain that he may sometimes nevertheless be required to pay for. See, e.g., Jules Coleman, *Corrective Justice and Wrongful Gain*, 11 J. Legal Stud. 421, 427 (1982). Also see Wendy J. Gordon, *On Owning Information: Intellectual Property and the Restitutionary Impulse*, 78 Va. L. Rev. 149, 187 (1992) (hereinafter *On Owning Information*).

[32] For example, the statute provides that any band can make a "cover" version of a song that has already been recorded simply by paying a statutory fee to the copyright owner. The composer who objects is powerless; he has no right to stop the making of a "cover" version that conforms to the provisions of the statute. *See* 17 U.S.C. section 115(a).

Incidentally, the compulsory license gives a privilege to *make* cover records, not to perform publicly. To *perform* a "cover", therefore, a band needs permission. It can be sought from the copyright owner, or (as occurs more often) a license can be obtained through BMI, ASCAP or other collective rights association that serves as the owner's representative.

In such instances, one might say that the only wrong would be a defendant's failure to compensate the plaintiff. Judge Keeton's term, "conditional fault", is useful to refer to such cases. As he pointed out, sometimes "[i]t is the moral sense of the community that one should not engage in [a particular] type of conduct, because of risk or certainty of losses to others, without making reasonable provision for compensation of losses."[34] My contention is that conditional fault, like other kinds of grounds for defendant liability, can be justified or excused.

Summary: For a market to serve as a socially acceptable mode of allocating resources, ideally (a) the available institutions and technology must provide the conditions for perfect competition, such as perfect knowledge and an absence of transaction costs,[35] and (b) society must want to distribute the resource in accord with efficiency criteria. Among academics, the dominant convention saves the term "market failure" for (a) the technical lack of perfect-market conditions. However, our pluralistic legal culture demands that we admit that markets can also fail when (b) the criteria that perfect markets maximize are simply not the criteria of most importance. Therefore it makes sense to use the term "market

---

[33] Campbell v. Acuff-Rose Music, 510 U.S. 569, 592 n. 10. To represent this graphically, here is the situation for a parody that is found to be a "fair use" before *Acuff-Rose*:

	Potentially Justified	Potentially Excused	Defendant loses
No permission	X		
No compensation	X		
Behavior	X		

Compare this with how such a parody could be treated after *Acuff-Rose* if the hint in the footnote 10 is taken up by later courts:

	Potentially Justified	Potentially Excused	Defendant loses
No permission	X		
No compensation			X
Behavior	X		

[34] Robert E. Keeton, *Conditional Fault in the Law of Torts*, 72 Harv. L Rev. 401 at 427–28 (1959). Please note that nothing in Judge Keeton's analysis (or in the instant article) suggests that because *some* harmful actions are permissible when compensation is paid, *all* harmful actions are permissible when compensation is paid. To the contrary, much of the literature on commodification and commensurability seeks to identify the actions whose permissibility should not be conditioned on compensation and, further, to identify the actions that can be *made wrongful* by introducing monetary compensation where it does not belong.

[35] These are the assumptions that economists following Adam Smith have posited as necessary for the attainment of perfect competition and achieving consistency between public and private interest. Notable among these assumptions are perfect knowledge, and the absence of transaction costs. See *Fair Use as Market Failure, supra* note 2, for a brief summary. One of the best books examining the limits of the market model is Michael J. Trebilcock, THE LIMITS OF THE FREEDOM OF CONTRACT (Harvard University Press 1993).

failure" broadly, whenever we have grounds to believe that bad results will follow from adhering to the rule of owner deference.[36]

One can develop rules about the likely failure of rules,[37] and as intimated there are at least two categories of occasions when an owner guided by self-interest is not likely to act in a way that society can tolerate. The simplest and most familiar category might be called, as mentioned above, market malfunction. This is when the facts of the real-world market at issue significantly fail to correspond with the factual assumptions behind the perfect market model.[38] We are in the domain of market malfunction if we feel that if only the deviation from the set of perfect market assumptions could be "fixed", the market would be a satisfactory method of making the needed decision.

By contrast, the presence of nonmonetizable interests and other non-monetary issues point up the inherent limitations of the market model. We can be in the domain of market limitation even if there is no technical problem to "fix" – if we would feel uncomfortable using the market to govern how the resource is used even if all the conditions of perfect competition were present and satisfied. I define cases of "justification" as cases of market limitation. There the market simply is the wrong place to look for answers.

Other kinds of excuse and justification may exist, as we will see when we come to assessing the tier I call "behavior". But from the perspective of the market, permission and compensation have particular roles: to help align private and public action. If the market cannot accomplish that task, either because of a lack of normative fit or a problem of technical market conditions, then a defendant might appropriately prevail despite a lack of permission and compensation.

Market limitations and the vocabulary of commodification

A definitional note regarding the connection between "market limitation" and "commodification" is in order. To say that economic norms are inapplicable to a

---

[36] This broad use was employed in *Fair Use as Market Failure;* see note 2, *supra*.

[37] This can occur in ethics too; situations of duress provide one such category. For example, the usual rule that prohibits lying may be a bad rule for a bank teller to follow when answering a robber's questions about how to how to shut off a police-warning system.

[38] In instances of market malfunction, facts fail to correspond to perfect-market facts. The decision-maker will face an initial normative inquiry – namely, whether a market norm should govern – but if she finds the market norm applicable, she will focus most of her efforts on the subsequent question of what empirical facts are presented by the given situation. In the case of market limitation, by contrast, the decision-maker sees the perfect-market norm as itself inadequate. She will focus much of her effort on identifying and clarifying alternative norms and deciding which one(s) should govern the presented situation.

given relation will often lead to the conclusion that the relation should not be commodified – which can involve denying a putative "owner" any right to sue in the given context.[39] This link between market limitation and commodification should hardly be controversial. Yet it may strike some readers that "things" rather than "contextual relations" are the appropriate focus of the commodification debate.

Admittedly, for reasons of academic path-dependence, debates over commodification often center on asking what "things" should or should not be commodified, as if resources could be permanently placed in one category (say, "property" or "commodity") or another (say, "personal" or "not tradable on a market"). However, as Margaret Jane Radin has pointed out, most resources are susceptible to varying categories,[40] with the result depending largely on the relation between persons, or between persons and the resource. I share Radin's relational perspective.[41]

When *most* of the relations regarding a thing are best handled outside the market, we are likely to place that "thing" in the category of things that cannot be owned. But that is only a presumptive categorization. It can be reversed. For example, consider the way that copyright protection extends to works of expression but does not extend to an author's ideas.[42] Just as "fair use" allows an exception to the usual presumption that works of expressive authorship *can* be exclusively owned, the presence of certain relations can undo the usual presumption that ideas *cannot* be owned.

It may be useful to explore this last example. In copyright, as I just suggested, people who create ideas have no property right to exclude others from using them, even if the ideas are embedded in a copyrightable work of expression. The reasons for so denying commodity status to ideas has both to do with economics (e.g., "ideas" are best exploited in diverse ways by non-centralized actors),[43] and with non-economic notions of personality, autonomy and fairness (e.g., "ideas"

---

[39] There are many aspects to making something a commodity: the right to sell is one aspect that is often discussed, and another is the right to sue to exclude others. A decision against commodification can affect one or many such characteristics.

[40] Margaret Jane Radin, *Market-Inalienability,* 100 Harv. L. Rev. 18 (1987); Margaret Jane Radin, *Justice and the Market Domain,* in MARKETS AND JUSTICE: NOMOS XXXI 165 (John W. Chapman & J. Roland Pennock eds., 1989).

[41] Persons adhering to a "thing" view of commodification might be said to have a "subject matter" perspective on the topic. Persons open to a "relational" view might be said to believe that "scope of rights" also matters for commodification. Since in most of intellectual property, subject matter and scope of rights always trade off against each other, cf., Robert A. Gorman, *Copyright Protection For The Collection And Representation Of Facts,* 76 Harv. L. Rev. 1569 (1963) at 1602, for intellectual property scholars a view of commodification that goes beyond "thingness" is practically inevitable.

[42] 17 U.S.C. section 102(b).

[43] *Compare* Edmund Kitch, *The Nature and Function of the Patent System,* 20 J.L. & Econ. 265 (1977) (patents are justifiable for those products whose exploitation is best managed by centralized decision-making).

become part of their recipients, and people who receive ideas should not be required to refrain from using parts of themselves.[44]) But although ideas are usually non-commodified, in some circumstances they can be bought and sold: namely, in negotiated two-party transactions between equals.[45] Thus, a screenwriter can "sell" his client an idea, and the two can agree in an enforceable contract that the client will not share the idea with others.[46] This is the law of "ideas" on which Hollywood operates.[47] Such two-party transactions are the "relational" exception to the rule that ideas are not commodities.[48]

Conversely, there can be relational exceptions to the presumption that certain things are usually commodities. In copyright, works of authorial expression are usually commodified.[49] Fair use is one of the doctrines that can negate this usual presumption that works of expression should be bought and sold.

Thus we have a trio of labels – market limitation, cases of possible justification, and non-commodified relations – that all make the same point: that there are many occasions on which a society cannot afford to rely on private ownership for its decision-making.

A related definitional note regarding "commodification" may also be helpful. When an item is a commodity, it means (among other things) that an owner can divest herself of ownership, and that an owner can stop other people from using the thing. In both instances – the owner's power to sell or give away the thing, and the owner's right to sue other people who injure or use the thing – we are concerned with someone losing access to the resource. To use Professor Radin's language of "human flourishing": in the case of the power to sell or give, we are concerned lest someone divest herself of something that is crucial to her *own* human flourishing. In the case of limitations on rights to sue, we are concerned lest someone divest others of something that is crucial to *their* human flourishing.

---

[44] *See* Wendy Gordon & Sam Postbrief, *On Commodifying Intangibles,* 10 Yale J. Law & Humanities 135 (review essay, 1998).

[45] The enforceability of shrinkwrap contracts raises a quite different set of issues.

[46] Similarly, in patent law there can be no ownership in ideas that are obvious, and in copyright there can be no ownership in non-creative lists. Nevertheless, the courts will routinely enforce contracts regarding non-patentable ideas, and lists of names, so long as the contracts are genuinely negotiated between equal parties. Moreover, such contracts can be backed up by trade secret law. See Kewanee Oil v Bicron, 416 U.S. 470, 482–3 (1974).

[47] See, e.g., Buchwald v. Paramount Pictures, 13 U.S.P.Q.2d (BNA) 1497, No. C 706083, 1990 Cal. App. LEXIS 634, 1990 WL 357611, (Cal. App. Dep't Super. Ct. Jan. 31, 1990). Not officially published (Cal. Rules of Court, Rules 976, 977), 13 U.S.P.Q.2d 1497, 17 Media L. Rep. 1257

[48] In turn, blackmail law is the relational exception to the rule that allows negotiated contracts over information to be enforced. In blackmail the purported contractual relation involves the infliction of unjustifiable harm and is socially wasteful in a particularly obvious and dangerous way. See Wendy J. Gordon, *Truth and Consequences: The Force of Blackmail's Central Case*, 141 U. Penn. L. Rev. 1741 (1993).

[49] 17 U.S.C. section 102(a): "Copyright protection subsists, in accordance with this title, in original works of authorship fixed in any tangible medium of expression ..."

The policies can be much the same.[50] Nevertheless, it should be noted that for "fair use", we are addressing only one part of the commodification conundrum: whether an owner should have a right to exclude *others* from the resource. Whether an owner should have a power to exclude *herself* from the resource – the issue of inalienability – is a separate question.

Examples of justifying and excusing

This distinction between justification and excuse now must be applied to the three-tier inquiry. As will appear, in copyright law the distinction has more "cutting edge" in regard to lack of compensation and permission than it does to behavior.

A. Behavior

In the analysis that follows, the term "behavior" is defined as the use that the defendant makes of the plaintiff's product. For example, in *Time v. Geis* the behavior was copying the Zapruder films in order to illustrate an argument about the Kennedy assassination. In the *Wind Done Gone* case, recently in the courts,[51] the behavior is a young novelist's borrowing of characters and plot structures from *Gone With the Wind* in order to criticize and parody Margaret Mitchell's famous work of popular fiction. In *Williams & Wilkins,* the behavior was a federal library photocopying medical articles for the use of researchers. In the case of a software pirate who mass-produces and sells copies of copyrighted computer programs, the behavior is the production and distribution of these additional copies. Whether it is justifiable or excusable for a behavior to occur can be separated from the question of whether it should have occurred only if the defendant had the copyright owner's permission (issue B, below), and from the question of whether the defendant should pay for the use (issue C, below).

Thus, for example, it may be very desirable that copies of the software be made and distributed (issue A), but if this could and should proceed only through the copyright owner's voluntary licensing (issue B), then fair use should be denied and

---

[50] For example: for reasons of both economics and human flourishing, sometimes society is unwilling to allow someone to divest herself of liberty to use her own ideas. For similar reasons, society might be unwilling to give owners rights to prohibit *others* from using ideas. See Gordon & Postbrief, *supra* note 44.

[51] Suntrust Bank v. Houghton Mifflin Co., 268 F.3d 1257, 60 U.S.P.Q.2d 1225, 14 Fla. L. Weekly Fed. C 1391 (11th Cir. 2001) and 252 F. 3d 1165 (11th Cir per curiam), reversing Suntrust Bank v. Houghton Mifflin Co., 136 F.Supp.2d 1357 (N.D.Ga. 2001). The case was settled after this article was written.

the defendant enjoined. Alternatively, should it be decided that the copies should be made and distributed (issue A), and that the owner's voluntary licensing is unlikely to function appropriately (issue B), a court may yet decide that the defendant should pay compensation (issue C).

For tangibles, the desirability of the defendant's behavior – isolated from questions of compensation – can be a matter of much dispute. This is true from the perspective either of market economics or of other norms. For tangibles, sometimes market failure can cause a lack of permission to be excused or justified, but the undesirability of the behavior itself can lead the court to find in favor of the plaintiff on the basis of an all-things-considered decision.[52] To put it another way, behavior is undesirable if we can say "even if the plaintiff was compensated, and even if the plaintiff gave permission, this behavior should not occur." With tangibles, therefore, much investigation is necessary to assess whether a behavior is value-maximizing or otherwise desirable.

For intangibles, by contrast, it is fairly hard to imagine a use that is *not* desirable so long as concerns regarding compensation are satisfied. Defendant's use usually does not interfere with plaintiff's ability to use the intangible. Because copyright like patent deals with inexhaustible public goods, we can light each other's candles without diminishing the light from our own.[53]

Admittedly, some speech can be undesirable on the merits. Consider, for example, hate speech. This is not desirable behavior. Nevertheless, it is unlikely to trigger legal sanction because of the First Amendment.

Interestingly, such treatment can be seen either through the lens of justification or excuse. Because of the First Amendment, judges are not likely to assess the merits of a defendant's *message* in deciding whether his copying is infringing or "fair". Rather, because of the free speech concerns, the defendant's behavior is likely to be assessed at a higher level of generality: say, his participating in public debate.[54] Viewed with such generality, the behavior is justifiable. Alternatively, focusing on the defendant's message itself, we might

---

[52] Whether or not compensation is paid to the injured party, a value-maximizer does not want wasteful acts to occur. Similarly, under other norms there are behaviors that cannot be made acceptable by having the gaining party pay the injured party.

[53] "He who receives an idea from me, receives instruction himself without lessening mine; as he who lights his taper at mine, receives light without darkening me." Graham v. John Deere Co., 383 U.S. 1, 9 n.2 (1966) (quoting VI WRITINGS OF THOMAS JEFFERSON, at 180–81 (Washington ed. 1903)).

Admittedly, one can imagine a contrary case: for example, if a software pirate creates three million copies while the copyright owner has already created three million copies, there will be wasted production costs if only four million people desire a copy of the software at or above marginal cost. But although such a case can be imagined, copying that is undesirable in itself is empirically likely to be rare.

[54] It is our institutional commitment to the First Amendment that allows such speech to be disseminated, rather than the merits of what is said.

Sometimes the law responds to harmful speech. For example, when someone quotes a target out of context in order to lie about him, the law of libel may respond, depending, inter alia, on

say that quoting from a copyrighted work as part of socially destructive speech is "excused" by the institutional considerations mandated by the First Amendment. Hate speech is not something we want to be emulated, but it is something to which our legal sanctions are not well suited.

Whether under the rubric of excuse or of justification, then, for copyright most of the difficult issues arise not with behavior, but with permission and compensation. This is the reason why it is particularly important for understanding intellectual property to divide the defense inquiry into three parts. Too often we think of defenses in terms of the rightfulness or wrongfulness of behavior. For copyright, the behavior of copying is almost always rightful, or at least institutionally excused. The hard issues arise in relation to *how* the copying should be done: pursuant to voluntary licensing under the market system, subject to an obligation to compensate the copyright owner, or freely. As to those issues, it can be helpful to identify if the market is functioning and whether market norms are applicable.

B. LACK OF PERMISSION

Assuming the goal of copyright is to achieve maximum social benefit, there is no reason to require a potential user of a work to ask the copyright owner's permission unless there is some way to believe the owner's self-interest is aligned with society's. When this is not the case – when for example social and private costs markedly diverge, or the interests involved are not monetizable – seeking permission should not be required.

As for justification, the commodification literature provides abundant examples of resources that justifiably should not be owned in the sense that they should not be subject to sale. Where the public interest cannot be evaluated in monetary terms, it makes no sense to treat owner self-interest as if it were likely to generate socially desirable outcomes.

When by contrast there is a technical failure of market functioning (typically, the presence of significant transaction costs), I would say the defendant who has not obtained permission is potentially "excused". He may be acting rightfully in

---

cont.
    whether the target was a public figure and whether the plaintiff spoke with reckless disregard of the truth.
    Note that elsewhere in this essay I recommend that judges allow themselves at least to admit when harm is caused by a work of authorship, and to allow speech in responses that mitigates harm. See the discussion *infra* accompanying footnotes 67–73 and accompanying text. One might debate whether that recommendation, and the caselaw on which it is based, is inconsistent with the supposed neutrality of the "marketplace of ideas" notion, and how the recommendation fits with alternative conceptions of the First Amendment.

not obtaining permission – or wrongly – but it is an empirical economist who can tell us if requiring permission would maximize value.

There are also cases on the borderline between excuse and justification. For example, sometimes we cannot trust the owner's judgment because there simply is no stable answer to "where is the highest valued use in monetary terms." Cases of unstable value could, on the one hand, be classified with cases of justification, since in the end a non-monetary metric will be needed. On the other hand, perhaps these should be classified as cases of excuse, since many such cases can still be fruitfully addressed through a quasi-economic consequentialist calculation. This issue will be discussed below, under the heading of "pricelessness."

C. LACK OF COMPENSATION

In the domain of market malfunction and "excuse", the desirability of compensation is by definition measured by economic effect. Here we can usefully borrow from Frank Michelman's classic treatment of the analogous question of whether governmentally inflicted injuries should be compensated.[55] He suggests there are at least two primary reasons why a value-maximizing economist might favor requiring the government to pay compensation for acts that, while facially desirable from a societal point of view, inflict injury on private parties.

First, paying compensation keeps the harm-causer honest. If the defendant (the government) has to pay, it will not use the plaintiff's resource without being sure that the behavior contemplated will in fact generate enough benefit to outweigh the costs.

Second, paying compensation averts the "demoralization costs" that can occur if the citizenry feels itself vulnerable to losing its investments at the whim of others. Professor Michelman suggests that the citizenry might work less hard in general if people thought their efforts might come to naught because of uncompensated governmental injury.

For copyright, we do not have to worry much about the first consideration. Given the inexhaustibility of intangible public goods, it will usually happen that copying and other uses of copyrighted works will in fact generate more benefits than costs. But the second consideration, what Professor Michelman called "demoralization costs", has great importance in the copyright area – though in copyright, demoralization costs go by their more familiar name, "incentive effects."

---

[55] Frank L. Michelman, *Property, Utility, and Fairness: Comments on the Ethical Foundations of "Just Compensation" Law*, 80 Harv.L.Rev. 1165 (1967)

In cases of excuse, where wealth maximization provides the appropriate norm, the incentive effects are likely to be crucial to the analysis. The legislature has presumptively decided what desirable incentive effects should be. If a grant of fair use substantially impairs those incentives, then a court might logically refuse to grant fair use treatment, or premise fair use on an obligation to compensate.

What of justification? If something we value is degraded by being priced, a judge may think it inadvisable to order compensation. Yet, ordering compensation may not be the same as selling.[56] Therefore, even in these cases, compensation might be a good idea if we made sure that any orders to pay were limited to cases where a defendant *reaped enough monetary benefit to pay and still find it profitable to make the use*.[57] Then plaintiff would be paid, and the defendant would be able to speak, and the realm of public discourse would still profit from defendant's work. However, as I suggest in the final section of this essay,[58] there can be significant problems even with such limited orders to compensate.

The chart on the next page may be a helpful summary of the discussion.

The justification of self-defense and its potential role regarding parody

One of the most interesting questions in "fair use" has to do with whether copyright owners should be empowered to enjoin persons who copy from their work in order to criticize, parody, or otherwise lampoon them. From a "justification" perspective, the answer seems clear: no such injunction should be

---

[56] See the discussion in Margaret Jane Radin, CONTESTED COMMODITIES at 184–205 (Harvard University Press 1996).

[57] If a defendant merely has to disgorge a *monetary* benefit, he or she is unlikely to be harmed.
   As scholars of restitution law have observed, one cannot always sell what one has received (services and goods may have been consumed; the markets may be distant; etc.) and no one can afford to pay for everything he or she might desire. Giving someone a service or a good and then requiring payment for it may make that person worse off than he or she would have been without the service or the product. Should a court require the defendant to pay for something non-monetary that he or she has gained, the defendant could indeed be harmed. Restitution law has long taken these considerations into account in an attempt to protect defendants from being made worse off after a restitution suit than they would have been had they never received a benefit from the plaintiff. See Gordon, *On Owning Information, supra* note 31 at text accompanying note 226 and following. The suggestion to utilize this approach for fair use purposes was made by Megan Richardson.

[58] See the Post-Script, *infra* at pages 188 *et seq*.

Summary of Analysis

	Potential justification: "inherent limitation" on market use	Potential excuse – "malfunction" in market	Neither excuse nor justification applies: Defendant loses
No permission	The market norm is not what should govern OR money is not a good measure of welfare in this context.	The market norm and monetary criterion are appropriately applied but the market is not working.[59]	Either the market norm and monetary measures are appropriate and the market is working, OR some other consideration[60] leads a court to favor honoring the owner's property right.
No compensation	Even if payment could be practicably made, it would be normatively wrong to make the defendant pay.	Market breakdown makes it difficult for defendant to pay.[61]	Either the market norm is appropriate and the market is functioning, or for some other reason (e.g., fairness) compensation is a good idea
Behavior	The defendant's behavior is desirable.[62] Still need to assess if permission or compensation is required.	Undesirable behavior might be excused for reasons other than its merits.[63]	Some behavior should be stopped[64] regardless of whether the harmed person consents or receives compensation.[65]

---

[59] Example: the defendant may be excused for not obtaining the plaintiff's permission if there is such a short period of time between the defendant realizing she will need to use the plaintiff's copyrighted work and the time when the use must be implemented, that she is unable to send a permission request capable of being acted on in a timely fashion.

[60] One example of such other consideration is autonomy. Another is Neil Netanel's "robust civil sphere". Netanel, *supra* note 6. Another might be Milton Friedman's notion that private property promotes political freedom.

[61] An example might be when the cost of contacting the owner is larger than the value of the use. As another example, consider a critic who generates significant positive externalities when he quotes from the copyrighted work.

[62] If defendant's behavior is desirable, one still needs to look at issues of compensation and permission to know whether plaintiff or defendant should prevail. Note: In copyright, this paper suggests, a defendant's behavior is likely to be desirable.

[63] As a possible example of speech that may be undesirable but excused by First Amendment and institutional considerations, consider a neo-Nazi who quotes from others' copyrighted works as part of a campaign of hate.

[64] The "undesirable behavior" could be stopped either by letting plaintiff win a civil suit against defendant, or by the government bringing a criminal or regulatory action, or by private self-help. The defendant's act might be cabined in many different ways.

[65] This is linked to issues of inalienability.

allowed. A paradigm instance of when we do *not* want a speaker to obtain a copyright owner's permission is when the speaker's use will be critical of the copyrighted work. If truth is a merit good that should be available without regard to payment, then a judge should not even order compensation.[66]

Further, many critical and parodic uses are essentially acts of self-defense, where someone who has been affected by an iconic work seeks to undo its negative effect on him or her.[67] This is the case with Alice Randall, author of *The Wind Done Gone*. Randall's novel seeks to undermine and parody Margaret Mitchell's *Gone With The Wind* through use of Mitchell's own characters. Randall in a recent interview made clear that *Gone With The Wind* had injured her, and many other African-Americans. Randall said she would rather have been "born blind" if blindness would have enabled her to avoid reading Mitchell's novel,[68] so great was the emotional harm she felt.

As a privilege allows one to respond to a threat of physical harm in the law of battery, self-help is also potentially justifiable in the law of copyright. This has been recognized in fair use case law under the label of "rebuttal". As the Ninth Circuit observed in a case where Jerry Falwell as part of a fund-raising effort sent his supporters photocopies of a Hustler magazine attack on him:

> [A]n individual in rebutting a copyrighted work containing derogatory information about himself may copy such parts of the work as are necessary to permit understandable comment. Falwell did not use more than was reasonably necessary to make an understandable comment when he copied the entire parody from the magazine. ... [T]he public interest in allowing an individual to defend himself against such derogatory personal attacks serves to rebut the presumption of unfairness.[69]

Thus, although the First Amendment barred Falwell from suing Hustler for the emotional damage the attack caused him,[70] the First Amendment did not bar the

---

[66] See the discussion of Posner, *infra* at note 124.

[67] I do not propose that one harm "justifies" the victim committing a responsive harm. I am *not* talking about revenge. Rather, I am talking about reducing the harmful effects caused by the copyright owner's work.

In the emotional realm, we acknowledge that merely speaking a trauma can help undo its effect. (See, e.g., the work of psychologist Alice Miller, FOR YOUR OWN GOOD (Farrar, Straus & Giroux 1984)). This is true in the cultural realm as well. Giving voice can be curative.

[68] *See* the Connection website for July 16, 2001 with guest Alice Randall talking about her book, THE WIND DONE GONE (Houghton Mifflin Company 2001), which criticizes GONE WITH THE WIND by means of writing a new novel that uses some of Mitchell's characters: < http://www.theconnection.org/archive/2001/07/0716b.shtml >

[69] Hustler Magazine Inc. v. Moral Majority Inc., 796 F.2d 1148 (9th Cir. 1986) at 1153.

[70] Hustler Magazine v. Falwell, 485 U.S. 46 (1988) (when *Hustler* made fun of Falwell in a lampoon that was both disgusting and untrue, the Supreme Court ruled that the First Amendment barred his suit for intentional infliction of emotional distress.)

court from giving Falwell a "self-help privilege" of self-defense assertable under the label of fair use.[71]

That the judge's self-defense argument puts us in the realm of inherent market limitation rather than market malfunction is patent. Nothing in the judge's discussion of the dispute between Hustler and Falwell's Moral Majority attempts to balance the harms and benefits.

To embrace self-defense within fairness does not mean the justification inquiry requires a judge to wander without guidance. Several articulable normative structures can give content to a notion of "fairness" that is sensitive to self-defense. One such structure is Lockean natural rights.

Locke suggested that property rights could arise from labor providing that the laborer left "enough, and as good" in the common for others.[72] Building on that Lockean proviso, I have argued that works of authorship that do harm (such as the Hustler attack and the racist portions of *Gone With The Wind*) should not have the aid of the law in doing so. That is, a copyright owner whose work has harmed someone has no natural right to prevent the harmed party from quoting or copying the injurious work in an attempt to undo its effects.[73] Such quotation or copying is justified.

It might be argued that behavior cannot be "justified" by reference to harms caused by speech, since the First Amendment requires all of us to bear most speech harms without legal recourse. But the caselaw seems to draw a dividing line between rights to sue (which the First Amendment can bar), and rights to self-help: While the First Amendment precluded Falwell from bringing suit for intentional infliction of emotional distress to recompense the injury he felt Hustler had caused him, the court under "fair use" gave Falwell a privilege to use self-help, and to quote or copy the injurious work in an attempt to undo its effect.[74] Lockean natural rights would come to the same result.[75]

---

[71] It might be argued that a personal attack (as by Hustler against Falwell) generates a self-defense privilege that is not available when a group is attacked. By contrast, I think the two cases sufficiently analogous – and the problem of cultural marginalization of minority groups sufficiently serious – that the Falwell case could be treated as suitable precedent for the privilege of group self-defense.

[72] John Locke, TWO TREATISES OF GOVERNMENT 287–88 (Peter Laslett ed., 2d ed. 1967) (3d ed. 1698, corrected by Locke) (bk. II, § 27).

[73] Wendy J. Gordon, *A Property Right in Self-Expression: Equality and Individualism in the Natural Law of Intellectual Property*, 102 Yale L. J. 1533–1609 (1993) (hereinafter *A Property Right in Self-Expression*).

[74] Although unable to sue *Hustler* for damages, Hustler Magazine v. Falwell, 485 U.S. 46 (1988), Falwell was held entitled under the fair use doctrine to photocopy the *Hustler* lampoon for purposes of raising money to defend himself. Hustler Magazine Inc. v. Moral Majority Inc., 796 F.2d 1148 (9th Cir. 1986) at 1153.

[75] Gordon, *A Property Right in Self-Expression*, supra note 73.

Pricelessness and private censorship

The above discussion suggests that some critics and parodists can use self-defense as an argument for fair use. Such an argument lies in the realm of justification. What I want to explore now is the possibility that even economic norms can lead to a substantial privilege for critics. That is, I aim to prove that for critical speech, a speaker who has not sought the owner's consent or who proceeds against an owner's consent has a potential excuse as well as a justification.[76] In instances of private censorship, free speech is not the only value that dictates a defendant victory. Economics, too, can lead to the same result. It will be useful to examine this example in some detail, borrowing both from the economics literature and the literature on commodification.[77]

In the most recent "fair use" case before the Supreme Court, the opinion indicated that fair use could be justified in part as a response to situations in which copyright owners are unlikely to give permission at virtually any price.[78] Other cases have taken the same position.[79] This position, advanced in a case involving a song parody, might strike the reader as inconsistent with the usual economic assumption that one must take preferences as a given. If one takes this notion seriously – it is sometimes known as the assumption of "consumer sovereignty" – then it seems the Court should have accorded as much respect to the copyright owner's desire not to be parodied as to any other value. After all, in theory, an unwillingness to sell or license merely indicates that the potential buyer/licensee is not the highest-valued user. So it may seem wrongheaded of the Supreme Court to suggest that it may be appropriate to give a parodist – a disappointed licensee – the liberty to copy for free on the ground that the owner would not sell him a license. Is the Court under-valuing the owner's preferences? Not necessarily; there are

---

[76] Also see the discussion of Richard Posner's position, see *infra* notes 80 and 124.

[77] The material on pricelessness and endowment effect borrows from my prior work, particularly Wendy J. Gordon, *On the Economics of Copyright, Restitution, and "Fair Use": Systemic Versus Case-By-Case Responses to Market Failure*, 8 Journal of Law and Information Science (Australia) 7 (1997) and Wendy J. Gordon, *Toward a Jurisprudence of Benefits: The Norms of Copyright and the Problem of Private Censorship*, 57 U. Chi. L. Rev. 1009 (review essay, 1990).

[78] *See* Campbell v. Acuff-Rose, 510 U.S. 569 (1994). In assessing the plaintiff's claim that the parody would impair their potential market, the Court responded: "[T]he unlikelihood that creators of imaginative works will license critical reviews or lampoons of their own productions removes such uses from the very notion of a potential licensing market." 510 U.S. at 592.

[79] The Ninth Circuit Court of Appeals made a similar point in Fisher v. Dees, 794 F.2d 432 (9th Cir. 1986) ("The parody defense to copyright infringement exists precisely to make possible a use that generally cannot be bought."). For other cases involving similar anti-dissemination motives on the part of copyright proprietors, *see* Gordon, *Fair Use as Market Failure*, *supra* note 2, and Gordon, *Toward a Jurisprudence of Benefits*, *supra* note 77 at 1632–33.

several explanations of the Court's approach that are consistent with the traditional economic deference to individual preferences.[80]

When a copyright owner refuses to let someone adapt her work for purposes of parodying it, or refuses to give an ideological opponent permission to quote lengthy passages, or insists on suing anyone who quotes passages of her memoirs that reflect unfavorably on her, she is using her copyright as a tool of suppression.[81] The question of whether authors should be entitled to refuse permission to those users of whom they disapprove is a complex one. For example, there can be practical problems in distinguishing improperly motivated suppression from a refusal to license motivated by a desire to maximize financial return.[82] More important than the practical problems may be a conceptual one. If the proper way to look at these problems were economic, then, as mentioned, the principles of consumer sovereignty would seem to dictate that governmental decision-makers should not question why someone refuses to sell or license.[83] Economics "assum[es] that man is a rational maximizer of his ends in life,"[84] and a desire to suppress would seem to be as rational an end as a desire for fame or fast cars.

Additionally, Ronald Coase has persuasively emphasized the importance of transaction costs by showing that, in their absence, the ultimate allocation of a

---

[80] Judge Posner admits, "it may be in the private interest of the copyright owner, but not in the social interest, to suppress criticism of the work", Richard A. Posner, *When Is Parody Fair Use*, 21 J. Legal Stud. 67 at 73 (1992). He also treats "reluctan[ce] to license" as a factor that should favor fair use, *id.* at 71. However, he is not clear as to what methodology he uses to reach that conclusion. His stated reason for his conclusion – that we should encourage the production of truth, *id.* at 74 – suggests that he is using a mixture of economic and noneconomic norms. See note 124 *infra*.

[81] Similar instances also appear in the corporate realm. For example, when a newspaper expanded its TV coverage it told its readership about the extended service in an advertisement that pictured a copyrighted TV Guide cover for purposes of comparison. TV Guide then sued for copyright infringement. Presumably the suit was motivated by something other than a desire for license fees. The comparative advertising was held to be a fair use. *See* Triangle Publications, Inc v. Knight-Ridder Newspapers, Inc., 626 F. Supp. 1171 (5th Cir. 1980).

[82] For example, it can be difficult to distinguish suppression from an attempt to direct the work into the most valuable derivative work markets. *See, e.g.*, Paul Goldstein, COPYRIGHT Vol I at 571–73 (Little, Brown and Company 1989) (rights over derivative works can affect the direction of investment and the type of works produced).

Similarly, in regard to unpublished works, it can be difficult to distinguish cases of suppression from cases of economically motivated refusals to license. An author accused of suppression may be simply trying to keep the work out of the public eye temporarily until it reaches its mature form and can be published.

Even if some practical means existed to distinguish all dissembling "suppressors" from those copyright owners who are genuinely motivated by financial return, some cases will present instances of truly mixed motives. For example, the owner of copyright in an out-of-print collection of letters might sue a biographer who extensively quotes the letters, not only out of a dislike for the biographer's message or perceived inaccuracies, but also out of a desire to preserve the reprint market for the letters. See Meeropol v. Nizer, 417 F. Supp. 1201, 1208 (2d Cir. 1976), *rev'd and remanded*, 520 F. 2d 1061 (2d Cir. 1977), *cert. denied*, 434 U.S. 1013 (1978).

[83] The discussion that follows draws in part on Gordon, *Toward a Jurisprudence of Benefits, supra* note 77 at 1042–43.

[84] Richard A. Posner, ECONOMIC ANALYSIS OF LAW 3 (5th ed. Aspen Publishers 1998).

resource will be efficient regardless of how entitlements are initially assigned.[85] So long as the parties can meet face to face, as in copyright a copyright owner and potential parodist or critic could often do, why should there be any need for the judiciary to do anything but enforce whatever property right is before it?

Whether suppression would or would not be economically desirable will depend in most cases on empirical analysis of the particular fact pattern.[86] But some general observations can indicate preliminarily why, when copyright owners seek to use the copyright law to enforce attempts at suppression, neither consumer sovereignty nor the Coase Theorem suggest that judges give the owners automatic deference.[87]

At least four reasons suggest that the market cannot always be relied upon to mediate attempts at suppression and that it might be economically desirable to refuse authors an entitlement to suppress.[88] The four reasons are the "suppression triangle"; pecuniary effects; managerial discretion; and what I call "pricelessness". In addition, of course, it is possible that economics is not the right way to view this matter at all. The four reasons are interrelated, and to explicate them let me begin with the "suppression triangle."

1. SUPPRESSION TRIANGLE

I use the term "suppression triangle"[89] to point to the fact that in cases involving

---

[85] See Ronald H. Coase, *The Problem of Social Cost*, 3 J.L. & Econ. 1 (1960). Efficiency will occur in the absence of factors such as transaction costs, wealth or endowment effects, and strategic behavior. See id. (transaction costs). See also, e.g., Donald Regan, *The Problem of Social Cost Revisited*, 15 J. Law & Econ. 427 (1972) (strategic behavior). Compare Ronald H. Coase, *Notes on the Problem of Social Cost*, in THE FIRM, THE MARKET, AND THE LAW 157 (University of Chicago Press 1988).

[86] Even if one interprets copyright's economic goal as being solely the use of incentives to "promote knowledge," so that satisfying the copyright owner's personal tastes would not count as an independent value, the empirical answer to suppression questions would not be easy: in a given case enforcing any particular type of suppression would both keep some knowledge secret, and yield long-term incentives that could aid knowledge in the long run (because authors who can suppress have a copyright worth more than authors who cannot). Cf., Michelman, *Property, Utility & Fairness*, supra note 55 (the effects of demoralization on productivity). Which of the two potential effects on knowledge would be greater (the loss from enforcing suppression or the gain from long-term incentives) cannot be determined *a priori*.

[87] For a fuller discussion of this issue, see Wendy J. Gordon, "The Right Not to Use" (unpublished manuscript).

[88] Additional reasons might include, e.g., the potential nonmonetizability of first amendment values. See, *Fair Use as Market Failure*, supra note 2, at 1631–32.

[89] I base this theory in part on the work of James Lindgren in the blackmail area. See James Lindgren, *Unraveling the Paradox of Blackmail*, 84 Colum. L. Rev. 670 (1984) (discussing the three-party structure involved). For an economic analysis of blackmail stressing other aspects of blackmail activity, see Ronald H. Coase, *The 1987 McCorkle Lecture: Blackmail*, 74 Va. L. Rev. 655, 673–74 (1988).

I am indebted to Warren Schwartz for suggesting the potential relevance of the blackmail literature to this problem.

the suppression of information or other intellectual products,[90] at least three parties are affected: (1) the person who seeks or threatens to make the contested use (for example, the potential parodist), (2) the copyright owner who wants to keep the material from being copied or adapted (the potential suppressor), and (3) the person or persons who would want to see the material (the potential recipients). This is the triangle of affected interests. Yet in the suppression transaction typically only two parties are present: the potential user (such as a parodist), and the copyright owner. Whether an attempt to suppress is likely to be value-maximizing will depend, inter alia, on how well the interest of the omitted third party, the class of potential recipients, is represented by the two immediate participants.

Theoretically, the more valuable the parody or other use is to the public, the more the public should be willing to pay for it, and the more the parodist should be willing and able to bid for permission. Thus, the notion of the Invisible Hand[91] expects that any market participant will be in a position to reflect the interests of affected third parties (that is, the public audience). Nevertheless, the Invisible Hand often falters, and the possibility of misallocation remains.

Consider a hypothetical novelist or moviemaker who wants to keep the world from knowing what a hostile critic or parodist has to say about his work. Assume also that the critic or parodist wants to quote from the work or use its imagery, and that use of the quotation or imagery is somehow essential to the comprehensibility or believability of the criticism or parody.[92] If the law required the critic or parodist to purchase licenses to quote or paraphrase, how sure could we be that the "highest-valued" use would ensue?

For purposes of mathematical example, assume that the critic or parodist stands to earn at most a $1,000 profit from even the best-written product. Assume that the novelist or film-maker would lose $50,000 if the criticism or parody were published. Since the copyright owner would charge at least $50,000 for a license to criticize or ridicule his work, and the critic or parodist stands to gain only $1,000 from publishing, it may look like the copyright owner holds the "highest valued" use when compared with the parodist or critic. But that may be an illusion

---

[90] Data can implicate different issues than can, e.g., literary expression. For purposes of this very general discussion, however, I shall group all together under the rubric "information."

[91] Adam Smith argued that people pursuing their self-interest will come to results that are in accord with social need, as if guided by an "invisible hand". Adam Smith, AN INQUIRY INTO THE WEALTH OF NATIONS 423 (Modern Library 1937).

[92] There is another factor that may be at work here as well: the idea/expression dichotomy. Since under current law copyright owners cannot prevent others from using their ideas, it could be argued that little suppression of note could occur. For simplicity's sake, therefore, assume that in the following examples whatever the defendant has taken from the first artist's work could be considered copyrightable expression rather than simply "idea" and that the use of the copyrighted expression is somehow essential to the effectiveness of the planned derivative work.

resulting from the fact that the third party (in the owner/user/public triangle) is not being counted as part of the deal.

The publishing of the review or parody might benefit the public (who would thus be warned off from, say, a much-hyped romance novel that does not really excite anyone who reads past page five). Perhaps the public gains something like that same $50,000, or perhaps even more. On these hypothesized facts, requiring the publisher to seek a license from someone who would not sell it is a bad idea, and giving the publisher (the critic or parodist) free use is a good idea. Both are consistent with economic measures of value. If the critic had been able to capture the full value that the review gave to the audience, then the novelist's $50,000 minimum asking price would have been met.

A parodist may similarly be unable to capture the full value that the work holds for the audience. This can occur for many reasons.[93] There may be significant positive externalities and surplus in the market for parodies, for example. There also may be other complications in the markets for reviews and parodies, such as pecuniary losses that diverge from societal economic losses.

2. PECUNIARY LOSSES

Much of the loss that can come from a critical review will often be merely pecuniary, reflecting not a net loss to society but rather a shifting of revenues from one novelist to another and possibly better one.[94] Say, for example, that after a negative review of the copyright owner's book, audiences turn to a better novelist's book. It begins to sell well and generates more than $50,000 in royalties that would not otherwise have been earned. It is as if the triangle now were a geometric figure with four points (the criticized novelist, the critic, the public, and the better novelist). If one could add to the $1,000 the reviewer could offer for a "license to criticize" the $50,000 that the better novelist would reap, plus the amount that consumers gain from avoiding a bad book, the total value generated by the review would be enough to outweigh the initial copyright owner's pecuniary loss. Since this hypothetical additur is highly unlikely to happen,[95] mere pecuniary losses may

---

[93] As economist Michael L. Katz writes of the similar problem in the research and development area: In the absence of perfect discrimination, the firm conducting the R & D will be unable to appropriate all of the surplus generated by the licensing of its R & D, and the firm will sell its R & D results at prices that lead to inefficiently low levels of utilization by other firms. Michael L. Katz, *An Analysis of Cooperative Research and Development*, 4 Rand J. Econ. 527, 527 (1986).

[94] *See* Richard A. Posner, "Conventionalist Defenses of Law as an Autonomous Discipline" 17 (September 21, 1987) (unpublished manuscript using pecuniary effects to explain why landowners who create certain positive spillovers are not entitled to payment from those who benefited).

[95] Journalistic ethics would undoubtedly forbid reviewers of a given book to accept subsidies from the authors of competing books.

take on an importance they should not have and they might prevent socially desirable licensing.

3. MANAGERIAL DISCRETION

Another possible complication has to do not with the potential buyer's inability to raise the appropriate amount of capital, but with the potential licensor's potential inability to know even a good deal when it comes along. This complication can be termed managerial discretion,[96] by which I mean to embrace all those agency problems that may make managers in complex corporations sometimes arrive at decisions that are less value-maximizing than they could be. I would include here, for example, personal risk aversion, bureaucratic structure, group dynamics, and laziness.[97] Thus, the officials of a company that owns a given copyright may refuse to license simply because the requested license is in an unfamiliar field and their particular bureaucratic structure penalizes unlucky risk takers more than it rewards lucky ones. When critical, parodic, or otherwise controversial licenses would be at issue, the human desire to "play it safe" might prevent value-maximizing transfers from occurring.[98] Managerial discretion is just one of many agency problems that can prevent the parties from dealing with each other like the unitary participants in the classic Coasian transaction.

4. PRICELESSNESS

All of the above are reasons why socially desirable "licenses to be critical" are not likely to be granted if left solely to the devices of copyright owners.[99] One additional and probably most important factor remains to be discussed: the difference between the minimum price a person would accept to sell something,

---

[96] There is a fairly extensive literature on the controversial question of whether managerial discretion exists and if so what impact it has and what should be done about it. I draw on it here only to make the most general point: that agency problems will often prevent value-maximizing choices from occurring.

[97] In an individual, a taste for risk or laziness might be a legitimate part of her personal utility curve, but a manager is supposed to maximize the utility of the corporation.

[98] *But see* Jennifer Arlen, Matthew Spitzer and Eric Talley, *Endowment Effects Within Corporate Agency Relationships*, 31 J. Legal Stud. 1 (2002) (Experimental evidence suggests that corporate agents may be *less* likely than ordinary persons to exhibit differences between willingness to pay and willingness to accept).

[99] Of course, such licenses might be granted; I offer here only an abstract analysis that would need to be empirically verified.

and the maximum amount that same person would pay if she wished to purchase the thing.[100]

The concept here basically refers to the fact that giving someone an entitlement makes that person richer, and this may change how the holder monetarily values both the entitlement and other resources, and this in turn may affect how entitlements are eventually allocated once bargaining between that person and other persons is completed.[101] Variations in buy and sell valuations do not retard resources from moving to hands where, given a particular entitlement starting-point, the resources have their highest monetary value. But the location of that highest value may depend crucially on starting point. Admittedly, these variations do not often make a difference; in instances where fungible commodities are sold in markets populated by many buyers and sellers, "buy" and "sell" valuations probably tend to converge. But, when the variations do have an impact, they have the potential of rendering the meaning of "highest-valued" use indeterminate in the sense that the location of the highest-valued use is not independent of the law. In such cases, everything can depend on the legal assignment of entitlements that form the transaction's starting point.

For example, you are unlikely to sell a privilege to inflict significant pain on yourself, no matter how much money another person offers for the privilege. Assuming you begin with such a right, you would not sell it to a sadist or a foe. By refusing to sell, you appear to be the highest-valued "user" of your body, and its continuance in a harm-free state seems to be the highest-valued "use" for your body as a resource. But consider what would happen if the entitlement were switched. If the law gave the sadist or foe liberty to inflict pain on you, he might refuse your monetary offers in preference to pursuing his pleasures. At that point the sadist or foe would appear to be the highest-valued user – and the highest-valued use of your body would appear to be serving as a pin-cushion.[102] The apparent location of "highest value" has switched.

When things like pain and bodily integrity are at stake, therefore, the notion of highest-valued use is dependent on legal starting points. It would be circular to

---

[100] I follow Mishan here. He used the term "welfare effects" to examine the allocative impact brought about by a change in wealth, including the change brought about by being given, or being denied, an entitlement. Mishan argued that one reason for this impact can be ability to pay. E.J. Mishan, *The Postwar Literature on Externalities: An Interpretive Essay*, 9 J. Econ. Literature 1 (1971) at 18–19.

[101] For an excellent numerical example, see *id.* at 18–21. It is well recognized that a divergence often exists between the price that a potential buyer would be willing to pay for a resource he does not own, and the price that the same person would demand before he would sell that same resource if the law had initially awarded its ownership to him. What is less clear is what terminology, explanations, and characterizations are best employed for discussing the phenomenon. For a valuable discussion, see Elizabeth Hoffman & Matthew Spitzer, *Willingness to Pay vs. Willingness to Accept: Legal and Economic Implications*, 71 Wash. U.L.Q. 59 (1993).

[102] See Mishan, *supra* note 100 at 18–19; Gordon, *Toward a Jurisprudence of Benefits*, *supra* note 77 at 1042–43; also see Alfred C. Yen, *Restoring the Natural Law: Copyright as Labor and Possession*, 51 Ohio St. L.J. 491, 518–519 (1990) ("flip-flop" of rights).

make the search for the highest-valued use the basis for assigning initial entitlements to such things. As Edwin Baker has pointed out, if we tried to assign a right in such things "to the party who would buy it from the other party if the party had the right", we could locate no such party. The answer is indeterminate: "neither party would buy because neither party would sell".[103]

Professor Coase showed that in a world without transaction costs, welfare effects or strategic behavior, resources will be traded to their highest-valued uses, so that, as between any two users of a resource, if A can use the resource more productively than B, A will end up with it.[104] Therefore, many scholars argue, in a real world full of transaction costs that can impede bargaining, it often makes sense to "mimic the market"[105] and assign legal rights to the highest-valued user in the first instance. This is a core insight of Law and Economics. Yet the Law and Economics argument largely depends on there being a stable highest-valued user. The injunction to "seek efficiency by mimicking the perfect market" only makes normative sense if the perfect market allocation is stable. If the allocation of rights significantly affects the monetary valuation that parties place on a resource, then there may be no stable economic reality for the law to seek to mimic.

There is at least one salient class of goods that lack this stability. These are the precious, personal, irreplaceable, crucial goods one thinks of as "priceless." Examples are many: the Dead Sea Scrolls; family heirlooms; one's children, health, reputation and peace of mind. The monetary value a person places on one of these goods may well depend on whether the person has a legal entitlement to it (whether she "owns" it) or whether she must purchase it.

Some of the change in monetary valuation may stem from differing psychological attitudes people have to things that are "theirs" versus things they have to purchase. Even with items as trivial as coffee mugs this endowment effect can be seen. (In experiments, college students were found to value mugs differently depending on whether the student's status was as an "owner" of the mug or as a "possible purchaser".[106]) But for many goods, like the coffee mugs, the effect is likely to be minor enough not to affect the identification of highest-valued use.[107]

---

[103] C. Edwin Baker, *The Ideology of the Economic Analysis of Law*, 5 Phil. & Public Aff. 3 at 12 (1975). This is perhaps the first legal article to discuss the relevance of such effects for the law.
[104] See Coase, *The Problem of Social Cost*, supra note 85.
[105] Assigning the legal right to the person who would purchase it saves society the costs of transfer, and ensures that the resource finds its way to the highest-valued user. However, there are many reasons to decline to mimic the market in this way. For example, a low-valuing user may nevertheless be morally entitled to payment for the resource, or incentive concerns may dictate giving the low-value user compensation for a resource he may hold.
[106] For further exploration, and for citation to relevant literature, see J.J. Rachlinsky & F. Jourden, *Remedies and the Psychology of Ownership*, 51 Vand. L. Rev. 1541 (1998) and Hoffman & Spitzer, *supra* note 101.
[107] See Coase, *Notes on the Problem of Social Cost*, supra note 85 at 157, 170–74.

The case is far different for things we think of as priceless. For them, adding to whatever endowment effect may exist, is the simple but immensely powerful constraint of a person's purchasing power, his or her ability to pay. For things of great value, ability to pay can interact with ownership status to yield obvious shifts in what appears to be the highest valued use.[108]

Consider health, for example. It is plausible that most people would be unwilling to sell their organs at any price, so that Jane Smith might turn down an offer of five million dollars from Billionaire X for one of her kidneys. Similarly, if Jane Smith has kidney failure and one of her dying relatives wills her a healthy kidney, she might well be unwilling to take the billionaire's five million dollars in exchange for her entitlement to it. If so, Jane Smith looks like the kidney's "highest-valued user." But should she have no entitlement to the kidney from the recently-deceased person (perhaps because the relevant jurisdiction does not recognize such bequests as enforceable), Jane Smith's own budget and health insurance will place a limit on how much she can spend pursuing the transplant. It is highly unlikely she will be able to outbid Billionaire X for the kidney. If so, Billionaire X will appear to be the "highest-valued user." One can draw from such a pattern no reliable information about whether the resource has its highest value in the hands of the billionaire or Jane Smith. This phenomenon might be called the "pricelessness effect."

The pricelessness effect is related to the phenomenon already mentioned: since assigning an entitlement to someone makes that person wealthier, it can affect the valuation the person puts on resources. For example, often "accept" and "offer" prices differ from each other. Many people hedge the Coase Theorem by noting it does not apply when significant effects of this kind are present. But usually such effects are so minor that they do not impair the reliability of using a market mimicry approach to model efficiency.[109]

The "pricelessness effect" deserves having its own name precisely because the subcategory of effects it denotes is likely to be significant. The "pricelessness effect" comes into play when the entitlement at issue pertains to a good that (1) an

---

[108] "[W]herever the welfare involved is substantial," Mishan points out, ability to pay may account for potent shifts in perceived value. "The maximum sum he will pay for something valuable is obviously related to, indeed limited by, a person's total resources, while the minimum sum he will accept for parting with it is subject to no such constraint." *See, e.g.,* Mishan, *supra* note 100, at 18–19.

[109] *See* Coase, *Notes on the Problem of Social Cost, supra* note 85 at 170–174 (discussing arguments re the presumed effect of changes in legal position on the distribution of wealth and on the allocation of resources).

Professor Coase argues that the impact of these effects can be overstated because, among other things, if the legal rules are known in advance, the prices of applicable resources will likely alter in a way that minimizes such effects; in addition, he suggests, contractual provision for contingencies may be available to mitigate some changes in legal rules. *See id.* at 157. *See also id.* at 170–174. Neither of these devices is likely to eliminate the effect – here called "pricelessness" – in the context of authorial suppression of embarrassing criticism, however.

individual or group values very highly and (2), which is virtually irreplaceable, and (3) when it is the allocation of that very good[110] which is at issue. As to such items, the initial placement of the entitlement is likely to have a sharp effect on the price and allocation of the resource, even in the absence of transaction costs.

In cases of parody or criticism – both areas where "fair use" treatment tends to be awarded to defendants – reputation may be at issue. To many, reputation is priceless in the sense we have been discussing. For example, a novelist who fears that a journalist will use extensive quotations from her book to bolster a hostile review will be most unlikely to sell the journalist a license to copy those quotations – regardless of the price offered. But that does not mean the author's preference is the "highest-valued use" in any meaningful sense, since that same author may be unable to buy silence if the law gives the journalist a "fair use" liberty right to publish. A similar analysis can be made of parody: since most people intensely dislike being ridiculed, the legal right may determine where the highest-valued use lies.[111] In such cases, the market is useless as a guide, and formal deference to owners' market powers is inappropriate.

For example, assume A is a novelist, a copyright owner who has an entitlement not to license and who is otherwise financially comfortable; she has perhaps $4,000 in the bank, a two-year old car and a prospect of steady royalties. She may be tempted by B's offer of, say, $10,000 for a license to use her work, but she can afford to say no without altering her lifestyle. If B's project is an ordinary commercial project and A will not be sacrificing more than $10,000 from foregoing alternative uses of the work, she will probably license. (It might also happen that B's project would not require an exclusive license and would not otherwise interfere with A's other licensing opportunities. If so, granting B permission to go forward would have no opportunity cost at all for A. She would be even more likely to license such a use.) However, if B's project is hostile toward A's work as a whole, A may well refuse the license, either to protect her long-term economic interest (which may be a mere pecuniary loss, remember), her aesthetic reputation, or her feelings.

If however the law gave novelist A no entitlement to prevent B's use, then she would have to persuade B not to publish (cf., "paying for silence," as in blackmail). The most A could offer B to persuade B not to make the critical use planned is the amount in her bank account, plus whatever she could sell her car for, plus whatever she could borrow on the strength of her expected royalty

---

[110] That is, while I predict that the law's assignment of rights in organs or free speech is likely to have a distinct effect on the allocation of kidneys or speech, it is a more complex question whether the law's assignment of rights in organs will have much of an effect on the allocation of *other* resources.

[111] These points are also explored in Gordon, *Toward a Jurisprudence of Benefits, supra* note 77 at 1042–43; also see *Fair Use as Market Failure, supra* note 2, at 1632–36 (anti-dissemination motives).

stream. The total may well be less than $10,000, and B will probably demand a price in excess of $10,000. Give A the entitlement and the highest-valued use of the contested expression is in her hands; give B the entitlement and the highest-valued use is in that licensee's hands. The locus of the "highest-valued use" has shifted as a result of where the law places its entitlement. In such cases, looking to the results of consensual transactions will not give us any information about who "should" have the right.

Another way to put the point is this:[112] Economics is sometimes used as a normative guide for good social policy. When it is used in this fashion, its primary claim to legitimacy stems from the links between economics and utilitarianism.[113] The more that income distribution restricts the expression of individuals' preferences, the shakier the link between economics and utility becomes. This linkage has the potential for completely breaking down in cases of "pricelessness." Though in such cases the parties' preferences may remain constant, both in their objects and in their intensity, a shift in who owns the entitlement may effectively disable one of those parties from effectuating that preference. Thus a legal regime that is committed (even in part) to utilitarian consequentialism would be unwise to rely upon a money-bound market model for normative guidance in cases of pricelessness.

In sum, refusing to allow a copyright owner to suppress a hostile use of the copyrighted work, in a case where the "pricelessness effect" is likely to make a determinative difference, does not necessarily contravene economic principles. In such an instance, it is appropriate for even an economically oriented court to refuse to defer to the copyright owner, and instead make an independent weighing of how enforcing the copyright in the given instance would affect welfare, and any other relevant consequentialist or nonconsequentialist policies.

Reconsidering the "substantial injury" hurdle to fair use

In *Fair Use as Market Failure,* I argued that fair use was and should be granted only if a three-part test were satisfied: that (1) defendant could not appropriately purchase the desired use through the market; (2) transferring control over the use to defendant would serve the public interest; and (3) the copyright owner's

---

[112] I am indebted here to Alan Feld.
[113] This belief is rather controversial. *See, e.g.,* such classic sources on the debate as the *Symposium on Efficiency as a Legal Concern,* 8 Hofstra L. Rev. 485 (1980) and Richard A. Posner, THE ECONOMICS OF JUSTICE 48–115 (Harvard University Press 1981) for further discussion of the question of whether utilitarianism and economics are truly linked in this way.

incentives would not be substantially impaired by allowing the user to proceed.[114] This current article is consistent with the first two prongs, but I would like to reconsider the third prong, the substantial injury hurdle, under which substantial injury to the plaintiff's incentives should ordinarily bar fair use.

As Neil Netanel has pointed out, the third prong of the test effectively forces all inquiries to be subordinated to the economic.[115] Yet there are instances where noneconomic values will be more important – a possibility for which the substantial injury hurdle leaves no scope. Since the whole point of singling out "justifications" is to help us see the occasions on which judges give fair use because economic value is not the proper metric, the excuse/justification distinction helped me understand that substantial injury to the plaintiff need not preclude fair use in all cases. In cases of "justification", we sometimes tolerate such injury in pursuit of other goals.

What happens to fair use when transaction costs decrease

In cases where fair use is premised on high transaction costs between owner and user, as arguably occurred in the *Williams and Wilkins* and perhaps even in the *Universal City Studios* cases,[116] the precedent is vulnerable to shifts in the institutional and transactional landscape: If changes occur that lower the transaction costs (whether through collecting societies, technological devices, or

---

[114] *Fair Use as Market Failure, supra* note 2.
[115] Netanel, *supra* note 6 at 330–331. (Thanks to Tom McNulty for this formulation of Netanel's point.)
[116] The following chart depicts the results in Williams & Wilkins Co. v. U.S., 203 Ct. Cl. 74 (1973), aff'd by an equally divided court, 420 U.S. 376 (1975) (per curiam) and Sony Corp. of America v. Universal City Studios, Inc., 463 U.S. 417 (1983):

	Potentially Justified	Potentially Excused	Defendant loses
No permission		W&W or SONY	
No compensation		W&W or SONY	
Behavior	W&W or SONY		

The next chart depicts *Williams & Wilkins* and *Universal Studios v Sony* as they could have been decided if the court had decided to "make a market" by imposing a monetary-only remedy:

	Potentially Justified	Potentially Excused	Defendant loses
No permission		W&W or SONY	
No compensation			W&W or SONY
Behavior	W&W or SONY		

otherwise), the increased ease in transacting should and does result in a lessened availability of the fair use defense.[117] This is appropriate, as I recognized in my original piece.[118] If fair use was granted because market conditions made it hard to consult the owner, but a market remained *desirable,* then there is every reason to return to relying on the market when owner and user are put in a position where they *can* consult. Relying on the market means fully enforcing the copyright.

In short, in many cases of "excuse" it will be possible for the facts to alter in a way that eliminates the desirability of fair use treatment. But the same is not true of cases of justification, for it is hard to see any factual change that could transform a decision governed by non-economic norms into something the market could adequately handle.[119]

Although market malfunctions can be curable, it is important to avoid exaggerating the extent to which even "excuse" cases will disappear. Consider the promise that the Internet and collecting societies may offer for lowering transaction costs. Much argument has centered on whether transaction costs will in fact grow low enough to allow markets to form between copyright owners and at-home occasional users, and what the impact will be on fair use.[120] But for all the debate, it

---

[117] See, e.g., three cases in which the availability of potential licensing helped persuade the courts against fair use: American Geophysical Union v. Texaco, 60 F.3d 913, 923 (2d Cir. 1994); Princeton University Press v. Michigan Document Services, Inc., 99 F 3d 1381 (6th Cir. 1996); Encyclopaedia Britannica Educational Corp. v. Crooks, 542 F.Supp. 1156, 1173–78 (W.D.N.Y. 1982). A graph for them would look as follows:

Texaco and *Princeton Documents* and *Britannica*:

	Potentially Justified	Potentially Excused	Defendant loses
No permission			x
No compensation		x	
Behavior	x		

The *Britannica* case is discussed in *Fair Use as Market Failure,* supra note 2 at 1629. For commentaries on how cases like *Texaco* may affect my *Market Failure* analysis, see, e.g., Edmund W Kitch, *Can the Internet Shrink Fair Use?,* 78 Neb.L.Rev. 880 (1999); Tom W. Bell, *Fair Use vs. Fared Use: The Impact of Automated Rights Management on Copyright's Fair Use Doctrine,* 76 N.C. L. Rev. 557 (1998); Loren, *Redefining The Market Failure Approach To Fair Use In An Era Of Copyright Permission Systems, supra* note 2; Merges, *The End of Friction?, supra* note 2.

[118] *Fair Use as Market Failure, supra* note 2, at 1629 & note 159 and 1645–57.

[119] See Michael Walzer, SPHERES OF JUSTICE: A DEFENSE OF PLURALISM AND EQUALITY (Basic Books 1983). He argues that to maintain some equality, it is necessary that some goods (e.g., political office) remain unavailable for purchase by money. By contrast, the instant article stresses *relations* rather than *things.*

As Margaret Jane Radin has pointed out, see *Justice and the Market Domain, supra* note 40, most of our life involves a mix of market and nonmarket relations, even in connection with the same objects.

[120] See, e.g., Bell, *supra* note 117; Edmund W. Kitch, *Can the Internet Shrink Fair Use?,* 78 Neb. L. Rev. 880 (1999); Loren, *supra* note 2.

185

must be stressed most cases of fair use are premised on factors *other than* transaction-cost barriers that keep copyright owner and potential licensee apart, and some of these other factors can be relevant to home copying. For example, a judicial and legislative unwillingness to impose copyright liability on individual at-home users has other, converging explanations, such as the desire to preserve privacy[121] and maintain a feeling of community.[122] These concerns will not disappear in the face of a reduction in transaction costs. Thus, many cases of excuse contain facts that are inextricably intertwined with non-economic normative judgments.

The latter point can be seen by considering the "external benefit" generated by a historian, critic or scholar who reproduces someone's words or images. In analyzing the case, we can move back and forth between the market and non-market normative realms. Let us focus on a scholar like the defendant in *Time v. Geis* who needs to copy some copyrighted text or image to convey his point. One way to look at the scholar's quandary is through the lens of justification: that he is furthering public debate in a way that is not monetizable. However, one could also see his position through the lens of excuse – that even if the benefits the scholar generates are capable of being put into monetary terms, the scholar's pocketbook is unlikely to reflect much of that benefit. Those benefits will remain *external* to him, so he will be unlikely to offer a license fee high enough to reflect the social benefit at issue. Conceivably the scholar's book could earn a million-dollar advance, which would "cure" the externality problem. But in reality, scholarly books rarely ever internalize much of the social benefit they generate, so that this kind of fair use is likely to be durable despite factual changes. The benefit given to the public by the historian, critic or scholar is unlikely ever to be reflected in his or her pocket.[123] And even if the historian, critic or scholar who quotes from a copyrighted work *did* capture a significant amount of the benefit she generates, a normative economist might still suggest exempting her from having to obtain permission from her target: Judge Posner has suggested that, "The social product is diminished if persons are able to exact compensation from truthful critics of their failings, for such a right reduces the incentive to produce truth."[124] One

---

[121] *See*, e.g., Jessica Litman, *Reforming Information Law In Copyright's Image*, 22 Dayton L.Rev. 587 (1997) (discussing privacy concerns).

[122] Maintaining gift relationships can be particularly important to maintaining *artistic* community and vibrancy. *See* Lewis Hyde, THE GIFT: IMAGINATION AND THE EROTIC LIFE OF PROPERTY 47, 272–82 (Vintage Books 1983).

[123] *See Fair Use as Market Failure, supra* note 2 at 1607, 1630–31 ("In cases of externalities, then, the potential user may wish to produce socially meritorious new works by using some of the copyright owner's material, yet be unable to purchase permission because the market structure prevents him from being able to capitalize on the benefits to be realized." *Id.* at 1631). *Also see* Loren, *supra* note 2.

[124] Richard A. Posner, *When Is Parody Fair Use,* 21 J. Legal Stud. 67 at 74 (1992). In the quoted passage, Judge Posner seems to be mixing norms. He seems to view truth as something whose value is absolute, rather than as something whose value is dependent on market preferences, but then he seems to use a purely economic model for its production. This is intriguing. Real-world

might add that the availability of receiving compensation from critics could also decrease the ordinary disincentives to produce flawed work.

For all these reasons, even market malfunction is not always curable. Many externalities will be unaffected by technological and institutional change. Further, many "excuse" cases are intertwined with issues of justification.

A possible danger of my approach

In copyright law, judges have developed a complex, largely unarticulated network of defenses under the rubric of "fair use."[125] This article suggests that, paralleling the common law distinction, some fair use cases involve "excuse" and some involve "justification". Because changes in circumstances are relevant to "excuse" in a way they are not to "justification", the distinction between the categories is particularly important for areas of law like copyright that involve rapid technological and institutional change. Some recent confusion may result from conflating cases of excuse and justification together.[126]

My analysis is not impaired by the fact that courts do not explicitly distinguish between justified and excused fair uses. What the common law judges accomplished over several centuries, copyright judges have had to develop over a much shorter time. It is no wonder that the separately delineated defenses of the common law are collapsed together in the copyright area, where the time to elaborate and distinguish the defenses has been so condensed.

The main problem with the analysis that I offer is that it leaves a myriad of decision points open for judges to resolve. Look at all the decisions that are open, and must be made by someone:

---

cont.
    policymakers do indeed regularly choose "goods" by means of nonmarket criteria, and then turn to pragmatic tools, including the economic, in order to secure the production of the good.
    Possibly Judge Posner is responding to the fact that "perfect information" (truth) is one of the pre-conditions for a perfect market. James Boyle has suggested that markets for information cannot be well addressed through a neoclassical lens since that lens presupposes an abundant supply of information whose scarcity is in fact something that needs to be remedied. James Boyle, SHAMANS, SOFTWARE, AND SPLEENS: LAW AND THE CONSTRUCTION OF THE INFORMATION SOCIETY (Harvard University Press 1996). While I do not share Boyle's pessimism about the uselessness of economics here – after all, no system can be validated by terms entirely within itself – he is right to emphasize that for a market, information has the dual role of precondition and product.

[125] In copyright law, a defendant is liable if her work is "substantially similar" to, and copied from, the plaintiff's copyrighted work. A finding that "substantial similarity" is lacking constitutes another place where doctrine hides a complex network of defenses and limitations.

[126] Thus, persons who believe that a decrease in transaction costs can eliminate fair use treatment may be seeing everything in terms of a narrowly-defined "excuse" type market malfunction, and ignoring the possibilities of justified fair use.

Someone (probably a judge, but "fair use" is usually considered a mixed question of law and fact) has to decide whether a defendant's use implicates only monetary values. Even if it is decided that the use implements solely monetary values, the Someone then has to decide whether or not the market can implement those values. If it is decided that the market suffices to achieve value maximization, then the plaintiff's right is enforced. If market norms are applicable but the particular market cannot be relied on, then the Someone has to decide whether the defendant's behavior is socially desirable on an economic metric, and, employing the same metric, whether it is appropriate that the plaintiff's consent was not sought and whether the defendant should pay compensation.

Conversely, the Someone may decide that the defendant's use does not implicate only monetary values. If so, then that Someone needs to address the values that are involved, and do so in relation to the three questions of behavior, permission and compensation.

The analysis makes clear – perhaps too clear – how many normative decisions the law of "fair use" requires. But the current doctrinal formulations for fair use involve no fewer normative choices – the choices are merely better hidden.

I do not think that requiring explicit normative choice means leading judges into a realm of pure judicial legislation. Rather, it leads them into a field of subtle cues that a judge can employ to navigate.[127] Nevertheless, it can be objected that such openness leaves the law too vulnerable to particular judges' idiosyncrasies. I know of no better preventative than to try to classify and define the choices involved, and the taxonomy of this article is intended as a contribution to that end.

Lawyers have known, at least since the Legal Realists and probably since law began, that the neutrality of the law is only partial, and that normative choice influences virtually all hard decisions. Is it more useful to explicitly name and organize those value choices, or is it better to promote law's perceived legitimacy by hiding them? That is, alas, an open question of its own. I suggest that much good can come from exposing the pluralism of our norms, even if that means the populace then loses its illusion that the law operates like a machine. Any narrower inquiry could impose great harm on nonmarket values, particularly free speech, and that would impose an even greater cost.

Post Script: thoughts on the issue of full fair use versus compensation

When a judge faces a fair use inquiry, she knows after *Acuff-Rose*[128] that she has

---

[127] See, e.g., Charles Fried, *Scholars and Judges: Reason and Power*, 23 Harv. J.L. & Pub. Pol'y 807 at 810–11 (2000).

[128] See note 33 and accompanying text, *supra*.

several options in regard to remedy. She can refuse an injunction (because she finds the defendant's use socially desirable and finds the neglect of the owner's veto power excusable or justifiable), but she is nevertheless free to give the plaintiff a reasonable royalty or other compensation. This is equivalent to the judge "making a market": the judge can decrease transaction costs by creating new points of contact between the parties. It can also be seen as a judicially imposed compulsory license.

Traditionally, judges in fair use cases faced a binary choice: either find fair use and give the plaintiff no remedy at all, or find infringement and give the plaintiff both injunctive and monetary relief. Now that their discretion is explicitly enlarged, should judges in fair use cases routinely give compensation to the plaintiff? Should they ever do so? A "compensation-only" or "liability rule" approach has the virtue of apparent compromise: it appears to encourage dissemination and discourse, while simultaneously preserving incentives.

The liability-rule approach is so attractive, that we may ask whether all copyright cases should be open to this route. In doing so, we must be wary of a likely corollary: if injunctions disappear in favor of monetary rewards, the scope of copyright is likely to expand. Congress has already been remarkably generous to the "copyright industries" (entertainment, media, and so on) at the expense of the public domain.[129] The demise of injunctions would let industry lobbyists more easily argue in favor of even greater copyright extensions. If so, much that is currently free will come to bear a price tag. Is this bad?

Of the many lessons the commodification literature has to teach copyright lawyers and theorists, let me single out two strands relevant to this issue. First, Titmuss in his classic and controversial work, *The Gift Relationship*,[130] suggested that for some products, *quality degrades* when they are commodified. His focus was on the market for human blood.

His research suggested that switching from a donor system to a sale system degraded the quality of the blood available for transfusions. People who sell blood are both likely to have questionable health histories (drug use corresponds with poverty) and a reason to lie about that health history. By contrast, people who donate blood are more likely to be healthy, and have fewer motives to lie.

Second, Titmuss and others have shown that over-commodification can have deleterious *systemic effects*. Thus, if a large proportion of blood begins to come from monetary purchase, the sheen of donative merit that now attaches to voluntary blood donation may diminish. Anything having to do with transfers of blood may begin to acquire an unsavory reputation, and voluntary donations may slow.

---

[129] *See* Jessica D. Litman, *Copyright, Compromise, and Legislative History*, 72 Cornell L. Rev. 857, 870–79 (1987); Pamela Samuelson, *The Copyright Grab*, 4.01 Wired 135 (1996)

[130] Richard M. Titmuss, THE GIFT RELATIONSHIP: FROM HUMAN BLOOD TO SOCIAL POLICY (Random House 1972). Whether or not Titmuss was correct as an empirical matter, the question of product quality is well raised by him.

For a more dramatic example of deleterious systemic effect, consider the following, drawn in part from a hefty science-fiction literature on commodification. If human organs could be freely bought and sold, persons might imperil their health in the efforts to help their families economically; people might make irreversible choices they come to regret because they may be unable to predict the way their preferences might be affected by selling parts of themselves; murders might increase as organ-nappers went into the chop-shop business. Even the state might increase the scope of crimes deemed worthy of capital punishment.[131]

Given the great attraction that the "no injunction/money only" remedy holds for copyright, we should consider some of its dangers. What kind of quality degradation or deleterious systemic effects could eventuate if liability-rule judgments of "compensation only" drastically increased? Let us look at an extreme: assume that fair use as free use disappears, that copyright expands, and that most of the public's current rights to "copy and to use"[132] have become conditional on payment.

Theresa Amabile and other social psychologists have determined that in some contexts, external motivation in the form of rewards can decrease the quality of creative work. Emphasizing monetary relief could conceivably have this effect. Injunctive relief is a "natural" outgrowth of an author's creating a work; with creation comes an instinct for control. If instead an author could only expect money, her perception of her task – and the quality of what she produces – could degrade.[133]

What of systemic effects? Imagine that technology increased to such an extent that all uses we made of each other's works would automatically trigger a change in our bank balances, and that copyright law had evolved to require payment on all such occasions. If I quote you – even a quote that would have been fair use to a prior generation – a nickel or a dollar flows from my account to yours. If I quote from a book written long ago – even a book that would have been in the public domain had there been no series of laws extending the copyright term – a nickel or

---

[131] In the future society of one science fiction story, a series of traffic violations was enough cause to sentence the violator to death, making his body available to the governmental organ banks. Larry Niven, *The Jigsaw Man* in DANGEROUS VISIONS 218–229 (Harlan Ellison ed., Berkley Books 1983). Consider also the recent revelations concerning China's use of executed prisoners. Craig G. Smith, *On Death Row, China's Source of Transplants*, N. Y. TIMES (October 18, 2001). (Thanks to David Koh for bringing this material to my attention).

[132] The phrase is Justice O'Connor's. Bonito Boats, Inc. v. Thunder Craft Boats, Inc., 489 U.S. 141, 165 (1989).

[133] Admittedly, the experiments of Amabile and her colleague are too limited to allow firm conclusions, particularly regarding adult artists. Teresa M. Amabile, Mary Ann Collins, Regina Conti, Elise Phillips, CREATIVITY IN CONTEXT: UPDATE TO THE SOCIAL PSYCHOLOGY OF CREATIVITY (Westview Press 1996) at 171–177. Further, my argument applies to works that are owned by their creators. For the large numbers of works written in work for hire contexts, monetization has to some extent already occurred.

Nevertheless, it is clear that a right to *control* can have effects different from a right to be *paid*, even outside the realm of creativity. See Rachlinsky and Jourden, *supra* note 106.

dollar flows from my account to the account of the authors' heirs. This is quite different from what happens today. But if in fact I have experienced monetary benefit in the amount of that nickel or dollar, would it not be safe to make me pay? After all, in such a case requiring payment will not impose a net harm. Yet even if the recipient is ordered to pay only a portion of the monetary benefit he or she has earned, some danger remains.

My space here is obviously too short to explore all the difficulties that might result with a regime where we pay for all the monetary benefits we receive from others. One salient danger is that a requirement of ubiquitous payment may erode everyone's sense of indebtedness to the community. In the literature on what motivates political morality,[134] the perception of reciprocity is key.[135] One reason we pay taxes without a policeman breathing down our shirts is that we see benefits the government gives us, and gives to others who in turn may benefit us. Our legal system would fall apart if we only paid taxes, and obeyed other laws, when a policeman looks over our shoulder. A pervasive system where we pay for each bit of what we use could give us the illusion that we are not net recipients. (I say "illusion", for only the labor and insights of generations has protected us from lives nasty, brutish and short. There is no way we can pay *everyone* we owe.) From this illusion that we have paid for everything we have, could come an unwillingness to give back to the community and an unwillingness to obey its laws.

Conclusion

In this essay, I have emphasized that sometimes our social goals aim at something other than "the maximization of value as measured by willingness to pay". On such occasions where the market shows its inherent limitations, it may be justifiable for a copyist not to ask permission from a copyright owner. It may still happen that a judge decides that the copyist should be considered an infringer, but the decision will be based on something other than a mere failure to obtain the copyright owner's consent.

I have also suggested that sometimes our social goals do indeed aim at "the maximization of economic value as measured by willingness to pay." On those occasions, the market is a presumptively useful way to proceed. However, sometimes the market cannot be relied upon to direct a resource to its highest-valued use because the conditions for perfect competition are absent. When a real-

---

[134] The phrase is Goodin's. *Robert E. Goodin*, MOTIVATING POLITICAL MORALITY (Blackwell Publishers 1992).
[135] Dan M. Kahan, *Trust, Collective Action, And Law*, in Symposium on Trust Relationships Part 1 of 2, 81 B.U. L.Rev. 333 (2001)

world market fails in this way to attain the conditions of a perfect market, we have market malfunction. In such cases, a copyist may be excused for not having sought a copyright owner's permission. It may still happen that a judge will decide that the copyist should be considered an infringer, but the decision should, again, be based on something more than a mere failure to obtain the copyright owner's consent.

Loosely, one can associate market malfunctions such as high transaction costs with "excuse", and inherent market limitations – where other, non-market norms should govern – with notions of "justification". "Excuse" fits those cases where economics appropriately governs, for there we would prefer the defendant to ask permission and pay if only circumstances did not make it inadvisable. By contrast, when alternative norms govern ("market limitation"), we may affirmatively want the defendant *not* to ask permission or *not* to pay. In such cases, failure of payment or permission is something we may want emulated, and if so, it is "justified".

In cases of both excuse and justification, it may be advisable to order compensation even if an injunction is denied. However, I have suggested one of several possible dangers in this tempting approach: That with the demise of the injunction we are likely to see an expansion in the scope of copyright, and as a result we may drift into a cash-and-carry mode of social interaction that could be destructive of creativity, community and respect for law.

How Much Solicitude for Fair Use is There in the Anti-Circumvention Provision of the Digital Millennium Copyright Act?

*David Nimmer**

In late 1998, the United States Congress enacted its most sweeping revisions ever to the Copyright Act of 1976.[1] Under the title Digital Millennium Copyright Act,[2] this amendment institutes radical changes, comprising a spectrum ranging from protecting boat hulls with *sui generis* rights to mandating respect for copyright management information. The most important feature of the Digital Millennium Copyright Act institutes anti-circumvention provisions into U.S. copyright law. The details of the resulting Section 1201 that it adds to the Copyright Act are fiendishly complicated. Even without canvassing all of the nuances, however, a philosophical issue emerges – how does this amendment affect one of the cynosures of copyright law, its fair use doctrine? This essay takes a few steps into that terrain.

I. The Digital Millennium Copyright Act

The millennial hope underlying the Digital Millennium Copyright Act is to bring U.S. copyright law "squarely into the digital age."[3] As part of the ceaseless

---

* © 2001 by David Nimmer. An expanded form of this article appeared in (2000) 148 U Pa L Rev 673.
[1] See D. Nimmer, "Puzzles of the Digital Millennium Copyright Act" (1999) 46 J Copyright Soc'y USA 401, 402.
[2] Pub L No 105-304, 112 Stat. 2860, 1 (short title).
[3] Report of the Senate Comm. on the Judiciary, S Rep No 105–190, at 2 (1998) [hereinafter S Rep (DMCA)].

N. Elkin-Koren and N.W. Netanel (eds.), *The Commodification of Information*, 193–221.
© 2002 David Nimmer. Printed in Great Britain.

struggle to keep up with constantly evolving technology,[4] this law proposes to "make digital networks safe places to disseminate and exploit copyrighted materials." The primary battleground in which the Digital Millennium Copyright Act achieved this goal is its first title, the WIPO Copyright and Performances and Phonograms Treaties Implementation Act of 1998 (the "WIPO Treaties Act").[5] This first title of the omnibus enactment brought U.S. copyright law into compliance with two treaties drafted at a Diplomatic Conference held in December 1996.[6] Foremost among its features is the new Section 1201 that the WIPO Treaties Act added to the Copyright Act of 1976.[7]

A. BACKGROUND – REGULATION OF DEVICES AND SERVICES

One of the most salient features of the Digital Millennium Copyright Act is that it serves several masters. In order to understand the thrust of the law, it is essential to appreciate Congress' concern with balancing the interests of copyright proprietors, on the one hand, against the interests of the community of users, scholars, equipment manufacturers, and on-line service providers, on the other.

During its deliberations through sequential referral to diverse congressional committees,[8] the bill for the Digital Millennium Copyright Act progressed from one designed solely to protect copyright interests into a more broad-based redress of various aspects relating to digital commerce.[9]

Historically, Congress has achieved the objectives of the Constitution's Copyright Clause "by regulating the use of information – not the devices or

---

[4] See id. at 2 ("Copyright laws have struggled through the years to keep pace with emerging technology from the struggle over music played on a player piano roll in the 1900's to the introduction of the VCR in the 1980's." (citations omitted)).

[5] Pub L No 105–304, 101, 112 Stat 2860, 2861 (1998) (short title).

[6] For this observer's perspective as a participant at that Conference, see the WIPO Treaty Triptych: D. Nimmer, "A Tale of Two Treaties" (1997) 22 Colum-VLA JL & Arts 1; D. Nimmer, "Aus der Neuen Welt" 93 Nw U L Rev 195,196–97 (1998); and D. Nimmer, "Time and Space" (1998) 38 IDEA 501.

[7] 17 USC § 1201.

[8] Even when reported out of the House Judiciary Committee, the bill was presented as a product of broadly supported compromises. See Report of the House Comm. on Commerce (1998) HR Rep No. 105–551, pt. 2, at 22 [hereinafter Commerce Rep (DMCA)]. Nonetheless, further hearings revealed that the bill "faced significant opposition from many private and public sector interests, including libraries, institutions of higher learning, consumer electronics and computer product manufacturers, and others with a vital stake in the growth of electronic commerce and the Internet." Id.

[9] The House Commerce Committee concluded that its revision to the bill previously reported on by the House and Senate Judiciary Committees "has appropriately balanced the interests of content owners, on-line and other service providers, and information users in a way that will foster the continued development of electronic commerce and the growth of the Internet." Id. at 21.

means by which the information is delivered or used by information consumers – and by ensuring an appropriate balance between the interests of copyright owners and information users."[10] The various provisions of the Copyright Act, on the one hand creating rights for proprietors but on the other hand delineating the scope of those rights, have as a unifying theme the fact that they are all "technology neutral."[11] That is to say, those laws do not regulate commerce in information technology, i.e., products and devices for transmitting, storing, and using information. Instead, they prohibit certain actions and create exceptions to permit certain conduct deemed to be in the greater public interest, all in a way that balances the interests of copyright owners and users of copyrighted works.[12]

New threats, however, sometimes necessitate new approaches. The Commerce Committee therefore concluded its examination by recognizing that the digital environment poses a unique threat to the rights of copyright owners, and as such, necessitates protection against devices that undermine copyright interests. In contrast to the analog experience, digital technology enables pirates to reproduce and distribute perfect copies of works – at virtually no cost at all to the pirate. As technology advances, so must our laws.[13]

The committee, therefore, incorporated anti-circumvention strictures into the WIPO Treaties Act. Those strictures target not only bad acts (the activity of copying itself), but also bad machines (devices that facilitate copying) and bad services (conduct that enables copying). In this manner, copyright law expands its reach.

B. SECTION 1201'S ANTI-CIRCUMVENTION BANS

Section 1201 separately defines three separate species of anti-circumvention violations – a basic provision, a ban on trafficking, and "additional violations." The core is the "basic provision" that provides: "No person shall circumvent a technological measure that effectively controls access to a work protected under this title."[14] The statute conditions this provision in numerous particulars, which form the bulk of the fair use discussion below.

Turning to the statutory text, the "ban on trafficking" provides as follows:

> No person shall manufacture, import, offer to the public, provide, or otherwise traffic in any technology, product, service, device, component, or part thereof, that

---

[10] Id. at 24.
[11] Commerce Rep (DMCA) at 24.
[12] Id. at 24.
[13] Id. at 25.
[14] 17 USC §§ 1201(a)(1)(A).

(A) is primarily designed or produced for the purpose of circumventing a technological measure that effectively controls access to a work protected under this title;

(B) has only limited commercially significant purpose or use other than to circumvent a technological measure that effectively controls access to a work protected under this title; or

(C) is marketed by that person or another acting in concert with that person with that person's knowledge for use in circumventing a technological measure that effectively controls access to a work protected under this title.[15]

In addition, the statute sets forth "additional violations" in provisions that are almost identically worded. Given that the statutory terminology used for the foregoing two provisions differs only subtly – and given that the face of the statute itself reveals no clue as to which variant is aimed against what type of infraction – one reverts to the legislative history to gain an idea of Congress' intent in adopting the language of the statute.

1. Breaking and entering

The basic provision and the ban on trafficking appear together in the same paragraph of the statute.[16] Essentially, they govern something equivalent to breaking into a castle – the invasion inside another's property is itself the offense.[17] Note that the gravamen here is not copyright infringement.[18]

---

[15] 17 USC § 1201(a)(2).

[16] See 17 USC § 1201(a).

[17] "Paragraph (a)(1) establishes a general prohibition against gaining unauthorized access to a work by circumventing a technological protection measure put in place by the copyright owner where such protection measure otherwise effectively controls access to a work protected under Title 17 of the U.S. Code." HR Rep No. 105-551, pt. 1, at 17–18 (1998) [hereinafter H Rep (DMCA)].

[18] As Congress itself recognized, "these ... provisions have little, if anything, to do with copyright law." Commerce Rep (DMCA) at 24. Instead, as 62 copyright law professors stated in a letter to Congress, they "represent an unprecedented departure into the zone of what might be called 'paracopyright.'" Id. at 24–25.

Although quoting the professors" terminology, Congress rejected the substance of their recommendation. See id. at 25. Turning to the substance of the professors" claim regarding "an unprecedented departure," those professors are undoubtedly correct in asserting that this zone represents a departure from traditional copyright interest. See D. Nimmer, "Aus der Neuen Welt" (1998) 93 Nw U L Rev 195, 204 ("[This feature] more closely resembles historic protection under the telecommunications law, or even more pointedly, the "Jesse James Act" forbidding armed postal robbery, than it does the balance of Title 17." (footnote omitted)). As to its being unprecedented, however, consideration of similarly extraneous amendments to the Copyright Act in 1984, 1992, and 1994 "shows that this departure is actually only too precedented." 3 *Nimmer on Copyright* § 12A.17[B] n.14 (referencing Semiconductor Chip Protection Act of 1984, Audio Home Recording Act of 1992, and Uruguay Round Agreements Act).

What of the trafficking ban? It targets not those who break into another's domain, but instead those who facilitate the process – say, those who market siege engines or catapults, devise ingenious infiltration strategies, and generally facilitate penetration of the stronghold.[19] This supplementary prohibition provides "meaningful protection and enforcement of the copyright owner's right to control access to his or her copyrighted work."[20] Building on previous doctrines of law outside the copyright arena (such as those barring manufacture of equipment to receive unauthorized cable television service and decrypting cable programming), the trafficking ban targets "'black boxes' that are expressly intended to facilitate circumvention of technological protection measures for purposes of gaining access to a work."[21]

2. Disorderly conduct

In contrast to invading the sanctity of another's castle (the basic provision), if a guest invited inside the manor contravenes the seigneur's edicts, then the trespass at hand differs qualitatively from breaking and entering.[22] Thus, the basic provision is inapplicable to "the subsequent actions of a person once he or she has obtained authorized access to a copy of a work protected under Title 17, even if such actions involve circumvention of additional forms of technological protection measures."[23] Instead, the statute's "additional violations" come into play here. They ban "circumventing protection afforded by a technological measure that effectively protects a right of a copyright owner."[24]

3. Distinctions between those schemes

Care must be taken to distinguish the ban on trafficking from the similarly worded additional violations.[25] According to the legislative history, "the two sections are not interchangeable, and many devices will be subject to challenge only under one of the subsections."[26]

The additional violations appear in their own statutory paragraph,[27] separate from the preceding paragraph of Section 1201 that contains both the basic

---

[19] 17 USC § 1201(a)(1).
[20] H Rep (DMCA) at 18; Commerce Rep (DMCA) at 38.
[21] Commerce Rep (DMCA) at 38.
[22] See id. at 19.
[23] H Rep (DMCA) at 18; see also S Rep (DMCA) at 28.
[24] 17 USC § 1201(b)(1)(C).
[25] See S Rep (DMCA) at 29.
[26] Id. at 12.
[27] See 17 USC § 1201(b).

provision and the ban on trafficking. The paragraph setting forth the additional violations contains nothing comparable to the basic provision. Accordingly, there is a marked contrast between the two schemes. As to prohibited access, the person engaging in that conduct has violated the basic provision; anyone assisting him or her through publicly offering services, products, devices, etc., to achieve the prohibited technological breach is separately culpable under the ban on trafficking. By contrast, a person who engages in prohibited usage of a work to which he or she has lawful access does not fall afoul of any provision of Section 1201. It is only someone who assists him or her through publicly offering services, products, devices, etc., to achieve the prohibited technological breach who becomes culpable under the additional violations. A chart sets forth the taxonomy.

The upper half of this table represents the two features found in the first paragraph of Section 1201. The basic provision sets forth a substantive offense, and the trafficking ban ensnares those who assist in violating the basic provision. The bottom half of the table represents the second paragraph of Section 1201. In this context, Section 1201 itself sets forth no basic ban; instead, that is the province of traditional copyright law. (For that reason, the lower left quadrant of the table remains blank.) However, the additional violations of Section 1201 hold liable those who aid that underlying conduct by helping to circumvent technological measures.

Why is it that Section 1201 is drafted, as the table illustrates, to set forth both an underlying basic provision and a complementary trafficking ban without any

Basic Provision No person shall circumvent a technological measure that effectively controls access to a work protected by [United States copyright.]	**Trafficking Ban** No person shall manufacture, import, offer to the public, provide, or otherwise traffic in any technology, product, service, device, component, or part thereof, that isprimarily designed or produced for the purpose of circumventing a technological measure that *effectively controls access to a work protected* under [United States copyright.]
	Additional Violations No person shall manufacture, import, offer to the public, provide, or otherwise traffic in any technology, product, service, device, component, or part thereof, that is primarily designed or produced for the purpose of circumventing a technological measure that *protects a right of a copyright owner under* [United States copyright] in a work or a portion thereof.

comparable underlying provision corresponding to its additional violations? The legislative history explains the rationale at work here:

> The reason there is no prohibition on conduct [as part of the additional violations] akin to the prohibition on circumvention conduct in [the basic provision is that the basic provision itself] is necessary because prior to this Act, the conduct of circumvention was never before made unlawful. The device limitation in [the ban on trafficking] enforces this new prohibition on conduct. The copyright law has long forbidden copyright infringements, so no new prohibition was necessary. The device limitation in [the additional violations] enforces the longstanding prohibitions on infringements.[28]

C. USER EXEMPTION

1. Theory

The vast bulk of Section 1201 comprises its numerous exemptions. For current purposes, the focus is on the user exemptions.

In adopting the WIPO Treaties Act, Congress evinced great solicitude for the role played by judicious application of the fair use doctrine.[29] That concern finds practical implementation in the instant domain through a "fail-safe" mechanism.[30]

To appreciate this mechanism, consider first how one can wax rhetorical about the great gains afforded by wide-scale access to copyrighted materials allowed by the Internet.[31]

> A plethora of information, most of it embodied in materials subject to copyright protection, is available to individuals, often for free, that just a few

---

[28] S Rep (DMCA) at 12. Given the stark contrast in how the two paragraphs are drafted, it would be improper for a court to construe § 1201 to bar the unenumerated behavior of one who engages solely in prohibited usage of a work to which he has lawful access. That is the function, instead, of traditional copyright law. To the extent that that individual capitalizes on his success, however, by offering comparable services to the public, at that point he incurs liability under 1201's additional violations. See 17 USC § 1201(b).

[29] The House Commerce Committee discussed this issue at length. See Commerce Rep (DMCA) at 25–26, 37–38, 85–87.

[30] See id. at 36 ("Given the threat of a diminution of otherwise lawful access to works and information ... a "fail-safe" mechanism is required."). The discussion below queries whether, as implemented, the mechanism truly qualifies for that billing.

[31] The growth and development of the Internet has already had a significant positive impact on the access of American students, researchers, consumers, and the public at large to informational resources that help them in their efforts to learn, acquire new skills, broaden their perspectives, entertain themselves, and become more active and informed citizens.
Commerce Rep (DMCA) at 35.

years ago could have been located and acquired only through the expenditure of considerable time, resources, and money. New examples of this greatly expanded availability of copyrighted materials occur every day.[32]

An undertow looms, however, when one reflects that the tide can as easily fall as rise. Future marketplace realities could "dictate a different outcome, resulting in less access, rather than more, to copyrighted materials that are important to education, scholarship, and other socially vital endeavors."[33] Such waning of the public's access to important works could stem from evanescence of hard copies in a world of pan-electronic access, from embedding into those electronic files encryption devices (that might remain active long after copyright protection has ceased), from new business models that call for "restricting distribution and availability, rather than upon maximizing it," or from factors not yet in evidence on the horizon.[34] Regardless of their provenance, the possibility of those scenarios calls forth the need to temper the categorical reach of the basic provision. As stated by the legislative history, it is "appropriate to modify the flat prohibition against the circumvention of effective technological measures that control access to copyrighted materials, in order to ensure that access for lawful purposes is not unjustifiably diminished."[35]

Toward that end, Congress devised an exemption for users.[36] In brief, this mechanism serves to "monitor developments in the marketplace for copyrighted materials, and allow the enforceability of the prohibition against the act of circumvention to be selectively waived, for limited time periods, if necessary to prevent a diminution in the availability to individual users of a particular category of copyrighted materials."[37] Implementation here depends on rulemaking undertaken pursuant to the Administrative Procedure Act.[38]

---

[32] Id. at 35–36.
[33] Id. at 36.
[34] Id.
[35] Id.
[36] As reported by the Judiciary Committee, the basic provision would have been absolute, with no solicitude for fair use. The Commerce Committee, however, approved an amended bill that "creates a rulemaking proceeding in which the issue of whether enforcement of the regulation should be temporarily waived with regard to particular categories of works can be fully considered and fairly decided on the basis of real marketplace developments that may diminish otherwise lawful access to works." Id. The latter approach carried the day.
[37] Commerce Rep (DMCA) at 36.
[38] See id. at 37.

2. Application

Having enunciated the basic provision,[39] Section 1201 continues to specify that the ban does "not apply to persons who are users of a copyrighted work which is in a particular class of works."[40] The statute itself does not give direct content to its enigmatic reference to "a particular class of works." But it does shed some light on that term insofar as it limits the foregoing release from the basic provision to the extent that "such persons are ... adversely affected by virtue of such prohibition in their ability to make noninfringing uses of that particular class of works under" U.S. copyright law.[41]

It would seem, therefore, that the language should be applied to discrete subgroups. If users of physics textbooks or listeners to Baroque concerti, for example, find themselves constricted in the new Internet environment, then some relief will lie. If, on the other hand, the only problem shared by numerous disgruntled users is that each is having trouble accessing copyrighted works, albeit of different genres, no relief is warranted.

Even if the adverse effect – whether on textbook readers or any other discrete class – does not currently pertain, that situation may not remain static. Accordingly, the statute provides for various periods of evaluation. The release from the basic provision applies not only to currently disadvantaged users, but also to the extent that they are likely to suffer that adverse effect during the succeeding evaluation period.[42] The first relevant period runs from enactment until two years thereafter (which translates to October 28, 2000). During that window, a rulemaking procedure had to take place, under the procedures described below.[43] Thereafter, during each three-year period, a new rulemaking proceeding must take place.

Considering first its bottom-line impact, each such rulemaking proceeding leads to publication of "any class of copyrighted works for which [the determination has been made] that noninfringing uses by persons who are users of a copyrighted work are, or are likely to be, adversely affected."[44] That publication makes the basic provision outlawing circumvention of technological measures inapplicable "to such users with respect to such class of works."[45] Thus, to continue the previous example, it may develop that users of physics textbooks are adversely affected by the new environment.

Apart from defending against a charge of an anti-circumvention violation, the

---

[39] See 17 USC § 1201(a)(1)(A) ("No person shall circumvent a technological measure that effectively controls access to a work protected under this title.")
[40] 17 USC § 1201(a)(1)(B).
[41] 17 USC § 1201(a)(1)(B).
[42] See 17 USC § 1201(a)(1)(B).
[43] For an analysis, see 3 *Nimmer on Copyright* § 12A.03[A][2][c].
[44] 17 USC § 1201(a)(1)(D).
[45] Id.

statute directs that neither the exception from liability, nor the whole rulemaking procedure, shall constitute a defense for any purpose.[46] Thus, for example, a defendant whose usage wins exemption in pertinent rulemaking does not thereby gain any mileage in urging a fair use defense to copyright infringement,[47] as opposed to a defense to the instant charge of violating the basic provision of Section 1201.[48] Likewise, a defendant who convinces the court that he or she falls within the exemption, even though not listed in the Librarian's published rules, should not be heard to make headway in any other feature of U.S. copyright law.

3. Effective date

Although the basic provision is framed in absolute terms, the statute delays its implementation. In fact, the provision *ex proprio vigore* remains in abeyance for two years following enactment of the WIPO Treaties Act.[49] Therefore, the circumvention ban did not take effect until October 28, 2000.

What was the reason for the delay? As we have just seen, the delay serves as a building block for the user exemptions. The main purpose for the delay "is to allow the development of a sufficient record as to how the implementation of these technologies is affecting availability of works in the marketplace for lawful uses."[50]

A separate issue arises in determining how long the protection lasts. Is circumvention of a technical process forbidden only so long as the work accessed thereby is subject to copyright protection, or does the prohibition continue longer? To appreciate this aspect of the matter requires an extended inquiry into the effective functioning of Section 1201. After considering other aspects of the statute, the discussion below reverts to that inquiry.

---

[46] See 17 USC § 1201(a)(1)(E).

[47] Would that conclusion follow in any event, because of the independent provision that "nothing in this section shall affect rights, remedies, limitations, or defenses to copyright infringement, including fair use, under this title"? 17 USC § 1201(c)(1). It would seem so, indicating that Congress adopted a "belt and suspenders" approach here.

[48] As previously noted, the field being plowed here is one of "paracopyright" rather than copyright proper.

[49] The basic provision provides that it "shall take effect at the end of the 2-year period beginning on the date of enactment." 17 USC § 1201(a)(1)(A). Both the trafficking ban and additional violations sections lack comparable language. See 17 USC § 1201(a)(2), (b). The conclusion thereupon follows that this delay applies to only one of the three bans.

[50] Commerce Rep (DMCA) at 37.

II. Fair Use

A. GENERAL SOLICITUDE FOR USER RIGHTS

The thrust of Section 1201, as explained above, is to create three anti-circumvention bans, in order to strengthen copyright proprietors. Other portions of that same section, however, also protect fair use. One subsection is designed to ensure that the judicial extension of fair use to reverse engineering not be undercut.[51] Previous case law safeguards over-the-air taping of analog television programming as within the fair use doctrine;[52] another aspect of Section 1201 ensures the continuation of that interpretation as well.[53] Of course, given how large fair use looms in copyright doctrine,[54] it received extended discussion in the legislative history for Section 1201, particularly in the Commerce Committee of the House of Representatives.

B. REACTING TO A "PAY-PER-USE" WORLD

As previously noted, Congress purported to adopt a "fail-safe" mechanism safeguarding fair use. An evaluation of that policy safeguard is necessary to test whether it meets its billing.

1. Background

Historically, copyright owners have always had the right to retain their works confidentially.[55] "The owner of the copyright, if he pleases, may refrain from vending or licensing and content himself with simply exercising the right to exclude others from using his property."[56] In this manner, United States law has accorded *de facto* recognition to the branch of moral rights called the *droit de divulgation*.[57] Once those same owners consented to initial publication of the work, however,

---

[51] See 17 USC § 1201(f).
[52] See Sony Corp. of America v. Universal City Studios, Inc. (1984) 464 US 417, 454–55.
[53] See 17 USC § 1201(k)(1).
[54] The Supreme Court has handed down more rulings on fair use than on any other aspect of copyright law. See 4 *Nimmer on Copyright* § 13.05[B][3] (reviewing a number of Supreme Court decisions on the scope of the fair use doctrine).
[55] See 4 *Nimmer on Copyright* § 13.05[A][2][b] ("The scope of the fair use doctrine is considerably narrower with respect to unpublished works that are held confidential . . . .").
[56] Fox Film Corp. v. Doyal (1932) 286 US 123, 127.
[57] See 3 *Nimmer on Copyright* § 8D.05[A]. ("The right [of the author to control initial dissemination] is nothing other than an American analog to France's *droit de divulgation*.").

they have historically lost control over its subsequent flow. The first sale doctrine prevented them from barring or demanding a royalty upon subsequent disposition of published copies.[58] The fair use doctrine prevented them from barring or demanding a royalty from such activities as miscellaneous quotations in the context of a review.[59] In this manner, traditional copyright law accorded the public substantial leeway in browsing published works.

The digital revolution places unprecedented stress on those browsing activities. Potentially, it allows copyright owners to control the flow not merely of their unpublished manuscripts,[60] but more importantly, of their published works as well.[61] If copyright owners package their "published"[62] goods in digital envelopes accessible only through passwords, then perhaps they can, indeed, levy a unilateral royalty upon such activities as resales and reviews.[63] At issue here are both factual and legal variables. The former involves a prediction as to the future of technology; the latter demands unprecedented attention to the legal status of such browsing activities as were previously simply beyond practical redress.

Consider first the factual angle. Publishers are free to take old works that have fallen into the public domain, to add a bit of original material to them,[64] and to claim a copyright in the newly released whole.[65] Thus, for example, they could collect all cookbooks published in the 19th century, write a new introduction to each, and then wrap the product in a digital envelope. The resulting product,

---

[58] See 17 USC § 109.

[59] See 17 USC § 107.

[60] Cf. Harper & Row, Publishers, Inc. v. Nation Enters. (1985) 471 US 539, 569 (holding that it is unfair, and therefore infringement, to copy an excerpt from President Ford's unpublished memoirs); Salinger v. Random House, Inc. (2d Cir. 1987) 811 F2d 90, 99 (holding that it is not a fair use to quote lengthy excerpts from private letters of reclusive author), cert. denied (1987) 484 US 890.

[61] If the basic provision of 1201 applied solely to unpublished works and the additional violations of 1201 applied solely to published works, then all fair use concerns would evaporate, given that the additional violations are already structured to safeguard legitimate acts of fair use. The problem, however, is that the basic provision can also apply to published but encrypted works. See WIPO Copyright Treaties Implementation Act; and Online Copyright Liability Limitation Act: Hearing Before the Subcomm on Courts and Intellectual Property of the House Comm. on the Judiciary (1997) 105th Cong 229 [hereinafter 1997 Hearings, Serial No 33] (statement of Rep.Frank).

[62] Though that word may be anachronistic in the Internet context, the policy implications are not. See D. Nimmer, "Brains and Other Paraphernalia of the Digital Age" (1996) 10 Harv JL & Tech 1.

[63] See 1997 Hearings, Serial No 33 at 291 (statement of Rep.Lofgren).

[64] Note that the standard for copyright ability is low. See Feist Publications, Inc. v. Rural Tel. Serv. Co. (1991) 499 US 340, 358 ("Originality requires only that the author make the selection or arrangement independently ... and that it display some minimal level of creativity."); L. Batlin & Son, Inc. v. Snyder (2d Cir. 1976) 536 F2d 486, 490–91 (en banc) ("While a copy of something in the public domain will not, if it be merely a copy, support a copyright, a distinguishable variation will.").

[65] See 17 USC § 101 (defining "derivative work" as "a work based upon one or more preexisting works, such as a translation, musical arrangement, dramatization, fictionalization, motion picture version ... or any other form in which a work can be recast, transformed, or adapted").

considered as a whole, would be subject to copyright protection.[66] Whether that product holds any promise or not, however, depends on how technology develops.

If lending libraries continue to flourish, then anyone with a burning interest in how shrimp was cooked in *fin de siècle* New Orleans could simply check out the relevant volume from his or her local repository. There is no reason for users to pay to access the digital product – unless they specifically wish to read the newly composed introductions, as opposed to the underlying books. Of course, to the extent that a user wants to review the copyrighted introduction, the law has every reason to validate charges that the copyright owner wishes to impose for that access.

On the other hand, if the world develops such that a trip to the library becomes as common as sending messages via the Pony Express, then a different dynamic pertains. If access to works via electronic or photo-optical means becomes the universal norm, and if the only way that the pertinent network allows users to view any instantiation of Louisiana cookbooks of the 1890s is through payment of a fee, then royalties to the publisher of the electronic cookbook would become essentially mandatory.[67] By the same token, if in tomorrow's world only antiquarians maintain phonographs and CD players, the sole effective way to hear an old recording of music might be through the same network service. To the extent that the service charged the same access fee for public domain jazz recordings of the 1920s as for new recordings subject to copyright protection, the effective result would be to convert public domain works into royalty-generating items.[68]

In short, depending on how the future unfolds, concern about fair use in the digital environment could range from pointless to vital. The latter scenario requires payment to gain access even to works that nominally lie in the public domain, such as works from centuries past, even if the purpose of the access is for one that the law favors, such as to quote a few sentences for scholarly purposes. Under that scenario, the work itself is effectively placed under lock and key, and

---

[66] Note that this copyright would not furnish any basis for protecting the underlying public domain materials standing by themselves. See 1 *Nimmer on Copyright* § 3.04[A]. By promiscuously mixing unprotected with protectible material, however, the publisher may attempt to ratchet up its rights. Cf. Matthew Bender & Co., Inc. v. West Pub. Co. (2d Cir. 1998) 158 F3d 674, 681 & n.4 (involving a case in which a party "claimed some creativity in its corrections to the text of opinions" and at one point claimed copyright protection on that basis over what otherwise would have been public domain judicial opinions), cert. denied (1999) 119 S Ct 2039.

[67] This nightmare scenario includes "the elimination of print or other hard-copy versions, the permanent encryption of all electronic copies, and the adoption of business models that depend upon restricting distribution and availability, rather than upon maximizing it." Commerce Rep (DMCA) at 36. For another view of the dangers, see D. Nimmer et al., "The Metamorphosis of Contract into Expand (1999) 87 Cal L Rev 19, 20–21, which offers a "Cautionary Tale" about the death of copyright in a completely wired world.

[68] Note that as a matter of copyright duration, music published in 1922 or earlier is entitled to no federal copyright protection. See 3 *Nimmer on Copyright* § 9.11[C].

the proprietor can charge simply for the initial act of access. Thus arises what one senator calls "the specter of moving our Nation towards a "pay-per-use" society."[69]

2. Digital First Sale?

In addition to the factual variables just encountered, the legal issue arises of how to conceptualize the browsing activities of users in decades past.[70] Copyright over the decades has matured in a universe in which authors disseminated works to the public, who typically acquired some physical manifestation containing the work. The "first sale" doctrine, in particular, arises out of the plurality of property interests at stake, tangible and intangible.

In a world of convergence, the physical recedes into insignificance, as all exploitations become ethereal. Within this new environment, it is difficult to distinguish the various strands of traditional law, such as fair use, the first sale doctrine, and matters inherent in the idea-expression dichotomy. Following the lead of the Copyright Office, "we will refer to all of these user privileges collectively as fair use interests."[71]

That terminology in turn leads to the substantive inquiry whether those old doctrines have now been rendered outmoded. To put it most pointedly, maybe users acquired interests during an era when they acquired tangible goods – books, discs, paintings, etc. – which simply do not arise in today's Internet environment.

The Chair of the House Judiciary Committee expressed himself forcefully on this issue: "In my opinion, this extension of the first sale doctrine [to the digital domain] is antithetical to the policies the doctrine was intended to further."[72] It remains to evaluate that point of view.

Let us start with the question whether making a copy in RAM implicates the copyright owner's rights. Some say that it does not.[73] It is submitted that the opposite result pertains – if Amalyah holds a copy of her favorite song in RAM, sends it to Benjamin's PC, who uploads it to Cindy, who transmits it to Davida's hard drive, it would seem that the copyright owner's rights have been implicated –

---

[69] 144 Cong Rec S11887 (daily ed. Oct. 8, 1998) (statement of Sen. Ashcroft).

[70] The legal questions actually run deeper. Before even reaching the fair use defense, how should one categorize the privileges that copyright law accords to authors themselves? To quote Macaulay's famous speech to the House of Commons on February 5, 1841, "Is this a question of expediency, or is it a question of right?" F.W. Grosheide, "Dutch Copyright: Right or Expediency (1817–1912 and After)" in J.J.C.Kabel and G.J.H.M. Mom (eds), *Intellectual Property and Information Law* 175, 176 (1998).

[71] 1997 Hearings, Serial No 33 at 48 n.1 (statement of Register of Copyrights Peters).

[72] See 144 Cong Rec H7098 (daily ed. Aug. 4, 1998) (statement of Rep.Boucher, quoting letter from Chairman Coble).

[73] See J. Litman, "The Exclusive Right to Read" (1994) 13 Cardozo Arts & Ent LJ 29.

in particular, "the right to reproduce the copyrighted work in copies."[74] Accepting this viewpoint, the user who obtains an authorized download cannot freely transmit multiple versions of it: to do so constitutes unlawful dissemination of "copies".

Let us imagine that Ursula pays the copyright owner $20 to obtain an authorized download of *The Art of War* starring Wesley Snipes. Some time later after tiring of it, she sells that file to Ulysses for $10. Simultaneously with sending the file containing that film to him, she expunges that same file from her own personal computer. Does that conduct implicate the "first sale doctrine"?

The provision at issue confers the right on "the owner of a particular copy ... lawfully made" to dispose of possession of that copy, "without the authority of the copyright owner."[75] Thus the question becomes whether Ursula qualifies as "the owner of a particular copy" of *The Art of War* that was "lawfully made." Given that we are dealing *ex hypothesi* with an authorized download, the last phrase appears to be satisfied. There can be little dispute as well that Ursula qualifies as the "owner" of her hard drive and RAM, and all the sectors contained therein. Accordingly, the remaining inquiry is whether Ursula is in possession of "a particular copy" of the subject film.

As already observed, to deny that RAM instantiations constitute "copies" is to give a free license to disseminate works willy-nilly over the Internet, notwithstanding the copyright owners' objection. If copyright is to have force in the Net environment – emphatically the notion on which Congress premised the Digital Millennium Copyright Act – then that file must qualify as a "copy" of the subject work, the reproduction of which is actionable.

It therefore follows that the authorization for owners to dispose of a "particular copy" of works in their possession extends to the digital sphere. By expunging the film from her own domain, Ursula has divested herself of that "particular copy" and hence would appear to fall within the statutory safe harbor.[76] Given that the Copyright Act of 1976 continues to govern, it is hardly surprising that its language maintains traditional distinctions – even in locales where, *a priori*, one might not expect to find them.[77]

---

[74] 17 USC § 106(1).
[75] 17 USC § 109(a).
[76] See D. Nimmer et al., "The Metamorphosis of Contract into Expand" (1999) 87 Cal L Rev 19, 39–40.
[77] See D. Nimmer, "Brains and Other Paraphernalia of the Digital Age" (1996) 10 Harv JL & Tech 1, 31 ("We have little choice but to use yesterday's heritage as the launch point to address tomorrow's needs.").

3. Constitutional Dimension

A further dimension arises out of the legal issue of how to conceptualize the browsing activities of users in decades past. Why is it that reviewers could traditionally quote scattered passages from copyrighted works? Is it because they had a *right* to do so?[78] Could chefs review the techniques of their predecessors as contained in published cookbooks of the past as a matter of *right*? If so, was the right of constitutional magnitude, safeguarding First Amendment interests of free speech and the advancement of knowledge? Or did the law simply allow those activities, as it would have been economically unproductive to pursue such small scale utilization?[79]

These fundamental questions exert practical consequences. Under the first point of view, any danger to the public's right to browse posed by the digital environment must be negated.[80] In other words, if users have a constitutional right to quote for fair use purposes, then Congress was under an obligation to frame Section 1201 in a manner that preserves that right.[81] Under the second point of view, by contrast, the marketplace can be left to develop;[82] if browsing rights are

---

[78] See Bateman v. Mnemonics, Inc. (11th Cir.1996) 79 F3d 1532, 1542 n.22 (Birch, J.) ("Although the traditional approach is to view "fair use" as an affirmative defense, this writer, speaking only for himself, is of the opinion that it is better viewed as a right granted by the Copyright Act of 1976.").

[79] See W.J. Gordon, "Fair Use As Market Failure: A Structural and Economic Analysis of the Betamax Case and Its Predecessors," (1982) 82 Colum L Rev 1600, 1605 (arguing that finding of fair use is appropriate when market failure is present).

[80] See J. Dowell, "Bytes and Pieces: Fragmented Copies, Licensing, and Fair Use in a Digital World" (1998) 86 Cal L Rev 843, 874–76 (arguing that use of copyright in the digital environment from an anti-dissemination motive should be subject to heightened fair use scrutiny).

[81] Barney Frank constituted a one-man cheering section for the First Amendment during deliberation of the Digital Millennium Copyright Act. On the House floor, only he called attention to the technological progression of speech from books to radio to the Internet, and the need to evince sensitivity to speech in the new environment. See 144 Cong Rec H7092 (daily ed. Aug. 4,1998) (statement of Rep.Frank); see also id. H7101 (statement of Rep.Frank) (juxtaposing the Digital Millennium Copyright Act against Communications Decency Act, and condemning "danger in some other legislation of our continuing the unfortunate tendency of holding electronically transmitted speech to a lesser standard of protection"); 144 Cong Rec H10618 (daily ed. Oct. 12, 1998) (statement of Rep.Frank) ("We are developing a second line of law which says electronically-transmitted speech is not as constitutionally protected."). Note, however, that another speaker expressed similar concerns, but without explicitly invoking the First Amendment: "These protections from a permanent pay-per-view world ought to be maintained. Copyright is not just about protecting information. It's just as much about affording reasonable access to it as a means of keeping our democracy healthy ...." Id. at H7094 (daily ed. Aug. 4, 1998) (statement of Rep.Bliley) (internal quotations omitted); see also N.W. Netanel, "Copyright and a Democratic Civil Society" (1996) 106 Yale LJ 283, 288 (showing how copyright, through its encouragement of the production of "sustained works of authorship," serves the underlying purposes of democracy).

[82] Moreover, the marketplace does not exhaust the *desiderata* at issue here. See J.E. Cohen, "Lochner in Cyberspace: The New Economic Orthodoxy of 'Rights Management'" (1998) 97 Mich L Rev 462, 552, 558 (stating that creative works implicate preferences "that are

extinguished in the process, the only lesson to derive is that the economics evidently have changed. Congress, under this viewpoint, need not embody into Section 1201 any special solicitude for user rights.

How did Congress actually view the matter in deliberating the WIPO Treaties Act? The exercise here is to test Congress' handiwork in the Digital Millennium Copyright Act against its self-stated goals.[83]

4. Formulation by Congress

The best expression of Congress' views on the subject are as follows:

> The Committee on Commerce felt compelled to address these risks, including the risk that enactment of the bill could establish the legal framework that would inexorably create a "pay-per-use" society. At the same time, however, the Committee was mindful of the need to honor the United States' commitment to effectively implement the two WIPO treaties, as well as the fact that fair use principles certainly should not be extended beyond their current formulation. The Committee has struck a balance that is now embodied in Section [1201](a)(1) of the bill, as reported by the Committee on Commerce. The Committee has endeavored to specify, with as much clarity as possible, how the right against anti-circumvention would be qualified to maintain balance between the interests of content creators and information users. The Committee considers it particularly important to ensure that the concept of fair use remains firmly established in the law. Consistent with the United States' commitment to implement the two WIPO treaties, H.R. 2281, as reported by the Committee on Commerce, fully respects and extends into the digital environment the bedrock principle of "balance" in American intellectual property law for the benefit of both copyright owners and users.[84]

---

cont.
   fundamentally external to the market," and drawing a distinction between maximizing the good of citizens as opposed to maximizing the good of consumers). See generally N.W. Netanel, "Copyright and a Democratic Civil Society" (1996) 106 Yale LJ 283, 288 (presenting "a conceptual framework for copyright that stands in opposition to both the expansionism of neoclassicist economics and the minimalism of many critics").

[83] The question at issue here arises not under international law, but solely as a matter of Congress' drafting choices, as "the treaties themselves...give us all of the latitude that we need to protect our traditional legal approaches to the fair use doctrine." S Exec Rep No 105-25, at 31 (1998) (statement of Alan P. Larson, Asst Sec of State for Economic and Business Affairs).

[84] Commerce Rep (DMCA) at 25–26 (citations omitted).

The ultimate bill did not contain simply a basic provision in Section 1201 protecting solely the technical processes used by those controlling content;[85] instead, Congress adopted that feature in tandem with the corollary features discussed above delaying its impact and providing an exception for adversely affected users.

However, the WIPO Treaties Act does not itself amend the fair use doctrine[86] as applied to copyright infringement.[87] The legislative history explains that Congress "determined that no change to Section 107 was required because Section 107, as written, is technologically neutral, and therefore, the fair use doctrine is fully applicable in the digital world as in the analog world."[88] Instead, vindication of user interest comes directly in Section 1201 itself and in other aspects of the Digital Millennium Copyright Act. In other words, there is no such thing as a Section 107 fair use defense to a charge of a Section 1201 violation; rather, Section 1201 itself includes provisions designed to aid the interests of users.

By the time the WIPO Treaties Act was enacted, solicitude for fair use in the digital environment exceeded support for mother's apple pie,[89] and "the specter of moving our Nation towards a "pay-per-use" society"[90] had become as popular in

---

[85] It would be inaccurate to refer to those in control of content as "copyright owners" (although the terms may overlap in large part) for the former category also includes those who have secured the technological means to control access to works that lie outside copyright protection. A low-tech example of that phenomenon would be one who unearths the sole surviving manuscript of a lost Shakespeare play. See 1 *Nimmer on Copyright* § 2.01[A] (hypothesizing such a manuscript in a British museum). Of course, as the cookbook example above illustrates, it is almost trivially easy to transform a public domain work into part of a larger whole that is itself subject to copyright protection.

[86] In addition, 1201 contains a provision specifically disclaiming any spillover onto a traditional fair use defense. 17 USC § 1201(c)(1). But that feature is merely negative. The provisions discussed above as to delayed effectiveness and exceptions for adversely affected users, by contrast, affirmatively import into the WIPO Treaties Act some solicitude for the fair use interest of those who access works of authorship.

[87] Note that 1201 deals with something that can be denominated "paracopyright," rather than with copyright infringement proper.

[88] S Rep (DMCA) at 23–24.

[89] See, e.g., 144 Cong Rec E1640 (daily ed. Aug. 4, 1998) (remarks of Rep.Tauzin) ("A free market place for ideas is critical to America. It means that any man, woman or child – free of charge!! – can wander into any public library and use the materials in those libraries for free."); 144 Cong Rec H7102 (daily ed. Aug. 4, 1998) (remarks of Rep.Hastert) (emphasizing that digitized products "should not hinder a child's learning...or complicate an academic's research...or prevent a high-tech engineer in Illinois from improving innovative products"); 144 Cong Rec H7093 (daily ed. Aug. 4, 1998) (remarks of Rep.Bliley) (stressing that a strong fair use provision was included "to ensure that consumers as well as libraries and institutions of higher learning will be able to continue to exercise their historical fair use rights").

[90] 144 Cong Rec S11887 (daily ed. Oct. 8, 1998) (remarks of Sen. Ashcroft).

Congress as the Mafia drug trade.[91] Not a single speaker in either the House or the Senate rose to express any other point of view.[92]

5. *Analysis*

With the adoption of the Commerce Committee's approach, praised by some as balanced while derided by others as inadequate, a question arises as to how well Section 1201 safeguards fair use and whether it successfully avoids the universally decried risk of a pay-per-use world. Based on the above analysis of Section 1201, we can now gauge the practical impact of the WIPO Treaties Act.

A. CASE STUDIES

Let us revert to the public domain cookbook or sound recording that has been combined with a new introduction or other material subject to copyright and brought under a technological protection measure. As of the year 2020, those works could be virtually unavailable through low-tech means yet accessible to those who have paid for the appropriate decryption algorithm or password. In such a world, let us further imagine that Alice hacks her way in, gaining access to the work to avoid paying the license fee associated with taking out an authorized password. Bob does the same but, instead, to determine if he likes the old jazz song enough to pay the freight for regular access to it. Carol is writing her Ph.D. dissertation on obscure diction and wants to quote archaisms and *franglais* from the mouths of Creole chefs, which she remembers (from browsing through a copy of the book long ago at a second-hand shop) are contained in the cookbook.

---

[91] As copyrighted works are afforded more protection, they will be encrypted in "digital wrappers" that make them impenetrable to anyone other than those who are willing to pay the going rate. While that may sound like the American way, it is not. United States copyright law historically has carved out important exceptions to the rights of copyright owners.
   144 Cong Rec H7099 (daily ed. Aug. 4, 1998) (remarks of Rep.Dingell); see also, e.g., 144 Cong Rec H7101 (daily ed. Aug. 4, 1998) (remarks of Rep.Stearns) (noting the inclusion of language to "protect consumers from a "pay-per-view" world in the digital area"); 144 Cong Rec E2144 (daily ed. Oct.13, 1998) (remarks of Rep.Tauzin) (describing pay-per-view as "profoundly antithetical to our long tradition of the exchange of free ideas and information").

[92] Even during deliberations on the bill, the hearings contain universal support for maintaining a robust fair use defense, even from witnesses on the "content side" as opposed to the "user side." For instance, in response to one of Representative Lofgren's frequent questions about how fair use would be safeguarded on the Internet, one witness supporting the Act testified that "my association is totally committed to and in favor of the doctrine of fair use." 1997 Hearings, Serial No 33 at 235 (statement of Michael Kirk, Executive Director, American Intellectual Property Law Association). See id. at 47 ("The challenge is how to [provide] ... protection to copyright owners, while avoiding chilling ... lawful uses of copyrighted works and public domain materials.") (statement of Register of Copyrights Peters); id. at 229 (suggesting that legislation should be amended to add to 1201(a) "without the authority of the copyright owner or in a manner that constituted fair use") (statement of Rep.Frank) (emphasis added).

Finally, Ted is a software virtuoso who boasts that he "can pick any lock."[93] How does their conduct stack up?

Alice is the quintessential violator[94] – hers is the precise conduct against which the basic provision is aimed. Accordingly, there is no question that her circumvention of a technological measure that effectively controls access to a work protected by a subsisting U.S. copyright places her in violation of the statute. Can she nevertheless take refuge in the fact that the publisher is actually charging for a work in the public domain rather than one protected by copyright? Inasmuch as the publisher has implemented a password scheme that prevents unauthorized access to its works, which themselves are subject to copyright by virtue of the new additions, that argument is unavailing. Although Alice would not run afoul of Section 1201 by hacking her way into a domain containing no copyrightable elements, the domain to which she in fact gained unauthorized entry does contain copyrighted elements – notwithstanding that the particular components that she ultimately wished to enjoy lie outside copyright protection. Given that the language of the statute is absolute – "[n]o person shall circumvent a technological measure that effectively controls access to a work protected under this title"[95] – Alice is culpable for the anti-circumvention violation.

What about Bob? Many publishers release shareware, which customers can "try on for size" during a test period. Shareware publishers do not fall within the framework of the anti-circumvention basic provision and its coordinate trafficking offense; instead, they fall under the "additional violations." In that context, there is no counterpart basic offense to dovetail with the additional violations, so Bob's conduct would be nonactionable against a shareware publisher. In effect, Bob has elected to treat the subject music as shareware; an honorable listener, he has an unblemished track record of paying for all recordings that he actually adds to his collection.

Ultimately, however, Bob too falls on the wrong side of the tracks laid by Section 1201. Although publishers are free to adopt the shareware paradigm, they are not obligated to do so. Bob cannot unilaterally pigeonhole purveyors of works into a category from which they have absented themselves – to make proprietary publishers into shareware publishers. Bob has no right to browse the access-protected works to determine if he wants to buy them. Section 1201 grants such browsing rights only to qualifying libraries and archives, not to individuals such as Bob.[96]

---

[93] See A.W. Branscomb, *Who Owns Information?* (1994), p. 90 ("For every technological lock placed within the work product, there will be a pirate locksmith ready and willing to break in...merely for the joy of accomplishment.").

[94] Note that the terminology here is not "infringer," inasmuch as 1201 does not safeguard copyright so much as something that can be termed "paracopyright."

[95] 17 USC § 1201(a)(1)(A).

[96] See 17 USC § 1201(d)(5) (granting an exemption from § 1201 to libraries and archives whose collections are either open to the public, or available to not only affiliated researchers, but also to "other persons doing research in a specialized field").

Bob, like Alice, cannot take refuge in the fact that the recordings themselves reside in the public domain, for the language of the statute is such that Bob runs afoul of it.[97] Given that the subject recordings are contained in a file that contains the copyrighted commentary of a renowned musicologist, that the file as a whole is protected by a technological measure that effectively controls access to it, and that Bob hacked his way into that file, all the elements for a Section 1201 violation are present – again, notwithstanding that the particular components that Bob ultimately wished to enjoy lie outside copyright protection.

The examples of Alice and Bob seem to bear out the Congressional critics who lamented that "the anti-circumvention language of [Section 1201] bootstraps the limited monopoly into a perpetual right."[98] To be sure, that bootstrapping is far from inevitable – it comes to bear only in a world in which the sole effective means of access to the subject cookbook and recording is through the encrypted methodology posited above. Hopefully, that state of affairs would never come to pass – just as one entity was able to obtain a copy of the subject works in order to upload them, so others should be able to do the same. The latter, moreover, can offer those works free of charge.[99] Therefore, it might be that the first publisher's efforts at constructing its own *domaine public payant*[100] will be doomed to failure. The point, however, is that the structure of Section 1201, despite protestations to the contrary (recall the purportedly "fail-safe" mechanism), does not categorically negate this baleful possibility – unless through the exception for adversely affected users,[101] to which the discussion turns below.

Before reaching those points, however, consider Carol and Ted. Not only is Carol (the Ph.D. candidate) using a public domain work – a circumstance that, as

---

[97] For Bob to interpose such a defense, the statute would have to read, contrary to fact, "no person shall circumvent a technological measure that effectively controls access to a work protected by this title except for the purpose of accessing uncopyrighted material." See also 1997 Hearings, Serial No 33 at 229 (containing alternative language that Rep.Frank mused Congress could have drafted).

[98] Commerce Rep (DMCA) at 85 (Additional Views of Representatives Klug and Boucher). In United States v. American Soc'y of Composers, Authors, and Publishers (SDNY. 1995) 902 F Supp 411, 422, a party challenged ASCAP's definition of "program subject to fee" that included material that was not subject to copyright protection. The court invalidated that construction under ASCAP's consent decree. Parallel logic would conclude that material subject to regulation under the Digital Millennium Copyright Act does not include material for which no license is required because it is no longer subject to copyright protection.

[99] Neither party had to undertake the cost of creating the underlying works, so there is little reason why a second comer cannot simply ignore the "value-added" introduction of the first party (which caused copyright protection to attach to its product) and offer the public domain work at a lower price – or for nothing.

[100] See J. Barta and R. Markiewicz, "Poland" in 2 International Copyright Law and Practice § 3[2][c] (1999); M.A. Emery, "Argentina" in id. § 4[3][d]; M. Ficsor, "Hungary" in id. § 4[3][f].

[101] Note that the statute also contains a safeguard for users by delaying the effective date of the basic provision for two years. See Commerce Rep (DMCA) at 37. Inasmuch as Alice's and Bob's conduct is posited to occur as of the year 2020, however, that grace period has long since passed.

observed in the cases of Alice and Bob, affords only cold comfort – but even such isolated quotation as she is drawing from the work, were it copyrighted, would itself find shelter under the fair use umbrella.[102] Does Section 1201 catch even her in its net? It does. For regardless of how lofty her purpose might be, she has violated the elements of the statute. Although, as noted in the discussion of Bob, Section 1201 contains no prohibition on disabling technological measures once access to a work has been lawfully gained, as critics specifically complained, efforts at "legislating an equivalent fair use defense for the new right to control access were rejected."[103]

But why does the fair use doctrine itself not come to Carol's rescue? Even though Congress did not add to Section 1201 a specific fair use provision that covers Carol, it at least left the existing provision undisturbed. Given that Carol's activities fall quintessentially within the protection of that defense, why is it inadequate to doom any cause of action against her? The answer lies in how the Copyright Act is structured. On the one hand, the Act forbids copyright infringement[104] subject to a fair use defense.[105] On the other hand, the WIPO Treaties Act adds a wholly separate tort of unauthorized circumvention,[106] to which the fair use defense is inapplicable.[107]

The upshot is that Carol, too, having circumvented a technological measure that effectively controls access to a work protected by U.S. copyright,[108] falls afoul

---

[102] The fair use provision singles out for special consideration "purposes such as...teaching [and] scholarship." 17 USC § 107 (1994). See also Sundeman v. Seajay Soc'y, Inc. (4th Cir. 1998) 142 F3d 194, 202–03 (holding a scholarly appraisal "from a biographical and literary perspective" to be fair use).

[103] Commerce Rep (DMCA) at 86 (Additional Views of Representatives Klug and Boucher) ("for reasons not clear to us").

[104] See 17 USC §§ 106, 501.

[105] 17 USC § 107 ("The fair use of copyrighted work ... is not an infringement of copyright.").

[106] For that reason, the legislative history refers to it as "paracopyright."

[107] Given that the hearings for the Digital Millennium Copyright Act contain endless complaints about this state of affairs, it scarcely can have arisen by oversight. Consider the following representative extract:

> By focusing on the technological act of circumvention in and of itself, as opposed to copyright infringement, the Administration bill creates a number of problems, among them the significant diminution of fair use. It is entirely possible that circumvention of a protection measure would enable fair use of the work. However, fair use is only relevant as a limitation on liability for infringement. If the new legislation does not use copyright infringement as the criterion for violation of the copyright act, then fair use is not a limitation on liability.

1997 Hearings, Serial No 33 at 260 (statement of Edward J. Black, President, Computer and Communications Industry Association).

[108] As previously noted in the context of both Alice and Bob, it is no help to Carol's defense that she was only seeking to obtain ultimate access to works in the public domain. In order to arrive at her goal, she disabled protection that excluded the public from access to the introduction to the 1875 cookbook, which introduction was written in 1999 and therefore subject to copyright protection.

of Section 1201. From a traditional copyright standpoint, the purportedly "fair" character of her utilization affords no defense to a charge that she is culpable of a new anti-circumvention violation.

At last reaching Ted (the hacker), to the extent that he advertises his abilities to, or performs services for, Alice, Bob, or Carol, he would thereby be aiding individuals who themselves fall afoul of Section 1201. As such, he would be culpable of a trafficking violation.[109]

As noted above, the House Commerce Committee, in order to balance user interests against owner interests, added two features to Section 1201. One of these features delays the application of the basic provision for two years. The other creates exceptions for the benefit of adversely affected users. If relief is to be found from the perpetual "lock up" of public domain works, its locus must lie in these two additions.

B. TWO-YEAR DELAY

As to the time limit, it offers no aid past 2000. As Congressional dissenters commented, it "simply delays this constitutional problem for a period of two years."[110] Given the hypothetical posture above, in which Alice, Bob, and Carol were acting in 2020, this feature offers no safeguard to their interests.

Nonetheless, it is still instructive to inquire how far the grace period goes in protecting user interests. Let us imagine that David wants access in 1999 to the same ancient recording posited above, and, further, that it is packaged with a musicologist's recent commentary. Because the basic provision is inapplicable during this time period, he can hack into the system to his heart's content without violating Section 1201.

Positing further, however, that the gregarious David knows the music he likes but lacks the technical wherewithal to access it, he must hire the withdrawn but brilliant Lisa to disable the encryption in which the music is currently wrapped. Imagine further that Lisa manufactures a device called JazzExtract that can indeed pluck out of its secure envelope the music that David wants; without the machine, however, the music lies beyond David's grasp. Selling a device falls within the statute's trafficking ban rather than the basic provision. That trafficking ban is not subject to a two-year delay; rather, it takes effect immediately. As a consequence, David cannot buy in 1999 the device that allows him to exercise the rights he possesses in 1999.[111]

---

[109] See 17 USC § 1201(a)(2).
[110] Commerce Rep (DMCA) at 85–86 (Additional Views of Representatives Klug and Boucher).
[111] The code that regulates Lisa, stopping her from helping David, is Title 17 of the United States Code, in which 1201 is codified. By contrast, the code that regulates David – who is under no comparable legal disability – forestalling him from obtaining the music he wants, is the computer encoding that encrypts that music or otherwise places it beyond his grasp. See L. Lessig, *Code and Other Laws of Cyberspace* (1999) [hereinafter: Lessig].

Does this statutory scheme make sense? As previously noted, the reason for the two-year delay in the basic provision "is to allow the development of a sufficient record as to how the implementation of these technologies is affecting availability of works in the marketplace for lawful uses."[112] Even before the game begins, however, users such as David, who lack technical expertise, are effectively checkmated.

As a result, Section 1201 produces a most curious state of affairs. It safeguards various rights to users but simultaneously bars third parties from assisting them to take advantage of those safeguarded rights. Although the WIPO Treaties Act forms an outgrowth of the law governing related defendants,[113] that amendment stands on its head[114] the proposition that related defendants cannot be liable for the offenses of others unless those others have actually committed an offense.[115]

C. STATUTORY EXCEPTION FOR USERS

The two-year delay thus cannot serve as the basis for justifying the Commerce Committee's claim that it has achieved balance, as applied to such cases as those of Alice, Bob, and Carol. More promising, though, is the exemption for adversely affected users of particular copyrighted works. To reiterate its rationale,

> the Committee is concerned that marketplace realities may someday dictate a different outcome, resulting in less access, rather than more, to copyrighted materials that are important to education, scholarship, and other socially vital endeavors. This result could flow from a confluence of factors, including the elimination of print or other hard-copy versions, the permanent encryption of all electronic copies, and the adoption of business models that depend upon restricting distribution and availability, rather than upon maximizing it. In this scenario, it could be appropriate to modify the flat prohibition against the circumvention of effective technological measures that control access to copyrighted materials, in order to ensure that access for lawful purposes is not unjustifiably diminished.[116]

---

[112] Commerce Rep (DMCA) at 37.
[113] See 3 *Nimmer on Copyright* § 12A.01[A].
[114] Do any facets of pre-existing law resemble this outcome? One case forbade the making of off-the-air videotapes for commercial purposes on behalf of clients who themselves would be privileged to do so acting in a private capacity. See Pacific & S. Co. v. Duncan (11th Cir. 1984) 744 F2d 1490, 1496 ("[A] commercial purpose makes copying onto a videotape cassette presumptively unfair." (quotations omitted)). But the reason for the discrepancy in *Duncan* is that the client's taping is saved from liability only because it is noncommercial, whereas the commercial taping is undertaken for pecuniary gain, and is liable on that basis. Here, by contrast, David's activity is noninfringing even if undertaken for commercial purposes because it falls into a statutory safe harbor. Yet Lisa cannot even give him *gratis* a device to help him attain his legitimate goal.
[115] See 3 *Nimmer on Copyright* § 12.04[A][3][a].
[116] Commerce Rep (DMCA) at 36.

Let us now add Harry and Sally to our cast of characters. Harry capitalizes on the statute's adverse effect on individuals such as Bob and Carol. He demonstrates to the satisfaction of the Register of Copyrights that 19th century cookbooks and vintage 1920s jazz recordings have been locked up with new copyrightable additions in digitally wrapped envelopes and are effectively unavailable for browsing and fair use quotation. As a consequence of Harry's proof, regulations emerge exempting those two categories of particular works from the anti-circumvention ban. Harry is now free to hack into those works; the content owners whose technological measures are thereby circumvented remain powerless to object. To this extent, the statute contains the safeguards for fair use that the Commerce Committee desired. As enacted, the WIPO Treaties Act therefore mollifies some of the concerns over fair use at which the committee aimed.[117]

Now imagine that Harry is himself a chef or musician who (like David confronted above) lacks the expertise to personally effectuate the access to which he is legally entitled. Sally is a whiz who can help him. Unlike Ted, who was hired to aid people to accomplish what Section 1201 forbids, Sally is to be hired to aid someone who has every right under Section 1201 to circumvent the technological protections in order to obtain access. It would seem, therefore, that her conduct should not only be exempt under the statute, but that it should be positively applauded – for it is necessary to vindicate the statute's policies, with respect to all but the most technically sophisticated users of copyrighted materials. Nonetheless, the statute as drafted bars Sally from aiding Harry because the user exemption applies solely to the basic provision and not to the coordinate trafficking ban. Sally's conduct in aid of Harry would seem to violate each of the three particulars of that latter ban, and thus to be triply barred. In particular, it:

1. is primarily designed or produced for the purpose of circumventing a technological measure that effectively controls access to a work protected under [U.S. copyright law];
2. has only limited commercially significant purpose or use other than to circumvent a technological measure that effectively controls access to a work protected under [U.S. copyright law]; or
3. is marketed by that person or another acting in concert with that person with that person's knowledge for use in circumventing a technological measure

---

[117] What if the feared "lock up" of works occurs not merely with cookbooks and jazz recordings, but across the board as to all works? In that event, the evil against which this exception is aimed would be at its most severe. Ironically, however, the Register of Copyrights would be powerless to act, inasmuch as the authority to issue regulations applies only as to "a particular class of works'" 17 USC § 1201(a)(1)(B).

that effectively controls access to a work protected under [U.S. copyright law].[118]

The problem in the statutory drafting is that none of the features quoted above contains an exception for a particular class of works to which consumers are denied access. Harry needs access to a work that is locked up; for that reason, Congress included a specific exemption to the basic provision of the three anti-circumvention bans. The only methodology that would afford Harry that right (short of putting him through years of schooling to develop his hacking skills up to world-class standards) is defined by the statute as trafficking. Unfortunately, Congress failed to include any complementary exemption to the trafficking ban in order to protect the likes of Harry! Because Harry needs help precisely "for the purpose of circumventing a technological measure that effectively controls access to a work protected under [U.S. copyright law],"[119] the peculiar upshot is that Sally would fall afoul of the ban on trafficking by helping Harry to act exactly within the scope of the user exemption.

* * *

Part of this state of affairs is eminently understandable. The need for balance here is, on the one hand, for the likes of Carol, David, and Harry who want access to a discrete category of works, and on the other hand, to proprietors who want to protect the vast bulk of works that may legitimately remain under lock and key. If a black box can lawfully be put on the market because it serves the narrow interests of Carol, David, and Harry that the law protects, then it can be sold to anyone. At that point, the exception threatens to swallow the rule, and the elaborate structure of Section 1201 could be rendered nugatory.

Nonetheless, the trafficking ban reaches too far to serve its stated purpose. Returning to our JazzExtract device, whose only purpose is to unlock 1920 recordings, there would be no need to suppress that particular machine, as consumers could not use it for a prohibited purpose.[120] More pointedly, if Harry

---

[118] 17 USC § 1201(a)(2). One witness urged Congress to solve problems arising out of regulating behavior rather than technology, by adding to the preamble for the trafficking ban: "For the purpose of facilitating or engaging in an act of infringement." 1997 Hearings, Serial No 33 at 250 (statement of Christopher Byrne, Director of Intellectual Property, Silicon Graphics). As Byrne elaborated, "we don't want black boxes out there that are only designed to steal intellectual property. When we cast that net, let's catch the tuna, but let's not drown the dolphins." Id. Ignoring that plea, Congress declined to adopt the proposed preamble (or another equivalent formula), thereby ensnaring Sally and fellow cetaceans.

[119] 17 USC § 1201(a)(2)(A).

[120] One witness claimed that the Commerce Department considered "a provision that would have provided a fair use exemption for devices that were limited to fair use uses, and, basically, they came to the conclusion that, kind of, too cute by half, because there isn't such a technology that exists." 1997 Hearings, Serial No 33 at 231 (testimony of Hilary Rosen).

hires Sally not to develop a machine that could be used generally for the nefarious goal of disabling general protections, but solely to perform the targeted service of hacking into a digitally wrapped file entitled Scott Joplin Recordings – pursuant to regulations that specifically authorize him to do so – then there is no reason at all to bar that conduct. To the contrary, Sally's service vindicates the lengthy mechanism inserted into the statute in order to protect adversely affected users. Further, the narrow focus of Sally's hacking means that, by definition, it cannot be subverted in the hands of third parties to defeat legitimate rights. In short, the reach of the trafficking ban is unjustifiably broad; Congress should have reconciled the trafficking ban with the exemptions that it placed on the basic provision.

By contrast to how Congress half-heartedly legislated protection to user interests in Section 1201, consider how Congress actually followed through to reconcile the various anti-circumvention bans with respect to other interests safeguarded by Section 1201. For instance, the statute creates an exception from the basic provision for the purpose of engaging in encryption research.[121] Standing alone, that safe harbor would be as feckless as the one protecting Harry. For the erstwhile researcher would only be allowed to act on his own, without benefit of help from others, such as Sally. For that reason, Congress also inserted into the statute a parallel exception from the trafficking ban for the purpose of facilitating encryption research.[122] The self-conscious goal of that latter addition was to permit "a person to provide such technological means to another person with whom the first person is collaborating."[123]

The same dynamic applies to the exception to the basic provision safeguarding reverse engineering;[124] Congress recognized in that context "that, in certain instances, it is possible that a person may need to develop special tools to achieve the permitted purpose of interoperability."[125] It therefore applied a separate exemption to both the trafficking ban and additional violations.[126] The contrast is striking between fully protected arenas, such as encryption and reverse engineering, and the user exemption invoked by Harry and Sally, which is not excepted from the trafficking ban as it is from the basic provision. Congress, in short, neglected to furnish the same measure of protection to adversely affected users as it did to other categories of users to whom it wished to show solicitude.

---

[121] 17 USC § 1201(g)(2).
[122] 17 USC § 1201(g)(4).
[123] Commerce Rep (DMCA) at 44.
[124] 17 USC § 1201(f)(1).
[125] Commerce Rep (DMCA) at 43. "The ability to rely on third parties is particularly important for small software developers who do not have the capability of performing these functions in-house. This provision permits such sharing of information and tools." Id. That language would appear equally applicable to the Harrys and Sallys of the world.
[126] 17 USC § 1201(f)(2).

Conclusion

Sadly, the lengthy analysis set forth above regarding how Section 1201 works in practice leads to the conclusion that its entire edifice of user exemptions is of doubtful puissance. The user safeguards so proudly heralded as securing balance between owner and user interests, on inspection, largely fail to achieve their stated goals. If the courts apply Section 1201 as written, the only users whose interests are truly safeguarded are those few who personally possess sufficient expertise to counteract whatever technological measures are placed in their path.

This defect is not a small one. Many legislators characterized the Digital Millennium Copyright Act as "probably one of the most important bills that we have passed this Congress."[127] The fair use issue constitutes "one of the most important provisions of this legislation."[128] Accordingly, it is a source of disappointment to be forced to disagree with the conclusion that Congress "mastered the intricate details of this complex subject and has produced a balanced result."[129]

Nonetheless, harm from that defect is not inexorable. For the pay-per-use world is not inevitable – for one thing, the technology to develop it may never come to bear.[130] Even if it did, market factors might preclude its exploitation.[131] Accordingly, the instant Wrap-Up cannot tie all the loose ends together. Only the passage of many years, decades in all probability, can reveal the ultimate contours of the world that the Digital Millennium Copyright Act will actually govern.

In the event that future technology and business models do indeed converge to produce such a pay-per-use world, then the structure of Section 1201, notwithstanding pious protests to the contrary, cannot meaningfully serve as the tool to defeat universal pay-per-use and *de facto* perpetual protection. Instead, courts at that juncture would be called upon to apply Section 1201 to that world of

---

[127] 144 Cong Rec H10618 (daily ed. Oct. 12, 1998) (remarks of Rep.Stearns); see also 144 Cong Rec S11889 (daily ed. Oct. 8, 1998) (remarks of Sen. Hatch) ("The DMCA is one of the most important bills passed this session ....").

[128] 144 Cong Rec H7094 (daily ed. Aug. 4, 1998) (remarks of Rep.Bliley); see also 144 Cong Rec E2144 (daily ed. Oct. 13, 1998) (remarks of Rep.Tauzin) (asserting that the fair use exception is "the most important contribution that we made to this bill").

[129] 144 Cong Rec H7096 (daily ed. Aug. 4, 1998) (remarks of Rep.Boucher).

[130] The architecture of the Internet will weigh heavily in this equation. See Lessig at 30–42.

[131] "In fact, there is some indication that copyright owners are nervous about their ability to impose technological controls to the full extent that they would like." J.E. Cohen, "Lochner in Cyberspace: The New Economic Orthodoxy of "Rights Management"" (1998) 97 Mich L Rev 462, 520. Even if copyright owners tried to impose such schemes, consumers might resist or reject them. See id. at 523 (providing examples of consumers' ability to affect product offering in high-tech markets). Consumers' prospects for success in that endeavor will rise, to the extent that the Internet of the future embodies open code. See Lessig at 100–08.

the future – whether by upholding it exactly as written, by interpolating[132] into it additional exceptions to give substance to the user exemption that it already contains,[133] or by making the determination that protection for user rights (traditionally protected in the analog world through such devices as fair use[134] and the first sale doctrine) rises to constitutional[135] levels.[136]

In any event, the issues ventilated herein seem unlikely to disappear quickly. They express conflicts latent in works of authorship and the tug-of-war that they generate between property rights and notions of access founded on public policy. The Digital Millennium Copyright Act will scarcely bring millennial expectations in this regard to permanent rest.

---

[132] Both the first sale doctrine and the fair use defense began as judicial constructions that Congress later codified. See Quality King Distribs., Inc. v. L'Anza Research Int'l, Inc. (1998) 523 US 135, 140 ("We first endorsed the first sale doctrine in a case involving a claim by a publisher that the resale of its books at discounted prices infringed its copyright on the books."); Castle Rock Entertainment, Inc. v. Carol Publ'g Group, Inc. (2d Cir. 1998) 150 F3d 132, 141 ("Until the 1976 Copyright Act, the doctrine of fair use grew exclusively out of the common law."). It remains to be seen whether courts may apply their common law powers to fashion a type of fair use defense to the anti-circumvention strictures of 1201, independent of the fair use defense that 107 codifies as to copyright infringement.

[133] "Courts interpreting Section 1201 may either be forced to find liability in some situations in which it would be inappropriate to impose it or to stretch existing limitations. Congress may eventually need to revise this provision to recognize a broader range of exceptions." P. Samuelson, "Intellectual Property and the Digital Economy: Why the Anti-Circumvention Regulations Need to Be Revised" (1999) 14 Berkeley Tech LJ 519, 538.

[134] It is to be noted that the Supreme Court recently had occasion to state that "from the infancy of copyright protection, some opportunity for fair use of copyrighted materials has been thought necessary to fulfill copyright's very purpose, 'to promote the Progress of Science and the useful Arts ....'" Campbell v. Acuff-Rose Music, Inc. (1994) 510 US 569, 575.

[135] Congress' efforts in parallel domains have not fared well under constitutional challenges. See Reno v. ACLU (1997) 521 US 844, 874 (striking down provisions of the Communications Decency Act of 1996, 47 USC 223 (1994 & Supp. 1997), as unconstitutional); ACLU v. Reno (ED Pa 1999) 31 F Supp 2d 473, 497–98 (striking down the Child Online Protection Act, 47 USCA. 231 (West Supp 1999), as unconstitutional).

[136] It is impossible to address, at enactment of the WIPO Treaties Act, what the resolution might be, in a future world, of a First Amendment challenge to technologies alleged to lock up works of public interest. For early ruminations on the subject, see Y. Benkler, "Free as the Air to Common Use: First Amendment Constraints on Enclosure of the Public Domain" (1999) 74 NYU L Rev 354, 420–29 (averring that anti-device feature of 1201 effectively violates freedom of the press, if not freedom of speech, and should be stricken on that basis.

Copyright Developments in Europe: The Good, the Bad and the Harmonized

David Vaver*

This chapter is in three parts. First, it provides some background for recent developments in European copyright law, including related and sui *generis* rights.[1] Secondly, it sketches some of those developments, namely:

- the Database Directive (1996),
- the proposed Copyright Harmonization Directive (2001),
- the E-commerce Directive (2000), and
- proposed greater access to governmental information.

Thirdly and finally, it makes some observations about harmonization and the commodification of information in the EU.

I. Background

Within the European Commission, copyright is promoted as critical to creativity and cultural development. In addition, EU policy aims to help local creators, information providers and packagers to compete adequately with their foreign counterparts, particularly those based in the United States. Copyright is a central policy instrument for these purposes.

---

* My thanks to my research assistant, Patrick Masiyakurima, at the OIPRC for his assistance in settling this version of the paper. An earlier version of part of this chapter appeared as "Copyright in Europe: The Good, The Bad and the Harmonised" in (1999), 10 Austr. I.P.J. 185.

[1] "Copyright" is used throughout in this extended sense.

N. Elkin-Koren and N.W. Netanel (eds.), *The Commodification of Information*, 223–237.
© 2002 *David Vaver. Printed in Great Britain.*

As the United States began developing its National Information Infrastructure policy in the early 1990s, Europe began planning for something even bigger, the "Information Society." In 1994, the European Council was told by a "High-Level Group" that Europe had to become an Information Society, and fast; else it would be Apocalypse Now:

> "The first countries to enter the information society will reap the greatest rewards ... By contrast, countries which temporize, or favor half-hearted solutions, could, in less than a decade, face disastrous declines in investment and a squeeze on jobs."[2]

According to this report (the "Bangemann Report"), individual European states were getting, or would get, up to speed, but Eurocrats had to ensure that Europe got there all together as a single unit. The benefits of this policy would flow through all of European society. Those benefits would, according to the report, be the following:

- **Europe's Citizens and Consumers:**
  "A more caring European society with a significantly higher quality of life and a wider choice of services and entertainment."
- **The Content Creators:**
  "New ways to exercise their creativity as the information society calls into being new products and services."
- **Europe's Regions:**
  "New opportunities to express their cultural traditions and identities and, for those standing on the geographical periphery of the Union, a minimizing of distance and remoteness."
- **Governments and Administrations:**
  "More efficient, transparent and responsive public services, closer to the citizen and at lower cost."
- **European Business and Small and Medium Sized Enterprises:**
  "More effective management and organization, access to training and other services, data links with customers and suppliers generating greater competitiveness."
- **Europe's Telecommunications Operators:**
  "The capacity to supply an ever wider range of new high value-added services."
- *the equipment and software suppliers, the computer and consumer electronics industries:*

---

[2] *Europe and the global information society: Recommendations to the European Council* (26 May 1994), chaired by Martin Bangemann (and including one Romano Prodi, who became chairman of the European Commission in 1999).

"New and strongly-growing markets for their products at home and abroad."[3] No supporting data accompanied these predictions. After all, the High-Level Group was providing Vision, and Vision needs only clear (perhaps appropriately tinted) spectacles, not numbers or charts. The drive to, and arrival at, this Eurotopia would produce only winners – unless one lacked the wisdom or foresight to join in the race.

Intellectual property was central to the Vision for the Information Society:

> "In this global information market place, common rules must be agreed and enforced by everyone. Europe has a vested interest in ensuring that protection of IPRs receives full attention and that a high level of protection is maintained."[4]

In advocating that what was good for IP for Europe was also good for everyone else, the Bangemann Report's vision nonetheless got a little cloudy. One could equally have argued that a different strategy would benefit Europe more: e.g., by ensuring that everyone else had worse intellectual property laws than Europe. Europe might be better off if others did not harmonize: the non-harmonizers would then become the temporizers that the report predicted would face "disastrous declines in investment and a squeeze on jobs." Presumably, the investments and jobs would flee for the richer IP climes of Europe.

Grand Visions, however, look and sound better if they are untrammelled by requirements of consistency. The general policy that has therefore developed is that EU law should become world law. Unsurprisingly, the EU has worked with WIPO to make WIPO's copyright agenda reflect that of the EU.[5]

European policy in copyright matters has involved the adoption and promotion of two Universal Truths:

1. If copyright is good – and the weight of history and of lobby group numbers says that it is – then more copyright is even better.
2. Those in Europe who are skeptical or agnostic about Truth No.1 are potential menaces to the common weal (or common market) and so must be "harmonized" into that truth. They might not become believers; but then law is law, and dis- and non-belief are mere bubbles in the breeze.

Such truths need respectable underpinning if they are to become legal policy. A typical early example is found in the recitals to the Semiconductor Topographies

---

[3] *Ibid.*, ch. 1 ("The information society – new ways of living and working together").
[4] *Ibid.*, ch. 3 ("Completing the agenda").
[5] The WIPO 1996 Treaties on Copyright and Performances also, naturally, reflect the United States" partly successful attempt to control the agenda.

225

Directive of 1986.[6] Those recitals appear *mutatis mutandis* in the boilerplate of each new directive that strives for harmonization of copyright and like rights, and run something like this:

(a) Widgets[7] have become important in European industry or culture; they cost lots to make and little to copy, so they have to be protected from unauthorized copiers.
(b) Member states don't protect widgets properly or coherently. Therefore:
(c) The EU should make states do what they can't or won't do by themselves, because otherwise the EU common market will not function properly.

The directives on computer programs (1991), rental rights (1992), satellite broadcasting and cable retransmission (1993), duration (1993), and databases (1996) all contain similar boilerplates, as does the new proposed Directive on Copyright Harmonization (2001).[8] By contrast, the E-commerce Directive (2000) is less *dirigiste*:

> "The approach is to interfere as little as possible with national legal rules and to do so only where it is strictly necessary for the proper functioning of the area without frontiers. In fact, the principal [sic] of mutual recognition and the body of existing Community law help reduce the need for new rules. Moreover, the parties involved can themselves deal effectively with many of the issues. This therefore reduces the remaining issues that call for regulatory intervention. Accordingly, the Directive does not cover complete areas of law, [sic] it can target specific aspects."[9]

Why minimalism is good enough for e-commerce but not for copyright remains tantalizingly unclear.

---

[6] *Council Directive on the legal protection of topographies of semiconductor products,* Dec. 16, 1986 (87154/EEC). One might go back even earlier to decisions of the European Court of Justice that recognize that copyrights cannot be exercised to impede the free movement of goods in the common market: e.g., *Deutsche Grammophon v.Metro-SB-Grossmarkte* [1971] E. C. R. 487.

[7] For "widgets", substitute one's technology of choice: semiconductors, databases, copyright material, sound recordings, etc.

[8] Proposal for a European Parliament and Council Directive on the harmonization of certain aspects of copyright and related rights in the Information Society COM(97)0628. As of January 1, 2001, a common position by the Council of Ministers and the European Commission had been reached on this directive, but the revised proposal reflecting that position draft was being subjected to extensive lobbying before the European Parliament.

[9] Proposal for a European Parliament and Council Directive on certain legal aspects of electronic commerce in the internal market COM(98)586.

II. Some Recent Developments

1. DATABASE DIRECTIVE (1996)

The Directive on the Legal Protection of Databases of 1996 is an example of the Universal Truths in action.[10] The success of the UK database industry[11] was not mirrored elsewhere in Europe, or in Europe"s overall position in relation to the United States. Since databases may be created, located and accessed from anywhere, standardized rules for protection, access and use should therefore benefit both users and producers, and even perhaps stimulate growth.

The directive meant to introduce two different levels of protection for databases, but in practice a more complicated system has emerged. Thus:

- Databases, which "by reason of the selection or arrangement of their contents, constitute the author's own intellectual creation" are protected by ordinary copyright for life-plus-70 years. National treatment is extended, as Berne and TRIPs require, beyond EU nationals.[12]
- Databases that are not such "intellectual creations" have a 15-year *sui generis* right against copying, but new 15-year terms (without limit) may run afresh each time the database is quantitatively or qualitatively updated substantially. This right extends only to EU nationals and corporations, but can be extended, presumably reciprocally, to others; hence one reason for the present U.S. push to create its own database protection scheme.[13]
- Pre-1998 databases that were protected by copyright in countries with low (sub-*Feist*) thresholds of originality (e.g., the United Kingdom and Ireland) may continue with that protection.[14]
- Databases that do not technically qualify as a "database" under the directive's definition may (or may not) be protected by copyright as compilations under ordinary unharmonized national copyright principles. [15]

---

[10] See generally B. Hugenholtz, Implementing the European Database Directive", a paper presented at an EIPR Conference held at London on December 4,1998. The UK implemented the directive as of January 1, 1998, by the Copyright and Rights in Databases Regs. 1997 (SI 199713032).

[11] Databases are big business. In the UK alone, the database market was said to be worth around £10 billion in 1997 and to be growing at 11% a year. See House of Commons Standing Committee on Delegated Legislation, <http://www.parliament.the-station...d/deleg4/st971203s01.htm>

[12] See Article 3(1) of the Directive.

[13] See Article 7(1) of the Directive.

[14] See Article 1(3) of the Directive.

[15] Under Art. 1(2) of the Database Directive, a database is "a collection of independent works, data or other materials arranged in a systematic or methodical way and individually accessible by electronic or other means." These adjectives and adverbs may arbitrarily put some classes of collected data outside the definition of a database.

- A single database may comprise some or all of the above classes of database, and thus different parts will be differently protected.[16]
- These protections are on top of the copyrights that may exist in the contents of the database or in the computer programs that drive it, even though these elements may be mechanically integrated into a database. The functionally integrated and seamless product that comprises a database is not matched by similarly integrated and seamless legal protection.

For the database owners, the benefits flowing from the directive have, however, so far been imperfectly realized. So far as database producers are concerned, protection is confusing and overlapping. On the user side, the benefits are, at best, fragmented and, at worst, illusory:

- Confusions in the scope of protection just noted create corresponding difficulties for users. The rights over database contents are unclear. This may impede scientific and other research. Additionally, users may be precluded from using information that is already in the public domain.
- Users have no guaranteed rights of access and use. An initial proposal for compulsory licensing was scrapped,[17] so refusals to deal by information monopolists or oligopolists must be handled under competition or human rights law (e.g., free expression). This provision may make it very expensive to obtain information from those owners who have a monopoly in certain databases, and thus runs counter to a central tenet of the Information Society, that information flows be unimpeded.

Users cannot extract or reuse anything that is "quantitatively and/or qualitatively" a substantial part of the database.[18] This vague test gives database operators almost unlimited rights of control, since almost any datum – e.g., a single stock quotation – may be substantial in a given case.

- The exceptions[19] granted to users are of little use. Harmonization is not assured since member states may not enact some of the optional exceptions. Even if enacted, the exceptions may be narrower than those for ordinary copyright works; they may differ depending on whether the database is protected by copyright or the sui *generis* right; and commercial use, even for research, is virtually banned.

2. COPYRIGHT HARMONIZATION DIRECTIVE (2001)

The Copyright Harmonization Directive ("Copyright Directive"), first issued as a

---

[16] See Article 3(2) of the Directive.
[17] The Council of Ministers deleted the compulsory licensing provisions from the final version of the Directive.
[18] See Article 7 of the Directive.
[19] See Article 9 of the Directive.

proposal by the Commission in 1997, aims to implement a 1995 EU Commission Green Paper[20] to continue copyright harmonization for the internal market, and also to implement the WIPO Copyright and Performances Treaties of 1996. Three years of the now familiar sort of controversy ensued. Some states wanted more stringent protection for their copyright industries; others were more concerned on the consumer side. A strong lobby mounted by the music industry caused the proposals for already quite narrow user rights to be narrowed still further by the European Parliament in February 1999 and by the EU Commission's acceptance in May 1999 of much of the Parliament's report.[21] The music industry may have persuaded France, Italy, Belgium and Spain to clamp down on user rights, but a strong counter-attack came from the United Kingdom, the Netherlands, Denmark and Sweden, who saw no good reason for this move. Mounting pressure to have a deal in place quickly caused the Council of Internal Market Ministers and an unenthusiastically backtracking Commission to reach a common position at the end of 2000,[22] under which member states may retain most of their existing exceptions if they so choose. This common position prevailed in the final Directive, even though the European Parliament was furiously lobbied to remain closer to its stance of 1999.

Despite the minor rebellion of the Council of Ministers, reluctantly joined by the Commission, the general trend toward broad rights and narrower exceptions seems irreversible and the only issue these days is how narrow narrow can be.

The key features of the Copyright Directive include:

- a reproduction right for works and sound recordings, first fixations of films, and fixations of performances and broadcasts, covering temporary or permanent reproductions by any means or in any form;[23]
- a similar right of public communication, covering cases of individual public access, e.g., on the Internet or a public electronic database;[24]
- a distribution right for works in any form, subject to EU-wide exhaustion for hard copies (but not for on-line services);[25]
- a ban on circumventing technological measures – e.g., by avoiding passwords or unscrambling material – that protect copyright or database rights. The ban covers any activity – including the manufacture or distribution of circumvention devices, products or components, or the provision of services – carried on

---

[20] COM (95) 382.
[21] EU Commission, Amended Proposal for a European Parliament and Council Directive on the harmonization of certain aspects of copyright and related rights in the Information Society, 97/0359/COD, COM(1999) 250 final (Brussels, 21 May 1999).
[22] The link to the common position and the commission's response can be found by searching at http://register.consilium.eu.int/scripts/isoregisterDir/WebDriver.exe? MIval=simple&MIlang=EN
[23] See Article 2 of the Directive.
[24] See Article 3 of the Directive.
[25] See Article 4 of the Directive and Recital 29 of the Directive.

by anyone who knows or should know that he or she is pursuing the objective of unauthorized circumvention. To offend, an activity, device or service must be promoted for the purpose of circumvention, must have only a "limited commercially significant purpose or use" other than for circumvention, or must be "primarily designed, produced, adapted or performed for the purpose of enabling or facilitating" circumvention;[26]

- a ban on removing or altering electronic rights management information – digital watermarking or otherwise identifying the work or rightholder – or on distributing or telecommunicating such doctored material, where the doer knows or should know that infringement of copyright or database rights is induced, enabled or facilitated.[27]

The anti-circumvention ban is not supposed to "hinder research into cryptography" or prevent the "normal operation" of electronic equipment, whatever "normalcy" may mean here.[28] The directive does not, however, suggest that circumvention could be necessary or desirable, e.g., for public security, administrative or judicial proceedings, or to advance legitimate purposes such as enabling fair dealing for teaching, criticism or review.[29] Further, although rights management information systems ought to comply with EU directives on privacy, the Copyright Directive does not encourage users to remove or alter information that is gathered by such systems and that may be used against users' wishes.[30]

Writing rights is easy, writing limits, less so – as the directive proves to the hilt. It provides a comprehensive list of exceptions and then requires member states to enact only one dealing with caching and browsing.[31] Member states have a discretion to enact the other exemptions but cannot make them wider than the Copyright Directive prescribes. So some states may continue with no, or very

---

[26] Copyright Directive, Arts. 6(1) & (2). Technological measures are defined to mean "any technology, device or component that, in the normal course of its operation, is designed to prevent or inhibit copyright infringement" art. 6(3).

[27] See Article 7 of the Directive.

[28] Both these limitations appear, oddly, merely in the recitals (No. 48 bis) to the Copyright Directive, not in its enacting language.

[29] Exceptions for public security, administrative and judicial proceedings appear in art. 5(3) of the Copyright Directive as allowable exceptions to copyright, but not to circumvention or management measures. Whether this omission is cured in the version agreed by the Council of Ministers is unclear.

[30] See, e.g., T.C.Vinje, "Should we begin digging copyright's grave?", [2000] EIPR 551. U.S. implementation of the WIPO, Treaties of 1996 by the Digital Millennium Copyright Act of 1998 includes exceptions along the lines in the text. U.S. implementation has nevertheless drawn criticism: P. Samuelson, Intellectual Property and the Digital Economy. Why the Anti-Circumvention Regulations Need to be Revised" (1999) 14 Berk. Tech. L.J. 519.

[31] Art. 5(1).

narrow, exemptions.[32] The directive at first required existing exemptions that were broader than those set out in the directive to be trimmed back but, faced with opposition within the Council of Ministers, a compromise was reached allowing the retention of most existing exceptions for both analogue and digital copying.[33] But just to make the task of national drafters akin to the camel's attempt to traverse the eye of a needle, the exemptions must be written in a way that does not "unreasonably prejudice" rightholders' legitimate interests or conflict with the "normal exploitation" of their material.[34]

The exemptions are as follows:

Caching and browsing. A mandatory exemption allows temporary reproductions "such as transient and incidental acts of reproduction which are an integral and essential part of a technological process, including those which facilitate effective functioning of transmission systems, whose sole purpose is to enable use to be made" of material and which have "no independent economic significance".[35] This much-amended language is supposed to exempt caching and browsing and "the phenomenon of temporary copying as carried out by networks".[36] Whether the tortuous wording in the operative articles of the directive actually effects this intent is debatable. Equally debatable is the question of whether the directive clearly exempts other copying practices that are part of the ordinary operating procedures of servers, search engines and other automatic data gathering agents.

The E-Commerce Directive adopted on May 4, 2000 may give Internet service providers (ISPs) clearer and more favorable immunity than the above rules provide.[37] Both directives were supposed to take effect simultaneously to "provide a harmonized framework of principles and provisions",[38] but this synchronicity is unlikely to occur. In any event, harmonization is best achieved by using common enacting language in both directives, rather than by talking generally about harmonization in recitals or press releases. Practical questions, such as which text

---

[32] In the initial 1997 version of the directive, the Commission justified this mixed approach by saying it is "taking due account of the principle of subsidiarity and proportionality", balancing Internal Market needs', "differentiating" according to the "acquis communautaire", but "enshrining a level playing field in copyright and related rights across Member States, whilst leaving Member States with sufficient room to keep their national legal and cultural traditions in place': Explanatory Memorandum to Copyright Directive (1997), Comment on Article 5. The kindest thing to be said of this passage is that it well illustrates how to say nothing with words.

[33] Copyright Directive, Arts. 5(2)(a)–(e), 5(3)(a)–(o) and 5(4), expanding the original list of 8 optional exemptions to 21.

[34] Copyright Directive, Art. 5(5).

[35] Ibid., Art. 5(1)(a).

[36] Recital No. (23) of the Copyright Directive; Comment on Article 5(1) in Explanatory Memorandum attached to the Copyright Directive.

[37] The rules proposed by the E-Commerce Directive are discussed below.

[38] Recital No. (16) of the Copyright Directive.

prevails in case of conflict, are currently left unanswered – leaving national courts to reach different unharmonious results.

Other limitations on the reproduction right.[39] Optional exceptions are allowed for reprographic reproduction (except for published sheet music) and for copying on audio, visual or audio-visual analogue media "made by a natural person for private and strictly personal use and for non-commercial ends". As mentioned earlier, however, the amendment proposed by the European Parliament, and adopted by the European Commission in 1999, that rightholders had to receive "fair compensation" for such uses ran into opposition at the Council of Ministers. The United Kingdom, for one, was firmly opposed to introducing the blank audio and videotape levies that it had deliberately omitted to enact in 1988. And so, a compromise position was reached allowing states "flexibility ... in accordance with their own legal traditions and practices" on how to assess "fair" compensation. In "certain minor cases", including time-shift recording, "fair" compensation might plainly be zero. More generally, existing exceptions could continue to be applied "in minor cases" for analogue copying.[40]

While subjecting digital recording to the same exemptions as analogue recording, the directive states that the exemption is "without prejudice to operational, reliable and effective technical means capable of protecting the interests of rightholders".[41] Thus, rightholders may use encryption to try to fend off all attempts at digital recording. Presumably, rightholders who are successful in this strategy should be excluded from any share in a blank recording medium levy: "no copying, no compensation" remains the rule.

Two minor exceptions allow ephemeral recording by broadcasters, and copying "for archiving or conservation purposes" by bodies such as non-profit libraries, archives, and other teaching, educational or cultural establishments.

Limitations on the reproduction and telecommunication rights. Relatively uncontroversial exemptions are provided for the visual- or hearing-impaired, for public security and administrative and judicial proceedings, for quotation for purposes such as criticism or review, and for excerpts for use in reporting current events.

Problems however lurk in some of the preconditions. Thus, illustration for teaching or scientific research is permitted, but only if:

(1) such illustration is the "sole purpose", and
(2) the use is "to the extent justified by the non-commercial purpose to be achieved".[42]

---

[39] Copyright Directive, art. 5(2).
[40] Commission statement, note 17 above, under headings Fair Compensation' and Exhaustive list of optional exceptions'.
[41] Copyright Directive, art. 5(2)(b)bis.
[42] Copyright Directive, art. 5(3)(a). The source must be indicated unless "impossible".

An amendment inserted by Parliament in 1999, that rightholders had to receive "fair compensation" for such uses, was dropped by the Council of Ministers. Even with that amendment, this exemption does not match the corresponding exemption in the Database Directive of 1996, which allows users to have mixed purposes – e.g., entertainment *and* research – if this mixture was already allowed under national laws.[43] Even without that further restriction, the limitation to "non-commercial purposes" is troublesome in policy and practice. The rationale for stigmatising commercial research – presently allowed in the UK if a "fair dealing" – is unclear,[44] especially in light of other EU policies encouraging collaboration between industry and universities and other public producers of research.

All in all, the effect of the Copyright Directive is captured neatly in the subtitle of a commentary: "Nice Rights, Shame about the Exceptions."[45]

3. E-COMMERCE DIRECTIVE (2000)

This directive, to come into effect toward the end of 2001, is designed to facilitate electronic commerce. It leaves electronic contracting rules largely to member states, insisting mainly that the contracting process be transparent and subject to "full and informed consent."

Perhaps of greater significance are provisions, loosely modelled on the U.S. legislation of 1998, limiting the liability of ISPs that are established within the EU.[46] An ISP's liability for hosting, caching, or just carrying material within an information network, including third-party material that infringes copyright,[47] may be limited to a prohibitory injunction. The ISP need not monitor information or actively seek out possible infringements. Immunity is, however, subject to conditions, such as the following:

When acting as a conduit, the ISP cannot initiate the transmission, select or

---

[43] Database Directive, arts. 6(2(b) & (d). The Copyright, Designs & Patents Act 1988 (U.K.), s. 29(1), presumably omits the word "sole" for the latter reason, in referring to the use of databases for research.

[44] Suppose that photo clips are proposed for use in an anthology: the extent of exempted use, if any, is unclear. If the anthologist receives royalties, or the anthology is used for a commercial training course or in a collaboration between industry and a non-profit school, the purpose may be considered "commercial" and so outside the exemption. Whether such a use might be permitted under the exception of "certain [existing] other cases of minor importance" in Art. 5(3)(o) is, at best, doubtful

[45] M. Hart, "The Proposed Directive for Copyright in the Information Society: Nice Rights, Shame about the Exceptions" [1998] E.I.P.R. 169.

[46] The proposed directive covers EU-established ISPs who use off-shore servers, but not ISPs established off-shore who use servers situated in the EU: see Explanatory Memorandum attached to the proposed directive, para. N(4), note 16. States should implement the directive a year after it comes into force.

modify its content, select the receiver, or store the material longer than is "reasonably necessary" for the transmission.

Caching must be for the sole purpose of making onward transmission of the information more efficient and must comprise only automatic, intermediate and temporary storage. The ISP must promptly remove the information that has, to its knowledge, been removed at source or that has been ordered removed by a competent authority.

Immunity from damages for storing a recipient's infringing formation lasts so long as the ISP does not know of the infringement or is not aware of facts or circumstances from which the infringement is "apparent".

As noted earlier, these immunities seem more generous to ISPs than the corresponding exemptions in the proposed Copyright Harmonization Directive. One hopes that the E-Commerce Directive prevails in any conflict between the two texts. An ISP's liability should remain harmoniously constant whether the content it carries is defamatory, criminal or an infringement of a copyright or trademark.

4. Proposed Greater Access to Governmental Information

In the EU, the concept of "open government" is still widely regarded, at least in government circles, as an oxymoron. Strong freedom of information laws are not the norm, and some states – e.g., the UK and Ireland – protect even basic material like legislation and judicial decisions by copyright. But, as much governmental information is made available on the Internet, pressure is mounting for wide access to become a legal standard. Thus, a recent European Commission Green Paper stated:

The ready availability of public information is an absolute prerequisite for the competitiveness of European industry. In this respect, EU companies are at a serious competitive disadvantage compared to their American counterparts, which benefit from a highly developed, efficient public information system at all levels of government. The timely availability of public sector information is also increasingly important to further the networked economy and valorise [sic] its economic potential.[48]

One issue the Commission highlighted was whether "different copyright regimes within Europe represent barriers for the exploitation of public sector information".[49]

---

[47] Annex to Explanatory Memorandum, see previous note, Commentary on Section 4, covering articles 12 to 14.

[48] European Commission, Public Sector Information: A Key Resource for Europe Green Paper on Public Sector Information in the Information Society, COM(1 998)585, Introduction, §3.2

[49] *Ibid.*, ch. 111.6, Question 6. The response of the UK, as well as other governments and organizations, may be found at <http://www2.echo.lu/info2000/en/publicsector/gp_comments.html>

In March 1999, the UK issued a White Paper on *The Future Management of Crown Copyright*. Its watchwords were, predictably, "evolution, not revolution".[50] Copyright would continue to be claimed over public sector information, subject to liberal rights of access and use. As an example of this relaxed policy, up to 1999 commercial republishers in print or electronic form could freely reproduce UK legislation but had to be accurate, acknowledge sources, and add value "by compilation with other related text, analysis, commentary, annotation, indexing or cross-referencing".[51] As of October 27, 1999, the requirement to add value was deleted and copyright was waived in favor of all users, all media and all purposes.[52] Various other notices waiving copyright over documents ranging from public records to ephemera such as press releases have also been issued.[53]

Significantly, the White Paper said nothing about judicial decisions, and no waiver concerning them has so far appeared. The copyright position of the opinions that judges write and deliver continues to be unclear in the UK. Private corporations claim copyright in any record that their reporters transcribe of oral judgments. Such claims might, until recently, have been met with arguments that copying is justifiable, either generally or in a specific case, on public interest grounds. This possibility now seems foreclosed in the United Kingdom. The English Court of Appeal has cut back the situations when the public interest defense can be run in a copyright infringement case,[54] and the Vice-Chancellor has followed a similar path in holding that freedom of expression guarantees in the European Human Rights Convention add nothing to the exceptions in the copyright legislation.[55] A further possibility of trumping the claim by invoking EU or local competition law, under which monopolists of legal information might be forced to license all comers on reasonable terms,[56] also exists; but this route is problematic and prohibitively dear to follow in most cases.

---

[50] March 26, 1999, chs. 1 & 5; <http://www.hmso..qov.uk/document/copmp.htm.>
[51] "Dear Publisher" Letter, <http://www.hmso._qov.uk/publet.htm>, clause 4.2.
[52] HMSO Guidance Note No. 6, Reproduction of United Kingdom, England, Wales and Northern Ireland Primary and Secondary Legislation, <http://www.hmso.gov.uk/g-note6.htm.>
[53] See generally HMSO Guidance Notes, *Publishing and Copyright,* <http://www.hmso.gov.uklguides.htm.>
[54] *Hyde Park Residence Ltd v. Yelland,* [2000] E.C.D.R. 275 (C.A.); cf. *British Columbia Jockey Club v. Standen* (1985),8 C.P.R. (3d) 283 at 288 (B.C.C.A.) (dicta).
[55] *Ashdown v The Daily Telegraph* and *Imutran Ltd v. Uncaged Campaigns Ltd & Daniel L Lyons*, both decided by Morritt V-C on January 11, 2001, <http://wood.ccta.gov.uk/courtser/judgements.nsf/.>
[56] RTE v Commission (Magill) [1995] ECR 1-743; cf. Philips Electronics v. Ingman [1999] F.S.R. 112 at 133 (Pat. Ct.).

III. Some Observations on Harmonization

The current drive for EU copyright harmonization may be applauded for the pragmatic reason that information today, more than at any other time in history, is boundless. Its place of production, distribution or reception is often a matter of sheer chance. So the rules about copyright and information should not differ according to such chance elements. Some EU initiatives – e.g., for open access to public sector information – deserve applause: without them, some member states might continue trying to operate as fiefdoms.

Nevertheless, harmonization is controversial for practical, political and instrumental reasons. While attractive to theoreticians who like their law tidy, it may sometimes lack real-world relevance. Thus, e-surfing and e-commerce may function marginally better with common rules, but – even without such rules – they may function well enough for all practical purposes.[57] Given a PC and some modest computer skills, any of us – in Europe, at least any of us with cable or deep enough pockets to afford the telephone charges – can surf the Web for our information and entertainment, and can order, pay for and receive products and services from anywhere without harmonized legal rules.

Harmonization is also politically charged. A body of public opinion within Europe favors trade in, but not necessarily rule by, Europe. Harmonization for harmonization's sake is a poor political sell to such people. It may, on the other hand be a boon for those lobbyists who prefer concentrating their efforts on one place, instead of retracing today's version of the Grand Tour to achieve their ends.

In principle, harmonization makes sense only if good rules are first chosen to be harmonized. Having one uniform, but bad, rule across a large territory seems a modest gain over having diverse, but equally or less bad, rules. The harmonized rule also needs to be clear. Sometimes, harmonization seems only to replace the complexity of territorial diversity with the complexity of harmonized obscurity.

Whether current harmonization trends have produced good rules depends on one's point of view. As currently practised, harmonization tends to extend or create rights for investors or creators of information products, while subtracting existing rights from users. Even in its diluted form, where states ... are given the option of how or whether to implement a provision, harmonization may iron out the bumps, but tends first to raise the field before the ironing is carried out.[58]

The perceived merits of harmonization are inevitably intertwined with the

---

[57] See, e.g., T. Anderson, "10 Simple Steps to Help Reduce Legal Disputes for E-commerce Entrepreneurs" (1999) 10:2 Computers & Law 27.

[58] See, e.g., the optional defence for scientific research in both the Database Directive and the proposede Copyright Directive, where commercial research is virtually eliminated as a fair dealing defence, even though in the UK, the right to do commercial research was deliberately retained in 1988 as an aspect of fair dealing when the UK's copyright legislation was debated.

perceived merits of the substantive rules that the process produces. Whether the utopian society that the Bangemann Report envisaged will likely result from the present round of EU copyright harmonization, and whether – if current Internet trends are anything to go by – that society will more resemble an Entertainment or Shopping Society than an Information Society, presently remain very much open questions.

Copyright and Freedom of Expression in Europe

P. Bernt Hugenholtz*

1. Free Speech and the Copyright Paradigm

INTRODUCTION

If anywhere, the commodification of information – the consistent expansion of intellectual property into areas traditionally considered public domain – is visible in Europe. Over the past 100 years we have seen a host of newcomers entering the intellectual property arena: performing artists, phonogramme producers, broadcasters, software producers, publishers of ancient manuscripts, and – more recently – database producers. The term of copyright has been extended from a European average of 50 years *post mortem auctoris* to 70 years. By virtue of the recently adopted European Copyright Directive[1] the scope of copyright protection appears to have increased as well: the reproduction right has been expanded to include acts of temporary digital copying and use. Limitations must comply with an exhaustive "shopping list" of possible exemptions, whereas the exhaustion rule, which limits the right of distribution, has been restricted to first sales in the community.

Not surprisingly, an increasing number of prominent European scholars and judges have expressed anxiety over the seemingly unstoppable growth of

---

* The author wishes to thank Neil Netanel, Aernout Nieuwenhuis, Jan de Meij, Diane Zimmerman, Tarlach McGonagle and Niva Elkin-Koren for useful comments, references and inspiration. This is a work in progress; an earlier version was published in: Rochelle Cooper Dreyfuss, Harry First and Diane Leenheer Zimmerman (eds.), *Expanding the Boundaries of Intellectual Property*, Oxford: Oxford University Press 2001.

[1] Directive 2001/29/EC of the European Parliament and of the Council of 22 May 2001 on the harmonisation of certain aspects of copyright and related rights in the information society, Official Journal No. L 167 of 22 June 2001, 10.

N. Elkin-Koren and N.W. Netanel (eds.), The Commodification of Information, 239–263.
© 2002 P. Bernt Hugenholtz. Printed in Great Britain.

intellectual property rights.[2] Can the rising tide of copyright and related rights be stopped? Recent court decisions from Europe seem to suggest that freedom of expression and information, as guaranteed inter alia by the European Convention for the Protection of Human Rights and Fundamental Freedoms (ECHR), may under specific circumstances pose a limit to overbroad protection. Article 10 ECHR,[3] long overlooked by courts and scholars, may serve, perhaps, not as a dyke, but as a lifebuoy for bona fide users drowning in a sea of intellectual property.

Whereas copyright grants copyright owners a limited monopoly with respect to the communication of their works, freedom of expression and information, as guaranteed under article 10 ECHR, warrants the "freedom to hold opinions and to receive and impart information and ideas..." Assuming that every copyrighted work, be it factual or artistic, falls within the broad category of "information and ideas",[4] the potential conflict between copyright and freedom of expression is immediately apparent.

In theory, if neither right nor freedom came with limitations or exceptions, copyright and free speech would be impossible to reconcile. In practice, of course, a variety of legal instruments and doctrines, ranging from the idea/expression dichotomy to the limited term of protection,[5] does allow copyright and freedom of expression to co-exist, albeit not always in a harmonious manner. The statutory limitations of copyright found in all copyright laws of the world are particularly well suited to accommodate free speech interests. However, situations may and will arise in practice where the absence or the inflexibility of statutory limitations – often drafted in outdated, technology-specific ways – makes the conflict between

---

[2] Among many others: J.H. Spoor, *De gestage groei van merk, werk en uitvinding* (The steady growth of trademark, work of authorship and invention), Zwolle: W.E.J. Tjeenk Willink 1990; D.W.F. Verkade, *Intellectuele eigendom, mededinging en informatievrijheid* (Intellectual property, competition and freedom of expression and information), Deventer: Kluwer 1990, 11–15; T. Koopmans, "Intellectuele eigendom, economie en politiek" (Intellectual property, economics and policy), [1994] *Informatierecht/AMI* 110–111; H. Laddie, "Copyright: Over-Strength, Over-Regulated, Over-Rated?", [1996] *EIPR* 253.

[3] European Convention on Human Rights (ECHR), signed in Rome on 4 November 1950. Article 10 ECHR reads: "1. Everyone has the right to freedom of expression. This right shall include freedom to hold opinions and to receive and impart information and ideas without interference by public authority and regardless of frontiers. [...]. 2. The exercise of these freedoms, since it carries with it duties and responsibilities, may be subject to such formalities, conditions, restrictions or penalties as are prescribed by law and are necessary in a democratic society, in the interests of national security, territorial integrity or public safety, for the prevention of disorder or crime, for the protection of health or morals, for the protection of the reputation or rights of others, for preventing the disclosure of information received in confidence, or for maintaining the authority and impartiality of the judiciary."

[4] See text accompanying note 33. For discussion of "informational" nature of work of authorship see P.B. Hugenholtz, *Auteursrecht op informatie*, Deventer: Kluwer 1989.

[5] See text accompanying note 47.

copyright and free speech very real and acute. Will copyright prevail in such situations, or is it trumped by freedom of expression and information?

The antithesis of copyright and free speech has been recognized and analyzed in U.S. legal doctrine since the early 1970s, even though U.S. courts have been reluctant to validate First Amendment defenses in copyright infringement cases.[6] In Europe, the "gathering storm" that was sighted above the horizon of American copyright as early as 30 years ago went largely unnoticed until the 1980s.[7] National courts have been equally slow to recognize the looming conflict between copyright and free speech.[8] In 2002, the European Court of Human Rights has yet to decide its very first case dealing with this issue.

There are a number of explanations for this lack of European interest. A factor which may have discouraged European courts from subjecting copyright to the test of freedom of expression is, perhaps, the natural law mystique that traditionally surrounds copyright (*droit d'auteur*) on the European continent. Unlike the law of the United States, where utilitarian considerations of information policy are directly reflected in the Constitution ("to promote the Progress of Science and useful Arts . . ."),[9] continental-European "author's rights" are based primarily on notions of natural justice; "author's rights are not created by law but always existed in the legal consciousness of man".[10] In the pure *droit d'auteur* philosophy, copyright is an essentially unrestricted natural right reflecting the "sacred" bond between the author and his personal creation.[11]

Another factor that might explain the paucity of copyright v. free speech case law is the absence, in many European countries, of constitutional courts with the power to subject rules of national law to the provisions of the constitution. An important exception is the Federal Constitutional Court in Germany, the *Bundesverfassungsgericht*, which, since its inception in 1948, has displayed a measure of constitutional activism comparable to that of the U.S. Supreme Court.

---

[6] Melville B. Nimmer, "Copyright vs. the First Amendment", 17 *Bulletin of the Copyright Society* 255 (1970); Lionel S. Sobel, "Copyright a the First Amendment: a gathering storm?", 19 *ASCAP Copyright Law Symposium* 43 (1971). For recent discussion see Stephen Fraser, "The Conflict between the First Amendment and Copyright Law and its Impact on the Internet", 16 *Cardozo Arts & Ent. Law J.* 1; Neil Weinstock Netanel, "Market Hierarchy and Copyright in Our System of Free Expression", 53 Vand. L. Rev. 1727–2254 (2000) .

[7] Early commentators include: E.W. Ploman and L. Clark Hamilton, *Copyright. Intellectual Property in the Information Age*, London 1980, p. 39; M. Löffler, "Das Grundrecht auf Informationsfreiheit als Schranke des Urheberrechts", [1980] *Neue Juristische Wochenschrift* 201; H. Cohen Jehoram, "Freedom of expression in copyright and media law", [1983] *GRUR Int.* 385; id., "Freedom of expression in copyright law", [1984] *EIPR* 3.

[8] See discussion of national case law below, § 2(C).

[9] U.S. CONST. Art I, § 8, cl. 8.

[10] Ploman/Clark Hamilton (note 7), 13; F.W. Grosheide, *Auteursrecht op maat*, Deventer: Kluwer 1986, 130.

[11] F.W. Grosheide, "Paradigms in Copyright Law", in: B. Sherman and A. Strowel, *Of Authors and Origins. Essays on Copyright Law*, Oxford: Clarendon Press 1994, 207. Admittedly, other rationales underlying the copyright equation (economic efficiency, protection of culture, dissemination of ideas) are recognized as well in Europe; see Grosheide (note 10), 129–143.

Moreover, because constitutional freedoms nearly always leave room for free speech restrictions imposed by national legislatures, courts in Europe have a tendency to turn a blind eye toward issues of constitutionality.

This article will describe the state of European law concerning the conflict between copyright and freedom of expression. The main part will consist of an overview of national case law that has emerged from a number of continental European countries (Germany, France, the United Kingdom and the Netherlands), and also from the former "gate-keeper" of the European Court of Human Rights, the European Commission of Human Rights.[12] By way of introduction, we will first describe the constitutional basis of copyright (or absence thereof) in various European countries, and briefly sketch the workings of Article 10 ECHR in general. In the final part of this article we will speculate, on the basis of general ECHR jurisprudence, how the European Court might eventually decide a case in which copyright and free speech interests are to be reconciled.

CONSTITUTIONAL BASIS OF COPYRIGHT IN EUROPE

The constitutional vesture in which copyright is clad in the United States (the Copyright Clause in the U.S. Constitution) does not as such exist anywhere in Europe. As a "natural" right based on a mix of personality and property interests, copyright in continental Europe has its constitutional basis, if at all, either in provisions protecting rights of personality (privacy) or property. The ECHR does not expressly recognize copyright or intellectual property as a human right. Neither the European Court of Human Rights nor the Commission has ever been called upon to consider copyright as such. Arguably, a fundamental rights basis for copyright may be construed both from the "property clause" of Article 1 of the First Protocol to the ECHR[13] and the "privacy clause" of Article 8 ECHR.[14]

---

[12] Until 1 November 1998 the European Commission of Human Rights decided over the admissibility of complaints of human rights infringement. Only cases deemed admissible by the Commission were brought before the European Court. The Commission has since become part of the European Court.

[13] First Protocol to the ECHR, Paris, 2 March 1952, Article 1 reads: "Every natural or legal person is entitled to the peaceful enjoyment of his possessions. No one shall be deprived of his possessions except in the public interest and subject to the conditions provided for by law and by the general principles of international law. The preceding provisions shall not, however, in any way impair the right of a State to enforce such laws as it deems necessary to control the use of property in accordance with the general interest or to secure the payment of taxes or other contributions or penalties."

[14] Article 8 ECHR reads: "1. Everyone has the right to respect for his private and family life, his home and his correspondence. 2. There shall be no interference by a public authority with the exercise of this right except such as is in accordance with the law and is necessary in a democratic society in the interests of national security, public safety or the economic well-being of the country, for the prevention of disorder or crime, for the protection of health or morals, or for the protection of the rights and freedoms of others."

Express references to copyright in national constitutions are equally rare. The Swedish constitution is an exception: Article 19 of Chapter 2 of the Instrument of Government (*Regeringsformen*) provides that "[a]uthors, artists and photographers shall own the rights to their works in accordance with provisions laid down in law."[15] According to the explanatory memorandum, the rationale of this constitutional provision is to promote "the free formation of opinion". Consequently, the constitutional protection does not cover producers' rights, such as the (neighboring) rights of phonogram producers or broadcasting organizations.[16]

Case law and doctrine on the constitutional underpinnings of copyright are particularly well developed in Germany.[17] The moral rights element, which according to German doctrine is an indivisible part of the ("monistic") concept of copyright, is deemed to be protected under Articles 1(1)[18] and 2(1)[19] of the Federal Constitution (*Grundgesetz*). The economic rights are protected by Article 14(1),[20] which secures private property subject to the limits set by the law. Article 14(2)[21] expressly recognizes the "social" nature of property, thus providing for a constitutional limit to over-broad copyright protection.

In a series of landmark cases initiated by right holders, the Federal Constitutional Court has tested the constitutional validity, in light of Article 14(2), of a number of copyright limitations that permitted the unauthorized use without compensation of copyrighted works for educational and religious purposes.[22] The Court confirmed that the "social" nature of copyright (*Sozialbindung*), in principle, justifies certain limitations to the right holder's monopoly. Thus, without directly considering free speech issues, the German

---

[15] Chapter 2, Article 19 of the Swedish Constitution (*Regeringsform*).
[16] Jan M. de Meij, "Copyright and Freedom of Expression in the Swedish Constitution: An Example for The Netherlands?", in: Jan J.C. Kabel and Gerard J.H.M. Mom (eds.), *Intellectual Property and Information Law – Essays in Honour of Herman Cohen Jehoram*, Den Haag/ Londen/Boston: Kluwer Law International 1998, 315.
[17] F. Leinemann, *Die Sozialbindung des "Geistigen Eigentums"*, Baden-Baden: Nomos 1998, 52–58; F. Fechner, *Geistiges Eigentum und Verfassung*, Mohr Siebeck 1999.
[18] Article 1(1) of the German Constitution reads: "The dignity of man is inviolable. To respect and protect it shall be the duty of all public authority."
[19] Article 2(1) of the German Constitution reads: "Everybody has the right to self-fulfillment in so far as they do not violate the rights of others or offend against the constitutional order or morality."
[20] Article 14(1) of the German Constitution reads: "Property and the right of inheritance shall be guaranteed. Their substance and limits shall be determined by law."
[21] Article 14(2) of the German Constitution reads: "Property entails obligations. Its use should also serve the public interest."
[22] See, e.g., *Kirchen- und Schulgebrauch*, German Federal Constitutional Court 7 July 1971, [1972] *GRUR* 481, 31 BVerfGE 229; *Kirchenmusik*, German Federal Constitutional Court 25 October 1978, [1980] *GRUR* 44, 49 BVerfGE 382 (statutory limitations allowing unauthorized use of copyrighted works for educational or religious purposes not deemed unconstitutional, if providing for equitable remuneration).

constitution requires that a balance be struck between protecting copyright and the public interest.[23]

In post-war German copyright doctrine, the concept of "Sozialbindung" has gradually given way to a more protectionist approach. As Leinemann observes, this development is against the tide of history. Whereas the scope of "true" property rights increasingly reflects the realities of the modern social welfare state, copyright just keeps on expanding.[24]

An additional constitutional basis for copyright can be found in the "freedom of art" and "freedom of science" protected expressly, together with the freedom of expression and information, in Article 5 of the German Constitution.[25] Ironically, the same provision provides a constitutional basis for *limiting* the scope of copyright to protect these freedoms.[26]

Elsewhere in Europe, the protection of copyright as a human right is, at best, implicit in constitutional provisions guaranteeing private property, rights of privacy and personality, artistic freedoms, et cetera. Additional bases may be found in Article 27 (2) of the Universal Declaration on Human Rights or Article 15(1)(c) of the United Nations Covenant on Economic, Social and Cultural Rights.[27]

FREEDOM OF EXPRESSION AND INFORMATION IN EUROPE

A right to freedom of expression and information has been codified in various international treaties and instruments. From a European perspective, Article 10 of

---

[23] Leinemann (note 17), 58.
[24] Leinemann (note 17), 163–164.
[25] Article 5 of the German Constitution reads: "(1) Everybody has the right freely to express and disseminate their opinions orally, in writing or visually and to obtain information from generally accessible sources without hindrance. Freedom of the press and freedom of reporting through audiovisual media shall be guaranteed. There shall be no censorship. (2) These rights are subject to limitations embodied in the provisions of general legislation, statutory provisions for the protection of young persons and the citizen's right to personal respect. (3) Art and scholarship, research and teaching shall be free. Freedom of teaching shall not absolve anybody from loyalty to the constitution."
[26] See e.g. *Germania 3*, Federal Constitutional Court, 29 June 2000, 1BvR 825/98, discussed below.
[27] Article 27 (2) of the Universal Declaration on Human Rights reads: "Everyone has the right to protection of the moral and material interests resulting from any scientific, literary or artistic protection of which he is the author." Article 15(1)(c) of the United Nations Covenant on Economic, Social and Cultural Rights reads: "The States Parties to the present Covenant recognize the right of everyone: [...] (c) To benefit from the protection of the moral and material interests resulting from any scientific, literary or artistic production of which he is the author." See F. Dessemontet, "Copyright and Human Rights", in: Jan J.C. Kabel and Gerard J.H.M. Mom (eds.), *Intellectual Property and Information Law – Essays in Honour of Herman Cohen Jehoram*, The Hague/London/Boston: Kluwer Law International 1998, p. 113; M. Vivant, "Le droit d'auteur, un droit de l'homme", [1997] 174 RIDA 60; A. Kéréver, "Authors' rights are human rights", [1999] 32 Copyright Bulletin 18.

the European Convention on Human Rights is, of course, particularly relevant. Both in its scope and in its wording, Article 10 ECHR is similar to Article 19 of the International Covenant on Civil and Political Rights (ICCPR).[28] The provisions of the Convention may be invoked directly before the courts of the states that are party to it, subject to review by the European Court of Human Rights.[29]

The freedom codified in Article 10 ECHR is a compound freedom, comprising the freedom to foster opinions, as well as to impart, distribute and receive information without government interference.[30] In addition to its primary "negative" function – to protect the citizens of Europe against undue state control and regulation – freedom of expression and information is held by many to serve a "positive" function as well, a mandate for government intervention (a "duty of care") aimed at preserving a plurality of voices in the media. The Committee of Ministers of the Council of Europe has described the government's duty of care as follows: "[states ...] should adopt policies designed to foster as much as possible a variety of media and a plurality of information sources, thereby allowing a plurality of ideas and opinions".[31] Indeed, European states share a tradition of activist media policies (supposedly) aimed at promoting access to the media and fostering plurality, especially in the field of public broadcasting. The European Court of Human Rights appears to have accepted this interventionist interpretation of Article 10 in a number of broadcasting-related cases.[32]

Article 10 ECHR is to be interpreted broadly. It is phrased in media-neutral

---

[28] International Covenant on Civil and Political Rights, G.A. res. 2200A (XXI), 21 U.N. GAOR Supp. (No. 16) at 52, U.N. Doc. A/6316 (1966), 999 U.N.T.S. 171, entered into force Mar. 23, 1976. Unlike the Covenant, the ECHR does not contain an expressly formulated right to *seek* information from sources accessible to the public (freedom of information *stricto sensu*); it is generally accepted such a right is implicit in the European Convention. See Dirk Voorhoof, "Critical perspectives on the scope and interpretation of Article 10 of the European Convention on Human Rights", Mass media files no. 10, Strasbourg: Council of Europe Press, 1995, 30. A right to seek or gather information, as protected under Article 19 ICCPR, might provide a fundamental rights underpinning for a right to remove technological protection layers from copyrighted works, claimed by libraries and other (institutional) users. Note that Article 5 of the German Constitution guarantees, inter alia, a constitutional right "to inform oneself, without impediment, from public sources".

[29] Note that the European Convention on Human Rights exists independently from the European Union and its instruments. However, the European Court of Justice, applying the EC Treaty, has incorporated the norms of the Convention into community law by holding that the general principles of community law comprise respect for fundamental human rights; *Stauder*, European Court of Justice 12 November 1969, Case 29/69, Jur. 1969, 419. See Egbert Dommering a.o., *Informatierecht. Fundamentele rechten voor de informatiesamenleving*, Amsterdam: Cramwinckel 2000, 108–110.

[30] Caroline Uyttendaele and Joseph Dumortier, "Free Speech on the Information Superhighway: European Perspectives", 16 John Marshall J. of Comp. & Inf. Law 905, at 912 (1998).

[31] Declaration on freedom of expression and information, quoted from: F. Vlemminx, *Een nieuw profiel van de grondrechten. Een analyse van de prestatieplichten ingevolge klassieke en zociale grondrechten*, Deventer: W.E.J. Tjeenk Willink 1997, 154.

[32] *Groppera*, ECHR 28 March 1990, Publications of the ECHR, Series A 173; *Informationsverein Lentia*, ECHR 24 November 1993, Publications of the ECHR, Series A 276.

terms and thus applies to old and new media alike.[33] The term "information" (in French: "informations") comprises, at the very least, the communication of facts, news, knowledge and scientific information. Whether or not, and to what extent, Article 10 ECHR protection extends to *commercial* speech has been a matter of some controversy.[34] However, the European Court of Human Rights has made it clear that information of a commercial nature is indeed protected, albeit to a lesser degree than political speech.[35]

The freedom of expression guaranteed by Article 10 ECHR is not unlimited. As stated in Article 10 (2) ECHR, its exercise "may be subject to such formalities, conditions, restrictions, or penalties as are prescribed by law and are necessary in a democratic society [...] for the protection of the [...] rights of others". What are these "rights of others"? According to Boukema, Article 10 (2) necessarily refers only to the fundamental rights recognized by the Convention itself. It would undermine the meaning of the Convention if human rights and freedoms could be overridden by any random subjective right.[36] However, doctrine and case law have never accepted this narrow interpretation. Instead, the "rights of others" are deemed to include a wide range of subjective rights and interests, including the rights protected under copyright.[37]

Judging from the European Court's case law, the "rights of others" criterion has lost much, if not all, of its specific meaning. For example, in the *Groppera* case the Court considered a government-imposed restriction of the retransmission of foreign radio broadcasts legitimized as protecting the "rights of others", because the restriction's alleged purpose was, inter alia, to foster pluralism on the airwaves.[38] As interpreted by the Court, the "rights of others" has become almost synonymous with the public interest at large. Commentators have concluded that it is no longer an important factor in the application of Article 10.[39]

The more important test, therefore, remains. Restrictions on the freedom of

---

[33] *Antelecom BV v. Els*, Supreme Court of the Netherlands 26 February 1999, [1999] *Nederlandse Juristprudentie* 716 (holding that Article 10 ECHR is applicable to public telephone network in view of its increasing importance for the exchange of information and ideas).

[34] J.J.C. Kabel, *Uitingsvrijheid en absolute beperkingen op handelsreclame*, Deventer: Kluwer 1981, 39.

[35] See e.g. *Barthold v. Germany*, ECHR 25 March 1985, Publications of the ECHR, Series A 90; *Markt intern*, ECHR 20 November 1989, Publications of the ECHR, Series A 165; *Casado Coca v. Spain*, ECHR 24 February 1994, Publications of the ECHR, Series A 285–A; *Hertel v. Switzerland*, ECHR 25 August 1998, Publications of the ECHR, Reports 1998–VI. See J. Steven Rich, "Commercial Speech in the Law of the European Union: Lessons for the United States?", 51 Federal Communications Law Journal 263.

[36] P.J. Boukema, *Enkele aspecten van de vrijheid van meningsuiting in de Duitse Bondsrepubliek en in Nederland*, Amsterdam: Polak & Van Gennep 1966, 258. See Article 53 ECHR, which reads: "Nothing in this Convention shall be construed as limiting or derogating from any of the human rights and fundamental freedoms which may be ensured under the laws of any High Contracting Party or under any other agreement to which it is a Party."

[37] *Chappell*, ECHR 24 February 1989, Publications of the ECHR, Series A 152A ("Anton Piller" order not considered infringement of privacy right protected under Article 8 ECHR).

expression and information must be "necessary in a democratic society". The European Court of Human Rights has granted parties to the Convention a measure of discretion in deciding what is "necessary", the so-called "margin of appreciation". Restrictions on freedom of expression and information are deemed "necessary in a democratic society" if they correspond to "a pressing social need" and are proportional to the legitimate aim of the restriction. In this regard the Court has to consider whether the reasons adduced by the national authorities to justify the restriction are "relevant and sufficient".[40]

In practice, the "margin of appreciation" that national legislatures enjoy varies from case to case, depending largely on the interests at stake and the composition of the Court. Even though Article 10 is drafted in content-neutral terms, and does not, as such, create a hierarchy of categories of speech, in its judgments the European Court has tended to prioritize different categories of speech. States enjoy a relatively wide latitude in cases involving morality and commercial speech. In cases involving the core freedoms protected under Article 10, such as political speech, the margin of appreciation will be drawn more narrowly.[41]

Free speech provisions found in many national constitutions in Europe pale in comparison to Article 10. Some of these date from the 19th century, and are phrased in antiquated, media-specific terms. In most states party to the Convention, instead of resorting to outdated "local" constitutional freedoms, citizens may invoke Article 10 ECHR freedoms directly before the national courts. The post-war constitution of the Federal Republic of Germany is a notable exception in that it provides for a sophisticated, three-tiered freedom formulated in abstract terms: freedom of opinion, freedom of the media and a right to be informed.[42] Another noteworthy exception is Sweden; besides a broadly worded provision protecting freedom of expression in the general constitution (*Regeringsform*), it provides for two special constitutions that contain elaborate provisions protecting the freedoms of the press and of the electronic media.[43]

An important question, especially in the context of copyright, is whether freedom of expression and information may be invoked directly ("horizontally") against other citizens. In view of the freedom's primary function as a safeguard against undue state intervention, horizontal application appears unlikely. Indeed, most commentators accept that constitutional freedoms only rarely affect or create rights and obligations between citizens directly. However, both doctrine and case law have gradually recognized that private relationships may be affected *indirectly*

---

[38] *Groppera*, ECHR 28 March 1990, Publications of the ECHR, Series A 173.
[39] E.A. Alkema, [1990] *Nederlandse Jurisprudentie*, 738.
[40] *Handyside*, ECHR 7 December 1976, Publications of the ECHR, Series A 24; *Sunday Times*, ECHR 26 April 1979, Publications of the ECHR, Series A 30.
[41] See text accompanying note 110.
[42] Article 5 German Constitution.
[43] See Jan de Meij, "Uitingsvrijheid naar Zweeds model: een overladen menu van grondwettelijke delicatessen?", [1998] *Mediaforum* 44.

under a variety of legal theories. This principle of interpretation "in conformity with the constitution" is widely applied by courts in Europe.[44] In addition, constitutional freedoms often serve as benchmarks for interpreting general notions of private law, such as unlawfulness (tort) or good faith. Constitutional freedoms may also play a role in assessing cases of abuse of law or abuse of a dominant position (competition law). In brief, even though horizontal application *stricto sensu* is probably ruled out, in practice freedom of expression may play an important role in relationships ruled by private law.[45]

Before the European Court of Human Rights, the question of horizontal application is rarely an issue. The Court does not deal with proceedings between private parties; complaints must be directed against member states that have allegedly failed to comply with the European Convention. Thus, before the Court, "horizontal" conflicts automatically become "vertical" ones.[46] Arguably, the same is true at the national level. Copyrights are state-created statutory rights; enacting and enforcing these rights in violation of constitutionally protected fundamental rights and freedoms may well be perceived as acts of unconstitutional state intervention.

2. Limits to Copyright Imposed by Free Speech Considerations

LATE RECOGNITION OF CONFLICT IN DOCTRINE

The potential conflict between copyright and free speech has long been denied in European doctrine. Most treatises on copyright are silent on the issue, or mention the freedom of expression only incidentally in the context of certain statutory limitations. The arguments of denial are well-known. Copyright does not protect "information".[47] Copyright does not create monopolies. Copyright and freedom of expression serve the same purpose, i.e. the dissemination of ideas. Last, but not least, a "free flow of information" does not require a "flow of free information".

Perhaps the most convincing argument is that copyright, as codified, already reflects a balance between protection and the public interest.[48] In other words, the

---

[44] See, e.g., Fechner (note 17), 188.
[45] J.M. de Meij, *Uitingsvrijheid*, 2nd ed., Amsterdam: Otto Cramwinckel 1995, 82.
[46] De Meij (note 45), 88.
[47] Contra: P.B. Hugenholtz, *Auteursrecht op informatie*, Deventer: Kluwer 1989.
[48] See L. Guibault, "Limitations found outside of copyright law", in: L.Baulch, M. Green and M.Wyburn (eds.), *The Boundaries of Copyright: its proper limitations and exceptions*, ALAI Study Days, Cambridge, 1998, Sydney: Australian Copyright Council 1999, 43: "Almost unanimously, the reports indicate that the copyright regime already addresses the public's claim for freedom of expression and a right to information, through the idea/expression dichotomy and the multiple statutory limitations."

conflict between copyright and freedom of expression has been "internalized", and presumably solved, within the framework of the copyright laws. Proponents of this argument point to various aspects of the copyright system: the concept of the work of authorship,[49] the idea/expression dichotomy,[50] the limits to the economic rights,[51] the limited term of protection[52] and, particularly, the limitations of copyright discussed below.

In more recent European literature on copyright, the independent relevance of freedom of expression is gradually being recognized.[53] Even the monumental German handbook on copyright, *Urheberrecht Kommentar*, contains an elaborate discussion of the limits imposed on the scope of copyright by freedom of expression.[54]

The expansion of the reproduction right, as provided for under the European Copyright Directive,[55] is of particular concern to legal commentators. In criticizing the Green Paper that preceded the directive, the Legal Advisory Board (LAB), the advisory body of the European Commission in the field of information law, observed:[56]

---

[49] Most European copyright laws protect only works that are "creations" in the sense that they are "original" and have "personal character".

[50] The idea/expression (or in Europe, the form/content) dichotomy implies that ideas, theories and facts as such remain in the public domain; only "original" expression/form with "personal character" is copyright protected.

[51] The economic rights protected under copyright normally include the rights of reproduction, adaptation, distribution and communication to the public (in all media), but not the reception or private use of a work.

[52] In the European Union the term of protection has been harmonised; copyright normally expires 70 years after the death of the author. See Article 1(1), Council Directive 93/98 harmonizing the term of protection of copyright and certain related rights, Official Journal No. L 290 of 24 November 1993, 9

[53] See, e.g., P.B. Hugenholtz, *Auteursrecht op informatie*, Deventer: Kluwer 1989, p. 150–170 (discussing potential conflict between copyright in information and freedom of expression and information); D.W.F. Verkade, "Intellectuele eigendom, mededinging en informatievrijheid", Deventer: Kluwer 1990, p. 38–39 (closed system of limitations may call for direct application of Article 10 ECRM); D. Voorhoof, "La parodie et les droits moraux. Le droit au respect de l'auteur d'une bande dessinée: un obstacle insurmontable pour la parodie?", in: *Droit d'auteur et bande dessinée*, Brussels: Bruylant 1997, 237, at 243–247 (Article 10 ECHR may provide defense in parody cases). For extensive discussion see Egbert Dommering a.o., *Informatierecht. Fundamentele rechten voor de informatiesamenleving*, Amsterdam: Cramwinckel 2000, 431–455.

[54] Wild, in: Schricker, *Urheberrecht Kommentar*, 2nd ed., München : Beck 1999, 1500–1504.

[55] Directive 2001/29/EC of the European Parliament and of the Council of 22 May 2001 on the harmonisation of certain aspects of copyright and related rights in the information society, Official Journal No. L 167 of 22 June 2001, 10.

[56] Legal Advisory Board, Reply to the Green Paper on Copyright and Related Rights in the Information Society, Brussels, September 1995, < http://www.ispo.cec.be/legal/en/ipr/ipr.html. > See generally P. Bernt Hugenholtz , "Adapting copyright to the information superhighway", in: P. Bernt Hugenholtz (ed.), *The Future of Copyright in a Digital Environment*, Information Law Series, Vol. 4, Deventer/Boston: Kluwer Law International 1996, 81–102.

"... the LAB notes with concern that considerations of informational privacy and freedom of expression and information are practically absent from the Green Paper. The LAB wishes to underline that these are basic freedoms expressly protected by Articles 8 and 10 of the European Convention on Human Rights, and therefore part of European community law. In the opinion of the LAB, the extent and scope of these rights are clearly at stake, if as the Commission suggests (Green Paper, p. 51–52), the economic rights of right holders is to be extended or interpreted to include acts of intermediate transmission and reproduction, as well as acts of private viewing and use of information.[...] *The LAB therefore recommends that the Commission give sufficient attention and weight to issues of privacy protection and freedom of expression and information when undertaking any initiative in the area of intellectual property rights in the digital environment.* [...] *According to the LAB, the broad interpretation of the reproduction right, as advanced by the Commission, would mean carrying the copyright monopoly one step too far.* Freedom of reception considerations may, perhaps, not carry much weight in respect of computer programs. However, the information superhighway will eventually carry the very works for which Articles 8 and 10 of the European Convention of Human Rights were written."

The Copyright Directive has caused additional free speech concerns in that it attempts to "harmonize" copyright limitations ("exceptions") in the European Union by providing an exhaustive list of exceptions that national legislatures may apply. Commentators are worried that the Directive leaves member states insufficient flexibility in accommodating the public interest, especially in the dynamic environment of the Internet.[57] It is to be expected that the absence of any such "safety valve" in continental European copyright law, where copyright limitations tend to be express, exhaustive and narrowly interpreted, will put the copyright/free speech issue more firmly on the map in Europe.

OPEN RIGHTS, CLOSED EXEMPTIONS

The essential difference between American-style "utilitarian" copyright and European-style "natural" author's rights, is immediately visible in the way continental Europe has given shape to its economic (exploitation) rights and corresponding exemptions. As Strowel has observed, in Europe economic rights are generally drafted in flexible and "open" terms, allowing for the exclusive rights to encompass a wide spectrum of exploitation acts.[58] On the other hand, copyright

---

[57] P. Bernt Hugenholtz, "Why the Copyright Directive is Unimportant, and Possibly Invalid", [2000] 22 EIPR 501.

[58] A. Strowel, *Droit d'auteur et copyright. Divergences et convergences*, Brussels: Bruylant 1993, 144–147.

limitations tend to be rigorously defined and "closed". The opposite is true for copyright in the United States. In Europe, economic rights are mostly narrowly defined, whereas the exemption of *fair use* leaves ample room for a variety of unauthorized uses.[59]

Courts and commentators in Europe also have a "natural" tendency to construe economic rights as broadly as possible, whereas limitations (or "exceptions") will be interpreted in the narrowest possible manner.[60] This approach, however, must be called into question. First, it is often merely a matter of legislative technique whether the copyright monopoly is limited by precisely defining an exclusive right (e.g. the right to publish, broadcast or rent) or by carving out detailed exceptions to a broadly worded exclusive right (e.g. the right of communication to the public).[61] In other words, copyright exemptions are not necessarily exceptions.[62] Second, and more importantly, since limitations more often than not reflect user freedoms constitutionally protected, they should be interpreted accordingly, i.e. in light of the constitution.[63] From this perspective, the opposite rule presents itself: limitations reflecting constitutional freedoms should be broadly construed.[64]

Not surprisingly, in light of the natural rights basis of *droit d'auteur* copyright, the list of limitations presently found in continental-European copyright laws is generally considered, both by courts and commentators, to be exhaustive.[65] Continental copyright laws do not contain "catch-all" provisions (like fair use) that may serve as "safety valves" in hard cases. Courts are generally reluctant to construe "unwritten" exemptions, or even to apply existing exemptions by analogy.[66] In this regard the landmark case decided by the Dutch Supreme Court

---

[59] A. Lucas, *Droit d'auteur et numérique*, Paris: Litec 1998, 173.

[60] See, e.g., A. Lucas (note 59), 171; G. Schricker (ed.), *Urheberrecht Kommentar*, 2nd ed., München: Beck 1999, § 45, no. 15, and § 51, nos. 8–9.

[61] *Kirchenmusik*, German Federal Constitutional Court 25 October 1978, [1980] *GRUR* 44, 49 *BVerfGE* 382.

[62] P. Bernt Hugenholtz, "Fierce creatures: copyright exemptions towards extinction?", IFLA/IMPRIMATUR Conference, 30–31 October 1997, Amsterdam, < http://www.imprimatur.net/legal.htm. > S. Dusollier, Y. Poullet and M. Buydens, "Copyright and access to information in the digital environment", Study prepared for 3rd UNESCO Congress on Ethical, Legal and Societal Challenges of Cyberspace, InfoEthics 2000, Paris, 17 July 2000, 14–17.

[63] See supra, text accompanying note 44. S. Macciacchini, "Urheberrecht und Meinungsfreiheit: Drei Thesen", [2000] 111 UFITA 683, 686.

[64] Arguably, limitations reflecting constitutional freedoms cannot be overridden by contract; see Lucie Guibault, "Contracts and Copyright Exemptions", in: P. Bernt Hugenholtz (ed.), *Copyright and Electronic Commerce*, Kluwer Law International: London/The Hague/Boston 2000, 128–134.

[65] Jaap H. Spoor, "General aspects of exceptions and limitaions to copyright: general report", in: L.Baulch, M. Green and M.Wyburn (eds.), *The Boundaries of Copyright: its proper limitations and exceptions*, ALAI Study Days, Cambridge, 1998, Sydney: Australian Copyright Council 1999, 30.

[66] Cf. *Manifest*, Supreme Court of Sweden (Högsta Domstolen) 23 December 1985, *GRUR Int.* 1986, p. 739 (even if infringing use were justifiable, courts are not allowed to overrule legislature).

in 1995, *Dior v. Evora*, may signify a breakthrough. The case involved the reproduction of copyrighted perfume bottles in advertisements by a retailer offering parallel-imported goods for sale. Having concluded that no statutory copyright exemption applied to the facts of the case, the Court accepted there was room to move *outside* the existing system of exemptions, on the basis of a balancing of interests similar to the rationale underlying the existing exemptions.[67]

According to some commentators, the *Dior v. Evora* judgment has opened the door to an American-style "fair use" defense. Others are more cautious and interpret the Court's decision merely as a form of reasoning by analogy well known in other areas of law.[68] The *Dior* decision has inspired the Dutch Copyright Committee, an advisory body to the Ministry of Justice, to propose the adoption of an open, fair-use type provision in copyright law.[69] The provision would allow for a variety of unspecified unauthorized uses, subject to a "three-step test" consistent with Article 9(2) of the Berne Convention.[70] Even though the Dutch Minister of Justice has expressed his interest in the proposal,[71] it is unlikely that it will ever be enacted, since Article 5 of the European Copyright Directive leaves little room for open-ended exemptions.

National laws in Europe currently reveal a bewildering variety of often very detailed limitations.[72] In many cases limitations are drafted as outright exceptions to the copyright owner's exclusive rights. Sometimes, limitations take the form of statutory licenses that provide for a right to equitable remuneration. Usually, such schemes are complemented by a regulatory framework for the collective administration of rights.

Many of the limitations found in European laws are inspired, either explicitly or implicitly, by freedom of expression and information concerns.[73] Permitted acts vary from country to country, but mostly include copying for personal use, news reporting, quotation and criticism, scientific uses, archival purposes, library and museum uses, access to government information, et cetera. Many of these limitations reappear in the European Copyright Directive's exhaustive list of

---

[67] *Dior v. Evora*, Dutch Supreme Court (Hoge Raad) 20 October 1995, [1996] *Nederlandse Jurisprudentie* 682.

[68] F.W. Grosheide, "De commercialisering van het auteursrecht", [1996] *Informatierecht/AMI* 43.

[69] Commissie Auteursrecht, Advies over auteursrecht, naburige rechten en de nieuwe media, The Hague, 18 August 1998.

[70] Article 9(2) of the Berne Convention reads: "It shall be a matter for legislation in the countries of the Union to permit the reproduction of such works in certain special cases, provided that such reproduction does not conflict with a normal exploitation of the work and does not unreasonably prejudice the legitimate interests of the author."

[71] Minister of Justice, Letter to the Second Chamber of Parliament, 10 May 1999, English translation at <http://www.ivir.nl/Publicaties/engvert1.doc.>

[72] P. Bernt Hugenholtz and Dirk J.G. Visser, *Copyright problems of electronic document delivery*, Report to the Commission of the European Communities, Luxembourg, 1995.

[73] Council of Europe Steering Committee on the Mass Media, Discussion Paper on the question of exemptions and limitations on copyright and neighbouring rights in the digital era (prepared by L. Guibault), Strasbourg, 1 September 1998, MM-S-PR (98) 7 rev, 22–27.

copyright limitations (Article 5 (2) and (3)), sometimes in the form of statutory licenses requiring "fair" compensation.

COPYRIGHT V. FREEDOM OF SPEECH: SELECTED DECISIONS FROM NATIONAL COURTS

The paucity of legal literature on the conflict between copyright and free speech is reflected in a dearth of relevant case law. Even so, national courts in Europe are beginning to recognize that existing copyright limitations must, under exceptional circumstances, be extended or supplemented by direct reference to freedom of expression, as guaranteed by national constitutions and the European Convention. The following inventory of case law indicates that national courts in Europe are increasingly inclined to curtail copyright claims in favor of free speech especially when freedom of the press, traditionally the "hard core" of the freedom of expression and information in Europe, is at stake. Not surprisingly, freedom of expression defenses have been particularly successful in cases where literal copying was considered inevitable, e.g. for purposes of quotation or in cases of "live" broadcasting of works of art.

Courts have applied constitutional provisions for freedom of speech freedoms, or Article 10 ECHR in different ways. Some courts have given direct effect to freedom of expression. Most courts, however, have shied away from direct application, treating freedom of expression instead as a normative principle of "interpretation" of statutory limitations.

Germany

The copyright versus free speech conflict was recognized in German case law at a relatively early stage.[74] As early as 1962, the Berlin District Court allowed an unauthorized re-broadcasting by West-Berlin television of parts of a DDR-produced news item, on the grounds that freedom of expression provided an extra-statutory justification of copyright infringement.[75] In 1968 the Berlin Court of Appeal found that the republication by a Berlin periodical of cartoons stereotyping students, published initially by (i.a.) Bild Zeitung, was justified in the given context, i.e. in a critical piece describing the way left-wing Berlin students were being portrayed by the Springer press. The Court held that the publication did not infringe the cartoonist's rights, even though the criteria of the statutory

---

[74] See generally Schricker/Wild (note 54), § 97, no. 24.
[75] *Maifeiern*, Landgericht Berlin 12 December 1960, [1962] GRUR 207.

quotation right[76] were not met. The Court insisted that the copyright law should be interpreted in light of Article 5 of the Constitution, and limited accordingly.[77]

Referring to the Springer decision, the Berlin Court in 1977 allowed a German public television broadcast of four copyrighted photographs of members of the Baader-Meinhof terrorist group (RAF), previously published in Der Spiegel, in a critical news report on Der Spiegel's purported role as a vehicle of RAF publicity. Again, the facts of the case did not meet the criteria of the statutory exemption, but in the particular circumstances freedom of expression prevailed over the photographers' copyright interests.[78]

Similarly, in 1983, the Munich District Court allowed a television station to transmit a photograph taken from a pharmaceutical brochure in the context of a program critical of pharmaceutical advertising aimed at juveniles. The Court accepted that Article 5 of the Constitution may also provide a defense in cases like these.[79]

In 1999 the Hamburg Court of Appeals let freedom of expression squarely prevail over copyright in a decision involving a book on former DDR dissident Prof. Havemann. The book contained extensive quotes from a brief prepared in Havemann's defense before a DDR court. The brief's author, Havemann's former attorney (now a prominent politician), objected to publication of the brief as a matter of principle. The Court considered that copyright, even if perceived as a right having constitutional underpinnings, should be balanced against (other) fundamental rights and freedoms, such as freedom of expression. In this case, the interest of the public to be informed in full about the Havemann trial justified extensive literal quotation from the brief, and therefore weighed more heavily than the author's copyright interest.[80]

The German Supreme Court (*Bundesgerichtshof*) has been more cautious in recognizing the potential conflict between copyright and free speech. Its *Lili Marleen* decision of 1985[81] concerned the unauthorized publication of the "Lili Marleen" song lyrics in newspaper articles on a forthcoming film picturing the life of the "real" Lili Marleen (Lale Anderson). The Court held that Article 5 of the Constitution did not provide a defense, since freedom of the press finds its limits in the general statutes, and the Copyright Act already dealt with the conflict between copyright and free speech.[82] Even so, the Court did accept that "under exceptional

---

[76] Article 51 of the German Copyright Act.
[77] *Bild Zeitung*, Court of Appeal (Kammergericht) Berlin 26 November 1968, [1969] 54 UFITA 296.
[78] *Terroristenbild*, Landgericht Berlin 26 May 1977, [1978] GRUR 108.
[79] *Monitor*, Landgericht München, 21 October 1983, [1984] Archiv für Presserecht 118.
[80] *Havemann*, Court of Appeal (Oberlandesgericht) Hamburg 29 July 1999, [1999] Zeitschrift für Urheber- und Medienrecht – Rechtsprechungsdienst (ZUMRD) 533.
[81] *Lili Marleen*, German Federal Supreme Court 7 March 1985, [1987] GRUR 34.
[82] The Austrian Supreme Court has similarly refused to accept free speech overrides of copyright law. Cf. *Head-Kaufvertrag*, Austrian Supreme Court 17 December 1996, [1997] Medien und

circumstances, because of an unusually urgent information need, limits to copyright exceeding the express statutory limitations may be taken into consideration".[83] However, in the present case no such circumstances were found.

The Supreme Court again refused to apply Article 5 of the Constitution in the two *CB-Infobank* cases decided in 1997. The defendant operated a commercial research database containing abstracts of articles published in professional periodicals, and offered a document delivery service providing full-text copies. According to the Court the public interest in accessing information, even in view of the needs of the emerging information society, could not justify derogating from the strict wording of existing limitations that should be narrowly interpreted. The Court stressed that since copyright does not protect information as such, information services remain free to provide facts, data and bibliographical information.[84]

The year 2000 brought the first decision of the Federal Constitutional Court on the conflict between copyright and free speech. Its landmark *Germania 3* decision concerned a play that contained extensive quotations, for a total of four pages, from a pair of Berthold Brecht plays. Again, the quotations did not meet the stringent test of the statutory quotation right. The Court, however, held that in light of the freedom of artistic expression embedded in Article 5(3) of the Constitution, the quotation right deserves broad application with respect to artistic works. Authors must, to a certain degree, accept that works of art gradually enter the public domain. Copyright exemptions should be interpreted accordingly, and reflect a balancing of relevant interests. In the case at hand, the Court considered, the commercial interests of the copyright owner should give way to the user's interest in providing artistic commentary.[85]

The Netherlands

Under Dutch law, acts of Parliament ("formal" laws) are not subject to constitutional review. Freedom of expression defenses against copyright-based claims, therefore, rely solely upon Article 10 ECHR, which has direct application

---

cont.
Recht 93, at 95 (freedom of expression does not justify curtailing copyright to a further degree than the statutory limitations allow); see critical comments by M. Walter, *ibid.*; and R. Schanda, "Pressefreiheit contra Urheberrecht", [1997] Medien und Recht 97; and *Karikaturwiedergabe*, Austrian Supreme Court 9 December 1997, [1998] GRUR Int. 896 (free speech values deemed incorporated in statutory limitation).

[83] Cf. *Pelzversand*, German Federal Supreme Court 10 January 1968, [1968] GRUR 645 (freedom of speech may impose limits on unfair competition).

[84] *CB-Infobank I*, German Federal Supreme Court 16 January 1997, [1997] GRUR 459 at 463; and *CB-Infobank II*, German Federal Supreme Court 16 January 1997, [1997] GRUR 464, at 466.

[85] *Germania 3 Gespenster am toten Mann*, Federal Constitutional Court 29 June 2000, [2000] Zeitschrift für Urheber- und Medienrecht (ZUM) 867.

and supersedes statutory and constitutional law. Courts in the Netherlands have long been hesitant to apply Article 10 ECHR directly in copyright cases. However, a number of recent court decisions may be symptoms of a gradual shift.

The potential conflict between intellectual property (both copyrights and trademarks) and freedom of expression was recognized in principle by the Dutch Supreme Court in 1995 in its *Dior v. Evora* decision, previously discussed.[86] However, having found sufficient room to accommodate the users' interests by construing an extra-statutory exemption, the Court saw no need for direct application of Article 10 ECHR.

The first Dutch copyright case where Article 10 was indeed applied directly was decided by the Amsterdam District Court in 1994. The case involved an interview with a well-known "corporate raider", published in the daily newspaper De Volkskrant,[87] which was illustrated by a photograph taken in the interviewee's office. The photograph prominently, and humorously, featured one of the many works of plastic art on display in the office, a statuette of an archer, aiming, as it would seem, at the head of its collector. The Dutch collecting society for visual arts claimed damages for copyright infringement. The Court agreed that no statutory copyright limitation was applicable to the facts of the case, but went on to hold that this does not preclude a conflict between copyright and freedom of expression, as protected by Article 10 ECHR. The Court then proceeded to subject the collecting society's claim to the test of proportionality inherent in Article 10 (2). Nevertheless, the Court found for the plaintiff; depicting the work of art in such a prominent manner was not deemed to be required for the purpose of De Volkskrant's news reporting.[88]

In a remarkable decision concerning the "missing pages" of Anne Frank's diary, reprinted without authorization by the Dutch newspaper Het Parool, the Amsterdam Court of Appeal in 1998 decided that Article 10 did not override the copyright claims of the Anne Frank Foundation, which owns the copyrights in the diary.[89] After carefully weighing the public interest in having the pages divulged against the interest of the Foundation in protecting, inter alia, the reputation of the Frank family members described in the diary fragments, the Court found for the Foundation, reversing the decision of the District Court.[90]

---

[86] *Dior v. Evora*, Dutch Supreme Court (Hoge Raad) 20 October 1995, [1996] Nederlandse Jurisprudentie 682.

[87] *Boogschutter*, District Court of Amsterdam 19 January 1994, [1994] Informatierecht/AMI 51; see comment P.B. Hugenholtz, [1994] NJCM Bulletin 673.

[88] Cf. *LiteROM*, District Court of The Hague 3 May 1995, [1995] Informatierecht/AMI 116 (exercise of copyrights in literary reviews not deemed disproportional in claim directed at library organisation producing unauthorised cd-rom compilation).

[89] *Anne Frank Fonds v. Het Parool*, Court of Appeal Amsterdam 8 July 1999, [1999] Informatierecht/AMI 116.

[90] *Id.*, President District Court of Amsterdam 12 November 1998, [1999] Mediaforum 39.

France

French courts have been very reluctant to accept free speech defenses in copyright cases. In the seemingly endless string of *SPADEM v. Antenne 2* cases concerning the scope of the freedom to (briefly) display protected works of art in television broadcasts, freedom of expression was not mentioned even once.[91]

Seen in this light the recent decision of the Paris Court of First Instance in the *Utrillo* case constitutes a minor revolution. The case was brought before the court by the Utrillo estate against the national television station France 2 for showing 12 copyrighted paintings in a two-minute news item on an Utrillo exhibition. The Court reminded that Article 10 ECHR is superior to national law, including the law of copyright, and concluded that in the case at hand the right of the public to be informed of important cultural events should prevail over the interests of the copyright owner.[92]

Not surprisingly, the *Utrillo* decision did not survive scrutiny by the Paris Court of Appeal.[93] According to the Court, copyright-related restrictions to freedom of expression and information are justified and proportionate, particularly since the law already provides for remedies against cases of copyright abuse or misuse. The Court also pointed to the "property clause" of Article 1 of the First Protocol to the ECHR, which protects both physical and intangible property, such as copyright. Finally, the Court observed that for France 2 to inform the general public of the Utrillo exhibition it was not indispensable to display the paintings.

United Kingdom

Direct references to freedom of expression as a limit to copyright are equally rare in United Kingdom case law,[94] even though doctrine has been more forthcoming.[95] However, the recent entry into force of the Human Rights Act 1998,[96] which incorporates the European Convention on Human Rights into U.K. law, is likely to raise human rights awareness among U.K. courts. Indeed, two recent

---

[91] *Du côté de chez Fred,* Court of First Instance Paris 15 May 1991, 150 RIDA 164, reversed Court of Appeal Paris 7 July 1992, 154 RIDA 161, affirmed Supreme Court (Cour de Cassation) 4 July 1995, 167 RIDA 263. The case eventually came before the European Commission, whose decision is discussed below. See also *Tuileries,* Supreme Court (Cour de Cassation) 4 July 1995, 167 RIDA 259.
[92] *Utrillo,* Court of First Instance Paris 23 February 1999, [2000] 184 RIDA 374, with note A. Kéréver; see also case note P. Kamina, Le Dalloz, 1999, No. 38, Jur., p. 582.
[93] *Utrillo,* Court of Appeal Paris 30 May 2001, Case 1999/07668.
[94] The potential conflict between copyright and freedom of speech was acknowledged, possibly for the first time in the U.K, in the *Alan Clark* case decided by the High Court on 21 January 1998; see Clive D. Thorne, "The Alan Clark Case – What It Is Not", [1998] *EIPR* 194.
[95] Sir Anthony Mason, "Developments in the law of copyright and public access to information", [1967] 19 EIPR 636 (1997).

decisions by the High Court give ample consideration to the copyright v. free speech dilemma. The first case, *Ashdown v. Telegraph Group*,[97] concerned an unauthorized publication by The Sunday Telegraph of confidential minutes from a meeting between the former leader of the Liberal Democrat Party, Paddy Ashdown, and the Prime Minister. The minutes revealed the true story of an attempt to create a coalition cabinet in 1997. Before the Court, Ashdown, the author of the minutes, complained of copyright infringement; the defendant invoked Article 10 ECHR. The Court recognized that copyright, in principle, amounts to a restriction on the right to freedom of expression. The Court also admitted that s. 171(3) of the Copyright, Designs and Patents Act 1988 expressly recognizes a public interest defense, but binding precedent limits this defense to cases in which a work is either (i) immoral, (ii) injurious to public life, public health and safety and the administration of justice, or (iii) incitant.[98] Consequently, the Court refused to accept that Article 10 (2) provides for a free speech defense, above and beyond existing statutory exemptions. Otherwise, the Court lamented, "the intellectual property litigation would burgeon out of control and the rights which the legislation apparently confers will be of no practical use except to those able and willing to litigate in all cases."[99] In another decision of the same date the Court similarly rejected a free speech defense in a case involving the divulgation of confidential information on "pig-to-primate" organ transplants by an animal warfare activist.[100] Again, the Court saw no room for a public interest defense based on free speech concerns.

COPYRIGHT V. FREE SPEECH BEFORE THE EUROPEAN COURT

Until today, the European Court of Human Rights has never been called upon to consider the conflict between copyright and freedom of expression, or opine on the potential "necessity" of copyright. The European Commission of Human Rights, the former gateway to the European Court, has however faced the problem twice.

---

[96] Human Rights Act 1998, as of 2 October 2000.
[97] *Ashdown v. Telegraph Group*, High Court, Chancery Division, 11 January 2001, Case No. HC 1999 05116.
[98] *Hyde Park Residence v. Yelland*, [2000] 3 WLR 215.
[99] *Ashdown v. Telegraph Group* (note 97), at § 13.
[100] *Imutran v. Uncaged Campaigns & Lyons*, High Court, Chancery Division, 11 January 2001, Case No. HC 0004406.

De Geïllustreerde Pers N.V. v. The Netherlands

The case of *De Geïllustreerde Pers N.V. v. The Netherlands*[101] concerned the Dutch public broadcasters' monopoly in radio and television program listings. Before the Commission, publisher De Geïllustreerde Pers complained that the Dutch copyright in (non-original) program listings, and the broadcasters' refusal to license, were at odds with Article 10 ECHR. The broadcasters' copyright monopoly arguably restricted the freedom to impart information in a way that was unnecessary in a democratic society.

The Commission did not agree. The broadcasters' copyright did not amount to a restriction of the freedom of expression and information in the first place, so no need to consider the "necessity" of the copyright in the listings could arise. Having recognized that the program listings were "information" within the meaning of Article 10, the Commission observed:

"In the first place, such lists of programme data are not simple facts, or news in the proper sense of the word. [...] The characteristic feature of such information is that it can only be produced and provided by the broadcasting organisations being charged with the production of the programmes themselves [...] The Commission considers that the freedom under Art. 10 to impart information of the kind described above is only granted to the person or body who produces, provides or organises it. In other words, the freedom to impart such information is limited to information produced, provided or organised by the person claiming that freedom being the author, the originator or otherwise the intellectual owner of the information concerned. It follows that any right which the applicant company itself may have under Art. 10 of the Convention has not been interfered with where it is prevented from publishing information not yet in its possession."

The Commission finally considered that "the free flow of such information to the public in general" was not at stake, since Dutch audiences could inform themselves of the information through a variety of mass media.

The *De Geïllustreerde Pers* decision has been criticized by many commentators.[102] The Commission's conclusion that third parties may not invoke Article 10 freedoms in respect of "single-source" data is obviously erroneous. The freedoms

---

[101] *De Geïllustreerde Pers N.V. v. The Netherlands*, European Commission of Human Rights 6 July 1976, European Commission of Human Rights Decisions & Reports 1976 (Volume 8), 5; cf. *KPN/Kapitol*, President District Court Dordrecht 8 September 1998, [1999] Informatierecht/ AMI 7 (copyright in telephone subscriber listings not deemed infringement of Article 10 ECHR because (a) freedom of the public to receive information not impeded, and (b) listings could be licensed).

[102] H. Cohen Jehoram, "Het Omroepbladenmonopolie", Ars Aequi 28 (1979), 153; P. van Dijk & G.J.H. van Hoof, *De Europese Conventie in Theorie en Praktijk*, 2nd ed., Nijmegen 1982, 358.

guaranteed under Article 10 are not confined to speech that is original to the speaker. Moreover, the Commission wrongly suggested that freedom of expression and information is not restricted as long as the free flow of information "to the public in general" is not impeded. The existence of alternative communications channels may be an element in measuring the "necessity" of a restriction, denying the restriction altogether is clearly at odds with the meaning and purpose of Article 10.

France 2 v. France

The second Commission decision involving potentially overbroad copyright claims is of a more recent date, but equally disappointing in its reasoning and outcome.[103] During a television news program broadcast by France 2 (Antenne 2), covering the reopening of the theatre on the Champs-Elysées after major restoration work, the camera focused several times, for a total duration of 49 seconds, on the theatre's famous frescoes by Edouard Vuillard. Before the French courts the visual arts collecting society SPADEM, representing the Vuillard estate, demanded and was eventually awarded compensation. The Cour de Cassation had held that France 2 could not invoke the statutory right to quote briefly from copyrighted works for informational purposes,[104] because showing an entire work cannot, by definition, amount to a brief quotation within the meaning of the law.

Before the Commission France 2 complained that the Cour de Cassation had failed to apply Article 10 ECHR. The Commission agreed that, in principle, copyright is a restriction of the freedom of expression and information that must pass the test of Article 10 (2). Having observed that copyright law is "prescribed by law", and serves to protect the "rights of others", the Commission applied the test of proportionality of Article 10 (2) – not without a certain reluctance:

> "... it is normally not for the organs of the Convention to decide, in respect of Article 10 (2), possible conflicts between the right to communicate information freely, on the one hand, and the right of the authors of the works communicated, on the other hand."[105]

The Commission then found sufficient proportionality by reducing SPADEM's claim to a matter of unpaid royalties. The Commission held "that under the circumstances of the case the French courts had good reason to take into account

---

[103] *France 2 v. France*, European Commission of Human Rights 15 January 1997, Case 30262/96, [1999] *Informatierecht/AMI* 115.
[104] Article 43–1 of the Act of 11 March 1957 (currently article L 111–1 of the Code of Intellectual Property).
[105] Translation from French by the author.

the copyrights of the author and the right holders in the works that were otherwise freely broadcast by the applicant." Again, as in the case of *De Geïllustreerde Pers N.V. v. The Netherlands*, the Commission sidestepped the essence of the conflict between copyright and Article 10, i.e. that copyright is, by its very nature, an exclusive right that may prevent any (further) communication of a work.

Conclusion

How will the European Court of Human Rights eventually decide a conflict between copyright and freedom of expression? Both the national cases and the decisions by the Commission of Human Rights discussed in this article provide a number of clues. Also, we may learn from the vast body of Article 10 ECHR cases decided by the Commission and the Court in non-copyright matters.[106]

The somewhat related field of unfair competition law has generated a number of interesting decisions by the European Court.[107] The case of *Hertel v. Switzerland* is particularly noteworthy.[108] Swiss scientist Hertel had published an article in a popular journal on the potential carcinogenic effects of microwave cooking. According to the Swiss courts, Hertel's publication amounted to an act of unfair competition, since it had a potential negative effect on microwave oven sales. Before the European Court, Mr. Hertel invoked his right to freely express his scientific opinions.

The Court reiterated that Member States enjoy a wide "margin of appreciation" in imposing restrictions on freedom of expression and information in the framework of unfair competition law. However, the Court did find that Mr. Hertel's freedom of expression was unnecessarily restricted because there was no evidence that microwave oven sales had effectively declined as a result of the publication.

The Hertel decision confirms that commercial speech enjoys only limited protection in Europe.[109] The European Court of Human Rights allows Member

---

[106] See generally Dirk Voorhoof, "Critical perspectives on the scope and interpretation of Article 10 of the European Convention on Human Rights", Mass media files, No. 10, Strasbourg: Council of Europe Press 1995.
[107] *Barthold*, ECHR 25 March 1985, Publications of the ECHR, Series A 90; *Markt intern*, ECHR 20 November 1989, Publications of the ECHR, Series A 165.
[108] *Hertel*, ECHR 25 August 1998, Publications of the ECHR, Reports 1998-VI. See A. Kamperman Sanders, "Unfair Competition Law and the European Court of Human Rights. The Case of Hertel v. Switzerland and Beyond", paper presented at 7th Annual Conference on International Intellectual Property Law and Policy, Fordham University School of Law, New York, 8–9 April 1999, paper on file with the author.
[109] See *supra* text accompanying note 41.

States a wide latitude in applying speech restrictions derived from commercial law and the law of unfair competition. This line of cases suggests that Article 10 will allow the unauthorized use of copyrighted works for predominantly commercial purposes only in exceptional cases.

Clearly, not all speech restrictions are treated equally by the European Court. In a long line of cases not concerning copyright, the European Commission and the European Court have consistently granted a higher level of protection to political speech than to "ordinary" kinds of expression. In doing so, they have either implicitly or explicitly recognized the democracy-enabling function of the freedoms protected by Article 10.[110] The Commission and the Court also appear to have given artistic speech a preferred position, even though artistic freedoms are not expressly recognized by the Convention, and an *exceptio artis* that would have made creative artists immune from restrictions has never been accepted.[111]

Not surprisingly, the traditional "core" of the freedom of expression and information, freedom of the press, has generally been well protected. In several cases the Court has emphasized the special role the press has to play in democratic society, e.g., as "public watchdog".[112] The Commission and the Court have been especially critical of acts of government censorship, even if Article 10, unlike many national constitutions, does not contain a ban on censorship.

In applying the test of proportionality (necessity), the following factors have been taken into account.[113] First and foremost, the public interest involved in the act of speech appears to play a crucial role; restrictions on political speech will more readily be found to be disproportionate than those on commercial communications. A second factor is the substantiality of the restrictions; minor impediments will more likely meet the test. A third factor is the "legitimate aim" involved; for instance, a restriction for reasons of national security will more readily be judged proportional than restrictions on other grounds. A fourth factor is the level of European consensus; if similar restrictions exist in most other Member States, the European Court will be hesitant to find an infringement of Article 10.[114] This does not mean, however, that national deviations will never meet the test of proportionality; especially in areas of the law where norms tend to

---

[110] Chr. McCrudden, "The Impact on Freedom of Speech", in: Basil Markesinis (ed.), *The Impact of the Human Rights Bill on English Law* Oxford: Oxford University Press 1998, 90.

[111] Voorhoof (note 106), at 35.

[112] *Handyside*, ECHR 7 December 1976, Publications of the ECHR, Series A 24; *Sunday Times*, ECHR 26 April 1979, Publications of the ECHR, Series A 30; McCrudden (note 110), 98–99.

[113] J.G.C. Schokkenbroek, *Toetsing aan de vrijheidsrechten van het Europees Verdrag tot bescherming van de rechten van de mens*, Zwolle: W.E.J. Tjeenk Willink 1996, 220 ff.

[114] Schokkenbroek (note 113), at 226; Colin Warbrick, ""Federalism" and Free Speech: Accommodating Community Standards – the American Constitution and the European Convention on Human Rights", in: Ian Loveland (ed.), *Importing the First Amendment*. Oxford: Hart 1998, 183.

diverge, such as morality and unfair competition, the Court will allow a wide margin of appreciation.

In sum, our analysis suggests that freedom of expression arguments are likely to succeed against copyright claims aimed at preventing political discourse, curtailing journalistic or artistic freedoms, suppressing government information or impeding other forms of "public speech". In practice, this might imply that the Court is willing to find infringement of Article 10 in cases of unauthorized uses of copyright material, if national courts fail to broadly interpret or "stretch" existing copyright limitations, such as those enabling quotation, news reporting, artistic use or re-utilization of government information. The Court might even be prepared to go one step further by finding national copyright laws to be in direct contravention of Article 10 for failure to enact limitations in certain cases, such as parody.[115]

However, the Commission has been reluctant to accept freedom of expression and information arguments in cases where copyrights are primarily exercised to ensure remuneration, and the flow of information to the public is not unreasonably impeded. For European courts and legislatures, the message is clear: as long as licenses are made available under reasonable conditions, or statutory licenses apply, the European Court is unlikely to let copyright and Article 10 collide.[116]

European case law also suggests that speech restrictions that are in line with European consensus will more readily be accepted than national particularities. Considering the increasingly important role of the European Union as pan-European copyright legislator, this is a sobering conclusion. Even if, as according to many commentators, recent European Directives have upset the "delicate balance" between copyright and the public interest, it is improbable that the European Court of Human Rights will be easily convinced to apply Article 10 to restore the equilibrium.

---

[115] Most copyright laws in Europe do not provide for parody exemptions. Article 5(3)(k) of the European Copyright Directive does expressly allow such exemptions.

[116] Cf. *KPN/Denda*, Court of Appeal Arnhem 15 April 1997, Informatierecht/AMI 1997, 218 (refusal to license telephone subscriber information deemed unautorized restriction of freedom of expression and information).

IV. MEDIA AND TELECOMMUNICATIONS

International Trade in Media Products[1]

C. Edwin Baker

Pressure from the United States to adopt free trade principles for mass media or "cultural" products almost derailed the Uruguay round of the GATT negotiations, seven years in the making and finally signed on April 15, 1994. Only an eleventh hour capitulation by the U.S. saved this defining trade agreement. After fierce negotiations, the U.S. also abandoned similar demands in the negotiation of NAFTA in 1992, repeating its failure to get free trade provisions for cultural products included in the 1988 Canada-United States Free Trade Agreement.[2] In the early 1980s, the U.S. feared and opposed UNESCO efforts that would support governmental involvement in creating better, more balanced and informative national media systems because these efforts would not rely solely on free trade principles. This opposition was possibly the principal reason for U.S. withdrawal from UNESCO in 1985.[3]

---

[1] This essay is based on C. Edwin Baker, "An Economic Critique of Free Trade in Media Products" (2000) 78 *North Carolina Law Rev.* 1358, which provides more complete notes and discusses additional issues; I also discuss the topic in C. Edwin Baker, *Media, Markets, and Democracy* (Cambridge U. Press, 2002). The essay applies an economic argument developed in C. Edwin Baker "Giving the Audience What It Wants" (1997) 58 *Ohio St.L.J.* 311.

[2] Although President Clinton asserted that trade in film and audio visuals was a "defining issue" that would "make or break" the negotiations, the US had to settle for an agreement to disagree, with newspapers reporting that "France defeated the film moguls of Hollywood," and the French Prime Minister telling the French Parliament that "[t]he European cultural identity has been saved." Bernard Weinraub, "Clinton Spared Blame by Hollywood Officials," *NY Times* (Dec. 16, 1993), D1; Steve Doughty, "Gentlemen, We Have a Deal," *Daily Mail (London)* (Dec. 15, 1993), 10; Scott Kraft, "In French Parliament, A Resounding "Oui' for Accord," *L.A. Times* (Dec. 16, 1993), A19. *But see* Sandrine Cahn and Daniel Schimmel, "The Cultural Exception: Does it Exist in GATT and GATS Frameworks? How Does It Affect or Is It Affected by the Agreement on TRIPS?," (1997) 15 *Cardozo Arts & Entertainment L.J.* 281 (offering much more skeptical view both of the European victory and of the degree free trade principles do not prevail).

[3] Given the voracious criticism coming from the United States, this may seem an overly benign description of the MacBride Commission Report and the New World Information and Communication Order (NWICO) to which the United States objected. Nevertheless, I think one of the chorus of American critics correctly described the Commission Report as "advocat[ing] the elimination of governmental interference and censorship, the decentralization of the mass

N. Elkin-Koren and N.W. Netanel (eds.), *The Commodification of Information*, 267–290.
© 2002 C. Edwin Baker. Printed in Great Britain.

These disputes represent, in part, the practice in many countries to adopt measures that promote the availability of domestic (or regional in the case of the European Community's Television Without Frontiers Directive in 1989) media or cultural products, such as broadcast or screen quotas requiring a minimum of local content or subsidy schemes to promote local media content creation, often paid for in part by tariff or tax schemes that discriminate against imported media products. On the other side, not only does the United States' second largest export industry stand to profit handsomely from implementation of free trade in this realm, but the United States has long asserted that *principle*, not merely self-interest, demands its free trade position. The U.S. argues that protectionism prevents people in importing countries from receiving the media or cultural products they want. Certainly economic efficiency, if not even more fundamental norms, which American advocates of free trade believe are encoded internally in the United States in the First Amendment, demand international free trade in these products. Thus, it might seem hard to find a benign explanation as to why so much of the world stands against principle, that is, stands against free trade in media or cultural products.

The standard presentation presents the debate as an opposition between economic principle and purported cultural values. U.S. representatives concede that economic efficiency is not everything. Still, they regularly exhibit skepticism about whether foreign invocations of cultural values represent anything other than a mask for the interests of influential domestic economic groups or the values of local elites. American commentators raise the issue of the paternalism of these elites deciding that the public should be fed cultural products which that public does not particularly want rather than receive the imported, often Hollywood, culture that their purchases in a free market would show they actually prefer.

Elsewhere I have commented more broadly on the legitimacy of the cultural claims often invoked by those favoring trade restraints.[4] In this essay, my primary goal is to dispute the American claim that either economic principle or the liberal normative principle of giving people the cultural products they want justifies free trade in media products. My economic argument must make two points. First, it must show that the market routinely fails to produce efficient results in the context of media products. However, this point is not enough. Responsive or corrective regulations might be applied equally to domestic and foreign media products. If to do so provided a good solution to the problem of market failures, free trade might not be a barrier to desirable results. Free trade principles generally permit regulatory interventions as long as they provide for "national treatment" of foreign products,

---

cont.
> media, high standards of professionalism for journalists, and a better balance in the contents and coverage of mass media reporting." Michael J. Farley, "Comment, Conflicts over Government Control of Information – the United States and UNESCO" (1985) 59 *Tulane Law Rev.* 1071, 1076. For further discussion, see Baker (2000), note 1 above, at 1430–34.

[4] Baker (2000), note 1 above.

that is, they only prohibit regulations that discriminate against foreign products. Thus, my argument must show, secondly, that international free trade exacerbates the problems created by the market and that, therefore, at times the most appropriate solutions will treat foreign media products less favorably than domestic products.

General arguments for and against free trade are legion. This essay is agnostic about such claims. Instead, here the question is whether special attributes of media or cultural products justify deviations from free trade *assuming* that a free trade regime is generally desirable. Of course, their special attributes could have the opposite force. One attribute discussed briefly in the conclusion, media products' capacity to bring new ideas and aesthetics into a society, makes trade in media products uniquely valuable (as well as threatening to some established elites). The essay's economic argument, however, focuses on three attributes of media products, presented in turn in the three central sections of the essay, that make unrestricted free trade especially problematic. These three – the high first copy cost as opposed to low reproduction costs of media products, the portion of media products' costs and benefits that consists of positive and negative externalities, and the appropriate method of identifying and measuring preferences for media products – cause markets to fail to efficiently supply people with media products they want.

Non-Rivalrous Use and Monopolistic Competition

Carol's consumption of an ice cream cone leaves nothing for Ed. Like ice cream cones, the cost of resources used in producing each iteration of most products is significant – despite economies of scale, each added item often costs almost as much as producing the first. In the idealized models of introductory economics texts, firms produce and sell typical products up to the point where the marginal cost is increasing and where the average cost, marginal cost, and demand curves intersect. Competition within competitive markets leads to that happy result.

This picture is not true for goods that, over the relevant range of production, have constantly declining average costs – a common characteristic of most media products. Media products typically have high first copy costs – the costs of idea development and of researching, writing, layout and editing or of scripting and filming are all necessary to have a newspaper or film or broadcast for the first person to consume. However, additional people can consume the same item or copies of it at little if any additional expense.[5] Of course, media products are not

---

[5] Marketing expenses complicate the story but for the policy purposes of this essay can be ignored.

unique in this quality of allowing "non-rivalrous use." It is, for example, a quality of all public goods. Once created (or maintained), national defense protects and beautiful scenery enriches multiple individuals. Markets, however, are not normally effective at producing an appropriate level of "public goods." Failure occurs because no potential buyer receives anywhere close to the full value of what is produced, while costs of getting all the beneficiaries together for joint purchases and the dysfunctional incentives for individual beneficiaries not to fully participate prevent voluntary action from achieving adequate "purchases."

Market failures in goods whose use is non-rivalrous is alleviated but not eliminated if the producer/seller can deny the goods to those who want the good but do not pay. "Pure" public goods are characterized by *non-excludability* as well non-rivalrous use. But many products, including most media products, permit at least partial exclusion of those who do not pay.[6] Still, as long as an additional user's consumption costs the seller/producer nothing (that is, as long as the marginal cost is zero) or at least costs less than the product's average cost (that is, the product's total costs divided among all users), there will be no single price for which the good can be sold that will result in economically appropriate levels or production and use. For such a product, assuming inability of the seller to fully *price discriminate* (that is, to charge different users different prices depending on their willingness and ability to pay), the market will fail.

The point is actually even more dramatic. Below, I will present a simplified example to illustrate three points, which I will then apply to the media context. Assuming inability to adequately price discriminate, although the market will occasionally work fine, often the market will: (1) inadequately make available those media products that it does produce; (2) fail to produce other media products valued by consumers; and, an often unrecognized point emphasized below, (3) sometimes allow products to succeed that produce less value for consumers than would the goods that these successful products drive out of existence.

As a hypothetical illustration of these possibilities, consider various possible combinations of consumer demand and product costs in a three-person society (see Table 1). The illustration maps a hypothetical demand for *Product A* at time T1, and then the demand for *Products A* and *B* after *Product B* is introduced at time T2. *Product B* in this hypothetical might be for example, a newspaper packed with features such that everyone can find something they want (hence bulkier and higher marginal costs) but without the expensive, more edgy, investigative material

---

[6] The main function of copyright can be seen as an effort to promote excludability, although copyright is only one mechanism – consider the walls that require a ticket to get into a theatre, cable rather than over-the-air broadcasting, or scrambling of either television or cable programs; moreover, copyright only aides some exclusions – consider, for example, inability to exclude access to unscrambled over-the-air broadcasting or further dissemination though (fair use) repetition in conversation.

of the original newspaper that made at least person 1 value *Product A* so much – or a parallel story could describe differences between films represented as *Product A* and *Product B*. Here (and in Table 2, below), I assume that the seller cannot price discriminate; that is, the seller must choose one price at which to sell the product to all who want to buy at that price. (This assumption will be relaxed with telling consequences later.)

With each level of demand, the seller tries to find a *selling price*, if any, that allows maximum profits. In this discussion, *actual surplus* equals the amount that the various purchasers value the product beyond what it costs to produce ($\Sigma D_i - \Sigma C_i$, where D is each person's demand for and C is the cost of each item actually purchased). This surplus becomes either "consumer surplus," the amount consumers value the product above what they pay, or "profit" ("producer surplus"), the amount the seller receives over what it costs to produce. (The distribution between these two makes a significant difference for distributive but not for efficiency purposes). *Potential surplus* equals the surplus that the most desirable or efficient level of production and distribution would produce.

The market achieves an *efficient* result if the demand curve for *Product A* takes the form of $T1_A$. However, if the demand for *Product A* were only slightly less, for example, if the demand was as represented in Table 1 by demand curve $T\text{-}2_A$, the result turns bad. Then, even though production and supply of *Product A* for the three people would produce a value of 36 (19 + 10 + 7) at a cost of 22 (20 + 1 + 1), potentially producing a surplus of 14 (36 – 22), no selling price exists at which the market will produce the good. Again assuming no ability to price discriminate, the possibilities are to sell to one person for 19 while the cost would be 20, to sell to two persons for 10 each or a total of 20 (10 × 2) while the cost would be 21 (20 + 1),

Table 1: Results of Demand for Media Products in Three-Person Society

	Product A			Product B	
	Cost	Demand		Cost	Demand
Person		$T1_A$	$T2_A$		$T2_B$
P1	20	19	19	19	10
P2	1	11	10	2	9
P3	1	8	7	2	8
For each demand set:					
Profitable Selling Price		8	—		8
Actual Surplus		16	—		4
Act. profit or producer surplus		2	—		1
Act. consumer surplus		14	—		3
Potential Surplus		16	14		4

or to three persons for 7 each or a total of 21 (7 × 3) while the cost would be 22 (20 + 1 + 1). The result is *inefficient non-production*.[7]

In non-media contexts, goods with declining marginal costs – usually goods that have a high cost to produce for the first beneficiary (consumer) but that can be supplied to others for little if any additional cost – are often handled inefficiently by markets, that is, either not produced or under-produced. Common examples include national defense, parks or utilities (for which a major cost is the infrastructure). If excludability allows private provision at all (given non-excludability, like for beneficiaries of national defense, usually *only* public provision is possible), the declining cost aspect of the goods' provision commonly results in so-called natural monopolies that lead to under-production. This situation is often thought to justify rate regulation with cross subsidies and, sometimes, additional public subsidies. In the media context, scholars have invoked declining average costs resulting from high first copy/low subsequent copy costs to explain the decline in competition in daily local newspapers in the United States and the development of local newspaper monopolies.[8] In such situations, the most appropriate economic analysis to apply is the "theory of monopolistic competition."[9]

Although the need for government subsidies and, sometimes, rate regulation is commonly recognized as appropriate in the context of goods with declining marginal costs (for example, for parks or utilities), commentators often do not note an additional feature of these declining-cost products. Specifically, they seldom note that the introduction of competition into the markets for these goods

---

[7] *Inefficient under-production* is just as likely as *inefficient non-production*. For example, if the demand of Person 3 is slightly less than is indicated in Table 1, namely 7 rather than 8, even though Person 3 would benefit by more than the cost of supplying her with the product (value of 7 generated by a copy produced at a cost of 1, generating a gain of 6), the selling price of 7 would not produce enough revenue to support the product. That is, supplying three people at that price would, again assuming no ability to price discriminate, produce a revenue of only 21 (7 × 3) while the cost would be 22 (20 + 1 + 1). Under these circumstances, the seller will still produce *Product A* but only two copies, selling it for 11 to two people, producing revenue of 22 (11 × 2) at a cost of 21 (20 + 1). The result is *under-production* since person 3 also should have been supplied.

[8] James N. Rosse and James Dertouzos, *Economic Issues in Mass Communications Industries* (1978); James N. Rosse, "The Decline of Direct Newspaper Competition" (1980) 30 *J. of Communication* 30. I have challenged the adequacy of this interpretation, arguing that it fails to explain why newspapers were once more competitive and showing how consideration of newspapers' increasing reliance on advertising revenue greatly improves the analysis. C. Edwin Baker, *Advertising and a Democratic Press* (1994), ch. 1.

[9] See Edward H. Chamberlain, *The Theory of Monopolistic Competition* (1960); Clement G. Krouse, *Theory of Industrial Economics* (1990), pp. 190–218; Robert D. Willig, "Consumer's Surplus without Apology" (1976) 66 *Amer. Eco. Rev.* 591. For application to media contexts, see Bruce M. Owen and Steven S. Wildman, *Video Economics* (1992); Baker (1994), note 6 above; Randolph E. Bucklin, Richard E Caves, and Andrew W. Lo, "Games of Survival in the US Newspaper Industry" (1989) 21 *Applied Economics* 631.

can itself be the cause of consumers getting less of what they want. That is, *competition can itself cause inefficiency*.

To illustrate competition that causes inefficiency, look back at Table 1. Assume that at Time 1, column $T1_A$ represents the demand curve for media Product A. Then, at Time 2, a competitor introduces new Product B with its demand curve $T2_B$, a curve that reflects that Product B can be sold to all three persons and produce a surplus of four. The availability of this new product (at a given price, say, of eight) is likely to affect the demand for other products, especially somewhat competitive products such as Product A. That is, the effect of introducing Product B at Time 2 could be to change the demand for Product A from what it was at Time 1 to the amounts represented by column $T2_A$. Now, at Time 2, Product A cannot be profitably sold at any set price, possible revenue will be lower than costs (that is, $1 \times 19 < 20$, $2 \times 10 < 20+1$, $3 \times 7 < 20+1+1$). Thus, Product A cannot be sold even though its production and distribution previously (at Time 1) produced a surplus of 16 and even now, with the decline of demand (at Time 2), could still produce a gain of 14. Given these demand functions, the result of introducing Product B into a free market is to change from a situation in which an expenditure of 22 (cost of producing Product A for three people) created a value of 38, generating a surplus of 16, to a situation in which an expenditure of 23 (cost of Product B) creates a value of 27, generating a surplus of four – a clear decline in value to the public. Despite the fact that Product A produces much more value, in market competition only Product B is profitable and can succeed. Here, the result of competition is to make people much worse off.

A further observation about inefficiencies potentially caused by monopolistic competition could be relevant to possible policy responses. In the above scenario, the only reason the new product's introduction generates a bad result is that it causes the competitive failure of Product A. Introduction of Product B would produce an overall gain if the government adopted an appropriate policy to prevent the consequent failure of Product A. It could do so, for example, by providing a one-unit subsidy to the producer for each sale of Product A she sells at a price of seven, causing the sale to three people to produce revenue of 24 ($3 \times 7 + 3 \times 1$) while the producer's cost is only 22. Given this interventionist policy, the availability of both Product A and Product B at Time 2 would generate a combined surplus of 18 ($14 + 4$), which is greater than the surplus for only Product A at Time 1 of 16. The ideal government policy would be free market entry combined with a carefully calibrated subsidy.

However, by assuming a more dramatic effect of the introduction of Product B on the demand for Product A, as represented by the new $T2_A{}^*$, Table 2 (which merely substitutes $T2_A{}^*$ for $T2_A$ from Table 1) illustrates a more demonic possibility. For example, if most people did not particularly want two media products, the introduction of Product B at an appealing price (e.g., 8) might have a larger negative effect on the demand for Product A than was assumed in Table 1.

Table 2: Results of Demand for Media Products in Three-Person Society

Person	Product A			Product B	
	Cost	Demand		Cost	Demand
		T1$_A$	T2$_A$*		T2$_B$
P1	20	19	14	19	10
P2	1	11	8	2	9
P3	1	8	5	2	8
For each demand set:					
Profitable Selling Price		8	—		8
Actual Surplus		16	—		4
Potential Surplus		16	5		4

At Time 2, a subsidy of *Product A* would still be better than mere reliance on the market (although the subsidy would have to be greater, about three units for each item to allow the sale of *Product A* for five). However, the best possible result after the introduction of *Product B* at Time 2 is a surplus of four from *Product B* and of five from *Product A*, or a total gain of nine. Thus, the best possible result (a gain of nine) given the introduction of *Product B* is less than the gain of 16 produced solely by *Product A* at Time 1. The competitively successful *Product B* results in people getting less of what they want whether or not the government introduces an ideal subsidy program. Given these demand functions, introduction of *Product B* necessarily results in a reduction of welfare (that is, a decline in the total surplus) generated by media product(s) – an example of *ruinous competition*.[10] In this case, the ideal government policy on efficiency grounds, the policy that would best serve consumers, would be to bar the introduction of *Product B* or to tax it at a level such that it would not be profitable to introduce.

The most relevant policy question is the likelihood of these various scenarios actually occurring or, for present purposes, the likelihood of international trade increasing this likelihood. Abstract theory cannot unambiguously answer these questions. Still, the central condition for "inefficient" results is clear – contexts where the seller is unable to capture enough of a product's potential surplus to pay for producing (or adequately producing) the product. These contexts are

---

[10] There are hidden complexities implicit in my suggestion of demand curve T–2$_A$*, e.g., why would person A buy both products if the result is to reduce the value she receives from *Product A* by so much – why would she not just buy *Product A* and receive the greater total surplus? Maybe she values the comics in *Product B* but its news, although a substitute for that in *Product A*, is not very good so she would still like to get *Product A*. Despite such possibilities, their empirical likelihood is not something that can be abstractly predicted. Here I merely note the complexity of possible ways competition – even without hypothesizing inefficient predatory or defensive strategies – can generate negative effects.

predictably more likely for goods that have a higher proportion of their value in the form of consumer surplus – leading to inadequate incentives to produce.

Three observations suggest that international trade can increase the contexts where these bad results occur, that is, to introduce goods such as *Product B* that cause the demand for goods like *Product A* to change from $T1_A$ to $T2_A$ or $T2_A{}^*$. First, the failure to produce an economically-valued good is most likely for goods with rather steeply declining demand curves, which at any given selling price results in a relatively high portion of the value being left in the form of consumer surplus. (As used here, a "valued good" is one whose production and distribution at an appropriate level would produce more value than it costs.) Second, steeply declining demand curves occur most often for products with comparatively small audiences. For example, in the above Table, if the number of people valuing *Product A* at each price doubled, the curve would flatten – it would have the same beginning and end point levels but would extend over a greater distance (a greater number of people on the horizontal axis). With this larger audience (and consequently flatter demand curve), a firm could profitably produce and sell *Product A* to all those desiring it (although the firm might generate even greater monopoly profits by charging a higher price and restricting sales). For example, for demand curve $T2_A$, with six rather than three people willing to pay at least seven, the producer could easily provide the product, where it could generate a revenue of 42 (6×7) at a cost of 25 ($20 + 5 \times 1$). Thus, public policy makers should worry most about smaller-audience, often diversity-producing media products. These are the economically valued goods that markets most likely will fail to produce. Since for most countries, the market for many domestic products will be much smaller than the international markets available to the main imports, the economically valued goods that fail due to a free trade regime will predictably be disproportionately domestic media products. This result may be even more characteristic of domestic media products serving distinct sub-parts of the domestic culture. That is, international trade is likely to introduce products such as *Product B* and to cause the failure of domestic products such as occurs in the change of demand for *Product A* between Time 1 and Time 2.

A third observation reinforces reasons to fear the economic consequences of free trade. Cheap and effective price discrimination by sellers reduces the likelihood of failing to produce and distribute up to an efficient level. Importantly, however, costless, effective price discrimination would lead to the commercial success even of goods that generate little surplus for either the seller or consumer. Thus, some of those products best able to price discriminate would produce little or no gain in social value while competitively destroying goods that would produce great gains for consumers (and society).

Sellers of media products have always been able to engage in *some* price discrimination. One of the most common means is by exploiting different "windows," for example, releasing a story creation at different times in video and print format, in first run movie theatres, VCR format, on premium cable, over-the-air TV, in hardback and paperback book formats, and with different language translations. Those consumers most willing and able to pay receive the product earlier or in a more preferred format, but price discrimination allows others eventually to receive it in some form. Two factors greatly increase sellers' opportunities to price discriminate. The first is the availability of more windows. The second relates to the typically significant cost of exploiting (or creating) windows or engaging in various other forms of price discrimination. The more purchasers over whom the seller can spread these costs, the more likely the seller will be able to profitably engage in price discrimination.

International trade creates advantage on both fronts. Different geographical areas, and especially different areas with clear borders, often constitute relevantly different windows. Selling prices can be calibrated to the level of wealth and product appeal in each country. In this way, geopolitical borders have long increased the number of available windows and, thus, the opportunity to price discriminate.[11] Likewise, since the potential international audience is overtly larger than the domestic audience, international trade increases the audience over which to spread the costs of a price discrimination strategy. More specifically, each window must be worth the cost of differentiating within a price discrimination strategy, which will be most true in the case of the blockbuster or mega hit movies, television programming, music, or translated books that are most prominently marketed internationally. Thus, the tendency is predictably for more price discrimination to occur with internationally traded media products than with domestic products, especially those smaller-audience domestic products whose economic viability international competition is most likely to undermine.

Of course, many international (as well as domestic) media products will only be *marginally* successful (in terms of proportion of revenue constituting profits, not in terms of audience size). That is, some media products will succeed not because they produce a large surplus, some of which becomes consumer surplus and some becomes producer surplus or profit but because, making use of price discrimination the producer is able to capture almost all the product's value and still just barely cover her costs. Thus, to the extent these products are only marginally successful (profitable) and that success is only due to considerable price discrimination, these products will have predictably produced rather little surplus, either consumer or producer. In contrast, the smaller-audience domestic products that these marginally successful products undermine, such as *Product A* in the move from demand curve $T-1_A$ to $T-2_A$ or $T2_A{}^*$, are likely to have relatively high proportions of potential surplus. In such cases, competition leads to inefficient outcomes – a scenario predictably created by a free trade regime.

---

[11] This ability to price discriminate is reduced to the extent that people can purchase a product in one country and then sell it in another – which is why the permissibility of engaging in "arbitrage" is an important trade issue that is especially relevant for intellectual property.

From a policy perspective of trying to maximize value as perceived by audiences, no blanket restriction on media imports can be justified (at least by the argument developed in this section). If an imported media product succeeds in the market, it will have produced more value than it cost *except for its potential detrimental effect on domestic products*. However, given this detrimental effect, eliminating marginally profitable international products can often produce a gain. Likewise, subsidies for potentially undermined domestic products are often justified. Although various coherent policy responses are possible, one obvious approach is to tax the revenue produced by the import (or impose a screen fee or screen percentage quota, which operates like a subsidy) and to use that revenue to subsidize marginal domestic products.[12]

Positive and Negative Externalities

The standard claim that the market provides people the goods they want is not a claim that it really provides them all the consumption items they want. Lots of people would want BMWs if provided for free but do not obtain them in the market – and if BMWs sold for $500,000, people would want less than the market currently provides. Rather the pro-market claim is that the market provides people with those goods that they want and for which they are willing to pay the "cost." This payment of the cost is the fact that, economists say, causes markets to lead to efficient allocations of resources. Crucial to the claim on behalf of the market is that products are properly priced, that is, priced at their real (marginal) cost. If some costs are not brought to bear on the purchaser (most often because these costs were not first brought to bear on the seller or producer), then the product will be sold too cheaply. The common example is the polluting factory (or the manufacturer of a polluting product, like cars with damaging emissions) that does not include in its cost calculations the damage caused by the pollution. This leads the manufacturer to sell too cheaply and consequently to produce too many of its products (whose price does not represent their real cost) as well as to cause too much pollution. There will be more polluting factories and more cars than there would be if people paid the full cost. Similarly, if the seller/producer cannot capture some benefits produced by the

---

[12] Interestingly, the notion of taxing block busters to pay for subsidies to smaller audience products is in some ways structurally comparable to the tax struck down in Minneapolis Star & Tribune v. Minnesota Comm'r of Revenue, 460 U.S. 575 (1983). On the other hand, it is arguably even more explicitly like the policy of a tax differential to support "fledgling publications" that in Arkansas Writers' Project v. Ragland, 481 U.S. 221 (1987), the Court hypothesized might be justified. *See* Baker (1994), note 6 above, ch. 4, for a similar proposal for a tax and subsidy scheme.

(marginal or last sold) good, then it will have inadequate incentives to produce and sell the product. The market will supply less than it would if the seller did not impose all the goods' costs on purchasers who receive only some of its benefits. People purchase less of these products because the products are priced too high. These observations explain why so-called negative externalities lead to too much and positive externalities lead to too little production.

Media products often generate huge positive and negative externalities. In fact, it is quite plausible to believe that most of many media products' value or disvalue goes to people other than the immediate purchaser/consumer. Elsewhere I have tried to catalogue the dominant categories of positive and negative externalities that different media products produce to varying degrees.[13] Here, I only note a few major categories and then suggest that, as compared to internationally traded media products, domestic media are likely to have comparatively high levels of certain positive externalities, meaning that they will be under-produced by the market. Moreover, international products will often have comparatively high levels of negative externalities and, hence, will be over-produced. To the extent these empirical predictions are right, a plausibly appropriate structural policy approach would duplicate the suggestion in the last section, namely, a regime, such as a tax and subsidy system, that disfavors imports.

Social science evidence is quite overwhelming that extensive exposures to some types of violent media content increases people's anti-social and violent tendencies.[14] There are plenty of reasons to conclude that this fact does not justify censorship. Still, injury to the victim is one "cost" of those media products that play a crucial part in the causal chain[15] leading to a copycat crime or to violent rape, robbery or murder. In fact, predictable harm to people other than the immediate consumer is involved in most categories of expression that are subject to serious social criticism and proposed regulatory suppression – for example, hate speech, war propaganda, political disinformation as well as much gratuitous violence in media content. Any market system that does not take these harms, these costs, into account will predictably produce more of such expression than it would if media products were priced at their true cost.

In contrast, people other than the immediate consumers often benefit from media products. A person often benefits from the knowledge, wisdom and sensitivity of those with whom she shares social space, and the media consumption

---

[13] Baker (1997), note 1 above.
[14] For a critical summary of evidence and references, see James T. Hamilton, *Channeling Violence* (1998), pp. 20–30. Like Hamilton, I will assume here that violent programming has at least some negative externalities and that policy should take this likelihood into account.
[15] To say "causal chain" means that in a meaningful number of cases, elimination of this factor would eliminate the violent or objectionable effect. It does not mean that the media content necessarily leads to violence or that the objectionable effect is not the result of additional factors including, in the final instance, a decision for which the person who commits the violence is responsible.

of those people can have huge consequences for their knowledge, wisdom and sensitivity. Sometimes people can even benefit from the media production process independent of any purchase by either themselves or others. Here the key is that potential exposure in media content can lead people – government officials or corporate executives, for example – to act more responsibly, honestly, and in the ways that others legitimately want. Both effects are intrinsic to the frequently asserted "checking function" or "fourth estate" role of the press.[16] Although characterization of a voter's use of the franchise as wise or intelligent is always contested, intelligent voting benefits not just the individual voter but all who gain from "good" governmental policies and practices. A person's purchase and consumption of media content that leads to better, more informed voting generates clear and, in the aggregate, potentially huge positive externalities. Media that leads to misinformed and misguided voting does the opposite. Likewise, media exposés showing corruption or the need for new and different governmental or corporate policies, to the extent that the story leads to corrective responses,[17] benefits many other than the direct purchasers/consumers of the media product. Even the mere existence of credible investigative media can be a major social force leading to better behavior by governmental, corporate and other power holders. When the potential of exposure leads to behavior that eliminates the need for exposure, the media produces a benefit without creating any content to sell. The better behavior is a positive externality of media presence that is independent of any exposé to sell – a benefit that goes to people beyond the media purchasers.

As noted, my empirical thesis is that international trade favors media products that produce comparatively more negative and less positive externalities. This claim hinges on international trade encouraging the production and distribution of media products that characteristically have relevantly different content than the domestic products with which they compete. Obviously, speculation about the consequences of different trading regimes is hazardous. Still, some observations have plausible theoretical and empirical support. Eli Noam offered a useful threefold categorization: domestic content (*D*), foreign content (*F*), and universal content (*U*).[18] *Domestic content* has special relevance or, because of its use of local cultural resources including local history and humor (as well as the local language), greater accessibility to domestic audiences. Although the exotic has

---

[16] *See* Justice Potter Stewart, "Or of the Press" (1975) 26 *Hastings L. J.* 631; Justice William J. Brennan, Jr., "Address" (1979) 32 *Rutgers L. Rev.* 173; Vincent Blasi, "The Checking Value in First Amendment Theory" [1977] *Amer. Bar Foundation Res. J.* 521.

[17] For evidence that corrective responses often occur, but occur independently of any public response (that is, response by readers or viewers), as if the media itself were the public to which the democratic process reacts, see David L. Postess et al, *The Journalism of Outrage: Investigative Reporting and Agenda Building in America* (1991).

[18] Eli Noam, *Television in Europe* 18 (1991). For a critique of other aspects of Noam's analysis, *see* Baker (2000), note 1 above.

always had appeal,[19] most evidence shows that people on the whole mostly prefer media representations and news about people like themselves or with whom they identify.[20] *Foreign content* is, basically, the domestic content of some other country or people. *Universal content* has the least domestic markers. Instead, it emphasizes elements that are easily translatable, understandable or appealing for people of widely varying local cultures and political circumstances.

Among most people, demand is greatest for *D*, is strong for *U*, and weakest for *F*. However, that which is *D* in the producer's home country will be the relatively unappealing *F* in the countries into which it would be imported (except maybe when serving the home country's diasporic population). And that which is *F* in the producer's home country will not appeal to the domestic audiences on which the producer dominantly relies for sales, at least if the home country offers a significant audience as it obviously does in the United States as well as in most countries producing significant media exports. Thus, the dominant incentive for a producer who wants to engage in international trade is to emphasis *U*.[21] High levels of *U* can be appealing both at home and abroad. This is especially true if slick content made with high production values, itself one version of *U*, makes up for any loss of appeal due to containing less *D*. Of course, expenditures on expensive production values are facilitated by the opportunity to spread costs over a larger audience. Thus, the market-created bias toward blockbusters is heightened by the expanded market made available through international trade.

The question is: in addition to U aspect of content with high production value, what types of content go into the categories *U* and *D*? No complete analysis is possible here – that is the task for which studio heads or top editors are handsomely paid to figure out. Still, several observations related to this section's concern with externalities are possible. First, content emphasizing action, violence and sex are normally easily translatable. Therefore, international trade predictably favors content focusing on these U qualities (except to the extent certain presentations of, say, sex are actually – not just purportedly – unacceptable in major export markets). George Gerbner concludes that violent programming has been overemphasized in American television scheduling due to the incentives to produce programming that also has appeal for export markets.[22] From research

---

[19] In conversation, Professor Mary Anne Case forcefully insisted on this point.
[20] *See, e.g.*, Steven S. Wildman and Stephen E. Siwek, *International Trade in Films and Television Programs* (1988).
[21] This incentive toward *U* is quite similar to the incentive experienced by newspapers that want to be local monopolies to favor "objective" journalism as opposed to partisan reporting. Partisan reporting that would be like *D* for its supporters but like *F* to others in the community, who would then be available to support a competing paper. Baker (1994), note 5 above, ch. 1. Another, more overtly disparaging name for both *U* and objective journalism is "lowest common denominator" media.
[22] George Gerbner, "The Hidden Side of Television Violence" in George Gerbner, Hamid Mowlana, and Herbert I. Schiller (eds), *Invisible Crisis: What Conglomerate Control of Media Means for America and the World* (1996), pp. 27, 32.

on audience ratings, Gerbner reports that American audiences generally prefer domestic programming with less violence, but he observes that this programming sells less well abroad. Combining these observations with the social science research indicating that violent content generates negative externalities suggests that international trade has, at least in this respect, deleterious effects both on the content provided to Americans and on the content that becomes prevalent elsewhere due to American exports. Note that this claim is not that producers force violent content on anyone or even that people do not find it appealing. Rather, the initial claim is that more violent content is produced and more is obtained by consumers because the producer (and hence the consumer) does not have to pay for its full cost. In addition, but more relevantly for trade policy, the claim is that international trade systematically exacerbates the problem because this U quality, which trade favors, has predictable negative externalities.

Second, the huge positive externalities associated with the press's checking function and fourth estate role are associated almost exclusively with D content. Clearly, any country committed to good government, especially any country committed to democracy, must place heavy value on encouraging and preserving robust domestic media. Although U content is not entirely irrelevant to democratic processes – and exclusion is sometimes an aspect of domination by particular entrenched interests – U (or F) content will seldom be the primary substance of domestic political debates nor will it be the content most focused on a people's cultural and identity discourses. Intelligent and informed outcomes to these debates and the existence of these discourses benefit many people other than the actual readers or viewers of the material.

International trade's tendency to replace domestic media with media containing primarily U can have predictably devastating effects on production of these positive externalities. For example, a country's magazine industry can contribute vitally to the country's cultural debates and to its political health. Canadian law, without restricting people's access to foreign magazines, prohibited importation (or heavily taxed versions printed in Canada) of magazines if the magazine was a special or "split" edition that contained advertising targeting Canadian consumers that differed from the advertising in editions designed for the home country. In effect, the law required that advertisers (primarily Canadian advertisers) that specially target Canadian consumers or purchasers, spend their magazine advertising dollars on Canadian rather than foreign (i.e., American) or split-run magazines. With the consequent support of this advertising "subsidy," Canadian magazines were quite successful, taking roughly two thirds of the Canadian market. In periods without such laws, Canadian magazines have been almost completely marginalized, obtaining only about a 20 percent audience share.[23] This

---

[23] Ted Magder, *Franchising the Candy Store: Split-Run Magazines and a New International Regime for Trade in Culture* 8 (Canadian-American Public Policy #34 1998), pp. 12–13. Magder's is one of a number of excellent accounts of the Canadian trade case.

legal attempt to preserve Canadian-oriented advertising as a subsidy for Canadian media, however, was found by a WTO panel and appeals board to violate international trade law.[24] The story illustrates that when U.S. magazines are left to depend on the appeal of its content, its advantages of economies of scale, and general *American* advertising support, Canadians dominantly choose Canadian magazines even though there is no limit on American magazines' access to Canada. Canadians want mostly American magazines only when the price of American magazines is determined not only by the advantages of scale but also by the support of advertising dollars (mostly Canadian advertising dollars) specifically aimed at Canadian consumers and when Canadian magazines have reduced support from Canadian-oriented advertising. That is, the magazines that Canadians want appear to depend, unsurprisingly to an economist, on the magazine's price and its related ability to generate revenue to support content creation. More relevant to the discussion here, however, is a second conclusion. The Canadian policy – supporting Canadian magazines by means of a structural rule that uses domestic advertising to create a domestic magazine subsidy – can be easily justified economically on the basis of the positive externalities that are predictably more associated with the Canadian than the American magazines.

The argument about externalities should not be overstated. People do value content received through trade. Even if its negative externalities were properly included in the price, people would often purchase foreign content. Moreover, new ideas and information that imports bring can often be characterized as significant positive externalities. Still, if I am right that generally domestic media as compared to imported media will tend to have more positive and less negative externalities, a structural policy granting some advantage to domestic media over imported media – for example, making domestic media somewhat cheaper or imported media somewhat more expensive – could be justified as a way of getting audiences more of the media that they would want if the different media were properly priced. Of course, calculations of the extent of the economically appropriate advantages (if any) for domestic media are specific to the circumstances of the individual country. For example, given the comparative lack of need to worry about the strength and health of the American media industries, the United States should find that imports add more to the diversity and to new ideas than it costs in terms of lost but valued domestic content – that is, for the United States, the externality

---

[24] World Trade Organization Report of the Appellate Body, *Canada – Certain Measures Concerning Periodicals*, June 30, 1997, WTO Doc. WT/DS31/AB/R, found at <www.wto.org/wto/ddf/ep/public.html> Canada's legislative resistance to the WTO decision was clear, but in 1999, "Canada was able to avert a trade war with the U.S. through an eleventh hour [Agreement on Periodicals]" between the US and Canada, that allows Canada to mandate that much advertising be channeled to Canadian magazines, an agreement giving Canada a lot of what it wanted but that is in quite doubtful conformity to the WTO decision. *See* Glenn A. Gottselig, "Canada and Culture: Can Current Cultural Policies Be Sustained in the Global Trade Regime?," (2000) 5 *Int'l J. Comm. L. & Pol'y* 1.

balance might tilt in favor of subsidizing imports. But the situation is not symmetrical. For most countries, the opposite is likely to be true. Thus, for most countries, limited discriminatory media taxes or import duties, screen and time quotas, targeted domestic subsidies, and channeling of advertising resources can be economically justified by the concern for audience's receiving the content they want. In fact, American audiences might also benefit from foreign burdens on American media exports to the extent that the reduced advantage of international trade leads American producers to emphasize more D content and less U content – like violence – for its American audiences.

Identifying and Weighing Audience Preferences

The market only satisfies preferences that it identifies and weighs. For this purpose, the market uses the criterion of willingness and ability to pay within market transactions. But what if a person's preference is to receive a story from a friend as a conversational "gift?" What if the person has preferences but has no money to register in the market's scales? There is nothing objectively correct or accurate – although also nothing objectively wrong – with the market's criterion for either identifying or measuring preferences. Moreover, people express preferences in many ways. Each way is likely to have normative significance and legal consequence for some but not other purposes. Neither the content, ordering nor strength of preferences need be the same for each method of expression. Although somewhat artificially, this point is worth making by separating it into two parts – contrasting the market (1) with other means of *identifying* and (2) with other means of *weighing or measuring* preferences.

People make different choices, express different preferences, depending on context – for example, after discussion or on impulse, in public or in private, in the voting booth or in the market. These differences are the basis for considerable legal policy. Sometimes law or practice requires that decision makers publicly identify their preference – for example, in the open, recorded voting common in legislative assemblies. Other times, as in the electoral voting of citizens in most democracies today, the law privileges private or anonymous expressions. Some market decisions are revocable for a period of time, thereby privileging the latter, possibly more reflective expressions. Purportedly to encourage reflection and deliberation, the law sometimes requires waiting periods – for example, before a woman can obtain an abortion.[25] In each case, the premise is that the preference

---

[25] *See* Planned Parenthood of Southeastern Pennsylvania v. Casey, 505 US 833 (1992). The dispute in this case was not about the legitimacy of this purpose but rather about whether this was the real purpose and actual effect of a mandatory waiting period.

may be different – and in some sense more valid – in the favored context. Moreover, factually, some preferences cannot be directly expressed in some contexts. As noted, the market cannot properly record a preference for a non-commodified, non-purchased product, service or experience – although various entrepreneurs work hard to provide close substitutes or even, as in the case of psychiatrists or paid romantic match-makers, to provide improved, commercialized versions or support for non-commodified interactions.

There is an essay to write, but not here, on the difficulty of economic analyses of communications that results because so much communication occurs in non-commodified forms and much of its value lies partly (often mostly) in its non-commodified quality. Terminology is emblematic here. The term "information," so often used, for example, in descriptions of the coming "information economy" or "information age," immediately suggests commodification. "Information" exists independently of relationships. Despite information's public good character emphasized in Part I, above, and despite current copyright law's refusal to provide ownership of information or ideas as opposed to their unique expression (but compare patent or trade secret law), information is a potentially own-able and clearly transferable resource. In contrast, the notion of "conversation" resists these reductions. Popular treatment of new technologies could thematize extending and transforming conversations rather than e-commerce or access to data banks. Web sites or home pages would vary in significance depending on which concept, information (often itself related to inducing other commodity transactions) or conversation, provided the focus of inquiry. With conversation, non-commodified relationships are often all important and clearly highly valued. Often subjecting them to overt market transactions would destroy their value.

"Communications" is a transition term. Sometimes "communications" refers primarily to the economic "instrumentality" or medium that either enables parties to transfer information or people to engage in conversation. At other times, the term – especially when used as a verb – more generically refers to the "activity;" or the reference is to the content of communication, which may or may not be part of a commodified interaction In any event, my impression is that the term "information," at least, is hermeneutically biased toward more commodified measures of value and conceptions of what is significant. That is, the market is more often well suited to value preferences for information than for conversation.

It might be argued that, although people often value activities and goods that exist only outside the market, since these occur on a "voluntaristic" basis, legal policy can ignore these non-commodified goods. That is wrong. First, market goods and non-commodified goods obviously compete for people's attention and time. The terms on which the alternatives are available predictably affect countless choices people make – from their choice of non-commodified or commodified communications to their decision to engage or not engage in money-making labor in order to satisfy their desires. The legal structure, however, affects these terms. It often favors or disfavors a particular form of communication, making it cheaper or easier to obtain or having the opposite effect, and thus making preferences for one or the other type of goods more or less realizable. Yochai Benkler, for example, has shown how the design of copyright law can favor not only the production of certain types of information but can also favor either non-commodified or commodified producers of information.[26] Early in U.S. history, the Postal System heavily subsidized delivery of newspapers, a commodified form of communication, by over-charging letter writers, a potentially non-commodified form (although at that time apparently most letter writing was as a part of a business). Whether broadcast rules should favor public or commercial broadcasting has been a contentious issue since the beginning of broadcasting. Since people engage in market (and non-market) expressions of preferences only within a market already structured by legal rules, and since this structure affects what preferences they express, reliance on market expressions is an overtly incoherent (as well as unjustified) means to determine whether to favor those structural rules that in turn favor commodified or those that favor non-commodified communicative goods or activities. Rather, these structural decisions would seem to be the type that should be made on the basis of value-based discussion within a democratic political sphere.

From the perspective of a country wishing to favor less commodified, more conversational or voluntaristic forms of communications, wariness about a free trade regime is warranted. Not only does free trade have the potential to directly favor commodified forms in the competition for people's time and attention, it is likely to lead to increased emphasis on subsidiary rules, such as more protective intellectual property rules, that burden non-commodified communications and advantage commodified expression. Nevertheless, I want to put aside both the problem of market *identification* of preferences and the related issues concerning policy choices to favor commodified or non-commodified expression. Here, instead, I want to briefly consider the other "arbitrary" aspect of the market criterion – its *measuring* preferences on the basis of "ability and willingness to pay."

Payment in a market is hardly an objective measure of how much a person values an item. Rather than "ability and willingness to pay given the existing distribution of wealth," the standard could be "willingness to pay given a just distribution" – or given an egalitarian distribution. A committed utilitarian might argue that the ideal standard would be to rely on some hypothetical "utility counter" attached to each person – although critics bemoan that this standard would result in people, already lucky enough to be specially able to draw joy or pleasure from almost any experience, then being allocated a disproportionately high proportion of society's goods. Or the standard might be that, without further

---

[26] Yochai Benkler, "Free as the Air to Common Use: First Amendment Constraints on Enclosure of the Public Domain" (1999) 74 *NYU L. Rev.* 354.

attempts at measurement, anyone's mere expression of a desire or preference for (or against) a particular item should count as being as great or as significant or as worthy of fulfillment as anyone else's – a criteria quite close to that used in one-person-one-vote decision-making. In any event, there is certainly no reason to believe that a rich person's expenditure of $150 on a French dinner, including the "moderately" priced half bottle of wine, necessarily fulfills 50 times as many or as strong of preferences as does the food on which a hungry homeless person, on days that she experiences as lucky, gets to spend $3. Putting aside the inadequacy of the market for identifying or ranking preferences of a single individual, the problem preliminarily addressed above, even market-oriented economists usually make no claim that "willingness and ability to pay" accurately or objectively measures the weight or significance of preferences interpersonally. Nevertheless, at least given a society's rough acceptance of the appropriateness or justness of an existing distribution of wealth, pragmatic reasons often support reliance on the market measure to distribute opportunities for preference fulfillment. That, at least, is what all market societies do.

In part because a market valuation is in no sense an objectively correct measure of value to the individual but at best a pragmatically useful allocative device, no democracy leaves all preferences to be fulfilled on the basis of willingness and ability to pay. Democracies vary as to what opportunities or benefits they exempt from solely market allocations.[27] Often included are food, housing, and medical care as well as individual rights (sometimes called "inalienable" rights, an overtly non-market terminology). But particularly common among items that democracies distribute more egalitarianly are access to the vote, a basic education and, sometimes, a variety of cultural opportunities. People's just claims to, as well as strength of their preferences for, these goods are thought to be adequately strong to justify their receipt of the goods if they merely make the effort to use the right or opportunity – although sometimes societies require the expenditure of other "currencies," such as the time or effort of queuing or the planning plus time and effort involved in registering to vote, before the person gets a particular "good."

Some media products have attributes similar to other goods or opportunities that most democracies distribute by market means. Many media products serve primarily as entertainment, for which market (or voluntaristic) means of distribution is widely accepted. Other media goods – some trade journals or flight charts or other technical specifications or lists of standards – serve primarily as inputs in commercial, productive activities, inputs that are also usually allocated by the market. However, other media products have characteristics more analogous to goods for which democracies usually measure preferences and then distribute more egalitarianly. With their inevitable guarantees of a "free press"

---

[27] Michael Walzer, *Spheres of Justice* (1983).

(compare a press that is economically "free" to recipients[28]), all democracies recognize that receipt of media goods is closely related to a democratic political process and a supposedly egalitarian voting process. For such goods, the argument for more egalitarian measurement of preferences and subsequent more egalitarian distribution of access is strong. Likewise, the media can play a quite crucial role in the educational process given that education is a lifelong process that often occurs outside school walls. Again, this arguably justifies a more egalitarian access to the relevant media. Finally, once democracy is recognized to extend beyond mere electoral processes to the building of the entire culture[29] and to the creation of mature public opinion on all sorts of issues, and once access to a society's cultural resources is seen, like education itself, as basic to full participation in a society,[30] a broad egalitarian argument can be made for access to various quality cultural as well as merely informative media content. Of course, the complexity of basing policy on these distinctions is increased both because different individuals will value the same media product for differing reasons and because the same individual will value it for multiple reasons.

I put aside here the unexpectedly puzzling issue of what "egalitarian" access to the mass media ought to mean.[31] Here the main point is that to some extent and for some media products, a market measure of preferences may be perfectly appropriate – for example, to the extent the audience values the media product simply for entertainment purposes; however, to some extent and for some media products, more egalitarian preference measurement and distributional principles are more justifiable. Even if free trade best provides for market-expressed preferences (an argument systematically critiqued above), there is no reason to expect it will best serve preferences if measured more egalitarianly.

On the whole, those products for which a more egalitarian distribution is justified not only will be domestic products but also are likely to be products especially disadvantaged by a free trade regime. For example, products with high levels of "domestic" as opposed to "universal" content will be particularly

---

[28] In 1832, Senators invoked the First Amendment's guarantee of a free press to justify a proposal to abolish postal charges for newspapers, a proposal that lost by one vote in the United States Senate. Richard B. Kielbowicz, *News In the Mail: The press, Post Office, and Public Information, 1700–1860s* (1989) pp. 58–61.

[29] Thomas I. Emerson, *The System of Freedom of Expression* 1970, p. 7.

[30] The Universal Declaration of Human Rights, U.N. Doc. No. A/810, at 71 (1948), art 27(1), provides that everyone "has the right freely to participate in the cultural life of the community," and the International Covenant on Economic, Social and Cultural Rights, Dec. 16, 1966, 993 U.N.T.S. 3, art. 15 (1), recognizes "the right of everyone ... to take part in cultural life." Interestingly given the US opposition to the cultural argument in the trade context, Rosemary J. Coombe, "Symposium: Sovereignty and the Globalization of Intellectual Property," (1998) 6 *Ind. J. Global Leg. Stud.* 59, 62, observes that the United States and Haiti are the only two of the about 120 countries that have ratified International Covenant on Civil and Political Rights that has not also ratified Covenant on Economic, Social and Cultural Rights.

[31] Baker (2000), note 1 above, pp. 1410–16; Baker (1997), note 1 above, pp. 393–396.

important for the political and cultural needs of a polity's members. Once the broader conception of democracy is invoked, this argument applies not merely for "news" and for explicitly political or viewpoint issue-oriented material, but also for a society's more cultural expression that relates to its *own* ongoing "conversation" about its identity and values. For this conversation to be the society's own, the (egalitarian) participants in the conversation must be the country's own people, both as speakers and listeners – although, of course, it is hardly improper for them to draw ideas and wisdom from elsewhere. Thus, this re-evaluation of what serving or satisfying preferences means to some extent challenges reliance on the market as a measuring device and suggests the need for government interventions. More specifically, it suggests the need for government intervention not only to favor more egalitarian access to certain media but in particular interventions to favor those domestic media products predictably disadvantaged by a free trade regime.

Conclusion

The claim has been that, for many countries and their residents, the nature of media products is such that a free trade regime would produce worse results from the perspective of economic efficiency or from the perspective of audiences receiving the media content they want than would a well-designed system of rules distinguishing between domestic and foreign media products. Nevertheless, three caveats, with the third being particularly important, should be emphasized. First, each of the essay's three arguments either depends on contingent empirical factors – such as the nature of people's demand curves or summations of negative and positive externalities – that could turn out differently than predicted here or depends on disputable normative judgments about appropriate standards for weighing preferences.

Second, as with all cases where government action is theoretically justified, is the question of whether actual governmental interventions will take an intelligent form. There is always a danger that it will instead be perverted toward the economic or ideological interests of the powerful. This point is very important – bad regulations are possible and can do serious harm. Of course, the point is perfectly general. "Free trade" itself is a particular legal form of regulation. Given the analysis here, it is plausible to conclude that the U.S. commitment to free trade in cultural or media products reflects not principle but the narrow rent-seeking activities of powerful corporate participants in the political process.

This essay has only explored the question of whether the *idealized* market, that is, the market that works in the way economic theorists would want, would produce ideal results – and answered "no." The actual market, of course, could be much worse. The same contrast can be made in respect to the political process. The essay has not made predictions about how the political process will actually work. Rather, it has asked whether, if the political process works ideally, that is, as an arena where people have an opportunity to democratically establish rules that ideally and fairly serve their values and interests, would it adopt rules other than mere reliance on the market that would produce preferable results – and answered "yes." Of course, in practice the political process might not work so well. Still, as the only arena that, if it works as it should, can give results that people want, the response to gloomy predictions about how it works in practice should be to consider how to improve the workings of this arena. Looking at actual practice rather than idealized possibilities, overtly illiberal media regulations are, unfortunately, not uncommon in today's world. They are, however, mostly adopted by undemocratic regimes and take an overtly censorious form. Moreover, they typically apply equally to offending domestic as foreign content and, hence, would not be blocked by a free trade regime that only requires national treatment. Although I cannot demonstrate the claim here, my sense is that the deviations from a free trade regime in media products that democratic countries have actually adopted fit quite closely the contours of what the economic analysis in this essay suggest are appropriate. That is, at least in this context, the fear of a malfunctioning political process as compared to a malfunctioning free trade regime may be considerably overstated.

Third, none of the economic arguments against a free trade regime suggest that outside ideas or content should be kept out. Such an illiberal goal obviously would be contrary to the preferences of those potential audience members who want access. Outside ideas and other imported media content both can be directly very valuable to recipients and sometimes can have very positive externalities, including positive political and culturally democratizing effects. Thus, the economic analysis arguably justifies only what Oliver Goodenough has called "weak protectionism," policies whose aim is to use subsidies and other legal or structural advantages to encourage and maintain local media content, especially content that predictably has the most positive externalities or democratic relevance.[32] The economic critique does not justify what Goodenough calls "strong protectionism," policies aimed at excluding outside content and ideas.

The second and third caveats combine in a way that leads to my final suggestion. Generally, a political entity should be slow to give up – to a Constitution or an international regime – the authority to make democratic decisions necessary to best advance the welfare, education or political participation of its citizens. On the other hand, devices like a properly interpreted First Amendment in the United States that bar illiberal legislative policies – for

---

[32] Oliver R. Goodenough, "Defending the Imaginary to the Death? Free Trade, National Identity, and Canada's Cultural Preoccupation" (1998)15 *Ariz.J.Int'l & Comp.L* 203.

example, policies that prevent access to new and different ideas and cultural possibilities – could offer a real gain for democratic processes even if they are seen as in some sense a restriction on parliamentary sovereignty. Free trade mandates in international agreements offend the first concern and fail to sensitively serve the second. The claim here has been that treaty-based free trade rules improperly restrict domestic legislative authority that should exist and that often should be used. And it is an especially blunt and arguably inappropriate and ineffective instrument for blocking illiberal legislation. Moreover, sociological considerations may counsel against reliance on trade law here. Trade lawyers and trade courts are occupationally skeptical of rules discriminating against imported goods and prone to see only their possible rent-seeking justifications. That is, even admitting that weak protectionism can be justified in the media or information or discourse realm, these trade lawyers are often likely to misidentify legitimate exercises of legislative authority as cases of strong protectionism.[33] For example, screen or broadcast quotas (typically requiring a minimum percentage of domestic content) do not require blockage of *any* outside content. At most, what they do is require that the outside content must "pay for" or "subsidize" domestic content by making it necessary to give screen or broadcast space to those domestic contents. Nevertheless, trade lawyers are particularly apt to fall into the easy trap of viewing these rules as "partial exclusions" of imports rather than structural subsidies of domestic content.

The goal of barring illiberal exclusions sounds more in terms of international human rights. The frequently asserted right of people to informational freedom is a part of this human rights system. I do not mean that current international human rights norms or, especially, current enforcement are adequate. Still, the more useful intellectual and political effort in behalf of preventing illiberal suppression may be to try to improve on such human rights doctrine and enforcement mechanisms rather than to seek an international free trade regime in media or cultural products. The latter, in fact, could impede adoption of policies that improve on consumers' access to media or informational content that they want and that democratic theory suggests citizens' need.

---

[33] I agree with Goodenough that weak protectionism is normally legitimate while strong protectionism is presumptively not. Goodenough, note 32 above. Nevertheless, I think he mischaracterizes his primary example, Canada's rules about magazine advertising, as strong rather than weak protectionism. If Goodenough makes this mistake, I worry even more that trade-oriented practitioners would often see improper exclusion in rules that are better described as attempts to promote local media.

A Speakers' Corner Under the Sun

Yochai Benkler

Introduction

Imagine that it was possible, from a technical perspective, to dedicate part of the radio frequency spectrum to a high-speed communications infrastructure that is not owned or controlled by anyone – not a government agency, not a media mogul, no one. In this paper I outline reasons why, if such a communications commons is technically possible, it's implementation better serves the democratic values of autonomy – in both its personal autonomy and political self-governance senses – than contemporary alternative approaches to regulating communications infrastructure. A society committed to these values would best serve them by investing in making the possibility of a spectrum commons a reality.

To make this a manageable paper on the normative underpinnings of spectrum policy, I make the following two factual assumptions that will not be defended here. First, it will become technically possible to provide access to large numbers of end users (more or less everyone) to high-speed data networks, using wireless communications techniques over license-free, unowned spectrum. Second, while these networks will not replace real-time networks with assured quality of service, they will enable a very wide range of uses, from Internet access, through online games, overnight (or over dinner) delivery of video on demand, to nonessential video conferencing. Following Baran,[1] Gilder,[2] and Noam,[3] I have elsewhere

---

[1] Paul Baran, Visions of the 21st Century Communications: Is the Shortage of Radio Spectrum for Broadband Networks of the Future a Self Made Problem? Keynote Talk Transcript, 8th Annual Conference on Next Generation Networks Washington, DC, November 9, 1994, available http://www.eff.org/pub/GII_NII/Wireless_cellular_radio/false_scarcity_baran_cngn94.transcript.
[2] See George Gilder, *The New Rule of the Wireless*, Forbes ASAP, March 29th, 1993.
[3] Eli Noam, Taking the Next Step Beyond Spectrum Auctions: Open Spectrum Access, 33 IEEE Comm. Mag. 66 (1995); Eli Noam, Spectrum Auction: Yesterday's Heresy, Today's Orthodoxy, Tomorrow's Anachronism. Taking the Next Step to Open Spectrum Access, 41 J. Law & Econ. 765 (1998) (hereinafter "Noam 1998").

N. Elkin-Koren and N.W. Netanel (eds.), The Commodification of Information, 291–315.
© 2002 *Yochai Benkler. Printed in Great Britain.*

suggested the basic technical and economic reasons for thinking that these assumptions are plausible.[4] The plausibility of attaining the assumed conditions is, however, contested,[5] and my purpose in this paper is not so much to defend this plausibility as to explain why it is normatively important to find out whether and how such a commons could be made operational.

My aim is to suggest why a nation committed to the democratic values of personal autonomy and the attainment and maintenance of robust, decentralized public discourse should make the investments necessary to create an infrastructure commons. In Part II, I outline the normative commitments that I take to be relevant to an analysis of information policy from a democratic perspective – focusing on personal autonomy, with some reference to political self-governance. In Part III I compare an infrastructure "commons," on the one hand, and an idealized "pure private property" infrastructure, on the other hand. I suggest that the private property approach suffers an autonomy deficit relative to the commons. In Part IV I introduce alternative models of regulation that constrain the pure property model, but do not implement a commons either, and I explain why these models do not serve the democratic values I posit as well as the commons does. I focus on the two models that present the most attractive, alternative solutions to the autonomy deficit of a pure private property system: privately owned infrastructure with heavy access regulation – *i.e.*, common carriers (and its cousin, publicly owned infrastructure, to which government has made a credible commitment not to censor – *i.e.*, public forums) and Noam's open access spectrum proposal.

The core claims are as follows:

First, both personal autonomy and collective self-governance are enhanced as individuals in society gain greater control over their own communicative environment. A system that widely distributes the capacity to acquire, manipulate, and communicate information (however encoded) is preferable, from the autonomy perspective, to one that concentrates control over these capacities, whether that control is concentrated in the hands of a governmental or nongovernmental organization. Such a system permits individuals to play a central role in defining their understanding of the world in which they must act and the range of possible options for actions open to them, and enables them to communicate to others and persuade them to accept their individual choices. Furthermore, a widely decentralized system entailing low cost access to information *production and distribution* facilities permits individual constituents

---

[4] Yochai Benkler, Overcoming Agoraphobia: Building the Commons of the Digitally Networked Environment, 11 Harv. J. L & Tech. 287 (1998) (hereinafter Benkler, Overcoming Agoraphobia).
[5] See Thomas Hazlett, Spectrum Flash Dance: Eli Noam's Proposal for "Open Access" to Radio Waves, 41 J.L. & Econ. 805 (1998).

of a polity to communicate their own beliefs and reduces the entry barriers to effective political speech prevalent in large democracies dominated by mass media.

Second, whether the capacity to control one's information environment is regulated by administrative processes or rules of property is less important, from an autonomy perspective, than the effect of the rules that govern information production and exchange on the pattern of distribution of this capacity. In other words, a system that is wholly owned by the public and administered by government officials may be more autonomy-friendly than one owned by nongovernmental actors. As a medium for public debate over local school board policies, for example, a public park subject to the public forum doctrine better serves autonomy, *in both its senses*, than a privately owned shopping mall protected by property law and controlled by a private actor not subject to the constraints of that doctrine.

Third, we now have a choice between a communications system designed to include *no* centralizing organizational authority, on the one hand, and communications systems that rely on centralized clearance decision makers – including those, like common carriers, required to clear communications indiscriminately – on the other hand. I argue that, given that choice, the system that lacks the centralizing organizational anchor will better serve autonomy. The reasons fall into two broad types. First, even where owners are required by law to grant access to their infrastructure – through a common carriage requirement – imperfections in the institutional details of the common carriage requirement can lead to both design and enforcement shortfalls that will lead to reassertion of control by owners. Second, the common carrier facility always remains an available locus for reassertion of control over information flow in a way that is impossible in a system that is designed from the ground up to be decentralized, as would the proposed spectrum commons. In other words, wherever it is possible to attain roughly similar efficiencies using any of a commons, a privately owned communications system, whether or not regulated as a common carrier, or a publicly owned facility, the first would be preferable to the latter two.

Part I: A Commons in the Air

The factual assumptions underlying my analysis are technological. Once upon a time, the only way for a receiver to receive a wireless signal was to have a transmitter transmit at sufficiently greater power than the sum of all other sources of electromagnetic radiation at a given frequency so as to drown out the "noise." If more than one transmitter tried to use this strategy, at least one, and usually both, would fail. We would get "interference." Hence the need for organizational/institutional determination of who will be the one permitted to drown out all others.

As a theoretical matter it has been understood for about half a century that this was not the only way to send electromagnetic signals over the air. As early as the 1940s spread spectrum techniques were theorized, permitting weak signals to share frequencies and be differentiated from each other by means other than relative strength. These techniques moved from the realm of theory (and military applications) to that of consumer applications with the radical decline in the cost of processors in the early 1990s, and are now the core techniques in the arsenal of the largest mobile communications providers.

Since 1993, Paul Baran, George Gilder, and Eli Noam have suggested that the availability of consumer products that utilize spread spectrum techniques alters the terms of the debate over spectrum management. The former two suggested that these techniques simply eliminate scarcity, and hence the necessity of treating spectrum as an economic good. Noam, on the other hand, assumed that scarcity would continue, and therefore suggested a way to retain a pricing system to clear competing claims to spectrum use, while eliminating spectrum ownership. He suggested that technology could be used to replace the auction system with a more efficient pay-as-you-go system in which each transmission bids in real-time for a slot in the spectrum, or calls on futures contracts for real-time delivery of transmission slots.[6] He called this approach "open access spectrum."

Like Noam, my own contribution to this literature has assumed that although spread spectrum techniques change the terms of the debate, some form of "scarcity". The "scarcity" that remains, however, is not correctly conceived as "spectrum scarcity", but as a more nuanced problem of how to allow multiple users to communicate in a system without wires. Unlike Noam, I proposed that the most important implication of these techniques is therefore not replacement of the market in licenses by a spot-market in "spectrum", but rather by a spectrum commons that anyone with the right equipment can use as and when they please, subject to sharing protocols embedded in the equipment. The idea is similar to the approach taken for Internet communications, where computer-communications are routed over the Internet using equipment-embedded collision and congestion control protocols, with no one controlling network traffic at an overall level. I argued that the efficiencies that proponents of property rights in spectrum seek to obtain from spectrum auctions, and for which Noam relies on real-time bidding, will be obtained in such a commons through investments by consumer equipment manufacturers and consumers.[7]

It is important to underscore that the claim is not that technology eliminates all

---

[6] Noam developed an approach based on automated bidding for each message slot, implemented by messages that carry their own tokens with which they bid on slots available through automated clearinghouses, with prices at any given moment, location, and frequency range reflecting demand for transmission capacity over that swath of frequencies, in that area, at that time. See Noam 1998, at 778–80.

[7] See Benkler, Overcoming Agoraphobia.

scarcity (in the economic, not in the discredited political-legal sense). Rather, it is that technology enables an allocation solution to scarcity that is at least as, and perhaps more efficient than the traditional approaches that rely on clearance of competing uses of spectrum by organizational mechanisms. Whether one uses a licensing scheme or a private property scheme, the core concept underlying both these traditional approaches is that conflicting uses are cleared by organizational decisions. Spread spectrum techniques, on the other hand, permit conflicting uses to be cleared by equipment-embedded protocols using computation and network architecture. These two approaches – organizational clearance and equipment-embedded collision avoidance and congestion control – compete in the relative efficiency with which they can clear millions of preferences about use of communications facilities. What is important to understand is that the tradeoff would be between identifying and serving communications preferences using, on the one hand, a market in large-scale infrastructure (*i.e.*, licenses), or, on the other hand, a market in end user equipment.

Suspend disbelief for a moment, and imagine how a network with no organizational center would look. Imagine that each piece of equipment can serve as either a transmitter or a receiver. Each node on the network can serve as either user or as network component. In a town, imagine the local school board deploying a license-free wireless network as a low-cost solution to connecting its schools to each other and the Internet,[8] individuals buy and install wireless modems on their computers, the local Blockbuster runs a VOD server, the public library runs an Internet access point, the bank an ATM, etc.[9] With existing technology, such a network could deliver up to 20Mbps data transmission rates (five times the speed most cable modems currently offer), to distances of 10–15 kilometers. While there is some disbelief among many orthodox regulators, economists, and engineers, there is also a growing number of people who argue the sustainability of many services on an Internet model relying on such decentralized, license-free wireless networks.

For purposes of this essay, I will assume, as I have already said, that such networks are technically and economically feasible. At the very least, I think it clear that we cannot tell *a priori* that such networks will be less cost effective for those uses that they could deliver with ease – data transmission, including non-real time video delivery, email, online games, community (voice and video?) chat rooms etc. Bear with me and imagine that, though these networks will not serve for real-time voice calls (we all have access to those over phone lines already), real-

---

[8] See descriptions of such systems implemented by David Hughes at http://wireless.oldcolo.com/.
[9] For the idea for this architecture of a license free wireless network, and the original illustration from which I borrowed my poor imitation in Figure 1, see D.Beyer, M.Vestrich, and JJ Garcia-Luna-Aceves. The Rooftop Community Network: Free, High-speed Network Access for Communities Rooftop Networks, < http://ksgwww.harvard.edu/iip/doeconf/beyer.html; > for current elaboration on this approach see generally < www.rooftop.com >.

time Super Bowl broadcasts, or micro-surgery by telemedicine, they will be capable of these non-time-sensitive services quite reliably.

The question that will be my focus here is whether attaining the deployment of such networks is a goal worth pursuing, from the perspective of democratic values. My main claim is this. To the extent that it is possible to implement a fully decentralized, unowned network such as the one I describe in this part, that network will be the communications infrastructure that best serves the values of personal autonomy and political self-governance. In a networked environment built on such an infrastructure, end user, equipment-embedded protocols avoid collision, and deal with congestion, using a preset, user- and content-independent protocol. In such an environment there is no design necessity for a point of centralizing decisions over infrastructure use, and hence no *potential* point of centralization. End user equipment clears competing uses by relying on more-or-less sophisticated queuing techniques recognizable and implemented by a fully decentralized network of end user equipment. There is no provider, no owner, no central network server that can say to any user; your communication may not pass. The remainder of the paper explains why such a decentralized spectrum commons is preferable, normatively, to any system that has such a center, and why the primary alternative approaches to infrastructure regulation do not provide a robust, decentralized infrastructure as does a spectrum commons.

Part II: The Stakes of Communications and Information Law

AUTONOMY AND POLITICAL SELF-GOVERNANCE

Why should we care about how people in society communicate? We might care because we believe that improving the communication of information will enhance general welfare by, for example, increasing the efficiency of markets or by increasing the rate of innovation, and hence of growth. But I would like to focus on why we should care as a matter of political morality.

The organization of the system of information production and exchange has implications for personal autonomy and political participation. The claim about the effects of the organization of information production on self-governance is more familiar than the claim about personal autonomy. It has been a consistent theme of the critique of media concentration for many years. Scholarship that followed Chafee's[10] pioneering work has developed a sophisticated set of

---

[10] Zechariah Chafee, Government and Mass Communications, 471–719, in particular 678–719 (1947).

arguments suggesting why a democratic system such as ours should seek to decentralize its information production sector.[11] The reasons fall into two broad categories. First, concentrated systems can be expected to produce different information than decentralized systems. They might simply reflect the views of their owners, but more likely, given their market-orientation, are likely to exclude challenges to prevailing wisdom that are necessary for robust political discourse. Second, concentrated commercial systems tend to translate unequal distribution of economic power in society into unequal distribution of power to express ideas and engage in public discourse. This inequality not only conflicts with our basic commitment in liberal democracies to equality in the political sphere, if not elsewhere, but also results in a diminution in the possibility of deep change through political discourse, which in turn diminishes the efficacy of, and engagement in, politics.

While this critique arises primarily in the context of mass media, the core analytic point transcends mass media. The point is that the organization of the means of communications play a central role in shaping political and cultural consciousness and shape a society's democratic processes. The degree to which the technical infrastructure of communications is controlled by a small number of actors or is widely dispersed among users-constituents in society, and the extent to which control over infrastructure permits, as a technical matter, and is used, as a practical matter, to control the content of communications, affect who gets to say what, to whom, and who decides who gets to say what to whom.[12] These questions go to the very core of who has an opportunity to participate in public discourse, and what they may say that will effectively be communicated to a large enough portion of the relevant constituency to make a difference to the collective decisions of the polity.

A parallel, but less often noted effect occurs at the level of personal autonomy.[13] By autonomy I mean something like Raz's "vision of people controlling, to some degree, their own destiny, fashioning it through successive

---

[11] The literature is very diverse, and includes significant internal variations. It includes Jerome A. Barron, Access to the Press – A New First Amendment Right, 80 Harv. L. Rev. 1641 (1967); Thomas I. Emerson, The Affirmative Side of the First Amendment, 15 Ga. L. Rev. 795 (1981); Owen M. Fiss, Free Speech and Social Structure, 71 Iowa L. Rev. 1405 (1986); Owen M. Fiss, Why the State? 100 Harv. L. Rev. 781 (1987); Jack Balkin, Some Realism About Pluralism, Legal Realist Approaches to the First Amendment, 1990 Duke L.J. 375, 383–86; C. Edwin Baker, Advertising and a Democratic Press 140 U. Pa. L. Rev. 2097 (1992); Cass R. Sunstein, Democracy and the Problem of Free Speech (1993); C. Edwin Baker, Private Power, the Press, and The Constitution, 10 Const. Comment. 421 (1993); Jack M. Balkin, Populism and Progressivism as Constitutional Categories, 104 Yale L.J. 1935 (1995); C. Edwin Baker, Giving the Audience What It Wants, 58 Ohio St. L.J. 311 (1997); C. Edwin Baker, The Media that Citizens Need, 147 U Penn L. Rev. 317 (1998).

[12] For a more detailed statement see Yochai Benkler, Communications Infrastructure Regulation and the Distribution of Control Over Content, 22(3) Telecommunications Policy 183 (1998).

[13] See Yochai Benkler, Siren Songs and Amish Children: Autonomy, Information, and Law, 76 N.Y.U. L. Rev. 23 (2001).

decisions throughout their lives."[14] While there are many inconsistent views of autonomy, some hostile to the type of definition of the term exemplified by Raz's, two types of effects of the organization of information production and exchange would, I believe, quite widely be considered to compromise personal autonomy. First, different patterns of information flow can have different systematic effects on the range of options known to individuals as open to them. As among any two systems of information production and exchange, that which will produce information about a more diverse set of life options is the system that better enables people to be their own authors, rather than being authored by the limited options they know to be open to them. Second, different organizational models of information production and exchange can give one group in society a systematic advantage in the ability to control the information environment within which others make their life choices. Parents, for example, care for their children partly by constraining their autonomy, and sometimes they do so by selectively revealing to them the range of options open to them, or perspectives on the values of different options. In the case of the parent-child relationship, we have many good reasons to tolerate this infringement on the immediate autonomy of the child in favor of education. But where a system of information production and exchange puts one set of adults in a similar relationship of power over information flow to another, as the parent is to the child in our example, personal autonomy is compromised.

These two normative strands – the commitment to political discourse and the commitment to personal autonomy – require that we ask specific questions when we evaluate a given information or communications policy. We must ask how the proposed policy will affect the structure of the primary means of communications in our large, complex democracies. Will it lead to a greater concentration of decisions about who gets to communicate with whom, or will it lead to decentralization of such decisions? Will the concentration be of a type that implies control over the flow of information? In other words, we must ask whether the policy increases or decreases the likelihood that some people could purposefully use control over information flow to manipulate the information environment of others so as to bend those others to their will.

---

[14] Joseph Raz, The Morality of Freedom 369 (1986).

Part III: A Simple Model of Ownership and Autonomy Comparing

INFRASTRUCTURE COMMONS TO UNREGULATED PROPRIETARY INFRASTRUCTURE

To frame the analysis, let me begin with two opposing ideal type approaches to regulating control or ownership over communications infrastructure: a commons and an idealized property regime.

A resource, in our case communications infrastructure, is a commons, or unowned, if everyone is equally privileged to use it, and no one has a right to prevent anyone else from using it. For purposes of this simple model, let's assume that "ownership" is Blackstone's "sole and despotic dominion," expressed as an unconstrained right of the owner to exclude anyone from using his or her owned infrastructure or to condition use of the infrastructure as the owner chooses.

Imagine a world with four agents, A, B, C, and D connected by a network that enables them to communicate with each other. Each component of the network could be owned or unowned. If unowned, each agent has equal privilege to use any route or component of the network to communicate with any other agent. If owned, the owner of any network component can deny to any other agent use of that network component to communicate with anyone else. If a network component is owned, it could be owned by any of the agents.

In this simple model, if the network is unowned, then all that is required for communication is a willing sender and a willing recipient. No third agent has a say as to whether any other pair will communicate with each other. Each agent determines independently of the others whether to participate in a communicative exchange, and communication occurs whenever all its participants, *and only they*, agree to communicate with each other. Say that A wishes to alter his information environment by exchanging information with B. A can do so if B lends her attention or agrees to communicate to him. In other words, the only person who can prevent A from receiving information from or sending information to B, is B, in the exercise of B's own autonomous choice whether to change her information environment. Under these conditions, neither A nor B are subject to control of their information environment by others, except where such control results from denial to them of the capacity to control the information environment of another.

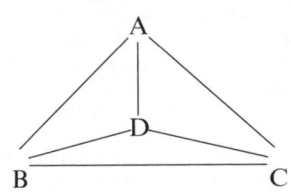

Figure 1

If all network components are owned, on the other hand, then for any communication there must be a willing sender, a willing recipient, and a willing infrastructure owner.[15] In a pure property regime, infrastructure owners decide whether, and under what conditions, others in their society will communicate with each other. It is precisely the power to prevent others from communicating that makes infrastructure ownership a valuable enterprise – one can charge for granting one's permission to communicate. For example, imagine that D owns all lines connecting the ADB triangle, and C owns both lines AC and BC. A wishes to change his information environment by communicating to B. In addition to B's consent to A's invitation to communicate, either C or D must also consent. So now there are two *types* of constraints imposed on A. The first as before, is a constraint imposed by B's autonomous choice. The second constraint is that A must persuade an owner of whatever carriage medium connects A to B to permit A and B to communicate. The communication is not intended to or from C or D. It does not change C or D's information environment, nor does A have any intention to do so. Their ability to withhold use of the infrastructure is based on a consequentialist calculus – namely, that such property rights create incentives to deploy infrastructure. It is not based on respect for their autonomy, for the autonomy of individuals cannot be served by giving them power over communications to which they are strangers.[16]

From a formal perspective, then, ownership of infrastructure entails curtailing the autonomy of users in order to obtain consequentialist goals. Imagine, for example, that D owns all infrastructure. If A wants to get information from B, or to communicate to C in order to persuade C to act in a way that is beneficial to A, A needs D's permission. D may grant or withhold permission, and may do so either for a fee or upon the imposition of conditions on the communication. For example, D might charge a fee, or impose constraints on communication that are

---

[15] Where a participant in the communication is also an owner of infrastructure we have a collapse back to two parties, and that is an example of the autonomy-loving effects of property ownership – the independence it gives one to act free of the decision making power of others.

[16] The point here is that property rights in communications infrastructure do not themselves serve autonomy, and to the extent they are supported on the basis of autonomy, this can be done only by derivation from the effects that the incentives they create will have on the capacities of individuals to communicate. There are, of course, non-consequentialist justifications of property rights in general that could be applicable to communications infrastructure as well. The importance of these, however, is largely undercut by the fact that almost all communications infrastructure is owned not by individuals whose interests bear moral weight, but by business organizations that serve a market purpose in communications infrastructure. See Yochai Benkler, Siren Songs and Amish Children: Autonomy, Information, and Law, 76 N.Y.U. L. Rev. 23 (2001). Even where infrastructure is owned by individuals, the aspect of property that entails control over the conditions of use by others is not a service to the owners' autonomy, but only of their well-being as an autonomous agents, in the sense of aiding them to pursue their life choices successfully. It would be difficult to defend as "autonomy enhancing" a rule that increased the welfare of some autonomous agents by giving them a degree of control over the lives of other autonomous agents to the detriment of the autonomy of those others.

likely to alter the information available to A so as to affect A's perception of options open to him in a way that increases the probability that A will behave in ways conducive to D's preferences. Or D may decide that B will pay more if all infrastructure is devoted to permitting B to communicate her information to A and C, rather than any of it used to convey A's statements to C. D might then refuse to carry A's message to C, and permit only B to communicate to A and C. The point is that from A's perspective, A is dependent upon D's decisions as to what information can be carried on the infrastructure, among whom, and in what directions. To the extent of that dependence, A's autonomy is compromised. It is compromised both through susceptibility to manipulation (D's imposition of constraints to manipulate A's behavior) and by the probability that D's judgments as to what information would be valuable to A as inputs into A's decision making process will diverge from what A's judgments would have been were A's decisions about the content of his communications wholly independent of D's (when D decides to carry B's, but not C's, messages to A). D becomes the sole agent who retains control over her own communications, independent of the permission of another.

Note that while the point has distributive aspects, it is primarily not about distribution. The object of assessment is a comparison between two states of the world as to the degree of freedom any person has, in each state, to author his or her life free of the decisions of another. The capacity of *each* of A, B, and C, to control their own information environment decreases with a shift from a commons to a property system. For D, there is an increase only in control of the information environment *of others*, which is not an enhancement of her autonomy, but only of her ability to control others.

Perhaps, one may argue, this is so formally, but what about market transactions for privately owned infrastructure? Before addressing this question in a competitive market context, one must first recognize the importance of the autonomy concern in explaining the widespread policy concern we have with media concentration. If an infrastructure owner like D has market power in the market for information infrastructure, there is no reason to think that D will allocate infrastructure to be used by A, B, and C in a way that maximizes their, or even their combined, welfare. In this sense freedom from constraint can be thought of as a dimension of welfare, and just as we have no reason to think that in a concentrated market total welfare (let alone consumer welfare) will be optimal, so too we have no reason to think that that component of welfare – autonomous choice as to one's communicative environment – will be optimal. The users' autonomy is diminished irrespective of whether D appropriates the rents available on the influence dimension by imposing its own views or by selling the ability to exert influence (*e. g.*, advertising). Moreover, when we count autonomy as a dimension of welfare our normative reasons to prefer "maximization" have a quite distinctive bias in favor of consumer, rather than producer surplus. For insofar as control over one's information environment is concerned as a problem of autonomy, it is only the "consumer surplus" side that counts as autonomy enhancing. Producer "surplus", on the other hand, translates simply into control exerted by some people (providers) over others (consumers).

Let's pause for a moment to consider how one might go about including an autonomy dimension in the analysis of how property affects the distribution of control over our personal information environments. Imagine that each agent's welfare is roughly composed of two types of parameters. Let's call them wealth and influence. By "wealth," I mean fungible commodities that can be translated into any other fungible, private, welfare-enhancing commodity. By "influence" I mean the ability to shape the behavior of people who share one's environment so as to make them play the role in one's own life plan that one prefers that they play. Politics, advertising, preaching, and selective disclosure of information are obvious instances of exerting influence on the information environment of others so as to make them conform their behavior to the pattern that would best fit one's own life story. In the case of D the monopolist, D might offer access to his infrastructure in return for any combination of wealth and influence. To the extent that D cannot effectively price discriminate among those who value freedom from his influence highly and those who do not, D will likely maximize the monopoly price attainable in both dimensions – wealth and influence.

But why is this analysis not *solely* about media concentration? Why is it also a valid concern when one compares private property and commons approaches to communications infrastructure regulation?

If we make the standard assumptions of competitive markets, one would think that the analysis must change. D no longer has monopoly power. We would presume that owners of infrastructure would be driven by competition to allocate infrastructure to uses that their users value most highly. If one owner "charges" a high price in terms of conditions imposed on users, say, prevents access to certain types of information – let's call this condition an influence exaction – then users will go to a competitor who does not impose that condition. This standard market response is far from morally irrelevant, if one is concerned with autonomy. If in fact every individual gets to choose precisely the package of influence exactions under which he or she will communicate, then the autonomy deficit created by privatization of communications infrastructure is minimal.

The reasons that the standard model that assumes perfect competition will not in fact eliminate the autonomy deficit of privately owned communications infrastructure fall into both familiar and unfamiliar categories.[17] The most familiar constraint on the "market will solve it" hunch is imposed by transaction costs, in particular information gathering and negotiation costs. To the extent that

---

[17] A wonderfully comprehensive consideration of the constraints of the applicability of the standard market model to media is C. Edwin Baker, Giving the Audience What it Wants, 58 Ohio St. L.J. 311 (1997).

influence exactions are less easily homogenized than prices expressed in currency, they will be more expensive to eliminate through transactions. Some people value information lobbed at them positively, others negatively. Some people are more immune to suggestion, others less. The content and context of an exaction will have a large effect on its efficacy as a device for affecting the choices of the person subject to the influence, and could change from communication to communication for the same person, let alone among different individuals. Users and providers have imperfect information about the users' susceptibility to suggestion by varying forms of exaction, and the value that each user would place on being free of this exaction or that in a given communicative context. Obtaining the information necessary to permit a tight fit between each consumer's preferences regarding the right level of influence-to-cash ratio to be paid for a given service and the service offered would be prohibitively expensive. Even if the information were obtained, negotiating the precise money to influence tradeoff would be costly.[18]

Communications services also have various economies of scale, be they first-copy costs in content products or infrastructure investments for carriage facilities, or demand-side effects like network-externalities. If price discrimination is costly, then providers are likely to court the widest audiences with standard influence/cash tradeoff bundles, and consumers/users are likely to choose the closest fit among a series of less-than-perfect bundles. In particular, those whose conception of the information environment they would choose are farthest from the norm are likely to find themselves with no service that resembles the information environment they would have elected given adequate choice.

No less important is the fact that the price component at stake expresses an effort on the part of producers to shape what in the standard model would be assumed as exogenous "taste" or "preferences". The standard model would have the service provider and the consumer negotiating with preferences carrying certain values at time T_1 about the extent to which the provider will alter the preferences the consumer will hold at time T_2, where the provider knows where it seeks to lead the consumer but the consumer knows only what the provider tells it about how the producer would like the consumer to be at T_2. Needless to say, once the transaction is complete, it is difficult to undo because, if successful, the consumer has adopted the preferences that the producer wanted them to adopt, not the person they thought they might agree to become when they entered into the transaction at T_1. (This is similar to Baker's point that since consumers seek

---

[18] That today we see relatively simple price discrimination schemes – email either with or without advertising; TV with advertising and no pay (over the air), advertising and pay (basic cable), or pay TV (HBO) – also suggests that the cost of identifying finer gradations of preferences individuals hold are costly relative to the gain that could be attained by offering finer-grained cash to influence tradeoff bundles. Communications capabilities therefore are generally priced with one option for no influence (which is priced at a rent maximizing price for the owner given its market power, as explained in the following text paragraph) – in effect charging the user the lost advertising revenues), and then a relatively small number of cash plus influence bundles.

information for, among other purposes, edification, it is impossible to obtain acceptable valuations of the value of information sought for that purpose in advance.)[19]

One might think as follows of the effect of introducing explicit recognition that providers can obtain welfare from exacting influence on users, not only from charging them a price. Each owner would offer infrastructure capacity at a price comprised of cash plus an influence exaction. Under perfect competitive conditions, this combined price will be driven to marginal cost. Users will therefore see a cash price composed of what a market-cleared price would have been in the absence of influence exactions, minus an amount up to the value to the infrastructure owner of imposing an influence exaction on users, plus the exaction. Depending on the relative elasticity of demand to the cash component and to the influence component of the price (which needn't be the same), we would likely see circumstances under which users communicate paying part of their carriage by subjecting themselves to the influence of infrastructure owners, rather than necessarily buying unencumbered access. Assuming a diminishing marginal utility for money, one would expect that poorer people would be willing to accept greater influence exactions than richer people, which is likely normatively relevant.

Where there are relatively high switching costs, or where it is costly to obtain information about the cost any given exaction imposes on a user (*i.e.*, it is hard to tell how much "autonomy" the user will lose from being subjected to this or that exaction in a given communicative context), one would expect the market to offer communications at a price composed of an exaction and a cash price set below the marginal cost of offering the service, where the discounting factor is the value of the exaction for the owner discounted by the probability that the user will be unaffected by the exaction. If the marginal cost of the communications service is lower than the average cost (as is often the case because of decreasing marginal costs and/or high fixed costs), then the relevant benchmark is the average cost, and we would likely see competitors price close to marginal cost while making up the shortfall by selling influence. If the marginal cost of communications is in fact, as it seems, approaching zero, influence exactions will be an important strategy to sustain an above marginal cost supply price that is necessary to sustain businesses who provide communications facilities with such a marginal cost structure. Just like broadcasters turned to advertisers to solve the public goods problem that over-the-air TV posed for them. If there is an equal probability that any given user will be unaffected by any given exaction, and there is competition among providers who place a positive value on their ability to exert influence on users, then each would be equally likely to recoup its costs by providing services with the exaction attached to them, at a price that is discounted by the value of imposing the exaction on the entire population of users given the probability that some of these

---

[19] Baker, Giving the Audience What it Wants, *supra*.

users will be affected by it. Providers can offer the power to determine the content of the exaction as a separate product – *e.g.*, they can sell advertising space. If it is costly to find out whether for a given communication a user values freedom from influence enough to pay the full marginal cost of carriage, or difficult to price discriminate among users along this dimension, or if the provider must sustain an above marginal cost price to cover average costs, we would expect a market to gravitate toward cash plus influence pricing.

The upshot is this. A system that permits owners of infrastructure to exclude anyone they choose to exclude from their infrastructure, or to impose conditions on their use of the infrastructure, creates a cost, in terms of autonomy, for users. One might call this effect an autonomy deficit imposed by privatization, caused by the introduction of a right to control use of resources that permits the owner to control the information environment of another.

Part IV: Alternative Models of Ownership and Control Compared to A Commons

Infrastructure ownership can be regulated by two primary categories of constraints on "pure" ownership rights. Ownership can be constrained either by restricting the owners' rights to control content or by restricting the owners' rights to control access by others to the infrastructure to communicate their preferred content. Moreover, ownership itself can be public, rather than private. When ownership is public, decisions can be treated as either made by agents with their own agenda, as positive political theory would have it, or as decisions "by the people." When the decision making practices of ownership are treated as separate from "the people," ownership is at least as constraining to autonomy as private property, or, if one subscribes to state-centric libertarian or liberal positions, even worse simply because the proprietor is a government agency. Even if public ownership is treated as ownership "by the people", decisions about the use of communications may at best be seen as an instance of political self-governance

Table 1: Alternatives Models of Ownership and Regulation

	Content	Access
Privately owned	Broadcast	Common carriage & cable access regulation; open access spectrum?
Publicly owned	Nonpublic forums; government as speaker	Postal service; public forums; open access spectrum?

through participation displacing personal autonomy. Personal autonomy is in all events displaced by the decision-maker.

When property rights are curtailed through content regulation there is usually no gain in the personal autonomy of users. Someone other than the end user is determining the content of communications over the infrastructure. That that "someone" is the government agency that passed the content control rule rather than the owner does little to aid the users' autonomy. Moreover, if the rule covers all private owners of infrastructure, then the government's content choice has the effects of the choice of a monopolist, and counteracts whatever autonomy benefits can be gained from the presence of competition, if any, in the regulated market. I say "usually" because it is not impossible that a content control rule could be autonomy enhancing – for example, a rule that prohibits certain kinds of selective disclosures of information that media owners could try to use to influence their users. Similarly, a requirement that broadcasters program a minimal number of hours of children's television might be understood as such an instance, because the educational content would be seen as enhancing the capacity for autonomy of the adults the children will become.

Access regulation consists in constraining the private property owner's use of its property right to exclude users from using the infrastructure, or to condition their use upon some influence exaction. In other words, the regulator is not placing its own preferred content or access constraints on the infrastructure. Rather, it is privileging users to use the communications medium to pursue their informational choices. And it attains this privileging of use by negating that aspect of the private property regime that creates the autonomy deficit under pure private property, namely, the absolute right to exclude from, or condition access to, the infrastructure. If we return to Figure 2, if A, B, and C are perfectly privileged to communicate as and when they wish over D's infrastructure, then the mere fact of ownership by D does not effect the autonomy of any of the users. A perfectly regulated common carrier regime should look to end users no different than a commons, as might Noam's open access spectrum approach. Whether a private party (the phone companies) or the state (the mail) owns the common carrier is less important. The primary difference between a common carrier and a public forum is that the latter, once declared or recognized, is constitutionally protected. It is therefore less susceptible to the problem of regulatory defection that common carriage suffers from, and to that extent (ironically, given traditional concerns with the state) is preferable to common carriage as a means of reducing the autonomy deficit of owned infrastructure.

In Part III we saw that, by comparison to a pure commons where all are equally privileged to use the infrastructure, and no one has a unilateral right to constrain that use, a pure private property regime exhibits an autonomy deficit. The alternative models we will now consider constrain the infrastructure owner's absolute right to exclude and condition access to its infrastructure, and hence seem to address the underlying cause of the autonomy deficit created by private property in communications infrastructure. There are, however, three reasons why access-focused constraints like common carriage, while helpful, do not entirely alleviate the autonomy deficit either. Mostly, these reasons reflect a concern that the common carriage regulation will be imperfect, but partly the concern is about the relative regulability of a network built for centralized clearance of communicative preferences as compared to a network built for decentralized clearance. First, the institutional details of the common carriage regime can skew incentives for what types of communications will be available, with what degree of freedom. Second, the organization that owns the infrastructure retains the same internal incentives to control content as it would in the absence of common carriage, and will do so to the extent that it can sneak by the carriage regulation intended to negate such control. And third, as long as the network is built to run through a central organizational clearinghouse, that center remains a potential point at which regulators can reassert control, or delegate to owners the power to prevent unwanted speech by purposefully limiting coverage of the common carriage requirements.

First, the common carriage regime would have to be not only entirely neutral as among content, format, medium, and identity of sender and recipient, but also would have to embrace them all. To the extent that the common carriage regime is partial in its application the deficit of proprietary infrastructure arises where common carriage is absent. For example, some courts held in the early 1990s that the first amendment prohibits the state from extending the common carriage requirement imposed on telephone companies from voice and data communications to cover video signal carriage as well.[20] The result is that information of a type that people seek to acquire through video communications, or that requires/benefits from utilizing video as a medium of expression, is subject to the proprietary infrastructure problem. If one held the view that given prevailing norms of information acquisition video programming had particularly important political and cultural ramifications in terms of shaping the perceptions of life choices available to individuals or of political choices open to our polity, such a deficit takes on significant proportions. If our assessment of the state of the law or of the politics of regulation is such that we think that extending common carriage to important areas like video programming is unlikely, then the common carriage option is less appealing than it might be in the abstract.

We might map this effect on Figure 2, but add an additional layer, where there are three types of communications, text (t), voice (vx), and image (i). The consequence of a common carriage regime that entailed poor design incentives, depicted in Figure 3, would be to cause the owner of the infrastructure to build a lopsided network. In such a network, some types of communications, in our example text and voice, would seem to the users as freely usable as though they

---

[20] Chesapeake & Potomac Tel. Co. v. United States, 42 F.3d 181 (4th Cir. 1994).

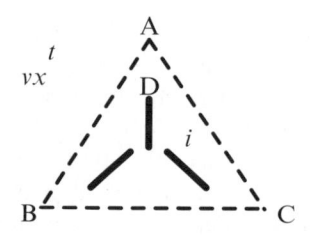

Figure 2

were unowned. Images, however, would be available to users only under conditions controlled by the infrastructure owner, which designs the network to take advantage of regulatory shortfalls. The consequence would be a network optimized to provide the communicative uses from which owners can extract the full private benefit, unconstrained by access regulation.

A parallel effect occurs if there are gaps in the coverage of the carriage requirement that permit organizations, whose incentives to control information flow over their networks do not change simply because a regulator has sought to neutralize them, to retain that control by circumventing the carriage requirement. Communications carried over these networks that do not fall under the carriage requirement will incur the autonomy deficit associated with proprietary infrastructure. For example, an FCC working paper on cable Internet access suggested that Internet access provided over a hybrid system with downstream information flow carried over coaxial cable, and an upstream return path over the public phone system, would plausibly qualify the service for regulatory treatment as cable service rather than a telecommunications service.[21] This was thought at the time to relieve cable providers of the possibility that they may be forced to provide competitors with access to their networks to provide competing Internet access services.[22] In other words, the legal definition of cable service could create incentives for carriers to design their systems so that high-speed internet access would be organized on an information retrieval model that is *not* subject to common carrier regulation, rather than an information retrieval *and dissemination* system that is relatively egalitarian in its capacity to deliver information produced by end users. By adopting this approach, the organizations that provide communications media could avoid the constraints of common carriage, and find themselves back where they would have been in a pure(r) private property regime. So would users. The actual practice of cable Internet access providers – prohibiting their users from operating servers and from streaming video[23] – suggests that the

---

[21] Barbara Esbin, Internet Over Cable: Defining the Future in Terms of the Past 91 (August 1998).
[22] Ironically, since that document was written, local franchising authorities have been much more aggressive than the FCC in imposing access requirements on cable broadband services.
[23] See Peter H. Lewis, Picking the Right Data Superhighway, NYT, Circuits, Nov. 11, 1999 (surveying broadband services and finding that "The two leading cable data services, Time

current freedom of the Internet, developed initially over telephone common carriage lines and university computers, is contingent and susceptible to change if the infrastructure owners decide to change it. It is precisely to avoid such an infrastructure-based change in the freedom that the Internet provides that a commons in the infrastructure layer is so important.

Third, common carriage leaves untouched, indeed relies on, the existence of an organizational center that controls the network. The persistent existence of such an organizational center to a network makes the network more easily subject to regulation.[24] The design concept underlying a common carriage regime is that there should be one organization that clears user preferences as to use of a communications infrastructure, in order to maintain efficient information flow. This design feature remains true even if there are redundant networks that compete with each other, because each network has an owner that controls it. The crux of common carriage requirements is to remove from that organization certain decision-making powers that would be inimical to the purpose of having a communications infrastructure to begin with. Most importantly, the common carrier is denied the option to select communications for carriage based on content. But this constraint on common carriers is a political choice, imposed by law. The architecture of the network remains centralized. And to the extent that the law can change, to that same extent the network remains susceptible to regulation by future choices of legislatures to change the parameters of common carriage.

The most egregious instance of such a legislative defection from a common carrier-like regime are sections 10(a) and 10(c) of the 1992 Cable Act, considered *and partly upheld* by the Supreme Court in *Denver Area Educational Telecommunications Consortium*.[25] In *Denver*, the Court dealt with an anti-indecency Act that took the form of content-based tweaking of access regulation provisions. The underlying access rule was that cable operators were required to set aside a number of channels for programming by unaffiliated programmers, commercial programmers in the case of leased access channels, and public, educational, and governmental programmers in the case of PEG channels. In the 1992 Act, Congress decided to regulate non-obscene, indecent programming on these access channels indirectly, by removing the carriage requirement from them. In other

---

cont.
Warner's Roadrunner and @Home, forbid residential customers to run Web server computers on the network."). See Phil Weiser, Paradigm Changes in Telecommunications Regulation, 71 U. Colo. L. Rev. 819, 835 (2000); *but see* James B. Speta, Unbundling and Open Access Policies: The Vertical Dimension of Cable Open Access, 71 U. Colo. L. Rev. 975, 1004–07 (2000) (arguing that cable operators have no incentives to prevent video streaming to protect their video programming services).

[24] Lawrence Lessig, Code and Other Laws of Cyberspace (1999) (defining the concept of "regulability" as the extent to which a given technical architecture is more or less easily subject to regulation by the state).

[25] 518 U.S. 727 (1996).

words, cable operators were still required to offer nondiscriminatory carriage to unaffiliated programmers on these channels, but they were *permitted* (not required) to exclude "indecent" programming. Under established first amendment law, Congress couldn't have itself *prohibited* such indecent, non-obscene material. But, in the name of respecting the infrastructure owners' right to speak over the network they own, a quilt of votes upheld Congress' power to exclude such undesirable but protected content from the carriage requirement. The intended effect of the removal from the carriage requirement was precisely that cable operators use their control over their systems, now freed from the access rule, to ban the material Congress disapproved. This provision was upheld, however, only with respect to commercial leased access channels. As to PEG channels, the court held that the regulation imposed too great a burden on speech. The reason was that as to PEG channels there were already publicly accountable bodies that controlled access to the infrastructure to assure that the content was appropriate, and hence there was no showing that the added layer of censorship imposed by the cable operators was necessary to attain Congress' legitimate goal of protecting children. It is hard to think of a clearer instance of self-conscious exclusion of certain content from coverage under a carriage requirement in order to squelch the unwanted speech. The risk of common carriage regime, then, as compared to unowned, fully decentralized networks, is that the common carrier always remains as an organizational center that is available as a locus of re-concentrating control over decisions about what information will or will not flow over the system. It is this susceptibility that makes a publicly owned public forum somewhat preferable to a privately owned common carrier, because of the clearer constitutional rules prohibiting content-based exclusion from access to the infrastructure.[26]

Insofar as implementing an autonomy-enhancing infrastructure, the most intriguing alternative to the spectrum commons is Eli Noam's proposal for an open access spectrum. Noam's proposal and the commons proposal share a number of crucial features. First, they both relate solely to communications by propagating electromagnetic signals at radio frequencies over the air. This aspect is crucial, because unlike other carriage media – twisted copper pair, coaxial cable, optic fibers – radio spectrum is available to carry signals by the grace of Mother Nature. The problem of radio communications, unlike all other communications, is therefore not how to create incentives for the building and maintenance of the carriage facility, but rather how to coordinate competing uses of an existing, inexhaustible, perfectly renewable carriage medium. This requires investments in equipment design to utilize more of this resource at increasing efficiency, and in technological or organizational means of attaining the most efficient coordination of utilization. While auctions are the "hot" technology for attaining efficient coordination, there is nothing holy about this organizational technology if others,

---

[26] See, *e.g.*, Justice Kennedey's dissent in *Denver*.

most notably technical innovations in equipment, can do the job. Second, both systems replace organizational clearance of decisions about spectrum use with equipment-embedded clearance mechanisms, and hence eliminate the need for owned spectrum. Third, both proposals must therefore predict that someone other than a "spectrum owner" will bear the incentives to develop the new equipment capable of utilizing ever higher frequency ranges, and utilizing frequency ranges already available for human communications more efficiently. My commons proposal suggests that the consumer equipment market will assure these developments, as equipment manufacturers seek to deliver machines that communicate with each other at the greatest efficiency over the unowned spectrum.[27] Noam's model assumes that service providers who will use the spectrum to sell communications services to users will do the ad hoc bidding for spectrum. These service providers, presumably, bear the incentives to optimize their use of spectrum.

The core difference between the commons I propose and Noam's open access spectrum concerns the question of how to clear competing preferences for using the communications infrastructure that has been liberated by technology from the need to have "an owner" (be it private property owner or government owner and its licensee). Noam seeks to maintain a pricing system, in order to assure that spectrum utilization using his approach can provide quality of service equal to that available over enclosed media and owned spectrum. I, on the other hand,

---

[27] I have explained in some detail why equipment manufacturers not only have incentives to develop better equipment, but would also likely push content decisions into the hands of users, whereas infrastructure owners have incentives to make these decisions themselves, in Overcoming Agoraphobia, *supra* note 5, at 348–52, 365–68. Like computer manufacturers, and unlike broadcasters or cable operators, equipment manufacturers can best capture wide variations in taste among users by providing a versatile, rather than special-purpose machine. This is because a versatile machine can be put by each user to its highest valued use for him or her as it changes over time, without the user needing to identify that use either to himself or to the seller, and hence with much lower information costs and a lesser degree of uncertainty about the value of currently-known uses in the future. The absence of a necessity to provide continuous service over time (e.g., as with cable or broadcast) removes opportunities, on the one hand, and incentives, on the other hand, to appropriate the value of the equipment over time, as opposed to ex-ante, at the time the equipment is sold. Equipment manufacturers therefore have an incentive to maximize user's capabilities so as to maximize the users' ex-ante valuation of the equipment as a reflection of their projections about how valuable unfettered use will be to them in the future. It is, nonetheless, quite possible that some users would prefer to pay with attention to influence than with cash – as in the case of free PCs. Nothing in a spectrum commons prevents this eventuality. But the outcome would not be the consequence of a regulatory decision that makes no infrastructure available that is control-free, as it is in the case of current spectrum management. Moreover, this influence-based equipment market would exist alongside a robust market in end user equipment whose primary means of extracting value is in giving users more, rather than less, choice. Compare this to the consequences of current spectrum policy. There is no alternative that allows one to buy a television set and thereafter enjoy influence-free use with no additional cost. But for the same or a lower price (as of this writing, "modems" that could utilize a spectrum commons have prices equivalent to low to mid-range television sets), one could buy a device that would thereafter enable influence-free use at no incremental cost.

proposed that some form of queuing be used to coordinate spectrum use. If the utilization of queuing means that the spectrum commons cannot be used for all communications available over an enclosed medium, that is an acceptable price to pay in return for eliminating the normative costs that maintaining pricing imposes.[28]

The normative costs of maintaining pricing as a means of clearing competing preferences is exacted in system design. Noam writes:

> Such an open-access system might look as follows: For packets of information to be transmittable, they would require to be accompanied by an access code. Such a code could be a specialized token, a general electronic cash coin. The token would enable its bearer to access a spectrum band (rather than a specific frequency), to be transmitted over physical network segments, and to be receivable by equipment. Price for access would vary, depending on congestion, and be determined by an automatized clearinghouse of spectrum users. Assured price, at a price certain, could be obtained from a futures market.
>
> For example, a mobile communications provider, A, might face heavy [demand] for its service during the post-Labor Day morning drive time. It would therefore buy access codes to that capacity from the desired band, to unlock spectrum usage in a network environment. The tokens are bought from an automatic clearinghouse market of all users. Firm A and its customers, when initiating transmissions, add the access token to blocks of their transmitted information. Without the access codes, information could not be passed on to other networks and might not be readable by their intended receivers, if user equipment requires these codes for activation or descrambling.[29]

Like the common carrier regime, this proposal has the attraction that it is blind to content when it assigns access to infrastructure. Only the value of the token a communication carries will determine its access to the network. But there are two ways in which this description threatens to make the open access system no better,

---

[28] One objection to my position is that if queuing degrades quality of service sufficiently, then the medium no longer significantly facilitates autonomy, at least not to an extent that makes it superior to a medium made much more efficient by relying on a pricing mechanism. The response is that the technological change that has made commons possible has caused a drastic reduction of the degradation in efficiency to be expected in the absence of property and pricing. While scarcity is not eliminated completely, non-price-based mechanism for allocating communications capabilities – like queuing – become more possible because their cost in terms of degraded service is acceptable. The Internet – a medium that uses queuing to clear competing uses – while imperfect, nonetheless permits diverse uses cleared in a completely different model than radio, cable, or telephone systems. The lost quality relative to the owned and centrally managed medium is made up for in the diversity of voices and autonomy it enables its users to exercise. As an infrastructure of last resort, a spectrum commons can provide unconstrained communications capabilities for many who would not have been able to use a pricing-based medium.

[29] Noam 1998, at 778–79.

and possibly worse, from the normative perspective, than a common carrier regime.

First, Noam appears to imagine a world in which spread spectrum technologies change the way *service providers* obtain spectrum access to serve consumers, but does not affect the way in which consumers communicate with each other – namely, through service providers. One might easily imagine how a system designed to assure quality of service could decide that, in order to cut down on the overhead involved in the bidding in the spectrum spot market, only "members" are permitted to bid. To the extent that this is so – either as a practical matter, or institutionally, because only providers who are, say, members can purchase tokens on the automated exchange – then in the relationship between consumers and service providers, and as among consumers, the autonomy deficit is recreated. If this institutional constraint in fact develops, then even if the cost of "a seat" on this exchange is low enough to permit greater competition than permitted by the costs of purchasing a spectrum license under the existing auction system, still one would see a class of "providers" develop, who manage "their" spectrum inventory as property vis-à-vis their customers. Whether Noam's system will then be better or worse than a common carrier system, from the normative perspective, will depend on whether these service providers are themselves, in turn, regulated as common carriers. Certainly his system could accommodate a world in which only providers bid on spectrum, and these providers are all contract carriers, such that, from the normative perspective, we are closer to the pure property regime than we are to the common carrier regime.

But there is nothing inherent in Noam's conception to prevent it from being implemented on a peer-to-peer network model, where users have equal ability to bid on slots as do providers. If it is indeed so implemented, and the clearinghouse is regulated so that it cannot bar a transmission on any basis other than failure to pay the value of the token necessary to transmit at the required frequency-time-space unit, then there is no reason to think that the system will be any worse than a common carrier system. Its advantage over such a system would be that it relies, technologically, on digital communications that can carry any type of communication format, and any kind of content, and does not differentiate them along any of these lines. Such a system could therefore be better than traditional common carriage over traditional media, insofar as assuring that the system is not built to serve only some types of communications on a common carrier basis.

There does, however, remain one significant risk to autonomy from the open access spectrum solution, as compared to the spectrum commons solution. In order to implement a pricing system, all transmissions must carry a code that determines whether they can or cannot reach their intended recipient. That code is issued by an automated process that determines on a moment-by-moment basis whether the code that any given transmission carries is of sufficient value to permit that transmission to reach its destination. In Noam's plan, the code reflects pure "cash" value. But there is nothing inherent in the system design he offers that makes it immune to enforcing any one of a number of "values" to determine access to infrastructure. One might imagine a law that requires all tokens to identify themselves in terms of sexual or violent content, V-chip style. Initially, such a law might take advantage of the existence of tokens to facilitate end user filtering. Then a following Congress will remove tokens bearing such markings from the clearinghouse's common carriage responsibility. The point should be clear. In order to affect a pricing system to clear spectrum uses, the open access spectrum approach requires that communications identify themselves, and be given permission to travel by a clearinghouse. That clearinghouse remains a center for reassertion of control over communications, either by government or by the owner-operator of the clearinghouse.

Part V: Conclusion

Implementing a wireless commons as part of our information infrastructure is a policy that faces formidable challenges. Most prominent among these is the intellectual entrenchment of what Noam called the orthodoxy of "licensed exclusivity"– the prevailing paradigms that hold that spectrum management must either be allocated administratively or privatized through auctions, but that by either of these mechanisms *someone* must control the airwaves for them to be usable. No less trenchant will be the resistance of those legislators who smell the red pottage of budget relief gained by spectrum auctions and cannot see the birthright of a public-domain communications infrastructure available for all to use on equal terms.

In this essay I have not focused on why the prevailing orthodoxy is wrong to think that a spectrum commons is impossible to implement. What is important to understand, however, is that the debate of *whether* a commons is possible, and how it can be implemented, should be of the highest concern to those who care about information and communications policy, and particularly those who care about how our society's communications infrastructure will enhance or degrade our democratic values.

Building a wireless commons will make available one component of our information infrastructure, call it our infrastructure of first and last resort that is equally available to all to acquire and disseminate information. Because of the unique characteristics of radio communications, wireless communications present the only possible source of such a commons, because the "airwaves" are the only carriage infrastructure created and replenished by nature. The policy problem we have with respect to radio frequency spectrum is not how to get it created, but rather how to use this environment in an efficient and sustainable manner.

Digital communications technology and the digitally networked environment have opened a window of opportunity to reverse the trend of the 20th century toward centralized, commercialized knowledge and cultural production. The Internet and its successors make it possible for our society's constituents to become makers of their own information environment, not only its consumers. But this opportunity will only materialize if the decentralizing potential of this new technology of communication is embedded in the network itself. The same digitization that creates the opportunities for decentralization also creates the potential for a new dimension of concentration, where commercial providers increasingly mass-customize the information environment of our society's constituents while retaining control over it. The result would be a system that seems much more diverse than the one we now have, but in fact would be equally controlled by a small number of market and government actors who together determine for us all what we see, when, and in some measure, to what effect.

A spectrum commons offers the best hope that at least some of our information environment will be truly decentralized and hence truly available for autonomous making of our information environment. What makes this environment unique among communications infrastructures is that it is unowned, uncontrolled, and therefore can be built using a completely decentralized architecture. The development incentives in this environment are located with end user equipment manufacturers, who in turn must compete by providing the greatest flexibility and value to end users from having unimpeded, equal access to the capacity to communicate with others. The content of the environment, in turn, is determined by end users themselves, on a transmission-by-transmission basis. Like a Speakers' Corner, and unlike any other medium, this wireless spectrum commons can provide each and every one of us with a space in our information environment wherein we can listen to our peers or jump up on our digital soapbox and speak our mind. In the absence of an organizational center, this medium would be more resistant to attempts to control it – whether by companies that seek to control our information environment so as to persuade us to act in ways conducive to their interests – or by governments that seek to impose their political will on us all.

Investing in an infrastructure commons is important because it serves the most basic values of democracy – our personal autonomy, and its political implementation through self-governance.

The Commercial Mass Media's Continuing Fourth Estate Role

Neil Weinstock Netanel

As James Madison aptly put it: "A popular Government, without popular information, or the means of acquiring it, is but a Prologue to a Farce or a Tragedy; or, perhaps both."[1] In our day, certainly in the United States and to a growing extent in other developed democracies, most citizens, most of the time, acquire information about political and social issues from the commercial mass media. It hasn't always been that way and, perhaps, need not be that way in the future. At one time, the party press and government-financed media dominated public discourse in democratic nations. And, in the view of some observers, peer-to-peer communication through digital networks might increasingly supplant commercial mass media in the not-too-distant future.

In this essay, I compare the commercial media with party press, government-financed media, and peer-to-peer alternatives for gathering and distributing information and opinion to citizens of advanced liberal democracies. I tentatively assess their relative advantages and disadvantages for popular governance in the liberal democratic tradition.

The role of commercial media in liberal democracy has been the subject of renewed controversy in light of peer-to-peer alternatives made possible by the Internet and other digital communications technology. I, and other commentators, have asserted that, despite all their imperfections, the commercial news media play and will continue to play an important "Fourth Estate" role in liberal democratic governance. Media critics have countered that (1) liberal democratic governance would be better off if peer-to-peer communications were to assume the primary role in the dissemination of information and opinion and (2) digital communications makes that transition possible.

I have no quarrel with much of the criticism levied at the commercial news

---

[1] Letter from James Madison to W.T. Barry (Aug. 4, 1822), reprinted in 9 *The Writings of James Madison* 103, 103 (Gaillard Hunt ed., 1910).

N. Elkin-Koren and N.W. Netanel (eds.), *The Commodification of Information*, 317–339.
© 2002 *Neil Weinstock Netanel. Printed in Great Britain.*

media. I also join with media critics in favoring various forms of structural regulation and government subsidization of noncommercial speakers in order to preserve media competition and expressive diversity. But to the extent media criticism calls for or, if taken to its logical conclusion, supports jettisoning the commercial-media-as-Fourth-Estate ideal and replacing it with an alternative vehicle for informing citizens, I think it important to consider potential shortcomings of proffered alternatives as well. I conclude that, at least at this juncture, advanced liberal democracies are probably better served by the continued preeminence of the commercial mass media, supplemented but not supplanted by non-market-based alternatives such as the party press, government-financed media, and peer-to-peer communication.

At the same time, I wish to emphasize, my brief study is meant more to raise questions and identify problem areas for further research than to espouse definitive conclusions. In particular, I briefly consider only three of the many possible market and nonmarket alternatives to the commercial mass media. In addition, I do not discuss which structural regulations might be warranted to foster the commercial media's better fulfillment of its Fourth Estate role and to preserve alternative discursive regimes in the face of commercial media aggrandizement.

My argument unfolds in six parts. Part I broadly outlines salient aspects of liberal democracy, focusing on those pertinent to comparing the performance of alternative discursive systems in informing citizens of advanced liberal democratic states. Part II describes the commercial media's purported "Fourth Estate" role and briefly notes the ways it falls short of realizing it. Parts III and IV limn two alternatives to the commercial media: political-party financed press and government-funded media. These Parts focus on the advantages and disadvantages of those alternatives as compared to the commercial media. Part V presents the proffered alternative of peer-to-peer communication. Part VI critiques that alternative. It argues both that peer-to-peer communication is probably incapable of serving as a substitute "Fourth Estate" and that such a substitution would be undesirable even if possible.

I. Liberal Democracy

"Liberal democracy" has multiple meanings and iterations. One's understanding of "liberal democracy" can heavily color one's view and expectations concerning the desired role of the commercial media and its alternatives.[2] Accordingly, I

---

[2] Ed Baker has convincingly detailed this point with respect to "democracy" and the media. *See* C. Edwin Baker, *The Media That Citizens Need*, 147 U. Penn. L. Rev. 317 (1998).

briefly outline my working understanding of "liberal democracy." In so doing, I build upon Ed Baker's model of "complex democracy," as distinct from elitist, interest group pluralist, and republican democracy.[3] This model, I believe, captures the most salient common characteristics and aspirations of advanced, developed-country democracies at the beginning of the twenty-first century.

Liberal democracy presents numerous fault lines. These include tensions between individual autonomy and democratic process and between interest-group pluralism and more republican notions of a common public good. Contrary to the view of some theorists, liberal democratic theory and practice incorporates and seeks to accommodate all of those elements.[4] It includes values and legal doctrine that highlight individual autonomy, interest group pluralism, and common public discourse. As Ed Baker puts it, contrasting his model of "complex democracy" with interest group pluralism, civic republicanism, and other unidimensional variants: "A more "realistic" theory would assume that a participatory democracy would and should encompass arenas where both individuals and groups look for and create common ground, that is, common goods, but where they also advance their own individual and group values and interests. Moreover, normatively, it is difficult to argue that either type of political striving is inappropriate for an ethical person or within a justifiable politics."[5]

Significantly, and this is certainly the experience of liberal democratic nations, complex democracy necessarily encompasses multiple concentrations of power. Interest groups, civic associations, business firms, political parties, labor unions, and government subdivisions and agencies vie and compete for power and influence in a wide variety of arenas.[6] The dispersion of power and consequent multiple concentrations of power are both inevitable to and part of the fabric of a pluralist, liberal democracy. They are part and parcel of divided and limited government and of individuals' right and ability to organize in common social, political, and commercial enterprise. As I will discuss below, in designing policies regarding the dissemination of information and expression in a liberal democratic society, we must take account of both the various values that comprise "complex democracy" and the fact of multiple concentrations of political and economic power.

---

[3] *See id.* at 335–43.
[4] For a cogent refutation of the notion that rights-based liberalism is inherently hostile to democracy, *see Stephen Holmes, Passions and Constraint: On the Theory of Liberal Democracy* 29–36 (1995). In addition, as Ed Rubin insightfully argues, the often overblown rhetoric of "rights" and "democracy" fails to capture the essence of most government decision making in a modern "liberal democratic" administrative state. *See* Edward L. Rubin, *Getting Past Democracy*, 149 U. Pa. L. Rev. 711 (2001).
[5] Baker, *supra* note 2, at 336.
[6] *See* notes 76–77 *infra*.

II. The Commercial Media's "Fourth Estate" Role

Echoing a widely held view of the role of the institutional press, I have argued elsewhere that "liberal democracy requires an institutional media that possesses the financial strength to reach a mass audience and engage in sustained investigative reporting, free from a potentially corrupting dependence on state subsidy."[7] Underlying that view is an understanding of the role that the commercial media plays in supporting liberal democracy. In acting as the "Fourth Estate," the press is said to fulfill three basic functions. These are watchdog, public discourse facilitation, and trustworthy supplier of information.

I use those three functions as the framework for my analysis. I posit that liberal democracy as I have described it requires some institution or combination of institutions that serve those functions. Accordingly, I assess the relative desirability of the commercial media and its alternatives by examining the extent to which they serve – or can be expected to serve – those functions. More particularly, I take the status quo – a system of free expression dominated by the commercial media – as my starting point. I take cognizance of the abundant criticism of the commercial media and agree that the media imperfectly serves as watchdog, public discourse facilitator , and trustworthy supplier of information. But I then look at some leading alternatives and ask whether they have performed or are likely to perform any better.

I begin by outlining the three functions. I first describe the ideal of the commercial media as Fourth Estate. I then briefly rehearse some of the ways in which the commercial media falls short of this ideal.

A. WATCHDOG

To the extent it fulfills the watchdog function, the commercial media catalyzes and, to a degree, embodies public opinion in the face of both government authority and private centers of power. It serves to check the power – and abuse of power – of government, business, political parties, interest groups, and associations.

The media acts as watchdog, first, by providing the public with information that the public can then use to judge the politically and economically powerful. Significantly in that regard, the media engages in investigative reporting.[8] It aggressively seeks out information and scrutinizes those in positions of power,

---

[7] Neil Weinstock Netanel, *Market Hierarchy and Copyright in Our System of Free Expression*, 53 Vanderbilt L. Rev. 1879, 1919 (2000).
[8] *See, generally,* David L. Protess et. al., *The Journalism of Outrage: Investigative Reporting and Agenda Building in America* (1991).

rather than merely acting as a passive conduit for relaying the information given to it by the powerful. Armed with that information, the public can then vote out elected officials whom the press exposes as incompetent, corrupt, or out-of-touch with majority views. Citizens can also boycott or otherwise organize against businesses or other associations that the press exposes as unworthy (as those citizens would define it). A prime, recent example is the reaction of the public and elected officials to media reporting of tobacco company executives' perjurous denials that they long knew of nicotine's addictive properties.[9]

In addition, the media fulfills its watchdog role by, in some sense, representing the public before public and private officials. Officials react to media reporting with the assumption that it reflects public opinion.[10] They also alter their conduct out of concern for the possibility of that conduct coming under press scrutiny. Thus, the mere presence of the media helps check public and private power. At times, of course, officials simply try to cover-up illicit activity. But overall, the ever-present glare of the media gives officials a strong incentive to desist from abuse of power.

B. PUBLIC DISCOURSE FACILITATION

In addition to their watchdog function, media enterprises help to lay a foundation for public discourse. Liberal democratic governance requires some measure of *public* discourse, some means for identifying issues of widespread concern and some forum for confronting opposing perspectives.[11] Individuals may have widely divergent interests and preferences. But democratic politics require at least some shared understanding about what are the most significant issues facing the polity as a whole. And in that regard, studies show that the public can converge upon only a half a dozen or so issues at any given time.[12] As a result, politics is not only about prevailing on contentious issues. It is, just as importantly, a struggle to place one's favored issues on the public agenda.

---

[9] See *infra* notes 78–86 and accompanying text (discussing 60 Minutes interview with tobacco company whistle blower Jeffrey Wigand).

[10] See *Protess et. al.*, *supra* note 8, at 244–49 (noting, on the basis of detailed case studies of investigative reporting, that government officials tend to respond to investigative reporters and media exposés before interest groups or the public take up the issue, treating the press as if it were the public).

[11] See *Cass R. Sunstein, Free Markets and Social Justice* 186–87 (1997) (contending that liberal democracy requires a realm of discursive exchange in which citizens can test their preferences and produce better collective decisions).

[12] See Maxwell McCombs, et. al., *Issues in the News and the Public Agenda: The Agenda-Setting Tradition*, in *Public Opinion and the Communication of Consent* 281, 292 (Theodore L. Glasser & Charles T. Salmon eds. 1995) [hereinafter *Public Opinion*] (noting that given competition among issues for saliency among the public, the public agenda typically consists of no more than five to seven issues).

The commercial media serve as conduits for discursive exchange. But, of course, they are not mere passive common carriers. Rather, they present a forum for mediated and edited deliberation and debate. In so doing, the media both delimit a range of passable opinion and actively contribute to shaping a rough consensus regarding what are the important public issues that need to be addressed.[13] Such media agenda-setting has positive as well as negative ramifications. The mass media narrow the public agenda to a limited set of resonant issues, which is in some sense antithetical to expressive diversity. But at the same time, public debate in a highly pluralistic, advanced democratic state cannot proceed without some measure of broad public consensus on the major priorities facing the polity at any given time.

Agenda-setting also has value for individual self-realization. We define ourselves within and against social groups. For that reason, we generally want to read, see, and hear at least in part what we think others of our social group are reading, seeing, and hearing.[14] We want to experience cultural events and phenomena jointly with others and to share a common basis for conversation with our friends and colleagues. We also want to know what others think is important, current, and of interest, and to show others in our social group that we are "in the know." The commercial mass media help to create a common culture that can be shared by many, to some extent even across ethnic and ideological subgroupings.

C. Trustworthy Supplier of Information

Inaccurate information has little or no value for either public discourse or individual autonomy.[15] Indeed, false and misleading statements of fact can be highly damaging to liberal democratic governance and individual well-being.

Trustworthiness and accuracy in the provision of news and information has

---

[13] For further discussion of this point, see Neil Weinstock Netanel, *Asserting Copyright's Democratic Principles in the Global Arena*, 51 Vand. L. Rev. 218, 263–67 (1998). See also Owen M. Fiss, *The Censorship of Television*, 93 NW. U.L. Rev. 1215, 1217 (1999) (noting that television, unlike today's computer communication, has the capacity to create a shared understanding among a mass audience).

[14] Cass Sunstein and Edna Ullman-Margalit label as "solidarity goods" those "goods whose value increases as the number of people enjoying them increases." Cass Sunstein & Edna Ullman-Margalit, Solidarity in Consumption, John M. Olin Law & Econ. Working Paper No. 98 (2d Series) (April 28, 2000), available at <http://papers.ssrn.com/paper.taf?abstract_id=224618.>

[15] As the Supreme Court famously noted in Chaplinsky v. New Hampshire, 315 U.S. 568, 571–72 (1942): "There are certain well-defined and narrowly limited classes of speech, the prevention and punishment of which have never been thought to raise any Constitutional problem. These include the lewd and obscene, the profane, the libelous, and the insulting or "fighting" words – those which by their very utterance inflict injury or tend to incite an immediate breach of the peace.".

long been a central component of journalists' professional standards.[16] Within the mainstream news media, the provision of "a truthful, comprehensive, and intelligent account of the day's events" is seen as the most important responsibility of the press,[17] and the principle of objectivity forms the core of the Code of Ethics of the Society of Professional Journalists.[18] In line with those principles, commercial news media devote considerable resources and professional commitment to checking facts and verifying sources.

D. THE COMMERCIAL MEDIA FALLS SHORT OF THE FOURTH ESTATE IDEAL

As numerous critics have pointed out, the commercial media's actual performance falls short – some would say "far short" – of the ideal I have just described. In performing its watchdog, discourse-enabling, and information-providing functions, the commercial media skews as well as narrows public debate. Commercial media, critics assert, routinely produce bland, uncontroversial expression, designed to put audiences in a buying mood and to attract a broad cross-section of viewers, readers, and listeners without unduly offending any of them.[19] At the very least, such mainstreaming is unlikely to provide adequate expression to minority interests and concerns. More insidiously, it might help to engender a widespread sense of complacency and a diminished capacity to envision potential challenges to the status quo.[20]

Part of the reason for media's failure to live up to the Fourth Estate ideal, and one that appears increasingly to be so as media enterprises consolidate into conglomerates with non-media corporate parents, is that media enterprise self-interest and concern for the bottom line pushes coverage to favor commercial

---

[16] U.S. journalists' emphasis on "objectivity" in reporting appears to have had its early beginnings with the penny presses in the 1830s with their self-announced mission to report the "news" and to have attained status as ideology and code of professional conduct after the Progressive Era in the late 19th and early 20th centuries. *See* Michael Schudson, *Discovering the News; A Social History of American Newspapers* (1978).

[17] *See The Commission on Freedom of the Press, A Free and Responsible Press: A General Report on Mass Communication: Newspapers, Radio, Motion Pictures, Magazines, and Books* 21 (1947), quoted in Baker, *supra* note 2, at 348–49.

[18] *See* Society of Professional Journalists, Code of Ethics, available at < http://spj.org/ethics/code.htm. >

[19] *See, e.g.*, Jerome A. Barron, *Access to the Press: A New First Amendment Right*, 80 Harv. L. Rev. 1641, 1641–47 (1967); *see also* James G. Webster & Patricia F. Phalen, *The Mass Audience: Rediscovering the Dominant Model* 101 (1997) (stating that "(m)any contemporary analysts from both ends of the political spectrum have portrayed the media as inexorably committed to the production of standardized content").

[20] *See* W. Russell Neuman, *The Future of the Mass Audience* 28–30 (1991) (summarizing the viewpoint of critical media theorists and other critics that commercial media trivializes political life).

interests.[21] Media's skewing also grows out of market dictate, both real and perceived. Sensationalism, mainstream worldview, and reporting that focuses on current political leaders and dominant institutions sell better to broader audiences than does alternative content.[22] Moreover, media exhibit considerable herd behavior, imitating the format of existing commercially successful movies, books, and TV shows, thus exacerbating the homogenized, uniform character of much media content.[23] Reporters' dependence on government officials and prominent, well-organized associations for raw material might also vitiate the media's watchdog bite.[24] Some commentators claim, indeed, that government officials exert such a powerful, albeit informal, influence on news coverage that the notion of autonomous media production and distribution of ideas is little more than a pipe dream.[25]

As a result of these factors and others, while the mainstream mass media may often exhibit moderate-reform-oriented norms, it rarely challenges our basic social, economic, and political structures.[26] Nor, for better or for worse, does it provide a full spectrum of fathomable expression and opinion.

Of course, to enumerate the commercial media's shortcomings is not to say that some other discursive institution or combination of institutions would better serve the needs of citizens of advanced liberal democracies. In a world of imperfection and scarcity, the question pertinent to any institutional analysis must always be not whether a given institution has failed, but rather whether another institution can do any better.[27] With that injunction in mind, I now turn to alternatives to the commercial mass media.

---

[21] *See* Burt Neuborne, *Media Concentration and Democracy: Commentary*, 1999 Ann. Surv. Am. L. 277, 280.

[22] As Ed Baker demonstrates, sensationalist violence, and sex sell particularly well across cultures, and thus assume greater portions of media content as markets for that content become increasingly global. C. Edwin Baker, *International Trade in Media Products*, in *The Commodification of Information* (Niva Elkin-Koren & Neil Netanel eds. 2002).

[23] See Neil Weinstock Netanel, *Copyright and a Democratic Civil Society*, 106 Yale L. J. 282, 333–34 (1996); Cass R. Sunstein, *Television and the Public Interest*, 88 Cal. L. Rev. 499, 515–16 (2000).

[24] *See, e.g.*, Clarice N. Olien, et. al., *Conflict, Consensus, and Public Opinion*, in *Public Opinion*, *supra* note 12, at 301, 306 (noting media dependency on power relationships); Jonathan Weinberg, *Broadcasting and Speech*, 81 Cal. L. Rev. 1103, 1154–55 (1993).

[25] See, e.g., Robert M. Entman, *Putting the First Amendment in Its Place: Enhancing American Democracy Through the Press*, 1993 U. Chi. Legal F. 61, 65–72; Steven Shiffrin, *The Politics of the Mass Media and the Free Speech Principle*, 69 Ind. L. J. 689, 702–11 (1994).

[26] Weinberg, *supra* note 24, at 1157. At the same time, critics charge that noncommercial, government-subsidized media also generally fall well within the mainstream.

[27] *See, generally*, Neil K. Komesar, *Imperfect Alternatives – Choosing Institutions in Law, Economics, and Public Policy* (1994).

III. Political Party-Financed Media

An alternative model to media that depend upon advertising and sales is media financed in part or in whole by political parties. Party affiliated newspapers dominated the American landscape through much of the first half of the 19th century.[28] The party press also played a major role in post-World War II Western Europe. In recent decades, however, the European party press, like its 19th century American counterpart, has significantly diminished in circulation and influence.[29]

Some commentators lament the passing of an openly ideological, partisan press.[30] They surmise that the politically aligned press brought about considerable political excitement and thus encouraged greater citizen participation in politics.[31] Concomitantly, a party press might also sharpen oppositional views and encourage more robust debate.[32] Partisan newspapers in the antebellum United States would not infrequently launch virulent attacks against newspapers of opposing political affiliation,[33] as well as against newspapers – the forerunners of today's commercial press – that charted a more independent course.[34] One might also imagine that an ideologically driven opposition press would act as a more vigorous watchdog against the government and party in power than does the commercial media.

Yet the party press system in the antebellum United States ultimately fell into disrepute because the parties in power used government patronage to purchase press loyalty. By the 1820's, newspaper editors regularly received government appointments and subsidies. Newspapers favored by those in power were also awarded lucrative government contracts. These ranged from contracts for printing laws and government documents to concessions for the supply of twine, printed

---

[28] Census data taken in 1850 showed that 95% of all U.S. newspapers had a political affiliation. C. Edwin Baker, *Advertising and a Democratic Press* 28 (1994), citing Hazel Dicken-Garcia, *Journalistic Standards in Nineteenth-Century America* 48–49, 114–15 (1989).

[29] *Council of Europe Publishing, Media and Elections Handbook* 11–12 (1999); Peter J. Humphreys, *Media and Media Policy in Germany; The Press and Broadcasting Since 1945*, 91 (2nd ed. 1994) (noting that in Germany, "[t]he established political press, with its explicit connection to the major parties, has all but disappeared").

[30] *See, e.g.*, Baker, *supra* note 28, at 41–43.

[31] *Id.* at 41, citing Michael E. McGerr, *The Decline of Popular Politics* 135 (1986).

[32] See Baker, *supra* note 2, at 358–59 (arguing in support of partisan journalism that "[p]articular groups, especially oppressed groups, ... need more segmented or partial dialogues in which to develop their self-conception and their understanding of their own interests").

[33] See Jason P. Isralowitz, Comment, *The Reporter as Citizen: Newspaper Ethics and Constitutional Values*, 141 U. Penn. L. Rev. 221, 225, 26 (1992) (describing vituperative debate among early American newspapers, characterized by close ties between editors and party machinery).

[34] *See Schudson, supra* note 16, at 54–57 (describing the 1840 "Moral War" of the New York party press establishment against the politically fickle, penny-paper upstart, the *New York Herald*).

forms, and wrapping paper for the Post Office.[35] Such patronage brought the press into a corrupt bargain. It transformed newspaper editors into "political professionals, people for whom printing was a way to make a living out of politics, rather than the other way around."[36] As John Quincy Adams described the alignment of newspapers behind presidential hopeful and then Adams ally, William Crawford:

> The *National Intelligencer* is secured to him by the belief of the editors that he will be the successful candidate, and by their dependence upon the printing of Congress; the *Richmond Enquirer* because he is a Virginian and slave-holder; the *National Advocate* of New York, through Van Buren, ... the *Democratic Press*, of Philadelphia, because I transferred the printing of the laws from that paper to the *Franklin Gazette*; and several other presses in various parts of the Union upon principles alike selfish and sordid.[37]

Opposition politicians railed against such patronage and its accompanying shackling of the press. They rightly charged that the patronage system transformed the party press into a "government press" and that press liberty is compromised when "the favor of power is essential to the support of the editors."[38] But once in power, those critics used the very same tools to reward their loyal supporters and curry favor with newspapers whose future support they sought.[39] It was not until the Civil War, the establishment of the Government Printing Office, and the emergence of a strong independent press that party press patronage as an overt federal government policy came to an end.[40]

To be certain, the party press patronage system in the antebellum United States gained momentum as a result of circumstances unique to that time and place. The high cost of producing and distributing printed material and the absence of a federal government printing office led to both the federal government's reliance on

---

[35] *See* Culver H. Smith, *The Press, Politics, and Patronage; The American Government's Use of Newspapers 1789–1875* (1977); Donna Lee Dickerson, *The Course of Tolerance; Freedom of the Press in Nineteenth-Century America* 65–71 (1990). The government also provided subsidies on a non-partisan basis for the press in general. Beginning soon after Independence, Congress heavily subsidized newspaper deliveries by imposing preferential postal rates, levying postal charges on subscribers rather than printers, intermittently collecting subscribers' postal charges, providing free newspaper delivery among printers, and maintaining postal roads for both post office and printers' private use. Richard B. Kielbowicz, *The Press, Post Office, and Flow of News in the Early Republic*, 3 J. Early Republic 255, 257–59 (1983).

[36] Jeffrey Lingan Pasley, "Artful and Designing Men": Political Professionalism in the Early American Republic, 1775–1820, at 336 (Doctoral Thesis, Oct. 1993).

[37] 6 *Memoirs of John Quincy Adams* 61 (Charles Francis Adams ed. 1874–77; reprinted, Books for Libraries Press, 1969), quoted in *Dickerson, supra* note , at 66.

[38] Duff Green, *U.S. Telegraph*, Feb. 9, 1826, quoted in *Dickerson, supra* note , at 69.

[39] *See Dickerson, supra* note 35, at 65–71 (describing criticism and subsequent use of press patronage by John Quincy Adams and Daniel Webster).

[40] *See Smith, supra* note 35, at 229–48.

the press for printing and distributing government documents and the press' financial dependence on government subsidy and patronage. But the antebellum party press' susceptibility to government influence presents a broadly cautionary tale nevertheless. Even short of systematic patronage, there are a multitude of ways in which the government can bestow favors upon media aligned with the party in power, ranging from preferential access to information to subtly discriminatory regulation. As a result, at the same time that the party press aligned with the government will have little incentive to scrutinize government officials and policy, the opposition press will have reduced ability to act as an effective watchdog. Nor will government-aligned or opposition press have an incentive to question fundamental components of the political system that benefit all major political parties.

Finally, at its extreme, a party-aligned press can lead to considerable polarization and insularity. At least within the mainstream of the political spectrum, the commercial press presents an exchange of views even while it supports a common language and understanding for political and social discourse. The party press might have the advantage of challenging mainstream assumptions, empowering marginal voices, and sharpening political debate. But it can also lead to the fragmentation of public discourse, a situation in which debate occurs only within the narrow province of like-minded people. That in turn can lead not only to insularity, but also to greater extremism and polarization.

Cass Sunstein has recently surveyed studies in individual and group psychology documenting the phenomenon of "group polarization."[41] Longstanding democratic theory holds that group deliberation produces better outcomes. But as Sunstein summarizes, when a group consists of individuals with predeliberation judgments that, on the whole, lean even moderately in a given direction, deliberation tends to move the group, and the individuals who compose it, toward a more extreme position. Thus, with striking empirical regularity, "people who are opposed to the minimum wage are likely, after talking to each other, to be still more opposed; people who tend to support gun control are likely, after discussion, to support gun control with considerable enthusiasm; people who believe that global warming is a serious problem are likely, after discussion, to insist on severe measures to prevent global warming; jurors who support a high punitive damages award are likely, after talking, to support an award higher than the median of their predeliberation judgments."[42] A partisan press that repeatedly presents like-minded opinion on a narrow set of issues might engender a similar movement toward the extreme.

In short, while our system of free expression might be enhanced by a resurgence

---

[41] Cass R. Sunstein, *Deliberative Trouble? Why Groups Go to Extremes*, 110 *Yale L.J.* 71 (2000).
[42] Cass R. Sunstein, The Law of Group Polarization 1 (U. Chi. Law School, John M. Olin Law & Economics Working Paper No. 91, 1999) available at <http://papers.ssrn.com/paper.taf?abstract_id=199668.> *See also* Cass R. Sunstein, *Republic.com* 65–84 (2001).

of ideologically motivated media, there is reason to think that the party press system should at most supplement, not replace, independent commercial media. A party press might provide a welcome antidote to the mainstream, market-oriented bias of the commercial media. But it should not be viewed as a panacea to commercial media shortcomings.

IV. Government-Funded Media

Government subsidy provides an opportunity for media to avoid the biases inherent in reliance on advertising and the market for financial sustenance. As such, government-funded media can be an important component of the system of free expression. They can serve both to engender a public discourse that is not skewed to the wealthy and provide a forum for minority views that receive little play in commercial media. Indeed, in many democratic countries, state-funded television and other media have played important, perhaps even vital, watchdog and discourse-building roles.[43]

However, incidents abound of even democratic governments seeking to use the power of the purse to extract influence over the speech of state-funded media. The problem is not merely the difficulty of setting rational, neutral criteria for the distribution of government subsidies to the press.[44] In addition, state efforts to insulate state-funded broadcasters from government and political party interference have proven to be only partly successful.[45] In some instances, public

---

[43] *See* Jay G. Blumler, *Public Service Broadcasting before the Commercial Deluge, in Television and the Public Interest: Vulnerable Values in West European Broadcasting* 7–21. (Jay G. Blumler ed. 1992). *See also* Elihu Katz, *And Deliver Us from Segmentation*, 546 Annals 22, 23–24 (1996) (depicting the pre-commercial regime, which dominated post-war Western Europe, of public broadcasting and party press as an ideal vehicle for both national integration and robust debate).

[44] *See* Anthony Smith, *The Politics of Information; Problems of Policy in Modern Media* 174 (1978) (noting that proposals for press subsidies in German have foundered on the difficulty of determining such criteria).

[45] *See* Eli Noam, *Television in Europe* 96–97 (1991) (chronicling decades of post-war French government attempts to influence coverage on state-run French television and radio); *Furor over IRA Film Could Put Peace Talks in Jeopardy, The Independent* (London), July 27, 1997, at 1 (noting that under a United Kingdom government ban, Sinn Fein representatives were not allowed to speak on British television until 1993); *see also* Frances H. Foster, *Information and the Problem of Democracy: The Russian Experience*, 44 AM. J. COMP. L. 243, 257–58 (1996) (detailing instances of government censorship in the supposed "defense of democracy" in post-Soviet Russia); *cf.* Frances Stonor Saunders, *The Cultural Cold War; The CIA and the World of Arts and Letters* (1999) (documenting the CIA's covert funding of select academic conferences, magazines, and cultural activities in post-war Europe in an effort to lure Western European intelligentsia away from its fascination with Marxism toward a more favorable understanding of the American worldview).

broadcasters' internal supervisory organs have become politicized along party lines.[46] In others, governments have exerted direct pressure on public broadcasters to alter broadcasting content.[47]

Further, critics charge that noncommercial, government-subsidized media also generally fall well within the mainstream.[48] In part, political pressures constrain public broadcasters from taking controversial positions or even tackling controversial issues.[49] In addition, the people who determine public broadcast programming are largely drawn from the same intellectual and social élites as their counterparts in the commercial media and thus tend to share the same mainstream orientation.[50]

This admittedly cursory review suggests that a discursive arena dominated by government-funded media would not better serve liberal democratic governance than does our current commercial-media-dominated arena. While government-funded media remain free from the market dictate that subverts the commercial media's force as Fourth Estate, government funding brings a vulnerability to government influence that seems to be widely present, to one degree or another, in public broadcasting systems even of liberal democratic states. As with the party press, government-funded media might optimally serve as a supplement to their commercial counterpart, each offsetting and acting as a counterweight and watchdog against the limitations of the others.

---

[46] See Humphreys, *supra* note 29, at 176–87.

[47] See note 45 *supra*.

[48] See Frank Webster, *Theories of the Information Society* 107 (1995) (noting that the BBC's presentation of public affairs has generally "limited itself to the boundaries of established party politics"). Indeed, as Monroe Price notes: "There has been, at times, a division over whether public service broadcasting is an instrument primarily for the broad center and the major cultural institutions that serve it or, in addition, one specifically designed to redress lacunae by programming for the cultural needs of underserved groups in society." Monroe E. Price, *Public Broadcasting and the Crisis of Corporate Governance*, 17 Cardozo Arts & Entertainment L. J. 417, 423 (1999).

[49] See Humphreys, *supra* note 29, at 321 (discussing German public broadcasting). In addition, particularly in the United States, but also in other countries, decreased government subsidies and competition from commercial media have led public broadcasters to be increased concerned with ratings and the bottom line. *See* Samuel G. Freedman, *Public Radio's Private Guru*, N.Y. Times, Nov. 11, 2001, at Sec. 2, p. 1 (describing controversy surrounding market researcher who advises public radio stations how to tailor programming to maximize listener donations).

[50] See Weinberg, *supra* note 24, at 1201 (noting that "publishers of public broadcasting are not themselves the "public," [but] [r]ather, they are a professional elite responding to their own values and institutional agenda").

V. Peer-to-Peer Model

Yochai Benkler has argued that a system of distributed, peer-to-peer information production and dissemination would better secure individual autonomy than does our current commercial-media-dominated regime.[51] As Benkler suggests, such a system would be a much-expanded version of non-centralized, peer-to-peer music exchange made possible through Gnutella and other such software.[52] It would entail the establishment of a commons for both content and communications infrastructure. In that way, all could produce and exchange expressive content, ranging from video to text, free from governmental or proprietary control.

For Benkler, individual autonomy in the communications environment is best served when individuals enjoy broad opportunities to disseminate expression – both their own creative expression and expression that others have created – to choose among a highly diverse menu of expression to hear, see, or read. The advantage of his peer-to-peer model is that it takes editorial control away from the commercial firms that currently own carriage media and expressive content. It allows individuals to upload, distribute, and receive the content of their choice.

While Benkler's focus is individual autonomy, a peer-to-peer model might also be seen to better serve democratic institutions by providing for greater expressive diversity and "bottom-up" discourse. Indeed, other commentators have looked to peer-to-peer communication as a vehicle for "democratizing" our system of free expression.[53] As Niva Elkin-Koren puts it: the "transformative power of cyberspace lies in its capability to decentralize the production and dissemination of knowledge".[54]

VI. Peer-to-Peer; A Critical Evaluation

Peer-to-peer communication, such as takes place on the Internet, raises staggering problems of information overload and credibility.[55] Without some vehicle for

---

[51] See Yochai Benkler, *Siren Songs and Amish Children: Autonomy, Information, and Law*, 76 N.Y.U. L. Rev. 23 (2001).

[52] *Id.* at 107–08.

[53] See, e.g., Dean Colby, *Conceptualizing the "Digital Divide": Closing the "Gap" by Creating a Postmodern Network that Distributes the Productive Power of Speech*, 6 Comm. L. & Pol'y 123 (2001).

[54] Niva Elkin-Koren, *Cyberlaw and Social Change: A Democratic Approach to Copyright Law in Cyberspace*, 14 Cardozo Arts & Ent L.J. 215, 217 (1996).

[55] See Andrew L. Shapiro, *The Control Revolution; How the Internet is Putting Individuals in Charge and Changing the World We Know* 133–36, 187–97 (1999); Neil Weinstock Netanel, *Cyberspace 2.0*, 79 Texas L. Rev. 447, 456 (2000).

filtration and accreditation, individuals would face the impossible task of sifting through vast quantities of expression to seek to determine which items are both of interest and reasonably trustworthy. Without tools and institutions for filtration and accreditation, we would be awash in a maelstrom of noise.

Part of the function of the commercial news media is filtration and accreditation. The press often serves as a source of trustworthiness, stability, and accountability, or at least some combination of those traits. Whatever their faults, traditional news media have the resources and professional commitment to check facts and verify sources, and we hold them accountable if they do not. In contrast, Matt Drudge and other individual online publishers have neither the financial wherewithal nor institutional aspiration to meet professional journalistic standards.[56] That is not to say that such gadflies can make no constitutive contribution to public discourse or that the media should hold a monopoly over speech. But full disintermediation of the kind some critics envision would leave us without any real possibility for assessing the reliability and import of the vast bulk of expression and opinion swirling around the Internet.

Benkler well recognizes the need for filtration and accreditation in all communication, including peer-to-peer networks.[57] He argues, however, that peer-to-peer networks can generate vehicles for filtration and accreditation that will better serve individual autonomy than filtration and accreditation performed by the commercial news media. First, Benkler argues that filtration and accreditation only enhance autonomy if the editor's notion of relevance and quality comports with those of the sender and recipient and if the editor is herself trustworthy. As he puts it: "To the extent the values of the editor diverge from those of the user, an editor does not facilitate user autonomy by selecting relevant information based on her values, but rather imposes her own preferences regarding what should be relevant to users. A parallel effect occurs with accreditation. An editor might choose to treat as credible a person whose views or manner of presentation draw audiences, rather than necessarily the wisest or best informed commentators."[58] Second, Benkler insists that, armed with the right kind of communications and processing capabilities, peer-to-peer communication can generate its own, bottom-up vehicles for relevance and accreditation.[59] These would include peer-to-peer rating systems, such as are possible with music search engines that track and poll user preferences.[60] In addition to such peer-to-peer rating and referencing, Benkler and others suggest, distributed network communication enables persons and entities to establish competing filtration and

---

[56] Shapiro, *supra* note 55, at 133–36.
[57] Benkler, *supra* note 51, at 105–06.
[58] *Id.* at 107.
[59] *Id.* at 107–08.
[60] *Id.*

accreditation services, giving individuals a broad spectrum of choice regarding on which such "authorities" they wish to rely.[61]

I will take Benkler's arguments in reverse order, first questioning the efficacy of peer-to-peer filtering and accreditation and then addressing the peer-to-peer model's relative benefits for liberal democratic governance.

A. THE EFFICACY OF PEER-TO-PEER FILTERING AND ACCREDITATION

Benkler's proffered peer-to-peer filtering and accreditation is of two types: peer-to-peer rating and freelance editing. Peer-to-peer rating might work well with music and other art forms. Music is an "experience good." I can tell what a given musical work is worth to me once I hear it. I might also be able to know from experience that certain persons or certain categories of persons share my musical tastes, such that I can generally rely on their recommendations regarding what music is worth my while to hear.

But the music rating model does not apply to news and other sorts of information. Information is essentially a "credence good."[62] Consumers have difficulty evaluating the value of such a good even after consuming it. Information has value only if it is accurate. And I generally have no means, short of relying on the trustworthiness of the source of information, of knowing whether information I receive about an event or phenomenon outside my personal experience is accurate. (Of course, if I have such personal knowledge, the report of information has no value to me either because I already know it.)

Peer-to-peer rating over vast communications networks has no mechanism for ensuring trustworthiness. How do I know whether a given piece of "information" is accurate or just rumor, libel, manipulation, or urban legend? Indeed, even music rating is subject to such a problem. I can rely on my peers' music rating only to the extent that the network provides me with accurate information about my peers' preferences. But I have no independent vehicle for judging the accuracy of that information. How do I know whether the ratings reflect true preferences or manipulation by certain groups or musicians, like that which has plagued online public opinion polls?[63]

---

[61] *Id.* at 108; *see also* Eugene Volokh, *Cheap Speech and What It Will Do*, 104 *Yale L.J.* 1805 (1995) (predicting that [I have only seen this word as one word: freelance] authors and critics will supplant media firms).

[62] *See* Mark R. Patterson, *On the Impossibility of Information Intermediaries*, Fordham University School of Law, Law and Economics Research Paper No. 13, August 5, 2001, at 5 note 21, available at < http://www.fordham.edu/law/faculty/patterson/workingpapers/infointer.pdf. >

[63] *See, e.g.*, *The 'Person of Century' Could Be . . . . Ataturk?*, *Chicago Tribune*, Nov. 7, 1997, at C2 (reporting Kemal Ataturk lead in voting for Time Magazine's "Person of the Century," following urging by Turkish journalists for their readers to write in his name). The problem of lack of trustworthiness guarantees in peer-to-peer networking has apparently affected music exchange as well.

Ratings reflecting music *purchases* might solve this problem, at least to the extent the search engine is trustworthy. But if music must be purchased, we might no longer have a non-proprietary information commons. Peers can also reliably rate peer commentators' credibility in close-knit communities of experts, as with the elaborate, multi-level rating system in effect on the "computer nerd" website, "Slashdot."[64] But such commentator rating is of doubtful scalability to general news and public affairs sites, where audiences lack the expertise and, often, the motivation to rate peer commentators' credibility.

Where peer accreditation mechanisms are unavailable, networks suffer from the paralysis common to communities that lack guarantees for mutual trust: everyone doubts others' statements, so no one finds it worthwhile to invest in producing verifiably accurate information. Faced with this collective action problem, peer-to-peer network users might, like similar social groups, turn to trusted institutions to provide credible information and trustworthy assessments of others' information.[65] Such institutions would consist of information intermediaries, like Internet search engines and Consumer Reports, as well as competing freelance editors, along the lines of Benkler's model.

But as Mark Patterson has demonstrated, it is highly unlikely that trustworthy information intermediaries would arise to any consistent, systematic extent in the information commons, peer-to-peer environment.[66] Part of the reason stems from the public goods quality of information. Information intermediaries either provide information about information produced by others or aggregate information that the information intermediary warrants as relevant and credible. But once information is released, recipients can pass it on to others at little or no cost. As a result, unless information intermediaries can exert proprietary control over their information, which under Benkler's information commons model they cannot, they will be unable to profit from all the information they produce and thus will likely produce far less information than socially optimal.

Even worse, information intermediaries have an incentive to profit from slanting the information they provide.[67] In order to maximize their revenue, information intermediaries are likely to sell their services to advertisers and information sources, whether instead of or in addition to selling information to consumers. That has already happened with Internet search engines like Yahoo. Such information intermediaries regularly sell prominent placement in search

---

[64] See http://www.slashdot.org. See also Yochai Benkler, Coase's Penguin, or, Linux and the Nature of the Firm 13–17 (2001) available at <http://www.law.duke.edu/pd/papers>.

[65] As Jarvenpaa and Tiller note: "Under the rational choice perspective, customers facing prisoner's dilemmas and collective action problems are often willing to trust only to the extent that trust can be fostered by institutions. In such situations, trust takes a form of institution-based trust." Sirkka L. Jarvenpaa & Emerson H. Tiller, *Customer Trust In Virtual Environments: A Managerial Perspective*, 81 B.U.L. Rev. 665, 673 (2001).

[66] *See, generally,* Patterson, *supra* note 62.

[67] *See id.* at 9–12.

results.[68] Even so-called "shopping bots," specialized search engines designed to compare prices and goods on behalf of consumers, have been modified to cater to merchants. Shopping bot sites increasingly offer merchants opportunities for partnership, affiliation, advertising, and, most insidiously, top ranking in search results in return for a fee.[69]

To be certain, information intermediaries face certain reputational constraints.[70] But especially where the information concerns the quality and accuracy of news reporting, consumers of information will likely never determine whether the information received was accurate. Given their inability directly to evaluate the quality and credibility of information intermediary services, consumers will need to rely on the same meta-filtration and accreditation tools that apply to the commercial mass media. These involve some combination of (1) information providers' professional ethics, which are already firmly in place in the case of the mass media but which would have to be developed for their peer-to-peer counterparts, and (2) meta-information-intermediaries, who report on the accuracy of information intermediaries and who suffer from the same infirmities as any other information intermediary.

Finally, even if commercial, but reasonably credible information intermediaries do emerge, they are unlikely to do so in a competitive market. Like all producers of information, information intermediaries tend to have cost structures characterized by economies of scale. This is especially the case on the Internet, where the marginal cost of information production is extremely low and fixed costs are extremely high. As a result, information industries, online as well as offline, face considerable centripetal force. As economists have long recognized, "where technology creates significant economies of scale, markets tend towards dominance by a few large players."[71] The ongoing consolidations within the media and telecommunications industry are a prime example of this phenomenon. And, as Mark Patterson points out, the market for information intermediaries in the traditional economy also tends strongly toward monopoly.[72] There is no reason to think that peer-to-peer, online networks would somehow spawn a competitive information intermediary market.

At bottom, the only information intermediaries in the peer-to-peer network

---

[68] See Lucas D. Introna & Helen Nissenbaum, *Shaping the Web: Why the Politics of Search Engines Matters* 16(3) *Information Soc'y* 169 (2000) (discussing the search engine bias toward firms with resources to gain prominent placement in search results).

[69] See Karen Solomon, *Revenge of the Bots*, The Standard, Nov. 15, 1999.

[70] See Patterson, *supra* note 62, at 12–14; Gary Charness & Nuno Garoupa, *Reputation and Honesty in a Market for Information* (Working Paper, Sept. 1998), <http://papers.ssrn.com/so13/papers.cfm?abstract_id=139695.>

[71] Julie E. Cohen, *Lochner in Cyberspace: The New Economic Orthodoxy of "Rights Management"*, 97 Mich. L. Rev. 462, 522 (1998); see also Philip E. Agre, *Life After Cyberspace*, 18 EASST Rev. (Sept. 1999) <http://www.chem.uva.nl/easst/easst993.html>.

[72] See Patterson, *supra* note 62, at 4.

world likely to be different in kind from today's mass media are non-profit watchdogs. Such entities already exist in the offline world. Some, such as the Consumers Union, are quite effective in their narrow areas. But non-profit entities are unlikely to assume the role that Benkler envisions in the area of news reporting. Most importantly, the verification of others' reporting requires much the same resources as the reporting itself. And these resources are considerable.[73] Indeed, media critics rightly point out that even the commercial mass media lack the resources to engage consistently in independent investigative reporting, without reliance on government sources to provide information. It is far more costly to track, investigate, and verify ongoing news reporting than to test the safety and reliability of consumer products. While non-profit media watchdogs can sometimes call media news organizations to task for inaccurate and biased reporting,[74] they lack the resources to do so on a consistent and effective basis.

B. Peer-to-Peer's Relative Benefits for Liberal Democratic Governance

Even if peer-to-peer networks could generate information producers and intermediaries along the lines Benkler suggests, we would not want to jettison the commercial mass media. To the extent peer-to-peer communication would supplant the commercial mass media, Benkler, it seems, imagines a two-dimensional speech universe populated entirely by volunteer individual speakers revolving around a benign government.[75] To my mind, however, liberal democratic governance requires, rather, a speech universe punctuated by bubbles, a universe that contains concentrations of private expressive power capable of standing up to government and, indeed, capable of standing up to General Motors, Mobil Oil, the Republican and Democratic parties, the World Bank, and other concentrations of private economic and political power. Democratic governance requires a free press not just in the sense of a diversity of expression. It requires the *institution* of a free press. It requires media with the financial wherewithal and political independence to engage in sustained investigative journalism, to expose the errors and excesses of government and other powerful political and economic actors.

The Benklerian republic of yeoman speakers presupposes a republic of yeomen, period. It imagines a world in which we earn our livings, communicate, and govern

---

[73] See Protess et. al., supra note 8, at 233–35 (describing significant investment of news organizations' resources in investigative reporting and in responding to counterattacks by government officials and private firms who are subjects of exposés).

[74] See, e.g., Fairness & Accuracy in Reporting, < http://www.fair.org >

[75] See Yochai Benkler, *Free as the Air to Common Use: First Amendment Constraints on Enclosure of the Public Domain*, 74 N.Y.U. L. Rev. 354, 400 (1999) (complaining that an expanded copyright "tends to produce market-based hierarchy, rather than to facilitate and sustain independent yeoman authors").

ourselves without mediating organizations and concentrations of wealth and power. But that is not our world, never has been our world, and, so long as we are organized in polities larger than the Greek city-state, never will be our world. In fact, I dare say, it is not a world to which we should aspire because in such a world, nothing would stand between the individual and an all-powerful state.

Our best hope for democratic governance in this world is far messier than the ideal republic of yeomen. It requires mediating institutions and associations, private and public concentrations of wealth and power, and varied mechanisms to maintain multiple balances of power within government, within civil society, and between government and civil society.[76] No less, it requires an expressive sector that mirrors that panoply of governing institutions. It requires independent, powerful media to guard against abuses of power on the part of other private and governmental entities. It also requires mechanisms to check and distribute the power of the commercial media.

Individual authors and web site operators lack the resources to fulfill the press' traditional, vital role of watchdog against government myopia and oppression. Nor can individuals adequately expose corporate unlawfulness, labor union corruption, and political party self-aggrandizement. Liberal democratic nations necessarily encompass multiple concentrations of power.[77] Only an equally powerful press can effectively check other entities' and associations' deployment of their power by exposing it to the light of public opinion. Indeed, only a *mass media*, capable of reaching a mass audience, can both catalyze and, to a degree, embody public opinion in the face of government authority and corporate fiefdom.

The story of former tobacco company researcher Jeffrey Wigand is a case in point.[78] While employed at cigarette-maker Brown & Williamson, Wigand discovered that, despite repeated public denials and testimony under oath to the contrary, leading tobacco company executives had long known that the nicotine in cigarettes is an addictive substance. In 1995 Wigand relayed his discovery to a reporter for the widely watched CBS news magazine, 60 Minutes, and agreed to be interviewed on the program. In so doing, Wigand violated his Brown & Williamson non-disclosure agreement and undertook considerable financial and

---

[76] Intermediate associations can also help to support a democratic culture by building participatory norms. See Grant McConnell, *The Public Values of the Private Association*, in *Nomos XI: Voluntary Associations* 147, 149 (J. Pennock & J. Chapman eds. 1969). My focus here, however, is on intermediate organizations as loci of power vis-à-vis other power centers.

[77] See Peter H. Schuck, *The Limits Of Law; Essays On Democratic Governance* 204–50 (2000); E. E. Schattschneider, *The Semisovereign People; A Realist's View of Democracy in America* (1960). See also Mark P. Petracca, *The Future of an Interest Group Society*, in *The Politics Of Interests; Interest Groups Transformed* 345 (Mark P. Petracca ed. 1992) (noting the continuing, vital role played by interest groups in the democratic process).

[78] My account of the Wigand story draws heavily upon Paul Starr, *What You Need to Beat Goliath*, Am. Prospect, Dec. 20, 1999, at 7.

personal risk. Instrumental in Wigand's decision to divulge the tobacco company misdeeds despite that risk was CBS's promise to indemnify him for any liability to his former employer and, no less importantly, the knowledge that he would have the opportunity to present his findings before millions of prime time television viewers.[79] It is highly unlikely that Wigand would have exposed Brown & Williamson at his own peril without the backing and mass audience of a major media outlet. And even if he had, perhaps by posting information and documents on his personal web page, his story may well have been lost in the chorus of tobacco company denials (if they had even bothered to respond) and against the backdrop of tens of thousands of crank web pages presenting sundry allegations that few find credible even when true.

Of course, there is more to the Wigand story. CBS management initially scuttled the Wigand interview shortly before it was to appear on 60 Minutes. Apparently, CBS did want to take the unlikely, but not immaterial risk of having to pay a multi-billion dollar damage award to Brown & Williamson, especially since that contingency would have reduced CBS's share price at a time when the company was negotiating to be acquired by Westinghouse. Additional, and more insidious, corporate entanglements might have also contributed to the decision.[80] Laurence Tisch, CBS's chairman at the time, was also an owner of Lorillard Tobacco Company, and his son Andrew was Lorillard's president. In fact, Andrew Tisch was one of the tobacco executives who had sworn before Congress that nicotine was not addictive, and Wigand was a witness in the perjury investigation regarding that testimony.[81] At that time, moreover, Lorillard was negotiating with Brown & Williamson to buy six of its brands.[82] In sum, CBS's broadcast of the Wigand interview might have caused CBS and Laurence Tisch considerable financial loss and might have helped send Tisch's son to jail, facts that could hardly have been lost on the CBS lawyers and executives involved in the decision to cancel the Wigand broadcast.[83]

The circumstances surrounding CBS's cancellation of the Wigand interview graphically illustrate the potential vulnerabilities and limitations of the media-as-watchdog model, especially in an age of increasing media consolidation and conglomeration. But some three months after the Wigand interview was to have been aired, CBS reversed its decision to scuttle the interview and did in fact broadcast it, and in so doing, it dealt a significant blow to the tobacco industry. Significantly, it was the presence and coverage of competing media that pushed a

---

[79] Some ten million households watch 60 Minutes each week. Owen M. Fiss, *The Censorship of Television*, 93 NW. U.L. Rev. 1215, 1217 (1999) (citing Nielsen Media Research, 1998 Report on Television (1999)).
[80] Starr, *supra* note 78.
[81] Id.
[82] Id.
[83] Id.

reluctant CBS into reasserting its watchdog role. CBS broadcast the Wigand interview only after the New York Times had detailed CBS's capitulation in a front page story,[84] the New York Daily News had obtained and reported on the transcript of the omitted interview,[85] and the Wall Street Journal had published Wigand deposition testimony containing his central allegations.[86] Moreover, critical media coverage did not end with the CBS broadcast. Most notably perhaps, in its 1999 motion picture, The Insider, Disney/ABC presented a widely-acclaimed dramatized version of the entire Wigand episode, castigating CBS for the network's striking, if temporary, abdication of its journalistic integrity. That contemporaneous and subsequent coverage by competing media enterprises, an instance of such enterprises exposing each other's wrongdoing, may deter such lapses in the future.

The moral I wish to draw from this story is not that "all's well that ends well," that we can complacently rely on an increasingly conglomeratized mass media to expose corporate wrongdoing. Rather, the Wigand story illustrates that, like a host of governmental and private institutions, media power has both a positive and negative face. There are no perfect solutions to this dual face of power. There are only partial solutions, most involving efforts to balance one power center against one or more others. State subsidies for non-commercial media, state-imposed limitations on media firm conglomeration, and state assurance of individual access to effective channels of communication constitute such partial solutions. These measures aim to provide for greater expressive diversity without undermining the media's constitutive force. They are not perfect solutions. But such measures, and others like them, are the best that we can or should hope to obtain.

Peer-to-peer communication can certainly prove to be a useful supplement to the commercial news media. In addition to constituting a vast forum for alternative discourses, the Internet spawns gadflies, media critics and others who may sometimes successfully bring a story to mass media attention or challenge media silence.[87] But that is not to say that we should aspire, even as a liberal democratic ideal, to an egalitarian expressive universe composed entirely of virtual and street-corner pamphleteers.

---

[84] Bill Carter, *"60 Minutes" Ordered to Pull Interview in Tobacco Report*, N.Y. Times, at A1 (Nov. 9, 1995).
[85] Joe Calderone and Kevin Flynn, *What "60 Minutes" Cut; Attack on Cig Maker Was Axed, Transcript Shows*, N.Y. Daily News, at 2 (Nov. 17, 1995).
[86] See Bill Carter, *CBS Broadcasts Interview With Tobacco Executive*, N.Y. Times, at B8 (Feb. 5, 1996) (reporting that CBS broadcast the interview a week after the Wall Street Journal had published the transcript of the Wigand deposition).
[87] An already classic example is Matt Drudge's web site scoop of the Monica Lewinsky story. *See Shapiro, supra* note 55, at 41.

Conclusion

Much of the criticism of the commercial mass media is well-founded. But that does not lead to the inexorable conclusion that we should aspire to jettison the commercial mass media from its dominant role as a supplier of information and opinion. Rather, our system of free expression must include a plurality of speaker types, including commercial mass media, government-subsidized noncommercial media, party press, independent publishers, political and nonprofit associations, universities, and individuals. To some extent, each of these speaker types offsets, complements, and checks the rest. Like other speaker types, the commercial media plays a unique and, I think, vital role within this complex mix. The key, this preliminary study suggests, is not to find substitutes for the commercial media, but to design regulatory frameworks that enhance the commercial media's Fourth Estate potential while insuring the vitality of other speaker types as well.

V. INFORMATION AGGREGATION

Hardware-Based ID, Rights Management, and Trusted Systems

*Jonathan Weinberg**

In early 1999, Intel announced a new technology: the Processor Serial Number. This hardware feature proved highly controversial, and by the end of the year, Intel had retreated. Yet Intel's Processor Serial Number was only one example of a larger, and important, class of technologies that assign a unique identifier to each Internet user. That identifier, in these implementations, can be tied to the person's real-world identity, and is available to a wide range of applications and content providers. The approach is designed to allow content providers easily to identify consumers accessing information and entertainment via the Internet, and to correlate information from and about those consumers with the material that the content providers release to them.

Technologies involving user identification along the lines of the Processor Serial Number may give providers of information goods extensive new capabilities. They provide an easy and straightforward way for publishers to verify the authenticity of messages claiming authorization to receive digital works, better enabling them to limit availability of their works to recipients who meet certain criteria. The technology dovetails with the use of trusted systems, enabling content providers to prevent recipients from passing usable copies of the work to anyone who has not paid the content provider, and giving content providers flexibility in specifying the nature of the event that will trigger a payment obligation.

The technologies, though, have other consequences as well. The most obvious relate to privacy: Trusted systems relying on transparent unique identifiers

---

* I owe thanks to Phil Agre, Karl Auerbach, Lorrie Cranor, Jessica Litman, Neil Netanel, Joel Reidenberg, and Paul Resnick. An earlier (and longer) version of this paper was published as Hardware-Based ID, Rights Management, and Trusted Systems, 52 Stan. L. Rev. 1251 (2000). Versions of this paper were presented at a Haifa University Conference on the Commodification of Information, the Telecommunications Policy Research Conference, and a Conference on Cyberspace and Privacy: A New Legal Paradigm?, at Stanford University. The information contained in this paper is current as of summer 2000.

N. Elkin-Koren and N.W. Netanel (eds.), The Commodification of Information, 343–364.
© 2002 Jonathan Weinberg. Printed in Great Britain.

threaten to sharply diminish anonymity and informational privacy on the Internet. They raise the prospect that a much larger proportion of ordinary transactions will require consumers to present unique identification numbers digitally linked to a wide range of personally identifiable information. They are well-suited to across-the-board use by a large number of unrelated information collectors, increasing the ease with which a wide range of information about a person can be aggregated into a single overall dossier.

Moreover, the combination of trusted systems technology that enables publishers to ensure that speech released to one consumer does not make its way via sharing or secondary markets to another, and the privacy effects of allowing publishers to collect extensive individualized information on consumers, will likely affect the economics and politics of speech markets. It will sharply enhance producers' ability to discriminate among individual consumers on price and other grounds in connection with the sale and marketing of information goods. Some commentators suggest that this concentration of control is desirable because the price discrimination it enables will broaden distribution of information goods. Yet the benefits of such a system are clouded; any increase in distribution due to price discrimination comes at the cost of shutting down the distribution that is generated, in today's less-controlled system, through sharing or secondary markets. It will likely be accompanied by increased media concentration and a self-reinforcing cycle of commercial pressure on individual privacy.

Publishers can reap the benefits of trusted systems without these socially undesirable consequences by relying on identification techniques that assure consumers a greater degree of privacy. Building trusted systems around hardware-based consumer identifiers not only carries with it a dystopian future of universal personal monitoring and identification, but also is unnecessary to meet publishers' legitimate needs.

In Part I of this paper, I explore the market incentives for the widespread deployment of systems under which information flows from consumers to content providers. In Part II, I discuss the blend of anonymity and identifiability presented by current Internet architecture, and in Part III, I focus on a particular technology – the Processor Serial Number built into the Intel chips powering most computing devices today. In Part IV, I discuss the implications of such technology for privacy and the economics and politics of communications markets. In Part V, I note that the negative consequences of this technology are avoidable: Content providers could rely on more sophisticated cryptographic techniques to manage access to their information goods. Such systems would allow content owners to exploit their intellectual property while avoiding the consequences described in this paper.

I. Rights Management and Trusted Systems

The most important concern driving the information flow from consumers to content providers relates to rights management. The term "rights management" is commonly associated with the protection of intellectual property rights, but it need not be so limited. One can think of rights management as covering any technological means of controlling public access to, and manipulation of, digital resources. That sort of control is basic to any system of network computing. At the heart of Unix, for example, is the concept of permissions, which define *which* users on a network can take *what* actions (read, write, execute) on *which* files and directories.[1] Networking would not be practical without a way of defining and limiting the set of people who can have access to particular documents and other network resources. Rights management techniques, in that sense, are simply a form of network security.

Those techniques demand a reliable way to match user names with real-world individuals. After all, it is the individual, not the user name, whose access to files is at issue. In the old days, when mainframe computers ruled the world, system administrators had little difficulty associating the individuals using their systems with unique user names, and thus using permissions or similar file access rights to enforce that aspect of system security. The systems administrators themselves had assigned those user names to the individuals in question.[2] The situation was not much different for a self-contained local area network.

But the Internet changed things: It has no system administrator. There is no reliable, automated way under current technology to determine which individual is associated with any given user name on an Internet-connected network.[3] Indeed, even your own computer does not know who you are; if you tell your PC that you are Napoleon or Joan of Arc, it has no reason not to believe you.[4] For this reason, ordinary Internet architecture stymies attempts at rights management beyond a given network. It provides no convenient set of options in the middle ground between blocking access by anyone outside one's own network and granting access to everyone in the world.

How can one extend sophisticated file access rights beyond the controlled

---

[1] *See* Matt Welsh & Lar Kaufman, Running Linux 104–09 (2d ed. 1996).
[2] See Philip E. Agre, The Architecture of Identity: Embedding Privacy in Market Institutions, 2 Info., Comm. and Soc'y 1, ¶ 25 (Spring 1999) <http://www.infosoc.co.uk/00105/feature.htm>.
[3] See generally S. Bradner, Source Directed Access Control on the Internet (Nov. 1996) <ftp://ftp.isi.edu/in-notes/rfc2057.txt> (Network Working Group RFC 2057). While Unix systems may supply such information in response to the "finger" command, there is nothing in the Internet architecture that requires them to do so, or to do so accurately. See Ed Krol, The Whole Internet User's Guide & Catalog 171–74 (1992).
[4] See Agre, supra note 2, at 11.

network environment into the Internet universe at large? Put another way, how can a local server extend secure control over the many interconnected networks that make up the Internet? To do that, it must be able to reliably identify everyone seeking access to its files, or at least, everyone to whom it is willing to grant access, and then be able to sort those persons by whichever of their characteristics it deems relevant. That is to say, it must have some way of reliably associating incoming packet streams with identified real-world individuals, and it must have – or be able to collect – enough information about each of those individuals to implement a set of rules determining whether to grant access.[5]

One way for a content provider to accomplish these tasks is to allow access only if the recipient's computer (or other device) incorporates hardware and software, meeting security specifications approved by the content provider, that enforces rules defining which individuals can access and use particular digital content. In such a case, technologists refer to the server and recipient as being part of a "trusted system."[6] The server can rely on "trusted" elements of the recipients' device to identify the recipient, to transmit only accurate information about the recipient, and to limit the recipient's ability to manipulate any content it receives from the server in ways that exceed its authorization.

Trusted systems enable the sophisticated network security I discussed above because they give the content provider a way to verify the authenticity of any message it receives that claims authorization to read a digital work. But their implications are broader. They allow the content provider to make the works available only to persons the content provider knows have paid for access. They allow the content provider to prevent the recipient from passing usable copies of the works to unauthorized persons. And they allow the content provider great flexibility in specifying the nature of the event that will trigger a payment obligation. For example, a content provider could allow a consumer to download a work for free, but require payment each time he or she reads or listens to it. In short, trusted systems have the capability to be an effective and profitable means of controlling and rationing access to works of information and entertainment.[7]

If trusted systems can be extended to the ordinary home computer, they will provide content owners with an important tool in the economic exploitation of their works. To that end, the industry must develop technology well-suited to

---

[5] This criterion is oversimplified, as Part V of the paper demonstrates, but it will do for now.
[6] See Mark Stefik, Trusted Systems, Sci. Amer., Mar. 1997, at 78, available at <http://www.sciam.com/0397issue/0397stefik.html>; see also Xerox Corp., The Digital Property Rights Language: Manual and Tutorial – XML Edition 5 (ver. 2.00 1998).
[7] See generally Xerox Corp., supra note 6; Mark Gimbel, Some Thoughts on the Implications of Trusted Systems for Intellectual Property Law, 50 Stan. L. Rev. 1671 (1998). Xerox's ContentGuard is an example of sophisticated trusted-system technology. See ContentGuard, Self-Protecting Document (visited Dec. 6, 1999) <www.contentguard.com/overview/tech_spd.htm>; Arun Ramanujapuram & Prasad Ram, Digital Content & Intellectual Property Rights, Dr. Dobb's J., Dec. 1998, at 20–26 (Dec. 1998).

feeding reliable, identifying information about consumers' home PCs back to content providers. In the next section of this paper, I will start by discussing the degree to which identifiability is inherent in Internet architecture. I will then discuss new identification technology that companies have sought to put in place.

II. Anonymity and Identifiability on the Internet

In the physical, face-to-face world, we encounter an imperfect blend of anonymity and identifiability. We do not all know everything about each other, nor are we all completely anonymous. In some respects, we are easily identifiable (a four-year-old cannot walk into a convenience store and buy a copy of *Playboy*); in others, we are not (an adult can, without showing identification). We know some things about each other but not others; we negotiate boundaries through social interaction.[8]

Internet architecture presents a different blend of anonymity and identifiability.[9] On one level, it provides for a higher degree of anonymity. "On the Internet," (as the old saw has Rover explain while sitting at his computer), "nobody knows you're a dog."[10] In ordinary social and commercial transactions, it is easy to conceal one's identity or to adopt a new one. Further, that anonymity is for the most part socially acceptable. This has important advantages: It means, as Larry Lessig has explained, that one can explore the Internet without an internal passport, without having to present credentials.[11]

On another level, this apparent anonymity is deceptive. The Internet monitors the origin and destination of the packets that traverse it. It is therefore, in fact, extremely difficult to conceal one's identity while engaging in Internet activities from a truly determined adversary (such as a law-enforcement agency armed with subpoena power). And once one's identity is revealed, extensive information about one's online activities may come with it.

The most important reason for the absence of profound anonymity lies in the Internet's reliance on IP addresses to get packets to their destinations. IP addresses are the unique numbers that identify each computer connected to the Internet. Just as it would be impractical for a person to receive postal mail without a unique

---

[8] See Agre, supra note 2, ¶ 16.
[9] I am indebted to Lorrie Cranor for emphasizing the points in the next two paragraphs.
[10] This joke has sunk into the public consciousness; it was originally penned by Peter Steiner in a cartoon in the NEW YORKER, July 5, 1993, at 61. I owe the citation to Joseph M. Reagle Jr., Why the Internet is Good: Community Governance That Works Well (Mar. 26, 1999) <http://cyber.law.harvard.edu/people/reagle/regulation–19990326.html>.
[11] See Lawrence Lessig, The Laws of Cyberspace 7 (Apr. 3, 1998) (unpublished draft), available at <http://cyber.harvard.edu/works/lessig/laws_cyberspace.pdf>.

name-and-postal-address combination, a computer cannot receive or send information over the global Internet without a unique IP address.[12] Further, every packet of information transmitted over the Internet contains its origin and destination addresses in plain sight in its packet headers.[13] Thus, when I undertake any transaction over the Internet, I transmit my computer's IP address to anybody listening in.

For most residential Internet users, this is only a limited concern. Most of us get IP addresses from our Internet service providers using Dynamic Host Configuration Protocol, so that we receive different IP addresses each time we log on.[14] While a law enforcement agency armed with Internet service provider records would be able to trace the IP addresses we used during different logons, and thus track our online activity, we are not at the mercy of the casual commercial or social observer.[15]

This concern may become somewhat more important with the introduction of a new Internet addressing structure known as IPv6.[16] IPv6 will incorporate an address configuration procedure under which if a computer is connected to the Internet via an Ethernet card or certain other hardware, and the IP address is not unilaterally set by a DHCP or PPP server, then the computer's IP address will automatically include the unique identifier associated with that Ethernet card or

---

[12] This is oversimplified: Network address translation can allow a computer to function using an address, assigned by the local network, that is not globally unique. More simply, a user can piggyback on the IP address of a remote computer by logging into a shell account on that computer. The extent to which such a user's traffic can be traced to him individually (as opposed to the remote server generally) depends on the information retained by that server. Finally, a particular computer's IP address may change over time.

[13] See Thomas Narten, Privacy Extensions for Stateless Address Autoconfiguration in IPv6, at 2–3 (Oct. 1999) <http://search.ietf.org/Internet-drafts/draft-ietf-ipngwg-addrconf-privacy-01.txt>.

[14] This is somewhat oversimplified. A DHCP server will sometimes return to an Internet user the same address that it had used previously, if that address is still available. In certain contexts, a client could use the same address for months at a time. See id.

[15] The situation is different if a computer's IP address is "static" as opposed to dynamic. In that case, the address will be associated with that computer for an extended period of time. Users with broadband, "always on" Internet connections are more likely to have persistent IP addresses.

Once a particular IP address is firmly associated with a user, it is easy to match that IP address with the entity (an Internet service provider, corporation, government agency, etc.) to which the relevant block of IP addresses was assigned. However, one cannot further match the IP address to the identity of an individual user without information supplied either by the intermediate entity or by the user himself (as in a registration database). See Electronic Privacy Information Center, Request for Participation and Comment from the Electronic Privacy Information Center (visited Dec. 6, 1999) <http://www.ftc.gov/bcp/profiling/comments/shen.pdf>.

[16] See R. Hinden Nokia & S. Deering, Cisco Systems, IP Version 6 Addressing Architecture (July 1998) <ftp://ftp.isi.edu/in-notes/rfc2373.txt> (Network Working Group RFC 2373); Steve King, Ruth Fax, Dimitry Haskin, Wenken Ling, Tom Meehan, Robert Fink & Charles E. Perkins, The Case for IPv6 (Oct. 22, 1999) <http://search.ietf.org/Internet-drafts/draft-ietf-iab-case-for-ipv6-05.txt>.

other hardware.[17] This will make it easier to match IP addresses to individual computers,[18] and will make it possible for observers to track a given device's Internet traffic even though the device is connected at different times to different networks at different physical locations.[19] On the other hand, it should not affect the identifiability of the Internet traffic of an ordinary user with a dial-up connection and no Ethernet card.[20]

In sum, it is inherent in Internet architecture that Internet traffic carries identifying information along with it. At the same time, though, this information is not cheaply and immediately useful on a commercial level. In particular, a mass-market content provider cannot rely solely on IP addresses to identify residential users.[21] Content providers want – and are beginning to develop – cheaper and more precise tools better suited to their needs.

Various companies have already put in place systems for feeding consumer information back to content providers. For example, each copy of Windows Media Player and RealNetworks' RealPlayer contains a globally unique identifier (GUID) that is transmitted to the provider when the user accesses streaming media.[22] More impressively, it recently became known that RealNetworks' RealJukebox player transmitted information back to its makers including the names of all the CDs the user played, the number of songs recorded on his or her hard disk, the brand of portable MP3 player the user owned, and the music genre he or she listened to most.[23] The information was tied to a unique identification number that could be mapped to the user's email address via the registration database. In short, RealNetworks had the capability to collect, in personally

---

[17] See King et al., supra note 16, at 10; Narten, supra note 13, at 4.
[18] That will especially be the case if business information-exchange standards encourage the matching of a person's name and address with the identifier of the Ethernet card preinstalled in the computer he buys. See James Glave, RosettaNet: Nothing Personal?, Wired News (Sept. 10, 1999) < http://wired.lycos.com/news/news/technology/story/21699.html >.
[19] See Narten, supra note 13, at 4–5. One of the developers of IPv6 has suggested changes in the IPv6 addressing architecture to ameliorate this concern. Id. at 5–11.
[20] See generally J. Bound & C. Perkins, Dynamic Host Configuration Protocol for IPv6 (Feb. 25, 1999) < http://search.ietf.org/Internet-drafts/draft-ietf-dhc-dhcpv6–14.txt>.
[21] Instead, online advertisers tend to rely on cookies accepted by users and stored on their hard disks. Firms use a technique called cookie synchronization to share cookies and their associated information across multiple sites. See Junkbusters, Profiling: Comments to the Dept. of Commerce and Federal Trade Commission § 2.2 (Oct. 18, 1999) < http://www.junkbusters.com/profiling.html >. The use and abuse of cookies is beyond the scope of this paper, but their importance in online privacy issues cannot be overstated. See Deborah Kong, Online Profiling on the Rise, San Jose Mercury News, Jan. 3, 2000, at C1.
[22] See Mark D. Fefer, Media Player and Privacy, Seattle Wkly., Apr. 8–14, 1999, available at < http://www.seattleweekly.com/features/9914/tech-fefer.shtml >; see also Peter H. Lewis, Peekaboo! Anonymity Is Not Always Secure, New York Times, Apr. 15, 1999, at G1 (repeating the conclusions of the Seattle Weekly report).
[23] See Richard M. Smith, The RealJukeBox Monitoring System (Oct. 31, 1999) < http://www.tiac.net/users/smiths/privacy/realjb.htm >; Sara Robinson, CD Software Said to Gather Data on Users: RealNetworks Receives Variety of Information, New York Times, Nov. 1, 1999, at C1.

identifiable format, information regarding the listening activities of each user of its software. Responding to negative publicity, RealNetworks made available a software patch to disable RealJukebox's data collection function,[24] and announced a new version of RealPlayer software that would not transmit a GUID unless the user affirmatively turned that feature on.[25] The company noted, though, that some content providers might require that consumers enable the GUID in order to access their content.[26]

Along similar lines, users discovered not too long ago that various Microsoft applications label each of the documents they create with a unique identifier. If the computer running the applications contains an Ethernet card, the document identifier incorporates that Ethernet card's unique identifier, and thus definitively identifies the computer in question.[27] As a result, documents created in Microsoft Word and Excel can be traced back to the originating computer.[28] Until recently, Microsoft's Windows 98 Registration Wizard transmitted the Ethernet card identifier to Microsoft upon software registration, along with the identification information (name, address, phone number, etc.) entered by the user.[29] Microsoft too has backpedaled somewhat in response to publicity: It announced that it would make a software patch available to prevent the insertion of the GUID into Microsoft Office documents, and would stop collecting the information during registration.[30] Office 2000, it added, would not insert the GUID at all.[31]

Each of these systems has powerful identification capabilities, but is limited in certain respects. Microsoft's is limited in scope because the GUID identifies an individual's computer only if that computer contains an Ethernet card.[32] The RealNetworks system is limited in a different respect: The GUIDs it assigns are not used by anyone other than RealNetworks.[33] Although RealNetworks was in a position to use the GUID to catalog an individual's listening information, the system was not designed to be used by a variety of content providers in multiple contexts.

---

[24] See Sara Robinson, RealNetworks to Stop Collecting User Data: Music Software Will No Longer Transmit Personal Information, New York Times, Nov. 2, 1999, at C2.

[25] See RealNetworks, RealNetworks Consumer Software Privacy Statement (visited Dec. 6, 1999) < http://www.realnetworks.com/company/privacy/software-privacy.html >.

[26] See id.

[27] See Junkbusters, Privacy Advisory on Microsoft Hardware IDs (visited Dec. 6, 1999) <http://www.junkbusters.com/ht/en/microsoft.html#advisory >.

[28] See id.; Chris Oakes, Sniffing Out MS Security Glitch, Wired News, Mar. 8, 1999, ¶ 3 <http://wired.lycos.com/news/news/technology/story/18331.html >.

[29] See John Markoff, Microsoft Will Alter Its Software in Response to Privacy Concerns, New York Times, Mar. 7, 1999, §1, at 1.

[30] See Microsoft Addresses Customers' Privacy Concerns, ¶ 14 (visited Dec. 6, 1999) <http://www.microsoft.com/presspass/features/1999/03-08custletter2.htm >.

[31] See id.

[32] See Junkbusters, supra note 27; Advanced Streaming Format – Specification – Appendix: GUIDs and UUIDs, ¶ 6 (visited Feb. 2, 2000) < http://www.microsoft.com/asf/spec3/c.htm >.

[33] Each RealNetwork GUID is randomly generated by a RealNetworks consumer application during installation. See Smith, supra note 23.

III. Intel and the Processor Serial Number

Intel, which manufactures the vast majority of the chips powering personal computers today, introduced a technology in early 1999 that it described as the foundation for a whole new world of trusted systems: the Processor Serial Number, or PSN. The PSN is a unique identification number burned into each computer's central processing unit as part of the normal manufacturing process.[34] Intel announced plans to incorporate the PSN into all of its products, including not only its Pentium III chips for personal computers, but also the microprocessors embedded in devices such as television set-top boxes, telephones, and "Internet appliances."[35] Applications running on any device equipped with a PSN could read the unique identification number and transmit it to any requesting remote server. Such a system would provide a foundation for the reliable flow of identification information from *every* consumer to Internet-based content providers.

In introducing the PSN, Intel Vice-President Patrick Gelsinger explained that the company was shifting its vision from "a world of a billion connected computers" to "a billion *trusted* computers."[36] A vision of a world fully populated with myriad personal computers, each communicating with the rest, he explained, is insufficient unless those connected computers are trusted, and the first step on "the road to ... trusted connected PCs" is the PSN.[37] Because each computer's PSN is unique, he continued, the PSN provides a hardware framework for treating the home PC as part of a trusted system – that is, to allow servers on distant networks to authenticate the identity of a home PC user, and administer authenticated permissioning and rights management.[38] It could thus create a "trusted virtual world" for secure virtual enterprises, business-to-consumer electronic commerce, and secure delivery of high-value digital media content like movies and music.[39]

---

[34] See Patrick Gelsinger, A Billion Trusted Computers, Speech at the RSA Data Security Conference and Expo '99, ¶ 96 (Jan. 20, 1999) (transcript), available at <http://www.intel.com/pressroom/archive/speeches/pg012099.htm>.

[35] See Robert Lemos, The Biggest Security Threat: You, ZDNet News (Feb. 25, 1999) <http://www.zdnet.com/zdnn/stories/news/0,4586,2216772,00.html> (referring to Intel's StrongARM embedded processor, and quoting Michael Glancy, general manager of Intel's platform security division). Intel purchased the StrongARM line of embedded processors in 1998; StrongARM processors are currently used in cellular phones and handheld computers, and are suitable for use in set-top boxes and other Internet-aware consumer electronics. See Lisa DiCarlo, Intel Seals StrongARM Deal, PC Week Online (Feb. 27, 1998) <http://www.zdnet.com/pcweek/stories/news/0,4153,288760,00.html>.

[36] Gelsinger, supra note 34, ¶¶ 3–4 (emphasis added).

[37] Id. ¶¶ 66, 93.

[38] See id. ¶¶ 61, 66–67, 99.

[39] Id. ¶ 17. On the other hand, the PSN was unlikely to achieve that result effectively. As noted cryptographer Bruce Schneier urged, PSN-based authentication is inherently insecure because a

Gelsinger explained that the PSN, "enabl[ing] platforms and the users that are on those platforms to be better identified,"[40] was Intel's first building block in constructing this system. "You think about this maybe as a chat room, where unless you're able to deliver the processor serial number, you're not able to enter that protected chat room ... providing a level of access control."[41]

Atop that hardware framework, Intel was constructing the Common Data Security Architecture (CDSA).[42] Gelsinger announced plans to add significantly to the PSN and the CDSA's capabilities the following year, "allowing ... trusted access, adding authenticated permissioning to PCs, [and] increasing levels of capability" in the security architecture.[43] He announced plans to add capability in 2001 relating to "platform and peripheral integrity," thus "accomplishing the trusted transactions [and providing] a platform strong enough to bring all forms of valuable content to the PC."[44] An architecture incorporating all of these capabilities might enable extensive control by the content owner: the hardware and software of the home PC might enable a remote server to query that PC for its unique PSN, determine whether the machine associated with that PSN has received rights to play a movie, and (if so) deliver the movie in a form such that the PC could play it a set number of times, but could not make a digital copy outside the control of trusted systems.[45]

The PSN excited considerable controversy. Privacy advocates requested that the Federal Trade Commission initiate an inquiry[46] and followed that up with a complaint formally asking the Commission to halt distribution of the Pentium III as a violation of individual privacy.[47] The Electronic Privacy Information Center

---

cont.
  remote site cannot know whether a home PC's software is accurately reporting the hardware PSN. See Bruce Schneier, Why Intel's ID Tracker Won't Work, ZDNet News (Jan. 26, 1999) < http://www.zdnet.com/zdnn/stories/comment/0,5859,2194863,00.html >.

[40] Gelsinger, supra note 34, ¶ 66.
[41] Id. ¶ 99.
[42] See Intel Architecture Labs, Common Data Security Architecture: Frequently Asked Questions (visited Dec. 6, 1999) < http://developer.intel.com/ial/security/faq.htm > (Question 1).
[43] Gelsinger, supra note 34, at 7.
[44] Id.
[45] This discussion to some extent elides the distinction between identification of computer platforms and identification of consumers. The distinction comes into play to the extent that (a) more than one consumer uses a single computer; or (b) a single consumer uses more than one computer. The latter case is most important in connection with consumer acceptance of trusted systems; consumers may be reluctant to accept systems that limit them to a single computer in viewing the works they purchase.
[46] See Letter from Jeffrey Chester et al. to R. Pitofsky, Chairman, Federal Trade Commission (Feb. 22, 1999) available at < http://www.bigbrotherinside.com/ftc-letter.html > (letter from eight consumer and privacy groups including the Electronic Privacy Information Center) [hereinafter Letter to FTC].
[47] See Center for Democracy & Tech., Press Release: Privacy and Consumer Groups File Complaint Against Intel at Federal Trade Commission (visited Dec. 6, 1999) < http://www.cdt.org/press/022699press.shtml >.

announced a boycott of Intel.[48] Large PC makers responded by announcing that, when shipping Pentium III machines for the consumer market, they would set the BIOS (the first software instructions a computer loads when it boots) to make the PSN invisible.[49] Intel announced plans to release software patches that consumers could use to do the same thing.[50] These developments, though, did not entirely quiet the controversy over the PSN: A unit of the European Parliament, for example, published a working paper urging that the relevant committees of the Parliament call upon the NSA and FBI to provide information on their role in the PSN's creation, and suggesting that the Parliament "consider legal measures to prevent PSN-equipped (or PSN-equivalent) chips from being installed in the computers of European citizens, firms and organi[z]ations."[51]

Chastened by the public reaction to the PSN, Intel retreated and regrouped. It announced that it would omit the PSN from its new 1.5 GHz Willamette chip.[52] But it has inaugurated a new initiative: the Trusted Computing Platform Alliance (TCPA).[53] The TCPA is a more sophisticated attempt to achieve the goals of the PSN: Like Intel's earlier trusted computing program, the TCPA seeks to deliver an "enhanced HW- [hardware] and OS- [operating system] based trusted computing platform" to ensure, among other things, "[p]latform [a]uthentication." That is, the TCPA is designed to provide a standard way for outsiders to query a computer and establish its owner's identity, thus establishing "confidence in interacting with [that] platform."[54] TCPA statements emphasize that computer owners must

---

[48] See Big Brother Inside, Protect Your PC's Privacy ¶ 35 (visited Dec. 6, 1999) <http://www.bigbrotherinside.com/#who>.

[49] See Robert Lemos, Big PC Makers Decide to Disable Chip ID: IBM, Dell, Gateway and Compaq Shipping PCs with the Technology Off, Letting Users Decide, ZDNet News (Feb. 26, 1999) <http://www.zdnet.com/zdnn/stories/news/0,4586,2217252,00.html>.

[50] See Robert O'Harrow Jr. & Elizabeth Corcoran, Intel Drops Plans to Activate Chip IDs, Wash. Post, Jan. 26, 1999, at E1, available at <http://www.washingtonpost.com/wp-srv/washtech/daily/jan99/intel26.htm>.

[51] Dr. Franck Leprevost, Development of Surveillance Technology and Risk of Abuse of Economic Information: Encryption and Cryptosystems in Electronic Surveillance § 8(D) (European Parliament Scientific and Technical Options Assessment Panel Working Paper No. PE 168.184 / Part 3/4, 1999), available at <http://www.europarl.eu.int/dg4/stoa/en/publi/pdf/98-14-01-3en.pdf>.

[52] See Declan McCullagh, Intel Nixes Chip-Tracking ID, Wired News (Apr. 27, 2000), <http://www.wirednews.com/news/politics/0,1283,35950,00.html>.

[53] See Trusted Computing Platform Alliance, Background (visited Dec. 6, 1999) <www.trustedpc.org/home/home.htm>. The TCPA was formed by Compaq, Hewlett-Packard, IBM, and Microsoft as well as Intel, id., but Intel appears to be providing at least the administrative infrastructure. See Building a Foundation of Trust in the PC 7 (Jan. 2000), <http://www.trustedpc.org/press/pdf/TCPAwp.pdf> (listing the TCPA's mailing address, at Intel); Register.com, Whois Results for Trustedpc.com (visited Dec. 6, 1999) <http://www.register.com/whois-results.cgi?> (illustrating that Intel registered the domain name for the TCPA's Web site).

[54] Trusted Computing Platform Alliance, TCPA Overview Presentation 3, 9, 10 (1999), available at <http://www.trustedpc.org/press.html> (emphasis omitted) (slide presentation).

control their personal information and the system's authentication capabilities.[55] The Alliance, however, has not yet released a detailed specification to the public.

IV. Trusted Systems and Common Identifiers

A. INTRODUCTION

How should we think about the PSN and its successor technologies? Two characteristics of the PSN are especially notable. First, the PSN is keyed to the holder's *identity*, rather than his or her characteristics. It enforces a particular model of trust: to learn the characteristics of a particular would-be information recipient, a publisher first ascertains that person's identity and then looks up the characteristics associated with that identity.

This model stands in contrast to an approach in which a person can present credentials verifying certain characteristics, such as country of residence, without necessarily disclosing his identity at all.[56] For example, consider an idea floated by Ira Magaziner in 1998.[57] Magaziner was looking for an answer to one problem presented by Internet anonymity: It undercuts the ability of geographic jurisdictions to tax because it may not be clear to the merchant and interested governments whether taxes are due and to whom. Magaziner suggested that consumers could make purchases online through the use of electronic "resident cards" encoding their country of residence, so that escrow agents could collect taxes associated with that jurisdiction.[58] The proposal was unworkable, but was in one respect privacy-friendly: It contemplated that people would reveal, and carry with them online, a single personal characteristic (their country of residence), without having to reveal any other characteristics. The merchant could learn a buyer's residence, but that information transaction would not reveal his name. The PSN, by contrast, eschews this approach. For the PSN to be used as the basis for a trusted system, the content provider must correlate the PSN with its other data

---

[55] See id. at 5, 12; see also Building a Foundation of Trust in the PC 1 (Jan. 2000), <http://www.trustedpc.org/press/pdf/TCPAwp.pdf.> A TCPA white paper notes that its approach is consistent both with a PC transmitting a statistically unique identifier directly to a content provider, and with the PC instead transmitting that information to a trusted third party. Building a Foundation of Trust in the PC at 5–6.

[56] See Agre, supra note 2, ¶¶ 18, 35; David Chaum, Security Without Identification: Transaction Systems to Make Big Brother Obsolete, 28 Comm. of the ACM 1030, 1030 (1985); Lawrence Lessig & Paul Resnick, Zoning Speech on the Internet: A Legal and Technical Model, 98 Mich. L. Rev. 395, 412–13 (1999).

[57] Ira Magaziner, at the time, was the President's Senior Internet Advisor.

[58] See Internet Taxation System is Mulled by White House, Wall St. J., Sept. 11, 1998, at B4.

relating to the individual owning that computer, by tying all of that data to the single identifier that the PSN represents.

The second notable characteristic of the PSN is that it is a *common* identifier. That is, it is well-suited for use by different information collectors in unrelated transactions, increasing the ease with which a wide range of information about a person can be aggregated into a single overall dossier.[59] The greatest obstacle to efficient aggregation and manipulation of data today is the need to reconcile inconsistent formats and identifiers; a standard, common GUID can eliminate that obstacle.[60] To the extent that a variety of content providers and other merchants have each collected information tied to individual PSNs, it is a simple matter to compile those files into larger databases.

B. Privacy

Widespread deployment of systems in which the user's computer identifies itself during every transaction to anybody who asks is pernicious from a privacy perspective. Such systems allow the user to be tracked through cyberspace more easily and thoroughly than is possible under current technology. They have the potential to make the Internet a forum in which database proprietors have what Phil Agre has referred to as a "God's-eye view of the world" – a perspective in which all things have their true names and our Internet representations can straightforwardly be traced back to our real-world identities.[61] Under such an architecture, a much greater proportion of ordinary transactions would require consumers to present unique identification numbers that would in turn be digitally linked to a much wider range of personal information. To the extent that collecting identification and assembling dossiers is easy, content providers may do so even when they have no compelling use for the information.

Advertisers and others already see great value in compiling dossiers of personally identifiable information for each of us, as the controversy over the recent Abacus-Doubleclick merger illustrates.[62] Systems facilitating the close

---

[59] See David Chaum, Achieving Electronic Privacy, Sci. Am., Aug. 1992, at 96, available at <http://ganges.cs.tcd.ie/mepeirce/Project/Chaum/sciam.html>.

[60] See Graham Greenleaf, "IP, Phone Home": ECMS, (c)-tech, and Protecting Privacy Against Surveillance by Digital Works 7–8 (1999) (paper presented to the 21st International Conference on Privacy and Personal Data Protection held September 13–15, 1999, in Hong Kong), available at <http://www2.austlii.edu.au/~graham/publications/ip_privacy>.

[61] Agre, supra note 2, ¶¶ 23, 26 (developing idea of God's-eye view in relation to computer representations of identity and privacy policy).

[62] See Courtney Macavinta, Privacy Fears Raised by Doubleclick Database Plans, CNET News.com (Jan. 25, 2000), <http://news.cnet.com/0-1005-200-1531929.html>; Diane Anderson & Keith Perine, Privacy Issue Makes Doubleclick a Target, Standard (Feb. 3, 2000) <http://www.thestandard.com/article/display/0,1151,9480,00.html>; Bob Tedeschi, In a Shift, Doubleclick Puts Off Its Plan for Wider Use of the Personal Data of Internet Consumers, New York Times, Mar. 3, 2000, at C5.

tracking of content – of what people read, view, or listen to – are particularly problematic. All of these are the constituents of human thought. In the analog world, information or entertainment goods are commonly sold on a cash basis, leaving no paper or electronic trail. The copies themselves have no surveillance capabilities, and cannot report back to their makers. The copyright owner, indeed, collects no information about the user at all.[63] Trusted systems threaten to abandon those rules, facilitating the monitoring of individual thought. They raise the specter of the Panopticon, and of subtle and not-so-subtle pressures on individuals to eschew socially or governmentally disfavored information goods.[64]

C. Communications Policy

Technology such as the PSN is also important from the perspective of the economics and politics of content markets. "Small-scale, decentralized reproduction of intellectual property" has long been a fact of life in markets for information, entertainment, and computer software.[65] People copy music tapes and CDs for themselves, family, and friends; they photocopy magazine articles; they allow family and friends to use and copy their computer software. They persist in doing so, notwithstanding the best efforts of the copyright industries to convince them that it is illegal, largely because they find it hard to believe that this is something the law does or should proscribe.[66] And that system seems to work – at least, it has not obviously injured in any palpable way producer incentives to create intellectual property.

A lot of sharing, indeed, does not implicate the copyright law at all. People lend each other analog copies of protected works, and read, watch, or listen to works they have borrowed. At least in a static analysis,[67] both of these sorts of sharing are good since they increase the distribution of information and thus social benefit

---

[63] See Greenleaf, supra note 60, ¶ 8.
[64] See Julie E. Cohen, Some Reflections on Copyright Management Systems and Laws Designed to Protect Them, 12 Berkeley Tech. L.J. 161, 184–85 (1997).
[65] Stanley M. Besen & Sheila Nataraj Kirby, Private Copying, Appropriability, and Optimal Copying Royalties, 32 J.L. & Econ. 255, 255 (1989); see also Yannis Bakos, Erik Brynjolfsson & Douglas Lichtman, Shared Information Goods, 42 J.L. & Econ. 117 (1999); Litman, Copyright Noncompliance (Or Why We Can't "Just Say Yes" to Licensing), 29 N.Y.U. J. Int'l L. & Pol'y 237 (1996–97); Michael J. Meurer, Price Discrimination, Personal Use and Piracy: Copyright Protection of Digital Works, 45 Buff. L. Rev. 845, 852–56 (1997).
[66] See Litman, Copyright Noncompliance (Or Why We Can't "Just Say Yes" to Licensing), supra note 65, at 252–53; Jessica Litman, Revising Copyright Law for the Information Age, 75 Or. L. Rev. 19, 40–41 (1996).
[67] But see text following note 81 infra.

without any social cost.[68] Put another way, sharing allows the distribution of information at the optimal demand price, because that price is equal to the marginal cost of distribution, which in this case is close to zero.[69] The most successful institutions in American life today that are based on such sharing are public libraries, which were established precisely to enable large-scale sharing of analog works.

In existing communications markets, in other words, technical inefficiencies make it difficult to disseminate speech to a dispersed but tightly controlled group. There is always some leakage: If you want to disseminate speech, you have to give up some control over its dissemination. For example, once a content owner distributes a copy of an analog work, it has no technological means of preventing the owner of that copy from selling, loaning, privately displaying, or giving away the copy as he chooses.[70] And the copyright law's "first sale doctrine" denies content owners the ability to impose such restrictions within the four corners of the copyright law.[71] These limitations on content owners' effective rights have helped democratize access to content.

Trusted systems could eliminate these avenues for royalty-free redistribution. The content provider's enhanced control over access to the work would allow content providers to limit sharply the small-scale copying of intellectual property that has become both accepted and commonplace among consumers today, but that producers contend violates their copyrights. It could also greatly limit the small- and large-scale lending and borrowing of intellectual property that takes place today and is unimpeachably consistent with the copyright laws. After all, the control given content providers by trusted systems does not rest on whether the content provider can assert intellectual property rights in the work, or whether a particular use of the work by a consumer would violate those rights.

The trusted system world also seems well-suited to facilitate discrimination on the part of the content provider, a change with more ambiguous results. Most obviously, trusted systems will facilitate price discrimination – that is, the content provider can ask different consumers to pay different prices, unrelated to the provider's own costs. As a general matter, if a seller wishes to engage in price discrimination, three conditions must be satisfied.[72] First, the seller must be able to prevent (or limit) arbitrage – it must ensure that buyers who paid a low price do not turn around and resell the information or entertainment to someone who

---

[68] See Kenneth J. Arrow, Economic Welfare and the Allocation of Resources for Invention, in The Rate and Direction of Inventive Activity: Economic and Social Factors 609 (1962); Yochai Benkler, Free as the Air to Common Use: First Amendment Constraints on Enclosure of the Public Domain, 74 N.Y.U. L. Rev. 354, 424 (1999).
[69] See Benkler, supra note 68, at 424 & n.273.
[70] See Litman, Reforming Information Law in Copyright's Image, 22 U. Dayton L. Rev. 587, 600–01 (1997)
[71] Id.
[72] See Meurer, supra note 65, at 870.

would otherwise be willing to pay the content provider the higher price. Otherwise, any attempt by the producer to partition the market would be unavailing. Trusted systems make this possible by greatly enhancing the content provider's ability to control any redistribution of the work.

Second, the seller must have market power. All copyright owners have some degree of market power because of the legal control that intellectual property law gives them; that is one reason they are able to charge prices in excess of marginal cost. Some, naturally, have more market power than others, based on the demand for the work and the availability of near-substitutes.

Finally, the seller must be able to set prices in a way that in fact reflects consumers' willingness to pay. Trusted system technology can make this possible in two ways. First, as noted above, a trusted online architecture based on global user or platform identifiers will allow content providers to tie each consumer to a wide range of personally identifiable information. For example, when the consumer presents her PSN to gain access to a digital work, the content provider will be able to pull up other information associated with that PSN in order to make a judgment about the particular consumer's willingness to pay.[73] Alternatively, the content provider can shift its payment model from the "sale" model prevalent today, in which the consumer buys a copy of the work and can then read, listen to, or watch that copy an unlimited number of times without further payment, to a "pay-per-read" system in which the customer pays a smaller amount on each occasion that he or she reads, listens to, or watches the work. This allows the content provider to collect more money from those customers who want to use the work many times and presumably are willing to pay more for that ability, and less from those who want to view the work only once. The difference between those prices is largely unrelated to the content provider's own costs.[74]

Is this price discrimination good or bad? Some have argued that price discrimination in information goods is socially useful, because it increases the distribution of information.[75] Without price discrimination, the content provider must charge a single market price, and people unwilling to pay that price will be shut out of the market entirely. If the content provider can engage in price discrimination, by contrast, it can charge every consumer the exact price that he or she is willing to pay, thus simultaneously maximizing profits and maximizing the number of people who will be exposed to the information and entertainment in question. "[W]e can say with confidence that many more consumers [will benefit] from the author's creation."[76]

---

[73] See W. Kip Viscusi, John M. Vernon & Joseph E. Harrington, Jr., Economics of Regulation and Antitrust 290–91 (2d ed. 1995) (third-degree price discrimination).

[74] See id. at 249–55, 290–91 (second-degree price discrimination).

[75] See, e.g., William W. Fisher III, Property and Contract on the Internet, 73 Chi-Kent L. Rev. 1203, 1239 (1998). But see Wendy J. Gordon, Intellectual Property as Price Discrimination: Implications for Contract, 73 Chi.-Kent L. Rev. 1367 (1998).

[76] Fisher, supra note 75, at 1239.

The matter, though, is not nearly so straightforward. Price discrimination is unquestionably good for producers since it converts consumer surplus into producer profits. But whether, as a general matter, price discrimination increases overall welfare is more difficult.[77] In thinking about whether the price discrimination enabled by trusted systems would be a good thing, we need to ask the question, "Compared to what"? One of the key reasons that trusted systems enable price discrimination is that they sharply decrease sharing; they are designed to eliminate any redistribution of the information goods beyond the control of the content provider. That is, price discrimination allows the sale of information to consumers willing to pay less, but at the expense of cutting off *existing* means, through sharing and secondary markets, of getting the information or entertainment at low or no cost to some of those same consumers. Indeed, from a static perspective sharing is a more efficient way of allowing the market to reach those consumers, since it makes the goods available to them at a price more nearly approaching the zero marginal cost of supplying it to them.

Secondary markets (involving redistribution of information goods after their first sale and outside the control of the initial seller) can do the same job as price discrimination of getting information goods at lower prices to lower-valuation users. That is what used bookstores are all about. The price discrimination that trusted systems may facilitate, therefore, may not increase the number of consumers getting the goods at all; it may simply ensure that the low-valuation consumers receive the goods from the initial seller rather than someone else.[78] Further, it does so at the distributional cost of shifting all surplus away from consumers.

The points I have made so far are open to a variety of counterarguments. First, it might be argued that price discrimination will do a better job of getting the information or entertainment to low-valuation users, many of whom may not have the opportunity to gain access to the work through resale or sharing. Yet it is unclear to what extent price discrimination in practice can achieve the advantages theory promises for it. It is difficult to gauge consumer preferences precisely, and publishers are unlikely to drop prices too far based on guesses about a particular class of consumers' willingness to pay. While theoretical perfect price discrimination promises perfectly efficient markets, any attempt by publishers to group consumers by proxy characteristics and set prices for each group will fall short of that ideal. Nor will consumers easily accept pay-per-read pricing: The splashy failure of DIVX should give rise to some doubt about the enthusiasm with which ordinary folks will embrace usage-based prices for digital works.[79]

---

[77] See Viscusi et al., supra note 73, at 290–95; Meurer, supra note 65, at 896–98.
[78] See Gordon, supra note 75, at 1378–89.
[79] The DIVX plan was that a user would purchase a videodisk for $4–5, and have free access for 48 hours after the first play. After that time, the user would pay a fee for every subsequent viewing; those viewings would be purchased through a central server connected to the DIVX

Next, one might argue that if sharing were technologically disallowed, then market prices would fall. Without the possibility of sharing, the argument runs, information goods are not as valuable to purchasers. Yet when the content provider must set a single market price, it cannot easily raise that price to take into account the benefits of sharing, because different buyers will place significantly different values on the ability to share (and will in fact share with markedly different numbers of people).[80] Moreover, the existence of leakage also acts to constrain prices, by providing a near-substitute for the purchased goods.[81]

Finally and most obviously, one might argue that this analysis overlooks the dynamic impact of sharing and the nature of secondary markets in digital works: Sharing and resale do not generate revenues to the content provider, so they do not provide incentives to stimulate production. More baldly, one might argue that my discussion is in essence an argument for piracy – which will certainly lower prices to the consumer, but at the cost of diminishing incentives to produce. Secondary markets in the digital world, the argument runs, may involve large numbers of illegal, perfect copies. Sale of those copies cuts directly into the profits, and thus the incentives, of the initial producer.

To be sure, producer incentives are necessary. Publishers must be able to sell information goods at a price sufficiently above marginal cost, and for a sufficiently long period of time, to recover their fixed (first-copy) costs. Otherwise, they will lose money. To that end, there must be sufficient entry barriers limiting other folks' ability to sell those works as cheaply. We do not know, though, how much in the way of incentives producers need.[82] Ordinary economic theory suggests that publishers will invest so long as they expect profits, taking into account normal rates of return. If publishers have adequate incentives even without the extra rents that price discrimination gives them, then we *may* get a better social result by reaching lower-valuation users through secondary markets, sharing, or even some degree of piracy than through the increased control that trusted systems bring.[83]

Price discrimination, further, may have other negative consequences. To the extent that sellers' ability to price discriminate will rest on their access to personally identifiable information about buyers, publishers with access to those databases will have a competitive advantage over those who do not. This may have

---

cont.
   player by telephone line. See David Dranove & Neil Gandal, The DVD vs. DIVX Standard War: Network Effects and Empirical Evidence of Vaporware 8 (Tel Aviv Univ. Eltan Berlgas School of Economics Working Paper No. 14–99, 1999). DIVX was discontinued, for lack of consumer interest, in June 1999. See Carl Laron, Of Edsels and DIVX, Electronics Now, Sept. 1, 1999, at 2.

[80] Bakos et al., supra note 65, at 122–27, engage in a much more sophisticated analysis of this phenomenon.
[81] See Benkler, supra note 68, at 433 n.302.
[82] See Litman, The Exclusive Right to Read, 13 Cardozo Arts & Ent. L.J. 29, 44–46 (1994).
[83] See Bakos et. al., supra note 65, at 148.

two negative effects. First, it will tend to concentrate media markets – and, to the extent those markets are characterized by winner-take-all dynamics,[84] will help determine who those winners are. Second, it will increase the value of the dossiers, and thus increase the commercial pressure on privacy.

The control facilitated by trusted systems and common identifiers will increase producers' ability to choose who will be allowed to view or read particular works. Given the power of a common identifier such as Intel's PSN to facilitate the association of a wide range of information with a given personal identifier, producers could use these tools to allow access to a speech work only by persons who live in preferred zip codes, or have certain levels of family income. There may be only limited circumstances in which a mass marketer of entertainment and information would have an incentive to impose such limits. From a free speech and communications policy standpoint, though, it seems disturbing to see extensive social investment in a technology built around the ability to *prevent* the movement of speech and information to the public at large.

For the most part, today, content producers and consumers share control over the uses and dissemination of speech works. Content producers have extensive control by virtue of their ability to produce and license the technological artifacts (such as film reels) embodying those works, reinforced by the rights granted them by the copyright law. Consumers have some control as well, by virtue of their own abilities to use, copy, and manipulate such works in ways that the copyright law either does not forbid or expressly privileges,[85] or in ways that have been effectively immune from copyright enforcement. And because these are speech works, that distribution of control has political consequences. It shapes the overall movement of information and expression within society. The rise of trusted systems based on common identifiers would shift that control.[86]

V. Identification and Credentials

In short, trusted systems based on common identifiers that are tied to consumers' real-world identities have plainly undesirable privacy consequences. Their consequences for the structure of content markets appear to be negative on

---

[84] See Lada A. Adamic & Bernardo A. Huberman, Xerox Palo Alto Research Center, The Nature of Markets in the World Wide Web (1999), available at < http://www.parc.xerox.com/istl/groups/iea/www/webmarkets.html >.

[85] See, e.g., 17 U.S.C. § 1008 (privileging consumers' noncommercial use of digital audio recording devices, digital audio recording media, analog recording devices, and analog recording media for making musical recordings); Recording Indus. Ass'n v. Diamond Multimedia Sys., 180 F.3d 1072 (9th Cir. 1999).

[86] See generally Lawrence Lessig, Code and Other Laws of Cyberspace 154–56 (1999).

balance. And yet, one might think, they are unavoidable if we are to allow content providers control over exploitation of their works in the networked digital environment. That statement, though, is not correct. In fact, the Internet's architecture can support trusted systems, and the concomitant control by content providers over works of information and entertainment, without any need for common identifiers.

Recall the original concern driving industry plans for unique identification of Internet-connected computers and consumers: Content providers wish to be sure that a packet stream requesting access comes from a person who has paid or is otherwise entitled to access. One way to accomplish that result is to tag every computer/consumer with a single identifier that shows up in the packet stream requesting access and allows the provider to reference a database of consumers' characteristics. But that approach conveys much more information to the content provider than the provider actually needs.

What the content provider needs is a way to verify that the user has specific credentials: that the user has paid, or that he has some other characteristic that the content provider desires in its readers. Establishing the user's identity is an instrumental step toward verifying his credentials. Yet it is well-established in the cryptography literature that one can prove credentials without proving identity: that is the basis for anonymous digital cash.[87] A person, for example, can interact with other entities through a "pseudonym"— a name that is reliably associated with that individual in a particular context through cryptographic techniques, but cannot be associated with other names the person uses in other contexts.[88]

The word "pseudonym" sounds vaguely disreputable, but the goal is simple and usually honorable – to allow the user to enter into transactions and relationships in which he or she can be held accountable, without allowing data miners to collect into a single global profile the universe of transactions that the user enters into. It is consistent with current rights-management technology[89] to build structures under which consumers interact with content providers anonymously or pseudonymously, without sacrificing content owners' ability to enforce contractual restrictions.[90]

This approach would address the privacy issues raised earlier in this article, by blocking the aggregation of a user's information across unrelated transactions. It

---

[87] See Agre, supra note 2, at ¶¶ 6, 35; Chaum, supra note 59; Chaum, supra note 56; see also Bruce Schneier, Applied Cryptography 112–14 (2d ed. 1996) (blind signatures); id. at 125–27 (secure voting); id. at 139–45 (digital cash).

[88] See Chaum, supra note 56.

[89] See, e.g., note 7 supra; R. Martin Röscheisen, A Network-Centric Design for Relationship-Based Rights Management (1997) (Ph.D. dissertation), available at < http://pcd.stanford.edu/~roscheis/dissertation.pdf >.

[90] Indeed, technologists are now building a variety of services that could offer such pseudonymity. See Chris Oakes, Pseudonymity Now, Wired News (Jan. 21, 2000) < http://www.wired.com/news/technology/0,1282,33805,00.html >; David Pescovitz, Undercover Agents, Standard (Jan. 3, 2000) < http://www.thestandard.com/article/ display/0,1151,8482,00.html >.

would not be impossible for a content provider to discriminate among users, but that process would have to be more open and public. Because the content provider would not know any information about the user that the user did not provide, it could discriminate on the basis of a particular characteristic only after expressly asking the user to provide credentials relating to that characteristic. Content providers would be reluctant to seek information where such requests would be unpopular in the marketplace or the forum of public opinion.

I do not mean to suggest that verification systems protecting user privacy would be the first choice of content providers. Publishers may find such systems significantly less profitable, and hence less desirable, than those that give them access to a greater range of user information. However, the feasibility of privacy-friendly systems means that from a social-policy perspective, building trusted systems around common identifiers is not merely undesirable; it is unnecessary.

VI. Conclusion

Technologies involving the assignment and use of global user IDs, enforced through hardware-based user identification such as Intel's Processor Serial Number, could give providers of information goods extensive new capabilities. Such technologies provide an easy and straightforward way for publishers to verify the authenticity of messages claiming authorization to receive digital works, giving them greater ability to limit availability of their works to folks who meet certain criteria. These technologies, though, will have other consequences as well. The most obvious relate to privacy: Trusted systems relying on common identifiers, and in particular systems built around hardware such as the PSN, threaten to sharply lessen anonymity and informational privacy on the Internet. They raise the prospect that a much larger proportion of ordinary transactions will require consumers to present unique identification numbers digitally linked to a wide range of personally identifiable information. They are well-suited to being used across the board by a large number of unrelated information collectors, increasing the ease with which a wide range of information about a person can be aggregated into a single overall dossier.

Moreover, the combination of trusted systems technology, which allows publishers to ensure that speech released to Bob does not make its way via sharing or secondary markets to Alice, and the privacy impacts of allowing publishers to collect extensive individualized information on consumers will likely affect the economics and politics of speech markets. It may sharply enhance producers' ability to discriminate among individual consumers, on price and other grounds, in connection with the sale and marketing of information goods. Some commentators suggest that this concentration of control is a good thing; the price discrimination it enables, they argue, will broaden distribution of information goods. Yet the benefits of such a system are clouded; any increase in distribution due to price discrimination comes at the cost of shutting down distribution that comes, in today's less-controlled system, through sharing or secondary markets. It will likely be accompanied by increased media concentration and a self-reinforcing cycle of commercial pressure on individual privacy.

It is important to remember, finally, that publishers can get the benefits of trusted systems without these socially undesirable consequences. Building trusted systems around common identifiers, in other words, is gratuitous.

Databases – In Search of the Free Flow of Information

Dr. A. Kamperman Sanders

Introduction

In view of widespread counterfeiting and in the TRIPs (Trade Related Aspects of Intellectual Property) infused desire to obtain international recognition from policy makers and investors alike, action has been taken to find solutions for piracy and market failure by stretching the boundaries of copyright and other IP rights. The expansion of the rationale of intellectual property rights is, however, a common trend. With new creative exploits in high technology and new methods of marketing intellectual property, statutes are seemingly continuously tinkered with in order to prevent piracy and market failure. A common trend is to combat market failure where it occurs by the introduction of *sui generis* legislation bearing the classic hallmarks of misappropriation theory. The expansion of the scope of copyright protection through the WIPO treaties,[1] the implementation thereof in the EU as set out in the Directive on Harmonization of Certain Aspects of Copyright and Related Rights in the Information Society,[2] as well as the emergence of database rights,[3] has prompted an increasing number of critics to voice concerns. They feel that creativity is under threat, simply because access to vital information or the exploitation thereof is hampered by monopolistic claims.

This contribution explores the economic justifications for the *law of unfair competition*.[4] In order to grasp these economic considerations, the economics of

---

[1] WIPO Copyright Treaty, and WIPO Performances and Phonograms Treaty of December 20, 1996.
[2] Directive 2001/29/EC of May 22, 2001, OJL 167/10.
[3] Directive 96/9/EC of March 11, 1996, OJL 77/20.
[4] See Besen S.M. and Raskind L.J., "An Introduction to the Law and Economics of Intellectual Property" [1991] *Journal of Economic Perspectives* 3.

N. Elkin-Koren and N.W. Netanel (eds.), *The Commodification of Information*, 365–393.
© 2002 Dr. A. Kamperman Sanders. Printed in Great Britain.

the statutory "property-rule" regimes of trademark, patent, copyright and database protection are contrasted with the economics of protection of confidential information and other forms of "liability-rules" that are employed to regulate competition. The effects of market dominance sustained by a property or a liability rule on competition are considered. Furthermore attention is given to the Treaty of Rome, which forbids the abuse of such a dominant position. It is submitted that there are compelling economic reasons to protect valuable assets that are prone to copying, but that there are equally compelling reasons to limit monopolistic claims and stimulate cross-licensing practices.

Another important category of information is public sector information. Whereas the U.S. Collection of Information Antipiracy Act contains a paragraph on government collections of information,[5] the EC Database Directive does not. At the implementation stage in the Member States, however, access to information has become a concern. An exception for public sector information was, for example, introduced in The Netherlands.[6]

Furthermore certain Member States have begun to examine the effects of new technologies on the public service, especially on access to and exploitation of public sector information.[7] The EC Commission has followed suit by publishing its *Green Paper on Public Sector Information in the Information Society*,[8] outlining its vision on affordable access for all, exploitation potential, and fair competition.

A further development for such a right of access to information may be found in the domain of human rights. Despite past reluctance, the European Court of Human Rights[9] restricted the application of the Swiss Unfair Competition Act[10] following publication of a scientific article stating that consumption of food prepared in microwave ovens was dangerous to human health, because of concerns over freedom of speech, as contained in Art. 10 of the European Convention on Human Rights. The ECHR does, however, not only guarantee the freedom of speech, it also recognizes the freedom to receive information. It may therefore be that the balancing of interests of the freedom to receive information versus the

---

[5] § 1204 (a) of H.R.354. Two versions of Bill Number H.R.354 were before the 106th Congress
  1. Collections of Information Antipiracy Act (Introduced in the House) [H.R.354.IH] January 19, 1999
  2. Collections of Information Antipiracy Act (Reported in the House) [H.R.354.RH] October 8, 1999
[6] Art. 8 (1) Databankenwet (Dutch Database Act) 8 July 1999, Stb. 1999, 303.
[7] In the UK, *Freedom of Information White Paper*; in The Netherlands, *Towards the Accessability of Government Information*; and France, *Preparing France's entry into the Information Society*.
[8] COM(98)585final, adopted on 20 January 1999.
[9] *Hertel* v. *Switzerland* (59/1997/843/1049) 25 August 1998. For an assessment of the case and its implications see Kamperman Sanders A., "Unfair Competition Law and the European Court of Human Rights,The Case of *Hertel* v. *Switzerland* and Beyond", 10 *Fordham IP, Media and Ent. LJ*, 305 (1999).
[10] Federal Unfair Competition Act of 19 December 1986.

intellectual property rights of others[11] will prove to be an issue that the Strasbourg Court will not shy away from. A recent Panel Discussion on Intellectual Property and Human Rights[12] suggests that WIPO is also developing an interest in the relationship between IP and human rights.

The guarantee for a free flow of information is therefore no longer an issue that is limited by the discussion on the scope of IP rights and the traditional exceptions thereto.

The Economic Justification of Intellectual Property Rights

Free and unrestricted competition lies at the heart of the generally accepted western economic theory. Free play of market forces, free competition between enterprises, is thought to be the best means to satisfy supply and demand and to maximize wealth in society as a whole. Central to this proposition is the axiom that market participants can compete on a level playing field, so that all competitors face the same market barriers, thus facilitating freedom of entry in the market. From this point of view legal interference in the market should be kept to a minimum. This does not, however, mean that the policy towards markets should be one of *laissez faire*. There is a compelling argument for *laissez faire* in that interference in the market brings with it administrative costs that are incurred to transfer the costs of competition from one market participant to the other. Market intervention should therefore result in a clear social benefit. In the competitive game, the process of spreading market information facilitates the shaping of the opinion of market participants with regard to profit making activities[13] and is seen as socially beneficial. Government intervention to enhance this aspect of competition is generally accepted, even in classical economic theory. This adage has given rise to the premise in neo-classical theory that perfect knowledge induces a situation in which the spontaneous interaction of knowledge possessors leads to a state of equilibrium, the optimum distribution of resources in society. This means that disturbances in knowledge creation, leading to imperfect knowledge,

---

[11] *Vide* art. 10(2) ECHR, setting out the restrictions to the freedom of speech.

[12] A Panel Discussion in commemoration of the 50th Anniversary of the Universal Declaration of Human Rights on intellectual property and human rights organized by the World Intellectual Property Organization (WIPO) in collaboration with the Office of the United Nations High Commissioner for Human Rights, November 9, 1998.

[13] Hayek F.A., "Economics and Knowledge", in *Individualism and Economic Order*, (1948, Chicago Ill., University of Chicago Press) says at 106: "Competition is essentially a process of the formation of opinion: by spreading information [i]t creates the views people have about what is best and cheapest".

need to be countered.[14] Legal intervention should therefore be aimed at providing a level playing field of "market information" in which perfect knowledge induces perfect competition. Laws on the protection of intellectual property and competition can be seen in this light. Entitlements are allocated to specific creators, to safeguard their information against expropriation, so that bargaining can facilitate an exchange and a market is created. With most intellectual and industrial creations, the establishment of a market for ideas is possible only if the value of the idea can be assessed in advance. This generally means revealing that idea to a potential buyer, who will then already have acquired the idea at no cost.[15] Government intervention by the creation of a property right facilitates the bargaining process and the creation of a market for copyright materials and the information contained therein. After the creation of the entitlement, the role of the State is finished, leaving the transfer of the entitlement to the market, where a voluntary bargain can be made between buyer and seller. This implies that the value of the entitlement is also determined by the market and not by the State. This means that the value determination and maximization require the least State intervention.[16] According to the Coase Theorem[17] even the allocations of initial entitlements by the State are unimportant, since they will be transferred to their highest value use through private bargainings, leaving the total output of the economy unaffected. One system of property rights is no more efficient than another in this view. This means, however, that the costs of transaction of the (re)allocation of property rights and the rules governing the exchange determine the efficiency of one system over the other.[18] In addition, the cost effectiveness of a protective regime depends on the social costs that are incurred when protection is afforded in error and when the likelihood of overprotection by the system is real.

The economic rationale for the patent system,[19] commonly described as a system of incentives and rewards, can, for example, more aptly be described as a monopoly that creates a barrier to entry,[20] forcing a licensing practice to evolve. This serves two ends. First, the competitor faces a market barrier equivalent to that encountered by the first market entrant, that the competitor would not

---

[14] Hayek F.A., "The Meaning of Competition", in *Individualism and Economic Order*, (1948, Chicago Ill., University of Chicago Press), 530.

[15] Arrow K., "Economic Welfare and the Allocation of Resources for Invention'" in *The Rate and Direction of Economic Activity Economic and Social Factors*, (1962, Princeton NJ, Princeton University Press), 609 at 615.

[16] Calabresi G. Melamed A. D., "Property Rules, Liability Rules, and Inalienability: One View of the Cathedral", 85 *Harv.LR* 1089 (1972), 1092 and 1105.

[17] Coase R.H., "The Problem of Social Cost", 3 *Journal of Law and Economics* 1 (1960).

[18] Merges R.P., "Of Property Rules, Coase, and Intellectual Property", 94 *Col.LR* 2655 (1994).

[19] For an overview see Kaufer E., *The Economics of the Patent System* (1989, Chur, Harwood Academic Publishers GmbH). See also Heald P., "Federal Intellectual Property Law and the Economics of Preemption" 76 *Iowa Law Review* 959 (1991), 962–965.

[20] Demsetz H., "Barriers to Entry'", 72 *American Economic Review* 47 (1982): "The problem of defining ownership is precisely that of creating properly scaled legal barriers to entry.'"

encounter as a free rider, thus levelling the playing field and inducing him to be creative himself. Secondly, the creator produces a wider variety of works that the public may be willing to pay for, since creativity is stimulated. This gives the consumer more choice and facilitates the creation of new markets. Without the protective regime of the patent system, which excludes free riders, a situation of asymmetric market failure could emerge. Market failure is a situation where creators are not rewarded for their creative efforts. This makes it economically more attractive to copy than to create, resulting in creators producing fewer works than the public would be willing to pay for. The aspect of asymmetry is the situation where one party, the creator, faces a market barrier and the other, a copyist, does not.[21] If a combination of the market failure and asymmetry occurs, a pattern emerges that holds true for all forms of intellectual property law.

Just like the patent system, which serves to stimulate disclosure of the invention and thus encourages further development, the copyright system[22] should allow for utilization of information, either by addition to the public domain or by rights acquisition on a licensing basis. Where new work relies on prior work and ideas, the new work should not benefit the copyright holder in monopoly rents in excess of the value the copyrighted work has added to total welfare.[23] The other situation would lead to wasteful competition[24] to gain those rights that dispel the value of the underlying work, which often consists of contributions by others that may already be in the public domain or have never been susceptible to copyright.[25] In addition, if there are many potential users of the work, which is especially true if works have become *de facto* industry standards,[26] it may become too costly to negotiate individual licenses for every use that is made of it. Disclosure of the information and the fair use doctrine in copyright law can redress the economic imbalance that this increase in transaction costs entails.[27] The trademark system displays different characteristics,[28] in that it was not envisaged as a system of

---

[21] For a definition of asymmetric market failure and the role of intellectual property law in providing a remedy against the resulting loss in wealth see Gordon W.J., "Asymmetric Market Failure and Prisoner's Dilemma in Intellectual Property", 17 *University of Dayton Law Review* 853 (1992), 854.

[22] For a representation of classical patent and copyright protection and the varying level of creativity required, see Mackaay E., "Legal Hybrids: Beyond Property and Monopoly?" 94 *Col.LR* 2630 (1994), 2633.

[23] See Landes W. M. and Posner R. A., "An Economic Analysis of Copyright law", 18 *Journal of Economic Studies* 325 (1989) at 347–353, where the economic rationale for not protecting ideas is given.

[24] Besen and Raskind, note 4 above, 5.

[25] Warren-Boulton F., Baseman K., and Woroch G., "The Economics of Intellectual Property Protection for Software: The Proper Role for Copyright", Paper prepared for the American Council on Interoperable Systems, June 1994, Washington D.C

[26] *US* v. *Microsoft* The findings of fact of the district court are reported at 84 F. Supp. 2d 9 (J.S. App. 46–246). The conclusions of law of the district court are reported at 87 F. Supp. 2d 30 (J.S. App. 1–43). The final judgment of the district court is reported at 97 F. Supp. 2d 59 (J.S. App. 253–279). The order of the district court certifying the case under the Expediting Act (J.S. App. 284–285) 20 June 2000. For further developments see < http://www.usdoj.gov/atr/cases/ms_index.htm >.

incentives and rewards, but as a regulation of marketing efforts. As an identifier of products and their sources, a trademark performs the role of a communicator, a messenger that spreads information about what is best, the level and consistency of quality, and what is cheapest. Protection of trademarks ensures that the consumer can make correct purchasing decisions,[29] thus lowering the transaction costs.[30] The confusion rationale is also expressed in the doctrine of passing off, where it also serves to prevent the consumer from incurring increased transaction costs, guaranteeing to the marketeer that his or her message is heard without interference.

Protection of trade secrets is again underpinned by the notion of incentives and rewards, but may be located in the realm of unfair competition law.[31] As an item of sensitive information it may have commercial value, so that it attracts the interest of competitors. Here lies one of the major differences from the fixed costs associated with obtaining a patent, in that the value of the trade secret and the costs that have to be incurred in order to protect it are directly related to the willingness of another to try to steal it. The parties do not bargain themselves, neither are they able to, since one of the parties intends to keep the asset secret. A regime that protects trade secrets, therefore, veers towards a liability-rule-based system in which the transfer of an entitlement is protected and its value is determined by the State. In the patent system, independent invention, reverse engineering, and public disclosure do not detract from the proprietary right in the patent,[32] but in the case of trade secrets they do. Someone who sets out to uncover and apply another's trade secret may bring about social gain by increasing competition, but he may equally reduce the incentive to invent by inducing asymmetric market failure.[33] Trade secrecy protection serves to reduce the social costs that comprise expenditures for protection of trade secrets on one hand, and

---

[27] See Gordon W. J., "Fair Use as Market Failure: A Structural and Economic Analysis of the *Betamax* Case and Its Predecessors", 82 *Col.LR* 1600 (1982) as to the extent of the fair use doctrine. See also Landes and Posner, note 23 above, 357–361.

[28] See Cornish W. R. and Phillips J., "The Economic Function of Trademarks: An Analysis With Special Reference to Developing Countries", (1982) 13 *IIC* 41; Economides N. S., "The Economics of Trademarks", 78 *TMR* 523 (1988) ; Landes W. M. and Posner R. A., "Trademark Law: and Economic Perspective", *IPLR* 229 (1989).

[29] See Diamond S. A., "The Public Interest and the Trademark System" (1980) 62 *JPOS* 528, noting at 529 that the consumer is the "unnamed third party in every action for trademark infringement", since the interest of the consumer lies in the ability of the trademark to facilitate choice on the basis that a trademark guarantees uniformity of quality at a consistent level.

[30] Akerlof G. A., "The Market for 'Lemons': Quality Uncertainty and the Market Mechanism", *Quarterly Journal of Economics* 488 (1970), demonstrated that this also applies to the quality function of the trademark. In his work he succinctly describes the market breakdown that occurs when the consumer can no longer trust the quality message a mark conveys.

[31] Besen and Raskind, note 4 above, 23–24.

[32] Provided that the entitlement is enforced by the state.

[33] Friedman D. D., Landes W. M., and Posner R. A., "Some Economics of Trade Secret Law", *Journal of Economic Perspectives* 61 (1991), 69–70.

the cost of "not investing resources designed to effect a transfer of wealth"[34] on the other. In balancing those associated with the upkeep of a protective regime and the costs associated with the absence of a market structure that facilitates bargaining and sale of information, trade secrecy protection is limited to tortious interference with an entitlement that is not absolute in nature. An inventor relying on a trade secret cannot prevent the application of independent research and, if the resulting invention is patentable, he cannot even prevent a second market entrant from patenting the invention, forcing the original inventor out of the market. At first instance all market entrants face the same market barriers. This places reverse engineering in a peculiar position. It is not a method of independent research and may be considered theft. Friedman and Landes[35] advance two reasons against liability for reverse engineering, namely the administrative cost associated with proof that independent research did not take place, and the public disclosure argument. The line between piracy and acceptable reverse engineering then lies in the presence of substantial investment and innovation. This means that reverse engineering does not create a monopolistic barrier to entry, and the investment and innovation associated with it do not induce asymmetry in the market since all market entrants face similar market barriers.

Property-rules and Liability-rules

The differing rationale of patent and trade secrets or confidential information regimes may also be used to demonstrate the justification for each particular protective regime in an economic sense. The incentive and reward rationale can be found in both the patent and confidential information regimes, but it is modified by the property rule and liability rule dichotomy, which underlines the varying economic considerations that shape either regime. The work of Guido Calabresi and Douglas Melamed[36] demonstrates the economic considerations that are relevant to make a considered choice between either regime.

The patent system is based on a property rule, where the State sanctioned monopolistic entitlement enables the proprietor in advance to set the price for the use of his asset by others. From an economic point of view this system makes sense if transaction costs are low, there are few parties, and the value of the asset is difficult to assess.[37] In view of a legal entitlement, legitimate use of

---

[34] Landes W. M. and Posner R. A., *The Economic Structure of Tort Law*, (1987, Cambridge Mass., Harvard University Press) ch. 6.
[35] Friedman, Landes and Posner, note 33 above, 70.
[36] Calabresi and Melamed, note 16 above.
[37] Ibid. 1092; Merges, note 18 above, 2664–2667.

the asset can be made only after bargaining with the owner of the property right.

A liability rule, on the other hand, does not rely on a bargaining process prior to the transfer of an intangible asset, but the situation is assessed *ex post* in order to determine the correct amount of compensation for appropriation. A liability rule is economically effective in those cases where there are many parties and high transaction costs that interfere with the bargaining process.[38] The economic efficiency of the liability rule is furthermore heightened if the value of the asset can be easily assessed by the arbiter who has to settle a dispute. In view of the valuation problems that courts face in liability and property rule systems alike, damages and restitution rates are often assessed on an equitable basis, resulting in the "reasonable royalty". The reasonable royalty should be set at a level that makes the copyist face the same market barrier as the creator does, by remedying the market failure the creator suffers.

In the free market, the property rule appears to be the most liberal, since it minimizes State intervention in the valuation of assets, leaving it to the market to maximize wealth by voluntary transaction. Despite the fact that a property rule is often the most cost effective, since it stimulates party autonomy as opposed to State intervention in the transaction process, the policing of the property rule may require so much State intervention that the system is less cost effective than in a liability-rule-based system. This is increasingly true in the information society, where assets develop the characteristics of public goods, due to the fact that information based assets are costly to develop, but vulnerable to rapid and widespread duplication.[39] Furthermore, within the property rule system, barriers to entry are created, which may stifle competition. The absolute nature of property rights also does not take into account that some forms of "infringement" may be economically desirable for society. Economic theory has come up with two tests to determine whether the act of appropriation of an asset in the face of a monopolistic claim is efficient. The first, the so called Kaldor-Hicks test,[40] is whether the "infringer" can pay off the inventor and still find parties who are willing to value the infringer's product more highly. If this is the case, the exercise of a monopoly to the detriment of another is not economically justifiable. Where protection of intangible assets is concerned, this means that an injunction preventing the appropriation of an asset is not a correct option. This test, however,

---

[38] High transaction costs induced by market failure lead to a situation in which a liability rule is more efficient. See Reichman J., "Legal Hybrids between the Patent and Copyright Paradigms", 94 *Col.LR* 2432 (1994); See also Merges, note 18 above, 2668, who distinguishes another situation in which an exception to the property rule for intellectual property rights is efficient. Compulsory license regimes defer the bargaining process and valuation of intellectual property away from party autonomy.

[39] Reichman, note 38 above, 2443.

[40] Kaldor N., "Welfare Propositions of Economics and Interpersonal Comparisons of Utility", 49 *Economic Journal* 549 (1939) ; J. R. Hicks, "Foundations of Welfare Economics", 49 *Economic Journal* 696 (1939).

does not take into account that benefits and costs are not independent of the distribution of wealth. If the asset is appropriated without compensation, wealth is redistributed, but this does not mean that the situation that then comes about is efficient. Efficiency may in fact dictate that the old monopolistic situation is restored, for example, because the original developer is better placed to benefit society in the light of incentive- and reward-based innovation considerations. To avoid this paradox one also has to test whether the monopolistic claimant can pay the potential "infringer" to cease and desist appropriation of the intangible that is the bone of contention. If the answer is negative, then exercising monopoly power is not economically efficient. This Scitovszky test[41] serves to remedy that asymmetry and can be taken in tandem with the Kaldor-Hicks test. If both tests are passed, appropriation of an intangible is efficient and monopoly power should not be exercised in order to obtain injunctive relief. In effect the tests serve to determine whether copying results in the creation of *new* products that society is willing to pay for, without destroying the market for the source product.

When making a choice between a liability and a property rule, the desirability of the application of the Kaldor-Hicks and Scitovszky tests is also a consideration. The absolute nature of intellectual property rights does not leave room for the tests. However, statutory exceptions to the monopoly are the elements that can be tested for their effectiveness. It is equally clear that the elasticity of the liability-rule-based doctrine of misappropriation facilitates the assessment of fact on the basis of the Kaldor-Hicks and Scitovszky tests in a way that property rule systems cannot. This means that if a choice is made for a liability rule, and party autonomy in the assessment of the value of an asset by means of transfer bargaining is diverted to an arbiter, the efficiency of the transfer as such can be tested.

Commodification of Information and Databases

The discussion on the protection of databases encompasses both the distinction between property and liability rules, as well as concerns over abuse of dominance in the exercise of database rights of access to information that is needed for the creation of *new* works that society is willing to pay for, but that do not undermine the market for the source database.[42] The data mining industry is growing in importance. In the electronic environment information is not just a means to do business, it is a business commodity in itself. Electronic commerce and the new

---

[41] De Scitovszky T., "A Note on Welfare Propositions in Economics", *Review of Economic Studies* 77 (1941).
[42] See notes 40 and 41 as well as the related discussion on the Kaldor-Hicks and Scitovszky tests.

economy are starting to have an increasing impact on public policy and human interaction. To an increasing extent value to the economy is represented by the accumulated knowledge present in the organization.[43] Information, the currency of the new economy, has the capacity to generate exponentially growing new amounts of information. This requires organizations to adapt their processes, and forces legislators to provide a legal, social and cultural framework for the new economy. In the interest of providing privacy and security to the citizen and industry alike, governments are pressed to regulate data processing industries.[44] Article 2(5) of the Berne Convention, as clarified by the WIPO Copyright Treaty (WCT) sets the scene for this next section. Article 5 WCT states: "Compilations of data or other material, in any form, which by reason of the selection or arrangement of their contents constitute intellectual creations, are protected as such", and is the guiding principle in civil law jurisdictions for the subsistence of copyright law, requiring some level of originality as the threshold for protection. This demarcation was, however, not always so clear. Under English copyright law, for example, "skill, judgment and labour", "selection, judgement and experience", but also "labour, skill and capital" were sufficient, making it possible to protect white-listed telephone directories. The implementation of the EC Database Directive[45] changed this situation, restricting the scope of UK copyright law for the future. To this date, however, databases created before March 27, 1996 may be subject to compilation copyright in the UK.[46] Before we come to the EC Database Directive, it is important to reflect upon the pivotal year 1991, because it was then that the U.S. Supreme Court in *Feist* v. *Rural Telephone Services*[47] set the threshold for copyright protection in a major common law system and drew a line between original and non-original works.[48] This provided clarity for international copyright, but uncertainty for producers of databases, who felt exposed to misappropriation. The irony is also plain to see. The more exhaustive you are (the more labour, skill and capital you invest) in compiling a database, the smaller one's chances of demonstrating that there is a sufficient level of original selection

---

[43] Stewart T., *Intellectual Capital* (1997, Doubleday/Currency).
[44] See the contributions of Reback G. and Kelly K. to *Wired*, August 1997; see also Kelly K., *New Rules for the New Economy* (1998, New York, Viking Press).
[45] *Directive 96/9/EC of the European Parliament and of the Council of 11 March 1996 on the legal protection of databases*, OJ L 77, 27 March 1996, p. 20. For a description of the Directive and other database protection initiatives see Reichmann J. and Samuelson P., "Intellectual Property Rights in Data?", 50 *Vanderbilt LR* (1997) 51; Gaster J., *Der Rechtsschutz von Datenbanken: Kommentar zur Richtlinie 96/9/EG, mit Erläuterungen zur Umsetzung in das deutsche und österreichische Recht* (1999, Köln, Heymanns Verlag); Kübler P., *Rechtsschutz von Datenbanken (EU-USA-Schweiz)* (1999, Zürich, Schulthess Verlag).
[46] The Copyright and Rights in Database Regulations 1997, SI 1997/3032 of 18 December 1997, entry into force 1 January 1998, S. 29(1)
[47] *Feist Publications Inc. v. Rural Telephone Service Company Inc*, 111 S Ct. 1282; 113 L Ed 2d 358; 20 IPR 129 (US Supreme Court, 1991).
[48] See in this respect also the *Van Dale* v. *Romme*, Dutch Supreme Court, January 4, 1991, NJ 1991, 608, in which protection was denied to a list of words in a dictionary.

or arrangement to warrant copyright protection. This combination explains why lawyers are being told by some that old rights need to be strengthened[49] and new ones need to be created[50] in order to combat market failure. Some even go so far as to assert that: "Intellectual property law cannot be patched, retrofitted, or expanded to contain digitized expression We will need to develop an entirely new set of methods as benefits this entirely new set of circumstances".[51] Whereas I do not wish to challenge here that protection is necessary in order to promote innovation,[52] use of information does not exclude or place any costs on others using the same information, and as such information is a public good.

At the end of the day, however, database producers found a willing ear in their combat against market failure with the European Commission, which incorporated a new *sui generis* database right in a Directive, and also initiated an, albeit failed, attempt to elevate this new right to the world stage.[53] The resulting Draft WIPO Treaty on Databases[54] was part of the Diplomatic Conference[55] that spawned the WCT and the WIPO Performances and Phonograms Treaty.

The EU learned its lesson in "gunboat diplomacy"[56] when the U.S. adopted legislation[57] concerning the protection of semiconductor chip designs. Appreciating the success of this approach to set global standards, the EC Database Directive[58] follows the example of the Council Directive on the legal protection of topographies of semiconductor products[59] and also contains a reciprocity clause.

---

[49] WIPO Copyright Treaty, and WIPO Performances and Phonograms Treaty of December 20, 1996.

[50] Directive 96/9/EC of Mach 11, 1996, no L 77/20, and S. 2291, July 10, 1998; See also Laddie H., "Copyright: Over-Strength, Over-Regulated, Over-Rated?" [1996] 5 *EIPR* 260.

[51] Barlow J., "The Economy of Ideas", *Wired*, March 1994, 85

[52] One only needs to look at critical appraisal of database protection to see that investment and reward theories legitimize the creation of incentives for innovation. See Reichman J. and Samuelson P., "Intellectual Property Rights in Data?" 50 *Vanderbilt L. Rev.* 51 (1997).

[53] WIPO, Committee of Experts on a possible Protocol to the Berne Convention, Third Session, Geneva, 21 to 25 June 1993, Memorandum on the Questions concerning a Possible Protocol to the Berne Convention, Part II, WIPO document ref. BCP/CE/III/2–II (12 March 1993).

[54] Basic Proposal for the Substantive Provisions of the Treaty on Intellectual Property in Respect of Databases to be considered by the Diplomatic Conference, prepared by the Chairman of the Committees of Experts on a Possible Protocol to the Berne Convention and on a Possible Instrument for the Protection of the Rights of Performers and Producers of Phonograms, WIPO document ref. CRNR/DC/6 (30 August 1996).

[55] The Diplomatic Conference on Certain Copyright and Neighboring Rights Questions was held in Geneva from 2 to 20 December 1996. <http://www.wipo.int/eng/diplconf/index.htm> (visited 15-01-2001)

[56] Lloyd I., *Information Technology Law* (2nd Edition, London: Butterworths, 1997) at p. 390. Lloyd comments that the use of this tactic backed by the threat of force has been proved effective (*ibid.* at p. 391).

[57] Semiconductor Chip Protection Act of 1984 (Pub. L. 98–620, 98 Stat. 3347, 3356), as incorporated in 17 USC Chapter 9.

[58] Note 45 above.

[59] Article 3.7 of the *Council Directive 87/54/EEC of 16 December 1986 on the Legal Protection of Topographies of Semiconductor Products*, OJ L 024, 27 January 1987, p. 36.

Since *sui* generis database protection was now "officially" outside of the scope of copyright, and therefore not subject to the Berne Convention's guiding principle of national treatment, this was not a problem. The EU Database Directive affords protection to individual database makers who are nationals or have their habitual residence in the territory of the Community.[60] Similarly rights are also granted to companies and firms formed in the Community that have their registered office, central administration or principal place of business within the Community.[61] However, mere registration of an office in the territory of the Community is not sufficient, as the firm's "operations must be genuinely linked on an ongoing basis with the economy of a Member State".[62]

Less clear is the status of foreign database producers. The Database Directive states that[63] "foreign" databases are eligible for protection afforded by the *sui generis* (sweat of the brow) right[64] only, if the Council concludes an agreement extending this form of protection for specified countries outside the European Union. In other words, the basis for the protection of foreign databases is reciprocity rather than the normal rule governing copyright of "national treatment".

It comes to no surprise then that the U.S. attempted to introduce in U.S. law the protection for databases that would fulfill the reciprocity requirement of the EC Database Directive on several occasions. Legal initiative is necessary because databases are merely protected as "compilations" or "collective works"[65] and a requisite of originality is a threshold for protection.[66] At present facts and mere data are excluded from the scope of copyright.[67] Although sweat of the brow or industrious collection protection has been accepted by some courts,[68] the case of

---

[60] EC Database Directive, note 45 above, Art. 11(1).
[61] EC Database Directive, note 45 above, Art. 11(2).
[62] *Ibid.*
[63] EC Database Directive, note 45 above, Art. 11(3).
[64] EC Database Directive, note 45 above, Art. 7.
[65] See, *Nimmer on Copyright* § 2.04 [C]: "The statutory definition of 'literary works' is broad enough to include computer data bases and programs ..." See, however *Joan F. Lane d.b.a. Lane & Co v The First National Bank of Boston and others*, 687 F. Supp. 11; [1988] Copyright Law Decisions 26,328 (Dist. MA, 1988) at p. 16 (compilation copyright can apply to databases); Denicola, Robert C., *Copyright in Collections of Facts: A Theory for the Protection of Nonfiction Literary Works*, 81 Columbia Law Review 516 (1981) (at p. 531 the author asserts that "databases are, in essence, automated compilations").
[66] The US Copyright Act requires a "selection, arrangement or co-ordination". See: 17 USC s. 103 (b).
[67] 17 USC s. 103.
[68] *Leon v. Pacific Telephone & Telegraph Co.*, 91 F.2d 484 (9th Cir., 1937), held that names and addresses taken from a telephone directory for compiling a directory arranged by telephone numbers infringed copyright in that source directory. On sweat of the brow see *Nimmer on Copyright* § 3.04 [B][1], where he comments:
> "Protection for the fruits of such research – for the 'sweat of the author's brow' – may in certain circumstances be available under a theory of unfair competition. But to accord copyright protection on this basis alone distorts basic copyright principles, in that it creates a monopoly in public domain materials, without the necessary justification of protecting and encouraging the creation of 'writings' by 'authors.'"

Feist v. Rural Telephone Services[69] put the matter to rest. In *Feist* the Supreme Court held:

> "As a constitutional matter, copyright protects only those elements of a work that posses more than de minimis quantum of creativity. Rural's white pages, limited to basic subscriber information and arranged alphabetically, fall short of the mark. As a statutory matter, 17 U.S.C. sec. 101 does not afford protection from copying to a collection of facts that are selected, coordinated, and arranged in a way that utterly lacks originality. Given that some works must fail, we cannot imagine a more likely candidate. Indeed, were we to hold that Rural's white pages pass muster, it is hard to believe that any collection of facts could fail."

This is affirmation that extraction of facts from a particular database, even for compiling a competitive database is permitted.[70] In *Warren v Microdos*,[71] compilation copyright was clarified with respect to a computerized database. Hence, a massive extraction of data items from a printed directory for compiling a database was allowed. The data entries are unprotected facts and therefore the plaintiff's "sweat of the brow" argument on this issue could not prevail in light of the Supreme Court's *Feist* decision, a decision that was later affirmed in *Campbell v. Acuff-Rose Music, Inc.*[72]

The *Feist* decision also cast a shadow over the methods available to the U.S. legislator to provide protection for databases on par with the EC Database Directive's *sui generis* right. Protection of databases can no longer be based on quasi-property, but has to be based on unfair competition law, based on the commerce clause.

The first attempt was the Database Investment and Intellectual Property Antipiracy Act of 1996.[73] This Bill, which was roughly drafted on the provisions of the Database Directive, went beyond the Directive's measures regarding its scope of protection. For instance, the proposed term of protection was 25 years[74] as compared to 15 years in the Database Directive. No corresponding Bill was

---

[69] Note 47 above.
[70] *Bellsouth Advertising & Publishing Corp v. Donnelley Information Publishing Inc and another*, 1999 F.2d 1436; 28 USPQ 2d 1001.
[71] *Warren Publishing Inc v Microdos Data Corp and others*, [1992] CCH Copyright Law Decisions 26,928; 3 CCH Computer Cases 46,683 (Dist., Northern District of Georgia, Atlanta Division, 1992). The judgment of the district court was affirmed in 52 F. 3d 950 (11th Cir., 1995) but that decision was subsequently vacated by a grant of rehearing in: 67 F. 3d 276 (11th Cir., 1995). Finally, the District Court decision was vacated and remanded, see: 115 F. 3d 1509; Copyright L.R. 27,667 (11th Cir., 1997). The petition for a writ of certiorari was denied by the Supreme Court, see: 118 S. Ct. 397 (1997).
[72] 510 U.S. 569, 575 (1994).
[73] H.R.3531, 104th Congress, 2nd Session (1996).
[74] *Ibid.*, § 6(a).

introduced in the Senate, no actions were taken in relation to this Bill, and eventually, this Bill failed.

H.R.354, which is currently being considered by the United States Congress, is the Collections of Information Antipiracy Act[75] and superseded H.R.2652,[76] a 1997 attempt at introducing database protection. H.R.354 is based on the concept of misappropriation and prohibits extraction of information from a database for the purpose of re-utilization, or dissemination for use in commerce, or use harming substantially the database producer's primary market. The proposal gives database owners the right to prevent certain acts of extraction of information from their database for uses of information into downstream products, whether or not they compete with the database.[77] It should be noted that in the drafts towards the enactment of the Digital Millennium Copyright Act,[78] the text of the U.S. Database Bill was incorporated.[79] However, this text concerning database protection was dropped as the final draft of the Act was passed.[80] Yet another addition to the spectrum of database initiatives is the Consumer and Investor Access to Information Act.[81] This Bill is an attempt to provide protection for databases by addressing direct competitors only. At first glance H.R.1858 is narrower in its scope of application than H.R.354. H.R.1858 affords protection against misappropriation to a limited range of subject matter only,[82] leaving a

---

[75] Note 5 above.
[76] H.R. 2652, 105th Congress, 2nd Session, introduced on October 9, 1997. The Bill was passed by the House of Representatives on May 19, 1998 (C.R. H3404), and was received in the Senate on May 20, 1998 for further legislative action.
[77] H.R.354.RH
Sec. 1402. Prohibition
'(a) MAKING AVAILABLE OR EXTRACTING TO MAKE AVAILABLE – Any person who makes available to others, or extracts to make available to others, all or a substantial part of a collection of information gathered, organized, or maintained by another person through the investment of substantial monetary or other resources, so as to cause material harm to the primary market or a related market of that other person, or a successor in interest of that other person, for a product or service that incorporates that collection of information and is offered or intended to be offered in commerce by that other person, or a successor in interest of that person, shall be liable to that person or successor in interest for the remedies set forth in section 1406.
'(b) OTHER ACTS OF EXTRACTION – Any person who extracts all or a substantial part of a collection of information gathered, organized, or maintained by another person through the investment of substantial monetary or other resources, so as to cause material harm to the primary market of that other person, or a successor in interest of that other person, for a product or service that incorporates that collection of information and is offered or intended to be offered in commerce by that other person, or a successor in interest of that person, shall be liable to that person or successor in interest for the remedies set forth in section 1406.
[78] H.R. 2281, 105th Congress, 2nd Session.
[79] *Ibid.* Title V.
[80] DMCA 1998, Public Law 105–304. The Act was signed by the President on October 28, 1998.
[81] H.R.1858 of May 19, 1999.
[82] H.R.1858 speaks of protection against misappropriation of securities market and real-time market information that is sold, distributed or disseminated without authorization.

large part of the real-time information database market exposed to misappropriation.[83] Furthermore H.R.1858 recognizes a limited form of protection of databases against slavish copying by duplication of extracted information. The definition of what constitutes a database, however, is so wide, bordering in the infinite, as it also encompasses discrete sections of databases that contain multiple discrete items.[84] Furthermore the wide definition of "in competition" when it comes to confining the unauthorized sale or distribution of a duplicate of a database that is essentially the same as the original is only off-set by the possible application of antitrust measures[85] and not by a limitation of term. Whereas the omission of term may be explained by a desire to take away any association with an intellectual property-like right, its potentially stifling effect and uncertainty in the market may indicate that this Bill is not well thought-through. What is clear, however, is that H.R.1858 cannot be considered as adequate equivalent protection to that of the EC Database Directive, which leaves H.R.354, the Antipiracy Bill, as the only likely candidate to provide a solution for the database industries. Although different in approach to the *sui generis* quasi-property right of the EC Database Directive, H.R.354 protects the producer of a database against extractions that cause harm to his primary market and against extractions to make available information contained in a database so as to cause material harm[86] to the primary or related market. The fact that the Antipiracy Bill may be less monopolizing than the *sui generis* database right due to the theoretical restraints and practical application of unfair competition law, as well as the more elaborate limitations and exceptions, the misappropriation right is something which the European Union should take in stride, especially since the EC Database Directive is up for reassessment in 2002.[87]

---

[83] One can think of exchange rates, score results in sports games, news feeds, etc..

[84] Congressional Record E1055 (May 20, 1999); H.R.1858 S. 101(1) states that a discrete section of a database may also be treated as a database. This means, for example that if a directory of restaurants in the District of Columbia is organized by type of food, the section comprising Italian restaurants could constitute a database within the meaning of the Bill, even though it is part of a larger database (i.e., the D.C. restaurant directory).

[85] H.R.1858 S. 107.

[86] Thus displacing the requirement set out in the hot-news case *National Basketball League v. Motorola, Inc.* 105F.3d 841, 845 (1997), requiring the plaintiff to show that use made by the defendant of the plaintiff's efforts would substantially threaten the existence or quality of the product or service provided.

[87] Art. 16(3) EC Database Directive, note 45: "Not later than at the end of the third year after the date referred to in paragraph 1 [1 January 1998], and every three years thereafter, the Commission shall submit to the European Parliament, the Council and the Economic and Social Committee a report on the application of this Directive, in which, inter alia on the basis of specific information supplied by the Member States, it shall examine in particular the application of the sui generis right, including Articles 8 and 9, and especially whether the application of this right has led to abuse of a dominant position or other interference with free competition which would justify appropriate measures being taken, in particular the establishment of non-voluntary licensing arrangements. Where necessary, it shall submit proposals for adjustment of this Directive in line with developments in the area of databases."

Whereas the problem of reciprocity with the EU may be guaranteed with the adoption of H.R.354.RH, constitutional challenges[88] to the Bill may present a problem. Intellectual property rights are based on the patents and copyright clause,[89] empowering Congress to legislate in this area. It is also clear that the intellectual property clause not only pre-empts State's efforts to create quasi-intellectual property rights,[90] but also limits the power of Congress itself to do so when it doesn't involve "original contributions to the wealth of human knowledge".[91] This limitation reiterated in the *Feist* decision,[92] forces database legislation to be based on the commerce clause.[93] It has been argued that the type of protection envisaged in the Antipiracy Bill surpasses the constraints of both the commerce and the intellectual property clause, because in functionality, it creates an intellectual property right in data.[94] The present author does not agree with the analysis that H.R.354 creates a property right in information. Much of the assertion that H.R.354 is functionally equivalent to intellectual property rights is based on the definitional notion that it is market creating, just like intellectual property rights.[95] It is clear to see that the Antipiracy Bill strives to be as functionally equivalent as possible to the EC Database Directive. Where

---

[88] See in this respect Pollack M., "The Right To Know? Delimiting Database Protection At The Juncture Of The Commerce Clause, The Intellectual Property Clause And The First Amendment", 17 *Cardozo Arts & Ent L.J..* 47 (1999).
[89] U.S. CONST. art. 1, § 8, cl. 8.
[90] Bonito Boats, Inc. v. Thunder Craft Boats, Inc., 489 U.S. 141 (1989); Sears, Roebuck & Co. v. Stiffel Co., 376 U.S. 225 (1964); Compco Corp. v. Day-Brite Lighting, Inc., 376 U.S. 234 (1964). For an assessment see Kamperman Sanders A., *Unfair Competition Law – The Protection of Intellectual and Industrial Creativity* (1997, Oxford, Clarendon Press), 12–9.
[91] See *Feist*, note 47 above.
[92] Ginsburg J., "No 'Sweat'? Copyright and Other Protection of Works of Information After *Feist v. Rural Telephone*", 92 Col. L.R. (1992) 338, 369–74, Pollack, note 88.
[93] U.S. CONST. art. 1, § 8, cl. 3.
[94] Benkler Y., "Constitutional Bounds of Database Protection: The role of Judicial Review in the Creation and Definition of Private Rights in Information", to be published in 15 Berkeley Technology Law Journal, < http://papers.ssrn.com/paper.taf?abstract_id = 214973 >, (visited 15-01-2001) who argues that H.R.354 is unconstitutional. See also Conley J., Brown M., and Bryan R., "Database Protection in a Digital World: Why the United States Should Decline to Follow the European Model", 9 *Information & Communications Technology Law* (2000) 27.
[95] Benkler, note 94, p. 33: "Intellectual property rights are in this sense market creating – they are constitutive of the properties of the goods sold in the market. Functionally, this distinguishes them from laws that are market-regulating, or that constrain behavior in a market for goods whose excludability is already defined by other rules – namely, property rights. Now, it should be clear that these definitions are provisional working definitions, and their borders are permeable. But they capture rather well the distinction between, for example, fair use, a limitation on all information product owners" ability to exclude users from their products, and hence a limitation on excludability, and misuse of copyright, a limitation on some owners" ability, under certain circumstances, to do things with their products that they are generally entitled to do to most users. The former is a part of the definition of property in information, even though it is formally a defense to a copyright claim, not part of the definition of the owner's exclusive rights. The latter – misuse – is a regulation of using already-defined property rights in certain market situations."

H.R.354.IH was drafted so as to cover competitive relationships only,[96] H.R.354.RH now also covers other extractions that materially harm the primary market of the producer of a database. This means that those extracting data not for competition, but to the extent that there is no further need to access the original find themselves within the scope of the Antipiracy Bill. It is this last addition, which not only provides functional equivalence with the EC Database Directive, but also raises questions about the placement of the Antipiracy Bill on the borderline between the competition and the intellectual property clause. The prohibition is, however, limited, because *de minimis* uses are excluded[97] by the requirement to show "material harm" to the primary market of the database producer.[98] Section 1402(b) of H.R.354.RH therefore addresses the specific needs of the online database producers that stand to lose their income should subscribers be allowed to plunder all or a substantial part of a database so that they have no need to consult the database again. It is hard to see that this form of protection is based on anything other than unfair competition market failure theory. Although the concept of misappropriation has enjoyed limited application since its inception in the case *International News Service* v. *Associated Press*,[99] it is clearly rooted in unfair competition law. Such protection is not dependent on proprietary concepts like other branches of protection of intellectual and industrial creativity, but on legal concepts such as unjust enrichment[100] and economic concepts such as asymmetric market failure.[101]

It is certainly true that S. 1402(b) of the Antipiracy Bill does not necessarily address direct competition, and may therefore be perceived as proprietary. It is nevertheless also true that the prohibition for the act of extraction is framed in misappropriation terms and is thus market regulating. Most unfair competition statutes and case law around the world,[102] and indeed also the WIPO *Model*

---

[96] See H.R.354.IH Sec. 1402, which was limited to extractions for the purpose of making them available in commerce.

[97] H.R. Rep. No. 106–349, pt. 1, at 18 (1999).

[98] See note 86 above.

[99] 248 US 215 (1918). For an overview of the nature and development of unfair competition law see Kamperman Sanders A., note 90 above; On legal reasoning in unfair competition law see Ohly A., Richterrecht und Generalklausel im Recht des unlauteren Wettbewerbs: ein Methodenvergleich des englischen und des deutschen Rechts (1997, Köln, Heymann); for France see Passa J., Contrefaçon et Concurrence Déloyale (1997, Paris, Litec) ; for Switzerland see Berger M., *Die funktionale Konkretisierung van Art. 2 UWG* (1997, Zürich, Schulthess); and Germany Beater A., *Nachahmen im Wettbewerb* (1995, Tübingen, Mohr).

[100] See Callmann R., "He who Reaps where He has not Sown: Unjust Enrichment in the Law of Unfair Competition", 55 *Harv. LR* 595 (1942); see also Kamperman Sanders A., note 90 above ch. 1.

[101] Kamperman Sanders A., note 90 above ch. 4; Gordon W., "On Owning Information: Intellectual Property and the Restitutionary Impulse" 78 *Virginia LR* 149–281 (1992); "Asymmetric Market Failure and Prisoner's Dilemma in Intellectual Property" 17 *University of Dayton LR* 853–69 (1992); Karjala D., "Misappropriation as a Third Intellectual Property Paradigm" 94 *Columbia LR* 2594–609 (1994); Reichman J., "Legal Hybrids between the Patent and Copyright Paradigms" 94 *Columbia LR* 2432–558 (1994).

[102] See note 99 above.

Provisions on Protection Against Unfair Competition,[103] use a wide notion of competition for the purpose of market regulation, addressing also acts where there is no direct competitive nexus, but where the plaintiff's primary market is nevertheless directly and fundamentally affected. Since much of the database producer's value added to the database consists in providing access and context (structure, reliability and exhaustiveness) to information, only parasitic acts of destruction to this qualitative or quantitative investment are to be regulated. It is submitted that it would be desirable if the EC Database Directive were to be amended so as to spell out its confinement to this principle.

Section 1402 H.R.354.RH also covers extractions used in enhanced or derivative products (i.e. databases that are not exact duplicates of the original, but add other information). An argument can be made that this type of protection falls within intellectual property, and not competition law.[104] Again this interpretation of unfair competition law is rather narrow, but it underlines the legitimate concern for pricing, as well as dependence on one or a limited number of relevant databases.[105] At one point the EC Database Directive was set to have its own provision on compulsory licensing[106] in relation to the *sui generis* right, but this was dropped. In European Union cases involving databases, however, the single source issue[107] has been raised in defence to *sui generis* database protection claims.[108] Whereas monopoly pricing is left to antitrust authorities, reliance on

---

[103] No. 832(e) (Geneva, WIPO, 1996, and also *Protection against Unfair Competition*, No 725(e) (Geneva, WIPO, 1994).

[104] See Benkler, note 94 at 36.

[105] One can think of the stranglehold some publishers have over academic publications, as well as certain professional disciplines that depend on information.

[106] Proposal for a Council Directive on the Legal Protection of Databases, Art. 8, COM (92) 24 def. At 70.

[107] See Hugenholtz, P., "The New Database Right: Early Case Law from Europe," (2001) available at < http://www.iviz.nl/publications/hugenholtz/fordham2001.pdf > and Maurer S., Hugenholtz P. and Onsrud, H., "Europe's Database Experiment", Science vol. 294, 26 October 2001, 789.

[108] *KPN Telecom B.V. v. Xbase Software Ontwikkeling B.V.*, Pres. Distr. Ct. The Hague, 14 jan. 2000, KG 99/1429, [2000] 2 Mediaforum 64, [2000] 4 Informatierecht/AMI 71 which involved a software program running on the world wide web that allowed users to extract information from the KPN database containing telephone numbers, bypassing the advertising banners. This was held to be a clear infringement of the Database right; conversely see *Vermande B.V. v. Bojkovski*, Pres. Distr. Ct. The Hague 20 March 1998, [1998] IER 111; *Denda v. KPN*, Court of Appeal Arnhem 15 April 1997 & 5 Aug. 1997, [1997] 5 Mediaforum B72, [1997] Informatierecht/AMI 214. In the telco cases the point was also advanced that the investments made were not primarily geared towards the creation of databases of phone numbers. The argument that spin-off databases should not be protected for lack of substantial investment was not accepted. See, however, *Telegraaf/NOS and HMG*, Netherlands Competition Authority, 10 September 1998, (1998) Mediaforum 304; and *NOS v. De Telegraaf*, Court of Appeals of The Hague 30 January 2001, (2001) Mediaforum 90, both cases involving a refusal to license broadcasting information. Ultimately the CoA held that the broadcasters did not enjoy database right protection for their listings, as substantial investment in the making of the database, above and beyond any investments in the programming as such, had not been shown. Copyright for non-original writings was, however, granted, but the refusal to license was held to constitute anti-competitive behaviour.

intellectual property rights to safeguard assets and associated pricing is generally left unaffected.[109] Intellectual property policy and anti-trust policy are still perceived as separate domains.

In Search of a Horizontal Right to Information – Competitors

Whereas monopoly pricing is left to antitrust authorities, reliance on intellectual property rights to safeguard assets and associated pricing is generally left unaffected.[110] Intellectual property policy and anti-trust policy are still perceived as separate domains. Protection against misappropriation, however, is a distinct branch of competition law in that it is based on investment and return analysis and market failure assessment. Disguised beneath all the proprietary language even the EC Database Directive demands such assessment when it comes to the question of qualification for the *sui generis* right, as well as that of assessment of infringement. It is submitted that, because of its roots in competition law, database protection should follow the contours of market reality, and should therefore, contrary to intellectual property rights proper, be subject to a higher level of scrutiny when it comes to anti-trust policy. Here again the U.S. choice to place database protection in the domain of competition law may prove to be a fortunate choice, as the interrelationship between the protection against market failure and market policy is much more clearly underlined in such a setting.

In their work *Information Rules*,[111] Carl Shapiro and Hal Varian succinctly describe the characteristics of the network economy, pointing to the fact that there are many more factors, such as network effects, tying, bundling, lock-in and switching costs, versioning, and encryption technologies[112] that may also serve as barriers to access to and free flow of information goods. Some argue[113] that in the

---

[109] The rightholder is therefore permitted to maximize income. Only on cases of price discrimination between classes of purchasers are authorities prepared to act. For an overview of the plethora of means a marketer has at his disposal and the way in which US courts have reacted see Shapiro C. and Varian H., *Information Rules: A Strategic Guide to the Network Economy* (1999, Harvard, Harvard Business School Press); Shapiro C., "Exclusivity in Network Industries" 7 *Geo. Mason L. Rev.* 1–11 (1999); Katz M. and Shapiro C., *Antitrust in Software Markets*, Paper presented at the Progress and Freedom Foundation conference, *Competition, Convergence and the Microsoft Monopoly*, February 5, 1998.

[110] The rightholder is therefore permitted to maximize income. Only on cases of price discrimination between classes of purchasers are authorities prepared to act. For an overview of the plethora of means a marketer has at his disposal and the way in which U.S. courts have reacted see Katz M. and Shapiro C., note 109 above.

[111] Note 109 above.

[112] These techniques may be applied to the underlying software, but also to the data itself.

[113] See the contributions of Reback G. and Kelly K. to *Wired*, August 1997; see also Kelly K., *New Rules for the New Economy* (1998, New York, Viking Press).

new economic reality old economic axioms do not apply, as new information products possess different characteristics, which means regulators should stay well away from this emerging market. Others[114] argue that normal scenarios still apply. The Microsoft case, however, shows that the latter position is still prevalent.[115] Whereas there may be a certain reluctance to impose a duty on intellectual property rightholders to provide essential facilities,[116] the creation of a horizontal right to information may be construed under the essential facilities doctrine when there is only veritable source available.

Monopoly Power – Abuse of a Dominant Position

Just as there are compelling arguments for the protection of a trader's market through property- or liability-rule systems, there is also a compelling argument for the curbing of abuse of monopoly power resulting from either system. Whereas any monopoly leads to a situation in which market entry for new entrants is restricted, the abuse of monopoly power does so without heeding the justifiable reasons for restricting market entry for new incumbents, which can be found in the incentive- and reward-based paradigms. Instead the undertaking uses its monopoly right to seek excessive rents in an abusive manner through its position of dominance. Article 86 of the Treaty of Rome has the effect that in those circumstances in which an undertaking abuses its dominant position in the market, that undertaking may be forced not to exercise its monopoly power.[117] In *United Brands Co. and United Brands Continental BV* v. *EC Commission*[118] a dominant position was described as: "a position of economic strength enjoyed by an undertaking which enables it to prevent effective competition being maintained on the relevant market by giving it the power to behave to an appreciable extent independently of its competitors, customers and ultimately of its consumers". It is appropriate to point out at this point that intellectual property rights may contribute to a large extent to the dominant market position an undertaking can achieve and lead to a situation where: an undertaking's market share, either in itself or when combined with its know-how, access to raw materials, capital or other major advantage such as trademark ownership, enables it to determine the prices or to control the production or

---

[114] Note 109 above.
[115] R.A. Posner, "Antitrust in the New Economy" Tech Law Journal 14 September 2000 < http://www.techlawjournal.com/atr/20000914posner.asp> (visited 15–01–2001).
[116] Katz M. and Shapiro C., note 109 above, at 39 when discussing interfaces in software markets.
[117] For a description see Korah V., *An Introductory Guide to EC Competition Law and Practice* (5th edn. 1994, London, Sweet & Maxwell).
[118] (Case 27/76) [1973] ECR 215.

distribution of a significant part of the relevant goods. It is not necessary for the undertaking to have total dominance such as would deprive all other market participants of their commercial freedom, as long as it is strong enough in general terms to devise its own strategy as it wishes, even if there are differences in the extent to which it dominates individual sub-markets.

The mere existence and exercise of an intellectual property right as such does not constitute an abuse, since it is a legally recognized exclusive right to reproduction, that is a restriction on competition which is devised to create a market for an intangible in the first place. This point can be found in many abuse cases.[119] It is therefore important to distinguish between the existence of intellectual property rights conferred by national legislation of a Member State, which is not affected by the Treaty of Rome, the exercise of the "specific subject matter", which is a justifiable restriction on the freedom of trade but may come within the prohibitions of the Treaty,[120] and the use of market power, which may also come within the prohibitions of the Treaty.[121] The line set out by the European Court of Justice (ECJ) is that of "immune exercise", meaning that an exercise of a right corresponding with the core of an intellectual property right cannot in itself constitute an abuse.[122] "Specific circumstances" are needed in order to make the exercise abusive. These additional "specific circumstances" may be abuses of market power that are clearly separate from the existence/exercise of an intellectual property right,[123] or certain exercises of rights related to intellectual property rights, such as licensing and demanding royalties, which fall within the subject matter of the right. With this latter category the boundaries of what is part

---

[119] *Etablissements Consten SA & Grundig-Verkaufs-GmbH* v. *EC Commission* (Case 56/64) [1966] ECR 299, [1966] CMLR 418; *Deutsche Grammophon Gesellschaft GmbH* v. *Metro-SB-Großmärkte GmbH & Co. KG* (Case 78/70) [1971] ECR 487, [1971] 1 CMLR 631.

[120] Ibid. See also Article 30–36 of the Treaty of Rome. For a description see Green N., "Intellectual Property and the Abuse of a Dominant Position under European Union Law: Existence, Exercise and the Evaporation of Rights" [1993] *Brooklyn Journal of International Law* 141; Tritton G., *Intellectual Property in Europe* (1996, London, Sweet & Maxwell), ch. 7.

[121] *Radio Telefis Eireann and Independent Television Publications* v. *EC Commission* (Cases C241 and 242/91) [1995] ECR I-743.

[122] *Parke Davis & Co.* v. *Probel* (Case 24/67) [1968] ECR 55, [1968] CMLR 54.; *Hoffman-La Roche & Co. AG* v. *Centrafarm Vertriebsgesellschaft Pharmazeutischer Erzeugnisse GmbH* (Case 102/77) [1978] ECR 1139, [1978] CMLR 217; *Consorzio Italiano della Componentistica di Ricambio per Autoveilici (CIRCA) and Maxicar* v. *Régie Nationale des Usines Renault* (Case 53/87) [1988] ECR 6039, [1990] 4 CMLR 265; *Volvo AB* v. *Erik Veng (UK) Ltd* (Case 237/87) [1988] ECR 6211, [1989] 4 CMLR 122.

[123] One can think of practices such as tying, discriminatory policies, refusal to supply customers who might resell, refusals to honour guarantees, and operating secretly and unilaterally a policy of differential discounts. This was the case in *Hilti AG* v. *EC Commission* (Case C-53/92P) [1992] 4 CMLR 16, an appeal from Commission Decision 22 December 1987, *Eurofix-Bauco* v. *Hilti AG* (Cases 30/787 and 31/488) [1989] 4 CMLR 677, where 8 distinct abuses were put forward, all of which were exercises of market power, not of patent rights, although one of the abuses consisted of the frustration or delay of legitimately available licenses under Hilti's patent, by demanding exorbitantly high royalties.

of the existence, the exercise, and the specific subject matter is not evident.[124] It is not at all clear to what extent such exercises are subject to Art. 86 of the Treaty. As a consequence the question of whether a refusal to license on the basis of an intellectual property right constitutes an abuse is not self-evident, for it presupposes that the aims of Community competition law are included in the essential function of an intellectual property right.

In *Volvo AB v. Erik Veng (UK) Ltd*,[125] rights within the specific subject matter[126] were exercised in "special circumstances".[127] Because he was refused a license, the defendant imported spare parts (front wings) for the Volvo 200 series from Italy and Taiwan via Denmark into the United Kingdom, where these parts were protected under the Registered Designs Act 1949. In considering the exercise by Volvo of its intellectual property right, the ECJ stated that to oblige "the holder of a protected design to grant third parties a license to supply products incorporating the design, even in return for reasonable fees, would result in depriving the holder of the substance of its exclusive right", but that nevertheless Volvo's refusal amounted to an abuse of its dominant position. This was because Volvo itself was no longer producing the parts in question and thus created market conditions that obliged the consumer to buy a new car, where the old model was still in circulation. Whereas in *Volvo* the "specific circumstances" elevate the exercise of a design right to an abusive exercise, the distinction between existence and exercise is not so clear in the *Magill* case.[128] The case concerned the exercise of copyright in broadcast listings in the United Kingdom and Ireland, which the television broadcasters RTE, BBC and ITV provided on a daily basis free to newspapers. Weekly listings were provided by each broadcaster in separate television guides. When an Irish publisher, Magill, launched its comprehensive weekly guide, it was faced with an injunction by the Irish courts on the basis of the broadcasters" respective copyrights. When the ECJ finally upheld the decisions of

---

[124] As was pointed out by Miller C., "Magill: Time of Abandon the 'Specific Subject-matter' Concept" [1994] *EIPR* 415.

[125] Note 122 above.

[126] For the definition of specific subject mater of patents as the reward for inventive effort, see *Centrafarm BV and De Peijper v. Sterling Drug Inc.* (Case 15/74) [1974] ECR 1147, [1974] 2 CMLR 480; For trademarks see *Hoffman-La Roche & Co. AG v. Centrafarm Vertriebsgesellschaft Pharmazeutischer Erzeugnisse GmbH* note 94 above, defining as the essential function of a trademark the guarantee of the origin of the product. See *Ciné Vog Films v. CODITEL (Compagnie Générale pour la Diffusion de la Télévision)* (Case 62/79) [1980] ECR 881, [1981] 2 CMLR 362, where the right to demand a royalty for the public performance of a work was held to be an essential function of copyright, a position rejected by the AG in Magill. The difference between "specific subject-matter" and the "essential function" of intellectual property rights is not always clear, nor is the relevance for making it. See in this respect on Gulmann AG's Opinion in *Magill*, S. Haines, "Copyright Takes the Dominant Position" [1994] 9 *EIPR* 401, 402.

[127] See the definition in *Hoffman-La Roche & Co. AG v. Centrafarm Vertriebsgesellschaft Pharmazeutischer Erzeugnisse GmbH*, note 122 above.

[128] Note 121 above.

the Commission and the Court of First Instance, both holding that the broadcasters had indeed abused their dominant position in holding that the reliance on copyright amounted to the monopolization of a derivative market, much thought was given by commentators to the question as to whether the ECJ's judgment presents an overly broad incursion into the "immune exercise" of the broadcaster's copyright.[129] It is important to note at this point that the protection of moral rights and the ensuring of a reward for creative effort were judged to be within the "essential function" of copyright, but that the approach taken in *Coditel*,[130] where the right to demand a royalty for the public performance of a copyright work was held to be an "essential function", was not adopted.[131] This factor notwithstanding, *Magill* prompts the question of what the "special circumstances" were that made the otherwise legitimate exercise by the broadcasters of their copyright in their refusal to grant a license an exercise of a dominant position that is abusive. Commentators have looked at *Magill* on the basis of parallels with *Volvo*,[132] stating the refusal to license in that case amounted to an obstruction of the reproduction of products; *Magill* involved the monopolization of a derivative market. By the exercise of its copyright, Magill would not only retain its primary product; it would also prevent the production of comprehensive television guides based on raw data, and thus impair the genesis of a new market.[133] This is why *Magill* is not so much a refusal to license case, as a refusal to supply case,[134] comparable to *Commercial Solvents Corp. and Istituto Chemioterapico Italiano SpA* v. *EC Commission*.[135] This distinction is important to

---

[129] See Miller, note 124 above; Van Kerckhove M., "Magill: A Refusal to License or a Refusal to Supply?" [1995] 51 June/July *Copyright World* 26; Calvet H. and Desurmont T., "The Magill Ruling (1): An Isolated Decision?" 167 [1996] *RIDA* 2.

[130] *Ciné Vog Films* v. *CODITEL (Compagnie Générale pour la Diffusion de la Télévision)* note 130 above; and *CODITEL (Compagnie Générale pour la Diffusion de la Télévision)* v. *Ciné Vog Films (No 2)* (Case 262/81) [1982] ECR 3381, [1983] 1 CMLR 49.

[131] See on this point note 124 above, 418, where Miller attributes much of the controversy surrounding the Magill case to the incorrect application, as he sees it, of this distinction by the ECJ. It can be suggested that the ECJ's assessment of the abusive adverse effects on competition, which according to the Court lay in the monopolization of a market in weekly television guides by exercise of copyright in raw data, was in fact a covert attempt by the ECJ to interfere with the immune exercise of UK copyright, which happens to grant protection, where other Member States do not. See also the Broadcasting Act 1990, s. 176.

[132] Note 122 above; Haines, note 126 above.

[133] Treaty of Rome Article 86(b) defines it as dealing with abuse consisting in "limiting production, markets or technical development to the prejudice of consumers".

[134] Van Kerckhove, note 129 above.

[135] (Cases 6 7/72) [1974] ECR 224, [1974] 1 CMLR 309, a case in which the applicants produced the raw materials nitropropane and aminobutanol, needed for the production of ethambutanol, which was subsequently used in the production of a tuberculosis drug. The applicant refused to sell aminobutanol to a competitor because they wanted to enter the derivatives market themselves. This refusal to sell essential raw materials to a competitor was held to be an abuse of a dominant position.

the Court's finding of "exceptional circumstances",[136] which rendered the broadcasters" behavior abusive. The fact that raw data are susceptible to copyright in the United Kingdom, if incorporated in an original literary work,[137] stems from a nationally recognized right, the exercise of which is within the essential function of copyright. This could not be seen to be the basis for the ECJ's decision. The Court is indeed silent on the matter, but one cannot help thinking that at the back of the Court's mind were the provisions on decompilation in the Council Directive on the Legal Protection of Computer Programs,[138] and the compulsory licensing provisions that were part of the Database Directive as proposed at the time.[139] Exercise of a dominant position supported by intellectual property rights, resulting in the creation of extremely high barriers to entry for new market entrants, can thus be mediated by Article 86 of the Treaty of Rome. It is, however, important to realize that the modifying effects of the essential facilities doctrine can only be relied upon if a refusal to license or supply results in an exclusion of competition in a secondary market.

In *Oscar Bronner* v. *Mediaprint*[140] the ECJ accepted that a supply service consisting of a home-delivery scheme for daily newspaper media constitutes a separate market. On the question of whether a refusal by Mediaprint, owner of the only nationwide Austrian home-delivery scheme, to allow rival publisher Oscar Bronner access to the service against payment of reasonable remuneration constitutes an abuse of a dominant position, the Court answered negatively. This is because Mediaprint's refusal was not likely to eliminate all competition in the daily newspaper market, and would also not create technical, legal or economic obstacles, making it impossible to establish a competing home-delivery scheme. Access to the home-delivery scheme was, in this sense, not an essential facility. In view of the emerging U.S. practice of patenting business methods, however, it is easily conceivable that even delivery schemes may become essential facilities.[141]

Meanwhile, the *Magill* decision[142] is a clear example of a situation in which

---

[136] It is interesting to note that the ECJ speaks of "exceptional circumstances" and not of "special circumstances". This displays the extraordinary position *Magill* takes in the Art. 86 case law and supports the position taken by Calvet and Desurmont, note 129 above.

[137] Mallet-Poujol N., "The Information Market: Copyright Unjustly Tormented..." [1996] 167 *RIDA* 92, 138: "[T]he Magill case reveals plainly the impasses to which an incorrect application of copyright leads, through a lax assessment of the originality of programme listings and doubtless a poor understanding of the implementation of the reproduction right".

[138] Council Dir. 91/250/EEC of 14 May 1991, [1991] OJ L122/42.

[139] See Cook T., "The Final Version of the EC Database Directive – A Model for the Rest of the World?" [1996] 61 *Copyright World* 24, 27, on the removal of the provisions relating to compulsory licensing of commercially exploited databases that form the sole source of data from the final Dir. in the light of the *Magill* decision

[140] ECJ Case C-7/97 26 November 1998.

[141] See *Amazon.com* v. *Barnesandnoble.com* 73 F. Supp.2d 1228, 53 USPQ2d 1115 (W.D. Wash. Dec. 1, 1999) and *State Street Bank and Trust Co.* v. *Signature Financial Group, Inc.* 927 F.Supp.502, 38 USPQ2d 1530 (D. Mass. 1996).

[142] Vide ECJ Cases C-241and 242/91 *Radio Telifis Eireann and Independent Publications* v. *EC Commission* [1995] ECR I-743.

intellectual property rights were relied upon in order to control, in this case, a derivative market. As cross-licensing practices have not yet developed in the copyright and database domain to the same extent as in the patent area,[143] the *Magill* decision reinforces the argument for the application of antitrust law. In the past the EC Commission has contributed to the development of licensing practice in the patent area by the creation of block exemption regulations pertaining to certain types of potentially restrictive licensing agreements.[144] Alternatively it may be feasible to explore a system akin to the decompilation system contained in the EC Computer Programs Directive.[145] The idea behind decompilation without the authorization of the rightholder is that compatible and derivative products that interoperate with the original computer program can be created unhindered. The proviso is, however, that the rightholder has not made interface code available and that the information obtained by decompilation is not used to develop a computer program that is substantially similar in expression to the original. As such article 6 of the computer programs directive aims to balance the interests of rightholders with that of competitors and the interest of society. The making available of essential facilities and an underlying licensing practice demonstrate that the scope and nature of intellectual property rights and their exercise are not necessarily unconditional. Similarly this balance of interests should be made visible in database legislation, so that the creation of derivative non-competing database works is stimulated. This means that there is a need for clarification of the interrelationship between intellectual property and competition law. Now that the Commission has adopted a White Paper[146] for the reform of the system for enforcement of EU competition rules, there may also be an opportunity to clarify and change the EC Database Directive.[147] It is at this point where policy makers in

---

[143] Dam K.W., "Intellectual Property and the Academic Enterprise", *John M. Olin Law & Economics Working Paper* No. 68 (2d Series) (1998, The Law School, The University of Chicago).

[144] Council Regulation No. 17/62 of 6 February 1962 – First Regulation implementing Articles 85 and 86 of the Treaty; Commission Regulation (EEC) No. 418/85 of 19 December 1984 on the application of Article 85(3) of the Treaty to categories of research and development agreements; Commission Regulation (EEC) No. 4087/88 of 30 November 1988 on the application of Article 85(3) of the Treaty to categories of franchise agreements; Commission Regulation (EC) No. 240/96 of 31 January 1996 on the application of Article 85(3) of the Treaty on certain categories of technology transfer agreements.

[145] Council Directive of 14 May 1991 on the legal protection of computer programs, OJ L 122, p. 42, Article 6.

[146] White paper on modernisation of the rules implementing articles 85 and 86 [*now 81 and 82*] of the EC Treaty – *Commission programme No. 99/027 – approved on 28.04.1999*. See also the Proposal for a Council Regulation on the implementation of the rules on competition laid down in Articles 81 and 82 of the Treaty – *COM(2000) 582 – 27.09.2000*.

[147] On re-assessment of the EC Database Directive see note 87 above. See also *NDC Health/IMS Health*, Case COMPD/338.044 (July 3, 2001), [2002] 4 CMLR 111 and *IMS Health v. Commission*, Cases T-180/01 R (August 10, 2001), [2002] 4 CMLR 46 and T-184/01 RII (October 26, 2001), [2002] 4 CMLR 58, involving a compulsory license on a database 'brick' structure, because it was held to have become a *de facto* standard and therefore an 'essential facility'.

the U.S. should try to explore the possibilities of negotiating the proper reciprocal arrangement with the EU that incorporates the adoption of robust statutory safeguards against abusive control over single source information, as well as the appropriate regime to stimulate cross-licensing for the benefit of creating new works. It is also an outcome that is crucial to any further development in the area of database protection, either for countries considering database protection, or for further initiatives at WIPO.

In Search of a Horizontal Right to Information – Non-competitors

Whereas anti-trust policy may solve problems where direct competition, derivative marketers, or second-generation creators are concerned, not all can rely on the essential facilities doctrine. Arguably one could stretch market definitions so that academic researchers, end-users and consumers are comprised in the equation. This may even work when certain types of data are concerned, such as government information.[148] However, it is submitted that such information should fall under a limitation or exclusion regime. The Collection of Information Antipiracy Act contains such a provision;[149] the EC Database Directive does not.[150]

The use of market arguments to support the boundaries of limitations and exceptions to intellectual property rights can, however, not be sacrosanct. The argument can therefore be made that the ever-strengthened position of the rightholder ought to be checked and balanced by criteria that go beyond an economic calculus. There is a market for ideas and data, but that the sole application of market theory to safeguard access has its shortcomings.[151]

A recent Panel Discussion on Intellectual Property and Human Rights[152]

---

[148] Note 8 above on the EC *Green Paper on Public Sector Information in the Information Society*.
[149] Note 5 above.
[150] Note 6 and 7 above. At the implementation stage in the Member States access to public sector information has become a concern. Member States have begun to examine the effects of new technologies on the public service, especially on access to and exploitation of public sector information.
[151] See Barendt E., "The First Amendment and the Media", in Loveland I. (ed.), *Importing the First Amendment – Freedom of Speech and Expression in Britain, Europe and the USA* (1998, Oxford, Hart Publishing), pp.29–50, at 43 *et seq.*, arguing at 47, that the alternative lies in the Madisonian model, treating the public not as consumers of information, but as "citizens, entitled to information and a vigorous exchange of ideas and opinion". See also Sunstein, C., "The First Amendment in Cyberspace" (1995) *Yale LJ* 1757, at 1759–65.
[152] A Panel Discussion in commemoration of the 50th Anniversary of the Universal Declaration of Human Rights on Intellectual Property and Human Rights organized by the World Intellectual Property Organization (WIPO) in collaboration with the Office of the United Nations High Commissioner for Human Rights, Geneva, November 9, 1998.

suggests that WIPO is aware of the relationship between intellectual property and human rights. The joint panel discussion organized by WIPO and the Office of the United Nations High Commissioner for Human Rights commemorated the 50th anniversary of the Universal Declaration of Human Rights, and addressed issues such as biodiversity, the protection of traditional knowledge and innovation, the right to culture, health, non-discrimination, and scientific freedom.

During the panel discussions it was emphasised[153] that the Universal Declaration of Human Rights International Covenant on Economic, Social and Cultural Rights (ICESCR) augments intellectual property law. Articles 27(1) of the Declaration, and 15(1)(b) of the ICESCR guarantee the right to participation in cultural and scientific life. It not only protects the creator to enjoy the fruits of his labor, but also requires the Member States to "facilitate and promote scientific progress and its applications and to do so in a manner that will broadly benefit members of society on an individual as well as a collective level".[154] The considerations of the ICESCR go well beyond a simple economic calculus. The approach taken with regard to cultural and scientific life is therefore a multifaceted one, describing the right both in terms as access to and engagement in scientific discourse, and the protection of the spiritual and earthly benefits of the creator. Intellectual property law in its narrow sense primarily addresses the rights of the individual creator.

Similarly article 10 of the European Convention on Human Rights lays down the right to freedom of speech as a multifaceted right that not only protects the positive right to expression, but also the right to receive information. Thus far the right to information, its free flow, and academic freedom has had limited application in disputes over the exploitation of intellectual property rights in Europe.[155] It has been an established case law of the European Court of Human Rights that Member States have a wide margin of appreciation in imposing restrictions on the rights contained in article 10 ECHR in commercial matters. The Court has shown itself particularly sensitive to the enforcement of intellectual property and unfair competition laws.[156]

---

[153] See most notably the document prepared by Dr. A. Chapman – as yet unpublished.

[154] Ibid. WIPO-UNHCR/IP/PNL/98/5 Abstract. For the purpose of this paper I will not discuss further issues which have closer links to the Universal Declaration of Human Rights, the draft UN Declaration on the Rights of Indigenous Peoples, the UNESCO Declaration on the Human Genome and Human Rights, the International Covenant on Economic, Social and Cultural Rights, or the UN Convention of Biological Diversity. For these issues I refer to the WIPO-UNHCHR publication.

[155] In the U.S. the situation is somewhat different in that courts are willing to intervene on first amendment grounds much more willingly. *Vide* Foerstel H.N., *Free Expression and Censorship in America – An Encyclopedia* (1997, Westport/London, Greenwood Press); and Loveland I. (ed.), *Importing the First Amendment – Freedom of Speech and Expression in Britain, Europe and the USA* (1998, Oxford, Hart Publishing).

[156] *Markt Intern Verlag GmbH and Klaus Beerman* v. *Germany*, case 3/1988/147/201 (20 November 1989); *Jacubowski* v. *Germany*, case 7/1993/402/480 (20 June 1994).

The case of *Hertel* v. *Switzerland*[157] may change this position, as this is the first case in which the ECHR feels competent to deal with issues of competition law regarding free speech. The European Court of Human Rights struck out the application of the Swiss Unfair Competition Act[158] following publication of a scientific article stating that consumption of food prepared in microwave ovens was dangerous to human health. It held that the statements involved were not purely commercial, but formed part of a larger debate taking place in society, reducing the margin of appreciation of the member state. The Court therefore felt free to examine whether the measures restricting the freedom of speech were proportionate to the aims pursued by the Unfair Competition Act. The *Hertel* decision may signal the involvement of the norms of the ECHR in unfair competition and intellectual property issues by ensuring academic freedom, freedom of speech, and freedom of access in the information society. As the judgments of the European Court of Human Rights are directed to the Member States to the Convention, the creation of a direct horizontal right to information derived from jurisprudence may take a long time to develop. The fact that the European Court of Human Rights saw itself fit to decide upon "commercial matters, in an area as complex and fluctuating as that of unfair competition'[159] is, however, encouraging for the development of unfair competition law and intellectual property law. The Hertel decision is a positive statement that fundamental rights and freedoms affect commerce. One can envisage, therefore, freedom of speech playing a more prominent role in the balancing of interest. This may be the case in, for example, disparagement of trademarks and imagery, trade libel, and defamation cases,[160] but also in cases in which the free flow of information is at stake. For the citizens of Europe this means that the right of access to information is not only enforceable against government institutions and the databases generated by or on behalf of governments, but may also be claimed in respect of databases compiled using public sector, or even single source information.[161] This does not mean that information must always be made available for free, but it will provide a means to assess the equitability of the remuneration that is demanded in return for legitimate user rights to a database.

---

[157] European Court of Human Rights, Strasbourg, 25 August 1998, (59/1997/843/1049).
[158] Federal Unfair Competition Act of 19 December 1986.
[159] *Hertel*, note 9 above and *Markt Intern Verlag*, note 156 above.
[160] Leigh L., "Of Free Speech and Individual Reputation: *New York Times* v. *Sullivan* in Canada and Australia", in Loveland I. (ed.), *Importing the First Amendment – Freedom of Speech and Expression in Britain, Europe and the USA* (1998, Oxford, Hart Publishing), pp. 51–68.
[161] In this respect one can think of information of fact, such as closing values of indexes generated at the stock exchange. Commonly this information is compiled and disseminated by contractors of the stock exchange authorities.

Conclusion

The guarantee for a free flow of information is therefore no longer an issue that is limited by the discussion on the scope of IP rights and the traditional exceptions thereto. Whether one uses a proprietary model or a misappropriation model to protect database producers does, however, influence the scope of protection and the way in which limitation and exceptions may be set to fit the circumstances. Moreover, the misappropriation model places database protection in the realm of competition law. This leaves more scope for the assessment of market distortions by anti-trust authorities where the protection of intellectual and industrial creativity is a factor contributing to the abusive behavior by a rightholder. There is clear scope for courts and policy makers to contribute to the development of an equitable licensing practice in the copyright and database market for the benefit of derivative marketers and second generation creators that are dependent on information.

With the Hertel decision the European Court of Human Rights has claimed a role for itself in commercial matters. In the future the Court may have a more fundamental role to play in the balancing of interests of individuals and society as a whole in the area of intellectual property. The European Convention itself leaves scope to develop case law and doctrine not only in the area of freedom of expression, but also when it comes to the free flow of information and the participation in academic life. Furthermore the fundamental decision of the European Court of Human Rights should prompt policy makers to take action to ensure the free flow of information.

VI. COLLABORATIVE PRODUCTION AND SCIENTIFIC RESEARCH

Commodifying Collaborative Research

*Rochelle Cooper Dreyfuss**

The commodification controversy is posited as a conflict between the users and creators of information products over modifying intellectual property law in the face of technological change. Commodification is said to help creators because it establishes a market for their work – a market that generates monetary incentives to innovate, measures consumer demand for new works, and facilitates information exchange. Since modern technologies of reproduction and dissemination make the public-goods character of information products more salient, it is argued that a new law is needed in order to maintain the level of exclusivity creators previously enjoyed.[1] At the same time, however, commodification is thought to harm users because it makes it more difficult for them to acquire knowledge. Enhancing legal and technological means for privatization is therefore questioned as going beyond the mere maintenance of exclusivity, instead allowing rights holders to charge for works that formerly fell into the public domain, price discriminate, and impose all sorts of new restrictions on use.[2]

Lost in this debate is the effect of technology on the ways that information and cultural goods are actually produced, particularly on the extent to which individual creativity has been replaced by collaborative effort. In fact, the artist starving in a garret, the scientist madly experimenting in the garage, and the

---

* I would like to acknowledge research assistance from the Filomen D'Agostino and Max E. Greenberg Research Fund and to thank Matthew Gabin, NYU Law School Class of 2002, for his research assistance.
[1] William W. Fisher III, Property and Contract on the Internet, 73 Chi.-Kent L. Rev. 1203 (1998); Robert P. Merges, Contracting into Liability Rules: Intellectual Property Rights and Collective Rights Organizations, 84 Calif. L. Rev. 1293 (1996).; Raymond T. Nimmer, Images and Contract Law – what Law Applies to Transactions in Information 36 Hous. L. Rev. 1 (1999); U.C.C. Article 2B Preamble (Annual Meeting Draft, July 24–31, 1998)
[2] See, e.g., Niva Elkin-Koren, Copyrights in Cyberspace – Rights Without Laws?, 73 Chi.-Kent L. Rev. 1155 (1998); Niva Elkin-Koren, Copyright Policy and the Limits of Freedom of Contract, 12 Berk. Tech. L.J. 93 (1997); Julie E. Cohen, Copyright and the Jurisprudence of Self-Help, 13 Berk. Tech. L.J. 1089 (1998); Jessica Litman, The Tales that Article 2B Tells, 13 Berk. Tech. L.J. 931 (1998).

N. Elkin-Koren and N.W. Netanel (eds.), The Commodification of Information, 397–413.
© 2002 Rochelle Cooper Dreyfuss. Printed in Great Britain.

reclusive professor burning midnight oil are all rapidly becoming myths.[3] In a world of increasing technical complexity and intensifying specialization, interdisciplinary investigation has become crucial to progress. With the globalization of the marketplace comes a need for multicultural input into product development. As private financing for technological start-ups increases (and public funding of basic research withers), economic factors prompt new alignments within the innovation industries. At the same time, digitization and the Internet facilitate interchange and present fresh artistic and scholarly opportunities. This new world is characterized by such phenomena as chain art,[4] interactive websites,[5] multi-authored scientific articles,[6] as well as corporate joint ventures and university distance learning initiatives.[7] As production methods have become increasingly complex, claims for creative recognition have also blossomed. By drawing attention to their contributions, graduate students, dramaturgs, statisticians, reviewers, editors, and the like have transformed social understanding of information production. Works that might once have been seen as individually created must now be viewed as the product of collaboration.[8]

---

[3] See, e.g., Elisabeth Crawford, Nobel: Always Winners, Never Losers, 282 Science 1256, 1257 (Nov. 13, 1998) (noting that "the idea of the lone discoverer lingers on as a myth").

[4] See Margaret Chon, Symposium: Innovation and the Information Environment – New Wine Bursting from Old Bottles: Collaborative Internet Art, Joint Works, and Entrepreneurship, 75 Or. L. Rev. 257, 266–272 (1996); Michiko Kakutani, Culture Zone; Never-Ending Saga, N.Y. Times, Sept. 28, 1997, at § 6, p. 40, col. 2. (describing chain novels). Chain art sites allow viewers to load down art work, revise it, and then post their revisions where others can do the same.

[5] See, e.g., <www.detritus.net> (online culture gallery) Cf. Los Angeles Times v. Free Republic, Case No. CV 98-7840 (C.D. Ca. Nov. 9, 1999), <http://www.techlawjournal.com/courts/freerep/19991108.htm> (holding that posting news articles for viewer comment is not fair use of the articles).

[6] See, e.g., Walter W. Powell, Inter-Organizational Collaboration in the Biotechnology Industry, 151 (No. 1) J. Instit'l and Theoretical Ec. 197, 205 (1996)(citing an article coauthored by 45 scientists); Canon Computer Systems, Inc. v. Nu-Kote Int'l, Inc., 134 F.3d 1085 (1998)(patent is not invalid on the ground that it names 16 inventors).

[7] See, e.g., Neil Hickey, Ten Mistakes That Led to the Great CNN/Time Fiasco, Colum. J. Rev. Sept./Oct. 1998 at 26 (describing NewStand, a coproduction of CNN and Time Magazine); Funding of Higher Education: International Perspectives (Philip G. Altbach and D. Bruce Johnstone eds. 1993); The British Academy, The Conference of Medical Royal Colleges, The Royal Academy of Engineering, National Academies Policy Advisory Group, Intellectual Property & the Academic Community 6–7; 33–35 (1995) (hereinafteer NAPAG Report); Paul Cox, Higher Technology Cyberdegrees: Who Needs a College Campus? Just Log in and Start Studying, Wall Street Journal, Nov. 17, 1997, at R26. See also Karen W. Arenson, Columbia University Explores How to Profit From Educational Offerings on the Internet, N.Y. Times, Ap. 3, 1999, at B3.

[8] See, e.g., Jesse McKinley, On Stage and Off: Suit! Anger! Agreement!, N.Y. Times, March 26, 1999, at § E, Pt. 1, p. 2, col. 3 (Joe Mantello's claim to rights in his staging of Love! Valour! Compassion!); Jesse McKinley, Family of "Rent" Creator Settles Suit Over Authorship, N.Y. Times, Sept. 10, 1998, at p. B3, col. 5 (dramaturg Lynn Thomson's claim to rights of authorship in the play Rent); Eliot Marshall, Fight Over Data Disrupts Michigan State Project, 251 Science 23 (Jan. 4, 1991) (describing delays in the Sudan Project, an international parasitology study funded by the National Institutes of Health caused by the sequestration of data by a graduate

This essay looks at the special challenges that commodification presents to participants in collaborative projects and examines the disjuncture between current U.S. intellectual property law and the issues of importance to collaborators. It ends with suggestions on the ways in which the law might be improved.

The Problems of Collaborative Production

As described above, the challenge of adapting intellectual property law to modern technologies has tended to center on the problem of balancing the proprietary interests of innovators against the access needs of users. In the general formulation of the problem, innovators are rights holders; would-be users are strangers to the creative process; and access issues are basically questions about authorization, price, and the effective functioning of information markets. A typical question is whether there is correspondence between the social value of a particular use and the potential user's willingness to pay the innovator's price. Under this formulation, the public-regarding provisions of intellectual property law are, essentially, devices fashioned to deal with the times when the answer to such questions is no. (Indeed, the commodification controversy is, basically, a debate over when the answer is no and whether the positive-law response is sufficient.)[9]

Resolutions of these standard commodification debates are not, however, always apposite to problems arising in the course of collaborative production. The reason is that the framework for disputes arising among collaborators can be quite different from the one outlined above. Admittedly, it can be described in the same words: someone owns the right to utilize the work, and an access problem arises – perhaps the right holder denies access or sets a price the would-be user cannot pay. But despite the formal similarity, there is a key feature that is different: in collaborative disputes, the party seeking access is not a stranger to the work, but rather one or more of the parties who participated in its development; a party who expended effort, but was not rewarded with an intellectual property interest in the work, either by reason of contract or through operation of law.[10] Because of that

---

cont.
   student who claimed to have received inadequate credit); Floyd E. Bloom, The Importance of Reviewers, 283 Science 789 (1999) (noting peer reviewers' contributions). See generally, Sandip H. Patel, Note, Graduate Students' Ownership and Attribution Rights in Intellectual Property, 71 Ind. L.J. 481, 507–509 (1996).
[9] See, e.g., Wendy Gordon, Fair Use as Market Failure: A Structural and Economic Analysis of the Betamax Case and its Predecessors, 82 Colum. L. Rev. 1600 (1982).
[10] Examples of owner-stripping devices include the work for hire doctrine, see pages 8–10, infra, and policies within the patent industries, see page 13, infra.

distinction, the claims of collaborators have a different flavor from those asserted in standard disputes; in many instances, their claims are also different in kind. The difference in flavor is best described in Prof. Margaret Jane Radin's terminology: for participants in the creative process there can be a personhood dimension to intellectual property that is absent in the relationship between that same property and a stranger.[11] Radin gives, as an example of the impact of personhood, the distinction between a tenant's interest in an apartment and that of its landlord.[12] The tenant, she argues, has moral claims involving values such as liberty, privacy, dignity, and freedom of association that the landlord cannot plausibly assert. The same is true here. A stranger denied access to a work can search for alternative sources for the same information or move on to other projects. But a creator is usually intimately tied to her work; her need to follow it up (with new editions, interpretations, experiments) is quite different from that of a stranger. If, for example, she wrote a novel, she may have unfinished business for her characters;[13] if a scientist, she may have additional insights that make revisiting and expanding upon earlier work an especially felicitous use of her energies. Even from a purely economic perspective, there is an important difference between strangers to a work and its creators. In the case of a creator, both human and social capital have already been expended; these sunk costs will be lost if the project must be changed and new skills and associations acquired. Just as Radin is right that the rules surrounding real property ownership do not fully take into account the tenant's moral claims, so too the debate over balancing producer and user interests in intellectual property rights will not always fully capture the intimate connection between creators and their own works.

The differences in kind are equally significant. The work (indeed, the very fact of collaboration[14]) may represent an important professional accomplishment. Accordingly, the creator will want to have his name associated with the work and will want to refer to it on his résumé and in job grant applications. The work's importance to career interests will also lead the creator to be concerned about the continued reputation of the work, giving rise to a desire to participate in decisions about placement, licensing, and other continuing usages. In trying to redeploy the skills developed in the course of producing the work, the creator may also need continuing use of unique tangible products generated by the collaboration – tangibles such as reagents, slides, cell lines, and genetically altered laboratory

---

[11] Margaret Jane Radin, Property and Personhood, 34 Stan. L. Rev. 957 (1982).
[12] Id. at 992–96.
[13] Cf. Warner Bros. Pictures v. Columbia Broadcasting System, Inc., 216 F.2d 945 (9th Cir.1954) (putting characters in public domain, where they could be reutilized by their creator).
[14] See Walter W. Powell, Kenneth W. Koput, and Laurel Smith-Doerr, Interorganizational Collaboration and the Locus of Innovation: Networks of Learning in Biotechnology, 41 Admin. Science Q. 116 (1996).

animals that are ordinarily protected by legal regimes outside intellectual property.[15]

And although these interests are described as those of collaborators, society is not indifferent to them. Later editions and improvements may be better (or cheaper) because of the initial creator's continued association with the project. When the human capital at stake has been acquired at public expense, society will have an interest in how the creator's skills are next utilized. The public resources devoted to creating the work similarly favor assuring that it is sensitively exploited and put to its best usage. Furthermore, attribution and compensation tend to go hand in hand with responsibility and accountability – a creator without reputational, financial, or other interest in a work may not be as careful about its accuracy as one who enjoys continued association with it.[16] The problems of collaboration have, in short, consequences for the creative process, for maximum utilization of social resources, as well as for the quality of the work that ultimately reaches public hands.

There is, of course, another major difference between disputes involving strangers and those involving collaborators: collaborators know one another. Following Coase and modern institutional theorists, the intuition may be that no special laws are needed to protect creative interests in the collaborative enterprise because (unlike strangers) collaborators can structure their relationships for themselves. Further, because they can tailor their agreement to their particular needs, it can be argued that it is superior policy to allow them (indeed, encourage them) to do so.[17] This thinking is, in fact, consonant with that of the scientific community (and, presumably, other professions), where the aspiration has been to

---

[15] See, e.g.,. Thomson v. Larson, 147 F.3d 195 (2d Cir. 1998) (right to attribution and royalties); Richard A. Kerr, Contacts with the West Bring Cultural Revolution; Russian and Western Earth Scientists Collaborate, 264 Science 1277 (May 27, 1994) (right to make publication decisions); Marcia Baringa, UCSF Case Raises Questions About Grant Idea Ownership, 277 Science 1430 (Sept. 5, 1997) (right to use the work in grant application); Weismann v. Friedman, 868 F.2d 1313 (2d Cir. 1989) (right to follow on); Randy Kennedy, Doctor's Effort to Move Practice Leaves Patients in a Tug of War, N.Y. Times, April 8, 1999, at A1, p.1, col.1 (right to continued access to patients in experimental study).

[16] See, e.g., Felicity Barringer, Career of a CNN Star Hangs in the Balance Over a Repudiated Report, New York Times, July 8, 1998, at p. A17, col. 1 (describing gross inaccuracies in joint production of CNN and Time Magazine; quoting Peter Arnett, the Pulitzer Prize winning reporter, as saying of his role, "They gave me the list. I asked these questions. The producers took the tape and I was gone. I was the face.").

[17] See, e.g., Julie E. Cohen, Lochner in Cyberspace: The New Economic Orthodoxy of "Rights Management," 97 Mich. L. Rev. 462, 475–480 (1998) (reviewing the literature); Carol M. Rose, The Several Futures of Property: Of Cyberspace and Folk Tales, Emission Trades and Ecosystems, 83 Minn. L. Rev. 129 (1998) (providing, among other things, an excellent review of the literature); Mark A. Lemley, Romantic Authorship and the Rhetoric of Property, 75 Texas L. Rev. 873, 896–98 (1997); Frank H. Easterbrook, Intellectual Property Is Still Property, 13 Harv. J.L. & Pub. Poly. 108 (1990); Edmund W. Kitch, The Nature and Function of the Patent System, 20 J.L. & Econ. 265 (1977); R.H. Coase, The Problem of Social Cost, 3 J.L. & Econ. 1 (1960). Cf. Elinor Ostrom, Governing the Commons 1 (1990) (on communal regimes)

iron out difficulties among collaborators through cultural change and education,[18] or through the intermediation of the institutions with which collaborators deal, such as universities, journals,[19] and funders.[20] Thus, there is a sense in which it may be thought that all that is necessary from the standpoint of law is that rights be clearly defined and that parties enjoy transactional freedom to reach satisfactory allocations *inter se*.[21]

Nonetheless, as many of the marginal notes attest, collaborative problems abound, and it is becoming clear that leaving matters to voluntary agreements, private institutions, and to the operation of traditional intellectual property law is not working. There are several reasons why actual experience differs so sharply from what institutional theory predicts. For one, much of the theoretical work on private arrangements involves tangible resources, like land and water.[22] In situations involving tangibles, the products at issue are relatively easy to evaluate, making such matters as sharing arrangements, royalty agreements, and milestone payments straightforward to negotiate. In contrast, the current crop of technology-driven collaborations is operating at the proverbial cutting edge. As Rebecca Eisenberg has demonstrated, it is unlikely that parties will easily agree on valuation when the potential uses for the work under development are largely unknown.[23] These valuation problems are, of course, even worse when the parties cannot even predict what output their collaboration will yield.[24]

There is also the question of transaction costs. Even when theorists examine intangibles, they tend to do so in the context of repeat players, who can use prior experience to anticipate, and therefore deal with, the sorts of problems that arise in

---

[18] Jon Cohen and Gary Taubes, The Culture of Credit, 268 Science 1706 (June 23, 1995); Bruce Alberts and Kenneth Shine, Scientists and the Integrity of Research, 266 Science 1660 (Dec. 9, 1994).

[19] See, e.g., Steven Bachrach, et al., Who Should Own Scientific Papers?, 281 Science 1459 (Sept. 1, 1998); Jon Cohen, Share and Share Alike Isn't Always the Rule in Science, 269 Science 1715 (June 23, 1995); Paul M. Rowe, Encouraging Good Scientific Conduct, 343 The Lancet 1627 (June 25, 1994).

[20] See, e.g., Jocelyn Kaiser, HHS Is Still Looking for A Definition [of Scientific Misconduct], 272 Science 1735b (June 21, 1996); Barbara Mishkin, Urgently Needed: Policies on Access to Data by Erstwhile Collaborators, 270 Science 927 (Nov. 10, 1995).

[21] See Raymond T. Nimmer, Images and Contract Law – What Law Applies to Transactions in Information 36 Hous. L. Rev. 1 (1999); U.C.C. Article 2B Preamble (Annual Meeting Draft, July 24–31, 1998).

[22] See e.g., Robert C. Ellickson, of Coase and Cattle: Dispute Resolution Among Neighbors in Shasta County, 38 Stan. L. Rev. 623 (1986); Ostrom, supra note 17.

[23] Rebecca Eisenberg, Bargaining Over the Transfer of Proprietary Research Tools: Is This Market Failing or Emerging?, in Expanding the Bounds of Intellectual Property: Innovation Policy for the Knowledge Society (Rochelle Cooper Dreyfuss, Diane Zimmerman, Harry First eds. (forthcoming, Oxford University Press)(hereinafter Innovation Policy).

[24] Cf. F.M. Scherer, The Innovation Lottery, in Innovation Policy, supra note 23 (arguing that potential payments must be very high when there is high dispersion in the potential value of the output).

the course of their ventures.[25] But collaborations in the innovation industry are often one-off deals. In biotechnology development, for example, work is taken out-of-house and done through temporary alliances precisely because the particular set of expertise required for one project will not be needed again.[26] In these situations, there are no standard contracts to rely on, nor will it make economic sense to forecast what could happen and negotiate over every contingency. Indeed, in some types of creative collaboration, the parties are more averse to lawyers than to risk; it is highly unlikely that they would even appreciate the advantages of advance negotiations.

Culture is another important factor. Institutional arrangements over the use of land or water are, in a sense, easy because they always involve people who live in proximity. The participants either start with the same values or transmit them in the course of their association. Collaborative creativity in international and interdisciplinary contexts can, by contrast, involve players who lack a common language, tradition, and background rules, and thus be unaware of each other's expectations.[27] In those circumstances, there is very little chance that they will succeed in negotiating over all contingencies – they may not even know what matters require their attention. And if the collaboration itself occurs long-distance (for example, via the Internet), there is not much likelihood that values will coalesce – or that problems will be identified and solved – during the term of the association.

There are two other problems with relying on the Coasian intuition. One is that it assumes that collaboration is volitional. In many collaborations, that is not the case for all participants. Graduate students are the consummate example. They require the approbation of their teachers in order to get good grades, earn their degrees, and receive the all-important letters of recommendation. As a result, they do not enjoy enough bargaining power to assure that their interests – and society's investment in their training – will be adequately protected when they become a part of a large-scale university venture. And although graduate students probably view professors as better positioned, similar comments can be made about them, particularly those who are not tenured, in departments where the dean has a great deal of unbounded discretion, or whose salaries are dependent on the funding provided by other participants in the alliance.

Second, society is not necessarily best off when a Coasian bargain is made.

---

[25] See, e.g., Victor P. Goldberg, Bloomer Girl Revisited or How to Frame an Unmade Picture, 1998 Wis. L. Rev. 1051; Victor P. Goldberg, The Net Profits Puzzle, 97 Colum. L. Rev. 524 (1997).
[26] See Powell, supra note 6.
[27] See, e.g., Kerr, supra note 15 (describing a controversy between American and Russian scientist on etiquette for handling the discredited work of senior colleagues). An example of differing expectations familiar to readers is this one: whose name goes first on a publication: the senior author, the person who did most of the work, or the one whose last name begins with the letter earliest in the alphabet?

Collaborators can, after all, agree to relinquish follow on rights, forebear from accepting employment by competitors of former collaborators, or keep information secret.[28] Such agreements can have significant social impact: they reduce competition in the innovation industries and slow information flows. They misuse expensive resources and reduce employment mobility. These agreements may dissipate more than just human capital; they can also waste social capital by foreclosing those with specific experience in collaborating from participating in new projects.

The Disjuncture of Current U.S. Law

These observations argue for an intellectual property law that strikes a balance not only between rights holders and strangers, but also between rights holders and creators. Such law would alert potential collaborators to issues requiring negotiation, give them a starting point at which to begin discussion, a sense of what a fair allocation might be, and set default rules for omitted issues. Most importantly, these rules would protect participants with lesser bargaining power, safeguard the public's interest in quality and efficient use of social resources, and protect the public from those collaborations that turn out to be overly cozy. Unfortunately, current intellectual property law does not adequately serve these functions.

On the copyright side, one obvious problem is that the Copyright Act has little to say on issues of accountability, attribution, and access to unique tangibles.[29] But the larger problem is conceptual. The Act structures rights over collaborative projects in two ways: either the work is viewed as produced by an "orchestrator," who chooses individuals to work for hire on particular aspects of the orchestrator's vision, or it is viewed as the product of a small group of individuals, working jointly. Neither paradigm maps well on the collaborative efforts of today.

The orchestrator paradigm is codified in the work for hire doctrine.[30] Under the

---

[28] See, e.g., Elizabeth K. Wilson, Quantum Chemistry Software Uproar, Chem. & Eng. News, July 12, 1999, at 27 (describing an agreement foreclosing the students of former collaborators from using software crucial to quantum chemistry research).

[29] There are no provisions on accountability. Tangible materials are mentioned in a few sections of the Copyright Act, 17 U.S.C. §§ 101–1101. Section 407 requires deposit of works published in the United States, unless the work is exempted by the Register. Section 202 provides that ownership of any of the exclusive rights of copyright are "distinct from ownership of any material object in which the work is embodied." Section 106A creates a right to protect the integrity of physical objects, but this right applies only to works of visual art, which are defined as paintings, drawings, prints, or sculptures and which exist in a single copy or in a limited edition of 200 copies or fewer, 17 U.S.C. § 101.

[30] 17 U.S.C. § 201.

Act, work can be classified as for hire if it is prepared in the scope of employment[31] or, for certain works, if the parties so agree in a signed writing.[32] Once a work is for hire under either classification, the employer is the author and owns the copyright; the employee's relationship to the work is suppressed. Certain features of copyright law – including the provisions that deal with reputational interests in the work, such as rights of integrity and attribution – no longer apply.[33] The employee's rights are limited to those of the employment or commissioning contract.[34] Thus, all exploitation decisions are put in the hands of a single entity – the employer. All rights to build upon the work are likewise the employer's alone.

At first blush, this doctrine may appear to offer a good fit with collaborative interests. Thus, the doctrine's authorship principle protects the public by putting someone (the employer) on "the hook" for the accuracy of the final product. The formalities involved in obtaining a contract (for the first type of work for hire) or a written instrument (for the second type) give collaborators a certain amount of leverage to protect their interest. If nothing else, they prompt a kind of "Coasian moment" in which expectations can be thrashed out, and rights to credit, royalties, or future creative opportunities can be exchanged for other forms of compensation. In fact, it is arguably significant that the film industry was one of the primary forces shaping the work for hire doctrine:[35] If Twentieth Century Fox thought these rules would facilitate the artistic process of making films, one might expect the creative enterprises of the 21st century to be equally enthusiastic about them.

Nonetheless, the problems with the work for hire doctrine are manifold. The notion of an orchestrator does not square with what actually goes on in many collaborations. To continue with the example of graduate students and professors: although universities increasingly seek to enrich their coffers by claiming that faculty and student work is for hire,[36] it is hard to see in the academic relationship any of the hallmarks of employment or agency required for first-category work for hire. Faculty work product cannot realistically be said to be produced in the course of employment because tenured faculty are not required to engage in scholarly activities beyond teaching; they devise their scholarly agenda on their own, and pursue it in their own time, and at places of their own choosing.[37] Normatively, interference by a university in these kinds of decisions might well be

---

[31] 17 U.S.C. § 101(1) (first definition of "work for hire"); Community for Creative Non-Violence v. Reid, 490 U.S. 730 (1989).
[32] 17 U.S.C. § 101(2)(second definition of "work for hire").
[33] 17 U.S.C. §§ 106A, 203, 304(c).
[34] 17 U.S.C. § 201.
[35] See Jessica D. Litman, Copyright, Compromise, and Legislative History, 72 Cornell L.Rev. 857, 888–93 (1987). See also Register of Copyrights, 88th Cong., 1st Sess., Copyright Law Revision Part 2: Discussion and Comments on Report on the General Revision of the U.S. Copyright Law 153 (Comm. Print 1963).
[36] See, e.g., Massachusetts Institute of Technology, Guide to the Ownership, Distribution and Commercial Development of M.I.T. Technology, at § 2 (last modified June 1999) <http://web.mit.edu/afs/athena.mit.edu/org/t/tlo/www/guide.toc.html>.

considered an impairment of academic freedom. And although signed writings could be obtained to turn some (but not all) such projects into work-for-hire under the second category, the signing would in no way protect untenured faculty or graduate students because of their overriding interest in academic advancement.

There is also a larger point. The truth of the matter is, most collaborative projects are nothing like making movies. Films have producers and directors with overarching visions of the products they are creating. Since other collaborative work does not necessarily have such singular vision, there is no reason to believe that the rules that are instrumentally desirable for films will work more generally. To put this another way, given that copyright's core goal is to foster creativity (rather than raw investment),[38] the law should be putting decisions on disseminating, revising, and building on works in the hands of the entity that will maximize creative value, rather than on the entity that bankrolled the production. Yet, it is a rare employer who is in the position to be a good value maximizer.[39] In fact, many projects proceed as collaborations for the very reason that no entity possesses the skills necessary to complete the entire project. If that is so, then it makes little sense for the law to behave as if there were a participant

---

[37] See, e.g. Hays v. Sony Corp., 847 F.2d 412, 416 (7th Cir. 1988)(high school teachers) (Posner, J.); Respect Incorp. v. Committee on the Status of Women, 815 F.Supp. 1112, 1118 (N.D. Ill. 1993). There is considerable debate on this issue in the literature, both here and abroad, see, e.g., see, e.g., Mark L. Meyer, To Promote the Progress of Science and Useful Arts: The Protection of and Rights in Scientific Research, 39 IDEA 1 (1998); Sunil R. Kulkarni, All Professors Create Equally: Why Faculty Should Have Complete Control over the Intellectual Property Rights in Their Creations, 47 Hastings L.J. 221 (1995); Pat Ks. Chew, Faculty-Generated Inventions: Who Owns the Golden Egg?, 1992 Wis. L. Rev. 259; Laura G. Lape, Ownership of Copyrightable Works of University Professors: The Interplay Between the Copyright Act and University Policies, 37 Vill. L. Rev. 223 (1992); Sherri L. Burr, A Critical Assessment of Reid's Work for Hire Framework and Its Potential Impact on the Marketplace for Scholarly Works; 24 J. Marshall L. Rev. 119 (1991); Margaret D. Smith and Perry A. Zirkel, The Implications of CCNV v. Reid for the Educator-Author: Who Owns the Copyright?, 63 Educ. L. Rep. 703 (1991); Estelle A. Fishbein, Ownership of Research Data, Acad. Med., March 1991, at 133, 129; Russ VerSteeg, Copyright and the Educational Process: The Right of Teacher Inception, 75 Iowa L. Rev. 381 (1990); Michael J. Lluzum and Daniel S. Pupel, Jr., Weinstein v. University of Illinois: The "Work for Hire" Doctrine and Procedural Due Process for Nontenured Faculty, 15 J.C. & U.L. 369 (1989); Philip S. Bousquet, Note, Externally Sponsored Faculty Research Under the "Work for Hire" Doctrine: Who's the Boss?, 39 Syracuse L. Rev. 1351 (1988); Rochelle Cooper Dreyfuss, The Creative Employee and the Copyright Act of 1976, 54 U. Chi. L. Rev. 590 (1987); Leonard D. DuBoff, An Academic's Copyright: Publish and Perish, 32 J. Copyright Soc'y 17 (1984); Todd F. Simon, Faculty Writings: Are They "Works Made for Hire" Under the 1976 Copyright Act?, 9 J.C. & U.L. 485, 488 (1982–83). For European views, see NAPAG Report, supra note 7, at 58-59; William R. Cornish, Ownership of Copyright in the Results of Academic Research: The Position in Common Law Countries and the EC, in European Structures – Changes and Challenges: The Role and Function of the Intellectual Property Rights [hereinafter European Structures] (Max-Planck-Gesellschaft 1994).

[38] See, e.g., Feist Publications, Inc. v. Rural Telephone Service, Co., 499 U.S. 340, 352–56 (1991).

[39] See, e.g., Weinstein v. University of Illinois, 811 F.2d 1091, 1094 (7th Cir. 1987) (noting that faculty ownership is an academic tradition) (Easterbrook, J.).

with sufficient understanding of the whole to make the right exploitation decisions, to vouch for correctness, or to make as good a future use of any element of the whole as the one who created that element in the first place.[40] In the case of sequential collaborations – chain art, for example – such an assumption is especially inappropriate. In these works, there is no unified vision – the whole idea is to see what output eventuates in the absence of such a vision.

If the problem with work for hire is viewed as imposing a hierarchical relationship among participants that distorts the account of their intellectual contributions, then it might be thought that the solution is to treat collaborative production under the Copyright Act's second paradigm, as jointly authored works. Under the Act, these are works "prepared by two or more authors with the intention that their contributions be merged into inseparable or interdependent parts of a unitary whole."[41] In some ways, this provision is a significant improvement over work for hire. All of the authors of joint works co-own the copyright, meaning that each has a right to fully exploit the work without the permission of the others. But since each participant has a duty to account for profits to the others, financial interests are protected.[42] Copyright ownership also facilitates attribution and confers a right to follow on with derivative works. Moreover, continued association encourages each author to safeguard quality. Finally, by giving full rights of authorship to each of the parties *ab initio*, each participant enters negotiations with power to bargain for a legal environment appropriate to his or her needs.

There are, however, significant problems with this approach as well. For one, the courts have interpreted the intent requirement as requiring that each author intend to be a coauthor.[43] Since that interpretation permits any single member of

---

[40] A concrete example is helpful. Compare the work of the composer of a motion picture sound track to the contribution that a statistician makes to a medical study. In the case of the composer, the point of the music is to emphasize the theme and mood of the film. The work is acceptable and complete when it does that final say about what goes into the film belongs to the studio, or its representatives, the producer and director. Since completion is a subjective determination of the studio, it is the studio that should be looked at by the public as responsible for the work. In the case of the statistical analysis, however, acceptability depends on whether the statistician has correctly applied statistical tools to the data presented. Whether another entity – the statistician's university or the project's principal investigator – "wanted" that result is completely irrelevant to the question whether the work is satisfactory. Thus, while the public may be able to look to the university or the principal investigator to determine whether the statistician is a good collaborator, it cannot view the university or PI as the guarantor of the statistical analysis. Nor can the public count on anyone other than the statistician to make further productive use of the work – no one else understands it the way the statistician does. Cf. Graham v. James, 46 U.S.P.Q. 2d 1760 (2d Cir. 1998) (finding that a computer programmer was an independent contractor allowed him to revise and improve his product).
[41] 17 U.S.C. § 101.
[42] 17 U.S.C. § 201(a); Community for Creative Non-Violence v. Reid, 846 F.2d 1485, 1498 (D.C. Cir. 1988), aff'd on other grounds, 490 U.S. 730 (1989).
[43] Thomson v. Larson, 147 F.3d 195, 200 (2d Cir. 1998); Childress v. Taylor, 945 F.2d 500, 507 (2d Cir. 1991).

the collaborative team to veto the full participation of all other members – and to do it *sub silentio* – participants who lack bargaining power can be in a worse position under the joint authorship provision than under the work for hire doctrine. They can wind up ceding rights over their work to someone who has ambitious intentions, but not the skills needed to complete the project alone or exploit it judiciously. In collaborations involving cultural differences and divergent disciplinary practices, where misunderstandings are particularly likely, the possibility that a participant will inadvertently lose the right to associate with his own work is especially high.

Another difficulty with the joint authorship standard is that courts require that each author make a copyrightable contribution to the work.[44] That eliminates the possibility that certain contributors – for example, statisticians who contribute only factual material – will be protected by the statute. An additional problem is that under this interpretation of joint authorship, there is a gap between the two multiple authorship provisions. That is, there are apparently multiply authored works that are not for hire because of the absence of an employment contract, agency relationship, or written commission, which are also not joint works because one participant lacked the intent to share the attributes of authorship with others. The status of such a work is, apparently, indeterminate.

Congress has done somewhat better for collaborators in the patent industries. Thus, the Patent Act requires that all inventors (that is, each person who helped conceive the idea and the final solution to the problem at issue) join in the patent application.[45] There is no work for hire provision, and thus no way for attribution to be suppressed. Rights to access tangible products are, to some extent, protected by disclosure and deposit requirements.[46] Most importantly, the definition of joint inventorship explicitly acknowledges the episodic nature of the collaborative process: it envisions the possibility that participants will work at different places and different times, and contribute different amounts to the patented invention.[47] Those who achieve inventorship status acquire full rights to utilize the work.[48]

But as good as patent law might look in theory, it too has its difficulties. Most troublesome are the rules on exploitation, which do not require inventors to account to one another for profits.[49] Although there is some dispute on this point,

---

[44] See *Thomson*, 147 F.3d at 200; *Childress*, 945 F.2d at 507.
[45] 35 U.S.C. § 111. See generally, Donald J. Chisum, Patents, § 2.02[2], at 2–5 (MB May 1987).
[46] 35 U.S.C. § 112; 37 C.F.R. §§ 1.801–.809 (PTO regulations on the deposit of biological materials); Chisum, supra note 45, at § 7.03[5][b].
[47] Patent Law Amendments Act of 1984, Pub. L. No. 98-622, §104(a), 98 Stat. 2284, 3385 (amending 35 U.S.C. § 116). Although § 116 is slightly ambiguous, other provisions of the Patent Act make it clear that the inventors must be working together. If the inventors were independent, then the other patentability requirements and the priority rules will single out one of these independent inventors (usually the first to invent) as the only one entitled to the patent, see 35 U.S.C. §§ 102 and 103.
[48] 35 U.S.C. § 262.
[49] Id.

each owner also appears to have a right to assign the patent to others.[50] Moreover, although enforcement actions require all patentees to participate in the suit, courts are reluctant to name absentees as involuntary plaintiffs.[51] Statutory co inventors are, in short, at one another's mercy.[52] If they cannot manage to cooperate, they and their assignees can easily compete the price of embodiments down to cost. Finally, there is a common law shop right doctrine, which gives an employer a nonexclusive license in any inventions made with his or her resources. While the employer is only allowed to use the invention for business purposes and shop rights are not assignable, they can be transferred in connection with the sale of the business.[53]

The result of these rules is a rivalry that is potentially so destructive, the need to consolidate rights in a single owner is overwhelming. After the fact, the temptation is to squeeze out less significant players.[54] Indeed, exclusivity is so important, investors often want it assured before significant costs are incurred. In most cases, this is accomplished by establishing an employment relationship and making the duty to assign inventions to the employer a condition of employment.[55] In that process, the "employees" tend to lose out. Often the obligation to assign is expressed in a form contract – in the university context, for example, it can be set out in the employee handbook and then incorporated into faculty contracts by reference. Such contracts are usually considered enforceable even though

---

[50] See generally, Robert P. Merges and Lawrence A. Locke, Co-Ownership of Patents: A Comparative and Economic View, 72 J. Pat. & Trademark Off. Soc'y 586, 588 (1990) (also citing some scant contrary authority on the issue of assigning).

[51] See Ethicon v. U.S. Surgical Corp., 135 F.3d 1456, 1468 (Fed. Cir. 1998) (citing Willingham v. Lawton, 555 F.2d 1340 (6th Cir. 1977)). Cf. Hydril Co. v. Baker Hughes Inc., 121 F.3d 728 (Fed. Cir. 1997) (unpublished opinion) (disposed of on inventorship grounds, but assuming joinder required) and Fed. R. Civ. P. 19. For a discussion of the question whether patentees can be joined as involuntary plaintiffs, see Dale L. Carlson and James R. Barney, The Division of Rights Among Joint Inventors: Public Policy Concerns After Ethicon v. U.S. Surgical, 39 Idea 251, 264 (1999).

[52] See *Ethicon*, 135 F.3d at 1468(citing Willingham v. Lawton, 555 F.2d 1340 (6th Cir. 1977)). See also Carlson and Barney, supra note 51, at 260–63; Merges and Locke, supra note 50.

[53] See Chisum, supra note 45, at § 23.03[3].

[54] See, e.g., Ethicon, Inc. v. United States Surgical Corporation, 135 F.3d 1456 (Fed. Cir. 1998). For what may be a particularly lurid example, see University of Colorado Found'n, Inc. v. University of Colorado, 974 F. Supp. 1339 (D. Colo. 1997), aff'd in part, rev'd in part, 196 F.3d 1366 (Fed. Cir. 1999).

[55] Indeed, the vast majority of inventions appear to be subject to assignment before patent issuance, most as a result of an employment relationship. See Lucy Gamon, Note, Patent Law in the Context of Corporate Research, 8 J. Corp. L. 497 (1983) (noting that patent assignment data show that inventors employed by others garner seventy-five percent of all patents, that one percent of the labor force receives half of all patents, and that engineers, most of whom are employed by corporations in order to invent, obtain forty times as many patents as all other occupational groups combined); Joseph Straus, Current Issues in Patenting Research Results Close to Industrial Application, in European Structures, supra, at 7, 12 & 15–16 (citing patent statistics in the United States).

negotiation can be quite minimal.[56] Moreover, whatever bargaining does take place occurs at the time the employee is hired, before there is any sense on the employee's part of what might be discovered or what its value is. Even employees who manage to avoid signing an express assignment may have a problem, as courts will generally infer from the fact that an employee was hired for the purpose of inventing, an obligation to assign rights to the employer.[57] In such cases, there are no negotiations, and thus no opportunity for employees to protect their interests.[58]

Patent law has other problems as well. Obviously, it applies to only a limited number of collaborations. Although patentable work often yields subject matter within the purview of copyright, the reverse is not true, except (perhaps) in the computer industry. Further, because the standard of creativity is higher in patent law than in copyright law, many intellectual efforts in the patent industries are not, in actual fact, patentable. The deposit requirement is also rather circumscribed. It applies mainly to biological materials and only to products needed to make or practice the actual patented invention. It does not apply to information produced in the course of testing the product or to other material produced at the time the invention was made.

Suggestions for the Future

In the end, intellectual property law, as currently constituted, does not go far enough to mediate among the interests of collaborators. Accordingly, it is no surprise that there are so many disputes. Intellectual property law does, however, contain many useful policies and practices: a demanding test for joint authorship and inventorship that filters out contributors who are not positioned to make the

---

[56] See Chew, supra, at 286–93; Wright v. United States, 164 F.3d 267 (5th Cir. 1999) (U.S. is the owner of an employee's invention even though it had no interest in patenting it); University Patents Inc. v. Kligman, 762 F. Supp. 1212, 1221 (E.D. Pa 1991) (university claim of ownership survives motion for summary judgment); Donna R. Euben, The Faculty Handbook As a Contract: Is It Enforceable?, Sept./Oct. 1998 Academe 87.

[57] See, e.g., Standard Parts Co. v. Peck, 264 U.S. 52 (1924); University Patents, 762 F. Supp. at 1228; Chisum, supra note 45, at §22.03[2].

[58] Because the factors that courts consider in determining whether to imply this obligation are so similar to the factors that courts use to determine whether work is for hire under the Copyright Act, the two situations almost converge. Compare Community for Creative Non-Violence v. Reid, 490 U.S. 730 (1989), with the factors listed in Chisum, supra note 45, at 22–30 – 22–33. See also Chew, supra, 265–69 (suggesting that university faculty are not hired to invent under these factors). But see Patel, supra note 8, at 497–501, who argues that faculty are not hired to invent, but that the copyrighted works notes they produce should be considered for hire.

best use of the work or guarantee its accuracy; some requirements that push the parties to negotiate and equalize their bargaining power; some provision for access to tangibles. What is missing is a realistic conception of what the collaborative process can entail. Collaboration is increasing because at this point in intellectual history, innovation may be done at a level at which individuals (and firms) lose the capacity to work alone. When many distinct contributions are required, the end result can be the complete blending of inputs, but it is just as possible that the result will not be smooth or seamless or homogeneous. It may have texture, a texture so loose that single strands can be separately identified and teased out for individual development. As now constituted, neither copyright law nor patent law takes the possibility of texture into account. Certain participants are credited with the whole cloth, while the distinctive (and distinguishable) contributions of others are ignored. Failure to appreciate the texture makes parties forget that attribution issues can be tricky and that each participant may start with a different idea about how his or her strand will be further utilized. Indeed, the difference between the assumed texture of collaboration and its reality may be responsible for a disconnection between the public's understanding of who is responsible for accuracy and the perceptions of the individuals actually involved.

But although this disconnection has yet to be recognized in American intellectual property law, it has been acknowledged in other places. Universities, journals, and various administrative agencies have considered features of the problem, including the issues of financial reward, accountability, access to tangibles, and – for graduate students – inequality in bargaining power.[59] The Europeans have also considered (and in some cases, adopted) proposals aimed at collaborative problems.[60] For example, German labor law treats many of these

---

[59] See, e.g., See Mario Biagioli, The Instability of Authorship: Credit and Responsibility in Contemporary Biomedicine, 12 Life Sciences Forum 3 (1998); Drummond Rennie, Veronica Yank, Linda Emanuel, When Authorship Fails: A Proposal to Make Contributors Accountable, 278 J. Am. Med. Ass'n 579 (Aug. 20, 1997); Cohen, supra note 19; Mishkin, supra note 20; Ellen Murphy, Agencies, Journals Set Some Rules, 248 Science 954, May 25, 1990; American Association of University Professors, Statement on Professional Ethics II (1987), reprinted in Bill L. Williamson, Using Students: The Ethics of Faculty Use of Student's Work Product, 26 Ariz. St. L.J. 1029 (1994); Penelope J. Greene, et al., Policies for Responding to Allegations of Fraud in Research, 23 Minerva 203 (1985). For a survey of university policies, see Rochelle C. Dreyfuss, Collaborative Research: Conflicts on Authorship, Ownership, and Accountability, Vanderbilt L. Rev. (2000).

[60] See, e.g., Dutch Copyright Act of 1912, Arts. 5–9, 26 (creating categories of works that are separable, created by an employee, and jointly created); 45a-g; 45h-n. An English translation of the Dutch statute can be found at <http://www.ivir.nl/documentation/legislation/copyright-act.html>; U.K. Copyright, Designs and Patents Act 1988 § 3 (1) (dividing up rights in musical works between the author of the lyrics and the composer of the melody); Hanns Ullrich, Rules on Ownership and Allocation of Intellectual Property in R&D Collaborations Between Science and Industry – Some Principles of Comparison, in European Structures, supra (discussing a proposal in the EU to promulgate a model collaborative contract and proposing a "partnership model" for the treatment of collaborative work under German law).

issues in the specific context of employment.[61] More generally, the EU has proposed a model collaborative contract to deal with specified arrangements.[62] However, as Hanns Ullrich has pointed out, there are several reasons to doubt that this approach will be of much utility as applied to ad hoc collaborations, especially when the collaborators are individuals. The agreements tend to be based on the collaborative methodologies that existed at the time of the drafting. They deal – sometimes in "microscopic detail" – with the needs of the specific entities that evolved them.[63] These entities are usually large commercial enterprises that are wary of the loss of control entailed in joint ownership. Thus, while it is true that the agreements facilitate the sharing of mutually developed technologies, mutual development is not their real goal. The real goal is to subdivide the work so that sharing is minimized. Although that makes it easier for the participants to decide who owns what, these arrangements inhibit information flow among creators. Most importantly, the models under consideration are essentially Band-Aids. They fail to articulate any kind of genuine normative view of the relationship between collaborators and a work product that none could have realized alone.

What would be better is the codification into intellectual property law of a new overarching concept – a principle of proportionality. This principle would acknowledge the special texture of collaborative work products and allocate rights and duties in ways that recognize the distinctive nature of each collaborator's contribution. In copyright, the idea would be to recognize a new category of multiply authored product, the "collaborative work," which would encompass works that do not qualify as for hire and do not meet the test of joint authorship. The new provision would recognize the authorship status of every participant who has contributed material to such work and give each author pecuniary interests in the work proportional to that party's input. Authors' rights to exploit and make derivative use of the product would also be divided proportionately. In addition to the right to utilize and develop her own contribution, an author would also enjoy an implied (compulsory) license to utilize the work of other contributors in so far as were necessary to fully exploit individual derivative work rights. Compensation for exercise of the license would be determined by private negotiation or arbitration.

For patent law, the proportionality approach would leave the definition of inventorship as it now stands. The law would also continue to deem as an inventor anyone who makes the statutorily required contribution. However, each contributor's rights would be limited to the claims to which that participant contributed. Each contributor's reward and access rights would be determined in a way analogous to that suggested for authors, including the right to be granted an

---

[61] See, e.g., Rudolf Krasser, The Law Relating to Employee's Inventions with Respect to Scientists at Universities and Research Institutions, in European Structures, supra, at 26, 32–33.
[62] A model EU contract is reproduced as an appendix to Ullrich, supra note 60, at 158–68.
[63] Ullrich, supra note 60, at 149–151.

implied license to use other inventions protected by the patent, and to utilize other patents based on the collaborative work, to the extent that were required for the inventor to exploit his own work. At the same time, shop rights could be eliminated and employers reimbursed for their resources or compensated in proportion to the benefits these resources bestowed.

The proportionality principle would give rise to other rights and duties as well. A depository system, along the lines currently in place for biologicals, could be used to protect collaborators' access to unique tangible products. Thus, each contributor could be granted access rights in the products she produced, along with an implied license to use any product necessary to continue with the research that inventor contributed. On the accountability side, responsibility for the quality of the collaborative product could similarly be allocated proportionately: just as each contributor enjoyed a right of attribution, each would take on responsibility for the accuracy of her piece of the project.

Of course, the devil in a proposal like this one is in its details. And since one of the main reasons for adopting a proportionality principle is to protect the interests of collaborators who lack bargaining power, there will also be tricky questions about the circumstances under which parties should be permitted to contractually opt out of statutory allocations of rights.[64] In light of these difficulties, it is worthwhile to consider a set of lesser interventions as well. These would include simple adjustments, such as changing the interpretation of intent in the joint authorship provision of copyright law or imposing a duty to account on the co-inventors of a patent. But what is required right now most of all is recognition that there is an issue that requires attention; that commodification does more than create new obstacles for user groups; it also interposes barriers between creators and their intellectual output.

Conclusion

Technological advances in the methods of reproduction and dissemination have provoked laws that increase the extent to which information goods have been commodified. This trend has drawn the attention of intellectual property scholars to the problem of readjusting the delicate balance between proprietary and access interests. But technological development has also had an impact on the way that information is produced. As innovation becomes dependent on collaboration, the structure of intellectual property law must also be modified to reflect the interests and expectations of those who participate in these endeavors.

---

[64] For further discussion of these issues, see Dreyfuss, supra note 59.

Patents on DNA Sequences: Molecules and Information*

*Rebecca S. Eisenberg***

As public and private sector initiatives raced to complete the sequence of the human genome,[1] patent issues played a prominent role in speculations about the significance of this achievement.[2] How much of the genome would be subject to the control of patent holders, and what would this mean for future research and the development of products for the improvement of human health?[3] Is a patent system developed to establish rights in mechanical inventions of an earlier era up to the task of resolving competing claims to the genome[4] on behalf of the many

---

* Copyright 2000 Rebecca S. Eisenberg. An earlier version of this paper appears at 49 Emory L.J. 783 (2000).

** I am grateful to Robert Cook-Deegan, Ronald Mann, Margaret Parr, and workshop participants at Haifa University, University of Washington, Harvard University, Lewis & Clark University, University of Minnesota, Emory University, University of Pennsylvania, Princeton University, Stanford University, and the University of California at Berkeley for helpful comments on earlier drafts of this article.

[1] See Nicholas Wade, 2 Groups in DNA Race Differ on Fixing Project's Finish Line, The New York Times, April 11, 2000; Philip E. Ross, The Making of a Gene Machine, Forbes (Feb. 21, 2000) at 98; Paul Smaglik, A Billion Base Pairs, Times Two 13 The Scientist (Dec. 6, 1999); Francis S. Collins, The Sequence of the Human Genome: Coming a Lot Sooner Than You Think, posted on the internet at <www.nhgri.nih.gov/NEWS> (visited Jan. 10, 2000); Justin Gillis & Rick Weiss, Private Firm Aims to Beat Government to Gene Map, The Washington Post, May 12, 1998, § 1 at 1 (LEXIS News Library); Nicholas Wade, Scientist's Plan: Map All DNA Within 3 Years, The New York Times, May 10, 1998, Section 1, p.1, col. 1 (Lexis).

[2] See Peter G. Gosselin, *Patent Office Now at Heart of Gene Debate*, L.A. Times (Feb. 7, 2000); Ralph T. King, Jr., *Code Green: Gene Quest Will Bring Glory to Some; Incyte Will Stick With Cash*, Wall St. J. (Feb. 10, 2000) at A1; Justin Gillis, *Md. Gene Researcher Draws Fire on Filings; Venter Defends Patent Requests*, Washington Post (Oct. 26, 1999) at E01.

[3] See Peter G. Gosselin & Paul Jacobs, *Clinton, Blair to Back Access to Genetic Code*, L.A. Times, March 14, 2000, at C1; Peter G. Gosselin, *Clinton Urges Public Access to Genetic Code*, L.A. Times, Feb. 11, 2000, at A1.

[4] See., e.g., Note, *Human Genes Without Functions: Biotechnology Tests the Patent Utility Standard*, 27 Suffolk U. L. Rev. 1631 (1993); Philippe Ducor, *Recombinant Products and Nonobviousness: A Typology*, 13 Computer & High Tech. L.J. 1 (1997).

N. Elkin-Koren and N.W. Netanel (eds.), *The Commodification of Information*, 415–431.
© 2002 Rebecca S. Eisenberg. Printed in Great Britain.

sequential innovators who elucidate its sequence and function,[5] with due regard to the interests of the scientific community[6] and the broader public?[7]

Given that applicants have been seeking and obtaining patent claims on DNA sequences for 20 years,[8] one might expect that the U.S. Patent and Trademark Office (PTO) and the courts would have resolved many of the legal issues surrounding this practice. The patent system has had many opportunities to apply traditional patent law principles to a broad range of issues involving genetic discoveries as the industry has pursued and litigated patent claims covering biotechnology products.[9] One might therefore expect that biotechnology patent law would now be entering a relatively mature phase in which fundamental questions have been resolved and the issues that remain to be addressed are incremental and interstitial. Instead, the patent system is struggling to clarify the ground rules for patenting DNA sequences, while years' worth of patent applications accumulate in the PTO. What accounts for this persistent lack of clarity about how patent law applies to these discoveries?

A significant part of the problem is that new technologies are rapidly changing how discoveries are made in genetics and genomics research. The patent system, which inevitably requires years to resolve even routine matters,[10] has so far focused primarily on the discoveries of the 1980s. DNA sequences that were the subject of patent claims in that era typically consisted of cloned genes that enabled the production of proteins through recombinant DNA technology. Patents on the genes encoding these proteins promised exclusivity in the market for the protein itself, equivalent to the protection that a pharmaceutical firm obtains by patenting a new chemical compound that can be used as a drug. From this perspective, patents on DNA sequences seemed analogous to patents on new chemical entities. The Court of Appeals for the Federal Circuit (Federal Circuit) accordingly turned to prior cases considering patents on chemicals in resolving

---

[5] See Stanley Fields, *The future is function*, 15 Nature Genetics 325 (1997); Rebecca S. Eisenberg, *Structure and function in gene patenting*, 15 Nature Genetics 125 (1997).

[6] See Martin Enserink, *Patent Office May Raise the Bar on Gene Claims*, 287 Science 1196 (2000).

[7] See Jon F. Merz et al., *Disease Gene Patenting Is a Bad Innovation*, 2 Molecular Diagnosis 299–304 (1997).

[8] See Rebecca S. Eisenberg, *Patenting the Human Genome*, 39 Emory L.J. 721 (1990).

[9] See, e.g., Amgen v. Chugai Pharmaceutical Co., 927 F.2d 1200 (Fed. Cir. 1991) (erythropoietin); Scripps Clinic & Research Found. v. Genentech, 927 F.2d 1565 (Fed. Cir. 1991) (Factor VIII:C); Genentech v. The Wellcome Found., 29 F.2d 1555 (Fed. Cir. 1994) (tissue plasminogen activator); Hormone Research Found. v. Genentech, 904 F.2d 1558 (Fed. Cir. 1990) (human growth hormone); Novo Nordisk v. Genentech, 77 F.3d 1364 (Fed. Cir. 1996) (human growth hormone); Genentech v. Eli Lilly & Co., 998 F.2d 931 (Fed. Cir. 1993) (human growth hormone); Bio-Technology General v. Genentech, 80 F.3d 1553 (Fed. Cir. 1996) (human growth hormone); Enzo Biochem v. Calgene, (Fed. Cir. 1999) (Flavr Savr tomato).

[10] Mark A. Lemley, *An Empirical Study of the Twenty-Year Patent Term*, 22 AIPLA Q.J. 369 (1995).

disputed issues about how patent law should apply to DNA sequences.[11] Whatever the limitations of this analogy, it provided a relatively clear point of departure for analyzing patent law issues presented by the first generation of biotechnology products – therapeutic proteins produced through recombinant DNA technology.

As DNA sequence discovery has moved beyond targeted efforts to clone particular genes to large-scale, high-throughput sequencing of entire genomes, new questions have come into view. The DNA sequences identified by high-throughput sequencing look less like new chemical entities than they do like new scientific information. From the perspective of patent claimants, the chemical analogy is of little value as a strategic guide to exploiting this information as intellectual property. From the perspective of the PTO and the courts, claims to these discoveries raise unresolved questions that strain the chemical analogy. The result is profound uncertainty concerning how to apply the doctrinal tools of patent law for determining what may be patented and for drawing boundaries between the rights of inventors and the rights of the public.

Patent Eligibility

A threshold issue that one might expect to have been resolved long ago is whether DNA sequences are the sort of subject matter that the patent system protects. The U.S. patent statute defines patent-eligible subject matter as "any process, machine, manufacture, or composition of matter,"[12] language that the U.S. Supreme Court has held indicates an expansive scope that includes "anything under the sun that is made by man."[13] Although cases have held that "products of nature" may not be patented, this exclusion has not presented an obstacle to patenting DNA sequences in forms that do not occur in nature as new "compositions of matter." On the threshold issue of patent-eligible subject matter, as on other issues, the analogy to chemical patent practice has supplied an answer.

The standard patent lawyer's response to the "products of nature" intuition is to treat it as a technical, claim-drafting problem. From this perspective, the prohibition against patenting products of nature only prevents the patenting of DNA sequences in a naturally occurring form that requires no human intervention. One cannot get a patent on a DNA sequence with claim language

---

[11] See, e.g., Amgen v. Chugai Pharmaceutical Co., 927 F.2d 1200, 1206 (Fed. Cir.), *cert. denied sub nom.* Genetics Institute v. Amgen, 502 U.S. 856 (1991) ("A gene is a chemical compound, albeit a complex one ...")
[12] 35 U.S.C. § 101.
[13] Diamond v. Chakrabarty, 447 U.S. 303 (1980).

417

that would be infringed by someone whose DNA continues to do what it has done for generations in nature. But one *can* get a patent on the same DNA sequence with more limited claim language that could only be infringed through the intervention of modern biotechnology.

Patents have thus issued on "isolated and purified" DNA sequences, separate from the chromosomes in which they occur in nature, or on DNA sequences that have been spliced into recombinant vectors or introduced into recombinant cells of a sort that do not exist in nature.[14] This is consistent with longstanding practice, even prior to the advent of modern biotechnology, of allowing patents to issue on isolated and purified chemical products that exist in nature only in an impure state, when human intervention has made them available in a new and useful form.[15] This is not simply a lawyer's trick, but a persuasive response to the intuition that patents should only issue for human inventions. It prevents the issuance of patents that take away from the public things that they were previously using (such as the DNA that resides in their cells), while allowing patents to issue on new human manipulations of nature. Those of us who simply use the DNA in our own cells, as our ancestors have been doing for generations, should not and need not worry about patent infringement liability. On the other hand, those of us who get injections of recombinant insulin or erythropoietin should in fairness expect to pay a patent premium to the inventors who made these technological interventions possible.

The patentability of DNA molecules in forms that involve human intervention appears to be well settled. But recent advances in DNA sequencing raise the question of patent eligibility in a new way that the courts have yet to address.

Molecules vs. Information

DNA sequences are not simply molecules; they are also information. Knowing the DNA sequence for the genome of an organism provides valuable scientific information that can open the door to future discoveries. Can the value of this information be captured through patents? Can information about the natural world, as distinguished from tangible human interventions that make use of that information, be patented?

---

[14] Amgen, Inc. v. Chugai Pharmaceutical Co., 13 U.S.P.Q.2d (BNA) 1737 (D. Mass. 1990) ("The invention claimed in the '008 patent is not as plaintiff argues the DNA sequence encoding human EPO since that is a nonpatentable natural phenomenon 'free to all men and reserved exclusively to none.' ... Rather, the invention as claimed in claim 2 of the patent is the 'purified and isolated' DNA sequence encoding erythropoietin.").

[15] See, e.g., Merck & Co. v. Olin Mathieson Chemical Corp., 253 F.2d 156 (4th Cir. 1958) (upholding the patentability of purified Vitamin B-12).

The traditional statutory categories of patent-eligible subject matter – processes, machines, manufactures, and compositions of matter – seem to be limited to tangible products and processes, as distinguished from information as such. Although many cases have used the word "tangible" in defining the boundaries of patentable subject matter, neither the language of the statute nor judicial decisions elaborating its meaning have explicitly excluded "information" from patent protection. Arguably, such a limitation is implicit in prior judicial decisions stating that the patent system protects practical applications rather than fundamental new insights about the natural world[16] and in cases holding that "printed matter" is ineligible for patent protection.[17]

The exclusion of information itself from patent protection is also at least implicit in the statutory requirement that patent applicants make full disclosures of information about their inventions, with no restrictions upon public access to the disclosures once the patents issue.[18] One important function of patent disclosures is to enable the public to use inventions freely as soon as the patents expire, but this function alone cannot explain why patent law requires that disclosures become freely accessible to the public at the beginning of the patent term. The timing of the disclosure requirement suggests another function that is inconsistent with patent claims that cover the disclosed information itself – in the words of a leading commentator, "full disclosure ... on issuance of the patent immediately increases the storehouse of public information available for further research and innovation."[19]

Patent claims on DNA sequences as "compositions of matter" give patent owners exclusionary rights over tangible DNA molecules and constructs, but do not prevent anyone from perceiving, using and analyzing information about what the DNA sequence is. Once the patent issues, this information becomes freely available to the world, subject only to the inventor's right to exclude others from making, using, and selling the claimed materials. For patents on genes that encode therapeutic proteins, the value of this exclusionary right over tangible composi-

---

[16] See, e.g., Diamond v. Chakrabarty ("Einstein could not patent his celebrated law that $E = mc2$; nor could Newton have patented the law of gravity. Such discoveries are 'manifestations of ... nature, free to all men and reserved exclusively to none.'"); Dickey-John Corp. v. International Tapetronics Corp., 710 F.2d 329 (7th Cir. 1983) ("Yet patent law has never been the domain of the abstract – one cannot patent the very discoveries which make the greatest contributions to human knowledge, such as Einstein's discovery of the photoelectric effect, nor has it ever been considered that the lure of commercial reward provided by a patent was needed to encourage such contributions. Patent law's domain has always been the application of the great discoveries of the human intellect to the mundane problems of everyday existence.")

[17] See, e.g., In re Russell, 48 F.2d 668 (1931); Guthrie v. Curlett, 10 F.2d 725 (2d Cir. 1926). More recent decisions, while not explicitly overruling these prior cases, seem to limit the vitality of the printed matter exclusion from patentability. See, e.g., In re Lowry, 32 F.3d 1579 (Fed. Cir. 1994) (reversing PTO "printed matter" rejection of patent claims to a data structure for storing, using and managing data in a computer memory).

[18] 35 U.S.C. §§ 112, 154(a)(4). See In re Argoudelis, 434 F.2d 1390 (Ct. Customs & Pat. App. 1970).

[19] 3 D. Chisum, Chisum on Patents § 7.01 (1999).

tions of matter has been sufficiently large relative to the value of the information that spills over to the public through the patent disclosure to motivate inventors to file patent applications rather than to keep the sequence secret.[20] The commercially significant aspect of these discoveries was not the informational value of knowing what the sequence was, but the tangible value of being able to use the DNA molecules in recombinant production facilities to make therapeutic proteins for sale. So long as patents permitted capture of this tangible, commercial value, there was no need to withhold the sequence information from the public.

By contrast, in the contemporary setting of high-throughput DNA sequencing, there is immediate commercial value to knowing what the sequence is, while the commercial value of using particular portions of the sequence as tangible templates for protein production is remote and speculative. There are two reasons why informational value looms large relative to tangible value in this context, in contrast to the targeted cloning projects of an earlier era that yielded sequences encoding products of known value. First, high-throughput DNA sequencing typically yields information about DNA sequences for which the corresponding biological functions are not yet understood. It is thus unclear at the time of sequencing whether a particular sequence will have tangible value. Second, high-throughput DNA sequencing typically yields considerable chaff (in the form of non-coding sequences and sequences that do not correspond to any apparent commercial products) along with the occasional bit of wheat (in the form of sequences encoding commercially valuable proteins or offering other uses in tangible form). What is most valuable about these research results, at least initially, is that they provide an information base for future discovery. DNA molecules corresponding to some portions of the sequence, such as those portions that encode valuable proteins or that are the site of diagnostic markers, may ultimately prove valuable as tangible compositions of matter. But it might not be immediately apparent just where in the sequence these nuggets of tangible value lie.

It is not obvious how an inventor might use patents to capture the value of DNA sequence discoveries under these circumstances. It may be difficult to draft claim language[21] that covers the portions of the sequence that prove to have tangible value without claiming either too broadly (rendering the claim invalid because it covers similar sequences that have already been disclosed in the prior

---

[20] Indeed, the scientists who cloned the genes encoding the first generation of biotechnology products typically published the DNA sequences they identified long before the corresponding patents issued (although after filing patent applications to avoid loss of patent rights outside the U.S.)

[21] The language of patent claims defines the scope of the patent holder's exclusionary rights. 35 U.S.C. § 112; Ex parte Fressola, 27 U.S.P.Q.2d (BNA) 1608 (Bd. Pat. App. & Interf. 1993).

art)[22] or too narrowly (rendering the claim easy to evade through minor changes in the molecule).[23] More importantly, claim language that is directed to tangible molecules fails to capture the informational value of knowing the sequence itself. If this informational value is large relative to the speculative value of tangible molecules corresponding to portions of the sequence, the more sensible strategy may be to sell access to a proprietary database of sequence information. So far, database subscriptions have been the principle source of revenue for most private firms involved in high-throughput DNA sequencing, although the same firms have also filed patent applications.[24]

Claiming Computer Readable Information

Another strategy that the PTO is currently facing but the courts have yet to consider seeks to capture the informational value of DNA sequences through patent claims directed toward DNA sequence stored in a computer readable medium. An early example of this strategy is the patent application filed by Human Genome Sciences (HGS) on the sequence of the *Haemophilus influenzae* Rd genome.[25] *Haemophilus influenzae* is a bacterial strain that causes ear and respiratory tract infections in humans. It was the first bacterium whose genome was fully sequenced,[26] and the fate of the related patent applications may offer a preview of how the patent system will allocate patent rights in future genomic

---

[22] A broad claim is a claim that has few limitations. One might, for example, seek a claim that covers any molecule that includes (or "comprises," in the vernacular of patent law) at least ten consecutive nucleotides from the disclosed sequence. If allowed, such a claim would be very broad in that it would be likely to cover any portion of the sequence that later proves to encode a valuable protein. But the breadth of the claim makes it more likely that it will be held invalid. The claim would be invalid if any previously disclosed DNA sequence included any 10 consecutive nucleotides that were identical to a portion of the sequence disclosed in the patent appplication. The shorter the portion of the disclosed sequence that is necessary to establish infringement, the broader the claim. But the broader the claim, the easier it is to find "prior art" disclosures that would fall within the scope of the claim, rendering the claim invalid. See, e.g., Titanium Metals Corp. v. Banner, 778 F.2d 775 (Fed. Cir. 1985) ("when ... a claim covers several compositions, the claim is [invalid] if *one* of them is in the prior art").

[23] A narrow claim is a claim that has many limitations. One might, for example, claim the entire disclosed sequence as an isolated molecule. Since every element of the claim must be present in a competitor's product to establish infringement, a competitor who made a DNA molecule that included only a portion of the disclosed sequence corresponding to a particular protein would not be liable.

[24] Ralph T. King Jr., *Code Green: Gene Quest Will Bring Glory to Some; Incyte Will Stick With Cash*, The Wall Street Journal, Feb. 2000, at A1.

[25] Nucleotide Sequence of the *Haemophilus influenzae* Rd Genome, Fragments Thereof, and Uses Thereof, WO 96/33276, PCT/US96/05320.

[26] Fleischmann, R.D., et al., *Whole-genome random sequencing and assembly of* Haemophilus influenzae *Rd.* 269 Science 496–512 (1995).

discoveries. HGS[27] filed a patent application setting forth the complete nucleotide sequence of the genome, identified as "SEQ ID NO.1." This patent application was published 18 months after its filing date under the terms of the Patent Cooperation Treaty, before it had been issued as a patent.[28] The application concludes with a series of claims representing the invention to which HGS seeks exclusive rights. The first of these claims reads as follows:

> "Computer readable medium having recorded thereon the nucleotide sequence depicted in SEQ ID NO:1, a representative fragment thereof or a nucleotide sequence at least 99.9% identical to the nucleotide sequence depicted in SEQ ID NO:1."

It bears emphasizing that this claim language does not appear in an issued patent. It is, in effect, the first item on the wish list of HGS for patent rights associated with the discovery of the *H. influenzae* genome. Recently, the U.S. PTO issued a patent to HGS with claims that were limited to tangible DNA molecules within the *H. influenzae* genome and related processes, although the title of the issued patent ("Computer readable genomic sequence of *Haemophilus influenzae Rd*, fragments thereof, and uses thereof") continues to reflect the applicant's original aspirations for claim coverage.[29]

This claiming strategy represents a fundamental departure from the previously sanctioned practice of claiming DNA sequences as tangible molecules. By claiming exclusionary rights in the sequence information itself, if stored in a computer readable medium, HGS sought patent rights that would be infringed by information storage, retrieval and analysis rather than simply by making, using or selling DNA molecules. It remains to be seen whether the PTO will eventually issue such a claim, or whether a rejection would stand up on appeal to the Federal Circuit.[30]

---

[27] Patent Cooperation Treaty of June 19, 1970, Art. 21(2).
[28] The sequencing was done at The Institute for Genomic Research (TIGR), a private, non-profit organization affiliated with Human Genome Sciences (HGS) at the time. Pursuant to an agreement between TIGR and HGS, patent rights in the *H. influenzae* genome were assigned to HGS.
[29] See U.S. Patent No. 6,355,450, issued March 12, 2002.
[30] An applicant whose claims have been rejected by a PTO examiner twice may appeal to the Board of Patent Appeals and Interferences, 35 U.S.C. § 134, and an applicant who is dissatisfied with the decision of the Board of Patent Appeals and Interferences may appeal to the United States Court of Appeals for the Federal Circuit. 35 U.S.C. § 141.

Expansive Trend of Case Law

Recent decisions concerning the patentability of computer-implemented inventions may provide more guidance than prior decisions concerning the patentability of discoveries in the life sciences in predicting whether DNA sequence information stored in computer readable medium may be patented. The overall trend of decisions in the Federal Circuit is toward expansive interpretation of the scope of patent eligible subject matter – even for categories of inventions that prior decisions seemed to exclude from the protection of the patent statute – in order to make the patent system "responsive to the needs of the modern world."[31] The most conspicuous recent example of this trend was the 1998 decision in *State Street Bank & Trust v. Signature Financial Group*[32] upholding the patentability of a computer-implemented accounting system for managing the flow of funds in partnerships of mutual funds that pool their assets. This invention arguably fell within previously apparent judicial limitations that excluded mathematical algorithms[33] and business methods[34] from patent protection. The Federal Circuit minimized the first of these limitations,[35] holding that it only excluded from patent protection "abstract ideas constituting disembodied concepts or truths that are not 'useful,'"[36] and repudiated the second, insisting that "[t]he business method exception has never been invoked by this court, or [its predecessor], to deem an invention unpatentable," and that other courts that had appeared to apply the business method exception always had other grounds for arriving at the same decision.[37]

Rather than seeing the language of § 101 of the Patent Act, which permits patents to issue for "any new and useful process, machine, manufacture, or composition of matter," as a significant limitation on the types of advances that might qualify for patent protection, the Federal Circuit characterized this language as a "seemingly limitless expanse," subject only to three "specifically identified ... categories of unpatentable subject matter: 'laws of nature, natural phenomena, and abstract ideas.'"[38] From this perspective, it is not obvious why DNA sequence information stored in computer readable medium – a product that requires human intervention and serves human purposes – would be categorically excluded from patent protection.

---

[31] AT&T Corp. v. Excel Communications, Inc., 172 F.3d 1352 (1999).
[32] 149 F.3d 1368 (Fed. Cir. 1998), *cert. denied*, 119 S. Ct. 851 (1999).
[33] See, e.g., Gottschalk v. Benson, 409 U.S. 63 (1972); Parker v. Flook, 437 U.S. 584 (1978).
[34] Hotel Security Checking Co. v. Lorraine Co., 160 F. 467 (2d Cir. 1908).
[35] The exclusion of mathematical algorithms from patent protection had already been substantially restricted by prior decisions of the Federal Circuit. See, e.g., *In re Alappat*, 33 F.3d 1526 (1996).
[36] 149 F.3d at 1373.
[37] *Id*. at 1375–76.
[38] AT&T Corp. v. Excel Communications, Inc., 172 F.3d 1352 (Fed. Cir. 1999), citing Diamond v. Diehr, 450 U.S. 175 (1981).

PTO Guidelines

Of course, DNA sequence information stored in computer readable medium is not the same thing as a computer-implemented business method, and it is certainly possible to define boundaries for the patent system that include the latter but not the former. Indeed, the PTO's Examination Guidelines for Computer-Implemented Inventions[39] exclude data stored in computer readable medium from patent protection. The Guidelines distinguish between "functional descriptive material" (such as "data structures and computer programs which impart functionality when encoded on a computer-readable medium") and "non-functional descriptive material" (such as "music, literary works and a compilation or mere arrangement of data [which] is not structurally and functionally interrelated to the medium but is merely carried by the medium").[40] Although functional descriptive material will generally fall within the statutory categories of patent-eligible subject matter, the Guidelines state that non-functional descriptive material will generally not meet the statutory limitations:

> Merely claiming non-functional descriptive material stored in a computer-readable medium does not make it statutory. Such a result would exalt form over substance.[41]

---

[39] 61 Fed. Reg. 7478 (Feb. 28, 1996), posted on the internet at <http://www.uspto.gov/web/offices/com/hearings/software/analysis/computer.html> (last visited Feb. 4, 2000).

[40] The focus on functional relationship between data and substrate echoes language from *In re Lowry*, 32 F.3d 1579 (Fed. Cir. 1994), in which the Federal Circuit upheld the patentability of a data structure for storing, using and managing data in a computer memory. In that case, the Board of Patent Appeals had reversed the examiner's rejection of the claims under 35 U.S.C. § 101 as claiming non-statutory subject matter, and the issue of patentable subject matter was therefore not properly before the court on appeal. Nonetheless, in its analysis of the remaining issues of patentability under 35 U.S.C. §§ 102 and 103, the court drew a distinction between claiming information content and claiming a functional structure for managing information:
> "Contrary to the PTO's assertion, Lowry does not claim merely the information content of a memory. Lowry's data structures, while including data resident in a database, depend only functionally on information content. While the information content affects the exact sequence of bits stored in accordance with Lowry's data structures, the claims require specific electronic structural elements which impart a physical organization on the information stored in memory. Lowry's invention manages information. As Lowry notes, the data structures provide increased computing efficiency."
>
> *Id.* at 1583.

[41] This qualification in the Guidelines responds to a rhetorical question posed by Judge Archer in his dissenting opinion from the *en banc* decision of the Federal Circuit in *In re Alappat*, 33 F.3d 1526 (1996). In that case a majority of the court upheld the patentability of a claim to a computer-implemented mechanism for improving the quality of a picture in an oscilloscope. Judge Archer cautioned against the potential implications of allowing patent claims on mathematical algorithms stored in computer-readable medium in his dissenting opinion, asking rhetorically whether a piece of music recorded on a compact disc or player piano roll would be patentable:

DNA sequence information stored in a computer readable medium seems to fall squarely within the PTO's definition of "non-functional descriptive material" that is "merely carried by" the computer readable medium and is not functionally interrelated to it.

If the PTO continues to follow these six-year-old guidelines, it should reject claims to DNA sequence stored in computer readable medium. But if a disgruntled patent applicant appeals to the Federal Circuit, that court might well reverse the rejection. The distinction between tangible molecules and intangible information may do little work today in delineating the boundaries of patent eligibility in the face of recent decisions deemphasizing the importance of physical limitations in establishing the patentability of computer-implemented inventions. This shift in emphasis is particularly apparent in *AT&T v. Excel Communications*,[42] in which the court explicitly declined to focus on the "physical limitations inquiry" that had played a central role in distinguishing between unpatentable mathematical algorithms and patentable computer-implemented inventions in its prior decisions. Instead, the court asked "whether the mathematical algorithm is applied in a practical manner to produce a useful result."[43] This approach seems to merge the issue of patent eligibility with the issue of utility, opening the door to patent claims to information so long as it is "useful."

Traditional Patent Bargain

If the Federal Circuit steps back from the momentum of its recent decisions expanding the boundaries of the patent system, it should not be persuaded that information stored in computer readable medium is patentable. Patent claims to information – even useful information – represent a fundamental departure from the traditional patent bargain. That bargain has always called for free disclosure of information to the public at the outset of the patent term in exchange for exclusionary rights in particular tangible applications until the patent expires. Patent claims that are infringed by mere perception and analysis of the information set forth in the patent disclosure undermine the strong policy

---

cont.
    Through the expedient of putting his music on known structure, can a composer now claim as his invention the structure of a compact disc or player piano roll containing the melody he discovered and obtain a patent therefor? The answer must be no. The composer admittedly has invented or discovered nothing but music. The discovery of music does not become patentable subject matter simply because there is an arbitrary claim to some structure.
    33 F.3d 1526, 1545, at 1554 (dissenting opinion).
[42] 172 F.3d 1352, 1359–60 (Fed. Cir. 1999).
[43] *Id.* at 1360.

preventing patent applicants from restricting access to the disclosure once the patent has issued.[44] The limitation that the information be stored in "computer readable medium" offers scant protection for the public interest in free access to the informational content of patent disclosures. Scanning technologies arguably bring paper printouts of DNA sequence information within the scope of the claim language, an interpretation that would make copying the patent document itself an act of infringement. Even if the claim language is more narrowly interpreted to cover only electronic media, numerous websites post the full text of issued patents, including a website maintained by the PTO.[45] Any claim that would count these postings as acts of infringement simply proves too much.

Patents on information surely represent a departure from tradition. But departure from tradition may not be a sufficient ground to reject them in light of the increasing importance of information products to technological progress. Perhaps the traditional bargain of free disclosure of information in exchange for exclusionary rights that are limited to tangible applications makes no sense in this new environment. If the value of unprotectible information gained from high throughput DNA sequencing is large relative to the value of tangible molecules that might be covered by established claiming strategies, patents that do not allow the inventor to capture the value of the information might not do enough to motivate investment in DNA sequencing. This may seem unlikely as an empirical matter, given the substantial investments made in DNA sequencing in both the public and private sectors with no clear precedent for capturing the informational value of this investment through the patent system,[46] but it is at least a logical possibility. A more plausible speculation is that inventors might forego the patent bargain if they are stuck with the traditional terms of that bargain, choosing instead to exploit their discoveries through restricted access to proprietary DNA sequence databases.[47]

Although the conventional wisdom in the patent community is that patent protection promotes the public interest in technological progress better than trade secrecy, it is by no means clear that the public interest in progress in genomics would be better served by issuing patents on DNA sequence information in computer readable medium than by relying on trade secrecy to

---

[44] See In re Argoudelis, 434 F.2d 1390, 1394–96 (C.C.P.A. 1970)(concurring opinion); Feldman v. Aunstrup, 517 F.2d 1351, 1355 (C.C.P.A. 1975), *cert. denied,* 424 U.S. 912 (1976).

[45] See <http://www.uspto.gov/web/menu/pats.html>.

[46] See, e.g., Barry A. Palevitz, *Rice Genome Gets a Boost: Private sequencing effort yields rough draft for the public,* The Scientist, May 1, 2000, at 1.

[47] In fact, private firms that invest in DNA sequencing appear to be pursuing a dual strategy of licensing access to proprietary databases while pursuing traditional composition of matter patents on particular sequences within those databases that appear likely to correspond to valuable tangible products. See Ralph T. King Jr., *Code Green: Gene Quest Will Bring Glory to Some; Incyte Will Stick With Cash, supra* note 2.

motivate investment in DNA sequence databases. If the terms of the traditional patent bargain are altered to allow patent holders to capture the informational value of their discoveries, the bargain becomes less attractive to the public. The public might be better off withholding patents and allowing others to derive the same information independently. Withholding patents makes particular sense if the efforts of the patent holder are not necessary to bring the information into the public domain. Much DNA sequence information is freely disclosed in the public domain, both by publicly-funded researchers and by private firms. If a discovery is likely to be made and disclosed promptly even without patent incentives, there is little point in enduring the social costs of exclusionary rights.[48]

Bricks and Mortar Rules for Information Goods

There are sound policy reasons to be wary of permitting use of the patent system to capture the value of information itself. The traditional patent bargain ensures that patenting promptly enriches the information base,[49] even as it slows down commercial imitation. This balances the interests of inventors in earning a return on past research investments against the interests of the larger public in promoting future research. If patent claims could prevent the perception and analysis of information, this balance would tilt sharply in favor of patent owners.

Even if some form of intellectual property protection for information is necessary to promote investment in the creation of new information products, one might question whether the patent system is a suitable model. Compared to other forms of intellectual property protection, such as copyrights and trade secrets, there are few safety valves built into the patent system that constrain the rights of patent holders in favor of competing interests of the public. Unlike copyright law, patent law has no fair use defense that permits socially valuable

---

[48] Normally the nonobviousness standard set forth at 35 U.S.C.§ 103 prevents the issuance of patents on inventions that are highly likely to be made independently by another inventor by excluding from patent protection inventions that would have been "obvious" to persons of ordinary skill in the field of the invention given the state of the art. This standard fails to serve this important function in the context of DNA sequencing because of decisions of the Federal Circuit upholding the patentability of newly identified DNA sequences discovered through routine work, so long as the prior art did not permit prediction of the structure of the DNA molecule. See In re Bell, 991 F.2d 781 (Fed. Cir. 1993).; In re Deuel, 51 F.3d 1552 (Fed. Cir. 1995).

[49] See *supra* notes 44–45 and accompanying text.

uses without a license.[50] Contrary to the understanding of many scientists, patent law has only a "truly narrow" research exemption that offers no protection from infringement liability for research activities that are commercially threatening to the patent holder.[51] Nor is independent creation a defense to patent infringement, in contrast to both copyright law[52] and trade secret law.[53] Unlike trade secret law, patent law has no defense for reverse engineering.[54] The most important concession to the competing interests of the public that is built into a patent, apart from its finite term,[55] is the disclosure requirement.[56] By requiring full disclosure of how to make and use the invention, and by mandating that this disclosure become freely available as soon as the patent issues, the patent system in effect permits unlicensed use of information about the invention, as distinguished from use of the tangible invention itself. But if patents issue that restrict the public from perceiving and analyzing information about the invention, the claim effectively defeats that safety valve.

If information is not appropriate subject matter for patent protection, does it follow that DNA sequences should not be patented at all? The foregoing discussion distinguishes between patent claims to DNA sequences stored in computer readable medium, which are tantamount to patent claims on information itself, and traditional patent claims to DNA molecules and constructs. But perhaps any principle that excludes information from patent protection has broader implications for patents on DNA sequences. DNA molecules may be thought of as a tangible storage medium for information about the structure of proteins. Cells read the information stored in DNA molecules to make the proteins that they need to survive in their environments, and they copy that information when they divide and reproduce. If DNA

---

[50] 17 U.S.C. § 107. For an interesting analysis of whether a fair use defense would make sense for the patent system, see Maureen A. O'Rourke, *Towards a Doctrine of Fair Use in Patent Law*, 100 *Colum. L. Rev.* 1177 (2000).
[51] The quoted words are from the opinion of the Court of Appeals for the Federal Circuit in *Roche Prods., Inc. v. Bolar Pharmaceuticals, Inc.*, 733 F.2d 858 (Fed. Cir.), *cert. denied,* 469 U.S. 856 (1984). For a fuller discussion of the research exemption, see Rebecca S. Eisenberg, *Patents and the Progress of Science: Exclusive Rights and Experimental Use*, 56 *U. Chi. L. Rev.* 1017 (1989).
[52] See 2 *P. Goldstein, Copyright* § 7.1.1 (2d ed. 1996) ("Infringement turns strictly on proof of copying and improper appropriation.").
[53] See, e.g., *Chicago Lock Co. v. Fanberg*, 676 F.2d 400, 404 (9th Cir. 1982).
[54] See *Kewanee Oil v. Bicron*, 416 U.S. 470, 490 (1974); *Rockwell Graphic Systems, Inc. v. DEV Industries, Inc.*, 925 F.2d 174, 178 (7th Cir. 1991).
[55] The rule for determining the expiration date of a U.S. patent was changed in 1995 by the Uruguay Round Amendments Act, Pub. L. No. 103–465 (H.R. 5110). Prior to passage of that Act, U.S. patents expired 17 years after the date that they were issued, regardless of their application filing dates. The new rule, applicable to U.S. patents issued on the basis of patent applications filed after June 8, 1995, provides for expiration twenty years after their filing dates. 35 U.S.C. § 154.
[56] 35 U.S.C. § 112.

sequence information is not patentable when it is stored in an electronic medium that is readable by computers, how can it nonetheless be patented when stored in a molecular medium that is readable by living cells?

A quick answer is that information stored in a computer readable medium is directed at the human observers who are the intended beneficiaries of the information spillovers that arise through patent disclosures. It is therefore *human* readable information that must not be patented as such in order to maintain a balance between the exclusionary rights of patent holders and the rights of the public to use the disclosures that are the *quid pro quo* of those exclusionary rights. But humans can direct queries to DNA sequence information whether it is stored in molecular form or in electronic form. One might, for example, use DNA molecules as probes to detect the presence of a particular DNA sequence in a sample. This sort of molecular query has diagnostic and forensic applications as well as research applications. Researchers seeking to learn more about the functional significance of DNA sequence information are likely to query the information in both computer readable and molecular form.[57] The distinction between computer readable and molecular versions of DNA sequence is particularly difficult to maintain in the context of DNA array technology. DNA array technology involves immobilizing thousands of short oligonucleotide molecules on a substrate to detect the presence of particular sequences in a sample using specialized robotics and imaging equipment.[58] In effect, this technology enables people to use computers to perceive information stored in DNA molecules in a sample. When contemporary technology blurs the boundaries between computer readable and molecular forms of DNA, what logic is there to drawing this distinction in determining the patent rights of DNA sequencers?

A pragmatic reason for maintaining this distinction is that patent claims to DNA sequences in molecular form have been and will probably continue to be crucially important in motivating costly and risky investments in the commercial development of new therapeutic proteins, which must be proven

---

[57] After sequencing DNA, researchers might analyze the sequence in computer readable form to identify similarities to known sequences, and then analyze the sequence in cell-readable form to observe the functional significance of different portions of the sequence in a living cell or organism. They might, for example, use DNA molecules as probes to determine when and where an organism expresses a particular portion of its DNA sequence, or they might induce a cell to express a particular DNA sequence in order to learn more about the protein that it encodes, or they might interrupt expression of a DNA sequence in an organism and observe the consequences in order to learn more about the functions of the corresponding protein. This sort of interaction between analysis of electronic information and observation of how cells use the information characterizes what in recent years has become known as "functional genomics" research. See Philip Hieter & Mark Boguski: *Functional Genomics: It's All How You Read It*, 278 Science 601 (1997); Stanley Fields, *The future is function*, 15 Nature Genetics 325 (1997).

[58] See R. Ekins and F.W. Chu, *Microarrays: their origins and applications*, 17 Trends in Biotechnology 217 (1999); B. Sinclair, *Everything's Great When It Sits on a Chip – A bright future for DNA arrays*, 13 The Scientist at 18, (May 24, 1999).

safe and effective in human clinical trials before they can be brought to market. The arguments for free access to DNA sequences as a means of promoting scientific progress may have equal force whether the sequence is claimed in electronic or molecular form, but the countervailing arguments for exclusivity are far more powerful for DNA sequences in molecular form. The importance of patents in motivating drug development is well established;[59] the importance of patents in motivating the development of information products is speculative.[60]

A final argument for maintaining a distinction between DNA sequence information and DNA molecules at this point is consistency with tradition and precedent. Any categorical exclusion of DNA molecules from eligibility for patent protection would contradict the practice of the PTO and the courts for two decades and would undermine the precedent-based expectations of a patent-sensitive industry. On the other hand, allowance of patent claims to DNA sequence information stored in computer readable medium would extend patentable subject matter beyond what the PTO and the courts have recognized thus far, departing from a long tradition of free access to the information disclosed in issued patents. Genomics investors might hope to receive such patents, but they can hardly claim to have relied on their availability.

This analysis may seem stubbornly "bricks and mortar" in its focus on tangibility as the touchstone for protection, and therefore out of step with the needs of the modern information economy. If a significant portion of the value of DNA sequencing resides in the information that it yields, rather than in the molecules that correspond to that information, then perhaps we should not assume that investments in creating that value will be forthcoming on the basis of an intellectual property system that limits exclusionary rights to tangible things and allows the information itself to spill over to the general public.[61] At some point, we may need intellectual property rights that permit the creators of information products to capture the value of the information itself in order to

---

[59] See generally R.C. Levin, A.K. Klevorick, R.R. Nelson, & S.G. Winter, *Appropriating the returns from industrial research and development*, 3 Brookings Papers on Economic Activity 783–820 (1987) (indicating that the importance of patents varies considerably across different industries and that patents are particularly important in the pharmaceutical industry).

[60] Proposals for special legislation to provide intellectual property protection for databases have provoked a lively debate concerning the costs and benefits of such protection. See, e.g., National Research Council, Bits of Power: Issues in Global Access to Scientific Data (1997); National Research Council, A Question of Balance: Private Rights and the Public Interest in Scientific and Technical Databases (1999).

[61] The classic argument for intellectual property is that exclusionary rights are necessary to motivate investments in the creation of goods that are costly to make initially, but cheap and easy to copy once someone else the made the initial investment. As growing volumes of information become freely available on the internet, this argument seems to be overlooking significant incentives to create and disseminate information outside the intellectual property system. See generally Carl Shapiro & Hal Varian, Information Rules (1999).

motivate socially valuable investments. But if we have arrived at that point, then we need to look beyond the patent system for a suitable model. The patent system was designed to serve the needs of a bricks and mortar world, and it would be foolish to assume that it can meet the changing needs of the information economy simply by expanding the categories of subject matter that are eligible for patent protection.

New Research Norms for a New Medium[1]

Helen Nissenbaum

Many who have worked in a medium of ink and paper look to a future dominated by a digital electronic medium with a mixture of awe and apprehension. Scholars and researchers are among them, hailing the shift from the largely paper-based infrastructure of publication, communication and archiving to a predominantly electronic one as a boon, but also recognizing the problematic potential. Economic uncertainties likely to face publishers trying to devise business models for the new terrain are certainly worrying, but more central to scholars and researchers is the quality and integrity of the published corpus of their respective fields of inquiry and, by implication, the quality and integrity of research and scholarship itself.

This paper addresses an aspect of the relationship between electronic publication and the quality and integrity of research by focusing on one of the important mediating influences of quality and integrity, namely norms and conventions governing research and scholarship. What concerns me particularly is how we ought to be thinking about adapting those entrenched norms and conventions whose characteristics have been shaped for a realm of ink and paper, to an environment in which the electronic medium reigns. I use the example of establishing priority for research results as a case study for a general approach I develop in this paper. What I propose is that communities of scientific research should put potential normative shifts to a test, evaluating the extent to which proposed new norms are as true to research values as the entrenched norms they would replace. In the case of priority, I analyze whether commodification, a close

---

[1] Early drafts of the paper were presented at the IEEE Workshop on Socioeconomic Dimensions of Electronic Publishing, Santa Barbara, 1998 and at the conference, The Commodification of Information; Political, Social, and Cultural Ramifications, Haifa, May 1999. Improvements were prompted by participants' comments at both events. I am grateful to Rochelle Dreyfuss and Seumus Miller for helping clarify aspects of patent law and philosophical thought on convention, respectively. Thanks also to Neil Netanel for more excellent suggestions than I was able to incorporate and to Sayumi Takahashi and Hyeseung Song for able research assistance. This work was supported by the National Science Foundation, Grant SBR-9806234.

N. Elkin-Koren and N.W. Netanel (eds.), *The Commodification of Information*, 433–457.
© 2002 *Helen Nissenbaum. Printed in Great Britain.*

cousin of priority, could feature successfully as a rival source of norms. On the basis of my test for evaluating new norms for the new medium, I argue that property norms [,] despite their long history and success in other spheres, are problematic as replacements for norms governing attribution of priority in spite of the latter's relative ambiguity and contextual dependence.

Research Norms: Attribution of Priority

Scientific research is constituted of an enormous array of practices. These practices are governed – implicitly and explicitly – by a set of interdependent norms, conventions and institutions that define standards and prescribe expectations within research communities. (From hereon I use "norms" or "conventions" as shorthand for "norms, conventions and institutions.") These norms regulate the basic methods of conducting research (in whatever the environments typical of various fields) and for reporting on the results of such research. In addition to procedural standards, norms regulate practices such as peer review, authorship, attribution of credit, research collaboration, mentorship, and more. In this paper, I am particularly interested in the subset of these norms that Seumus Miller, in his work on social norms and conventions, would conceive as having "moral or quasi-moral normative force" (1997, p. 213). According to Miller, norms, conventions and institutions acquire this moral or quasi-moral force in the extent to which they help people or communities realize moral or morally relevant values, ends and purposes.

Among these norms, some more than others are likely to be affected by a shift to the medium of electronic publication, communication and archiving – perhaps those governing authorship, peer review, and collaboration, for example. The goal of this paper is to offer a systematic approach to the challenge of devising new norms and reshaping old ones for the context of the new medium. I will use as a case study for this approach norms governing the attribution of priority, which, surprisingly, will call for adjustment as our reliance on the electronic medium of publication grows.

To have priority for a significant idea, result, discovery or invention (henceforth I use "result" as a generic term), is to have one's name associated with it and to be recognized as the first to have produced, invented, or discovered it. Many researchers, for whom priority is the "holy grail," will fight priority disputes with a fierceness and enmity not usually associated with the genteel hallways of academe. Some of these disputes have reached outside the research communities playing out in the public eye, for example, Robert Gallo of the National Cancer Institute fighting Luc Montagnier of the Pasteur Institute of Paris over priority for the discovery and isolation of the AIDS virus. The fight persisted for more than a decade and involved Gallo and his co-workers in accusations of gross misconduct. In another dispute a few decades ago, the South

African surgeon Christian Barnard performed the first ever heart transplant on a human, infuriating his mentors at Stanford University who believed that in exploiting the less stringent criteria for experimental medical treatment of his home country, Barnard had stolen their own clearly deserved priority.

Examples could be spun out indefinitely: the race to the double helix, Newton competing with Leibniz over calculus, Pasteur's dubious victory in the discovery of an anthrax vaccine and so on (See Geison). I will here briefly describe only one more, to use as a case study for the themes I wish to explore in this paper. The case involves mathematicians in the 19th century.

In 1832 a young mathematician, Janos Bolyai, published a treatise on a theory of non-Euclidean geometry, known today as hyperbolic geometry. Because at the time he had not yet established a reputation as a scholar, his father published the work as an appendix to an essay the father himself had written. When the senior Bolyai communicated his son's result to Carl Friedrich Gauss, the pre-eminent mathematician of their day, Gauss responded with words that mathematicians today are fond of quoting and frequently parodying. Reacting to Bolyai's work, Gauss wrote: "To praise it would amount to praising myself. For the entire content of the work ... coincides almost exactly with my own meditations which have occupied my mind for the past thirty or thirty-five years."

As it turns out, a third name, Nikolay Ivanovich Lobachevsky, is now also associated with the discovery of hyperbolic geometry. Lobachevsky had pre-empted both Gauss and Bolyai with his result published in 1829. Nevertheless, surprising as outsiders may find it, many mathematicians consider the attribution of priority for hyperbolic geometry to be genuinely controversial. Although some are ready to be strictly guided by publication date and find this enough to establish Lobachevsky as the discoverer, others argue for priority of one of the other two, or both, or all three. So the dispute continues to fester long after its protagonists have passed on. We will return to this case later in the paper.

Although disputes over priority are more common in science and engineering, they are not unheard of in other fields. In philosophy, for example, priority over the so-called "New Theory of Reference" is hotly disputed. Although most philosophers acknowledge Saul Kripke as discoverer, the philosopher Quentin Smith raised a storm of controversy by arguing that some of the fundamental ideas in Kripke's theory had been discovered and articulated eight years earlier by Ruth Barcan Marcus (Smith, 1995). As in the hard-fought priority disputes of science and engineering, this one involved hostile exchanges, careful retracing of historical milestones, and a thorough study and reanalysis of the disputants' relevant key works. At the writing of this paper there is still no closure to the debate, though several leading philosophers of logic and language have claimed to have debunked Smith (Burgess, 1998; Holt, 1997).

This paper, nevertheless, is tuned primarily to the context of science and engineering partly because priority and priority disputes are a more common feature of the science and engineering landscape, where research efforts regularly converge on a number of widely recognized ends. Another, pragmatic reason for focusing on science and engineering is to reduce variation; even within the various sub-fields of science and engineering there is a degree of variability which I am not able fully to accommodate in what follows.

Publication and Priority

Before considering how attribution of priority may be affected by electronic publication, let us first consider the relationship of priority to publication generally. To earn priority, researchers (or a team of researchers) typically need, in the first place, to persuade their communities that their results are correct, sound, valid; that is, meet the standards of their fields for establishing the integrity of results, processes, discoveries, procedures, etc. One of the most common ways to establish integrity of results is to submit a written report for publication so that reviewers – usually accomplished members of a research community – may evaluate it. In judging a work worthy of publication, these respected peers accord public recognition of its quality. In the second place, researchers must persuade their peers of the primacy of their claims; that is, that they are the first to have proved, discovered, demonstrated, etc. the result. Publication frequently plays an important role in this, too, as researchers typically demonstrate that a thorough search of published works has not yielded the same result.

People credit Henry Oldenberg, who served from 1662–1677 as secretary of the Royal Society of London for Improving Natural Knowledge, with cementing the connection between priority and publication. Oldenberg, who opposed the secrecy that shrouded scientific discoveries and believed in the power of critique-and-rebuttal, started the Society's *Philosophical Transactions: Giving Some Accompt of the Present Undertakings, Studies and Labors of the Ingenious in Many Considerable Parts of the World* to promote these commitments. To encourage scientists in Europe and England – among them the young Isaac Newton – to publish their results in the *Philosophical Transactions*, Oldenberg offered prompt publication. He also promised that the Royal Society would stand behind these scientists' claims to being first to discover the phenomena in question. Thus, in March 1665, Oldenberg initiated the convention that priority goes to the person who publishes first (or now, more precisely, the person who first submits the finding for publication), rather than the person who first makes the discovery.[2]

---

[2] Discussed in Whitbeck, C. (1998). *Ethics in Engineering Practice and Research*. Cambridge University Press, New York p. 267; and *Dictionary of Scientific Biography*, Volume X, 200–203, American Council of Learned Societies, New York: Charles Scribner 1974. In reading up on Oldernberg, during my stay at the Institute for Advanced Study, I had the remarkable

A few qualifications and caveats are in order: (1) What I have described is a somewhat idealized version of actual practice. In the real world of research there may be significant compromises – some necessary, others regrettable: reviewers may not be as careful as they ought to be, acknowledgment of prior work not as comprehensive as it ought to be and so forth. (2) The details of practices may vary among distinct fields and disciplines: for example, in some fields conference proceedings (or other pre-publication reports) do not "count" as publications as much as polished journals, whereas in other fields, articles in polished journals are viewed as already "old." I do not expect that all such variations will affect my central claims. But in the cases where they do, it is quite possible that the broader picture I describe below will not apply. (3) Although publication is one of the predominant vehicles for establishing priority for results, I do not maintain that it is the only vehicle. Particularly in applied or practical fields it may be that what matters is not publication but being first to build a prototype, or perform a procedure (e.g., heart transplant surgery). Other exceptions may occur in fields that are willing to attribute priority even when researchers have not offered the full disclosure of publication but have only managed to convince key peers through informal channels that their priority claims are valid.[3] I merely claim that publication, for many fields of research in science and engineering, is one central vehicle for establishing or brokering priority and it is important, at least in these fields, to understand the expected impact of a shift to the electronic medium.

The Puzzle

Consider how electronic publication may affect conventions for establishing priority. As we have heard repeatedly, electronic publication "democratizes" publication, meaning that there are many more avenues for publication, including self-publication, that do not involve clearing the usual hurdles of peer review. This prospect has caused widespread concern that in eroding the traditional means of control, electronic publication will lead eventually to a declining quality of published work, resulting in an enormous but untrustworthy body of work unless we find ways to carry forward mechanisms or conventions of review. Although there are good reasons to worry about this problem, it takes us too far from the

---

cont.
    experience of paging through several of the delicate, yellowed three-hundred year-old volumes of Transactions, published around 1667. I am grateful to the librarian for pointing these out to me in the Institute's rare books collection.

[3] Robert Merges (1996) discusses several such scenarios, especially in high-stakes biomedical research.

current thread. Its relevance to priority is that the loss of one of the established mechanisms for assessing the correctness of results means we undermine one of the two crucial elements involved in validating the priority claims of aspiring researchers and scientists.

Although of enormous importance, it will not be the first but the second element – namely, establishing primacy – that will be my primary focus. Here, electronic publication poses a curious puzzle. Here, too, the backdrop is what people call the "publication explosion." If we construe publication in terms of its natural meaning – to cover the activity of preparing material for presentation and distribution, sometimes for sale, in public – we see that information and communications technology throws wide open the possibilities for publication.[4]

Currently the most prominent venue for publishing works in the electronic realm, the World Wide Web ("the Web")[5] has inspired a sense of excitement and prospects of revolutionary change. For many, the Web represents an ideal – a readily accessible medium without entry barriers imposed by the traditional gatekeepers, such as commercial publishers. Everyone who has access to the Web and some know-how can publish. Cited as key evidence for the democratizing tendency of information technology, this broad access to a medium of publication enables vast numbers of people to speak out, be heard by others, hear others speak and communicate to one and to many. Taking advantage of this novel opportunity, participants and contributors have built the Web into a virtually endless mélange of text, sound, images and information. It ranges over the polished, commercially produced websites of corporations (some costing millions of dollars) and government agencies, as well as the eccentric, highly personal websites of lone individuals. All of this constitutes the realm of electronic publication. These compelling but phenomenologically-based impressions of size and scope are given quantitative measure by researchers like S. Lawrence and C.L. Giles who, in 1999, using statistical sampling methods, estimated the lower bound size of the total indexable web to be 800 million.[6] In two years, this number has surely grown to above one billion. (see Ziman, 1998).

As noted earlier, scientific researchers claiming priority need to convince their peers that they have scrutinized the relevant body of published works and have ensured that they are first, that no others before them have obtained the same or very similar results. In opening wide the possibilities for publication, the electronic medium poses enormous challenges to locating the relevant body of published works. In addition to the standard journals, of which many are published on-line,

---

[4] In using the term "natural," I refer to the meaning of the term as conveyed in general conversation and captured by definitions given in any of the standard English dictionaries, such as Oxford or Webster.

[5] Although electronic publication may occur in locations other than the Web, this possibility only exacerbates and does not diminish the puzzle I describe below.

[6] S. Lawrence and C.L. Giles, "Accessibility of Information on the Web," *Nature*, 400, 107–109, 1999.

there is a wide range of new kinds of publications whose very possibility was unthinkable in the paper-based medium. Specialists in library and information science have identified various forms of emergent non-traditional species of electronic publication. B.J. Wyly calls attention, for example, to "wildcat electronic publications," a term he coined to describe the products of "small, single journal electronic publishers of free electronic journals" (1998). Like his namesake in the oil business, an "independent entrepreneur who has the daring to drill an exploratory well on a hunch about a possible oil field," the wildcat publisher creates exploratory scholarly communication tools based on some sense of the needs of scholarly communities and based on a hunch about the possibilities of electronic publishing. A generic term of trade, "gray literature" covers a broad range of material found on the Web that is not published by established publishers. This includes electronic preprints, locally published reports placed on the Web by institutions like universities or corporate research centers, and reports of work that individual scientists and engineers place on their personal web pages (see Gelfand and King, 1998; Sonkkila, 1998).

The puzzle of priority is this: in the face of the dramatic publication explosion, what will become of the norms governing priority? What will become of the systematic expectations we have of researchers claiming priority? How do we revise entrenched norms, how do we devise new norms, for a research environment built upon an electronic substructure? Will the burden upon those claiming priority be that they now must search all electronic publications to assure colleagues that they have a well-grounded conviction that no one, anywhere, has previously published similar results? Do we expect them to conduct a search of literally all publications, including every John Doe's and Jane Roe's personal Web pages? If not, then what?

Research Norms and Research Values

Rather than answer the question about priority norms directly, consider the question in terms of research norms (conventions and institutions) generally. Setting out to understand the rationale for existing norms, we surely will find a complicated picture. Sure to feature into this picture is the role of research values, ends and purposes in determining the shape of these norms, conventions and institutions. (From hereon I mainly use "values" as an abbreviation for "values, ends and purposes.") Take for example, the practice of peer review in which a paper is distributed according to certain rules for evaluation by several experts in the field. We can understand norms governing peer review as a way to promote and maintain the soundness and integrity of a body of research results. Blind review, a special form of peer review, seeks similar ends, trying in addition to correct for the tendency of personal ties to obscure or bias objective considerations. Norms that prescribe replication of experimental results serve to promote the ends of objectivity and fidelity in a world where researchers, even in good faith, are all too vulnerable to bias and accident. Conventions of authorship can be understood as designed to nourish and give recognition to promising researchers.

There is an important distinction to bear in mind between values, ends and purposes attributable to all humanity, serving, as it were, general welfare and those of subgroups within the general. In imagining ends of scientific and engineering research serving general welfare we might include the creation of a body of reliable and trustworthy work, the capacity to respond effectively and engage productively within the world, the ability to manipulate the world in service of important human needs. Even more fundamentally, we may also include ends such as: knowledge, truth, progress, social welfare, and the betterment of the human condition.[7]

By contrast, one can imagine a different set of purposes serving specialized subgroups like scientific researchers, universities, industrial organizations and non-governmental funding agencies, whose interests are not always identical or even compatible with those of the general. Any one of the subgroups may wish to steer scientific research practices, via norms, conventions and institutions, in directions that serve its own parochial interests, and, as a matter of fact, probably has succeeded in doing so in many cases. A descriptive or historical study of scientific research could chart the important place of parochial interests in determining the shape of conventions and institutions (and no doubt parochial interests have carried the day for particular practices). This paper, however, is primarily normative and primarily concerned with conventions responding to the general welfare. In other words, it is concerned with norms and conventions that carry moral weight; those that serve parochial or special interests, to the extent that they serve solely special or parochial interests, do not.

Although in some cases, it may be possible to understand a given norm as optimal, or near-optimal, in achieving certain ends or promoting certain values, it may be the case that the shape of research and publication norms will require more than an accounting of the relationship of norms, on the one hand, to values, on the other. Many other factors can influence the character of norms – some quite idiosyncratic. In some cases – ones I would judge pathological – a community may

---

[7] There is bound to be considerable disagreement over precisely what constitutes the goals, ends, values and purposes of scientific and engineering research, especially given skeptical appraisals of many sociologists, historians, philosophers and anthropologists. A discussion and defense of my proposed list extends beyond the scope of this paper and I must, therefore, let it stand as a basic assumption. For readers who fundamentally disagree with my characterization of the "values, ends and purposes" of scientific research, the central claims of this paper will most likely appear inadequately defended. Others who merely find the list incomplete, or mistaken in detail, may find that this does not detract from the central claims and arguments.

accept norms that are not optimal for achieving stated values because, for example, members systematically misjudge the way the norms operate on practices, or because it is corrupt, or because it is excessively influenced by parochial interests. Although in these pathological scenarios we should take corrective steps, in others, there are unavoidable but legitimate co-determinants of scientific norms and conventions that are non-moral in nature. To these I now turn.

The context for scientific research is ultimately the real world. If we wish to understand the factors that shape, or co-determine, the character of research norms, we must look beyond underlying values and ends, to contextual constraints of the research environment itself. These constraints may be as general as the political and educational backdrop of research, or as mundane yet as compelling as economic contingencies and speed of the local postal service. For example, the conventions governing recognition of scientific work and career development in the Soviet Union, several decades ago, systematically would take into account whether a researcher was Jewish. In other words, one would understand the shape of these norms only if one took into account certain features of the political context. In understanding norms of peer review, one needs to bring into account a number of detailed, practical factors such as overwork and the cost and difficulty of distributing copies. These factors may work against an ideal driven only by considerations of, say soundness and integrity, and can determine limits on features like the numbers of reviewers, degree of diversity and level of expertise, amount of time, etc. Similarly the convention calling for replication of experimental results is softened by practical factors such as funding limits and the general sense in many scientific communities that those who choose to replicate results are not engaged in what is seen as the exciting pursuit of novel research.[8]

In sum, successful norms (successful as norms with moral force) are ones that for a given environment are optimal with respect to values; they are likely to be shaped also, but not overly compromised by, external factors including environmental constraints and parochial influences. At any given time these norms will reflect a balance between the idealized pursuit of values, on one hand, and contextual constraints, on the other.

Over time, norms – even those that are for the most part successful – may change, evolve. From the model I have described, one can predict what some of the precipitating factors of change might be. It may be that a research community, finding that its record of stated ends and promoting recognized values falls short, makes a dedicated effort to improve via an adjustment of norms. It may be that change is precipitated in a shift in the nature of the values themselves. Or it may be

---

[8] David Baltimore discusses this point in his Tanner lectures (1992).

that non-moral features of the research context change, requiring a shift in norms.[9] These changes in norms may be gradual, occurring over the course of years or even centuries; or they may be sudden, a response to a significant discontinuity in either context or values.

In the case of attribution of priority, we have a case where changes in non-moral features of the research environment challenge entrenched conventions. These changes, as mentioned earlier, occur as a result of the shifting from a mode of publication, communication, collaboration and archiving that is paper-based to one that is largely electronic. If prevailing commentary and predictions are borne out, the shift will be swift and radical (some might even say revolutionary) and will demand swift and sometimes radical adjustments in norms, conventions and institutions. The puzzle of priority is a symptom of the need to adjust entrenched norms because of changes brought about by electronic publication. In this case we shall not have the luxury of waiting centuries for new norms to evolve, but will need to take explicit and active steps to adjust them to the new context. In the following section, I suggest a strategy for responding to such needs to revise norms.

The Test

I put forward attribution of priority as an example of a practice that is likely to be disturbed as a result of a move to a digital electronic medium of publication, communication and archiving like the Internet and the World Wide Web. Conventions that worked reasonably well in the past may give rise to challenges, like the puzzle, when they are embedded in a new context. Instead of a quick resolution to the puzzle, I outline a systematic approach to devising and evaluating new research norms for a digital age, drawing on the model I have sketched above of the relationship among norms, values, and contextual factors. The terms of the model offer a vocabulary for framing a fundamental test of any proposed norms (that is, new norms that would replace entrenched norms). The test to which we put new norms is to evaluate whether, and to what extent, they promote the values, ends and purposes that inspired the entrenched norms in the first place.

In practice, establishing that norms have "passed" the test is not a straightforward affair. To demonstrate that the proposed new norms serve the values served by the norms they replace, and serve them as well as, or better than,

---

[9] In The United States we are currently seeing a spate of interest in norms and conventions governing scientific research coming in the wake of much publicized cases of so-called scientific misconduct. A large literature discusses this trend. See as an example, Caroline Whitbeck (1998).

these norms, calls for an acquaintance with, and at least some understanding of, complex social, intellectual and historical factors driving the research endeavor, as well as an ability to reason about considerations of value. Once we have explicated the relationship between proposed new norms and values and ends, and compared this with the relationship of entrenched norms and values and ends, we must be prepared to consider how efficacious proposed norms would be in comparison with competing contenders. (Readers familiar with traditional utilitarian analysis will be familiar with the formal characteristics of this demand: a moral prescription to act, or not to act, in a certain way should not only maximize the balance of happiness over unhappiness but must do so optimally.)

In spite of these complexities, it is worthwhile submitting proposed norms to the test because the alternatives are in all likelihood worse. One alternative is that under pressure a community would adopt new norms prematurely without consideration for values and ends. This would leave the community, and society at large, vulnerable to the possibility that these new norms are suboptimal in a variety of ways, involving, for example, rigors that are arbitrary and not necessarily conducive to the values, ends and purposes of scientific research. Or they may involve an excessive compromise of values in favor of practical convenience. Another danger of adopting norms without submitting them to the test is that the scientific community might allow a tilting of purposes away from general societal needs toward parochial interests of specialized groups. In any of these cases we will have weakened the moral content, the moral force, of norms, conventions and institutions governing scientific and engineering research.

One final point to note is that the test need not be conservative; it need not limit possibilities to norms that do as well but no better than predecessors. Indeed, the appeal of information technology as a medium for research publication, communication and so forth is that it promises more; it offers the prospect of a less constraining research environment and potentially a more effortless, less costly, more efficient path than previously possible to realize the ultimate ends and values of scientific and engineering research.

Now, armed with the test, let us return to the puzzle of priority, at the same time trying to learn something about adapting research norms, in general, to contextual changes brought about by new and powerful technologies. In order to demonstrate how the test may be applied, I have narrowed my focus to two possible lines of response that both seemed to be plausible contenders. The one that occupies most of my attention is a wholesale shift in normative framework to that of intellectual property as a means of reducing some of the fuzziness and ambiguity in current norms of attribution of priority that the puzzle demonstrates. I will argue that this move fails the test and will briefly consider an alternative approach. This plan is inspired by two goals. One is that it offers a vivid illustration of how one may use the test as a tool for crafting and evaluating new research norms for the information age. The other is to mount a challenge, in this one small corner, against the looming dominance that intellectual property seems to have acquired as an omnibus solution to a broad range of problems in this era of information and information technology.[10]

Allure of Intellectual Property

There are a number of reasons why intellectual property may seem attractive as a replacement regime. Norms and conventions in research and scholarship are unquestionably imprecise, even sometimes ambiguous. As has happened in other domains, the arrival of information technology can spell opportunity for much needed change. In this case, one could argue, it triggers a need to impose order on an archaic, motley family of norms, particularly those guiding the allocation of entitlements, under the rubric of our rational system of property rights. Entrenched conventions that have guided the attribution of priority, as well as authorship, peer review, collaboration and so forth, evolved in a far different context and cannot automatically be expected to remain effective in the electronic realm. Why force from traditional conventions more than they are naturally able to yield when the conceptual framework of intellectual property, refined and adapted for the infrastructure into which research is sinking its foundations, is ready at hand? The institution of intellectual property has the further advantage of many years of explicit formal development within the legal system. Through it we could avoid the fuzziness and ambiguity of many of the entrenched conventions guiding scientific research that evolved only implicitly through years of use and practice.

Another reason to consider a role for intellectual property in rationalizing research norms and conventions is less normative and more historical. It points to the prominence of intellectual property in our thinking about information technology generally. In the past roughly two decades, intellectual property has been a central preoccupation of a number of constituencies involved in the development and use of information technology. Almost as soon as the commercial promise of information technology was recognized, lively debates erupted over the nature and extent of private ownership that could and ought to be exercised over a variety of aspects of the technology. Hardware and software developers, creators and distributors of content, economists, philosophers, scholars and practitioners of law and policy, motivated by concern over their and other stakes in the question, argued over the ownability of everything, from chip design to source and object code to algorithms. These arguments gained momentum and urgency as their scope extended to the many forms of intellectual

---

[10] It has emerged as a solution – misguided, I think – also in the context of protecting privacy.

work expressible in electronic form such as text, images, movies, music, information and more. The digital electronic format offered unprecedented tools for creating works of art and intellect embedded in a technology whose very nature is to provide easy, widespread and virtually instantaneous access to these works, as well as a power to manipulate vast troves of material. A clear blessing for many, such capabilities create headaches for those who seek to control and profit from these creations. The institution of intellectual property was seen, and continues to be seen, as a robust answer to this conundrum.

There remain several unsettled controversies, several highly charged questions about the appropriate extent and strength of intellectual property rights in cyberspace (see, for example, McCullagh, 1997; Samuelson, n.d.; Samuelson et al., 1994), and some important challenges to traditional regimes of intellectual property, most notably the open source movement. Nevertheless, it is fair to say that norms and policies defining the institution of intellectual property are – for better or for worse – a defining part of the culture that has emerged with the electronic medium as we know it today. As anecdotal evidence of this progression, I note the considerable familiarity many academic computer scientists have with the intricacies of intellectual property, as compared with their relative innocence of such matters, say, fifteen years ago. Also anecdotally, with other norms of authorship, it is common for people to express their disgust over plagiarism as a wrong involving a violation of property rights.

In progressively moving its center of gravity to the electronic media, the research enterprise is not merely adopting a set of bare tools and technological capabilities; it is adopting a technological system that is rich with values, culture and conventions of its own.[11] This shift to an electronic infrastructure of publication is not merely a matter of the world of scientific research adopting and adapting a set of neutral tools for its use. It is a matter of two worlds meeting – one, research, the other, information technology – both replete with their own sets of values, purposes, norms, practices, conventions and meanings. In the case of information technology this culture and these values powerfully reflect those of the communities that have developed the technology, as well as the communities in whose service the technology was initially developed. For the most part these communities have embraced intellectual property into their culture and viewed it as a boon.[12]

Another reason is more specific. The reason we think of intellectual property at all has to do with the very nature of a priority claim, which is after all a claim of

---

[11] The idea of values embedded or embodied in technological systems has been discussed quite actively in recent decades, first within the area known as Science, Technology and Society (STS) and more recently applied specifically to computer systems. (Bijker et al., 1987, Nissenbaum, 1998; Winner, 1986).

[12] I say "for the most part" because this is not true universally. Richard Stallman, through the Free Software Foundation, and many others continue to propound a view of computer software as a public good.

entitlement that an individual (or group) makes over an intellectual work. There are suggestive similarities between attribution of priority, on one hand, and allocation of intellectual property rights, on the other, more specifically, between the meaning conveyed in a priority claim and that conveyed in a patent claim. Both attach to the authors of inventions serving as public recognition of those authors. Both place demands on the quality and nature of a work in question. Both demand primacy of discovery. Both demand evidence of a search for prior similar work.

Intellectual Property and Research Norms

On the basis of these considerations, importing a patent-like system into the realm of research and scholarship holds promise. Moreover, in replacing norms governing priority, it offers needed precision to deal with difficult questions raised by our "puzzle." Beyond the potential efficiencies of such a switch, we may be interested in whether it is morally compelling. And to satisfy this interest, we need to submit the proposed change to the test; that is to say, evaluate whether the proposed new norms sustain and promote values, ends and purposes as well as their entrenched counterparts.

I see two perfectly good strategies for carrying out the test. In one, we first spin out the relationship between entrenched conventions and values and new conventions and values, respectively. Next we compare the results. In another – the one I pursue here – we take a shortcut by first identifying key differences between proposed (new) conventions and entrenched (existing) conventions and next analyzing how these differences might impinge upon the attainment of ends and values. In carrying this out, this second mode of analysis, I note two differences between patents and priority:

> Difference I: Patents do not tolerate independent invention, discovery, performance, etc.[13] By contrast, under entrenched conventions, priority can be shared.

---

[13] The prevailing patent system in the United States is committed to a distinction between discovery (e.g. discovery of pre-existing facts of nature) and invention (of processes, methods, machines, etc.). The second delimits a category of patentable works the first delimits one that is not. Although there may be utilitarian reasons for insisting that some works ought not be patentable, I do not see that the distinction can sensibly be based on the distinction between discovery and invention which has been given dubious interpretation, in my opinion, in the context of patents. It is not central to my paper that this matter be settled so I propose to finesse it.

Difference II: A patent must be formally applied for and registered with a legally sanctioned body (in the United States, The Patent and Trademark Office). No strict equivalent exists in research, where publication serves a similar function.

These differences, in themselves, do not imply superiority of one approach over the other. We need to look beyond the mere presence of difference, beyond formal disparities between institutionalized conventions of patents, on one hand, and conventions of priority, on the other, toward the question of their respective functional implications for values, ends and purpose. Before taking the two points of difference in turn, I need to prepare the ground by acknowledging key substantive presumptions upon which my analysis rests.

The first concerns the moral foundations of intellectual property, and property in general. While acknowledging the enormous depth of thinking on this subject, for the sake of simplicity (and progress on core issues of this paper), I adopt a utilitarian approach.[14] Accordingly, I take general welfare as the key measure for deciding among alternative regimes of intellectual property.

According to utilitarian reasoning, intellectual property produces utility by investing intellectual property owners with control over intellectual works. This they exercise by limiting access to the work, and setting conditions of sale, transfer, duplication and so on. In the case of patents, control is monopolistic – at least, for a period of time. Received wisdom has it that investing property holders – in this case patent holders – with control creates favorable conditions for investment because property holders, assured of protection, are ready to invest in bringing inventions, etc. to the public – paying for development, manufacture and so forth – will be protected. In turn, the promise of profit and other success, serves as encouragement to further inventiveness, creativity and bold investment in projects that might otherwise seem risky. The potential gains are thought far to outweigh the recognized costs to individuals and societies in the forms both of restricted freedoms and also the costs of enforcing property rights. In the patent system, for example, many see a system that has been finely calibrated (and continues to be adjusted) to yield on balance – through the direct benefits of innovative products and indirect benefits of wealth – a substantial increase in social welfare.[15]

My paper also rests on certain beliefs concerning the ends and purposes of research in science and engineering, and conditions necessary to nurture them. As noted earlier, I take the ends and purposes to include such things as the advancement of knowledge and understanding; attainment of truth; the ability to interact with and successfully manipulate the world; and so forth. They are best

---

[14] A large and daunting literature addresses the question of how to construe moral justifications for intellectual property. Jeremy Waldron (1988) provides an excellent historical overview.

[15] For an elaboration of these and other aspects of intellectual prop", see, for example, two recent articles (Eisenberg, 1989; Hughes, 1988).

served by an environment of openness, that is, an environment in which researchers freely share ideas, results and even primary data (with suitable caveats and limitations); where scientific researchers engage in active evaluation and critiquing of the work of others; where researchers may learn from others and teach them; where they are allowed to build, or piggy-back, freely upon the ideas, results, efforts and accomplishments of others. Such conditions of open exchange offer the greatest hope for successful cumulative efforts and rapid progress and have been expressed, or embodied, in the design of many of the dominant institutions in which cutting-edge research is housed and discussed – most notably, the university, professional organizations, research conferences, and open research publications.[16]

By contrast, at the heart of the institution of intellectual property, in general, and patents, in particular, is a fundamentally different idea. The insight here is that monopolistic control over intellectual property gives a head start to patent owners, thereby encouraging both intellectual effort and investment. This head start is important, if not essential, for the commercial viability of investment in innovative technologies. In the realm of research, however, such control is neither universally needed nor is beneficial for the attainment of values and ends. Progress in research is facilitated not by allowing researchers to limit and control access but by the possibility of free and ready access to the results of others, and the ability to build, without obstacle, upon them. Even as we hail the pursuits of commercial activity, and accept patents as an essential vehicle for promoting it, we can question the efficacy of patents in research. The key difference, the reason for the mismatch, is the divergence of their respective purposes, ends and values. The test thus implies caution against norms and practices being welcomed into the realm of research that were developed in the service of commercial viability, for these norms and practices are unlikely to promote the distinctive ends of the research realm.

By now I am sure many readers will be bursting with a mixture of cynicism and doubt. Even those who are not adherents of so-called postmodern or social constructivist depictions of scientific research and its ends might characterize my account as an impossible idealization, a roseate caricature of the real state of scientific and engineering research. A nuanced and historically detailed account would yield a different picture, shaped by the following observations:

1. Scientific researchers, as a matter of fact, are not nearly as generous with their results and know-how as I have suggested. This is due in part to the intense competition among scientists and laboratories, which is driven by the ambition (some may say even egomania) of scientists. But it is also due in part

---

[16] See Clarisa Long (1999) for an excellent and balanced discussion of the efficacy of intellectual property norms in a research context, problems as well as promise.

to what Robert Merges has described as a "creeping propertization" of scientific research. Contrary to traditional views, researchers and the institutions that house them are eager to jump onto the property bandwagon and embrace an intellectual property framework for the products of their research. Perhaps because they perceive in it the possibility of personal advantage – material wealth, control over further research, professional advancement and so forth – they are increasingly seeking property rights in fundamental ideas and discoveries.[17] This notion that intellectual property rights might serve the personal or "home team" interests of scientific researchers might well have featured as an important consideration in my discussion above of the allure of intellectual property.

2. Again, as a matter of fact, patent authorities seem to show an increasing tolerance for patent applications that by conservative standards might have been judged to contain unpatentable content (too distant from application, containing fundamental ideas, etc.). Controversial areas in which such patents have emerged include the biomedical sciences and "the patenting of life," and in computer science and engineering, the algorithms. This also demonstrates that the sharp line I draw between commercial efforts and research, even if it once did exist, is fast fading.

3. Although some research – especially "basic" research – is conducted in educational institutions and patronized by government (that is, public) funds, a great deal of research is – and has been for many decades – conducted for profit corporations. Although some may even argue that public funding does not necessarily imply a duty to forgo property-like control over their work, few have expressed doubt that research conducted in corporate, industrial settings is proprietary.[18] John Ziman, who applies the label of "academic science" and "industrial science" to identify not only two distinct funding sources but two distinct cultures, notes that, "In recent years, however, these two cultures have begun to merge. This is a complex, pervasive, irreversible process, driven by forces that are not yet well understood." (1998, p. 1814) If true, this observation would mean that there is, at best, only a fuzzy line between commercial, proprietary research and open, free academic research. This suggestion should, at least, serve as a caution against sweeping idealizations concerning the ends of scientific research and the motives of its researchers.

---

[17] Merges (1996) offers both historical and legal insight into this trend toward reliance on property for establishing claims over scientific results. Although Merges' discussion is clearly inspired by the model of research found most commonly in the biological and biomedical areas, it has implications for all science. Also see work by Rebecca Eisenberg (11989) which warns of potential harm to research resulting from excessive propertization.

[18] Merges discusses this claim in his article (1996).

449

Each of these three observations conveys important insights about contemporary institutions and practices of scientific research and deserves a more extensive and detailed response than I shall provide here. I do not find them to be fatal, however, with respect to the core claims of this paper though a full rebuttal (not possible here) would require at least that I would need to qualify the scope of my conclusions, to recognize fuzzy borders, and admit variation at the level of individual cases. Because a complete discussion would take me too far from the main course of the paper, I offer some stopgap responses; I hope they satisfy most readers, at least for the moment.

As a start, I would deflect at least some of the force of the observations by reiterating that my picture of research practices and institutions and of ends, purposes and values is sketched in broad brushstrokes only; it is intended to map compelling trends in general terms only and cannot, at the same time, account for the full range of variation within the realm of actual practice. Furthermore, it will not accurately reflect the substantial body of research that is conducted squarely within the corporate, for-profit sector (Ziman's "industrial science").

Second, I note that my purpose here is normative. When I declare the values and ends toward which scientific activity is directed, I describe not necessarily that which actually motivates every individual scientist and research institution, but the values and ends to which the endeavor of scientific research, and the surrounding society, publicly subscribe. I aim to identify those values and ends held out in the public eye as ideals both by participants in scientific research and by surrounding societies that sponsor it. It is in relation to these ends that I evaluate norms, conventions and institutions governing research – both those entrenched and those proposed to replace them. That some (or even a majority) of scientific researchers embrace property rights because they see them as an effective vehicle for transforming ideas and other intellectual accomplishments into material wealth, or personal advantage, does not in itself lend moral weight to an observed trend, or current, in the direction of increased propertization.[19] (Just because it is so does not imply it ought to be so.) To the detractor who points out that certain conventions would be preferred by scientific researchers and scientific research institutions, because they serve to advance parochial interests by promising personal and institutional wealth or power, I would argue that such conventions are simply not morally compelling. My prescriptions are not proffered as prudential advice for any particular interest group within scientific research, but as suggestions of general policy for a society intent on furthering general social welfare through scientific and engineering research, and for members of the

---

[19] Merges also discusses the regrettable scenario where even researchers who are in principle opposed to staking private ownership over basic scientific results may find themselves compelled to do so or be driven out of the business of research altogether, if others around them "defect" to a property framework in significant numbers (1996).

scientific community (individuals and institutions) who remain eager to ground their norms and conventions in morally compelling terms.

We now return to consider the two points of difference between the conventions of priority and the conditions of patents, and to evaluate how these differences bear on values and ends.

Concerning Difference I: In this point we observed that built into the patent system is protection against the threat of independent co-discovery. Conventions governing priority, by contrast, regularly admit shared priority. Priority is readily shared when discovery is simultaneous, but may be shared even when one discovery indisputably precedes the other. This may occur under one, or more, of the following conditions: the second discovery was independently achieved; the time difference was not excessively large; the method of achieving the result was significantly different; and the second researcher was not negligently unaware of the first's result. In the discovery of hyperbolic geometry; for example, Bolyai is acknowledged as one of the discoverers even though there is no doubt that his work was published three years after Lobachevsky's. Should we consider this as evidence that conventions for the attribution of priority are vague, misguided, internally inconsistent, etc.? I think not. In the commercial realm it is arguably essential for patent holders to know that there will be a period in which no others will compete in the manufacture of their inventions. Without such assurance, investment – especially large investment – might always seem excessively risky. In research the need to identify a unique discoverer may at times be outweighed by the advantage of linking more than one researcher with a result. The possibility of shared priority serves important ends: it highlights, or helps reify, successful lines of attack, effective or powerful techniques, and promising schools of thought. There need not be only one and indeed, if there are more, then it serves scientific research if all are kept in clear sight.

Another reason for embracing shared priority is that priority serves to highlight promising members of a community, constituting an important currency of community approval. Priority thereby helps forge careers in research. Whereas the monopolistic aspect of patents helps attract investment in a particular invention, priority contributes toward the needs of a research community to identify its ablest members – those who produce consistent, excellent, reliable work, those who will ultimately form the corps of peers whose judgment is trusted and who undertake the responsibilities of mentorship, review and so forth. These trusted members also serve as leaders not only in defining the directions of research that should be patronized but in carrying out, or managing, the work that happens to be patronized. The demand for uniqueness that is characteristic of a system of patents – and works so well to realize its ends – could, therefore, work against the purposes served by the looser requirements of conventions of priority.

Concerning Difference II: It may be difficult to appreciate how the second point of difference – the absence of an authorized body, and an explicit, formalized procedure for recognizing priority – reflects anything but a weakness in conventions of priority. Is it not due to the vagueness in the conventions guiding priority that we are led to such strange results as the confusion over priority for the discovery of hyperbolic geometry? Skeptical outsiders may want to set "straight' the misguided mathematicians who continue to maintain that Gauss be recognized as a co-discoverer, based only on his flimsy claim that the work "occupied his mind" for several decades. Explicit guidelines, or an authorized body, could draw clear and unambiguous lines between acceptable and unacceptable grounds for priority claims.

The test guides us to frame a question along the following lines: does the explicit, authority-driven procedure of patent allocation serve the same ends of research, and as well, in the electronic age, as the entrenched norms have served until now? The answer, I think, is no. What appears as ambiguity and unclarity in conventions for attributing priority is, rather, a sensitivity to contextual factors that is well-suited to promoting ends for which these conventions were designed. In the case of hyperbolic geometry, we observe an exceptional tolerance to the unusual priority claim made by Gauss. Mathematicians who show forbearance for Gauss' priority claim do so not because they are confused by a fuzzy convention but, rather, because they are swayed by Gauss' extraordinary stature within the mathematical community. These mathematicians could argue that allowing for convention to be sensitive to such considerations is neither irrational nor grossly unjust (as we might say of a patent system that allowed for such favoritism). In any given time communities of researchers recognize a few of their members as enlightened leaders, who usually have earned their stature on the basis of exceptional work. The community accords these leaders tremendous trust – trust that is not easily, blindly or irrationally accorded. The rewards the community expects to reap are what all of us seek from enlightened leadership. We value it not because the paths it takes are already evident to those who follow, but because it takes paths and offers the possibility of insights that are frequently not evident to others. For many mathematicians Gauss' well-earned stature means that even his mere meditations promise fruitful avenues of study.

We must conclude, then, that a patent-like system does not pass the test. An explicit authority-driven procedure, not sensitive to such needs, offers decisiveness at the cost of inspiration and serves different ends to the ones that have guided entrenched norms. This is not to say that some ends might not be served by a patent-like system of priority for intellectual work, but they are not likely to be the same ends that norms, conventions and institutions governing practices in research currently serve. The test indicates that researchers should not rush to these new property-like norms simply because they are already embedded in information technology, or because they hold the allure of personal profit.[20]

---

[20] Contextual factors are an important backdrop for this claim. It assumes, for example, that some form of public support is available for scientific research. Robert Merges describes a compelling scenario in which strong property claims to results have become the norm and researchers may be forced to assert strong property rights or be driven out of research altogether (1996).

Other Approaches

Where does this conclusion leave us? It is all very well to reject the more rigorous patent-like system for the idealistic reason that values and purpose of research will not be as well served by it as they are by the current norms, but this does not make the puzzle go away. Pressure to adjust priority norms for the electronic medium is still with us; what alternatives do we have?

A direct approach to the puzzle is to hone in on the scope of a search for prior work. At one conservative extreme, we may propose simply to "bite the bullet," making no change whatsoever in the literal framing of the norms and conventions governing priority. Naturally, although the stated requirements remain unchanged, their meaning has changed considerably: researchers would still be responsible for searching for prior work in all publications, but now the search ranges over a great deal more than before, including not only traditional works published electronically, but also all the new forms of publication such as gray literature, wildcat publications, and every last arcane homepage upon which someone may have posted materials. This position is problematic.

Although it adheres to the letter of the old convention, it involves a radical semantic shift. Because the term "publication" now spans a far wider domain, a hapless priority seeker would face the daunting challenge of searching a virtually endless domain of publication. To make matters worse, according to the study by Lawrence and Giles cited earlier, the technology for conducting these searches is still relatively unthorough. In addition to estimating the sheer size of the Web, Lawrence and Giles studied how effectively the major search engines indexed it.[21] Of the search engines they studied, they found that none, taken singly, indexed more than one-third of the Web, and, in combination, all covered approximately two-thirds. This means that even the most vigorously pursued search is unlikely to yield all relevant material.

Aside from these practical obstacles critics could argue that the requirement is unfair: in pre-electronic days no-one expected priority seekers to hunt for results in desk drawers, privately owned filing cabinets, backs of envelopes and past conversations. Similarly we should not now expect them to search, literally, *all* electronic publications. Even if improved and refined search engines could assure better results (whatever that may amount to), we may still worry about the quality and reliability of the publications in the gray literatures and personal home pages. Should they count? Because these considerations indicate that conventions based on a bite-the-bullet approach would in all likelihood hamper progress, the test would weigh against its adoption.

---

[21] When users run a search using a search engine, the search will yield results only from the sites indexed by that search engine.

An attenuated or less extreme version of the approach may seek to define a more restricted scope of search; a revised convention in this spirit would demand a search for prior work only within a circumscribed range of pre-approved publications. Although more reasonable than a bite-the-bullet version and less disturbing of fundamental values than a framework of intellectual property, this promising alternative would stand or fall on the basis of satisfactory answers to questions like what the subset would be, how it would be defined, and who would be responsible for defining it. Philosophical analysis alone is unlikely to offer much more than general guidelines, for example, that the definition ought not be arbitrarily drawn, and that it should not be so limiting or conservative that it stifles the exciting, novel creations of electronic publication. It might also point out that care should be taken in identifying who has discretion over setting boundaries: a professional organization, a committee, an individual. Finally, any proposal must pass the test. That is to say, careful consideration must be given to the consequences on values and purposes of research.

Beyond these quite general directives, any concrete interpretation – I believe – requires a degree of familiarity with actual practice that most likely inheres with participants themselves in the various areas of research, including researchers and high-level administrators. Specific answers will be forged by those with the deepest understanding of the real meaning of various options, familiar with practices and conventions, and best able to anticipate how particular conventions for delineating the scope of the search would affect the attainment of values. To the extent that this paper can contribute to the important process of revising and adapting to the demands of the new situations and challenges of electronic publication, communication and collaboration, it is to warn against rushing to new norms and conventions merely because they appear most similar to the old, nor because they happen to come along with the technology (though developed to serve values that are not their own). Nor should they pursue parochial interests, however alluring these prospects might be. They should approach important questions about revising norms, practices, institutions and conventions with an eye to underlying values, ends and purposes. Where the electronic environment demands new norms, or new interpretations of traditional norms, these values, ends and purposes should be their paramount consideration.

Conclusion

A great deal of social activity is governed by norms and conventions, some trivial, some grave, some regulated by law, some not: from stopping at red, to driving on the right (or left), to addressing strangers in particular ways, to "ladies first", to not talking in theatres. Many conventions are so entrenched and so effective that we barely are conscious of them, we rarely question their hold over us, and in some cases we forget that we adhere to them not as ends in themselves but as means of promoting other valued ends. It is frequently only as a result of change or disruption that we "notice" a convention and understand its operation. Disruption may force us to dissect a convention and gain insight into its functioning.

This paper has drawn attention to conventions of scientific research publication, suggesting that the shift toward the electronic medium constitutes one of these convention-disrupting changes. The puzzle of priority is an example of conventions disrupted and the need to put new ones in their stead. Calling attention to the need is an important first step, but as important is delineating a reasonable process for determining the shape of new conventions. In what I call "the test," I attempt to do so by outlining a systematic approach to evaluating proposed new norms. The test demands that we dissect entrenched conventions to discover the ends, purposes and values they serve. When proposing conventions to replace entrenched ones, we must evaluate proposed conventions according to their likelihood of achieving these same ends, purposes and values. When, for example, traffic lights are replaced by traffic circles, we establish new rules by making sure that the ends are served as well if not better; when gender roles are re-examined for ideological reasons, we try to re-engineer conventions of who goes first that "work" to serve other ends and so forth. We may happily discover that the new conventions serve valued ends even better than the old, but we should be wary of results showing that proposed conventions are inefficient, arbitrary or biased. In the case of electronic publication I have argued that conventions will maintain moral force only if they continue to serve, and serve justly, the fundamental ends of scientific and technical research.

References

Baltimore, D. (1992). "On Doing Science in the Modern World! The Tanner Lectures on Human Values. Delivered at Clare Hall, Cambridge University.

Bijker, WE., Hughes, T.P. & Pinch, T.J. (1987). *The Social Construction of Technological Systems: New Directions in the Sociology and History of Technology.* MIT Press, Cambridge, MA.

Burgess, J. (1998). "How Not to Write History of Philosophy: A Case Study," Humphreys, PW & Fetzer, J.H. (eds), *The New Theory of Reference.* Kluwer Academic Publishers, Dordrecht, pp. 125–136.

Eisenberg, R. (1989). "Patents and the Progress of Science: Exclusive Rights and Experimental Use," *University of Chicago Law Review, Vol. 56.*

Geison, Gerard. "The Secret of Pouilly-le-Fort: Competition and Deception in the Race for the Anthrax Vaccine." In *The Private Science of Louis Pasteur*, 145-76. Princeton, NJ: Princeton UP, 1995.

Gelfand, J. & King, J.L. (1998). "Grey Market Science: Research Libraries, Grey Literature, and the Legitimization of Scientific Discourse in the Internet Age," *Proceedings of the Socioeconomic Dimensions of Electronic Publishing Workshop.*

Gordon, W.J. (1993). "A Property Right in Self-Expression: Equality and Individualism in the Natural Law of Intellectual Property," *The Yale Law Journal,* Vol. 102, pp. 1533–1609.

Holt, J. (1997), "Whose Idea Is It, Anyway? A Philosopher's Feud", Lingua Franca Archive, Lingua Franca Classics, < http:/www./linguafranca.com/ >.

Hughes, J. (1988). "The philosophy of Intellectual Property," *Georgetown Law Journal,V61.* 77, No. 2, pp. 287–365.

Lawrence, S. & Giles, C.L. (1998). "Searching the World Wide Web," *Science.*

Long, C., (1999) "The dissonance of scientific and legal norms," *Social Epistemology*, vol. 13, no. 2, 165–181

McCullagh, D. (1997). "Copyrights and Wrongs," < www.netlynew.com >.

Merges, RY (1996). "Property Rights Theory and the Commons: The Case of Scientific Research: *Social Philosophy and* Policy, Vol. 13, No. 2.

Miller, S. (1992). "On Conventions," *Australasian Journal of Philosophy, Vol.* 70, No. 4.

Miller, S. (1997). "Social Norms" in Holmstrom-Hintikka, G. & Tuomela, R. (eds), *Contemporary Action Theory.Vol.* 2, Kluwer Academic Publishers, Dordrecht.

Nissenbaum, H. (1998). "Values in the Design of Computer Systems," *Computers in Society,* March, pp. 38–39.

Samuelson, P., Column: Legally Speaking, *Communications of the ACM* (numerous discussions of property rights in the context of information technology).

Samuelson, P., *et al.* (1994). "A Manifesto Concerning the Legal Protection of Computer Programs," *Columbia Law Review,* 2308.

Smith, Q. (1995). "Marcus, Kripke, and the Origin of the New Theory of Reference: *Synthese,* 104, pp. 179–189.

Sonkkila, T. (1998). "From Generic to Descriptive Markup: Implications for the Academic Author: *Proceedings of the Socioeconomic Dimensions of Electronic Publishing Workshop.*

Waldron, J. (1988). *The Right to Private Property,* Oxford University Press, Oxford.

Whitbeck, C. (1998). *Ethics in Engineering Practice and Research.* Cambridge University Press, New York. Winner, L.(1986). Do *Artifacts Have Politics? The Whale and the Reactor,* University of Chicago Press, Chicago, IL.

Wyly, B. J. (1998). "Overcoming Intellectual and Virtual Access as Barriers to Utilization of Electronic Publications," *Proceedings of the Socioeconomic Dimensions of Electronic Publishing Workshop.*

Ziman, J. (1998). "Why Must Scientists Become More Ethically Sensitive than They Used to Be" *Science,* Vol. 282.

VII. MARKET PRACTICES

Network Effects, Standardization, and the Internet: What Have We Learned from the DVD vs. DIVX Battle?

David Dranove and Neil Gandal

I. Introduction

The theoretical literature on network effects has extensively examined the tradeoff between "standardization" (all consumers adopt compatible products) and "variety" (several incompatible products have positive market shares). Two important welfare implications of this tradeoff are

- Market forces often result in suboptimal standardization, that is, left alone the market may fail to achieve standardization when standardization is socially desirable.[1]
- Even if the market settles on a standard, the standard may be inferior, that is, social welfare would have been higher had an alternative standard been chosen.

Some policy makers have interpreted these results to mean that when there are strong network effects, regulators should play an active role in setting standards.

---

* We are grateful to Severin Borenstein, Dennis Carlton, Luis Cabral, Richard Gilbert, Shane Greenstein, David McGowan, Paul Gertler, Michael Riordan, Carl Shapiro, Catherine Wolfram and seminar participants at New York University, UC-Berkeley, the 2nd CEPR Conference on Applied Industrial Organization, the IDEI (Toulouse) Conference on Competition in Internet and Software Industries, the Tel Aviv University Conference on Antitrust and Regulation, the Haifa University Law School Conference on the Commodification of Information, and the Telecommunications Policy Research Conference for helpful comments.

[1] This result is robust to both physical networks and virtual networks. For the physical networks case, see Farrell and Saloner (1986). For the virtual network case, see Chou and Shy (1990) and Church and Gandal (1992). The latter shows that suboptimal standardization is most likely to occur when consumers place a relatively high value on software variety.

N. Elkin-Koren and N.W. Netanel (eds.), *The Commodification of Information*, 461–477.
© 2002 *David Dranove and Neil Gandal. Printed in Great Britain.*

This is especially true when a new technology emerges and backwards compatibility is an issue.[2] Others have urged regulators not to intervene despite the presence of network effects,[3] unless owners of proprietary standards take strategic actions to influence the adoption decisions of consumers. One such action that has raised regulatory (antitrust) concerns is strategic product preannouncements or "vaporware." According to the 1991 Microsoft Press Computer Dictionary, vaporware is defined as "promised software that misses its announced release date, usually by a considerable length of time." Thus vaporware includes products that simply arrive significantly late due to unexpected technical difficulties and products that arrive late because of strategic preannouncements. Anticompetitive vaporware allegations refer to the latter.

In this paper, we empirically test for network effects and preannouncement effects in the DVD market and examine the role played by the Internet. We do this by measuring the effect of potential (incompatible) competition on a network undergoing growth. We find that there are network effects in the DVD market and that the preannouncement of DIVX somewhat slowed down the adoption of DVD technology. This suggests that preannouncements can indeed affect the outcome of a standards competition.

The paper proceeds as follows. In section II, we provide an introduction to network effects, while section III briefly discusses vaporware and preannouncement effects. In section IV, we describe the DVD market. Section V describes our data and section VI contains our empirical results. Section VII provides brief conclusions.

II. A Brief Introduction to Network Effects

A network effect exists when the value that consumers place on a particular product increases as the total number of consumers who purchase identical or compatible goods increases. In the case of an actual (or physical) network, such as

---

[2] Recently, the FCC set down the guidelines for the new digital television (HDTV) standard. NTSC televisions will be able to view new broadcasts with a "down-converter" box, which will provide a somewhat improved image. New HDTVs will be able to watch old NTSC programs if they have a second (analog) tuner built-in. The speed of adoption of HDTV has some ramifications; the FCC has scheduled an end to NTSC broadcasts by the year 2006. (See "HDTV: How the Picture Looks Now," *Business Week*, May 26, 1997, and "Should you Roll Out the Welcome Mat for HDTV?" *The New York Times*, April 27, 1997.

[3] Leibowitz and Margolis (1994) criticize the literature on network effects in part because it cannot tell us whether effects identified by the theoretical literature (such as the failure to achieve compatibility) are privately or socially important. They argue that until the literature is able to estimate such effects in a meaningful fashion, the public policy debates are premature.

the telephone network, the value of the network depends on the total number of subscribers who have access to the network.

In the case of virtual networks, that are not linked physically, the network effect arises from positive feedback from complementary goods. Examples of virtual networks in which the value of the "base" product increases as the variety of complementary products increases include computer operating systems, videocassette recorders (VCRs), compact disc players (CD-players), and Digital Versatile Disc players (DVD-players). In the case of computer operating systems, the complementary goods are the applications software programs, while in the case of VCRs, the complementary goods are the VCR cassettes or tapes; similarly in the case of CD-players, the complementary goods are the compact discs, while in the case of DVD-players, the complementary products are the DVD-discs.

The positive feedback mechanism works as follows: the value of the base product is enhanced as the variety of (compatible) complementary products increases; hence consumers will be more likely to purchase a base product with many compatible complementary products. The variety of complementary products, in turn, will depend on the total number of consumers that purchase the base product. As the number of consumers that purchase the base product increases, there is a greater demand for compatible complementary products. This increases the profitability of supplying complementary products. Since there are typically fixed or sunk entry costs, production of the complementary products is characterized by increasing returns to scale. Hence more complementary products will be produced or developed for a base product with a large share of the market. This further enhances the value of the base product. Thus, there is positive feedback in such a system: an increase in the sales of the base product leads to more compatible complementary products, which further increases (the value of and) sales of the base product. See Chou and Shy (1990) and Church and Gandal (1992).

As Katz and Shapiro (1994) note, the positive feedback means that there is a "natural tendency toward *de facto* standardization" (p.105). They note that these system markets are often characterized by tipping: once a system has gained an initial lead, there is a snowball effect. One system ends up being the market standard with large amounts of compatible complementary products; the other system has a very small market share, if any at all. The value of the base product with little or no complementary software is essentially zero, since the base product itself provides little or no stand alone benefits.

A small but growing literature has empirically (statistically) found evidence of virtual network effects. See Greenstein (1993), Gandal (1994, 1995), Brynjolfsson and Kemerer (1996), and Gandal, Greenstein, and Salant (1999) for empirical evidence of network effects in the computer software industry. Other papers that provide empirical evidence of virtual network effects include Saloner and Shepard (1995), the ATM industry, Park (1997), the VCR market, Shankar and Bayus (1997), the Home Video Game Industry, and Gandal, Kende, Rob (2000), the CD industry.

III. Vaporware and Preannouncement Effects

In most cases, the premature announcement of a future product is not anticompetitive. As Fisher, McGowan, and Greenwood, (1983,p. 289) note "In general, there is no reason to inhibit the time when a firm announces or brings its products to the marketplace. Consumers will be the final arbiter of the product's quality and the firm's reputation ... Advance announcements of truthful information cannot be anticompetitive." Farrell and Saloner (1986, p.942) note, however, that when there are strong network effects, "the timing of the announcement of a new incompatible product can critically determine whether a new product supersedes the existing technology." Lemley and McGowan (1998, p.505) remark, "by preannouncing a product, a large company may therefore influence the outcome of a standards competition in an industry characterized by network effects."

Anticompetitive vaporware allegations have been leveled at IBM and Microsoft. Claims of anticompetitive vaporware were leveled against Microsoft in the 1994 antitrust case. One of the main claims in the IBM case was that IBM increased its market share by preannouncing products that were in very early stages of development (see Fisher, McGowan, and Greenwood (1983)). In April 1990, DR-DOS 5.0 was introduced and received positive reviews. Baseman, Warren Boulton, and Woroch (1995) noted that "within a month of DR-DOS 5.0's inauguration, Microsoft reported development of MS-DOS 5.0. Curiously, it boasted nearly all of the innovative features of the DRI product (p.7)." MS-DOS 5.0 was eventually released in June 1991.

Concerns about vaporware led the Software Publishers Association (the computer software industry's largest trade association) to include prohibitions in February 1998 against vaporware in the associations' eight principles of competition.[4] Despite the antitrust concern about vaporware and preannouncement effects, there is no empirical work on the issue. (See Levy 1996 for a recent theoretical manuscript on vaporware.)

IV. The Development of the DVD Market

Throughout the 1990s, video hardware and software manufacturers sought a digital format to replace videocassettes. Keen to avoid another Beta/VHS format

---

[4] See McWilliams, B., "Industry Group Issues Software Competition Guidelines," PC World Communications, February 2, 1998 at <http://pcworld.com/news/daily/data/0298/980202164433.html>.

war, hardware manufacturers led by Sony, Toshiba, and Panasonic, in conjunction with movie studios led by Warner and Columbia (a division of Sony), worked together to establish a single standard. The result was the DVD (digital video disc or digital versatile disc). DVD discs are identical in appearance to compact discs, but store ten times as much information – more than enough for a feature film with twice the visual clarity of a videocassette – as well as providing a five channel surround soundtrack.

In September 1996, the "DVD forum" of hardware and software firms published the DVD specifications. DVD would be an "open format", meaning that all machines carrying the DVD logo could play all DVD discs. All DVD discs would be encoded with the Dolby Digital sound process, and could also be encoded with other sound processes, such as Dreamworks' DTS surround process, as they became available. All DVD players would be capable of outputting the Dolby Digital bitstream to external decoders; some manufacturers included internal decoders as an added feature of their DVD players. DVD-ROM drives for computers would also be able to play DVD movies (though DVD video players need not be able to play DVD software designed specifically for the personal computer.) All DVD discs would be forward compatible with the soon to be launched high definition television, through a technology known as progressive scan.

Warner Home Video (and its sister companies such as HBO and New Line), Columbia Tri-Star, MGM/UA, and Polygram committed to providing DVD videos even before there were any DVD players available. (See Table 1.) Smaller firms that held distribution rights to movies, documentaries, and IMAX films, also committed to the format. When the first DVD players were released in the U.S. in early 1997, there were 40 software titles to choose from, including Batman, Blade Runner, Singing in the Rain, and the IMAX film Africa: The Serengeti. In July and August 1997 respectively, Universal and Disney's live-action Buena Vista division entered the market.

Some studios held back support for DVD because of concerns about whether the technology would succeed and because of concerns about piracy. Because DVD is digital, it offers opportunities for pirates to make perfect digital copies. The DVD consortium had included some protection against piracy in the DVD format, including Macrovision, which prevents direct copying onto videotape or a recordable DVD player. They also adopted regional coding, so that players designed for sale in the U.S. region could only play discs designed to play in the U.S. (There are seven regions altogether.) But many studios were concerned that these precautions were inadequate, and were reluctant to release films on DVD unless demand from the installed base of DVD players was large enough to offset the risks of piracy. Paramount only committed to DVD provision in April 1998, while 20th Century Fox did so in August 1998.

Despite the lukewarm support of several studios, DVD was cautiously welcomed by "early adopters" – electronics enthusiasts who derive utility from being the "first on their block" to own a new technology. Most of the early adopters were among the two million Americans who owned laserdisc players, which came close to matching DVD's visual clarity and sound. Early adopters established several Internet "chat sites," in which they debated the relative merits of DVD and laserdisc, and speculated about the future of the new format. All agreed that DVD had two advantages over laserdisc. First, it was much cheaper to master and produce DVD software. DVD software retail prices range from $10-$30 per movie, compared with $30-$70 for films on laserdiscs. Second, the laserdisc market had peaked without becoming mainstream, leaving laserdisc enthusiasts searching for stores that rented or sold discs. With lower prices and renewed interest from hardware and software makers, DVD held out the promise of finally replacing the inferior videocassette format. When Best Buy (the nation's second largest electronics retailer) indicated that it would fully support DVD with special in-store displays, wide selections of hardware and software at discounted prices, and heavy advertising, many believed that the format would quickly become mainstream.

Sales of DVD hardware (Figure 1) in the first few months were well within industry expectations, and much higher than sales of CD players during its first few months on the market. As the market grew, more brands of hardware became available, and most major electronics retailers, including Circuit City (the nation's leading electronics retailer), jumped into the market. By the end of 1997, manufacturers introduced second generation DVD players with enhanced features such as a higher video bitstream rate for superior video imaging, 96/24 audio resolution for playing DVD audio (expected to eventually replace CDs), and component outputs for direct connection to projection televisions. In early 1999, manufacturers introduced third and fourth generation machines, the latter using progressive scan technology to provide the resolution available on high definition television.

During this time, a DVD culture was emerging over the Internet. Early adopters tended to be frequent Internet users, and it was no surprise when several on-line hardware and software vendors established DVD-related sites. The most popular DVD chat sites received more than 1,000 posts weekly, many from individuals who did not own a DVD player. (By late 1998, there were at least four on-line chat sites receiving as many as 10,000 postings weekly.) At the same time, new Internet vendors emerged, offering discounted prices on DVD hardware and software sales.

Tempering this early enthusiasm were occasional rumors about a competing technology known only as "zoom," which was supposed to be a pay-per-view alternative to open DVD. Rumors on the Internet about zoom died down during the summer of 1997, only to come true on September 8, 1997, when Circuit City announced the introduction of DIVX (Digital Video Express).[5] DIVX players

---

[5] DIVX is a joint venture between Circuit City and the law firm of Ziffren, Brittenham, Branca & Fischer.

would play all DVD discs. But they would also play special DIVX discs (that could not be played on DVD players). DIVX discs are "locked" by an encryption technology. They are unlocked when the user starts playing them, and remain unlocked for 48 hours. Once time expires, the user can replay the disc by contacting a computer operated by a firm working for Circuit City. (This is done via a modem connection that comes with the DIVX player.) Circuit City planned to charge $4 - $5 for the first time use of each disc, with a similar fee for each reuse. In this way, DIVX offered an alternative to rental.

The DIVX announcement shocked DVD enthusiasts. Circuit City was the leading seller of home electronics in the U.S. and could be expected to heavily promote DIVX. It also had commitments from Disney, Paramount, Universal, and Dreamworks to release DIVX discs "day and date" with VHS tapes. (Table 1 lists the major studios and the dates on which they committed to "open" DVD and DIVX.)

One Internet site summed up the problem this way: "The confusing situation where two formats exist, supported by different companies, was what DVD was supposed to avoid. The DVD forum was set up to stop a format war but it now looks like the introduction of DIVX could result in just that ... The fact some studios are supporting only open DVD and some are supporting only DIVX will lead to confusion and ultimately be harmful to DVD."[6] To add to the confusion, there seemed to be no technological reason for studios to support only one format. Once a digital master is created for either format (at a cost ranging from $50,000 to a few hundred thousand dollars per movie), the incremental cost of creating a disc in the other format was negligible. The studio merely had to add or delete the encryption code. Apparently, the only reason that certain studios, notably Disney, released any titles exclusively in DIVX format was that Circuit City had paid them handsomely to do so.

Many suspected that Circuit City prematurely announced DIVX in order to slow the growth of DVD. A December 13, 1998 editorial in the popular Internet site DVD Resource Page noted that the DIVX preannouncement created "confusion in a marketplace a year ago (fall of 1997) when DVD sales SHOULD have taken off, but did not because people wanted to know how they were going to watch movies on a format not supported by all the studios."[7] The editorial also noted that while DIVX attempted to "submarine DVD in September of 1997," DIVX actually embraced DVD a few months later (in January 1998) as a basic component in the DIVX system.

Circuit City had two reasons to prematurely announce DIVX. First, if DVD established itself too quickly, it would all but eliminate the market for DIVX. Second, Circuit City rival Best Buy had embraced DVD from the beginning, and

---

[6] DVD Centre Webpage at < http://web.ukonline.co.uk/Members/s.roberts/index.htm >.
[7] DVD Resource Page at < http://www.dvdresource.com >.

was firmly established as the nation's leading seller of DVD hardware and software. If DVD continued to grow, electronics shoppers would be drawn to Best Buy, costing Circuit City sales in other categories.

Although DVD supporters were disappointed by the DIVX announcement, investors were reasonably pleased. In the three trading days surrounding the announcement, Circuit City's share values increased by 17.6 percent. In contrast, Best Buy's shares increased by 13.6 percent. Investors might have even reacted more favorably to the announcement had Circuit City offered more concrete plans for DIVX. Indeed, claims of vaporware appeared almost immediately after the DIVX announcement. For months after the announcement, Circuit City had neither DIVX hardware nor software to demonstrate.

Finally, on January 17, 1998, Circuit City CEO Dick Sharp made an announcement that seemed to settle the DVD market. He demonstrated a DIVX prototype to the media, but announced that test marketing of DIVX (in San Francisco and Richmond, Virginia) would not begin until the summer, with a nationwide release expected in the fall. He also indicated that initially all DIVX players would be manufactured by Zenith, which was not a significant force in the audio/video hardware market and was on the verge of bankruptcy; he also announced that only one retailer (The Good Guys) had agreed to join Circuit City in offering DIVX products. Finally, he indicated that DIVX would be marketed as an advanced feature of DVD, rather than as an alternative standard. Indeed, some Internet reports suggested that DIVX owners used their players solely to play "open" DVD disks.

With this second announcement, fears of format wars seemed to die down. Investors seemed resigned to the fact that Circuit City would not become the dominant force in the digital video market. In the three-day window surrounding the January 17th, announcement, Circuit City shares lost 0.35 percent of their value while Best Buy shares climbed 3.2 percent. Numerous press reports attributed a substantial portion of Circuit City's woes to the unsuccessful launch of DIVX.[8]

DIVX did reach the market in the fall of 1998, but it faced an uphill battle. Studio support for DIVX had weakened (no new studios had come on board and some of the fence-sitting studios had begun releasing in open DVD). Circuit City still could not convince competitors to carry the product. While Circuit City reported that it sold as many as 80,000 DIVX players in the crucial Christmas 1998 shopping season, this represented less than 25 percent of the sales of open

---

[8] According to "Still, business booms for Circuit and others," by David J. Elrich, June 4, 1999 (from e-town.com), Circuit City had invested more than $207 million on DIVX (as of February 28th, 1999), nearly seven percent of the firm's total assets. The article also notes that quarterly earnings per share were off by 16 cents due to charges for DIVX. During the time that Circuit City was launching DIVX, it had a difficult time digesting its acquisition of the CARMAX Group. This further suppressed the share value.

DVD players during the same period. The handwriting was on the wall: at best, DIVX would be a niche format.

In early June 1999, rumors swept the Internet that Circuit City would soon pull the plug on the DIVX format; those rumors came true on June 16, 1999. The facts on the ground justified the decision. By the end of 1998, the installed base of DVD players (shipped to retailers) was approximately 1.32 million. During the first 20 weeks of 1999, at least 572,000 additional players were sold to retailers, yielding a DVD installed base of at least 1.9 million through mid -1999. The DIVX installed base through that time was at most 165,000. As of May 31, 1999, there were 3,317 software titles available on the DVD format and only 471 titles available on DIVX.[9]

In the remainder of this paper, we determine whether Circuit City's September 1997 preannouncement did, indeed, have a chilling effect on DVD sales. We also explore whether the entry of DIVX into the market in the fall of 1998 and the June 1999 official announcement of the demise of DIVX affected DVD sales.

V. Data

The dataset was compiled from several sources, as described below. We collected monthly data from April 1997 (the first month DVD players were available) through June 2000. We have more than three years of data. We now describe the variables used in the study. (Descriptive statistics are in Table 2.)

- We have monthly data on the sales of DVD players (denoted SALES) from manufacturers to dealers. We are grateful to the Consumer Electronics Manufacturing Association for supplying these data and the data on prices.[10] Monthly DVD player sales are shown in figure 1. The natural log of this variable is denoted by LSALES.
- The variable LPRICE is the natural log of the average monthly price (denoted PRICE) of DVD players to retailers. Monthly prices of DVD players are shown in figure 2.

---

[9] It is interesting to ask whether the DIVX strategy (of marketing its player as an advanced feature of DVD, rather than an alternative standard) was a mistake. Theoretical models show that a base product that is more compatible with a second base product's software will have less software written in its format and this in turn will decrease it's hardware (base product) market share. We leave this question for future research.

[10] The sales data also include DIVX sales. DIVX sales began on a trial basis in June in the San Francisco and Richmond Va. markets. According to "How Circuit City Can Fix What Ails DIVX," Computer Retail Week,} September 14, 1998, there were very few sales of DIVX players during the trial period. DIVX was launched nationally on September 25, 1998. As noted above, the DIVX installed base through the first 20 weeks of 1999 was at most 165,000, while the installed base of DVD was at least 1.9 million. through the same period.

- One measure of software availability is when a particular studio committed to releasing films in DVD technology and the importance of that studio as measured by the 100 most successful box office releases of all time. (The box office data have been adjusted for inflation. Since DVD sales began in 1997, we use data on box office releases through 1996 for the construction of this variable.) These data are displayed at the Mr. Showbiz website under the Movie Guide Box Office Leaders category. (See < http://mrshowbiz.go.com/reviews/moviereviews/numbers/top100adjusted.html >).

We sorted the movies by studio and added up the box office revenues in order to obtain an impact measure for each studio. We then constructed the studio impact measure (denoted SOFT) by using the dates at which each studio committed to DVD. (See table 1 and figure 3.) The variable LSOFT is the natural log of the studio impact measure.

- Another measure of software availability is the percent of U.S. Box Office top 100 films (adjusted for inflation) that had been released in DVD format by each point in time. This measure of software availability is denoted BOA. See figure 4.
- q^i is a dummy variable that takes on the value 1 if the data is from quarter i. The quarterly dummies adjust for seasonal effects.
- The dummy variable DIVX takes on the value 1 from September 1997 (the preannouncement date of the DIVX technology was September 8, 1997) through December 1997, just before the DIVX demonstration.
- The dummy variable ENTRY takes on the value one for the three-month period (October–December 1998) following the entry of DIVX into the market.
- The dummy variable DEMISE takes on the value 1 from June through August 1999. The Demise of DIVX occurred on June 16, 1999, but the announcement had been expected for several weeks.

VI. Estimation and Empirical Results

Like other electronics products, consumer demand is likely a function of price and the availability of software as well as seasonal effects and shocks (such as the DIVX announcement). We employ the following consumer adoption equation:

(1) $\text{LSALES} = \beta_0 + \beta_1 \text{LPRICE} + \beta_2 \text{LSOFT} + \beta_3 \text{BOA} + \beta_4 \text{DIVX} + \beta_5 \text{ENTRY} + \beta_6 \text{DEMISE} + \beta_7 Q^2 + \beta_8 Q^3 + \beta_9 Q^4 + \varepsilon$

The coefficient β_1 is the price elasticity of demand. The coefficient β_2 is the elasticity of DVD player sales with respect to studio support for the DVD standard, while ß₃ measures how increases in the availability of box office hits in DVD format affect DVD player sales. The coefficient ß₄, the DIVX parameter, measures how the DIVX preannouncement affected DVD adoption. β_1 should be less than zero while β_2 and β_3 should be greater than zero. β_4, the DIVX parameter, should be less than zero if the DIVX preannouncement slowed down DVD adoption.

Although we do not estimate the software entry equation (with LSOFT as the dependent variable) or the software supply equation (with BOA as the dependent variable), LSALES is a right-hand side variable in both of these equations. This is because studios likely made their decision to release films in DVD format in part on the number of DVD player sales. Hence the variables LSOFT and BOA are endogenous. Given that increased DVD sales likely lead to increases in both LSOFT and BOA, the sign on the LSALES coefficient is positive in both the software entry and software supply equations. LPRICE itself may be endogenous, since the firms likely have some market power. This discussion suggests that the Ordinary Least Squares estimates of the "ß" parameters will be biased. See Dranove and Gandal, (2000) for details.

To obtain consistent, i.e., asymptotically unbiased estimates of the coefficients, we employed instruments for LPRICE, LSOFT, and BOA, the endogenous variables on the right-hand side of equation (1). Since DVD technology is based on, in part, VCR, CD and camcorder technologies, we used the installed base of these technologies (denoted VCRINSTALLED, CDINSTALLED, CAMINSTALLED) and the logarithm of installed base (denoted LVCRINSTALLED, LCDINSTALLED, LCAMINSTALLED) as instruments. In particular, DVD, VCR, and CD technologies share sound decoding and interconnection technologies. These technologies were steadily evolving during the late 1990s. Additionally, "S-video" connections became standard on DVD players, VCRs and camcorders. So it is reasonable to argue that there are some scope economies among the technologies and that the installed bases of VCRs, CD players, and camcorders are appropriate instruments.

The results of the instrumental variable regression are contained in Table 3. The estimated price elasticity is negative as expected, although not statistically significant. The estimated coefficients of LSOFT and BOA are positive as expected. BOA is statistically significant (at the 99 level of confidence), while the coefficient on LSOFT is quite small and not significant. These results mean that as the important studios began to release their films in DVD format, the number of consumers adopting DVD players also increased. This suggests that there are positive virtual network effects.

Table 3 also shows that the DIVX preannouncement slowed down the adoption of DVD technology. The coefficient estimate on the DIVX dummy variable – which is statistically significant at the 90 percent level of confidence using a one sided test – suggests that the preannouncement reduced DVD sales by approximately 20 percent. (This follows from the fact that $\exp(-.22) = .80$.) Hence the econometric results confirm the simple time series graph of DVD sales (figure 1) in which there was no fourth quarter Christmas blip in sales in 1997.

This is a lower bound on the preannouncement effect. Since movie availability (as measured by studios supporting DVD and the number of box office hits released in DVD format) is endogenous, studio support for DVD might also have been affected by the preannouncement. In order to precisely measure how much faster DVD technology would have been adopted without the DIVX preannouncement, we would have had to estimate the "studio supply" equation. The DIVX effect is likely underestimated for an additional reason. If the DIVX preannouncement was strategic and was based on the early success of DVD, the DIVX variable itself is endogenous. In such a case, it can be shown that without correcting for the endogeneity, the estimated DIVX coefficient is biased toward zero.

As expected, Table 3 shows that there is a large positive fourth quarter effect (sales of consumer electronic durables usually increase significantly in the fourth quarter of the year) and that the second and third quarter sales are higher than first quarter sales (typically the low point of the year).

Note that the demise of DIVX had essentially no effect on DVD sales. In contrast to the preannouncement in September 1997, this announcement had been expected for some time and its effect on sales of DVD players was minimal. Table 3 shows that the entry of DIVX into the market had a positive but insignificant effect on DVD sales. Although it is insignificant, the sign of this coefficient makes sense because DIVX sales are included in DVD sales, and this period is where DIVX had its only real success.

VII. Conclusion

We established that there are network effects in the DVD market and that the preannouncement by DIVX somewhat slowed down the adoption of DVD technology. While we cannot say whether the preannouncement was strategic or whether the release of DIVX was delayed due to technical difficulties, we have quantified the effect of the preannouncement.

In the case of DVD vs. DIVX, the product preannouncement was made by an entrant, rather than an incumbent firm, and there were clearly benefits from the preannouncement. For example, it's likely that the DVD rental market emerged more quickly due to the DIVX preannouncement; consumers certainly benefited from the rental market. Nevertheless, the result that the product preannouncement by an entrant had such a large effect suggests that a product preannouncement by an incumbent would likely have a much larger effect; hence the general antitrust concern about vaporware and preannouncement effects seems justified.

Finally, the Internet played a key role in helping consumers communicate information and coordinate actions. Since many of the early adopters were also Internet users, the large number of active DVD and DIVX web sites conveyed very useful information to potential adopters in real time. The ability of the Internet to convey information quickly and inexpensively may reduce market failures (such as suboptimal standardization and the adoption of an inferior standard) associated with competition between incompatible technologies.

References

Baseman, K., Warren-Boulton, F., and G. Woroch, 1995, "Microsoft Plays Hardball: The Use of Exclusionary Pricing and Technological Incompatibility to Maintain Monopoly Power in Markets for Operating Systems," *Antitrust Bulletin*, 40: 265–315.

Brynjolfsson, E., and C. Kemerer, 1996, "Network Externalities in Microcomputer Software: An Econometric Analysis of the Spreadsheet Market," *Management Science*, 42: 1627–1647.

Chou, C. and O. Shy, 1990, "Network Effects without Network Externalities," *International Journal of Industrial Organization*, 8: 259–270.

Church, J., and N. Gandal, 1992, "Network Effects, Software Provision and Standardization," *Journal of Industrial Economics*, XL: 85–104.

Dranove, D., and N. Gandal, 2000, "The DVD vs. DIVX Standard War: Empirical Evidence of Preannouncement Effects," UC Berkeley IBER Working Paper # E00-293.

Farrell, J. and G. Saloner, 1985, "Standardization and Variety," *Economics Letters*, 20: 71–74.

Farrell, J., and G. Saloner, 1986 "Installed Base and Compatibility: Innovation, Product Preannouncements, and Predation," *American Economic Review*, 76: 940–955.

Fisher, F., J. McGowan, and J. Greenwood, "Folded, Spindled, and Mutilated: Economic Analysis of U.S. v. IBM," Cambridge, MA: MIT Press, 1983.

Gandal, N., 1994, "Hedonic Price Indexes for Spreadsheets and an Empirical Test for Network Externalities," *RAND Journal of Economics*, 25: 160–170.

Gandal, N., 1995, "Compatibility Standards and Complementary Network Externalities in the PC Software Market," *Review of Economics and Statistics*, 77: 599–608.

Gandal, N., S. Greenstein, and D. Salant, 1999, "Adoptions and Orphans in the Early Microcomputer Market," *Journal of Industrial Economics*, XLVII: 97–106.

Gandal, N., M. Kende, and R. Rob, 2000, "The Dynamics of Technological Adoption in Hardware/Software Systems: The Case of Compact Disc Players," *RAND Journal of Economics*, 31: 43–61.

Greenstein, S., 1993, "Did Installed Base Give an Incumbent any (Measurable) Advantages in Federal Computer Procurement," *RAND Journal of Economics*, 24: 19–39.

Katz, M. and C. Shapiro, 1992, "Product Introduction with Network Externalities," *Journal of Industrial Economics*, XL: 55–84.

Katz, M. and C. Shapiro, 1994, "Systems Competition and Network Effects," *Journal of Economic Perspectives*, 8: 93–115.

Lemley, M., and D. McGowan, 1998, "Legal Implications of Network Economic Effects," *California Law Review*, 86: 481–611.

Levy, S., 1996 "Vaporware," mimeo.

Park, S., 1997, "Quantitative Analysis of Network Externalities in Competing Technologies: The VCR Case," SUNY- Stonybrook mimeo.

Rohlfs, J., 1974, "A Theory of Interdependent Demand for a Communications Service, *Bell Journal of Economics*, 5: 16–37.

Saloner, G. and A. Shepard, 1995 "Adoption of Technologies with Network Externalities: An Empirical Examination of the Adoption of Automated Teller Machines," *RAND Journal of Economics*, 26: 479–501.

Shankar, V., and B. Bayus, 1997, "Network Effects and Competition: An Empirical Analysis of the Home Video Games Industry," mimeo.

Figure 1. DVD Player Sales

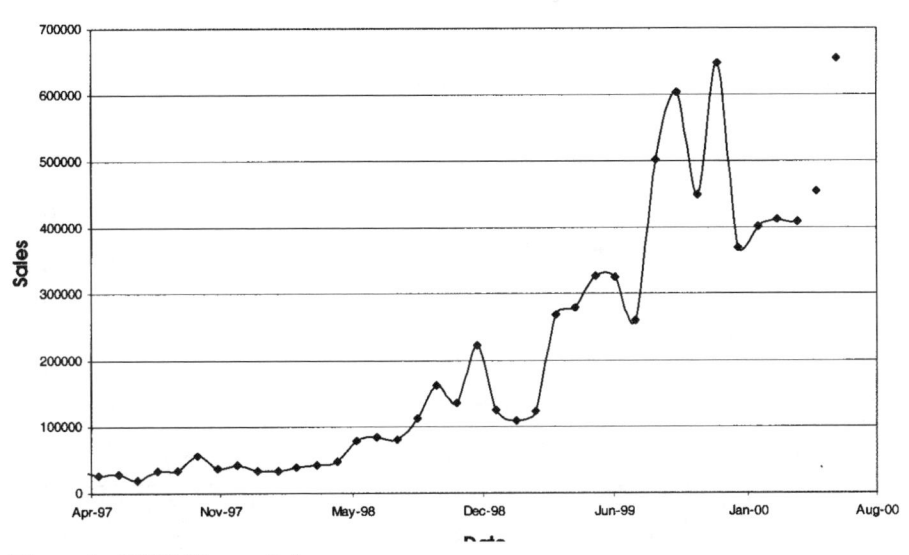

Figure 1: DVD Player Sales

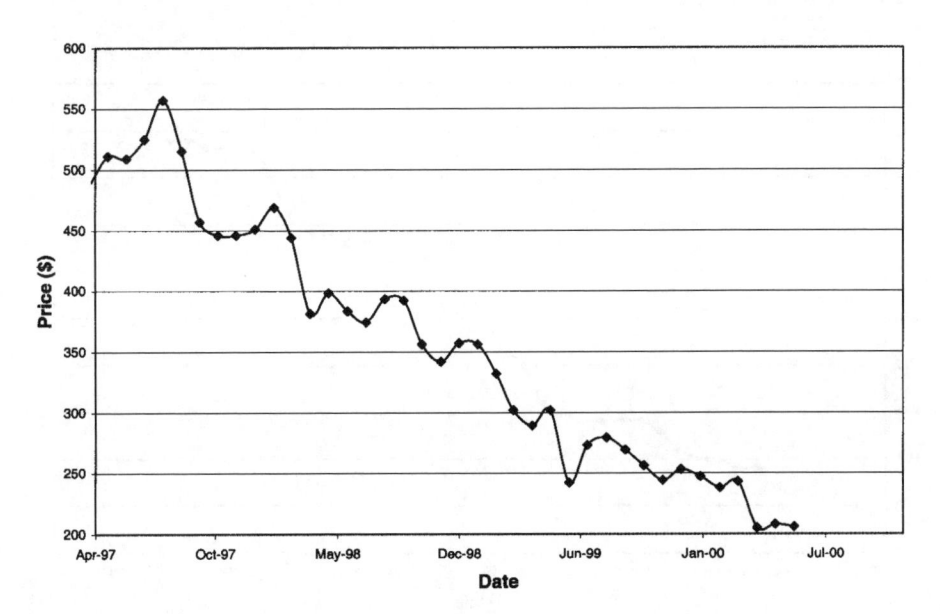

Figure 2: Average Sales Weighted Prices for DVD Players

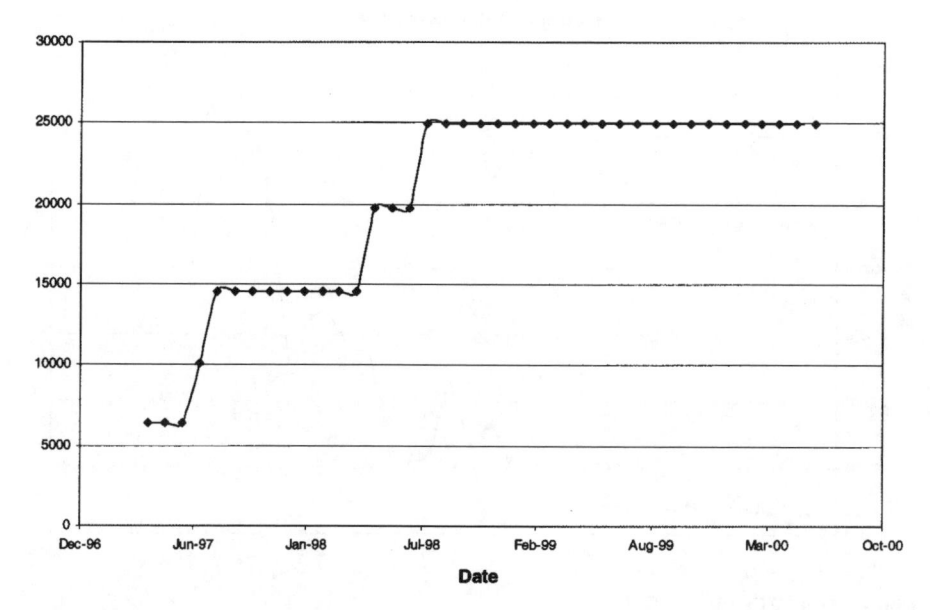

Figure 3: Studio Impact Measure (SOFT)

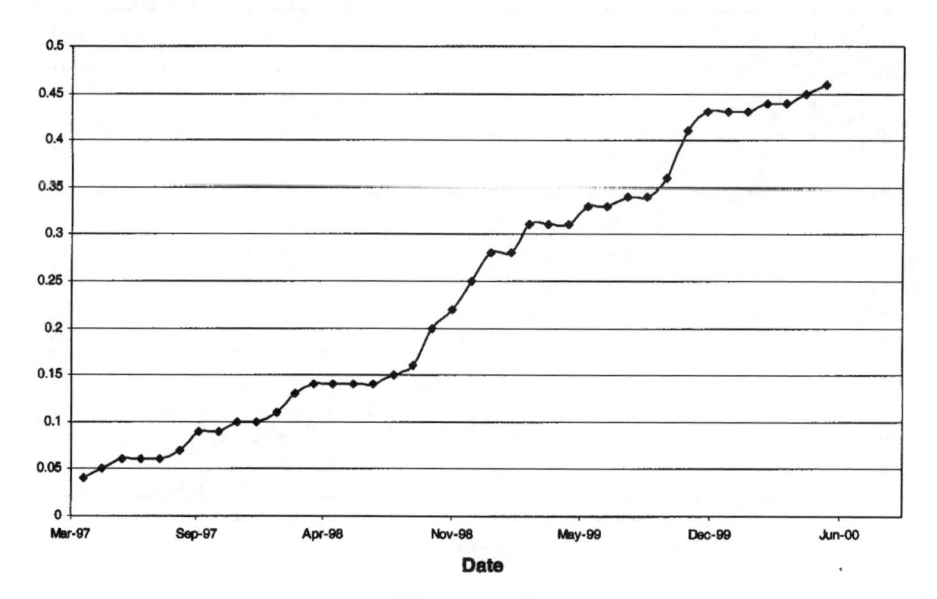

Figure 4: Percentage of top 100 Box Office Hits Released in DVD format (BOA)

Table 1: Studio Impact Measure and Dates the Studios Committed to DVD & DIVX Formats

Major Studio	DVD Date	DIVX Date	LSOFT
Warner (HBO, New Line)	Before DVD players were available	Did not release in format	2022
Columbia	Before DVD players were available	Did not release in format	1865
MGM/UA	Before DVD players were available	March 1998	2544
Universal	July 1997	September 1997	3702
Disney (Buena Vista)	August 1997	September 1997	4422
Paramount	April 1998	September 1997	5218
20th Century Fox	August 1998	February 1998	5204

Table 2: Descriptive Statistics

Variable	Mean	Std. Dev.	Minimum	Maximum
SALES	208,070	194,510	19,146	654,687
PRICE	357.4	103.2	205.0	557.0
SOFT	20,364	3,524	6431	24977
BOA	0.24	0.14	0.04	0.46
DIVX	0.10	0.31	0	1
ENTRY	0.08	0.27	0	1
DEMISE	0.08	0.27	0	1

Table 3: Instrumental Variable Results: Dependent Variable LSALES: (Instruments: CAMINSTALLED LCAMINSTALLED, VCRINSTALLED, LVCRINSTALLED, CDINSTALLED, LCDINSTALLED)

Independent Variables	Coefficient	T-statistic
CONSTANT	15.55	1.92
LPRICE	−1.20	−1.24
LSOFT	0.18	0.65
BOA	4.71	3.05
q^2	0.25	1.44
q^3	0.46	3.41
q^4	0.58	5.22
DIVX	−0.22	−1.51
ENTRY	0.082	0.60
DEMISE	−0.016	−0.10
N of observations	39	
Durbin-Watson	1.82	

Vaporware, the Internet, and Consumer Behavior

David McGowan[1]

In his lecture accepting the Nobel Memorial Prize in economics, Ronald Coase argued for "studies which increase our understanding of how the real economic system works" and a corresponding "reduction in that elegant but sterile theorizing so commonly found in the economics literature on industrial organization."[2] The need for hard data sensibly analyzed is of course not limited to the economics of industrial organization. It is particularly acute in law, where judges and legislators have to make decisions that move money from the pockets of one party (or class of parties) to the pockets of another. Within law, one could make a good case that antitrust has a particular need for data and analysis. Antitrust is, as Herbert Hovenkamp has said, "an extreme case of 'applied' economics"[3] and, on at least one view of the law, the question whether the law has been broken depends on the economic consequences of a party's acts.

And within antitrust, one could make a good argument that claims based on network economic theory are particularly in need of empirical study. If one identifies a market with strong network characteristics – where the proportion of a product's value that is derived from its being part of a network is high relative to its value standing alone – what follows from this fact? Judges and parties quickly realize that the fact of high network value may cut both ways. Microsoft will say the high network value of its operating system explains why it needs to be so aggressive in controlling the application and user interfaces: Standard interfaces make the operating system more valuable to users, and someone has to maintain

---

[1] My thanks to David Dranove, Dan Farber, Neil Gandal, and Dan Gifford for their comments. Mistakes that remain are my fault.
[2] Ronald H. Coase, *The Institutional Structure of Production*, in *Essays on economics and Economists* 14 (1994).
[3] Herbert Hovenkamp, *The Areeda-Turner Treatise in Antitrust Analysis*, 41 *Antitrust Bull.* 815, 821 (1996).

N. Elkin-Koren and N.W. Netanel (eds.), *The Commodification of Information*, 479–492.
© 2002 *David McGowan. Printed in Great Britain.*

and improve the standard.[4] Netscape or Sun will say the operating system's high network value means that original equipment manufacturers and software developers can be cowed into obeying Microsoft's dictates, even if some other course would increase surplus more. Who is to say who is right, and on what basis? The answer to the first question, of course, is that both parties may have legitimate theoretical points, which is to say the theories alone will not tell courts what to do. If neither argument can be rejected as a matter of theory, judges will want to know whether the effects each side claims can be reliably measured to see which is stronger.[5] These questions are not easy, and the law can use all the help it can get from investigation and analysis intelligently done.

For these reasons Professors Dranove and Gandal's study of the competition between DVD and DIVX is most welcome. Theirs is the kind of work that can help lawyers, legislators, and judges better understand how competition works in a strong virtual network market. I will here briefly discuss vaporware claims, the complex interactions among consumers that the Dranove–Gandal study depicts, and what these interactions imply for the law.

I

"Vaporware" is not a well-defined term, and the DVD/DIVX story provides a good example of some of its ambiguities. In its brief to Judge Sporkin on the vaporware questions he raised before rejecting Microsoft's 1995 consent decree with the Justice Department,[6] the Antitrust Division said the term had "no single precise meaning" and concluded that the various definitions had in common only their reference to "a 'preannouncement,' e.g., a statement, before the product is available for purchase, regarding the features or expected release date of the product."[7]

Some definitions of vaporware are satisfied if a product is announced long before it is to be available,[8] though these definitions tend not to say how far in front of the

---

[4] For more on this point *see* Daniel J. Gifford and David McGowan, *A Microsoft Dialogue*, 44 *Antitrust Bull.* 619 (1999); Mark A. Lemley and David McGowan, *Could Java Change Everything? The Competitive Propriety of A Proprietary Standard*, 43 *Antitrust Bull.* 715, 731 (1998).

[5] One might also want to know whether benefits claimed for a practice could be had by conduct entailing fewer costs.

[6] United States v. Microsoft Corp., 1995-1 Trade Cases 70,928 n.4 (D. D.C. 1995).

[7] Memorandum of the United States of America in Response to the Court's Inquiries Concerning "Vaporware," January 27, 1995 (available at <www.usdoj.gov/atr/cases/f0000/0050.htm)> (visited September 9, 1999).

[8] *E.g.*, Steven C. Salop, R. Craig Romaine, *Preserving Monopoly: Economic Analysis, Legal Standards, And Microsoft*, 7 George Mason Univ. L. Rev. 617, 637 n. 57 (1999) ("'Vaporware' refers to the practice of announcing software well in advance of it becoming available, if it ever becomes available").

product the preannouncement must be.⁹ Other definitions, such as one of Judge Sporkin's, require that the preannouncement be "misleading."¹⁰ Still others, such as another of Judge Sporkin's, require that the announcement be strategic – that is, "for the sole purpose of causing consumers not to purchase a competitor's product that has been developed and is either currently available for sale or momentarily about to enter the market."¹¹ One website offers a particular definition with a cover-all-bases fallback: "Vaporware is software or hardware that is either (1) announced or mentioned publicly in order to influence customers to defer buying competitors' products or (2) late being delivered for whatever reason."¹² This site goes on to state that, so defined, "most computer companies have from time to time delivered vaporware, either by calculation or unintentionally."¹³

The term's ambiguity carries over to its use in a legal context: "Vaporware" is shorthand for objectionable conduct, and what counts as legally objectionable depends on the claim at hand. For example, before Judge Sporkin the Antitrust Division argued that "product preannouncements do not violate the antitrust laws unless those preannouncements are knowingly false and contribute to the acquisition, maintenance, or exercise of market power."¹⁴ The requirement that the announcement be false is interesting, and we will return to it in a moment. But if we accept this as a workable definition when the question is whether conduct harms competition, then preannouncements by firms without market power (or a dangerous probability of getting it) would not be "vaporware" in an antitrust sense. Preannouncements by such firms might still support a claim under the Federal Trade Commission Act, however, such as the complaint the Federal Trade Commission brought against Dell Computer for advertising a system with a software CD-ROM but shipping a system with a coupon for the software "when available."¹⁵ And facts establishing a claim under the FTCA may or may not be enough to establish a "vaporware"-based securities claim.¹⁶

---

[9] In the dispute between MCI and AT&T, for example, the trial court instructed jurors that it could find an antitrust violation based on a price reduction announcement "by a firm with monopoly power" if the announcement came "a long time before [the firm] intends to put the reduction into effect." MCI Communications v. American Tel. & Tel. Co., 708 F.2d 1081, 1129 n. 69 (7th Cir.), modified, 1983-2 Trade Cas. (CCH) 65,520 (7th Cir.), cert. denied, 464 U.S. 891 (1983). The instructions went on to add that the announcement would have to have been made "not for legitimate reasons, but for the purpose of maintaining a monopoly." The circuit court disapproved of the instructions because they made "no mention of deception or misleading conduct." Id.

[10] United States v. Microsoft Corp., 159 F.R.D. 318, 326 n.15 (D. D.C. 1995).

[11] Id. at 334.

[12] See www.whatis?.com (visited September 10, 1999).

[13] Id.

[14] Memorandum, *supra* note 7.

[15] United States of America v. Dell Computer Corp., Complaint for Civil Penalties, Injunctive and Other Relief, 7 (available at < www.ftc.gov/os/1998/9804/complai6.htm) > (visited July 29, 1999).

[16] See, e.g., Robert A. Prentice & John H. Langmore, *Beware of Vaporware: Product Hype and The Securities Fraud Liability of High-Tech Companies*, 8 Harv. J. L. & Tech. 1 (1994). These

Professors Dranove and Gandal are concerned with market structure and they therefore refer to vaporware as the "strategic preannouncements of products." This definition excludes negligent preannouncements (though it probably includes reckless ones), but it does not say whether the term should be reserved for lies or whether truthful preannouncements qualify as well. This ambiguity does not impair their data or findings, which pertain to whether and how the DIVX announcement affected consumer behavior. But whether true preannouncements can support a claim is important to the law. In defending its consent decree with Microsoft, the Justice Department added falsity to its proposed test for liability because "courts have refused to find that product preannouncements violate the antitrust laws unless they are knowingly false."[17] Judge Sporkin called this a "rather narrow view" of a "highly questionable practice."[18] Though his concerns might have traced more to his experience with the Exchange Act than the Sherman Act,[19] the question whether a "vaporware" claim can be based on a true preannouncement is interesting and the Dranove-Gandal data provide a good example of why.[20]

The DIVX case confirms that true (or at least roughly true) preannouncements may affect consumer behavior. DIVX was announced at the beginning of the Fourth Quarter of 1997, before the Christmas shopping season, even though the DIVX camp admitted that no product would be ready until 1998. (The *Wall Street Journal* reported on September 9, 1997 that "the first Divx players and accompanying software will begin appearing in some areas next spring.")[21] In a

---

cont.
 authors cite In re Apple Computer Sec. Litig., 886 F.2d 1109 (9th Cir. 1989), *cert denied* 496 U.S. 943 (1990), as an example of a vaporware-based securities case. *Apple* dealt with optimistic statements about a technology that was delivered late and was bad, though it is not clear that the statements were strategic in the same way as the DIVX preannouncement.

[17] Memorandum, *supra* note 7. For this point the Justice Department cited MCI Communications v. American Tel. & Tel. Co., 708 F.2d 1081, 1129 (7th Cir.), modified, 1983-2 Trade Cas. (CCH) 65,520 (7th Cir.), cert. denied, 464 U.S. 891 (1983); ILC Peripherals Leasing Corp. v. IBM Corp., 458 F. Supp. 423, 442 (N.D. Cal. 1978), aff'd sub nom. Memorex Corp. v. IBM Corp., 636 F.2d 1188 (9th Cir. 1980), cert. denied, 452 U.S. 972 (1981).

[18] United States v. Microsoft Corp., 159 F.R.D. at 336.

[19] Judge Sporkin had been the head of the SEC's enforcement division before becoming a judge. See <www.lawschool.cornell.edu/lawlibrary.ssbio.html> (visited October 4, 1999).

[20] For purposes of this discussion I do not attempt to answer the question whether firms might have the right under the speech clause to make true preannouncements; I consider only questions of competition policy. If one decided that true preannouncements could serve as the basis for antitrust claims, one would then have to confront questions based in the commercial speech doctrines. *See*, *e.g.*, Central Hudson Gas & Elec. Corp. v. Public Service Comm'n, 447 U.S. 557 (1980).

[21] Bruce Orwall, *A 'Disposable' Videodisk Threatens To Undercut Nascent Market for DVDs*, Wall Street Journal September 9, 1997. The *Los Angeles Times* reported the same day that "hardware and software is planned to be available by summer 1998" while the *St. Louis Post Dispatch* reported that "movies and discs are expected to be available in test markets by the spring of 1998, and nationwide next summer."

post-Christmas press conference, the DIVX camp pushed the dates back to testing in the summer of 1998 with wider release in the fall. The timing suggests the DIVX preannouncement was strategic, but it may not have been deliberately false.[22] (The post-Christmas slip in the date suggests the pre-Christmas announcement was too optimistic, but the date did not slip very far and the inference of a deliberate lie is correspondingly weak.)

A monopolization or attempted monopolization claim against Digital Video Express might have failed on a number of grounds.[23] But is the antitrust question automatically put to rest if we assume the announcement was true, even though the Dranove-Gandal data show that the announcement altered consumer behavior? Based on our knowledge at present, yes. A knowing or reckless falsity requirement should be imposed as a matter of existing precedent and for reasons of efficiency and practicality.

Antitrust is in general concerned with competition, not truthfulness, which is mainly the province of fraud or false advertising rules.[24] But a truthful preannouncement could stifle competition as well as a false one, maybe better. The more credible the preannouncement is, the more likely it will be to persuade consumers not to buy a competitor's product. If we assume firms can signal that their true preannouncements are true, then true preannouncements will be more powerful tools in a standards competition than false ones. Indeed, if we assume that false preannouncements harm the reputation of the announcing firm, as they probably do to some degree when their falsity is found out, then rational consumers would discount the statements of at least repeat liars. Statements made by repeat liars would therefore be less worrisome from a competition policy point of view than either true preannouncements or statements by liar-initiates.[25]

Efficiency concerns suggest several arguments for penalizing only false statements, however. Investors are keen to get a look at a firm's future, which is

---

[22] Dranove and Gandal prudently stick to their data and draw no conclusions on whether the preannouncement was strategic. Common sense suggests that it was, though my willingness to say so may mean only that lawyers are more willing than economists to draw conclusions without conclusive proof.

[23] See infra Part III.

[24] This general statement should be qualified to the extent one believes deceit may be used to harm competition in general, rather than consumers or individual firms. Though some have argued that this is possible, see Mark R. Patterson, *Coercion, Deception, and Other Demand-Increasing Practices In Antitrust Law*, 66 Antitrust L.J. 1 (1997), it is probably not a common problem.

[25] We still have a problem with the false preannouncement that seems credible, of course. False product announcements serve only to increase demand out of proportion to the benefits of the good demanded, and they might create cynicism generally, leading consumers to give too little weight to true preannouncements. But this is true regardless of the market position of the false preannouncers, suggesting that laws other than competition policy might do a better job of policing the truthfulness of such statements. Either way, the case for scrutinizing true preannouncements under the antitrust laws would seem strong, while reputational effects reduce the problem of false preannouncements to some degree and falsity might be better tackled with better-tailored laws.

why the federal securities laws have over the past 20 years taken steps to encourage firms to make forward-looking statements about events important to the firm's business.[26] Product preannouncements may fall into this category, which is why vaporware is a term familiar to securities law as well as competition policy. To the extent one believes that disclosure of accurate forward-looking information makes capital markets more allocatively efficient,[27] a falsity requirement is a good thing and should be applied to all vaporware-based claims.

And if we assume that a product is legal in itself – it is not a pretext for an unlawful tie, or something of that sort – a truthful preannouncement will help consumers decide what they want to do. A consumer told in September 1997 that DIVX would appear in June 1998 could weigh the benefit of having a DVD player in hand against the risk of its obsolescence if DIVX prevailed and the cost (lost use) of waiting. Consumers probably would prefer to judge for themselves the risk of being stranded on a niche technology rather than being blindsided by DIVX after they had bought DVD players. The DIVX preannouncement gave consumers information they needed to make such decisions. True preannouncements also warn advocates of a competing technology that they might have to fight for their standard. So from an efficiency angle, the falsity requirement can be defended if, and to the extent that, we believe the benefits of true preannouncements generally outweigh the costs.

Against this it might be said that while a true preannouncement might increase the wealth of the preannouncer's shareholders, investors in a competitor might lose as much or more. A trade-off between investors is a wash as far as social welfare is concerned, but a true preannouncement that heads off adoption of a potentially leapfrogging technology in theory might serve to maintain a monopoly position or otherwise reduce welfare. Consumers might prefer the preannouncement to being surprised and then stranded with a new but dying technology, but they might prefer even more a rule giving the new technology a chance to become popular and perhaps set a standard of its own. The Dranove-Gandal data suggest early DVD adopters in particular might favor a rule preventing DIVX from announcing its technology too far in advance. On this view, it should be enough for a vaporware-based antitrust claim to allege that a preannouncement was strategic; an allegation that it was false would not be needed.

These thoughts bring us to three practical and, in my view, compelling arguments for a falsity requirement. The first is that the argument in the last

---

[26] *E.g.*, 15 U.S.C. §77z-2 (Securities Act Safe Harbor for forward-looking statements); 17 C.F.R. 230.175 (safe harbor for forward-looking statements in certain documents filed with the SEC).

[27] For more on this question, *see* Lynn A. Stout, *The Unimportance of Being Efficient: An Economic Analysis of Stock Market Pricing and Securities Regulation*, 87 Mich. L. Rev. 613 (1988) (arguing that market efficiency has only a weak connection to allocative efficiency); Marcel Kahan, *Securities Laws and the Social Costs of "Inaccurate" Stock Prices*, 41 Duke L.J. 977 (1992) (discussing examples where market efficiency has allocational effects).

paragraph, stated in concrete terms, is really a defense of ignorance: Consumers would be less confused if they had less information. One could reply that the argument does not really defend ignorance for its own sake, but rather points to a coordination problem that consumers would be better off without. Because it is information that creates this problem, the reply would go, removing information is the logical solution. I do not find this argument persuasive, though some might. Either way, we should be clear what we are talking about, which is keeping consumers in the dark in the hope that it will be for their own good.

The second argument concerns the time limit. How far in advance is too far? A rule that announcements not precede the actual product by more than six months, say, might seem reasonable at first. (One could even add some flexibility for costly products that required consumers to plan their purchases farther in advance.) Yet a six-months rule would have had the DIVX announcement occurring at Christmas or only shortly afterwards, a result that could arguably have caused more confusion than the nine-months preannouncement that was made. A three-months rule would have solved the problem of the Christmas crunch in this case, but either number is largely arbitrary, and it is hard to see how courts or legislatures could choose a time limit that was reasonably related to market structure and which firms could actually use.

The third argument is based on the risk of error. If the welfare loss depends on the entrant's product being in some way better than the incumbent monopolist's, we must ask how courts are to decide this. If consumers decide to wait for the monopolist's product to come out, is this because they would prefer the entrant's but do not want to run the risk of being stranded with losing technology, because they fear that other consumers will think this way, or because they decide the monopolist's product sounds better than the entrant's – better enough to make it worth the wait? These are hard questions to answer – if there are any answers that hold for any large number of consumers – and a courtroom is probably not the best place to try to answer them. So while true preannouncements might in theory reduce social welfare, it would be very hard to know when this had happened. Because we can be fairly confident that true preannouncements enhance welfare to some degree, we could not evaluate a vaporware-based antitrust claim sensibly unless we had a sense of how severe the harm was.

The elements of a vaporware claim should reflect our best theory and evidence on whether true preannouncements are, on balance, more likely to increase welfare or to reduce it. At the moment, the instincts of courts that have considered the question weigh in favor of punishing only false claims. These instincts are logical and should prevail until proved wrong by analysis based on reliable data. Courts therefore should dismiss vaporware-based antitrust claims unless plaintiffs can show the preannouncements in question were knowingly or recklessly false.[28]

---

[28] This approach is for the most part consistent with the suggestion of Professors Areeda and

That being said, the Dranove-Gandal data show that this is a discussion worth having. The DIVX statements in the fall of 1997 were not obviously false, and may not have been false at all, but they launched a brief standards competition and affected the behavior of potential DVD consumers. On constitutional or other grounds we may conclude that true preannouncements may not be challenged, but our conclusions will be better if we know what they cost. In this regard, Dranove and Gandal's work contributes importantly to a job on which work needs to be done.

II

Dranove and Gandal's findings are based primarily on hard data concerning the number of DIVX and DVD players shipped to retailers, but I wish to discuss for a moment the event studies they performed on the share prices of Circuit City and Best Buy. These studies allow us to consider some legal principles that will help place the relationship between the DIVX preannouncement and consumer behavior in context. Event studies are probably most often used in the law in securities fraud cases, where a class of plaintiffs claims that a statement or omission moved the price of a firm's securities away from the "true" value.[29] The

---

cont.
Hovenkamp that "no liability should attach to" preannouncements that "truly reflect the monopolist's expectations about future quality or availability where that expectation is both actually held in good faith and objectively reasonable." IIIA Phillip A. Areeda & Herbert Hovenkamp, *Antitrust Law* 267, 782j (1996). A point of difference is whether liability should be imposed for unreasonable preannouncements or only for those made with reckless disregard for their accuracy. The former standard leaves open the possibility of a negligent violation of the antitrust laws – for the unreasonable preannouncement that is truly believed – while the latter comes closer to punishing only deliberate lies. The reasonability standard corresponds to the negligent misrepresentation tort while recklessness corresponds with the scienter requirement for securities fraud announced in *Ernst & Ernst v. Hochfelder*, 425 U.S. 185, 193 n.12 (1976), as interpreted by the circuit courts. The court in *MCI v. AT&T*, 708 F.2d at 1128, quoted the Areeda and Hovenkamp standard with approval but went on to say that the preannouncement at issue "must be found to be knowingly false or misleading before it can amount to an exclusionary practice." *Id.* at 1129. The court said the claim never should have gone to a jury because it saw "no deliberate deception or misleading conduct here." *Id.* In actual cases, the difference between reasonability and recklessness might not lead to different results very often. Still, I favor a recklessness standard because courts have some experience with such inquiries under the securities laws, because it is hard to determine what an organization's state of mind is, and because there are many unobjectionable reasons why product shipment dates might slip. The latter two facts make the risk of error a real one. Because preannouncements are often desirable, the cost of erroneous liability findings could be significant, which counsels in favor of a more lenient standard of liability.

[29] *See, e.g.,* Eckstein v. Balcor Film Investors, 8 F.3d 1121, 1130 (7th Cir. 1993)(Easterbrook, J.); Green v. Occidental Petroleum Corp., 541 F.2d 1355, 1341 (9th Cir. 1976) (Sneed, J., concurring).

essential question is one of the relationship (or lack of one) between information and investor behavior.[30] Data from event studies can be open to different interpretations. If a plaintiff claims that information was concealed, and a security's price did not change by a statistically significant amount when the "truth" came out, the lack of a reaction may mean the market already knew the information, or that the information was not material, or that its price effects were offset by other information. Substantially equivalent interpretations exist if the market did not respond to an alleged lie.[31]

These concepts provide an interesting perspective on the way event studies tell the DVD/DIVX story. In September of 1997, when DIVX preannounced its technology, the price of stock in both Circuit City and Best Buy increased. Assuming these increases were statistically significant for each firm, the increase implies that investors considered the announcement good news for both, though better news for Circuit City than for Best Buy. Why? Why didn't the prices move in opposite directions, with investors bidding up the price of Circuit City and dumping Best Buy? DIVX players could play DVDs, though the reverse was not true, so perhaps investors thought DIVX purchasers were only buying insurance against being stranded on a losing format. On this view DIVX purchasers would still add to the demand for DVD content, and good news for DIVX might be only slightly less good news for DVD. Or perhaps investors thought Best Buy would do well no matter which format won, so long as it could sell the hardware (which DIVX would have wanted it to do, though Best Buy would not have agreed unless the market forced it to). Perhaps investors thought Circuit City's margins on the new technology would be higher than what Best Buy earned on DVDs, or that the risk associated with Circuit City's future returns was lower because DIVX players could also play DVD content. (Circuit City did sell DVD players, and its chairman said its stores would not promote DIVX at the expense of DVD.)[32]

The January 1998 DIVX announcement is also interesting. Following the announcement Circuit City's share price fell by .35% while Best Buy's increased by 3.2%. The movement in Circuit City's share price was much smaller than for the September announcement and may imply that the market had anticipated the January information.[33] If it had, though, why the increase in Best Buy's share price? Perhaps neither price movement was statistically significant, or perhaps investors felt Best Buy would get a boost from confirmation that DIVX would be marketed as an enhanced feature of DVD technology. Such reasoning has

---

[30] *E.g.*, Weilgos v. Commonwealth Edison, Co., 892 F.2d 509 (7th Cir. 1989)(Easterbrook, J.).
[31] Goldberg v. Household Bank, FSB, 890 F.2d 965 (7th Cir. 1989) (Easterbrook, J.).
[32] *Orwall, supra* note 21.
[33] It is not clear how much of an effect this statement should have had (depending on one's view of market efficiency), because reports of Circuit City's original announcement made clear that DIVX machines would play DVDs.

ambiguous implications, though, because it implies strong DVD revenues and Circuit City sold DVD machines as well.

Complicating matters further is the datum that between September 1997 and January 1998 Circuit City's share price fell by 5.5% while Best Buy's increased by 153%. One could read this to imply that the DIVX announcement did not slow the adoption of DVD technology, though Dranove and Gandal's data on actual shipments refute any such reading. An acquisition appears to have dragged down Circuit City's share price during this period, which may account for its numbers, though the increase in Best Buy's share price still needs explaining. If the increase was due to anticipated sales of DVD players, the Circuit City numbers look even more significant. Either way, the shipment data are a caution to courts that share prices should not be used as evidence of how consumers behave: such prices may be evidence of how investors think consumers will behave, but they are no substitute for direct evidence.

Dranove and Gandal base their finding that the DIVX announcement reduced DVD sales by approximately 24% on the actual number of DVD and DIVX machines ordered by retailers. Their approach allows for variables that might affect an analysis of this market, such as the number and popularity of movies available in each format. Because their data show that DVD sales increased with the availability of popular movies on DVDs – indicating that virtual network effects were at work in this market – this reduction could be due to the choice of Paramount and 20th Century Fox to back DIVX before DVD, as well as to consumer confusion or risk aversion. And because DIVX players would also play DVDs, it is possible that some DIVX sales were actually to consumers who did not intend to use the DIVX feature but could not find DVD players during high-demand periods.[34] Because DIVX players cost more and there is no evidence of severe shortages, however, this sort of confounding behavior was probably not significant.

Dranove and Gandal's concluding point is worth emphasizing. These data were generated by an announcement from an entrant attacking a technology that had been in the works for years and on which major hardware and software suppliers had done their best to coordinate in supporting a standard. The howls the DIVX announcement brought from the DVD camp suggest that market participants took the announcement seriously. (For example, Warner Home Video's Warren Lieberfarb denounced DIVX as "obsolete before its introduction" and fought

---

[34] There is anecdotal evidence of a shortage of DVD players during the fourth quarter of 1998. *See DIVX Blitz May Be Helping Regular DVD, Video Store*, January 17, 1999. This article states that DIVX reported sales of 87,000 units through January 1999 but declined to report how many buyers had registered with DIVX to use the DIVX feature of the players. Buyers would not have had to register to use a DIVX player to play DVDs, and DIVX probably would have reported the number of registrations if the percentage had been favorable to DIVX. So there is some basis for speculating that some DIVX buyers had no interest in the feature, though I know of no actual evidence of such confounding behavior.

against DIVX for the entirety of its brief life on the ground that it would confuse consumers).[35] Dranove and Gandal are right to say that a similar announcement by the owner of an incumbent standard probably would have a stronger effect. A false preannouncement through which a firm got, kept, or extended market power could state a claim under the antitrust laws, assuming one could trace the power (or a dangerous probability of getting power) to the preannouncement.[36] Dranove and Gandal's study is the type of work courts should consult to determine whether preannouncements have had the necessary effects. Their data are valuable confirmation that product preannouncements in a market with strong network effects may affect consumer behavior and are a legitimate subject of concern for the law.

III

So why didn't it work? As Dranove and Gandal report, DIVX was a memorable failure, folding its tent and slinking from the scene in June of 1999. On some accounts, the DIVX threat actually helped the DVD cause by spurring firms in the DVD camp to greater efforts.[37] Warner Home Video was reported to have begun a campaign to persuade video stores to rent DVDs, and major DVD hardware manufacturers began giving away five free movies with each unit sold.[38] Perhaps such firms should have been doing these things anyway, and DIVX was only a wake-up call reminding them that nothing in business is inevitable. The DIVX preannouncement may have reduced DVD sales in the fourth quarter of 1997, but it also gave the DVD coalition time to plan their response and have it in place when DIVX machines actually began to arrive in stores.

And, apropos of this point and of any discussion of the commodification of information, whose interests did DIVX serve? As Dranove and Gandal report, movie studios were concerned that movies distributed in digital format could be pirated with ease. With its lock-out and pay-per-view features, DIVX provided one apparent answer to this problem. One commentator argues that the DIVX idea "was to protect the rights of the content producers and stop piracy at all costs" and that DIVX failed because this single-minded focus ignored the interests

---

[35] *Confusion fear in DVD market*, Financial Times, September 9, 1997.
[36] *See* Areeda & Hovenkamp, *supra* note 28.
[37] *See* Joel Brinkley, *Few Tears Are Shed As DIVX Joins The 8-Track*, New York Times, June 24, 1999 ("Paradoxically, Divx actually hastened acceptance of DVD"); Laura Heller, *DIVX We Hardly Knew You*, Discount Store News, July 12, 1999 (quoting a NationsBanc Montgomery securities analyst who argued that "DIVX was a real positive last year for open DVD" because "It got everyone real aggressive").
[38] Brinkley, *supra* note 37. On Warner's efforts, *see, also, DVD Report* July 12, 1999.

of consumers who, after all, were the ones expected to buy the machines and the movies.[39] This is a bit too strong, for DIVX might have offered some benefits to consumers – at least the forgetful among us would like to avoid fees for the late return of rented movies – but the main point is valid.[40]

These sorts of arguments will suggest to some that the law need not worry about vaporware. I do not agree with this as an absolute statement, but before explaining why I will mention one more argument on that side of the ledger. The concern over preannounced technology is largely a problem of coordination among consumers. From a market structure point of view, the problem is one of getting the relevant consumers together to compare the benefits of the entrant's preannounced product with that of the incumbent and to decide which they prefer. For this to happen, the relevant consumers have to find each other and exchange ideas, which is costly. I say the relevant consumers because, as Dranove and Gandal point out, the early buyers will be a relatively discrete group with a particular interest in the type of technology at hand – audiophiles, computer geeks, etc. At least in the case of a new product market, where most potential consumers have not decided what to buy, the purchases of early adopters may signal to both software vendors and other consumers which technology is likely to win out.

One of the most intriguing aspects of the story Dranove and Gandal tell is how consumers used the Internet to fight DIVX. As they point out, early DVD adopters and others in the DVD community made heavy use of pro-DVD websites to discourage adoption of DIVX. Both adopters and potential adopters could use these, of course, making it easier (cheaper) for consumers to share information and judge whether a consensus was forming about whether DVD was better than laserdisc technology and, later, DIVX. Dranove and Gandal report that by the end of 1998 – as DIVX was beginning to get as established as it got – these sites were seeing 10,000 postings per week. And this during a several-week period when only 87,000 DIVX machines and 320,000 DVD machines were sold. (Many messages were no doubt repeat posts from particular persons, but the number of messages relative to the number of sales is impressive nevertheless.) The Internet made it easier for early adopters and potential adopters to find each other and share information. To the extent a coordination problem created by a preannouncement rests on the cost of communicating, the Internet lowers the costs and makes the problem better. (This is not to say the Internet can or will solve such problems entirely.) The DVD/DIVX battle offers an example of how preannouncements can impede adoption of a technology, but it also offers an example of how consumers can use technology to decide what their interests are and, voting with their wallets, to assert them. To the extent technology makes it easier for consumers to coordinate their decisions in markets where consumer

---

[39] David Thompson, *The Lessons of DIVX*, PC Week, July 26, 1999.
[40] It should surprise no one that a product whose main purpose was the protection of copyrights was the brainchild of a law firm that became a joint venturer in developing the technology.

coordination may be desirable, there is a less compelling case for legal intervention to protect these consumers from behavior that seems designed to create or play on coordination problems. By the same token, rules that make coordination more effective – such as rules that increase the legal reliability of information introduced to the market – become more important. I return to this point in a moment.

But first, what does all this mean for competition policy? DIVX was an entrant technology pushed by a firm holding contractual rights with complementary hardware and software producers.[41] DIVX never had market power, nor did its preannouncement pose a dangerous threat that it would monopolize a relevant market. For these reasons, an antitrust claim based on the preannouncement would have failed even if the preannouncement had been recklessly false.[42]

But while no antitrust claim could have been stated on these facts, it does not follow that the evidence Dranove and Gandal present is of no interest to the law. They have shown how one type of market behavior can affect actual consumers making decisions in actual markets. Though the relatively blunt, structural tools of antitrust might not be suitable for such a case, these data make a case for considering whether other sorts of legal rules might be called upon to protect consumers, even when announcements are made by non-dominant firms. There is a good case to be made that in network markets the truthfulness of product announcements should be closely scrutinized and firms should be held to promises made to persuade consumers to adopt a technology (contract or other theories might be employed to this end).[43] This study provides welcome empirical support for that idea; it also suggests a potentially useful role for oft-abused state unfair competition laws. Though in some cases their breadth renders these laws all but content-free, they might legitimately be applied to prevent consumers from being sandbagged by preannouncements.

---

[41] Any questions about the agreements themselves should be analyzed under the rule of reason. *See* William F. Baxter & Daniel P. Kessler, *Toward A Consistent Theory of the Welfare Analysis of Agreements*, 47 *Stan. L. Rev.* 615, 630 (1995).

[42] *See* Spectrum Sports v. McQuillan, 506 U.S. 447 (1993) (monopolization claim requires the plaintiff to show a dangerous probability of acquiring a monopoly); Adsat v. Associated Press, 181 F.3d 216, 226, 229 (2d Cir. 1999) (no dangerous probability of monopolization where defendant's market share was below 30%).

[43] *See* David McGowan, *Free Contracting, Fair Competition, and Article 2B: Some Reflections on Federal Competition Policy, Information Transactions, and "Aggressive Neutrality,"* 13 *Berkeley Tech. L.J.* 1173, 1224-37 (1998).

IV

Professors Dranove and Gandal have improved our understanding of competition in virtual network markets and shed light on many legal questions pertaining to "vaporware." Their work shows us both that product preannouncements present complex questions for many fields of law and that these problems are important. Finding the mixture of legal doctrines that best preserves the benefits of preannouncements while minimizing their costs is a delicate task that lawyers and judges should undertake with care and humility, with an eye always on guidance of the kind of data Dranove and Gandal have given us.

About the Contributors

C. EDWIN BAKER, Nicholas F. Gallicchio Professor, University of Pennsylvania School of Law, is a graduate of Stanford University and Yale Law School. He has taught at New York University, Chicago, Cornell, Texas, Oregon, and Toledo law schools and at Harvard's Kennedy School of Government and was a staff attorney for the ACLU. He regularly teaches Constitutional Law, Mass Media Law, and related courses. He is the author of three books: Media, Markets, and Democracy (Cambridge, 2001), Advertising and a Democratic Press (Princeton, 1994), and Human Liberty and Freedom of Speech (Oxford, 1989), and numerous articles about free speech, equality, property, law and economics, jurisprudence, and the mass media.

YOCHAI BENKLER is a Professor at the New York University School of Law. He is the Director of the Engleberg Center for Innovation Law and Policy, and of the Information Law Institute at NYU. His research focuses on the effects of laws that regulate information production and exchange on the distribution of control over information flows, knowledge, and cultural production in the digital environment. Before coming to NYU, Benkler clerked for Justice Stephen Breyer of the United States Supreme Court, and had earlier been an associate in the corporate practice group of Ropes & Gray in Boston. He received his J.D from Harvard Law School and his LL.B. from Tel-Aviv University.

DAVID DRANOVE is the Walter McNerney Distinguished Professor of Health Industry Management at Northwestern University's Kellogg Graduate School of Management, where he is also Professor of Management and Strategy. He has a Ph.D. in Economics from Stanford University. Dranove's research and teaching focus on problems in industrial organization and business strategy with an emphasis on the health care industry. He has published more than 70 research papers, monographs, and book chapters, and is coauthor of the popular textbook *The Economics of Strategy*. His most recent book is *The Economic Evolution of American Health Care: From Marcus Welby to Managed Care*, published by the Princeton University Press.

ROCHELLE COOPER DREYFUSS is the Pauline Newman Professor of Law at N.Y.U. School of Law, where her research and teaching interests include intellectual property, civil procedure, privacy, and the relationship between science and law. After a career as a research chemist, she entered Columbia University School of Law, where she served as Articles and Book Review Editor of the Law Review. A former law clerk to Chief Judge Wilfred Feinberg of the U.S. Court of Appeals for the Second Circuit and to Chief Justice Warren E. Burger of the Supreme Court, she is currently a member of the American Law Institute and a National Academy of Sciences panel on intellectual property. She was a consultant to the Federal Courts Study Committee and to the Presidential Commission on Catastrophic Nuclear Accidents, and a Chair of the Intellectual Property Section of the American Association of Law Schools.

REBECCA S. EISENBERG is the Robert and Barbara Luciano Professor of Law at the University of Michigan Law School. She has written and lectured extensively about patent law as applied to biotechnology and the role of intellectual property at the public-private divide in research science, publishing in scientific journals as well as law reviews. Professor Eisenberg has received grants from the program on Ethical, Legal, and Social Implications of the Human Genome Project from the U.S. Department of Energy Office of Biological and Environmental Research for her work on private appropriation and public dissemination of DNA sequence information. She has played an active role in public policy debates concerning the role of intellectual property in biomedical research. She is a member of the Advisory Committee to the Director of the National Institutes of Health, the Panel on Science, Technology and Law of the National Academies, and the Board of Directors of the Stem Cell Genomics and Therapeutics Network in Canada.

NIVA ELKIN-KOREN is a Senior Lecturer at the University of Haifa School of Law. She received her LL.B from Tel-Aviv University School of Law in 1989, her LL.M from Harvard Law School in 1991, and her S.J.D from Stanford Law School in 1995. She teaches Contract Law, Intellectual Property, Electronic Commerce and related courses and seminars. Her research focuses on the legal institutions that facilitate private and public control over the production of information. She has written and spoken extensively about the privatization of information policy, copyright law and democratic theory, the effects of cyberspace on the economic analysis of law, liability of information intermediaries, and the significance of the public domain. She was a visiting professor at Villanova University School of Law during 1997 and at the George Washington University Law School during 2001.

NEIL GANDAL is an Associate Professor of Economics in the Department of Public Policy at Tel Aviv University. He is also a Research Fellow at the Centre for Economic Policy Research, and has been a visiting professor at the University of California at Berkeley, and the University of Texas at Austin. Gandal is an Associate Editor of the *Journal of Industrial Economics*, and the *International*

Journal of Industrial Organization. His research interests include Industrial Organization, Network Economics, and the Economics of Language. His research has appeared in the *RAND Journal of Economics*, the *Journal of Public Economics*, and the *Journal of International Economics*. Gandal received his Ph.D. in Economics in 1989 from the University of California at Berkeley.

WENDY J. GORDON is Professor of Law and Liacos Scholar in Law at Boston University School of Law. She is General Secretary of the Society for Economic Research on Copyright Issues, is a member of the Editorial Board of the Encyclopedia of Law and Economics (Edward Elgar) and is a former Chair of the Intellectual Property section of the AALS. In 1999-2000 she was a Fulbright Scholar in England, elected to the Visiting Senior Research Fellowship at St. John's College, University of Oxford. Her publications include An Inquiry into the Merits of Copyright (Stanford Law Review), Fair Use as Market Failure (Columbia Law Review), On Owning Information (Virginia Law Review), A Property Right in Self-Expression (Yale Law Journal), and On Commodifying Intangibles (with Sam Postbrief, for the Yale Journal of Law and Humanities).

BERNT HUGENHOLTZ is Professor of Law and Co-Director of the Institute for Information Law of the University of Amsterdam. He has written extensively on a range of copyright-related topics, with particular emphasis on the problems of the digital networked environment. At the University of Amsterdam he teaches courses in copyright law, international copyright law, industrial property law and information law. Hugenholtz is chairman of the Intellectual Property Task Force of the Legal Advisory Board of the European Commission, and Editor-in-chief of the Information Law Series, published by Kluwer. He has been on several international missions representing WIPO, and is a regular speaker at international conferences. His most recent publications are available at <www.ivir.nl/staff/hugenholtz.html>.

JESSICA LITMAN is a Professor of Law at Wayne State University in Detroit, Michigan, where she teaches courses in copyright law, Internet law, and trademarks and unfair competition. Before joining the Wayne faculty in 1990, she was an Associate Professor at the University of Michigan Law School. Litman is the author of the recently published book, "Digital Copyright" (Prometheus 2001). She has also published many articles on copyright, trademark, and Internet law, and is the co-author of the third edition of Ginsburg, Litman & Kevlin, Trademark and Unfair Competition Law (Foundation 2001). Litman is a past trustee of the Copyright Society of the USA and a past Chair of the American Association of Law Schools' Section on Intellectual Property. She has testified before Congress and before the White House Information Infrastructure Task Force's Working Group on Intellectual Property. She currently serves on the advisory board of Cyberspace Law Abstracts, the National Research Council's

About the Contributors

Committee on Partnerships in Weather and Climate Services and the American Civil Liberties Union (ACLU) Committee on Intellectual Property and the Internet.

EJAN MACKAAY, LL.M. (Toronto), LL.D. (Amsterdam), is Professor of Law at the University of Montreal and Director of the Public Law Research Centre. He is correspondent of the Royal Netherlands Academy of Sciences. Professor Mackaay teaches contracts, law and economics, new technology law. His recent publications include Les droits de propriété, Pierre Lemieux and Ejan Mackaay, in Daniel Vitry (ed.), *Dictionnaire des Sciences Économiques* (Presses Universitaires de France, 2001), *Analyse économique du droit — I. Fondements* (Éditions Thémis, 2000), and The Economics of Emergent Property Rights on the Internet, in P. Bernt Hugenholtz (ed.), *The Future of Copyright in a Digital Environment*, The Hague, (Kluwer Law International, 1996).

DAVID MCGOWAN is an Associate Professor of Law at the University of Minnesota Law School. He teaches and writes in the areas of competition policy and intellectual property, contracts, electronic commerce, corporations, and securities regulation. He has written several articles concerning the intersection of antitrust and intellectual property policy, with particular emphasis on markets characterized by network economic effects. Before joining the University of Minnesota, McGowan practiced law in San Francisco.

EBEN MOGLEN is Professor of Law at Columbia Law School. His JD and PhD in history were earned during what he sometimes refers to as his long dark period in New Haven. He served as law clerk to Judge Edward Weinfeld of the Southern District of New York and Justice Thurgood Marshall. Before and during law school he was a designer and implementer of advanced computer programming languages at IBM's Santa Teresa Laboratory and Thomas J. Watson Research Center. Since 1993 he has served pro bono publico as General Counsel of the Free Software Foundation. His writing can be read at < http://moglen.law.columbia.edu >.

NEIL WEINSTOCK NETANEL is the Arnold, White & Durkee Centennial Professor of Law at the University of Texas, where he teaches copyright, international intellectual property, intellectual property theory, and property. Professor Netanel's scholarship, which has appeared in the Yale Law Journal, Stanford Law Review, California Law Review, and other leading law journals, has focused on copyright's historical and theoretical foundations, from both a domestic and comparative law perspective. His most recent articles examine the tension between copyright and free speech and critique the notion of cyberspace self-governance. Professor Netanel has also taught at the law schools of the Hebrew University of Jerusalem, Haifa University, Tel-Aviv University, and New York University.

About the Contributors

DAVID NIMMER is Visiting Professor, UCLA School of Law; Distinguished Scholar, Berkeley Center for Law and Technology; and Of Counsel to the Los Angeles law firm of Irell & Manella LLP. Since 1985, he has revised *Nimmer on Copyright* semi-annually, in order to keep that 10-volume treatise up to date. In 2001, he published a book-length analysis in the Houston Law Review of *Qimron v. Shanks*, the so-called "Dead Sea Scrolls Copyright Case." That piece melds literary theory with categories of religious interpretation to yield a multi-faceted critique of the Israeli Supreme Court's decision in the case. An anthology of his articles is forthcoming from Kluwer Law International, under the title *Copyright: Sacred Text, Technology, and the DMCA*.

HELEN NISSENBAUM is Associate Professor in the Department of Culture and Communication and a Senior Fellow of the Information Law Institute, New York University. She specializes in social, ethical, and political dimensions of information technology. Her published works on privacy, property rights, electronic publication, accountability, the use of computers in education, and values embodied in computer systems have appeared in scholarly journals of philosophy, applied ethics, law, and computer science. She is author of *Emotion and Focus* (University of Chicago Press), co-editor (with D.J. Johnson) of *Computers, Ethics and Social Values* (Prentice-Hall), and a founding co-editor of the journal, *Ethics and Information Technology* (Kluwer Academic Press). Grants from the National Science Foundation and Ford Foundation have supported her research and she has served on committees of the National Academy of Sciences, National Science Foundation, UNESCO, AAAS, and the ACM. Before joining NYU, Nissenbaum was a Member of the School of Social Science, Institute for Advanced Study, Associate Director of Princeton University's Center for Human Values, and Postdoctoral Fellow at the Center for the Study of Language and Information, Stanford University. She earned a B.A. (Honors) from the University of Witwatersand, Johannesburg and a Ph.D. in philosophy from Stanford University.

ELI M. NOAM is a Professor of Economics and Finance at Columbia Business School since 1976. After having served for three years as Commissioner with the New York State Public Service Commission, he returned to Columbia in 1990. He is Director of the Columbia Institute for Tele-Information, a university-based research center focusing on strategy, management, and policy issues in telecommunications, computing, and electronic mass media. Chairman of MBA concentration in the Management of Entertainment, Communications, and Media at the Business School, Noam has also taught at Columbia Law School and Princeton University's Economics Department and Woodrow Wilson School. Noam published more than 20 books and 400 articles in economic journals, law reviews, and interdisciplinary journals and served on the editorial boards of Columbia University Press and other academic journals. He was a member of the advisory boards for the Federal government's FTS-2000 telecommunications network, the IRS's computer system reorganization, and the National Computer Systems Laboratory. He received an AB (*Phi Beta Kappa*), MA, Ph.D. (Economics) and JD from Harvard University.

MARGARET JANE RADIN is the William Benjamin Scott and Luna M. Scott Professor of Law at Stanford University, and Director of Stanford Law School's Program in Law, Science and Technology. She received her A.B. from Stanford, where she was elected to Phi Beta Kappa, and her J.D. from the University of Southern California, where she was elected to Order of the Coif. She also holds an honorary LL.D. from Illinois Institute of Technology/Chicago-Kent, and an M.F.A. in music history from Brandeis University. Radin is the author of two books on property theory: *Reinterpreting Property* (University of Chicago Press 1993) and *Contested Commodities* (Harvard University Press 1996). Her current research involves intellectual property, information technology, electronic commerce and the jurisprudence of cyberspace.

PAMELA SAMUELSON is Chancellor's Professor of Law and Information Management at the University of California at Berkeley. She has written and spoken extensively about the challenges that new information technologies pose for traditional legal regimes, especially for intellectual property law. She is a Director of the Berkeley Center for Law & Technology, a Fellow of the John D. and Catherine T. MacArthur Foundation, and a member of the Board of Directors of the Electronic Frontier Foundation. A 1971 graduate of the University of Hawaii and a 1976 graduate of Yale Law School, Samuelson practiced law as a litigation associate with the New York law firm Willkie Farr & Gallagher before turning to more academic pursuits.

ANSELM KAMPERMAN SANDERS Ph.D (Lon) is Associate Professor in Trade and Intellectual Property Law at Maastricht University, The Netherlands. He was a Marie Curie Research Fellow and still is an Adjunct Research Fellow at Queen Mary, University of London. Research and editorial affiliations comprise the International Institute of Infonomics http://www.infonomics.nl, the Maastricht Journal of European and Comparative law, and the Intellectual Property Quarterly. He is the author of Unfair Competition Law, The Protection of Intellectual and Industrial Creativity (1997, Oxford, Clarendon Press) and co-editor (with C. Heath) of and contributor to Intellectual Property in the Digital Age (2001, The Hague, Kluwer Law International) He can be reached by e-mail at a.kampermansanders@pr.unimaas.nl.

DAVID VAVER is Reuters Professor of Intellectual Property and Information Technology Law in the University of Oxford, and the Director of the Oxford Intellectual Property Research Centre at St Peter's College, Oxford, where he is also a Professorial Fellow. He previously taught in New Zealand and Canadian law schools. His writings include Intellectual Property Law: Copyright, Patents, Trade-marks (1997) and Copyright Law (2000) in Irwin Law's Essentials of Canadian Law series, and (until 1998) the section on Canada in Nimmer & Geller's International Copyright Law & Practice (Matthew Bender, N.Y.). Previously an advisor to the Canadian government on copyright law reform, Vaver is currently a member of the UK Minister of Trade & Industry's Intellectual Property Advisory Committee.

JONATHAN WEINBERG is a law professor at Wayne State University in Detroit, Michigan. He has been a legal scholar in residence at the FCC's Office of Plans and Policy; a visiting scholar at Cardozo Law School; a professor in residence at the U.S. Justice Department; a visiting scholar at the University of Tokyo's Institute of Journalism and Communication Studies; a law clerk to U.S. Supreme Court Justice Thurgood Marshall; and a law clerk to then-Judge Ruth Bader Ginsburg. Weinberg recently chaired a working group created by ICANN (Internet Corporation for Assigned Names and Numbers – the international body seeking to order the domain name system and other aspects of Internet infrastructure) to develop recommendations on the creation of new Internet top-level domains.

Index

abuse of dominant position 384–9
access
   anti-circumvention rule 211, 212, 214–15, 217–18
   commons concept 54
   communications infrastructure 292, 305, 306–7, 310, 312–13, 314
   control over 91–4, 96, 97–8
   file access rights 345–6
   Internet 199–200, 308–9, 345–6
   patent disclosures 419, 426
   payment for 205–6
   political participation 101
   public sector information 234–5, 366, 390n150
   U.S. Act 378–9
Adams, John Quincy 326
advertising 7, 44, 305, 325
   Internet 25, 30, 41n102
   television 48
agenda-setting 322
Agre, Phil 355
Agreement on Trade-Related Aspects of Intellectual Property Rights (TRIPS) 69–70, 110, 365
alienation 99–100, 104–5
Amabile, Theresa 189
anonymity 344, 347–8, 354, 362, 363
anti-circumvention rule 70, 72–3, 75–6, 82, 90–1, 99
   DMCA x, 82, 193–221
   DVD case 92
   EC Copyright Directive 229–30
anti-commons 134, 141
antitrust 53, 80, 382–3, 389, 390
   Microsoft 44, 53
   vaporware 464, 479, 481, 483–4, 485, 489, 491

AOL-Time-Warner 68
Apache 122
Areeda, P.A. 485n28
Ashdown, Paddy 258
association rules 138, 140
AT&T 44, 119, 425, 481n9, 486n28
audience preferences 279–80, 281, 283–8
   see also consumer preferences
authorship 163, 249, 405, 407–8, 410, 412–13, 440, 445
autonomy x, 80, 102, 103, 319
   communications infrastructure 291–3, 296, 297–304, 306–7, 313–14, 316, 330
   peer-to-peer networks 331

Baker, C. Edwin x, 179, 267–90, 304, 319
Bangemann Report (1994) 224–5, 237
Baran, Paul 291, 294
Barlow, John Perry 144
Barnard, Christian 435
Baseman, K. 464
Benkler, Yochai x, 65, 68, 285, 291–316, 330–2, 334–5, 380n95
Berne Convention 252, 374, 376
Best Buy 466, 467–8, 487–8
Bidder's Edge 94–6, 98
biotechnology 144, 403, 415–31
blood donors 188–9
Bolyai, Janos 435, 451
books 48–9, 66–7
Boyle, James 68, 186n123
branding 44, 49, 95–6
Branscomb, A.W. 212n93
broadcasting 86, 232, 285, 290, 306
   EC case law 259, 386–7
   government-funded media 328–9
browsing 208–9, 212, 230, 231
burglary concept 73

501

C language 119, 121n19
cable services 53, 54, 87, 308–9, 310
caching 230, 231, 234
Calabresi, Guido 157n24, 371
Canada 87n23, 281–2
capitalism 49, 50, 106
case law
  abuse of dominant position 384–9
  behavior 164–5
  common carriage regimes 310
  compensation 159
  copyright exemptions 251–2
  databases 374, 376–7, 380, 382
  DNA sequence patents 416–17, 422–3, 425
  DVD case 92–3, 106n78
  eBay case 94–8
  fair use 9–10, 158, 183–4, 185
  free expression 63, 64, 253–61, 391–2
  Groppera case 246
  hyperlinks 90
  MP3.com case 88
  Napster case 74, 89
  safe harbor provision 33
  self-defense 170–2
  Sony case 93, 137
CBS 336–8
CD players 109
censorship 262, 278, 310
  copyright issues 66–7, 73, 76
  Internet 27
  private 63, 64, 75, 153, 172–4
centralization 100, 102–3, 105
cheapness of information 48–9
Circuit City 466–9, 487–8
civic virtue 103–4, 105
Clinton, Bill 24, 31, 38, 267n2
Coase, Ronald 174, 179, 181n108, 401, 479
Coase Theorem 174, 177, 179, 180, 368
COBOL (Common Business-Orientated Language) 114
Cohen, Julie E. 65, 72, 220n131
collaborative research 397–413
Collections of Information Antipiracy Act (U.S., H.R.354) 378–82, 390
Columbia Tri-Star 465
commercial media vii, 317–39

commercial speech ix, 42, 246, 247, 261–2
commercialization ix, 7, 45, 49–52, 83, 97, 323–4
commodification 5, 8, 21, 43–59, 83n13
  collaborative research 397, 399, 413
  communications 284–5
  copyright 13, 106
  definitions 44–5, 46–55
  fair use doctrine 9, 10–11, 150
  lack of quality 188–9
  market limitation relationship 162–4
  market rhetoric 3–4
  open source software 13, 14
  privacy 16, 20
  research norms 433–4
common carriers 292, 293, 306–10, 311, 312, 313–14
commons 54–5, 125, 141, 143
  communications infrastructure 291–2, 299, 301, 306–12, 314–15, 330
  spectrum 293, 294, 296
  see also anti-commons
communications infrastructure 291–316, 330
community 190
compensation 79, 84, 88, 106
  fair use 150–1, 156, 157, 165–6, 186, 187
  lack of 159–60, 162, 167–9
  reproduction rights 232, 233
  where no injunction 188, 189–90, 191
competition 49, 302–3, 305, 391–2
  databases 365–6, 367–9, 381–2, 383, 393
  eBay case 96, 98
  intellectual property rights 384, 385, 386, 389
  media products 269, 272–3, 274, 276
  new information markets 79, 80, 81
  use of copyright law 84–5
  see also antitrust; unfair competition
computer technology
  computer readable information 421–2, 423, 424–5, 426, 428–9
  development 115–18
  identifiability 347–50
  Processor Serial Number 343, 351–5
  programming 13, 65, 113–15, 119, 120, 121, 127, 142–4

502

computer technology, *cont.*
   rights management 345–6, 351, 362
   trusted systems 343–4, 346–7, 351, 354–61, 362, 363–4
   see also digital communications technology; information technology; Internet; personal computers; software
conditional fault 160
consent *see* permission
consequentialism 167, 300, 301
consolidation 68
constitutional issues 241–4, 247–8
Consumer and Investor Access to Information Act (U.S., H.R.1858) 378–9
consumer preferences 303, 304
   see also audience preferences
consumer sovereignty 172–3, 174
contract 15–16, 83, 136, 137–8
   collaborative research 409–10
   freedom of 72, 137, 140
   legal rules 111
   online commerce 18
control over information 79–106, 361
   communications infrastructure 298, 299–302, 305, 308, 316
   media companies 44, 52–3
   state 58
copyleft 13, 15n40, 124, 126
   see also General Public License
copyright vii–viii, 4n5, 6, 79–106, 134, 285, 361
   Antipiracy Bill 379
   cases 376–7
   collaborative research 404–5, 406, 407, 412
   computer software 115, 116, 118, 124, 126
   databases 374–5
   digital numeric information 109, 110
   DMCA anti-circumvention provision 193–221
   EC Copyright Directive 228–33
   essential function 387–8
   Europe 223–37, 239–63
   excludability 270n6

first sale doctrine 204, 206, 207, 221, 357
free expression relationship ix, 63–77, 106
Internet 23, 32–5, 136–7
licensing 369
limitation 133, 249, 250–1, 252–3
market perspective 154–6
noncommodification 5
open access goods 143
open source licensing 13
patent law 410
private performance 152n7
trusted systems 356, 357–8
   see also fair use doctrine
Copyright Act (US, 1976) 9n22, 87, 194, 207, 404, 407
Copyright Harmonization Directive (EC, 2001) 228–33, 234, 239, 249–50, 252–3, 365
Corley case 74, 75–6
corporations 8, 105, 335, 336–8, 449
costs
   cheapness of information 48–9
   communication services 304–5, 312–13
   externalities 277–8
   intellectual property rights 370–1
   Internet 25, 29–30, 49, 334
   large media companies 52–3
   media products 269–77, 278
   patent system 447
   production 82n5
   see also transaction costs
cover versions 160n31
credentials 362–3
criminal penalties 73, 154
critical reviews 175–6, 181
cross-licensing 389–90
cultural products 267–90
cultural software 109
culture 104–5, 403
cyberspace 3, 4, 94, 98, 330
   commons 125
   intellectual property rights 445
   utopian vs dystopian visions 7–8
   see also Internet

data privacy 17–18, 19n46, 20, 24

503

Database Directive (EC, 1996) 227–8, 233, 366, 374–7, 379–83, 389–90
databases x, 255, 355, 360, 362, 365–93
 DNA sequence patents 421, 426–7
 eBay case 94–5
decentralization 56, 292, 297
 decision-making 299
 Internet 81–2, 330
 networks 295, 296, 315
DeCSS 75–6, 90, 91–3, 133–4
Dell Computer 481
democracy 7, 80, 100–2, 103–4, 286–8, 296
 autonomy 291, 292, 316
 'complex' 319
 see also liberal democracy
democratization 330, 438
demoralization costs 168
Depoorter, B. 141
derivative works 109, 115, 117, 119, 173n81, 204n65, 407, 412
DHCP protocol 128, 348
digital communications technology viii, 195, 315, 317
Digital Millennium Copyright Act (DMCA, 1998) 4n5, 12n35, 32–3, 82, 99, 133, 378
 access control 93
 anti-circumvention rule x, 73–4, 75–6, 82, 90–1, 92, 193–221
 exemptions 199–202, 215, 216–18, 219, 220, 221
 fence-cutting 140
digital revolution 107–8, 123, 131, 204
Disney 68, 126n27, 130, 338, 465, 467
distribution 12–13, 14, 15
 channels 81, 85–91
 rights 229, 239
DIVX (Digital Video Express) 359, 462, 465–73, 477, 480, 482–91
DMCA see Digital Millennium Copyright Act
DNA sequences xi, 415–31
domain names 37–41
downloads 207
Dranove, David xi, 461–77, 480, 482, 486, 488–90, 491–2

Dreamworks 465, 467
Dreyfuss, Rochelle Cooper x–xi, 397–413
DVD (Digital Versatile Disc)
 DeCSS program 75–6, 90, 91–3
 DIVX conflict 462, 463, 464–73, 475–7, 480, 484–91
dystopian vision 7, 8

e-commerce ix, 23–42, 81, 83n9, 236, 373–4
E-Commerce Directive (EC, 2000) 226, 231, 233–4
eBay 94–8
ECHR see European Convention on Human Rights
ECJ see European Court of Justice
economic rights 249, 250, 251
economic transactions 43, 56, 57, 59
economics 104, 179, 383–4, 479
 free trade in media products 268, 289
 intellectual property rights 367–71
 property v. liability rules 371–3
 unfair competition 365–6
 utilitarianism 182
 welfare effects 167, 178, 180
efficiency 10, 146, 155, 161, 179, 180, 268, 373
egalitarianism 287
Eisenberg, Rebecca S. xi, 402, 415–31
electronic commerce see e-commerce
electronic publication 433, 434, 436–9, 442, 445, 453–5
Elkin-Koren, Niva 63, 65, 79–106, 330
employees 14, 409–10
enclosure of the commons 54
encryption 136, 140, 232, 344
 anti-circumvention rule 200, 215, 216
 DeCSS program 75–6, 90, 91–3
 DIVX 466
 MP3 files 35–6
 research 219
enforcement 16, 66, 72, 83, 99
Enron 44
essential facilities doctrine 384, 388, 389, 390
EU see European Union

Europe
  collaborative research 411–12
  copyright 223–37, 239–63
  freedom of expression x, 239–63
European Commission 223, 231n32, 234, 249–50, 366, 375, 388
European Commission on Human Rights 242, 258–61, 262, 263
European Convention on Human Rights (ECHR) x, 235, 366
  copyright 242
  freedom of expression 240, 244–8, 250, 253, 255–61, 263, 391–3
European Court of Human Rights 241–2, 245–8, 258, 261–3, 366, 391–2, 393
European Court of Justice (ECJ) 245n29, 385, 386–8
European Union (EU) 223, 225, 226, 227, 263, 365
  collaborative research 412
  databases 375, 379, 382, 389
  harmonization 236–7
  open government 234
  privacy 18
exceptions
  DMCA 199–202, 215, 216–18, 219, 220, 221
  EC Copyright Directive 230–3, 250
  EC Database Directive 228
  European case law 251–2
  parody 263n115
  patent law 423, 428
  see also fair use
excludability 97, 116, 117, 270n6, 272
exclusivity 314, 397, 409, 416, 430
excuse 150–2, 153–4, 156, 183, 184–6
  market malfunction 191
  permission/compensation 157–62, 166, 167–9
expressive authorship 163
externalities 277–83, 289

fair use ix–x, 8–12, 53, 64, 93, 138, 149–91
  demise of doctrine 69
  DMCA 33, 202–6, 209, 211, 214, 218n120, 220, 221

Europe 251, 252
Napster case 89
patent law 427–8
transaction costs 141, 146, 183–6
under attack 65
WIPO Treaties Act 199, 210, 217
Falwell, Jerry 170–2
Fanning, Shawn 36
Farrell, J. 464
Federal Trade Commission Act (US) 481
fencing 136–7, 139, 140, 142, 145
film industry 92–3, 405, 406, 465, 467, 477
  see also DVD
firmware 107n1, 108n3
First Amendment 65, 76, 166, 169n62, 171, 208, 241, 289
first sale doctrine 204, 206, 207, 221, 357
Fisher, F. 464
Fourth Estate vii, x, 279, 317–39
France 257, 260–1, 267n2
Frank, Barney 208n81
free software ix, 119–22, 123, 124–5, 126–9, 130
Free Software Foundation 13, 109n6, 120, 121, 122, 143, 445n12
free speech 20–1, 151, 187, 208, 366
  copyright 106, 240–1, 242, 247, 248, 253–61
  ECHR 391–2
  electronic commerce ix, 23–42
  First Amendment 166
  private censorship 172
free trade
  market preferences 285, 287
  media products 267–9, 275, 276, 288, 289, 290
freedom 80, 102, 103
freedom of contract 72, 137, 140
freedom of expression x, 3, 5, 7, 235
  copyright relationship 63–77, 106
  ECHR 391, 393
  electronic commerce 23–42
  Europe 239–63
  propertization conflict 11–12
freedom of information 240, 244–6, 247, 259, 366–7, 391

505

freedom of the press 254, 262, 286–7, 335
Friedman, D.D. 371

Gallo, Robert 434
Gandal, Neil xi, 461–77, 480, 482, 486, 488–90, 491–2
Gates, Bill 111, 118, 124, 131
Gauss, Carl Friedrich 435, 452
Gelsinger, Patrick 351, 352
General Public License (GPL) 121, 122, 124–5, 128–9
  see also copyleft
Gerbner, George 280–1
Germany 241, 243–4, 247, 253–5, 411–12
Gilder, George 291, 294
Giles, C.L. 438, 453
Ginsburg, Jane 76
globalization 18n44, 398
globally unique identifier (GUID) 349–50, 355
GNU 119–22, 124, 127, 134, 143–4
Goodenough, Oliver 289, 290n33
Gordon, Wendy J. ix–x, 10n28, 141, 149–91
governance 335–8
government-financed media 317, 318, 328–9, 339
GPL *see* General Public License
Grateful Dead 129–30, 144
Greenwood, J. 464
group polarization 327
Guibault, L. 248n48
GUID *see* globally unique identifier

hackers 8, 127, 144, 212, 217, 219
Hamilton, Marci 68
Hardin, Garrett 54, 143
hardware 107, 108, 116, 346, 351, 352, 363
harmonization
  Bangemann Report 225
  EC Copyright Directive 228–33, 234, 239, 249–50, 252–3, 365
  merits 236–7
Hart, H.L.A. 153n14
hate speech 166, 169n62, 278
hegemony 123

Heller, M.A. 141
Hermitte, Marie-Angèle 136, 138
HGS *see* Human Genome Sciences
highest-value use 178–9, 180, 181, 182, 191
homogeneity 47–8
Hovenkamp, Herbert 479, 485n28
Hugenholtz, P. Bernt x, 239–63
Hughes, Howard 64
human capital 400, 401, 404
human genome 415–16
Human Genome Sciences (HGS) 421–2
human rights 244, 257, 290, 366–7
  intellectual property relationship 390–1
  privacy 17, 18, 19, 20
Hurd, Heidi M. 151n6
hyperlinks 90–1
hypertext 26

IBM 115–16, 119, 122, 464
ICAAN *see* Internet Corporation for Assigned Names and Numbers
ICCPR *see* International Covenant on Civil and Political Rights
ICESCR *see* International Covenant on Economic, Social and Cultural Rights
ideas 12, 64, 163, 175n91, 249
identifiability 344, 347–50
identification of Internet users 343–64
incentives 44, 58, 79, 111–12, 168
  common carriage regimes 307
  communications infrastructure 307, 311, 315
  copyright law 84, 106
  intellectual property 123
  producer 360
  property rights 135, 136, 300
  scientists 144–5
inequalities 101–2, 297
influence 302–3, 304, 305
information
  autonomy 298
  cheapness of 48–9
  commodification of 43–59
  computer readable 421–2

506

information, *cont.*
  control over 79–106, 361
    communications infrastructure 298, 299–302, 305, 308, 316
    media companies 44, 52–3
    state 58
  databases 373–83
  DNA sequence patents 418–21
  free flow of 248, 260, 309, 391, 392, 393
  influence 302–3
  intellectual property 135
  intermediaries 333–4
  market 368
  media 52–3, 322–3
  non-commodified 284, 285
  overload 330–1
  peer-to-peer rating 331, 332–3
  personal 344, 349–50, 355–6, 358, 363
  production of 397–8
  propertization of 6
  public sector 234–5, 366, 390n150, 392
  search engines 94–8
  sharing 134, 142, 144–5, 146, 356–7, 359–60
  see also freedom of information
information age 79
information economy 59, 79, 81, 106, 284, 430–1
Information Society 80, 224, 225, 228, 237, 372
information technology 195, 443, 444–5
  see also computer technology
infrastructure, communications 291–316, 330
Intel 343, 351–4, 361, 363
intellectual property 51, 53–5, 154n18, 356
  censorship 153
  Europe 225, 239–40
  freedom of expression conflict 256
  Internet 32, 39, 41, 133–46
  law 80, 375, 382–3
    collaborative research 397, 399, 400, 401, 404–13
    origins of rights 71, 72
    research norms 443–9, 454
  rights ix, 43, 365, 383, 393

commodification 44
databases 379
distribution 81
DNA patents 427, 430
dominant market position 384–90
economic justification 367–71
human rights relationship 390–1
originality 70–1
TRIPS Agreement 69–70, 110, 365
unequal advantages 68
US legislation 379, 380–1
trusted systems 357, 358
see also copyright; patents; trademarks
interests 104, 206, 427
  balancing 194–5, 215, 220, 255
  researchers 440
International Covenant on Civil and Political Rights (ICCPR) 245, 287n30
International Covenant on Economic, Social and Cultural Rights (ICESCR) 244, 287n30, 391
international trade in media products 267–90
Internet viii, 51, 199–200, 291, 331, 338
  access 199–200, 308–9, 345–6
  'copy' definition 207
  costs 25, 29–30, 49, 334
  decentralized nature of 81–2, 295
  diversity 312n28
  domain names 37–41
  DVD/DIVX 465, 473, 490
  e-commerce 23–42
  expropriation of the commons 55
  intellectual property 133–46
  Linux 121
  narrowcasting 48
  network resistance 112
  online services 99
  propertization 4
  protocols 294
  streaming 86–8
  transaction costs 185
  user identification x, 343–64
  see also computer technology; cyberspace; websites; World Wide Web

507

Internet Corporation for Assigned Names and Numbers (ICAAN) 39–40
internet service providers (ISPs) 33, 99, 231, 233–4
IP addresses 128, 347–9
ISPs *see* internet service providers

Jarvenpaa, Sirkka L. 332n63, 333n64
Jaszi, Peter 70
Java language 142–3
joint works 407–8, 410–11, 412, 413
judicialization of information 99
justification 150–2, 153–4, 156–7, 184, 186, 191
 permission/compensation 158–62, 164, 166, 167–9
 self-defense 153–4, 170–2
 substantial injury 183

Kaldor-Hicks test 372–3
Katz, M. 463
Keeton, Robert 160
knowledge 5, 144–5
knowledge-based economy 52, 107n2
Kripke, Saul 435

Landes, W.M. 371
languages, computer programming 113–5, 119, 142–3
Lawrence, S. 438, 453
legal regimes 110–11, 182
legislation 4n5, 99, 139–40
 common carriage regimes 309–10
 EC Directives 225–6, 227–34, 263
  Copyright Harmonization Directive 228–33, 234, 239, 249–50, 252–3, 365
  Database Directive 227–8, 233, 366, 374–7, 379–83, 389–90
  E-Commerce Directive 226, 231, 233–4
 English copyright law 67
 Federal Trade Commission Act 481
 illiberal 289–90
 market failure 365
 Statute of Anne 67–8, 154n17
 Treaty of Rome 366, 384, 385–6, 388

United States
 collaborative research 404–10
 Copyright Act (1976) 9n22, 87, 194, 207, 404, 407
 database protection 377–82, 390
 DMCA 4n5, 12n35, 32–3, 82, 99, 133, 378
  access control 93
  anti-circumvention rule 73, 74, 75–6, 82, 90–1, 92, 193–221
  exemptions 199–202, 215, 216–18, 219, 220, 221
  fence-cutting 140
 Internet regulation 32–4, 40
 WIPO Treaties Act 194–5, 199, 202, 209–11, 214, 216–17, 229, 375
 see also regulation
Lemley, Mark 65, 464
Lessig, Lawrence 65, 141n21
liability rules 106, 138, 157n24, 188–9, 366, 370, 372–3
liberal democracy 317, 318–19, 320, 321, 329, 335, 336
licensing 10–11, 83n11, 84, 91, 181–2, 369
 compulsory 87, 151, 160, 188, 228, 382, 388
 computer software 119
 cross-licensing 389–90
 DVD case 92
 European copyright law 253, 263
 inventorship 412–13
 open source 12–16
 parody/critical review 176, 177
 pricelessness 178–82
 pricing 71
 search engines 96–7
 transaction costs 152
 TV retransmission 87
 UCITA 74–5
 voluntary 165, 166
limited common property 134, 142
Linux 14, 93, 120–2, 124, 125, 127–9, 134, 143–4
Litman, Jessica ix, 23–42, 72
Lobachevsky, Nikolay Ivanovich 435, 451
Locke, John 171
Loren, Lydia Pallas 150n

McGowan, D. xi, 464, 479–92
McGowan, J. 464
machine language 113n11, 114
Mackaay, Ejan ix, 133–46
Madison, James 317
Magaziner, Ira 354
managerial discretion 177
Marcus, Ruth Barcan 435
margin of appreciation 247, 261, 263, 391
market concentration 80, 91, 302, 315
market failure 140, 155n21, 165, 365, 369, 381
  market limitation 150–1, 161, 162–4, 171, 190, 191
  market malfunction 150–1, 156, 161, 167, 186, 191
  media products 268, 269, 270
market rhetoric 3–4, 18, 154–6, 191
markets vii–ix, 51, 53, 58, 79–82, 100, 102–3
  barriers to entry 25n14, 368–9, 371, 372, 384, 388
  consumer decisions 491
  distribution channels 85
  free competition 367
  idealized 288
  information 368
  market valuation 285–6
  privately-owned infrastructure 301–2
  secondary 359, 360, 363–4, 388
Marx, Karl 45, 50
mass production 45, 46–7, 81
MCI 44, 481n9, 486n28
media vii, x, 52–3, 68, 278–9, 297–8
  concentration 302, 344, 361, 364
  control of information 44, 52–3
  Fourth Estate role vii, x, 279, 317–39
  freedom of the 247
  government-financed 317, 318, 328–9, 339
  Internet 28–9, 86–8
  pluralism 245
  political party-financed 317, 318, 325–8, 339
media products x, 267–90
Melamed, Douglas 157n24, 371
Merges, Robert 152n9, 449, 450n19, 452n20
metacrawlers 94–5, 96, 97
MGM/UA 465

Michelman, Frank 167, 168
Microsoft 14, 15, 44, 53, 143, 384
  identifiability 350
  software 109, 110, 117–18, 121, 122, 128–9
  vaporware 462, 464, 479–80, 482
Miller, Seumus 434
Milsom, Toby 111n8, 124
Mishan, E.J. 178n99, 180n107
Moglen, Eben ix, 107–31
monetary benefit 188, 189–90
monopoly 117, 272–3, 334, 372–3
  abuse of dominant position 384–9
  vaporware 485
Montagnier, Luc 434
moral rights 203, 243, 387
Mosaic 55
Motion Picture Association 85, 86–7, 92–3
movies 92–3
MP3 format 34–7, 87–8, 89, 91n40, 130, 133
Mulgan, Geoffrey 52
music 112, 130, 160n31
  MP3 format 34–7, 87–8, 89, 91n40, 133
  patentability 424n41
  peer-to-peer rating 331, 332–3

nano-transactions 57
Napster 26n21, 28n31, 36, 74, 79, 89
national treatment 268–9, 289, 376
negligence law 157, 158
Netanel, Neil 63, 65, 183, 317–39
Netherlands 251–2, 255–6, 259–60, 366
Netscape 15, 55, 122, 480
network effects xi, 53, 383, 461–77, 479, 488, 489
network externalities 59, 303
networked digital technology 25
networks 14, 118, 291, 299–301
  common carriage regimes 307, 308, 309–10
  decentralized license-free 291, 295, 296, 310, 315
  packet-switched 56–7
  peer-to-peer communication 88–9, 314, 317, 318, 330–8
  rights management 345
  see also digital networks

news media 49, 130, 317, 320–4, 325–6, 331, 335, 336–8
Nimmer, David x, 193–221
Nissenbaum, Helen xi, 433–57
Noam, Eli ix, 43–59, 279, 291, 292, 294, 306, 311–14
noncommodification 4, 5, 9, 14, 21
norms 433–57

Oldenberg, Henry 436
oligopolies 53
online services 99
open access 142–4, 146, 292, 294, 306–7, 311–14
open source code 121–2, 143–4
open source movement 12–16, 445
originality 70–1
overpropertization 6–7
ownership 137, 154, 164, 293
 communication networks 299–301
 information technology 444–5
 public 305–6, 310

packet-switched networks 56–7
Panasonic 465
Paramount 465, 467, 488
Parisi, F. 141
parody 10, 158, 160n32, 170–1, 172–3, 175–6, 181, 263
party press 317, 318, 325–8, 339
passing off 370
patents 5n5, 6, 23, 53, 163n45, 371–2
 Antipiracy Bill 380
 biotechnology 144
 business method 5n5, 53, 146, 388, 423
 collaborative research 408–10, 412
 costs 370
 digital numeric information 109, 110
 DNA sequences xi, 415–31
 economic rationale 368–9
 research norms 446–52
Patterson, Mark 333, 334
pay-per-use society 205–6, 209, 210–11, 220
PCs *see* personal computers
pecuniary losses 176–7
peer review 437, 439–40, 441

peer-to-peer communication 88–9, 314, 317, 318, 330–8
permission 150–2, 156–7, 165, 187, 190
 lack of 158, 159–60, 162, 166–7, 169, 191
 private censorship 172–3
perpetual copyrights 70
personal computers (PCs) 116, 117–18, 121, 345, 346–7, 351–2, 353
piracy 72–3, 165, 195, 360, 365, 371
 DVDs 465, 489
 Internet 28–9, 30, 32, 34, 139
pluralism 187, 245, 246, 319
politics
 EU harmonization 236
 government-financed media 317, 318, 328–9, 339
 liberal democracy 319
 party press 317, 318, 325–8, 339
 public discourse 321–2
 self-governance 291, 292, 296, 297–9, 306, 316
Polygram 465
pornography 23, 27–8
Posner, Richard A. 155, 173n, 186
post-modernism 73–4, 76
power 101–2, 104, 297, 319, 320–1, 336, 338
PPFK *see* private-property-plus-free-contract
price discrimination 270–1, 275–6, 302, 304, 305
 commodification 397
 trusted systems 344, 357–61, 363–4
Price, Monroe 329n48
pricelessness 167, 178–82
prices 52, 53, 71
priority 433, 434–9, 442–4, 445–7, 451–3, 455
privacy 16–20, 185, 230
 ECHR 242, 250
 Internet identifiability 343–4, 352–3, 355–6, 361, 362–3
private enforcement 66, 72
private sector 24, 37
private-property-plus-free-contract (PPFK) 4, 6, 13, 15, 16, 17–20
privatization 50, 140, 146, 303, 305, 397

Processor Serial Number (PSN) 343, 351–5, 358, 361, 363
profit maximization 6, 69, 84, 104, 358
propertarianism 122, 123, 125–6, 127
propertization vii–viii, 3, 4, 6, 21, 96, 97
  freedom of expression conflict 11–12
  scientific research 449, 450
property 138, 139, 143–4, 145
  pure private 292, 306–7, 309, 313
  rights x, 58–9, 72, 106, 134–7, 142, 145
    alternatives 51
    communications infrastructure 300, 306
    economic rationale 368
    expiration of 52
    privacy 17–18, 19, 20
    research 450
    United States 20, 21
  rules 8, 111, 123, 157n24, 366, 371–2, 373
  slippage 139, 140–1
  software as 112, 113–15, 116, 117, 123
  see also intellectual property
proportionality 231n32, 256, 260, 262–3, 412–13
protectionism 68, 72, 244, 268, 289, 290
pseudonyms 362
public discourse 292, 293, 297, 298, 319
  facilitation by media 321–2
  fragmentation 327
  government-funded media 328
public domain 3, 138
  copyright issues 70, 71, 212, 213
  payment for access 205
public good 11, 135, 270, 319
public interest 167, 183, 195, 248–9
  European copyright cases 254, 255, 256, 257, 258, 262, 263
  genomics 426
  German doctrine 244
public ownership 305–6, 310
public sector information 234–5, 366, 390n150, 392
public sphere 53, 54–5, 80, 100–2, 100–5
publications 46, 52–3
  see also electronic publication

quality of content 47

Radin, Margaret Jane viii–ix, 3–21, 162, 164, 184n118, 400
radio communications 291, 293–4, 311, 315
Randall, Alice 170
Raymond, Eric 13–14, 126, 127n29
Raz, J. 298
RealNetworks 349–50
rebuttal 170–1
recording industry 34–7, 69, 85n17, 87–8, 130
Recording Industry Association of America (RIAA) 28n31, 35, 85, 87–8, 90
Reed Elsevier 68, 70, 71
Register of Copyrights 217
regulation 54, 194–5, 461–2
  communications infrastructure 292, 306–7, 308, 310
  Internet 31, 32–4, 40
  see also legislation
remedies 159, 188
rent-seeking 137, 139, 140, 142, 145, 146, 290
representations 80, 85
reproduction rights 229, 232, 239, 249, 250
reputation 14, 127, 145, 146, 181, 400
research viii, x–xi, 5n5, 51, 54, 144–5, 219, 433–57
  biotechnology patenting 415–31
  collaborative 397–413
  Europe 232–3, 236n58
reverse engineering 75, 110, 138, 203, 219, 428
  DeCSS 92
  liability rules 370, 371
Rifkin, Jeremy 49–50
rights 51, 71–2, 84, 229
  browsing 208–9, 212
  codification of 138, 145, 146
  collaborative research 412–13
  contractual 137–8
  distribution 229, 239
  exclusionary 419–20, 422, 425, 426, 427, 429, 430
  Lockean natural rights 171–2
  "of others" 246
  reproduction 229, 232, 239, 249, 250
  see also human rights

rights management 11, 230, 345–7, 351, 362
royalties 84, 176–7, 204, 372, 385
Rubin, Ed 319n4

safe harbor provisions 33, 219
Saloner, G. 464
Samba 122
Samuelson, Pamela ix, 63–77
Sanders, A. Kamperman x, 365–93
Schiller, Herbert 49
science viii, 46, 144–5, 415–31, 433–57
Scitovszky test 373
SDMI *see* Secure Digital Music Initiative
search engines 40–1, 90, 94–8, 331, 333–4, 453
secondary markets 359, 360, 363–4, 388
Secure Digital Music Initiative (SDMI) 35–6, 130
self-defense 153–4, 157, 158, 170–2
self-governance 291, 292, 296, 297–9, 306, 316
service marks 39, 40
service providers 311–14
Shapiro, Carl 141, 383, 463
shareware 212
sharing 134, 142, 144–5, 146, 356–7, 359–60
Smith, Quentin 435
social capital 105, 400, 404
social goals 190–1
social groups 322
social policy 57
social welfare 154–5, 244, 440, 447, 450, 461, 484–5
software 65, 72, 107–31, 142–4, 353
  availability 469–71
  open source licensing 12–16
  piracy 165
  vaporware xi, 462, 464, 468, 472, 480–92
Sony 93, 465
source code 12–13, 109–10, 113, 115, 119–22, 124–6, 128
Soviet Union 441
spectrum commons 292, 293, 294–5, 296, 306–7, 311–14, 315–16
spheres 184n118
Stallman, Richard M. 13, 119–20, 121, 124, 126, 143, 445n12

standardization 18n44, 461, 463
Statute of Anne (1710) 67–8, 154n17
Strowel, A. 250
subsidiarity 231n32
subsidies 57, 272, 273, 274, 277, 281, 283, 289, 290
substantial injury 183
Sun 142–3, 480
Sunstein, Cass 104n73, 322n14, 327
suppression triangle 174, 175–6
Sweden 243, 247
Switzerland 261, 391–2

20th Century Fox 465, 488
TCPA *see* Trusted Computing Platform Alliance
technical protection measures 70, 72, 99, 195–8, 212, 213, 217–18
technology 82, 98, 343–4, 397–8
  communications infrastructure 293–5, 311
  DVD v. DIVX 461–77, 480, 482–91
  see also computer technology; digital communications technology; information technology
television 46, 47, 48, 49, 86–7
Third Party Neutrality 55
Tiller, Emerson H. 332n63, 333n64
Titmuss, Richard M. 188–9
tort law 111, 150, 154, 157
Torvalds, Linus 120–1, 127
Toshiba 465
trade
  economy 144–5, 146
  law 290
  media products 267–90
  see also free trade
trade secrets 92, 109, 110, 370–1, 426–7, 428
trademarks 37–41, 234, 369–70
traditional patent bargain 425–7
trafficking 73n56, 195–6, 197–8, 215, 218–19
tragedy of the commons 54, 143
transaction costs 11, 131, 174, 179, 191, 303
  absence of 161, 181
  collaborative research 402–3
  excuses 152, 156

transaction costs, *cont.*
   fair use 141, 146, 183–6, 188
   intellectual property rights 370, 371
   licensing 97
transactions 43, 55, 56, 57, 59
Treaty of Rome (1957) 366, 384, 385–6, 388
TRIPS *see* Agreement on Trade-Related Aspects of Intellectual Property Rights
trust 104, 105, 332–3, 452
Trusted Computing Platform Alliance (TCPA) 353–4
trusted systems 343–4, 346–7, 351, 354–61, 362, 363–4
two-year delay 215–16

UCITA 74–5
Ullman-Margalit, Edna 322n14
Ullrich, Hanns 412
UNESCO 267
unfair competition 83, 96, 365–6, 370, 379, 381–2, 392
   European cases 261, 262
   leaks xi, 138, 491
United Kingdom
   audio/video levies 232
   copyright issues 236n58, 257–8, 374, 388
   fair dealing 233
   public sector information 235
United States
   Constitution 67–8
   copyright system 8–9, 10, 11, 69, 70–1, 82, 149
   database protection 376–82, 383, 389
   DNA sequence patents 417
   Europe comparison 250–1
   Internet 23–4, 25, 31–3, 37–40, 133
   legal doctrine 241
   mass production of information 46
   media products 267–8, 280–1, 282–3, 288
   party press 325–7
   patents 146, 427n48, 428n55, 446n13
   privacy 18
   property rights 20, 21
   research 404–10, 442n9
   semiconductor chips 375

TV audiences 47, 48
   see also Digital Millennium Copyright Act
Universal 465, 467
Universal Declaration on Human Rights 244, 287n30, 391
Unix 119–20, 121, 122, 345
user identification x, 343–64
utilitarianism 67, 69, 161n36, 182, 285, 443, 447
utopian vision 7–8

Vallopillil, Vinod 125, 128–9
values
   cultural 268
   research 439, 440–2, 443, 446, 448, 450, 454–5
vaporware xi, 462, 464, 468, 472, 480–92
Varian, Hal 141, 383
Vaver, David x, 223–37
video 307–8
virtual networks 463, 488, 492
Volokh, Eugene 26, 65
Volvo 386

waiver of rights 17, 18–19, 20
Walzer, Michael 184n118
Warner 465, 489
Warren-Boulton, F., 464
watchdog function of media 320–1, 324, 325, 335, 336
watermarking 136, 140, 230
websites 18, 284, 426, 438
Weinberg, Jonathan x, 343–64
welfare effects 167, 178, 180
welfare maximization 302
Wigand, Jeffrey 336–8
will formation 101, 102
Williamson, Oliver 59n52
Windows 93, 117, 120n19, 122, 134, 143, 350
WIPO *see* World Intellectual Property Organization
the work 68–9
work for hire doctrine 69, 404–6, 407
World Intellectual Property Organization (WIPO) 225, 229, 365, 367, 390

Copyright and Performances and
   Phonograms Treaties
   Implementation Act (1998) 194–5,
   199, 202, 209–11, 214, 216–17,
   229, 375
Copyright Treaty 374
Model Provisions on protection Against
   Unfair Competition 381–2
World Trade Organization (WTO) 282

World Wide Web 438–9
Woroch, G. 464
WTO *see* World Trade Organization
Wyly, B.J. 439

Yen, Fred 65

Ziman, John 449

Information Law Series

1. *Protecting Works of Fact: Copyright, Freedom of Expression and Information Law*, Egbert J. Dommering and P. Bernt Hugenholtz (eds)
   ISBN 90-6544-5676
2. *Information Law Towards the 21st Century*, Willem F. Korthals Altes, Egbert J. Dommering, P. Bernt Hugenholtz and Jan J.C. Kabel (eds)
   ISBN 90-6544-6273
3. *Challenges to the Creator Doctrine*, Jacqueline Seignette
   ISBN 90-6544-8764
4. *The Future of Copyright in a Digital Environment*, P. Bernt Hugenholtz (ed)
   ISBN 90-411-0267-1
5. *From Privacy Toward a New Intellectual Property Right in Persona*, Julius C.S. Pinckaers
   ISBN 90-411-0355-4
6. *Intellectual Property and Information Law: Essays in Honour of Herman Cohen Jehoram*, Jan J.C. Kabel and Gerard J.H.M. Mom (eds)
   ISBN 90-411-9702-8
7. *Copyright and Photographs: An International Survey*, Ysolde Gendreau, Axel Nordemann and Rainer Oesch (eds)
   ISBN 90-411-9722-2
8. *Copyright and Electronic Commerce: Legal Aspects of Electronic Copyright Management*, P. Bernt Hugenholtz (ed.)
   ISBN 90-411-9785-0
9. *Copyright Limitations and Contracts: An Analysis of the Contractual Overridability of Limitations on Copyright*, Lucie M.C.R. Guibault
   ISBN 90-411-9867-9
10. *Data Protection Law: Approaching its Rationale, Logic and Limits*, Lee Bygrave
    ISBN 90-411-9870-9
11. *The Commodification of Information*, Niva Elkin-Koren and Neil Weinstock Netanel (eds)
    ISBN 90-411-9876-8